Bohemia in America, 1858–1920

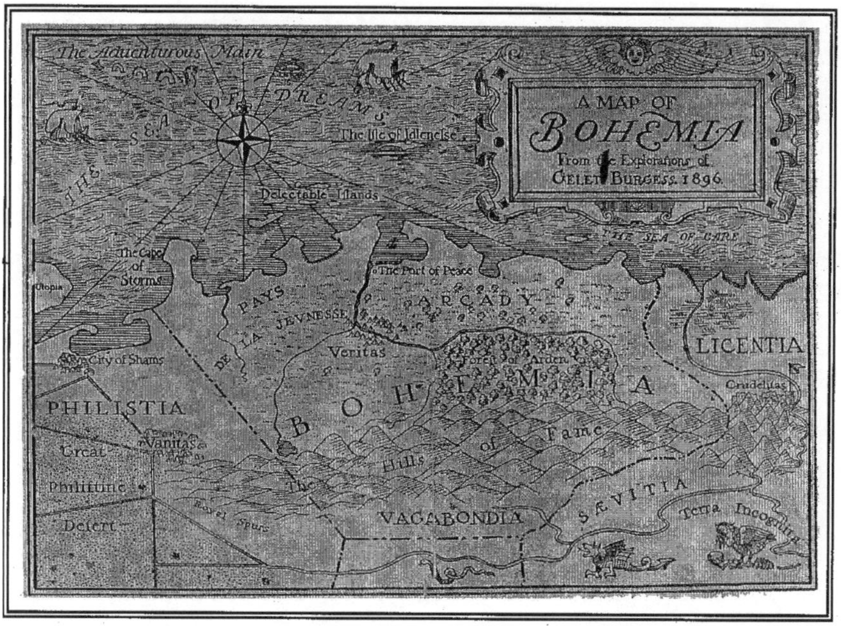

"A Map of Bohemia," by Gelett Burgess, *The Lark* (1896)

Bohemia in America, 1858–1920

Joanna Levin

Stanford University Press
Stanford, California

Stanford University Press
Stanford, California

This book has been published with the assistance of Chapman University.

Printed in the United States of America on acid-free, archival-quality paper

Library of Congress Cataloging-in-Publication Data

Levin, Joanna.
Bohemia in America, 1858–1920 / Joanna Levin.
p. cm.
Includes bibliographical references and index.
ISBN 978-0-8047-6083-6 (cloth : alk. paper)
1. American literature—19th century—History and criticism. 2. American literature—20th century—History and criticism. 3. Literary movements—United States—History—19th century. 4. Literary movements—United States—History—20th century. 5. Bohemianism—United States—History—19th century. 6. Bohemianism—United States—History—20th century. 7. Bohemianism in literature. I. Title.
PS217.B65L48 2010
810.9'11—dc22 2008055818

Typeset by Westchester Book Group in 11/13.5 Adobe Garamond

Contents

Acknowledgments

THIS PROJECT HAS GROWN (and grown!) out of the advice, support, and examples of so many scholars that I scarcely know where to begin acknowledging their contributions. I will limit my acknowledgments to those most directly concerned with this book, with the caveat that there are many other teachers and friends who have provided vital guidance. I am extremely grateful to have had George Dekker as my advisor. I have continually benefited from his remarkable generosity of insight, knowledge, and time, and will always be deeply thankful for his friendship, faith, and support. Albert Gelpi provided crucial advice, support, and inspiration, and his commitment to this project has made all the difference. Susan Gillman, Ramón Saldívar, and, in the early stages of the project, the late Lora Romero, helped me to conceptualize this project and attend more closely to its details. For their generous insight and careful reading, I am most thankful. I am also extremely grateful to Norris Pope at Stanford University Press for his support and belief in this book, and to Robert C. Leitz III and Jonathan Freedman for generously offering their time, encouragement, and important suggestions. I also wish to thank Carolyn Brown, James Cappio, Barbara Goodhouse, and Sarah Crane Newman for their excellent work throughout the editorial process.

There are other friends, colleagues, family members, and mentors whom I must mention, and I hope they know how much their support, examples, and suggestions have meant to me over the years. I would like to thank Ken, Adele, and Bob Levin, Alan Babb, David Cantrell, Ellie Amel, Logan Esdale, Melissa Goldman, Sylvia Greenbaum, Kent Lehnhof, Christina Mesa, Anne-Marie Pedersen, David Riggs, Eileen Jankowski, Tracey

Swan, Emma Teng, Justine Van Meter, Pavel Machala, Kevin O'Brien, Sarah Hepler, and Bob and Wendy Warner. I am also very grateful for fellowship support from the Stanford English Department, the Stanford Humanities Center, the Cogswell and Colin Higgins Foundations, a Copeland Fellowship from Amherst College, and a scholarly research grant from Chapman University.

I have been blessed with the best and most generous of parents, and I want to dedicate this book to my father, Gordon Levin, who has always guided my intellectual development and inspired me through his brilliant example (and tracked down many sources for this book!); to the memory of my loving mother, Elayne Levin; and to my husband, Farrell Warner, a constant source of love, humor, and support throughout the writing of this book.

Bohemia in America, 1858–1920

Introduction

"BOHEMIA ONLY EXISTS AND is only possible in Paris," declared Henri Murger, the writer credited with popularizing and largely inventing the romance of Bohemia in mid-nineteenth-century France.[1] Yet, a decade later, a group of U.S. writers, painters, and actors assumed the mantle of Bohemianism and sought to create a self-consciously American version of *la vie bohème.* The irony of this endeavor appealed to U.S. Bohemians and informed their own self-representations: from its beginnings, American Bohemianism has seized upon the foreignness of Bohemia as a means of launching cultural criticism, expanding aesthetic possibilities, and promoting cosmopolitan aspiration. "Transplanted from the mother asphalt of Paris," Bohemia entered American culture, first becoming the province of small artistic coteries and ultimately inspiring a popular vogue replete with "Bohemian" restaurants, clubs, neighborhoods, hotels, novels, poems, paintings, and periodicals.[2] By the 1890s, the recitation piece "I'd rather live in Bohemia than any other land" could be heard in even the most decorous bourgeois drawing rooms.[3] Part literary trope, part cultural nexus, and part socioeconomic landscape, *la vie bohème* existed both within and without literary narrative, enabling and shaping dramas of artistic and countercultural experience.

Murger immortalized Bohemian Paris in a series of sketches written in 1845 and 1846, and in *La Vie de Bohème*, a popular musical melodrama staged in 1849. Defying convention and poverty, dedicating themselves to love and creativity, transforming necessity into art and carefree abandon, and outwitting *les bourgeois* (in the form of soulless landlords and creditors), Murger's Bohemians set the stage for an enduring romance that has spurred countless representations and lived experiences, inspiring endless convolutions of art imitating life and life imitating art. Transposed into U.S. contexts, this literary romance quickly became an integral part of America's social and cultural geography.

Despite its vibrant presence, however, previous literary histories have minimized the role of Bohemia in the United States. Most commentators view American Bohemianism as a feeble imitation of a more vital European phenomenon (at least until the Greenwich Village of the second decade of the twentieth century). In Robert E. Spiller's *Literary History of the United States* (1948), Harry T. Levin articulates this perspective: "The *vie de Bohème* was deeply rooted in the interstices of European society, in the rift between artists and Philistines, between a radical intelligentsia and a predominant bourgeoisie. In America, where expansion left further room for individualism, the tensions were less explicit and the protests more superficial."[4] For Levin, the concept was simply redundant in a nation that gave the "bourgeois" a greater scope for individuality. In the recent *Cambridge History of American Literature* (2005), Richard H. Brodhead also insists that "in comparison with contemporary France, which had a stratified reading culture, nineteenth-century America is conspicuously lacking a Bohemia, a prestige-bearing *milieu artiste* defined in opposition to social respectability. In America high art was founded within, not in opposition to, the milieu of an *haute bourgeoisie*."[5]

Yet Bohemianism did take root in nineteenth-century American culture, and the very popularity and mobility of the phenomenon suggests that we should take it more seriously—without discounting its value as a form of play and humor. Alongside the revisionist histories that have dismantled the mythos of American "consensus," a new history of *la vie bohème* in the United States must address the many social and cultural differences that Bohemia both shaped and dramatized. Though comparatively mild when measured against some European varieties, American Bohemias offered a variety of oppositional standpoints. In America, as in Europe, Bohemia charted and tested "the boundaries of bourgeois life." Always opposed, the Bohemian and the Bourgeois nonetheless occupy "parts of a single field" of overlapping trajectories: they are, as Jerrold Seigel reminds us in his study *Bohemian Paris* (1986), the "positive and negative magnetic poles" that "imply, require, and attract each other."[6] In the U.S. context, I argue, the persistent differences between (and within) the categories of the Bohemian and the Bourgeois—including those based on race, ethnicity, class, gender, and regional identity—ever complicate the familiar opposition. Foregrounding these many differences, the cultural geography of Bohemia has subjected the traditional binary to many temporal, ideological, and aesthetic remappings.

Some critical accounts exaggerate Bohemian oppositionality, while others collapse the Bohemian into the Bourgeois.[7] This study reveals that, in all its manifold forms, the Bohemian and Bourgeois opposition produced important material and symbolic effects: it must be questioned but not elided. In all its many expressions, "Bohemia" never became an arbitrary or empty signifier. Instead, Bohemia offered a second and even a third term, continuing to challenge dominant ideologies and to mediate a series of social and cultural divides. Navigating between naturalistic "real life" and romantic enchantment, Bohemia moved in and out of literary genres, styles, cultural institutions, and social geographies. Bohemia appears in the writings of such disparate figures as Walt Whitman, Bret Harte, William Dean Howells, Willa Cather, Frank Norris, Henry James, Abraham Cahan, and James Weldon Johnson, as well as in numerous guidebooks, periodicals, popular novels, and memoirs. This study investigates the many textual and geographic spaces in which Bohemia was conjured.

How did these American Bohemias reinterpret *la vie bohème*? What was the role of Bohemia in negotiating between diverse cultural formations, both within and outside the United States? To answer these questions, we must pay close attention to how participants and critics imagined "Bohemia" and to how they charted its textual, visual, and performative coordinates. As Seigel has argued, "defining Bohemia's significance was a crucial way of participating in it"; *la vie bohème* was "at once a form of life and a dramatized interpretation, both of itself and of the society to which it was a response." Proceeding inductively, Seigel's study admits:

> There is no action or gesture capable of being identified as Bohemian that cannot also be—or has not been—undertaken outside of Bohemia. Odd dress, long hair, living for the moment, having no stable residence, sexual freedom, radical political enthusiasms, drink, drug taking, irregular work patterns, addiction to nightlife—all were Bohemian or not according to how they were meant or how they were taken, Bohemian at some moments and not at others.[8]

Like Seigel, I have also eschewed the search for an essential "Bohemia" or "Bohemian," focusing instead on the types of cultural work that these terms enabled.

Albert Parry, still the foremost chronicler of U.S. Bohemianism, recognized that "a book on Greenwich Village and what came before Greenwich

Village must necessarily discuss all those who designate themselves or were designated by others as Bohemians." His flexible approach was hobbled, however, by his conclusion that such analysis shows "that many of these were mere poseurs or slumming bourgeois rather than true gypsies of art."[9] In effect, Parry presupposed that we knew what Bohemia was, or at least what it should have been. His *Garrets and Pretenders: A History of Bohemianism in America* (1933) recounts many amusing anecdotes of Bohemian "pretenders" (and has been indispensable for my own research), yet, measuring all successors against Murger's prototype, he dismisses most as inauthentic or hypocritical, thus failing to analyze their social and cultural import. For Parry, as for other literary historians, "the mighty development of capitalism" in the United States impeded the development of Bohemia and muted its radical potential.[10]

There was, of course, a world of difference between the "Bohemian" as starving, consumptive artist and the "Bohemian" as consumer of exotic commodities and racy leisure activities. This study will not try to minimize the socioeconomic chasms that existed between these and other Bohemian prototypes. Yet it is only by exploring what Bohemia meant to both the putative "poseurs" and the "true gypsies of art" that we can understand why the concept of Bohemia has had such multiple resonances and lasting effects. By reconstructing what Bohemia meant in a variety of literary and social contexts, we gain a better understanding of how the mythic territory of *la Bohème* reconfigured social and cultural divisions, anticipating ongoing countercultural ideals and heralding new social expectations. Whether invoked in Richmond, Fort Worth, or Cincinnati (via literary periodicals) or in restaurants, clubs, and cafés in San Francisco and New York (by way of guidebooks, club annals, city sketches, stories, and novels), Bohemia amply demonstrates one of the central axioms of cultural geography: "place making always involves a construction, rather than merely a discovery, of difference. . . . Identity neither 'grows out' of rooted communities nor is a thing that can be possessed or owned by individual or collective social actors. It is, instead, a mobile, often unstable relation of difference."[11]

Bohemia stood for and produced such mobility and internal difference. Metonymically linked to the Gypsies (once thought to have migrated from the central European country of Bohemia), *la Bohème* moved within and without national borders: in the spirit of Shakespeare's famous "mistake" in *The Winter's Tale*, Bohemia might have a seacoast,[12] exist amongst the struggling artists and writers of the nineteenth-century Parisian Latin Quarter, or take up residence in Walt Whitman's "Vault at Pfaff's," the German beer hall that housed the first self-proclaimed American Bohemians. Always portable and shape-shifting, Bohemia was the place that, for many nineteenth- and early-twentieth-century Americans, promised to connect (and at times disconnect) the regional and the national, the national and the cosmopolitan, the modern and the traditional. During a period in which national boundaries and populations were in a state of flux and constant redefinition, Bohemia—that "wonderful land in which all conventions are despised and art and genius take precedence over rank, wealth and fashion"—was repeatedly called upon to chart a wide range of social and cultural destinations.[13] "The strange career of American Bohemia" becomes even stranger and more interesting when we explore the "lanes and byways" of this expansive cultural geography.[14]

Part I of this study investigates how the earliest groups of U.S. Bohemians defined themselves through the imagined community of Bohemia, first in New York City and then in San Francisco. Chapter 1 details the emergence of New York's Bohemia in the late 1850s. This Bohemia clustered around Henry Clapp Jr., an iconoclast who had recently returned from Paris with the idea of recreating *la vie bohème* in Pfaff's beer cellar. His circle included Walt Whitman, whose unfinished poem "The Vault at Pfaff's" gives the chapter its title. By comparing the Bohemians' self-descriptions to less favorable representations of the group, the chapter provides a case study in the (mutually constitutive) relationship between the Bohemians and their "bourgeois" antagonists.

Chapter 2 moves to the West Coast and explores how "Bohemia" figured in the early writings and careers of Bret Harte and other *Golden Era* authors, including the "Sage-Brush Bohemian," Mark Twain. The chapter focuses on Harte, who from 1859 to 1863 used the pseudonym "The Bohemian" in a regular column. Styling himself a Bohemian flâneur, Harte approached San Franciscan life through the discursive framework of Bohemian-Bourgeois opposition, all the while recognizing both the allure and the impossibility of positing a distinct, aestheticized realm "above and beyond convention." His columns ironize and critique the city's emerging commodity culture, question bourgeois divisions between the "separate spheres," and express a fascination with such ethnic enclaves (and alternatives to the city's dominant ethos) as Chinatown and the Mexican Quarter. The columns promote the increasingly potent, and popular, ideology of the alienated, unconventional Bohemian artist—an ideology that such writers as Harte and the Pfaffians used to express and renegotiate the relation between artists and their culture.

Part II explores the romance of Bohemia after it had become more broadly disseminated throughout the United States. After 1870, Bohemia ceased to be the exclusive province of struggling artists and writers. *La vie bohème* gained an ever wider appeal, entering both art studios and genteel drawing rooms, leaky garrets and opulent club rooms, popular novels and little magazines, ethnic quarters and the lush redwood forest of Northern California's "Bohemian Grove."

Chapter 3 introduces the stock Bohemian settings and plots that American writers and artists sought to dramatize and experience. In increasingly greater numbers, novels, dramas, and city sketches recycled and recontextualized Murger's *Scenes*; this popular vogue culminated in the "Trilbymania" of the 1890s and the revival of Murger in Puccini's *La Bohème* (first performed in New York in 1898). These narratives all convey a consistent message: to live with the utmost intensity and spirit, one must live in Bohemia. When the title character of *Phyllis in Bohemia* (1897) demands "a plot to live around," she knows where she must go. Most travels to Bohemia first occurred through the medium of print. These many narratives demonstrate the wide range of social conflicts that "Bohemia" continued to chart and negotiate: Bohemian plots routinely involve overlapping tensions between artists and "Philistines," wealth and poverty, women and men, "feminine Bohemianism" and traditional womanhood, propriety and license, America and Europe, and art and life. In all cases, Bohemia is either identified with one of these binary terms or it functions as a third term, capable of mediating (if only temporarily) between these conflicting forces. Highlighting these conflicts, the chapter weaves together such canonical texts as Henry James's *The Ambassadors* (1903) and numerous stories, sketches, and popular novels.

The Bohemian "plot to live around" continuously moved on and off the written page and took root in contemporary social geographies. Chapter 4 concentrates on the elite, all-male Bohemian Club of San Francisco, a group that included wealthy businessmen, leading politicians, Stanford and Berkeley professors, and such writers and artists as Frank Norris, Jules Tavernier, and Jack London. The formal invitations to the club's midsummer encampments at what would soon become known as the "Bohemian Grove" all proffer hope of a personal and collective transformation. The emphasis and imagery shift over the years, yet each invitation promises that the annual encampment will redress psychic strain, and answer longings for a world elsewhere—both within and without the self. Analyzing the club's rhetoric and rituals, recorded in its yearly annals, and focusing on its summer retreat to the "Bohemian Grove," the chapter demonstrates how the promise of "Bohemia" intersected with a range of emerging therapeutic discourses. Most commentaries on the Bohemian Club stress only the irony of the club's name. Yet in a limited and contradictory way, the club fostered alternatives to dominant cultural norms. An answer to fin-de-siècle malaise, this "Bohemia" (and other such clubs) became a locus of bourgeois desire and social experimentation: it enabled a rethinking of bourgeois work and leisure ethics, gender roles, and spiritual commitments.

During the heyday of the Bohemian vogue, the desire to "live in Bohemia" extended throughout the country and appeared in a number of unexpected locales. Chapter 5 demonstrates the extent to which Bohemia functioned as a liminal terrain, mediating between national and regional cultures, and, in so doing, complicating standard literary and social geographies. In most accounts, the regional metonymizes the provincial and upholds traditional values, while Bohemia represents urbane and risqué metropolitanism. Mapping a spatial and temporal split between the rural/regional and the urban/national, Bohemia aligns with the latter. Yet, during this same period, Bohemia also functioned to reject such antinomies. Regional variants of *la vie bohème* often took the form of periodicals, ones that flaunted "Bohemia" in their very titles. These regional *Bohemians* aggressively and explicitly sought to counteract the cultural hegemony of the Northeast; they also proved to be especially important to a number of women writers, enabling them to embrace the modernity of the "New Woman" from within their local cultures.

At the turn into the twentieth century, Bohemia mediated between the regional and the national. During the same period, I argue, this mobile geography also functioned to articulate and displace the cultural divide between the national and the global. Chapter 6, "Cosmopolitan Bohemias," focuses on the territories that contemporary guidebooks designated as "neither strictly native nor wholly foreign."[15] From its very beginnings in the 1850s, American Bohemianism had represented an international mixture of cultural styles. Invoking the Gypsies by way of the Parisian Latin Quarter, Bohemia signified both sophistication (for supporters) and cultural decadence (for critics). The stakes behind these two opposing views of *la vie bohème* only increased at the turn of the century, a period in which twenty million "new immigrants" entered the nation and Jim Crow laws reinstitutionalized the color line. In this cultural climate, the standard opposition between the Bohemian and the Bourgeois often functioned to underscore a conflict between more restrictive and more cosmopolitan and multicultural visions of national identity.

The final chapter examines what remains the most legendary of American Bohemias. The much-touted Bohemian "spirit" promised to defy geographic boundaries, even as it became increasingly identified with Greenwich Village. Here, many of the trends pioneered by earlier American Bohemias came to fruition. Negotiating between art and life, capital and labor, women and men, the modern and the genteel, the spiritual and the commercial, the Village popularized new forms of political activism, artistic expression, and "free love." Though variously contained and co-opted, the "spirit" of the Village nonetheless continues to inspire new countercultural visions and adventures.

From the basement at Pfaff's to the redwood forest of the Bohemian Grove, the cultural geography of Bohemia has occupied a vital intersection between the romantic and the real. Both a "real-and-imagined" place (in geographer Edward Soja's terms), Bohemia marks the crossroads between "the forms and patternings of 'real' material life" and the "mental and ideational worlds of abstract or 'imagined' spaces."[16] As such, Bohemia has offered its citizens (as it still offers its historians) an important site for the "encounter between geography and literary history"—a meeting that, as Sarah Blair has recently argued, "holds out the possibility for more intimate and more precise understandings of human praxis and of imaginative productions as social forces."[17] Because "living in Bohemia" was, by definition, an encounter between geography and literary history, *la vie bohème* helps us to think about how the categories of the mimetic, the material, and the imaginative continually inform one another. By complicating and defamiliarizing "traditional categories of US space and place, [including] nature, region, landscape, pastoral, the frontier,"[18] and even "America" itself, Bohemia offers a site from which to replot these territories, situating them along both national and transnational axes.

A mythic "republic within the republic," Bohemia provides a particularly useful standpoint for thinking outside the constraints of the American liberal consensus. Whether or not such a cultural position exists in American literary history remains controversial. In an influential argument, Sacvan Bercovitch maintains that the limitations of our classic American writers relate to their inability to imagine "perspectives radically other than those implicit in the vision of America": instead, "their works are characterized by an unmediated relation between the facts of American life and the ideals of liberal free enterprise." This study argues that for some American writers, "Bohemia" provided one form of mediation, however partial and limited. It was a realm within and without the United States where a "symbolic play between cultural options" could be performed.[19] Never admitting easy resolution, the dialectics of Bohemianism destabilize any reduction of the real to the ideal, the Bohemian to the Bourgeois, the ethnic to the national, the regional to the provincial, the gendered to the biological, or the aesthetic to the commercial. This book seeks to restore this complexity to the counterculture known and experienced as Bohemia.

Part I "Transplanted from the Mother Asphalt of Paris": Importing Bohemia, 1858–1870

William Dean Howells meeting Walt Whitman at Pfaff's. From William Dean Howells, *Literary Friends and Acquaintance* (New York: Harper and Brothers, 1900).

1

The "Vault at Pfaff's": Whitman, Bohemia, and the *Saturday Press*

The Bohemian cannot be called a useful member of society, and it is not an encouraging sign for us that the tribe has become so numerous among us as to form a distinct and recognizable class who do not object to being called by that name.

New York Times, January 6, 1858

Bohemia is a fairy land upon the hard earth. It is Arcadia in New York or London, in Paris or Rome. Hereabouts you may find it in painters' studios, and in the rooms of authors. Often enough its denizens are clad loosely—seedily, in the vulgate—and they are shaggy as to the head, with abounding hair. Whatever is not "respectable" they are. Respectability is the converse of the Bohemian idea. There are plenty of men among them worthy of respect—but none who are technically respectable. If they are the lees of society, as has been injuriously urged, then they are the richness which settles at the bottom of the cup. Respectability is the pale, thin, emasculated liquor that floats upon the surface and is easily seen through. Bohemia is the nimble essence, the fat substantiality, which "ascends me into the brain," and begets there glorious phantasies.

Harper's Monthly Magazine, 1859

THE YEARS PRECEDING THE CIVIL WAR witnessed many attempts to define the "Bohemian," the new urban type imported from Paris onto the streets of New York. Newspapers from New York to San Francisco reported the advent of an American Bohemia, and sought either to embrace or to censure the phenomenon. Yet, as columnists extolled the virtues or denounced the sins of the Bohemian, they also delineated the contours of that protean category: the American Bourgeois. Upheld or degraded as the antithesis of the Bohemian, the Bourgeois, further designated in mid-nineteenth-century America by such terms as "the respectable sort," the "Pharisee," and "Mrs. Grundy," was also undergoing a process of historical redefinition. Straining against and implicated within governing ideologies of class, race, gender, and nationality, Bohemianism provides an integral standpoint from which to view the development of American urban life and class formation. To discover the first self-identified American Bohemians is to explore the counterculture unstably contained within the national geography of bourgeois identity, consciousness, and expression.

The Bohemian-Bourgeois divide has long since entered the realm of the cliché, and it is a matter of course that "the style of life of a bourgeois" can "be set against that of an artist or an intellectual, representing order, social convention, sobriety and dullness in contrast to all that was seen as spontaneous, freer, gayer, more intelligent."[1] Yet the Bohemian-Bourgeois dichotomy quickly regains its interest and importance once we begin to specify its historical referents and identify the actors, passions, and ideologies that originally produced this well-known opposition. This history also reveals how the opposition first functioned—the types of social criticism, literary and artistic productions, and disparate lifestyles that the Bohemian-Bourgeois divide both enabled and curtailed.

Historicizing the Bohemian-Bourgeois divide, especially within the American context, requires the reconsideration of two opposing historiographical traditions that variously interpret the meaning of the bourgeoisie or the middle classes within the United States. On the one hand, the influential tradition known as the "consensus" model argues that the term "bourgeois" functions as a synonym for American culture at large; in Louis Hartz's words, "Americans, a kind of national embodiment of the concept of the bourgeoisie, have . . . rarely used that concept in their social thought," because a "triumphant middle class . . . can take itself for granted."[2] For the consensus scholar, then, the phrase "American bourgeois" is simply redundant. While acknowledging the reality of distinct classes throughout American history, subsequent commentators have preserved "consensus" as a crucial ideological category, emphasizing the extent to which the American political imaginary has depended upon an exceptionalist view of the nation's common "middle-classness"—defined "not as a relative position in the state but as an absolute state of mind," one ever open to individual aspiration and mobility.[3] On the other hand, recent studies of nineteenth-century America insist that, in Stuart Blumin's words, "however broad the bourgeois consensus may have been in comparison to European societies, it did not preclude the formation of distinct classes within American society."[4] Thus opposing consensus historiography, Blumin argues that "Americans diverged widely in their economic circumstances, and . . . they translated their economic differences into significant differences in life-style, outlook, and aspiration." For Blumin, then, "the [supposedly] all-encompassing American bourgeoisie . . . may well have been a class after all—the power of its values serving to reinforce rather than to destroy social class boundaries."[5]

These varying conceptions of the bourgeoisie in America focus the question of how the first American Bohemians defined their social antagonists: In their efforts to distinguish their own behavior from dominant social mores, did the first American Bohemians pitch themselves against an all-pervasive American bourgeoisie, or did they view the bourgeoisie as a distinct socioeconomic class? Did America itself function as the Bohemian antithesis, or did the Bohemians identify a particular class or classes as their foes? The Bohemians generally referred to their chosen nemesis as "respectability" or "humbuggery," and they alternately located the dreaded qualities of hypocrisy and respectability within the larger national culture *and* within specific social groupings that, during this period, were establishing themselves as either a haute bourgeoisie or an emerging middle class. Paradoxically enough, this developing class, especially in its upper reaches, often offended the Bohemians not because of its essential Americanness, but because it betrayed "American" ideals of democratic equality; in effect, the Bohemians sought to preserve (and contribute to) American "consensus" by challenging some of its most cherished social representatives. Though at times the nation itself appears in early Bohemian discourse as the ultimate bourgeois opponent, more often than not the Bohemians sought to defend their country from the socioeconomic dominance of its haute bourgeoisie, proposing themselves as the more appropriate heirs to the revolutionary tradition.

Specifying the objects of Bohemian rancor enables us to define how particular coteries of nineteenth-century American writers conceptualized bourgeois or "respectable" culture, and how they related it to their world and nation, to emerging class distinctions, and to questions of gender, race, and ethnicity. As the Bohemians elaborated their identities and staged their dissent, the opposition between the Bohemian and the Bourgeois occurred in multiple registers, and was often reconfigured as a conflict between radical individualism and reform movements, the public and the private, immigrants and nativists, the competing values of leisure and the Protestant work ethic, and even between the cities of New

York and Boston. Most crucially, the Bohemians spoke to tensions between the cosmopolitan and the national, the democratic and the elite. The shifting, overlapping terms of these various oppositions all amplify (and at times undermine) the Bohemian-Bourgeois divide and reveal its historical production: in so doing, these terms help expose both the ideological force and the limits of consensus. Ever critiquing and negotiating a range of often contradictory bourgeois values, the first U.S. Bohemians ambivalently located themselves within and without America.

Bohemia and "Myriad Rushing Broadway"

Bohemia's presence in an American metropolis suggested a double displacement, a cosmopolitan mixture of cultural styles. As such, Bohemia struck many early commentators as scandalously disrupting the integrity of the nation's bourgeois values. Almost as soon as the first group of self-identified American Bohemians began to congregate at Pfaff's saloon in 1858, the *New York Times* called attention to this threatening hybridity: that paper referred to the Bohemians as a "gipsy tribe" with a "loose and desultory nature," and in so doing highlighted the racialized origins of the Bohemian type.[6] The *Oxford English Dictionary* traces the English word "Bohemian" to a French usage that began in the fifteenth century when the gypsies (erroneously thought to have migrated from the central European kingdom of Bohemia) began to settle in regions of Western Europe.[7] It was not until the mid-nineteenth century, however, that Parisian artists first identified themselves with the gypsies and classified themselves with those who appeared "outside the law, beyond the reaches of society."[8] Indeed, it was not until Murger's popular musical *La Vie de Bohème* of 1849 that the term "Bohemian" achieved widespread currency as the appellation for idealistic, struggling artists and cultural outsiders. After Murger had popularized the term and extended its meanings, the gypsy or bohemian "race" continued to serve as the etymological, cultural, and even biological point of origin for artistic Bohemianism and its opposition to bourgeois life; similarly, the Parisian Latin Quarter beckoned as the quintessential Bohemian locale. To invoke Bohemia, then, necessarily conjured visions of gypsy life and its reinterpretation in Murger's Paris. This mythic realm, this cosmopolitan hybrid thus precariously positioned itself in the United States. For adherents, it intensified the nation's own (wavering) drive to embrace the nomad and transplant foreign traditions; for detractors, it threatened America's republican—as well as ethnic and racial—purity.

Bohemianism extended an earlier literary preoccupation with gypsy life as an alternative to a bourgeois society founded on state and individual property rights—and, contradictorily enough, with gypsy life as representative of the liberty idealized by bourgeois politics. This preoccupation alternately produced both repulsion and fascination, and if Enlightenment poets looked askance at the "vagabond and useless tribe" that remained "self-banish'd from society," preferring "squalid sloth to honourable toil," many Romantics admired "the gypsies' camp still free."[9] In the United States, the split between typical Enlightenment and Romantic responses reasserted itself in relation to Bohemian artists and writers—like the gypsies, artistic Bohemians were seen either as a threat to bourgeois values or as their purest expression. Thus, while the *Times* reasoned that participants in this latter-day "gipsy tribe" could not be called "useful member[s] of society," the first group of American Bohemians romantically celebrated their status as a free and independent "gypsy camp."[10] A "New Theory of Bohemians," published in the popular *Knickerbocker Magazine* in 1861, specifically invoked gypsy life as an inspiration for latter-day nonconformists in a ballad titled "Three Gypsies": "Three fold they showed me, as there they lay, / How those who take life in the true sense, / Fiddle it, smoke it, and sleep it away, / And trebly despise its nuisance."[11] Translated from a German ballad by a writer only tangentially acquainted with the "gypsy camp" at Pfaff's (he was none other than Charles Astor Bristed, the grandson of that quintessential self-made bourgeois, John Jacob Astor), this verse nonetheless expresses the traits that Bohemians typically valued in the gypsies: their allegedly free, noninstrumentalized existences and their pursuit of pleasure over and against the "nuisance" of a bourgeois work ethic.

Yet for the first American Bohemians, this cult of the gypsy was ever mediated by Murger and French Bohemian life. (Charles Astor Bristed was himself one of Murger's first English translators.)[12] Of course, Murger had maintained, with requisite chauvinism, "Bohemia only exists and is only possible in Paris."[13] Less than a decade after Murger penned these words, however, a group of American writers, painters, and actors assumed the mantle of Bohemianism and sought to create their own version of *la vie bohème*.[14] These Bohemians embraced and celebrated precisely the recalcitrant "Frenchness" of Bohemia as a way of distinguishing themselves, performing cultural criticism, and promoting an ideal cosmopolitanism. If the French artists who described themselves as Bohemians felt that they were opposing bourgeois routine, materialism, and mediocrity,

American Bohemians regarded themselves as doubly subversive. At a time and in a country in which France, with its "residual" aristocratic culture, was itself often associated with immorality, decadence, and vice, a sophisticated, French-inspired Bohemianism received the most vituperative attacks in the mainstream press.[15] Coupled with suggestions of an even more alien, gypsy lifestyle, the scandalous Frenchness of Bohemia further disturbed notions of a national, Anglo-American consensus.

The "loose and desultory" Bohemians of New York City first emerged in the late 1850s and clustered around Henry Clapp Jr., an iconoclast who had just returned from Paris with the idea of emulating *la vie bohème*, the mode of artistic and cultural life that he had encountered both on the streets of the Latin Quarter and through Murger's famous representations. In a complex and characteristically Bohemian convolution of life imitating art, of art imitating life, Clapp and his cronies sought to create their own Bohemia at Pfaff's saloon. Clapp seized upon Pfaff's because of its excellent coffee and beer and, most likely, because of its foreign ambiance. As one of the frequent "puffs" of the saloon printed in the Bohemians' own weekly paper, the *Saturday Press*, advertised, "this modest restaurant and Lager Beer saloon, at 647 Broadway, is extensively patronized by young literary men, artists and that large class of people called Germans."[16] Even more to the point, the poet Bayard Taylor noted that the saloon reminded him of a similar cellar in Leipzig and mused that the "mild potations of beer and the dreamy breath of cigars delayed the nervous, fidgety, clattering-footed American hours."[17] As Taylor indicates, Old World romance in the form of Pfaff's enabled the Bohemians to separate themselves from the time sequences of bourgeois life, here broadly equated with American national culture. Pfaff's delayed the realities of contemporary America, promoting the quintessential Bohemian goal of leisure in opposition to the dominant nineteenth-century work ethic.

Even when comically staged as an opposition between Pfaff's and the national marketplace, the Bohemian-Bourgeois divide only went so far. Pfaff's inaugurated the American Bohemian tradition of patronizing (sometimes in multiple senses of the word) "ethnic" restaurants and creating a symbiotic relationship. Clapp "puffed" Pfaff's, and Pfaff's extended generous credit. In this way, if the German beer cellar aided in the Bohemian fantasy of escape from bourgeois America, the Bohemians also helped this establishment to become commercially viable; in so doing, they also quite literally located and promoted *themselves* as cultural spectacles. To "delay" the "clattering-footed American hours" was not to negate or fully to transcend such time, but rather to bargain with it more effectively. Pfaff's thus helped facilitate the doubleness—the sense of being both within and without the dominant national culture—that Bohemia required. Indeed, the Bohemians—and the Bohemian character—of the region around Broadway and Bleecker became sufficiently well known for a guidebook to comment in 1869 on both their mystery and visibility:

The denizens of Bleecker Street are in the shadow. If the broad sunlight streamed upon them, something morally unpleasant might be discovered. It more resembles some of the streets in Paris than any other in New York. It is the haunt of ultra Bohemians of both sexes. . . . No street is more thoroughly cosmopolitan, more philosophic, more romantic. It is the Great City in miniature. . . . A walk through it any day, from Eighth avenue to the Bowery, will convey to an observer and man of the world, much of its hidden meaning. He will see strange characters and strange places that he does not notice elsewhere. A certain free and easy air will strike him as pervading the houses and shops and people.[18]

One William Winter, a drama critic, poet, and sometime editor of the *Saturday Press*, further reveals the spectacular design of the Bohemian's self-staging in his memoirs, highlighting Bohemia's complicated position within the American marketplace. "Beneath the sidewalk of Broadway," Winter dramatically recounts, "there was a sort of cave, in which was a long table, and after Henry Clapp had assumed the sceptre as Prince of Bohemia, that table and cave were pre-empted by him and his votaries, at certain hours of the day and night, and no stranger ventured to intrude into the magic realm."[19] Winter's recollection points to the Romantic myth the Bohemians strove to embody. They were not merely struggling artists but Bohemians, and as such elaborated a new, somewhat mysterious, artistic identity that mediated between that of established "men of letters" and the less "respectable" penny press journalists and popular performers. Further attesting to the Romanticism evoked by the beer cellar, the journalist Charles T. Congdon states that the low ceilings, stone walls, and stacks of barrels reminded him of Auerbach's Cellar in *Faust*.[20]

Yet, qualifying this Romanticism, Winter also notes that "most of [these writers] were poor and poorly paid."[21] They struggled to make a living through journalism while they pursued other more "literary" works. Such hardships only seem to have made the Bohemian identity all the more inviting, however, glamorizing and endowing a sense of purpose to a life that might otherwise have been experienced as an American Grub

Street.[22] For the writers and performers clustered at Pfaff's, Bohemianism emerged in part as a mode of self-promotion and of solidifying their fledgling and insecure social and artistic statuses. As Winter's and other accounts suggest, part of this identity was bound up with an international Romantic cult of the medieval. Even as they poised themselves to take advantage of new literary markets in the Midwest and to pioneer new marketing techniques (or perhaps as one of the means by which they marketed themselves), the Bohemians harkened back to a premodern vision of community, to a feudal realm replete with votaries and a Prince of Bohemia. However playful and ironic they might have been, such cults enacted the Bohemians' characteristically ambivalent relation to bourgeois America and to the cultural position of its writers.

The precarious position of Bohemia within and without the national marketplace is also the subject of Walt Whitman's own unfinished poem about Pfaff's. Drawing on the saloon's literal location within the urban geography, Whitman describes: "The vault at Pfaff's where the drinkers and laughers meet to eat and drink and carouse, / While on the walk immediately overhead, pass the myriad feet of Broadway / As the dead in their graves, are underfoot hidden."[23] Wielding the most absolute of binaries, life and death, Whitman goes on to describe a communal underground world that—however decadent, removed from and disregarded by the dominant culture—serves as a paradoxically vital antithesis to the "living" inhabitants of the city who rush above. In ghostly form, the vault at Pfaff's safeguards the values for which "America" ostensibly stands but that the commercial marketplace denies.

The vault at Pfaff's—"the capital of Bohemia"—regularly accommodated (or incited) those variously estranged from a settled bourgeois or American existence. According to one patron, this Bohemia offered itself as "the trysting place of the most careless, witty, and jovial spirits of New York—journalists, artists, and poets."[24] Many of these Bohemians wrote for, or illustrated, *Vanity Fair*, *Harper's*, the *New York Leader*, and the *Saturday Press*, which became the house organ of the circle. The New York Bohemians included, among many other writers, artists, and stage performers, the author Fitz-James O'Brien, an Irish immigrant who wrote Poesque horror stories; Fitz-Hugh Ludlow, author of "the Hashish Eater," a book David Reynolds calls "the most bizarre work by a nineteenth century American";[25] and as mentioned, Whitman, who, though long a canonical writer of the "American Renaissance," was regarded as "one of the most indecent writers who ever raked out filth into sentences" by many of his contemporaries.[26] Such eventual mainstays of the "genteel tradition" as Thomas Bailey Aldrich, E. C. Stedman, Bayard Taylor, and R. H. Stoddard (all particularly influential in the postbellum years) occasionally joined the circle; they did not fully embrace *la vie bohème* (some later tried to disassociate themselves from Pfaff's), yet in their antipathy toward bourgeois materialism they helped to define the genteel Bohemianism that would come into fashion in the 1870s and 1880s.[27] Also fraternizing with the writers and artists at the beer cellar were German immigrants, medical students, and, according to the *New York Times*, a number of "unemployed doctors and blighted lawyers" (ruined in the wake of the Panic of 1857)—as well as, via Whitman, a group of working-class stagecoach drivers.[28] Several women also frequented Pfaff's and viewed themselves as Bohemians. Female Pfaffians included Ada Clare, essayist, novelist, and actress who was perhaps best known for her notorious love affair with the pianist and Byronic sex symbol Louis Gottschalk. This affair resulted in an illegitimate son whom Clare then brandished in the face of conventional mores. Another famed female Bohemian was Adah Isaacs Menken, a sometime poet and successful actress who, in 1860, achieved international fame as the star of a melodrama in which, in the last scene, clad in flesh-colored tights, she rode into the horizon lashed to the back of a horse.[29] Yet it was chiefly Clapp who set the tone for the group and created a self-conscious Bohemian spirit. Explaining Clapp's charisma, Winter notes: "He was wayward and erratic; but he possessed both the faculty of taste and the instinctive love of beauty and essentially, he was the apostle of the freedom of thought."[30]

These qualities also determined the mood of the *Saturday Press,* the paper Henry Clapp started in 1858 and that, due to financial difficulties, only lasted until 1860 (save for a brief reappearance in 1865). Within the *Saturday Press*, Bohemian "freedom of thought" often translated into a scathing critique of what the Pfaffians took to be one of the central banes of bourgeois existence: humbuggery. "The purpose of *The Saturday Press* was to speak the truth," Winter remembers, "and to speak it in a way that would amuse its readers and would cast ridicule upon as many as possible of the humbugs then extant and prosperous in literature and art."[31] Promising to see beneath deceptive appearances and uncover social contradictions, the paper helped to popularize notions of Bohemianism and its position within American culture; it circulated throughout the country, and though it never acquired a broad subscription base, the *Press* was sufficiently influential for William Dean Howells to say that at the time, it "represented New York literature to my imagination" and "embodied the new literary life of the city."[32]

However "new," this literary life both extended and rejected earlier traditions of American reform. Alternately representative of the proto-Bohemian and the restrictive Bourgeois, antebellum reform movements allow us to chart the position of the first American Bohemia more precisely within the temporal and ideological "borders of bourgeois life."

From Reform to Bohemia

Whitman and Clapp provide direct links between antebellum reform and Bohemia. Before entering Bohemia, Whitman produced several temperance writings, and Clapp lectured and wrote on behalf of Abolitionism, Temperance, Fourierism, and Free Love. The transformations occurring between their earlier reform efforts and their later Bohemianism help to underscore the social energies that the later phenomenon both absorbed and counteracted.

Antebellum reform enjoyed widespread popularity and reflected a growing uneasiness about recent social, political, geographic, and economic dislocations. Industrialization, growing class divisions, Manifest Destiny, Evangelical Protestantism, urbanization, mass immigration, a transportation revolution, slavery, and sectional conflict, as well as the vagaries of party politics, all transformed the country and left many confused about their own social positions and moral directions.[33] Of all antebellum reform movements, Temperance enjoyed the broadest popularity and served as one of the more pivotal, and ironic, preconditions of American Bohemianism. To a large extent, Temperance served to reinforce rather than to oppose bourgeois values, particularly those of the emerging evangelically oriented middle class. The Temperance movement enjoyed two waves of enthusiastic support: first in the early 1830s, under the bourgeois leadership of the evangelical American Temperance Society, and again in the early 1840s with the advent of the working- and lower-middle-class Washingtonian movement. The earlier, elite-based organization operated in a hierarchical, top-down fashion, linking temperance, bourgeois respectability, and social control; it played on upper- and middle-class fears of becoming proletarianized by alcohol consumption—whether as a result of the bourgeoisie's own drinking or through the specter of an unruly, drunken working class.[34] The Washingtonians relied on similar themes of self-control and extolled bourgeois domesticity and individual responsibility, but as several commentators have noted, their discourse was double-edged, also exploring a "range of counter-discourses of perverse, orgiastic sexuality, morbid sentimentality, and the cultivation of loafing rather than utilization of the self as a marketable commodity."[35] Whereas the earlier Temperance Society's meetings had been devoted to addresses by doctors and clergymen who preached the virtues of temperance, the Washingtonians inaugurated evangelistic "experience meetings" in which the members announced themselves as reformed drunkards and recounted, often with titillating detail, their former battles with the bottle, or, in the words of one contemporary critic, their "spicy narratives of drunken orgies."[36] Such narratives, uttered in the context of a working-class movement, disturbed the very bourgeois ethos Temperance allegedly consolidated, and genteel response to the Washingtonians foreshadowed later critical views of Bohemianism.

Henry Clapp and Walt Whitman both wrote for the Washingtonian movement in the 1840s, and Whitman's temperance writings represent the sort of "return of the repressed" counterdiscourse that adumbrated his later Bohemianism. Two such publications were Whitman's novel *Franklin Evans* (1842) and the story "The Madman," both written on commission by the New York Washingtonians. The subject of both works was the emerging male subculture of the cities, a subculture that helped to determine the shape of American Bohemianism. Because industrial expansion forced more and more young men to relocate in cities, and because the decline in the apprenticeship system created what the reformers termed a new class of "masterless" young men, the boardinghouse, the saloon, and the brothel emerged as potentially dangerous sites of degenerate behavior and were targeted by both genteel and working-class reformers.[37] Like the reformist tracts, Whitman's novel and story ostensibly elaborated the evils of drink, but, like the "experience meetings," they also turned into something resembling the opposite—"a gloating over the details of vice."[38] Indeed, as Michael Warner demonstrates, Whitman progressively revised temperance out of *Franklin Evans*; when he republished the novel in his own paper, the *Brooklyn Daily Eagle*, he dropped Franklin's final conversion to the total abstinence pledge, and changed references to "drunkenness" to the more generalized term, "dissipation."[39] Still, it was in the context of Temperance that Whitman first developed a space in which to explore, via the medium of print, the world of New York nightlife, a world scandalously removed from bourgeois ideals of domestic security. Upon entering a saloon, Franklin declares: "Oh fatal pleasure! . . . Never in my life [was I] engaged in such a scene of pleasure." Later, though with more ostensible disgust, Whitman describes the goings-on in a boarding-house:

> A wretched scene! Half a dozen men, just entering the busy scenes of life, not one of us over twenty-five years, and there we were, benumbing our faculties, and confirming ourselves in practices which ever too surely bring the scorn of the world. . . . It is a terrible sight . . . to know the blood is being poisoned, and the bloom banished from the cheek, and the lustre of the eye dimmed, and all for a few hours' sensual gratification.[40]

These symptoms—the dimmed eye, ominous pallor, and poisoned blood—stand out as signs of drunkenness, but they were also associated with onanism in the contemporary sexual purity movement; and onanism, Michael Moon reminds us, not only signified autoeroticism, but "stood for a whole range of emergent social forms of male autonomy, including male homosexuality."[41]

This discourse also informs Whitman's most direct statement about Bohemianism, and as in his temperance writing, onanism threatens the bourgeois ideals that Whitman purportedly advocates. In September 1858, at the beginning of his tenure at Pfaff's, Whitman editorializes in the *Brooklyn Daily Times*: "We suspect that the reason why so many literary men make bad husbands, and do not properly appreciate the softer sex, arises from the infection of 'Bohemianism' by which most authors become tainted in their introduction into the literary guild; and which creates a restless craving for mental excitement unsuiting them to breathe the clear and tranquil atmosphere of home enjoyment."[42] By the time Whitman eulogized Pfaff's in his unpublished poem of 1860, however, his Bohemians were free from the taint of onanism: "Beam up—brighten up bright eyes of beautiful young men," Whitman writes, thereby distinguishing the brightly ascendant Pfaffians from the young men of *Franklin Evans* whose eyes exhibit that telltale "dimmed lustre."[43] It was also in 1860, near the end of his patronage of Pfaff's, that Whitman added the "Calamus" and "Children of Adam" poems to *Leaves of Grass*, and further divested his vision of homosociality and eroticism from signs of disease.

When Whitman wrote of his desire "To tell the secret of my nights and days, / To celebrate the need of comrades" in the 1860 edition of *Leaves*, he was spending most of his nights and meeting most of his comrades at Pfaff's.[44] Reminiscing about his Bohemian days, Whitman told Horace Traubel that Henry Clapp was "always loyal—always very close to me—in that particular period—there in New York," and added, "We were very intimate at one time."[45] Similarly, Whitman's letters refer to the "sparkle" a group of young men called the Fred Grey Association lent to Pfaff's, and mention numerous other men he hobnobbed with in the beer cellar. A letter from his close friend and possible lover Fred Vaughn, a New York stagecoach driver, also specifies Pfaff's as a favorite meeting place,[46] and this companionship may inform the contentment described in "Calamus" no. 29:

> One flitting glimpse, caught through an interstice,
> Of a crowd of workmen and drivers in a bar-room, around the
> stove, late of a winter night—And I unremarked, seated in a corner;
> Of a youth who loves me, and whom I love, silently
> approaching, and seating himself near, that he may hold me
> by the hand;
> A long while, amid the noises of coming and going—of drinking and
> oath and smutty jest,
> There we two, content, happy in being together, speaking
> little, perhaps not a word.
>
> (371)

Just as "Two Vaults" juxtaposes the interior of Pfaff's with the exterior of "myriad rushing Broadway," so does "Calamus" no.29 reinforce the distinction between a privileged inner realm (located in, and figured as, a barroom) and a cold exterior (the poem is set on a wintry night). The "split subject-position"[47] of the poem furthers this divide, briefly aligning the reader's perspective with the "one flitting glimpse, caught through an interstice," and then with the intensified emotional responsiveness of the "unremarked" first-person speaker. Such splitting ultimately protects the "I" from the voyeuristic moralizing that Whitman had himself advanced in his 1858 editorial, and, after the completion of the "flitting glimpse," the poem concentrates on a loving, "adhesive" immediacy.

Beyond blocking the anti-onanist gaze, the poem complicates the 1858 editorial by eschewing the opposition between tranquil feminine domesticity and feverish male Bohemianism. Despite the "noises of coming and going—of drinking and oath and smutty jest," the poem conjures a prototypically domestic scene centering on the warmth of a stove. That this scene happens to take place in a bar challenges the logic of separate domestic and public spheres, as well as the dichotomous gender identities such spaces allegedly fostered. The poem thus answers critics who (like

Whitman himself) complained that "our boarding-house system of living" offered "very little to make the fireside attractive" and threatened to turn men into "undomesticated animals."[48] To so question the divide between the public and the private was to disrupt the foundations of contemporary bourgeois discourse more fully than Washingtonian doubleness. At a time when shifts in the urban economy—including the decline of family farms and artisanal production, the growth of nonmanual, proto–white-collar jobs, the rise of the factories—increasingly moved male occupations from the home into the public marketplace, and concurrently inspired upper- and middle-class women to develop a complementary (and sometimes oppositional) realm of morally elevating and nurturing domesticity, the notion of "separate spheres" proved the linchpin of bourgeois identity, for men and women alike.[49] Severing the public from the private, the ideology of separate spheres also sought to locate love and romantic attachment more firmly within the bourgeois, normatively heterosexual home. Whitman's earlier editorial scandalously posits Bohemian sociability as the antithesis of such "home enjoyment," but by invoking a domesticated barroom his poem even more thoroughly unsettles the boundaries between the public and the private, men and women, the homosocial and the erotic, and even the Bohemian and the Bourgeois.

Whitman's exchange of Temperance for Bohemianism enabled a greater acceptance of homoeroticism and a more thorough rethinking of bourgeois norms. Resisting a straightforwardly progressive narrative development, the relation between Henry Clapp's early politics and his later Bohemianism was more complicated and oblique: To a degree, Bohemianism seems to have represented a disillusioned turn for Clapp, and he often used Bohemianism to articulate an agonized "politics of anti-politics."[50] Still, much continuity existed between his earlier visions of reform and his Bohemianism.

Like Whitman, Clapp wrote for the Washingtonian movement in the 1840s, but while Whitman's transition toward Bohemianism was foreshadowed by his "dark-temperance" rhetoric, Clapp manifested no paradoxical signs of reveling in the very behaviors he would oppose. With evangelical zeal, Clapp concluded his address to the "mass meeting of Suffolk, Norfolk, Plymouth and Bristol County Washingtonians," declaring: "We feel it is good to be engaged in such a cause . . . and more than at any other time can we enter upon it when our hearts are warm with the spirit of our holy religion." The future imbiber of Pfaff's beer further asserts, "Anyone who persists in an occupation which saps the foundation of public morals, is an enemy to his race. That the man who sells intoxicating liquors as a drink is engaged in such an occupation, he does not himself deny."[51]

If Clapp's reform writing unambiguously embraces Temperance, it nevertheless has other hallmarks of his later Bohemianism. With shades of his Bohemian cosmopolitanism, Clapp cheers advances in transportation that are "drawing the heart of men more nearly together and release men from the thralldom of 'state lines' and national prejudices" and that "lessen the distance between the Old World and the New."[52] Similarly present is his continuing antipathy to Bostonian elites, those he eventually regarded as the ultimate exemplars of the dreaded bourgeois ethos. Describing the Washingtonian Jubilee of May 1844 on Boston Common, Clapp announces that the "Boston politicians, clergymen, and 'world-lings' must feel ashamed that so mighty a battle has been fought, and they have been worse than Tories."[53] His later critique of the institution of marriage and unequal property laws, revealed in such combative statements as "I look on marriage as the upshot and catastrophe of civilization,"[54] is also present in the pointedly titled free love pamphlet, *Husband vs. Wife*.[55] And in an essay entitled "Self-Reliance," Clapp voices the contempt for organized politics that will become one of the mantras of his later *Saturday Press*: "Sign no creeds; bind yourself to no constitutions, choose to yourself no kings or Presidents; submit your judgment to no committees; engage in no political tactics; and submit to no party, congressional or (for they are all of a piece) constabular discipline."[56] Voiced within the context of the antislavery movement, these words constituted a "politics of antipolitics." Clapp was presumably following the tactics of prominent abolitionists like William Lloyd Garrison who, in the late 1830s, embraced a "no-government" philosophy and urged abolitionists to abstain from voting or otherwise participating in a corrupt political system.[57] Clapp too was willing to renounce the Union if it would halt the spread of slavery, dramatically stating, "I say if the Union cannot stand except upon the necks of these millions of men and women, let it fall. Such a Union is a covenant with death and an agreement with hell."[58]

How did Clapp's abolitionist Christian anarchism translate into Bohemianism during the course of the intervening decade? To be sure, certain principles, such as those sketched in his "Self-Reliance," continued to inform his writing—with the significant omission of any extended discussion of slavery. David Reynolds characterizes Clapp's Bohemianism as being "without political direction," consisting of an iconoclastic, desperate individualism that involved "kicking off political authority and living for the moment" and "standing for little besides a love of fine coffee, strong liquor, and lively repartee." In sum, Reynolds concludes that their "carefree, carpe diem attitude showed that fifties individualism had sunk toward anarchic decadence."[59] This assessment, as we will see, discounts the extent to which the *Saturday Press* upheld Clapp's earlier commitments to women's rights and free love, and advanced many other political stances made in the paradoxical spirit of antipolitics.

Yet it is true that at least on paper, the Bohemians virtually ignored slavery, the most pressing issue of the day, and, taking antipolitics to the extreme, even went so far as to repudiate existing forms of antislavery agitation. After Lincoln's 1860 election, the *Saturday Press* editorialized, "We are opposed to slavery of every kind, but we are even more opposed to what is stupidly called anti-slavery, for the simple reason that it has no distinct aim or purpose, and consists of nothing but a series of noisy and unmeaning howls." As for Lincoln, in the *Press*'s cynical estimation, he "merely used the Negro as a stepping-stone to power, and is now ready to kick him aside, and let him go to the devil."[60] And Clapp, the man who had once declared that "Slaveholding is a sin, and like all sin, should be immediately abolished; nowhere in the Scriptures . . . do I find anything said of 'gradual' repentance or gradual reform,"[61] went on to publish an article from the New York Ethnological Society that maintained: "The most conflicting of human acts and influences do not interrupt the progress of natural laws." The law in question was supply and demand, and the article insisted that slavery would wither away only with the development of alternative sources of labor and resources. In a strange fusion of Romanticism, laissez-faire economics, and Shakespearean drama, the article asserted that "notwithstanding our political and cultural machinery, it is Nature that shapes our ends, bend and rough-hue [*sic*] them as we will."[62]

Appeals to supposed natural laws often occur at times of growing cynicism about the possibilities of contemporary human agencies, and the 1850s certainly proved disillusioning to many antebellum reformers. Rampant government corruption and political compromises led to fears of a "slaveholding conspiracy," and increasing class divisions as well as infighting (often class-based) within reform organizations dampened faith in the possibility of a harmonious America or ruling bourgeois consensus. The financial Panic of 1857 further eroded faith in the country. As a *Saturday Press* editorial (likely written by Clapp) phrased it, "Somehow, the age seems pretty much resolved to do its own moving. It is more and more inclined to look upon all organized and official attempts to move it with suspicion."[63] Even Whitman, the former spokesman for the Democratic and Free Soil parties, declared: "We want no reforms, no institutions, no parties—we want a living principle as nature has, under which nothing can go wrong—this must be vital through the U.S."[64]

Unsurprisingly, since Bohemianism was a distinctively urban phenomenon, the "nature" to which it appealed was a Romantic human nature. Echoing the title and thesis of Emerson's own essay, Clapp's early reformist tract titled "Self-Reliance" emphasized the "unfaltering reliance on one's highest convictions and purest instincts." For the Bohemian Clapp, however, the "purest of instincts" did not demand an "unnatural ascetic[ism]." It was here that Clapp parted company with the famous American Romantics, Emerson and Thoreau, who felt, in Emerson's words, that "the sublime vision comes to the pure and simple soul in a clean and chaste body."[65] Seeking to retain kinship with the other Romantics, however, one *Saturday Press* article noted that Bohemia was simply an urban variant within a larger framework of "vagabondage": "If [the vagabond] lives in the country, he will love Nature and be sober like Thoreau; if in the city, he will drink beer and perhaps see other than painted Bacchantes."[66] Urban "vagabonds," the Pfaffians espoused a more decadent Bohemianism over and against the forebodings of our "lugubrious advisors" as a way of expressing "natural laws": "There is enough yet to do before the world becomes perfect, and to further that end, the best way is to give free scope to the development of human nature, such as it was wisely created."[67]

Valuing self-development over asceticism, Clapp thus located Bohemia at the intersection of several overlapping yet distinct bourgeois discourses. He pitched himself against the bourgeois molds of the moralizing evangelical and the abstemious, self-restrained individual—but espoused another, namely the cultivation of free subjectivity, or in the *Press*'s own formulation, the "force of Nature in mankind."[68] It is because of similar tensions *within* the category of the bourgeois that Jerrold Seigel argues that French Bohemia "grew up where the borders of bourgeois existence were murky and uncertain."[69] Yet, like Seigel, we must be careful when we label different types of discourse "bourgeois" not to seek to create an homology between them; indeed, one of the reasons that the term "Bohemian" gained its initial force was that it helped distinguish those who would give "free scope to the development of human nature" from those who emphasized strict conformity and self-control. Like the Bohemians themselves, contemporary critics were quick to recognize this Bohemian difference.

The Bohemian and the Sunday Papers

The *Saturday Press* devoted considerable space to articulating its vision of Bohemianism. Many of these manifestos were written in response to the depictions of Bohemianism advanced by contemporary "Sunday Papers" like the *New York Times*, and reveal the extent to which Bohemianism self-consciously defined itself against the opposition of a bourgeois press dedicated to cataloguing urban types and assessing their relation to desirable social norms.[70] At a time when cities, and especially New York City, were expanding at an unprecedented rate, encompassing growing immigrant populations and seeing class divisions widen, journalists increasingly contrived to expose such urban "mysteries" as Bowery B'hoy, the "high life," "life among the lowly," and "the Great Bear of Wall Street."[71] Bohemia quickly emerged as another urban phenomenon inspiring interpretation and critique, and as we have seen papers like the *Times* editorialized against this "loose and desultory" group almost as soon as the Pfaffians began to congregate. Elucidating their opposing commitments, the ensuing dialogue did much toward fortifying the division between the Bohemians and their bourgeois antagonists.

The Pfaffians contributed a series of columns to the popular *Harper's Weekly* in the winter of 1858 as part of their campaign to justify and promote their Bohemianism. The columns' prominent position on the third page of one of the first widely circulated periodicals in itself argued against Bohemian marginalization, and strove to gain attention and respect for *la vie bohème*. Entitled "Bohemian Walks and Talks," this series addressed the social status of the Bohemian, and as it elaborated the Bohemian typology and its relation to bourgeois life an inchoate class analysis further emerged. *Harper's* explicitly addressed the *New York Times*'s editorial, ultimately contesting the very terms of the *Times*'s conclusions. When the *Times* claimed that "the Bohemian cannot be called a useful member of society,"[72] its judgment expressed the morals of a culture still dominated by republican aspiration and the Protestant work ethic—by the belief, in the words of a fictional Yankee hero, that "this trifling away of time when there is so much to be done . . . is inconsistent with that principle of being useful, which every republican ought to cherish."[73] Further, despite the liberalization of Protestant theology in the nineteenth century, historian Daniel T. Rodgers demonstrates that "the ascetic injunctions of the Protestant ethic retained and multiplied their force in the mid-nineteenth century."[74] Such moralizing increased as the North distinguished itself from the antebellum South in the years preceding the Civil War, and further stigmatized leisure with the taint of aristocratic pretension; as Rodgers contends, "the work ethic radiated . . . from all the institutional fortresses of the middle class"[75] and was codified by the churches, the schools, and genteel magazines and newspapers like the *Times*. The Panic of 1857 gave further impetus to the ideology of work, and to a suspicion of overextended credit and unsound speculation. According to the *New York Times*, Bohemia expressed and recapitulated the very conditions of the Panic itself; not only did it harbor "unemployed doctors and blighted lawyers" and those whose "special aversion is work," but it encouraged its affiliates to be "perfectly reckless as to money, and decidedly given to debt." Additionally, the Bohemian was responsible for his or her own condition: "With talent enough to gain wealth and reputation, he must always live next door to beggary."[76] As representatives of, and contributors to, a depressed economy, the Bohemians thus threatened the integrity of bourgeois America; resisting Discipline and Thrift, they were an enactment or parody of the bourgeois economy gone awry.

Harper's "Bohemian Walks and Talks" defends "the distinguished confraternity of Bohemians in this city" against such a characterization. Extending this confraternity to the likes of Dumas, Gautier, Dickens, and even Shakespeare, the *Harper's* Bohemian asks, "Have these men shown any aversion to work?" and maintains that "the simple difference between the Bohemian worker and other workers is that the former takes, sometimes, rather odd hours in which to do his work."[77] If this defense accepts the value of work as a given, another column mounts a more direct protest against the very foundation of the work ethic: "And when we are sufficiently civilized to recognize the golden mean between the idolatry of labor and the idolatry of sloth, perhaps we shall return to the simple acknowledgment that labor is not an end but a means."[78] The *Saturday Press* also endorsed this critique of the work ethic, partially opposing the doctrine of usefulness with a belief in the "fruitfulness of idleness" and reveries like George Arnold's "Cui Bono": "A harmless fellow, wasting useless days / Am I: I love my comfort and my leisure / Let those who wish them, toil for gold and praise, / To me, this summer-day brings more pleasure."[79]

Further elaborating this idealized "golden mean" between the idolatry of labor and sloth, the *Press* excerpted Balzac's *Treatise upon the Life of Elegance*. In this work, Balzac posits the "poetic and vagabondish romance of Bohemia" as the ideal medium between the "Life of Occupation" and the aristocratic "Life of Elegance." The Bohemian artist is the beneficiary of this ideal and is one for whom "his laziness is labor and his labor repose."[80] Glossing this text, Pierre Bourdieu has argued that the *Treatise* acts as a "performative" statement, one that, "under the guise of saying what is" aims to make the life of art (specifically its conjunctions between work and play, lower- and upper-class life) into "one of the fine arts," and to equate such art with "this new social entity": Bohemia.[81] Excerpting Balzac's *Treatise*, the Pfaffians implicitly hoped that this Ur-Bohemian text could perform similar cultural work within the context of the *Saturday Press* and unsettle reigning distinctions between work and leisure, along with related class-bound expectations. Able to exchange intersecting signifiers of class position, work, and idleness, the Balzacian artist "puts on, according to whim, the laborer's smock, or decides on the tail coat worn by the man of fashion."[82] Class position, the privilege of leisure, and the necessity of work become, for the ideal Bohemian, a matter of individual agency. The Bohemian artist is, in effect, the self-made man *par excellence*—but rather than representing middle-class aspiration and mobility, Balzac's "golden mean" seeks to put the artist quite literally in a class by himself.

This positioning of Bohemia as a liminal (but not explicitly middle-class) space between the aristocrat and the worker further explains the animus of the *Times*, and no doubt complicated contemporary attempts to position the Bohemian according to social class. On one level, the *Times* raised the specter of a Bohemian *lower* class, analogous to Marx's description of French Bohemians as "ruined and adventurous offshoots of the bourgeoisie."[83] Stressing Bohemian debtorship, the *Times* also noted that this new urban type was "not far removed" from the "loafer." And a "loafer," a *Times* editorial from 1856 specified, resided in the working-class neighborhood of the Bowery, refusing to cultivate "useful" behavior.[84] Such an association may well have satisfied the poet who would "loaf and invite [his] soul," and who "sometimes amused [himself] with picturing out a nation of loafers,"[85] but, in the context of the *Times* editorial, it impugned Bohemianism's proximity to New York street culture and its pursuit of a more relaxed and reflective existence.[86] Conversely, the *Times* also questioned the Bohemian's proximity to the loafer's would-be socioeconomic antithesis: the aristocrat.

Articulating the republican and specifically Northern distrust of aristocratic manners, the *Times* objected to Bohemia's liminal social status, and in particular to its pseudo-aristocratic, dandified posturings. "Refined and artistic," the *Times*'s Bohemians "are seductive in their ways, and they hold the finest sentiments, and have a distinct aversion to anything that is low or mean, or common and inelegant." Rather than condoning such behavior, the *Times*, as we have seen, rejected it with recourse to the bourgeois standard of usefulness. Not only did the Bohemians renounce the work ethic and help foster the conditions of economic collapse, but their threat to bourgeois life lay in their alleged adherence to aristocratic tastes. Indeed, the *Times*'s critique of Bohemian refinement, leisure, and debtorship echoed many early postrevolutionary republican diatribes against aristocratic gentility: "A man who has been bred a gentleman cannot work, . . . and therefore lives by borrowing without intending to pay, or upon the public or his friends. . . . His hands and his legs are often as useless to him as if they were paralytic."[87]

Fitz-James O'Brien was the Bohemian most likely to inspire comparisons to both the working-class loafer and the aristocratic dandy. O'Brien alternately performed different class identities. An Irishman with "expensive tastes and already settled habits of extravagance," O'Brien would often aspire to the role of a social "aristocrat," spending his paycheck at Delmonico's even when he "lived nowhere in particular" and was "thoroughly well acquainted with hard times."[88] Alternatively, on occasion, O'Brien assumed a proletarianized stance, picketing *Harper's* when the magazine denied him a twenty-five dollar advance, and wielding a sign stating, "One of *Harper's* authors. I am starving."[89] He was, in effect, an individual embodiment of that constant threat to bourgeois life: the boom-and-bust economy.

Other Bohemians also identified with the loafer, the worker, and the aristocrat as part of their critique of bourgeois life and its ideology of work, using these different figures to expose the failure of their culture to recognize (and adequately reward) the labor of writers and artists. As César Graña has argued, the mythos of Bohemia allowed writers to "retain the mystical glamour of aristocracy as the source of a special cultural legitimacy," especially, of course, in France.[90] The Pfaffians hoped that their identification with Bohemian Paris would foster this legitimacy.

Along with Balzac's *Treatise*, the Pfaffians also translated Balzac's *Prince of Bohemia*, an account of a dispossessed aristocrat, and to a point such a characterization undergirded the Pfaffians' own imagined relation to bourgeois culture.[91] In another time or place, the Bohemians implied, they would have received the patronage that they deserved. If they sometimes represented themselves as part of an intellectual proletariat, their alternate pose as quasi aristocrats only served to emphasize the injustice of their precarious social position. They were dispossessed of a history they never had.

Nonetheless, the aristocratic dandy generally remained a distinct type in the contemporaneous catalogue of urban personalities, as well as in most Bohemian self-representations (and self-defenses). On occasion, the two personae merged. For example, despite Whitman and the Bohemians' penchant for the loafer, the frontispiece of the 1860 edition of *Leaves of Grass*, published during Whitman's period as a Pfaffian, imaged the poet not as the working-class rough of the 1855 edition, but as an elegantly dressed, well coifed, almost dandified presence. Similarly, the Bohemian of "Bohemian Walks and Talks" describes his experiences "flaning" on Broadway with an aspiring man of fashion. Yet, if united in the experience of flaning, the Bohemian and the dandy remain separate figures within the column. Designated as "Asterik," the dandy functions as a kind of "asterisk" or reference mark (for the missing aristocracy?) whose very name denotes an absurd absence of substance. Further, this dandy "does nothing but smoke pipes and read French novels, which he conceives to be the whole duty of man." In effect, this Bohemian ultimately echoes the *Times*'s critique of useless activity, yet he deflects this criticism by offering, and distinguishing himself from, a worthier target.[92]

While eschewing the Dandy's antidemocratic elitism, the Bohemians repeatedly used their multiple class affiliations to bolster their effort to expose and critique "distinctions of class." In his "Ethnography of the Street," the *Harper's* Bohemian archly observes that there are "as many distinctions among bagages [*sic*] as among persons": there is, for example, a "low order," a "patrician," an "aristocratic" and "shabby-genteel" trunk. The Bohemian observer then castigates the owner of the latter trunk for his cruel behavior toward his black servant, implicitly suggesting that such racist brutality serves to bolster the tenuous class identity conveyed by the hyphenated term "shabby-genteel."[93] Another *Saturday Press* article bemusedly asks, "What is an American Lady?"—ironically highlighting the confusion that attended emerging class distinctions. The disingenuousness of the author dramatizes her rhetorical point:

I would like an answer as soon as possible, because our minister, Mr. Hyde, last Sunday requested the "ladies" of his congregation to meet him this week to devise means for spreading the gospel among the "laboring classes" of his parish, and I wish to know if I am expected as a lady to attend the call, or if I am one of the "laboring classes" to whom the gospel is to be brought.[94]

As such articles imply, the Bohemians questioned the existence of an American bourgeois or republican consensus that obviated differences of social class, and they frequently anatomized the signs of social position. In so doing, they upheld Bohemianism's multiple, even mutually exclusive class references as a means toward the transcendence of class divisions—and ultimately toward the creation of that essentially classless America that the nation's bourgeois ideology prematurely celebrated.

At times, however, the Bohemians presented their socioeconomic indecipherability, as well as their disdain for the dominant work ethic, in a more sinister fashion. Indeed, O'Brien—who reportedly liked "to appear not to work at all" and who would "saunter down town as if time-killing were his only object in life"[95]—critiqued the Bohemian persona more scathingly than any Sunday paper in a story entitled "The Bohemian" (1855), which concerns a self-proclaimed Bohemian whose personal "seediness" is at odds with his aristocratic sentiments. He is also "what is vulgarly called 'a mesmerist.'"[96] Linking mesmerism's science of the unconscious with Bohemianism, the titular character hopes to eschew work altogether and to enter an ideal realm of nonnecessity; as he tells his pawn, an unsuccessful lawyer,

I don't want a profession. I could make plenty of money if I chose to work, but I don't choose to work. I will never work. I have a contempt for labor. . . . Why should we, —who are expressly and evidently created by nature to enjoy, —why should we, with our delicate tastes, our refined susceptibilities, our highly wrought organizations, spend our lives in ministering to the enjoyment of others? (287–91)

This bombastic speech seduces the lawyer into allowing the Bohemian to mesmerize his fiancée, whom the Bohemian suspects "is a clairvoyante of the first water" (292), so that she might be able to reveal the site of a long-buried treasure. When Annie, the fiancée, learns of the proposed psychic adventure, she pleads the values of the work ethic in protest: "Have a true heart, and learn to labor and to wait. You will be rich in time; and then we will live happily together, secure in the consciousness that our means have been acquired by honest industry" (297). The story bears out her fear, and, following the somnambulist trance that allows her to locate the treasure, Annie collapses, dead from nervous exhaustion, from an improper balance between means and ends; the lawyer enunciates the final moral: "I felt, as I knelt by her father and kissed her cold hand in the agony of my heart, that I was justly punished" (308). The very bourgeois work ethic that eluded the erratic O'Brien triumphs in his story, fully freighted with moralistic power. Instead of inaugurating a Romantic utopia beyond instrumentality, Bohemia, aligned with the occult forces of the unconscious, proves anarchic and mercenary.

The darkest of all mid-century U.S. Bohemian self-representations, "The Bohemian" was not alone in critically assessing the phenomenon and questioning the extent to which Bohemia could transcend a bourgeois existence. If the Bohemians sought to create a space separate from the imperatives of the bourgeoisie and its work ethic, they often acknowledged that this space could not function outside of the dominant culture. Whitman's own early journalistic celebration of the loafer acknowledges that his utopia requires its own antithesis. Addressing the conservative Whigs, the victors of the 1840 presidential election, Whitman demands, "Give us the facilities of loafing, and you are welcome to all the benefits of your tariff system, your manufacturing privileges, and your cotton trade."[97] Implicitly, the facilities of loafing could only exist if subsidized by a conservative bourgeois economy. Similarly, turning his ever-present irony on his own ideal, Clapp analogized the Bohemian to the ultimate vampiric parasite, the mosquito, whom he termed the "little Bohemian," and proceeded to sketch the type: "Like many other very excellent persons, he has no idea of letting anybody work in his presence. He belongs to the extensive class of non-producers who, though they have no objection to consuming the productions of the opposite class (without whom, indeed, they might find it difficult to live) have an elegant dislike to witnessing the processes of production."[98]

Clapp's "Night with a Mosquito" furthers the alliance between the Bohemian and the aristocrat, emphasizing their mutually "elegant" disdain for the processes of production. Yet Clapp distinguished his mosquito/Bohemian from other "non-producers," noting, however ironically, the power of his song: "For though thy orgies fret the drowsy night / To sing and sup thou hast a poet's right."[99]

If Clapp promoted (while ironizing) the Bohemian sense of artistic entitlement and exemption from the requirements of bourgeois life, his experience of Bohemia largely belied his own representation of a carefree *vie bohème*. Far from strictly being a playful consumer, loafer, or aristocrat, Clapp must also have been a diligent worker, writing several articles a week and editing a weekly paper. The Bohemians could not avoid the strictures of the capitalist economy. Much of the work may have been accomplished in a beer cellar and perhaps some of it realized Balzac's ideal of fusing labor and leisure, but Clapp and his staff nevertheless experienced many desperate moments as, in Whitman's words, they engaged in "the most heroic fight right along to keep the *Press* alive."[100] Clapp's correspondence with Whitman reveals his desperation over debts incurred by the paper: "I am so busy that I hardly have time to breathe. . . . I must have one hundred dollars before Saturday night or be in a scrape the horror of which keeps me awake 'o nights."[101] Such sentiments sparked earnest appeals in the *Press* and *Harper's* for the funding of the arts. If at times the Bohemians saw themselves as parasites, at other moments they passionately argued for their importance to American culture.

Pointing to a bourgeois paradox par excellence, the Pfaffians complained that Bohemian "free development" was misunderstood by the very republican society that should, theoretically, have been its patron. One *Harper's* column defended the group against the charge that they defrauded their creditors by protesting that literary men and artists simply did not have creditors "in a thoroughly money-grubbing community like this."[102] Similarly, the *Press* complained of Bohemian social alienation: "The prevalent idea of a Bohemian, especially in New York, is that of a man who, from circumstances beyond his control, doesn't happen to move in what is called 'society'." In contrast, the *Press* lauded French culture, stating, "In Paris, on the contrary, the Bohemian is courted by society, for he possesses preeminently those charms of character which among cultivated people in France are mostly in demand."[103] French Bohemians probably would not have agreed with this characterization of their place in French society,[104] but such a description crystallizes the importance that the Frenchness of Bohemianism had for the Pfaffians: France represented the very possibility of cultural sophistication and artistic appreciation, thus serving as the Bohemian answer to the limitations of their own national culture.

The Bohemian "Cosmopolite" and the "Narrow-Minded" Bourgeois

The Bohemians elaborated a view of themselves as consummate "cosmopolites" as part of their self-defense. "I cannot appreciate the definition of the Bohemian with which our Sunday papers ring," Ada Clare proclaims:

> They lead us to suppose that the Bohemian must be poor. That he must take pleasure in keeping his boots and his cheese in the same drawer. That he delights in cooking upon his shovel and tongs, and in eating out of the coal-scuttle. That he essentially drinks very much, and becomes affected by liquor. That he must go about, making himself ridiculous, by exposing his private views and feelings to the public, which cannot understand him. That he must shock people's religious and social sentiments by all sorts of harsh, anathematizing onslaughts upon such sentiments. That he should prefer to spend his money on bad liquor, instead of defraying the just debts which he necessarily contracts. That he should speak sneeringly of women; and that he should willfully let go the true paradise of the body, by sinking himself into a mere slough of carnalism.[105]

That the papers would ring with such characterizations of the Bohemian demonstrates the visibility of the Pfaffians, and the extent to which Bohemianism appeared as an assault against conventional morality, as a new, distinctively urban threat to social mores. This burlesqued characterization also has much to do with images popularized by Henri Murger's *Scènes de la vie de Bohème.* Yet, as Clare suggests, the first American Bohemians, perhaps in partial agreement with the more moralistic American society, tended to deemphasize the association between "dissolution" and Bohemianism. (Indeed, upon his visit to Pfaff's, William Dean Howells notes, perhaps with some disappointment, that the orgy "went but slowly for an orgy"—though he does comment on the "awful appearance" of some Bohemians who "were just recovered from a fearful debauch.")[106] Rather, Clare goes on to clarify what she sees as the true "nature" of the Bohemian:

> I thought the Bohemian was by nature, if not by habit, a Cosmopolite, with a general sympathy for the fine arts, and for all things above and beyond convention. The Bohemian is not, like the creature of society, a victim of rules and customs; he steps over them all with an easy, graceful, joyous unconsciousness, guided by the principles of good taste and feeling. Above all others, essentially, the Bohemian must not be narrow-minded; if he be, he is degraded back to the position of a mere worldling.[107]

"Wordlings" inhabited a realm of social artifice, but Bohemian "Cosmopolites" embraced a higher worldliness; their catholic and romantically natural sensibilities let "the world's masks drop from their faces" and enabled the would-be Bohemian to disregard "all social distinctions of rank and wealth."[108] (The *Oxford English Dictionary* similarly notes a divergence in the meaning of the two terms, defining the "wordling" as a pleasure-seeker and the "cosmopolite," more neutrally, as "an inhabitant of the world.")[109] Thus revealed, the inner "Bohemian" would represent the natural rights of man (and, as we shall see, woman).

The injunction that the Bohemian must be a "cosmopolite" and "must not be narrow-minded" did have many political ramifications within the *Saturday Press*. Most centrally, the paper identified itself with immigrant cultures and politics, perhaps tacitly regarding the immigrant as the ultimate symbol for the Bohemian, gypsylike nomad. For example, in an article entitled "The Freedom Not to Worship" the *Press* pitched itself against "that bigoted portion of the city of New York" whose "chief victims of their crusade have been that large class of people called Germans who have been hunted from pillar to post by irate ecclesiastic and their tools, with a view to force them into worshipping gods in whom they do not believe."[110] Similarly, the *Press* protested the "celebrated battle-axe City Reform," whose Sunday blue laws discriminated, in particular, against Catholic immigrants. Such laws, the *Press* insisted, had a tendency to inspire the support of the prototypical bourgeois hypocrite—whom the *Press* identifies in one article as "Dives." Though his head-clerk "sometimes tells queer stories of the 'old man' in former days," Dives purported to be "struck dumb with astonishment when he learned that 100,000 Germans insisted upon drinking the bier, singing the songs, seeing the plays, and indulging in the games of the Fatherland on Sunday as well as on any other day of the week, and chose that day with the absurd and ridiculous apology for a reason that they had none other."[111]

Often scathingly ironic, some such defense of immigrant cultural practices over and against moralizing reformers and city officials occurred weekly in the *Saturday Press*. At a time when the congressman for New York City was advocating nativist restrictions and sabbatarian laws to protect the city from "those malcontents of the Old World who hate monarchy, not because it is monarchy, but because it is restraint," the significance of Pfaff's as a Bohemian haunt becomes all the more apparent. Representing a desire to align with German immigrants, the patronage of Pfaff's opposed the City Reformers who would impose "strict Calvinist preaching" on an increasingly "heterodox" population. This identification with the Germans is manifest in the frequent "puffs" that the *Press* gave to Pfaff's: one such notice, quoted earlier in the chapter, explicitly aligns "young literary men, artists, and that large class of people called Germans."[112]

Such identifications are further explained by the extent to which Bohemian-Bourgeois conflict corresponded to tensions between German immigrant and Anglo-American cultures. Along with the Bohemians, German immigrants complained about the excessive practicality and materialism of American society: as one German American commentator noted in 1856, "Everything here becomes profane and common. . . . The American cannot get enthusiastic about anything; he can't even enjoy himself." Alternatively, German ethnic culture in mid-nineteenth-century America emphasized festivity and recreation, and in cities and towns throughout the country, German immigrants organized numerous *Feste*, parades, excursions, picnics, musical performances, and gymnastic exhibitions. German beer halls and gardens similarly encouraged festive culture. Itself largely middle-class, this festive culture nonetheless opposed a bourgeois American life that swung "between the market and the church."[113] Temperance, Sabbatarian, and Know-Nothing crusades no doubt further convinced the Bohemians that here was a cultural ally, one similarly persecuted by the "Bourgeois." Of course, like Bohemianism itself, German festive culture became more and more a part of mainstream American culture as the century progressed (and, conversely, the Germans became more and more "assimilated"), but the terms of its acceptance further reveal the extent to which this culture had once appeared as an assault upon Anglo-America. By 1883, the *New York Times* (the same paper that had editorialized against Bohemian "uselessness") concluded:

> The German immigration has been an unmixed good to the United States. Whatever tends to make life better worth living they have not left behind them, and it would be difficult to compute the good that German immigration has done us in importing German music and German beer, and in the labors of the German immigrants as social missionaries, practically showing . . . that it is possible on occasion to be idle and innocent.[114]

Bohemian cosmopolitanism also sought other cultural allies. Pitching themselves against a complacent and often hypocritical bourgeois respectability, the Bohemians championed the urban poor—perhaps viewing "vagrants, and persons of no reputable employment" as authentic analogues to the Bohemian, as they viewed immigrants. After condemning recent police raids against the poor and homeless, for example, the *Saturday Press* suggests that the people "force the rich and religious Corporation of Trinity Church to devote a part of its funds and attention to improving the wretched houses filled with the poor from the rent of which it derives a part of the income it squanders in deceptive monuments to suppositious revolutionary heroes."[115] Democratic equality, the paper implies, could not be achieved through the reification of the revolutionary past, but must serve as an ongoing impetus to social change. The self-satisfied bourgeois should not be permitted to claim identity with alleged revolutionary heroes simply through the act of monumentalizing history. In contrast, the Bohemians celebrated "a new general" in the current war on poverty; though "only a mechanic," this man, John Washington Farmer, "fitted up a neat room, where, from six in the morning till eleven in the evening of every day, he dispense[d] good, plain dinners to all who are poor and hungry."[116]

As the cases of both "Dives" and "the rich and religious Corporation of Trinity Church" suggest, the Bohemians' bourgeois antagonists often occupied a specific socioeconomic position: they were urban elites attempting to exert social control rather than American Everymen democratically expressing national values or even a middle-class order. At times, however, it was the privilege of maleness, and not necessarily of riches, that the Bohemians felt most exemplified "sham" respectability and exerted an undeserved social dominance. The ideal Bohemian cosmopolite, the *Press* argued, also represented the rights of women.

The *Saturday Press* continually championed women's rights and the abolition of a double standard of bourgeois sexual morality. Just one example occurred in response to a series of editorials in other New York papers condemning one Mrs. Gurney, who had left her husband and run off to Paris with another man and who then had the audacity to write a public letter in her defense. Dripping with irony, the *Press*'s editorial observes:

> Man has from the beginning been so scrupulously just to women, has been so careful at all times to make the laws as favorable as possible to her interests, and in his capacity of husband has so uniformly been a model of fidelity, that if, in face of so brilliant an example, she will depart from the paths of chastity, she must of course expect that he will boil over, as he is now doing, with "virtuous indignations."[117]

The alleged moral hypocrisy of the bourgeois had, of course, long been a target for ironic censure—the *Harper's* Bohemian, for example, declared himself the sworn enemy of "humbugs or shams, or false pretenses or nonsense of any kind."[118] However, the Bohemians further complicated the standard critique by locating the effects of humbuggery within unjust social relationships. They identified hypocrisy within sexual double standards: the point of the Mrs. Gurney editorial is not simply that men don't practice what they preach, but that they unfairly hold different expectations for male and female conduct. Even more radically, the editorial assumes that women have a right to retaliate against such corrupted standards. Another editorial states the point even more directly, encouraging the "Dishonored Wife" to "avenge the wrongs of her sex, by exposing the horrible state of public opinion, which, for the same offence, brands the wife with infamy, and leaves the husband untainted even in reputation!"[119]

Further, the Pfaffians welcomed such women as Clare and Menken into their coterie, and encouraged women writers; as one female correspondent noted, the *Saturday Press* was very active in "giving us womenfolk a lift into literature, especially through the columns of your bright little journal."[120] Attempting to promote similar commitments, Clapp punningly editorialized that the *Nation* should change its name to "The Stag-Nation," on the ground that "there are no lady writers on its list."[121] On the pages of the *Saturday Press*, Clare, in particular, wrote editorials advocating such feminist issues as dress reform, again calling attention to unreasonable double standards: "I would be pleased to see the young men who would walk the length of Broadway with a female, reasonably dressed, according to the male standard [for women]." Such dress, she suggests, itself limited the ability of women to move into a public sphere.[122]

Not every self-described New York Bohemian of this period wanted to encourage female Bohemianism, however. For example, Charles Astor Bristed of the "Three Gypsies" ballad announced in his "New Theory of Bohemianism" that "women are not fit Bohemians." Voicing a perspective that would be repeatedly reiterated in the ensuing decades, he insisted: "They are flowers too delicate for the violent extremes of the Bohemian climate. Moreover, it is difficult for a woman, without some loss of delicacy, to be very unconventional, and that is just what a Bohemian is apt to be." Indeed, further demonstrating the conservatism of his *vie bohème*, Bristed views the ideally *domesticated* woman as the desirable counterpoint to the male Bohemian: "It is better for him and for society that he should light upon a wife of rather anti-bohemian tendencies to keep his house in order." As we have seen, Whitman's most direct written statement about Bohemianism further amplified (and complicated) the distinction between a male Bohemia and a feminized bourgeois domesticity, but his poetry argued against such a dichotomy. Indeed, so did his experience at Pfaff's and with the *Saturday Press.*

In the space of Bohemia, Whitman regularly met with such female Pfaffians as Clare and Adah Isaacs Mencken, and later admitted that these women, along with several others who reviewed his poetry for the *Saturday Press,* had been among his most devoted readers: "It is very curious that the girls have been my sturdiest defenders, upholders. Some would say they were girls little to my credit, but I disagree with them there, and I suppose that's not the only place where we disagree either!"[123] These women strongly promoted the poet whose frank sexuality rendered him, in Mary Chilton's subversive formulation, "the apostle of purity, the teacher of the most vital, and hence the most Divine truth."[124] Further explaining the appeal of his book to these protofeminists, Whitman later insisted, "To the movement for the eligibility and entrance of women amid new spheres of business, politics, and the suffrage, the current prurient, conventional treatment of sex is the main formidable obstacle."[125] In its apotheosis at Pfaff's, the physical space of Bohemia also allowed women an entrée into a new sphere. Defining themselves as Bohemians, women like Clare and Menken created a certain sexual license, a license that enabled them to flaunt and justify their alleged improprieties or immoralities and that permitted them to move freely and independently in a public space without incurring the assumption, at least with regards to the other Bohemians, that they were in fact "public women" or prostitutes.[126]

These women not only challenged conventional sexual morality by their sheer presence in the public space of Pfaff's or the stage, but also through their writings in New York magazines and in the *Saturday Press.* That paper frequently inveighed against the very notion of "separate spheres," insisting: "Our notion is that woman's peculiar sphere is whatever field of action she finds herself best adapted to, and in which she can maintain herself, if need be, in entire independence of man." The *Press* further exposed the brutal patriarchal logic of separate spheres, ridiculing an article that claimed a woman should cook in order to minister to the health of her husband: "Observe that the effect of bad food on the *wife* is not alluded to,—in fact, is not of importance enough to be alluded to: it is the *husband* alone who is to be cared for." Instead, the *Press* advocated female "emancipation from the silly laws of society, which prescribe to them, now, as their first duty, to learn the art of administering to the pleasures of a sex which does all in its power to degrade them."[127]

On the pages of the *Saturday Press*, the championing of women, the poor, and immigrant groups all furthered the cause of "Bohemia." The paper's cosmopolitan, democratic impetus served to prove, in the words of Ada Clare, that "artists are less subject to blind prejudice than most classes of men. From that fact I infer that their art is set higher than other things, that from a greater eminence, a larger horizon passes under their eyes."[128] In such statements, Clare pays tribute to the artist as an elite cosmopolitan and Romantic hero, and also articulates the romance of culture that led to the formation of distinct cultural "brow" levels during this time, and to aestheticist projection of the autonomy of art in the coming decades. More will be said about such cultural hierarchies in a later section of this chapter, but for now it is worth noting that Clare conceives of the "greater eminence" of art as an active counter to larger social prejudices rather than as their guarantee.

Its cosmopolitan "greater eminence of art" located Bohemia in an ambiguous position with respect to American literary and cultural nationalisms. The Pfaffians championed a more cosmopolitan America, but in so doing they often rejected (if ultimately to affirm) what they saw as the dominant national culture. Part of that rejection lay, as we have seen, in their confirmed Francophilism. Often appearing to be "more a Frenchman than an American" (according to Winter),[129] Clapp questioned whether or not *la vie bohème* was even viable within bourgeois America: "The Bohemian requires a peculiar kind of esprit, not to say of culture, which is found with us [Americans] only in the case of those few individuals who by extensive travel, or by natural good taste, have become, in the best sense of the word, cosmopolitans." Except for these exceptional cases (the Pfaffians) or in locations (like Pfaff's) that both simulated foreign travel and encouraged what we might anachronistically call cultural pluralism, "the Bohemian [could] not exist in this country ruled by Mrs. Grundy."[130] A character from the eighteenth-century British play *Speed the Plow*, "Mrs. Grundy" represented the essence of the moralizing bourgeois matron; "ruled" by such characters, America's dominant bourgeois ethos, the Pfaffians insisted, militated against a sophisticated, European-inspired Bohemianism. Still, the Pfaffians' version of the proverbial Bohemian-Bourgeois dichotomy cannot be fully subsumed into an opposition between Europe and the United States; rather, Bohemian cosmopolitanism continued to admit a strongly nationalistic dimension.

Indeed, paradoxically enough, the "cosmopolite" Clapp viewed a "distinct national character" as the very condition of a future, more broadly based American Bohemianism:

> If in the progress of things there shall ever be formed in this country a distinct national character—and we are far enough from it, as yet—it is not impossible that out of it will grow a condition of society equal [to France] in independence and real culture. . . . Then we may have among us a type of character as fine in temper and as elevated in tone as that which in Paris goes by the name of Bohemian.[131]

A later article signed "Silver White" makes this argument somewhat less self-contradictory by noting that, as in all new countries, "society in this country is not favorable to the vagabond" since "everything here commands us to attain, confirm, establish."[132] Perhaps, the two articles suggest, new societies first require a strong material base at the national level; with such a foundation, an elevated "real culture" could eventually emerge. Such a culture would then transcend the bourgeois economic and political imperative to "attain, confirm, establish," and would allow for an ideal realm of cultural "independence" and "national character."

Clapp's cosmopolitanism, then, implied a prior nationalism: it demanded the exchange of refined national characteristics and not their dissolution. Noting the power of the electric telegraph, newspapers, and "fast times for travel" to set "the world on the jog, all mankind in a jumble," Clapp muses:

> Strange tongues touch each other and run together; and the word "foreigner" becomes invidious or obsolete. Steam is at work and sweats us out of our prejudices. Manifest Destiny becomes a religion. Old England annexes the Indies and Young America stretches her bony arms and gives the grip to Japan. The nations come to know each other; come to embrace each other. They group together in families; cultivate corn and good neighborhood together; see that the balance of power is the balance of trade; and learn to play our American game of swap. They swap corn, coal, iron, silk, literature, religion, and fancy goods, as unsuspecting young people swap hearts, jackets, and jackknives. All this is hopeful, and out of it may some day grow cosmopolitan nations composed of the elect of the people.[133]

This outpouring implicitly recognizes how easily cosmopolitanism could become nationalism and imperialism, and how fully it admitted an economic motive—the very motive that "real culture" allegedly transcended. Listing "literature" along with exportable natural resources and "fancy goods," Clapp understood the extent to which culture itself functioned as a commodity. Clapp's ever-present irony renders his own judgment of the dynamics he described somewhat opaque: Did he really believe that nations could "embrace" after one has been locked in the other's "bony grip?" Could "unsuspecting" swappings really foster a "hopeful" cosmopolitanism? In all likelihood, Clapp remained suspicious of the extent to which cosmopolitanism relied upon the "balance of trade," but he could not foresee any other mechanism by which international culture in general, and Bohemianism in particular, might flourish. Just as Clapp's "little Bohemian," the mosquito, parasitically lives off bourgeois "producers," so must Bohemian cosmopolites play an "American game of swap" as they cultivate the social goods of worldliness. Once again, Clapp eschewed a simplistic opposition between Bohemianism and the (national) bourgeois marketplace in favor of a more nuanced and agonized view that allowed for both their conflict and their interdependence.

Other articles resolve the tension between nationalism and a Bohemian cosmopolitanism more easily, insisting that in America, the national *was* the cosmopolitan and the universal. Whitman, of course, often espoused this developing American liberal ideology, reconciling his nationalism and his internationalism by representing the United States as an ideal microcosm of a cosmopolitan community, as a "teeming nation of many nations."[134] Signed "D.D," a *Saturday Press* article stresses the congruence between Bohemian cosmopolitanism and American nationalism, declaring, "The grand work of Bohemianism in our own day is our United States." Yet, in making this argument, the article belies its own cosmopolitan aspirations, revealing that "Mrs. Grundy" was not the only figure against whom the Bohemians defined themselves: the Jews, the article insists, "were never Bohemians," and "they are not to this day, except in rare cases, where the Artist-inspiration overcomes the Jewish tendency. . . . A Jew makes his small nationality a pride. He is not large-hearted enough or human enough to be a Bohemian." Conversely, the article implausibly insists: "In the present century, the great manifestation of Bohemianism was Napoleon's French army. Their valor, their daring, their good fellowship, their enthusiastic love and reverence for their leader, their devotion to their country, came from their Bohemianism."[135] Clapp appears to have shared some of this anti-Semitism, noting: "Jews excepted, I have from my youth up had a lively sympathy for all creatures who are the victims of a general persecution."[136] When a correspondent later complained about this statement, Clapp clarified his logic, insisting that Jews would "make as good folks as anybody" if they would only "leave off being Jews and turn mankind."[137] As we have seen, Clapp held a general antipathy for all political parties and religious sects, but he clearly singles out the Jews as examples of parochialism; further, even if his statements resist a racialist logic that would deny Jews the ability to "turn mankind," his wording nevertheless insists that "being Jews" and being members of "mankind" are mutually exclusive, ontological conditions. Still, such sentiments did not prevent the Bohemians of Pfaff's from welcoming the openly Jewish actress Adah Isaacs Menken to the beer cellar.[138]

Within the *Saturday Press*, the tension between the nationalistic and the cosmopolitan (and, by extension, the Bohemian and the Bourgeois) also surfaced in relation to literary culture. The conflict between cosmopolitan and nationalistic literary agendas went back at least as far as 1800 with the foundation of the *North American Review*, and sparked continual controversy between Democratic and Whig magazines. Represented by such magazines as the *Knickerbocker*, the Whig (and generally Anglophilic) cosmopolitans conflicted with the Democratic Young Americans and their advocates in the *United States Magazine and Democratic Review* and *Literary World*. The latter magazines promoted the search for an "American Genius," and in opposition to the Whigs, advocated an international copyright law that would raise the price of British literary imports.[139] The *Saturday Press*, from its inception, declared itself "independent" from all party politics. To be sure, the Whigs had already dissolved and the Democrats had fragmented by the time the *Press* began, but the conflict between literary nationalism and cosmopolitanism remained—however muted—and the *Press* alternately associated its Bohemianism with both positions. As we have seen, the very premise of a Bohemian press was Francophilic, and the *Press* highlighted this foreign influence by publishing a weekly "Dramatic Feuilleton" reviewing various dramatic and social happenings about town. The *Press* also published a weekly account of new books in print; by dividing them into the categories "English" and "American," the periodical most likely kept former Whigs and Young Americans equally happy (especially given that both columns were generally of comparable length). Still, with the arrival of Walt Whitman, the *Press* reasserted a full-blown literary nationalism. In a review of *Leaves of Grass* (most likely written by Whitman himself) the *Saturday Press* declares:

> You, bold American! and ye future two hundred millions of bold Americans, can surely never live, for instance, entirely satisfied and grow to your full stature on what the importations hither of foreign bards, dead or alive, provide—nor on what is echoing here the letter and spirit of foreign bards. No bold American! Our own song, free, joyous and masterful! Our own music raised on the soil of the wondrous all-America![140]

Sufficiently effusive to have been written by Whitman (in unintentional self-parody), this review was endorsed by the entire editorial staff, and another review written for the *Saturday Press* further declares, "Whoever has felt in the past that the originality of American Genius among her poets had never been fully justified, no longer has occasion to think or feel so."[141]

Notwithstanding such nationalist sentiments, the Bohemians retained their reputation for Francophilic cosmopolitanism. Ironically enough, nowhere is this more apparent than in an advertisement for the 1860 edition of *Leaves of Grass* that was printed in the *Saturday Press*, and that, so positioned, ultimately served as an advertisement for the Bohemians themselves. This blurb excerpts various reviews of Whitman's latest edition and includes one anti-Bohemian diatribe from the *New York Illustrated News.* Though Whitman himself had long been a fixture at Pfaff's and was championed almost every week by the *Saturday Press*, the reviewer for the *New York Illustrated News* distinguishes Whitman from "the flippant young gentlemen of the French school who do the brilliant for Bohemian clubs and newspapers":

> We can see that whatsoever appertains to the honor, interest, learning, literature, culture, manners, laws, and government of America, is very dear to him, dearer than all the world besides, and we love him for his love of the great and magnificent land. Legislators and literats, and office-seekers, and brilliant lager-bier drinkers, and grog-drinkers and the mob who hate law and government, may forget that they are Americans, may defame and traduce their country, sell its honor for a mess of pottage, or try to make it a French stew by inoculating us with French notions, French books, and French morals and habits—but not so Whitman! True as the needle to the North is he true to his country, to the brave mother language, and to the American people.[142]

This attack on "literats" suggests something of the cultural force of the first American Bohemia. Placing the Bohemians in the same company with the very office seekers and legislators whom they repeatedly denounced, the *New York Illustrated News* posits a large subculture of traitors who would inundate the country with all things French. Whitman, however, is excluded from the very company he kept.[143]

Whitman: American and Bohemian

While Whitman retained his "love of the great and magnificent land," he increasingly struggled with the question of how to position himself in relation to American culture. As the nation approached the Civil War, his sense of himself as the poet of American democracy began to fracture along with the Union. In Betsy Erkkila's words: "Despite the impulse toward union, fusion, and artistic resolution . . . there is in the 1860 *Leaves*—even more than in the 1856 volume—a disquieting undercurrent that registers the throes of personal and public dissolution. Published on the eve of the Civil War . . . the 1860 *Leaves* is divided between the desire to celebrate and the desire to mourn."[144] Part elegy and part spiritual guide to a renewed democratic faith, the 1860 edition frequently displaces Whitman from "the center to the margins of American democratic culture." Especially in the "Calamus" poems, as Erkkila notes, Whitman alternates between a "separatist impulse toward a private homosexual order" and a drive toward a public culture of democratic brotherhood.[145] His understanding of the relationship between these two impulses also wavers. In his more hopeful moments, Whitman imagines that the first impulse might ultimately sustain the second, and that homoerotic desire could intensify democratic bonds in the culture at large. In his darker moments, he experiences a disjuncture between the personal and the political—a rupture he links to the failures of democracy and the impending national crisis.

Locating Whitman in the Bohemia at Pfaff's underscores his sense of rupture and displacement at the time of the 1860 edition, enabling us to appreciate better how Whitman revised his perspective on American culture in this edition. In "Two Vaults," the unpublished poem written around the time of his tenure at Pfaff's, he describes his position in the German beer cellar in terms that resonate with the imagery of other poems in the 1860 edition. Though cited earlier in this chapter, the poem is worth quoting in full:

—The vault at Pfaffs where the drinkers and laughers meet to eat and
drink and carouse

While on the walk immediately overhead pass the myriad feet of
Broadway
As the dead in their graves are underfoot hidden
And the living pass over them, recking not of them,
Laugh on laughers!
Drink on drinkers!
Bandy the jest!
Toss the theme from one to another!
Beam up—Brighten up, bright eyes of beautiful young men! . . .
Drink wine—drink beer—raise your voice,
Behold! Your friend, as he arrives—Welcome him, where, from the
upper step, he looks down upon you with a cheerful look
Overhead rolls Broadway—the myriad rushing Broadway
The lamps are lit—the shops blaze—the fabrics vividly are seen
through the plate glass windows
The strong lights from above pour down upon them and are shed
outside,
The thick crowds, well-dressed—the continual crowds as if they would
never end
The curious appearance of the faces—the glimpse just caught of the
eyes and expressions, as they flit along
(You phantoms! Oft I pause, yearning, to arrest some of you!
Oft I doubt your reality—whether you are real—I suspect all is but a
pageant.)
The lights beam in the first vault—but the other is entirely dark
In the first[146]

Here, in the Bohemia at Pfaff's, there is a constant tension between stable identity and dissolution, between community and crowd. All boundaries are confused, even the most mysterious of all: life and death. Who are the living and who are the dead? Which vault is dark? Which phantasmagoric? At the outset of the poem, it is the Bohemians who are likened to the "dead in their graves," but, by the end of the poem, it is the faces in the crowd that appear as spectral presences. Like the "phantoms" that "cover all the land, and all the sea" and "spring as from graves" in "Out of the Cradle Endlessly Rocking" (titled "A Word out of the Sea" in the 1860 edition), the crowd also bespeaks "Death—ever Death, Death, Death" (277). With all light and animation displaced onto vivid fabrics and blazing shops, the disembodied expressions of the members of the crowd signal the end of Whitman's "democracy en masse." Threatened by impending Civil War and—the poem suggests—an alienating marketplace, the crowd no longer represents democratic substance.

Yet, within "the vault at Pfaff's," the Bohemian "dead" are laughing, drinking, and bandying jests. Thus, even within this one unfinished poem, there is the "compensatory rhythm of life and death, love and loss" that Erkkila identifies in the 1860 edition: here, as in other poems of the period, Whitman "locates the source of his songs not in democratic presence, but in absence and death, in the 'unsatisfied love' and 'unknown want' that he seeks to articulate in song but that can never be fully satisfied in the social world."[147] "Calamus" no. 2, for example, apostrophizes:

> Give me your tone therefore O death, that I may accord with it . . .
> Nor will I allow you to balk me any more with what I was calling life,
> For now it is conveyed to me that you are the purports essential,
> That you hid in these shifting forms of life, for reasons, and that they
> are mainly for you,
> That you beyond them come forth to remain, the real reality,
> That behind the mask of materials you patiently wait . . .
>
> (344)

Just as the "dead" Bohemians of "Two Vaults" form a vibrant, homosocial community, so does the "death" invoked in "Calamus" no. 2 convey a "real reality" imbued with love and comradeship. Conversely, the "living" consumers and commodities that "pass over" the Bohemians in "Two Vaults" suggest the uncanny "mask of materials" and "shifting forms of life" of "Calamus" no. 2. This reversal of signification between life and death projects an alternative reality, the "purports essential" aligned in "Two Vaults" with the Bohemia at Pfaff's. Still, punctuated by a series of successive exclamation points, the imperative need to drink, laugh, and jest appears as a desperate surge against time.

First appearing in the 1860 *Leaves*, the "Calamus" poems sought a new poetic destination, a "secluded spot" in which the poet could "respond as I would not dare elsewhere":

> In paths untrodden,
> In the growth by margins of pond-waters,
> Escaped from the life that exhibits itself,
> From all the standards hitherto published—from the pleasures, profits,
> conformities . . .

> I proceed, for all who are, or have been, young men,
> To tell the secret of my nights and days,
> To celebrate the need for comrades.
>
> (341–42)

"Two Vaults" indicates that, at Pfaff's, Whitman had found such a spot—however subterranean—in which "the need for comrades" could be duly celebrated.

Yet could a marginal community, such as that of the Bohemia at Pfaff's, underwrite a renewed democratic faith? Could the "intense and loving comradeship, the personal attachment of man to man" that Whitman found at Pfaff's help to "solve . . . the problems of freedom"? (349).[148] Written on the eve of Civil War, "Two Vaults" is, appropriately enough, left unfinished, raising more questions than it can answer. Located in a basement underneath Broadway, in a German beer cellar inside the United States, Pfaff's was positioned both within and without the dominant society. As Whitman turned both toward and away from the public culture of mid-nineteenth-century America, Pfaff's provided a literal and symbolic realm, an interstitial space that mediated between "desire and history, between the poet's democracy of the imagination and the fact of a disintegrating world":[149] between what Whitman conceptualized as the gap between the real and the ideal America.

"But where is what I started for, so long ago? / And why is it yet unfound?" (312). This question, posed in poem no. 10 of the 1860 *Enfans d'Adam* section ("Facing West from California's Shores"), imaginatively catapulted the poet to the western edge of the continent in the search for a still "unfound" America—just at the time the nation's constitutional "foundations" were becoming unmoored. Yet, from within his underground Bohemia, Whitman still tried to imagine a social space that would realize his visionary democracy.[150]

Understanding Whitman as a Bohemian not only highlights his vexed relation to American society at the time of the 1860 edition, but also encourages us to locate him in the international context that his fellow Pfaffians so eagerly fostered. If Whitman emphatically addressed himself to "You bold American!" it is also true that his poetry strove to speak "Not of one nation only—not America only," and his writing explored or exemplified many of the tensions between the cosmopolitan and the nationalistic found in the *Saturday Press*. Whitman, as noted, often reconciled his

Americanism and his internationalism by representing America as a "teeming nation of many nations,"[151] and further, by endorsing an imperialistic rhetoric of Manifest Destiny: at the conclusion of the Mexican War in 1847, Whitman wrote, "It is for the interest of mankind that [America's] power and territory should be extended—the farther the better."[152] Yet poems like "Salut au Monde"[153] and lines like "The Asiatic and African are hand in hand . . . the European and American are hand in hand"[154] have caused many critics to claim that his work "reaches beyond the very national literary boundaries he himself is credited with having established."[155]

To avoid the process of "nationalist 'hypercanonization,'" Jonathan Arac has encouraged critics "to link Whitman, through a global process of capitalist modernity, to great French poetry quite contemporary with his own activity"[156] Arac proposes Charles Baudelaire as an appropriate poet for such a linkage, and takes the growth of commercial-industrial urban centers as the topoi shared by Whitman and his French contemporary. And since Baudelaire also identified himself as a Bohemian, I would add that the common terrain of "Bohemia" focuses the comparison, revealing how two poets' various interpretations of *la vie bohème* responded to the "global process of capitalist modernity." Such a comparison partially brackets the tension between a self-conscious nationalism and cosmopolitanism, revealing the extent to which capitalism nullified this apparent opposition.

Baudelaire identifies Bohemia as a kind of perverse version of the bourgeois economy: it hyperappropriates the logic of the commodity and allows that logic to territorialize even the realms of sexuality and thought. In an early poem not included in *Les Fleurs du Mal*, Baudelaire describes the world of Parisian prostitutes, and writes "*Cette bohème-la, c'est mon tout.*" Baudelaire elaborates: "I [cannot] play the hypocrite and mimic loftiness, I who sell my thought and want to be an author."[157] This process involves the breakdown of a prior wholeness, creating a "vaporization of the self." Such self-dissolution takes place both on the streets of Paris and through the medium of print, and can be as exhilarating as it is disturbing—hence the oxymoron the "divine prostitution of the soul." Such divine prostitution feeds off fragmentation and alienation, and enables the poet to become "like those wandering souls who go looking for a body, entering as he likes into each man's personality. For him alone everything is vacant. . . . The man who loves to lose himself in a crowd enjoys feverish delights. . . . He adopts to his own all the occupations, all the joys and sorrows that chance offers." For Baudelaire this immersion is "the vagabond life, and that which may be called Bohemianism: the cult of multiplied sensation."[158]

Whitman's poetry often involves a similar response to the phantasmagoria of urban stimuli: "Myself effusing and fluid, a phantom curiously floating, now here absorb'd and arrested."[159] Indeed, "Two Vaults" often approaches a Baudelairean vision. Expanding and contracting, the rhythm of these lines provides an expressive parallel to Baudelaire's observation that perception in the metropolis involves a constant "interchange" (to use a Whitmanian term) between the "vaporization and the centralization of the Self."[160] As we have seen, at the outset of the poem, it is the Pfaffians who are likened to "the dead in their graves," but by the end of the poem it is the faces in the crowd that are phantasmagoric. Above ground, only the fabrics behind the plate glass are described as vivid; only the commodity "in the age of high capitalism" retains the vital spark. Or, perhaps, the commodified Bohemians who are similarly poised within and without the crowd?

The decadence of the poem allows for the Baudelairean comparison. Both Whitman and Baudelaire position their Bohemian selves within an urban crowd, both image the relentless commodification of bourgeois life, both use Bohemia as a trope for modernity's radical confusion of boundaries, and both ultimately liken Bohemia to a condition of death. For Baudelaire, as an instance of the "divine prostitution of the soul," Bohemianism is the ultimate expression of modern fragmentation and a way of endowing those fragments with significance. As such, Bohemianism compensates for the "death" of the soul by enabling the poet to experience multiple selves. Yet, if Baudelaire's Bohemian is "like those wandering souls who go looking for a body," Whitman's Bohemian "dead" are, conversely, the epitome of robustness and members of a situated community. Their "deaths" may be caused by modern alienation, but their Bohemianism ultimately counters such morbid fragmentation. Contained within, facilitated by, and yet antithetical to the "myriad rushing Broadway" above, Bohemia both preserves an older, even a "dead" mode of communal life, and, less nostagically, imagines how, through establishments such as Pfaff's, commercial conditions might actually reconstitute and extend the sort of pastoral ideal that they ostensibly destroyed. Thus, if Baudelaire's Bohemian functions as the quintessential modern individualist whose ephemeral contacts with other selves only serve to disperse his own fragmented ego, Whitman's Bohemian concentrates the self in and through a localized community.

In practice, Bohemia provided Whitman with a supportive community that operated both within and without the commercial marketplace. The Pfaffians congregated beneath the shops of Broadway, but, in this subterranean retreat, they also plotted effective marketing strategies for *Leaves of Grass*. Baudelaire's writings on Bohemia emphasize that it is the province of the isolated, alienated artist, yet Whitman's Bohemia at Pfaff's emphasizes camaraderie and shared purpose (for a time, centered around Whitman himself). In particular, Whitman later stressed his debt to Henry Clapp:

> Henry was my friend: he had abilities way out of the common. . . . Someday somebody will tell that story to our literary historians, who will thenceforth see that Henry cannot be skipped, for the *Press* cut a significant figure in the periodical literature of the time. I have often said that my own history could not be written with Henry left out; I mean it—that is not an extravagant statement.[161]

We can only speculate about the extent to which the Bohemians supported Whitman as he wrote the 1860 edition and continued his struggle to gain a national audience; what we do know is that following the publication of the third *Leaves of Grass*, the *Saturday Press* assiduously promoted him through weekly reviews, publications of his poetry, advertisements, and even parodies of the poet's style. Slyly undercutting Whitman's stance as an all-American poet, Clapp insisted that they make a "napoleonic thing"[162] out of publicizing Whitman, even invoking the wisdom of bourgeois economics and new marketing techniques in this struggle: "It is a fundamental principle in political economy, that everything succeeds if money enough is spent on it." Clapp's marketing campaign also involved insight into the power of the Romantic outcast; realizing, perhaps, that Bohemia at large only achieved its fame by inciting bourgeois opposition, Clapp applied this principle to Whitman, publishing both laudatory and scathing reviews of *Leaves*. Whitman later acknowledged the wisdom of this approach: "Henry was right: better to have people stirred against you if they can't be stirred for you—better that than not to stir them at all."[163] Whitman's (frequently ignored) contention that his "own history could not be written with Henry left out" amplifies his poetic affirmation of "the vault at Pfaff's."

The difference between Baudelaire's and Whitman's views of Bohemia is further revealed by their conflicting responses to Poe. Baudelaire identifies Poe as a fellow "Bohemian," and represents him as the ultimate decadent. "In the restless sport of this dying sun certain poetic spirits will discover new delights—dazzling colonnades, cascades of molten metal, fiery Elysiums, melancholy splendours, the sensuous pleasures of regret, all the magic of dreams, all the memories of opium," Baudelaire writes, singling out Poe as such a spirit.[164] Whitman depicts a similar Poe, yet he censures the very qualities that the French poet esteems. With explicit reference to Poe, Whitman describes "the inevitable tendency of poetic culture to morbidity, abnormal beauty—the sickliness of all technical thought or refinement in itself—the abnegation of the perennial and democratic concretes at first hand, the body, the earth and sea, sex and the like—and the substitution of something for them at second or third hand." Well before Max Nordau, he refers to such a decadent culture as "pathological." Baudelaire's Poe offers transcendence and Whitman's represents sickly distortion. Baudelaire and his Poe embrace the dream state while Whitman longs for the concrete. Of course, through its system of monetary equivalencies, capitalism itself effects the "second or third hand" substitutions that Whitman attributes to Poe and his poetic culture. For Baudelaire, the task of Bohemia is to accelerate the process that capitalism sets in motion, setting the two on a kind of collision course. For Whitman, the task of Bohemia is to penetrate surface pageantry, to find an essential basis of shared humanity beneath the "lurid dream" of "myriad rushing Broadway."[165]

These discrepant Poes are also informed by the two poets' respective attitudes toward the United States. According to Baudelaire, Poe's Bohemian life indicted American civilization, that "rabble of buyers and sellers" and "bourgeois mediocrity." Moreover, "Americomania" (or bourgeois capitalist society) had become a "transatlantic ideal," one that Bohemia needed to guard against. By contrast, just as Whitman never sought to dissolve the national fully into the global (unless in the name of an imperial Americanism), his Bohemia never supplanted his "America" as an ideal poetic territory. Bohemia, as localized in the beer cellar, may have helped Whitman to penetrate beneath the "petty grotesques, malformations, phantoms" which played upon the "surface of our republican States this day" (in the words of his later *Democratic Vistas*)—but in so doing, the primary function of *la vie bohème* was to reveal the inner depths within the outer layer of the "dry and flat Sahara" that America had become. For Whitman, Bohemia thus enabled the "prospecting" of a future America, one that would reveal the transcendental core of its "golden fruit."[166]

New York and Boston

As a group, the Pfaffians dedicated themselves to the creation of such a future America. Like Whitman's, their dedication to Bohemia did not ultimately conflict with their Americanism. Indeed, most of the Bohemians used that badge of cosmopolitanism as a way of establishing the critical authority necessary for entering into national social and cultural debates, as a way of pressuring rather than escaping their nation. Their cosmopolitanism often translated into advocacy of the urban poor, immigrants, and women, yet it also had another target. Perhaps most centrally, these early Bohemians sought to oppose the cultural hegemony of the American haute bourgeoisie—especially the social dominance of the formidable Boston Brahmins and their cultural establishment. In so doing, the Bohemians hoped to forge a more inclusive national narrative.

Directly after having made his first literary pilgrimage to Boston from the Midwest, a young William Dean Howells then traveled to New York in 1860. Some of his poetry had been published in the *Saturday Press*, and Howells set out to meet the Bohemians.[167] Once at Pfaff's, however, Howells quickly established himself as a representative Bostonian. In so doing, he discovered and ultimately helped to perpetuate the Bohemians' antipathy toward his chosen city. This conflict, always present in the *Saturday Press*, not only encompassed a literary rivalry between the two cities but also reasserted the classic opposition between the Bohemian and the Bourgeois. Cast as an opposition between New York and Boston, the dichotomy between Bohemian and Bourgeois became all the more focused and intense (though still characteristically unstable), and its basis in class conflict became all the more apparent.

Both at Pfaff's and in the offices of the *Saturday Press*, Howells discovered "a bitterness against Boston as great as the bitterness against respectability." Indeed, Howells recognized the extent to which the Bohemians aligned and conflated "Boston" with this dreaded "respectability." Henry Clapp, Howells noted,

> walked up and down his room saying what lurid things he would do directly if any one accused him of respectability. There were four or five of his assistants and contributors listening to the dreadful threats, which did not deceive even so great an innocence as mine. They probably felt the fascination for him which I could not disown, in spite of my inner disgust; and were watchful at the same time for the effect of his words with one who was confessedly fresh from Boston.[168]

As Howells no doubt realized, Clapp most likely subjected him to this diatribe because he *was* fresh from Boston, the city most connected to the nation's Puritan inheritance. Underscoring the extent to which the two cities appeared to embody Bohemian-Bourgeois opposition, Bayard Taylor observed in 1860, the year of Howells's visit: "The general impression which Boston and its environs made upon my friends was that of substantial prosperity and comfort. They also noticed its prim, proper English air, so strongly contrasted with the semi-Parisian vivacity of New York."[169]

Among the Pfaffians, Howells dutifully embodied the role of the Bostonian Bourgeois (and as later accounts reveal, the Bohemians also cast him in this part, referring to him as a "Prig").[170] Howells's own retrospective account reinforces the impression that this was his role, and helps to reveal the content of Bostonian "respectability": "I remember that as I sat at that table under the pavement at Pfaff's beer cellar, and listened to the wit that did not seem very funny, I thought of the dinner with Lowell, the breakfast with Fields, supper at the Autocrats', and felt that I had fallen very far."[171] Howells disparaged the (literally) subterranean Bohemians by contrasting them with the institutions of a culture increasingly constructed as "high" and consummately respectable—indeed with the very progenitors of such a cultural hierarchy.

By the middle of the nineteenth century, Boston had emerged as the home of an increasingly self-conscious literary culture, and as the widely acknowledged acme of American cultural life. As the residence of such "august luminaries of literature" as Emerson, Longfellow, Hawthorne, Thoreau, Whittier, Holmes and Lowell, Boston and its environs struck Howells and other aspiring "literati" as the principal location of literary excellence, as an "American Athens"; even the Bohemian William Winter later admitted sardonically, "All of the angels, of course, lived in Boston at that time."[172] Such angelic statures, whether deserved or not, were carefully cultivated by the Boston publisher James T. Fields, the very Fields with whom Howells had breakfasted before journeying to New York. By 1860, the firm of Ticknor and Fields had published all of the luminaries mentioned above, and had pioneered innovative marketing techniques. Emerson attested to the results of such publicity, writing to Fields, "your brilliant advertising and arrangements, have made me so popular."[173] Fields began advertising beyond local markets and encouraged editors (through the incentive of purchasing their advertising space) to vouch for the books he published or even to print reviews he himself had composed.

Yet as Richard Brodhead has argued, "Fields's real accomplishment [was] less that he saw how to market literature than that he established 'literature' as a market category."[174] At a time when technological advances in printing, new commercial organizations, and growing railroad networks expanded the reading public and, in particular, increased the demand for "popular" fiction, Fields sought to distinguish his authors and announce their literary quality; such production values as fine paper and elegant brown-board covers displayed the "elevated, here even sanctified, character" of a Ticknor and Fields book, and helped Fields to "identify and confirm the literary *as* a difference before the market."[175] The *Atlantic Monthly*, the Bostonian literary periodical that Fields took over in 1859 (and that James Russell Lowell edited until 1861), furthered such conceptions of the literary as a distinct and rarefied category of writing. As Howells (himself a future editor of the periodical) observed, the *Atlantic* "adventured in the fine air of high literature," and, we might add, helped to define "high literature" as such.[176]

The Bohemians, in turn, defined themselves and their paper against such exclusiveness. The *Saturday Press* often editorialized against the development of a restricted high culture (in Clapp's words, the "Procrustean standard of what is called High Art"), implicitly connecting Bohemianism with a democratic egalitarianism.[177] Unlike many French Bohemians who, along with Baudelaire, often lamented "the rising tide of democracy, which invades and levels everything," the American Bohemians sought to link their aesthetic postures to democratic freedoms, to their nation's putative social and political mission.[178] Bohemia, they often suggested, was less a foreign currency than a concentrated, even purified expression of American ideals. To this end, the *Press* announced that it would not admit the presence of a literary aristocracy, vowing not to "assume because [a work was] written by Longfellow, Emerson, or Taylor, that it is not trash."[179] Yet, as the *Press's* printed correspondence reveals, many of its readers already aligned elitism and excellence. One letter advises that "if unpopular, [the *Saturday Press*] should be indispensable. . . . Never ask for a moment how it will do or take, but make it do and take. Do not, like a physician, feel the pulse of your public and administer accordingly." Another reader writes that he admires the *Saturday Press* but "fears for its continuation" since it cannot appeal to a popular audience. Still, the reader was cheered by the "fixed success of the *Atlantic Monthly*" and expresses hope that the *Saturday Press* can find an equally loyal, if relatively small, readership. But the editorial response, sufficiently trenchant to have been written by Clapp, contests such notions of elite readership and affirms a Bohemian inclusiveness:

> For our own part, we are disposed to judge the public by ourselves, and we take the liberty of recommending the same course to our correspondents. It is not probable that wisdom will die either with them or with us. So far from being concerned lest we issue a paper too good for the public, our only fear is that we shall be unable to issue one good enough for them. With the daily and weekly trash which they are accustomed to receive, they have for a long time been utterly disgusted; they buy it for the same reason that sailors eat mouldy bread, because they don't know where to get anything better. If the *Saturday Press* furnished them with anything better (and it is a very modest assertion to say that it will) of course they will prefer to buy and read that.[180]

Though the *Press* distinguishes itself from "the daily and weekly trash," it refuses to grant that such trash actually reflects that taste of the general public. Unlike many priests of high culture who either maintained that the average mind could not adequately appreciate fine art and literature or who took it upon themselves to elevate the popular taste, the *Press* insists that the public is already quite capable of preferring quality publications. To think otherwise, the *Press* argues, would constitute "a gross insult to the intelligence and good sense of the whole American people."[181] Similarly, the *Press*'s theatre critic maintains that the public's "consumption of what is presented to them, however great, is not a test of their judgment." On the contrary, the critic democratically defends the public's "instinctive penetration" (though with enough condescension toward "the people" to justify his own professional expertise): "The people always detect imperfection in what is presented to them. They are not analysts, it is true, and cannot, at all times, lay their fingers on the weak spot; but they experience a vague dissatisfaction, which attests—if not to a high order of education—at least to an instinctive penetration."[182]

The Bohemians' attack on cultural elitism and defense of literary democracy helps to explain their antipathy toward Boston and many of its writers, but does not fully reveal how they came to view the northern city as the very embodiment of bourgeois "respectability." This "respectable" ethos no doubt included literary elitism, but only as a component of a larger class identity; indeed, the Bohemian hostility toward many Bostonian literati no doubt reflected an awareness of the degree to which the leading cultural and socioeconomic establishments in Boston intersected and mutually supported one another. As we reconstruct the many links between high cultural institutions, Bostonian society, and the ideology of respectability, the identity of the Bohemians' bourgeois antagonist becomes increasingly apparent. More than American national culture at large, the urban marketplace, or even the emerging middle class, it was the urban upper class, especially in Boston, that most aroused Bohemian rancor. More than American crudeness and materialism, more than middle class evangelical piety and morality, it was genteel superiority that most affronted our first Bohemians.

In the mid-nineteenth century, the very term "respectability" had specific class connotations that it has subsequently lost and that are crucial to an understanding of Bohemian dissent. Like the terms "genteel" and "gentility," "respectability" originally denoted the gentry and the wellborn. To be sure, popular etiquette books sought to teach the middle class how to emulate the cultural styles of the wealthy, and in so doing helped to democratize the concepts, or at least to extend their applicability beyond the upper class. Older definitions persisted, however, and were employed by contemporary representatives of differing social classes.[183] For example, Charles Astor Bristed, the grandson of John Jacob Astor and chronicler of the "Upper Ten Thousand" in New York (and, if we remember, an anomalous self-declared "Bohemian"), elides the word "respectable" with such terms as "good society," "fashionable," and even "Upper Ten," using all as apparent synonyms in a single paragraph.[184] Elsewhere, Bristed also promises to introduce the reader to New York's first set, "the real respectable, fashionable, exquisite part of New York society, the very cream of the cream."[185] This lexicon also appears in a self-consciously working-class publication, the *Mechanic's Free Press.* One article protests the privileges of the "rich and opulent, consequently the respectable" and another further reveals the class content of the term, referring to a "scale of respectability" that puts the laborer at the very bottom. As these disparate examples suggest, the association between the "respectable" and the upper class still retained its currency.[186]

In mid-nineteenth-century America, the most "respectable" members of the haute bourgeoisie resided in Boston. It was this class that Oliver Wendell Holmes first designated as "Brahmin" in 1860,[187] and by this time the mercantile and industrial elite in Boston had broadened into what historian Frederic Jaher describes as a "multi-faceted upper class."[188] An economic elite, this class also had "extensive intergenerational continuity, clan clustering, common birthplaces, and integration with the social and cultural patriciate."[189] It controlled a large proportion of the public offices and taxable wealth of the city (in 1860, the top 1 percent of the population owned two-fifths of that wealth),[190] and dominated the professions of law and medicine as well as Boston's philanthropic and cultural establishments, including Harvard University, the Massachusetts Historical Society, the Athenaeum (an elite subscription library), the Lowell Institute, Unitarian churches, the *North American Review*, and the more liberal *Atlantic Monthly*. Indeed, many of the "august luminaries of literature" themselves descended from Brahmin stock: historians Francis Parkman and William H. Prescott and writers James Russell Lowell and Oliver Wendell Holmes all descended from prominent mercantile families, and Longfellow married the daughter of the renowned mercantilist, Nathan Appleton. Lowell, Holmes, and Longfellow were also professors at Harvard, an institution that perhaps more than any other helped to consolidate and extend an elite class consciousness.[191]

A Harvard faculty member described the cultural work that the university ideally accomplished, insisting in 1849 that Harvard united its students into a "great family." Even if the students later became "rivals in business, struggling hand in hand in the competition for wealth," the professor maintained that their collegiate experience would ensure that "when they meet . . . they are indeed on common ground, with common tastes, feelings, and hopes."[192] Most contemporary Harvard students were "one of a great family" in more than a metaphoric sense: as one mid-century critic noted, most were "sons of rich men."[193] The Harvard Corporation, the primary governing board of the university, and the faculty also came increasingly from this class, or at least subscribed to its conservative expectations. One professor, seeking a law position, assured the corporation that he would avoid discussing "everything 'peoplish' or agrarian in character" or encouraging the "destruction of vested rights."[194] The increasing elitism of Harvard alarmed many non-Brahmins, especially since the university still possessed its original charter from the Massachusetts government, received some financial support from the state legislature, and was still supervised by a board of overseers drawn partially from that legislature. In the 1850s, however, the collapse of the Whig Party, the subsequent rise of Democratic Free-Soilers and the early Republican Party caused the Brahmins to lose their dominance of the legislature temporarily, and the new representatives began to attack that "certain class of individuals, who seem to think that they own the institution, president, corporators, overseers, and all, —a class of individuals who assume it to be their mission to keep Harvard College from the influences of the outside barbarians."[195]

From New York, the Bohemians echoed such attacks, and, in so doing, further revealed their anti-Brahmin animus and the extent to which that hostility was connected to their democratic ideals. On the pages of the *Saturday Press*, they lobbied for a Harvard that would "fitly represent the active energy, the movement, and the progress of this age and this country" and rise to the democratic task of "educating a free people."[196] Similarly, once again highlighting Harvard's social elitism, the Bohemians maintained that, after Lowell had become a Harvard professor, he had "buried himself in a university, and consequently ceased to be universal."[197] The *Press* also frequently disparaged Edward Everett, a former Harvard president and former editor of the *North American Review*, representing this elite social and literary figure as the ultimate bourgeois:

> Mr. Everett figures in American literature as the foremost representative of those writers who, trimming and veering with the currents of conventionality, build up fictitious reputations on the strength of a solemn outside, an imposing presence, and certain well-cultivated, but quite ordinary mental faculties. Most of the literary men congregated in and about Boston are of this kind. . . . In our view of the facts, such persons are only a congregation of inflated bladders, and the sooner they are punctured the better it will be, we think, for the growth and purity of American literature, and the integrity of American life.[198]

To deflate the likes of Everett, the *Press* advocated the quintessential democratic concept of "common sense." An article entitled "The Sage" argues that men such as Everett who attempt to "apply the old laws to the new order of things" are "ruined" by their experience, by their inability to use "Common Sense to comprehend and meet the unexpected exigencies and demands of the times." But, the article prophesies, "Soon Common Sense shall assert her rightful sway. Soon Humbug shall be banished" and soon men will "dare to say that they do not believe in Everett."[199] By reviving the revolutionary potential of common sense, the Bohemians proposed to debunk the evasive morality or "humbug" underlying the genteel hegemony of Everett and his class; the "elaborate commonplace respectability" of the Brahmins became their sworn foe.

If Boston, with its powerful Brahmin class, represented "respectability," how did the Bohemians regard their own metropolis? In many ways, they seem to have viewed New York as Bohemian in relation to Boston's Bourgeois. When Howells visited Pfaff's, he remarked on Clapp's sense that it was "proof of the inferiority of Boston that if you passed down Washington Street, half a dozen men in the crowd would know you were

Holmes, or Lowell, or Longfellow, or Wendell Phillips; but in Broadway no one would know who you were, or care to the measure of his smallest blasphemy." Howells then muses:

> I have since heard this more than once urged as a signal advantage of New York for the aesthetic inhabitant, but I am not sure, yet, that it is so. The unrecognized celebrity probably has his mind quite as much upon himself as if some one pointed him out, and otherwise I cannot think that the sense of neighborhood is such a bad thing for the artist in any sort. It involves the sense of responsibility, which cannot be too constant or too keen. If it narrows, it deepens; and this may be the secret of Boston.[200]

Even though he eventually moved to New York and wrote for a number of mass-circulation periodicals, Howells never ceased to protest the loss of earlier communal codes and ethics; for Howells, New York—and the increasingly urban and commercialized conditions of authorship that helped to foster Bohemianism—encouraged a fall from an earlier ethic and aesthetic of responsibility and indicated the emergence of a laissez-faire economy of the self. Though poised as social elites, the Boston literati, according to Howells, maintained a connection with the larger community; the Bohemians remained relatively anonymous, at least beyond the bounds of (the increasingly well known) Pfaff's.

The "secret of Boston" with its "sense of responsibility" that "narrows" and "deepens" of course pertained most fully to the noblesse oblige of the Brahmin class, the very class Howells encountered at the Autocrats Club and when breakfasting with Fields. Not all members of the Brahmin class shared Howells's favorable assessment, however, and Henry Adams perhaps best articulates how the Bohemians must have regarded "respectable" Boston. In a letter to Henry James, Adams maintains: "The painful truth is that all of my New England generation, counting the half century, 1820–1870, were in actual fact only one mind and nature; the individual was a facet of Boston. We knew each other to the last nervous centre . . . Harvard College and Unitarianism kept us all shallow." Indeed, Adams even identifies the object of his "antipathy" as the "Type *bourgeois-bostonian*!"[201] When discussing his generation, Adams of course refers to his own Brahmin class, and acknowledges the extent to which that class dominated the city's (and to a large extent the nation's) social, cultural, and economic institutions, and, despite some aristocratic tendencies, promoted strict bourgeois values. As Jaher attests, "all segments of proper Boston—scions of old families, new business titans, and members of the intelligentsia—supported commercial achievement, technological change, and the Protestant ethic."[202]

While the Bohemians opposed their city favorably to bourgeois Boston, many "Proper Bostonians" disparaged New York society. George Ticknor (of Ticknor and Fields) maintained that New York lacked the Brahmins' "severity towards disorganizers and social democracy," and Henry Lee noted that the city was without "our standard of morals."[203] These statements help to reveal how New York as a whole could have exemplified a tinge of Bohemianism, at least in comparison with contemporary Boston. Further, though somewhat beyond the Brahmin purview, an article from the *Gloucester Telegraph* (republished in the *Saturday Press* and so implicitly, if ironically, endorsed by that publication) noted that the Bohemian weekly was a "good representative of [its] incongruous metropolis, blending, most strangely, an elevated literary tone with the rankest of rant and the lowest and loosest scraps of penny-a-liners—just as the glitter and gayety of Broadway is in close proximity to the rags and wretchedness of Thomas Street."[204]

For the most part, the first Bohemians took less umbrage at the local New York elites. The prerevolutionary Knickerbocker upper class had not been able to retain the same level of prominence as the Boston Brahmins, nor were they able to incorporate new economic elites into their patriciate as successfully: to a large extent, the upper class divided into an Old Guard and a parvenu "smart set," though both, in comparison to the Brahmins, cultivated lavish tastes.[205] Bristed's Knickerbocker hero of the Upper Ten occupied rooms "overflowing with foppery"[206] and a visiting European writer for the *Saturday Press* noted that the more he "mixed in New York society, the more [he] was startled at the persistent efforts of everybody about [him] to appear of aristocratic lineage."[207] As we have seen, the Bohemians were themselves attracted to extremes of "high" and "low" society, and the dramatic presence of both in New York may partially explain their sense of the city's superiority. Also, elites and immigrants alike tended to come from more diverse backgrounds in New York, a condition that would obviously appeal to the Bohemians;[208] as a contemporary article in the *Atlantic Monthly* itself admits: "New York, in its various phases and developments, its crowded and cosmopolitan population, its out-door kaleidoscopic splendor, is indeed a representative of the entire country, . . . perhaps more of a representative city than any other in the land." (Of course, the article also contends that New York "has not the purely literary life of Boston," and that the latter expresses the "cultivated side of our nationality.")[209] Further, the New York economic elites also coincided less with the political and cultural leadership of the city, and perhaps this is one of the reasons that Clapp felt New York offered a liberating anonymity to its "aesthetic inhabitants," allowing them greater independence from bourgeois mores and control. New York did not have "a cultural establishment of interrelated publishers, writers, and merchant Maecenases like the Brahmin intelligentsia," and publications like *Harper's* catered to a wider audience than Boston's *Atlantic Monthly*.[210]

Still, the Bohemians also objected to haute bourgeois leadership in New York, singling out the rich philanthropist "Dives" and his army of "commercial chivalrie," as well as the wealthy congregation of Trinity Church, as we have seen. The *Saturday Press* did praise the cosmopolitan character of "New York Society," though not without a counterthrusting gibe: "Were it not for its cosmopolitan character, and the large admixture of foreigners, it would be intolerable for its snobbishness."[211] Yet in general, the mid-century haute bourgeoisie exerted a less comprehensive influence upon New York culture than the Brahmins did upon Boston, and New York offered greater scope for the sort of democratic culture the Bohemians idealized; they hoped, in the words of Whitman's later *Democratic Vistas*, that culture should not be "restricted by conditions ineligible to the masses," and that it should not be "for a single class alone, or for the parlors or lecture-rooms."[212]

Such critiques of cultural elitism invite the question how the New York Bohemians were themselves categorized within the developing cultural hierarchies of the mid-nineteenth century. All accounts suggest that the *Press* achieved a high level of prestige: though it never acquired a broad subscription base, it did circulate throughout the country (one letter to the editor even hailed from Peoria); in later years, Whitman maintained that "the *Press* cut a significant figure in the periodical literature of the time";[213] and no less a custodian of culture than Howells wrote in his retrospective of "literary New York" that "young writers throughout the country were ambitious to be seen in [the *Saturday Press*]" and they "gave their best to it."[214] Howells then bestowed what must have been his ultimate compliment: "It is not too much to say that it was very nearly as well for one to be accepted by the *Press* as to be accepted by the *Atlantic*, for the time there was no other literary comparison."[215] (Howells served on the editorial board of the *Atlantic* between 1866 and 1881.) The fact that Howells would align the *Atlantic*, one of the central Bostonian institutions dedicated to the pursuit of the "literary," with the *Saturday Press* attests to the latter's cultural influence. Indeed, despite the Bohemian opposition to Boston, the *Atlantic* published the work of several Bohemians, including Whitman and Fitz-James O'Brien, and conversely the *Saturday Press* often excerpted articles from its prestigious counterpart. (What is more, the assistant editor of the *Saturday Press*, Thomas Bailey Aldrich, himself eventually became the editor of the *Atlantic.*) Still, Howells nevertheless calls attention to one important difference between the two periodicals: noting the discrepancy between the two magazines' endowments, Howells maintains that "the *Saturday Press* never paid in anything but in hopes of paying."[216] Thus, Howells confirms that, in relation to the eminent *Atlantic,* the *Saturday Press* finally emerged as an insolvent Bohemian in relation to a more respectable Bourgeois.

Some have argued that the Bohemian antipathy toward Boston stemmed primarily from a sense of relative socioeconomic marginalization. The "literati" belonged to Boston, and most Bohemians had to resort to hack writing to earn their livelihoods. At a time when the absence of an international copyright law caused the American market to be flooded with inexpensive editions of British books and articles, few American men of letters subsisted on their literary output. As the Bohemian William Winter retrospectively noted: "The conditions of literary life in America, certainly, were not propitious. . . . The number of writers who were obtaining a subsistence from distinctively literary labor was small. Dana was a man of fortune. Halleck was an accountant. Bryant was an editor. Longfellow was a college professor."[217] Yet, unlike these members of the Bostonian literati who supplemented their literary income with other genteel professions, many Bohemians were reduced to seeking "Bonner-like patronage."[218] The latter phrase refers to Robert Bonner, the editor of the *New York Ledger*, a popular weekly newspaper. Bonner strictly regulated contributions to his paper: as one literary observer noted, "a great many of the highly moral and instructive effusions that were an important feature of the paper were prepared by ungodly and happy-go-lucky Bohemians, who were glad to eke out the livelihood earned by reporting with an occasional 'tenner' from Mr. Bonner's treasury."[219] Such practices led the *Round Table* to refer to the Bohemians as "hireling hacks led by a moral hyena."[220]

Accordingly, Christine Stansell has argued that the significance of Pfaff's and the *Saturday Press* lay in allowing "hack writers, unconnected to the powerful institutions of literary taste and approbation, to begin to conceive of themselves as artists. . . . The gatherings at Pfaff's thus coalesced a sense of literariness among men who, from most other perspectives, were simply working stiffs."[221] For Stansell, Bohemianism thus served as a less elite version of such "powerful institutions of literary taste" as the *Atlantic Monthly,* instead of constituting a more distinct cultural ethos.

This argument contains some truth, but it is important to recognize that the very meaning and scope of the "literary" and the "artistic" were in question during this time, and that these meanings changed according to the contexts of their expression. Bohemia was one such important context, and, as a "commercial democratic cultural space," Bohemia not only passively embodied but also strenuously championed the cause of democracy.[222] If it affirmed a category of "literary" writing, it generally sought to promote the representative quality of such writing, and to protest the widening gap between the literati and the populace. In both life and literature, the Bohemians objected to a culture that was growing "excessively grandiloquent and florid"; and at a time when Brahmin literati like Charles Eliot Norton maintained that, though deserving of respect, Whitman's writing contained "passages of intolerable coarseness," and even Emerson encouraged Whitman to censor the 1860 edition, the *Press* embraced *Leaves*' "new wild strain, grand and lofty, sweet and harmonious, then again rash and tumultuous."[223] In so doing, the Bohemians opposed Brahmin "high" culture by championing a new, Bohemian aesthetic, one that they hoped would not and could not "be tolerated for an instant if viewed from the commonest social standpoints"; this aesthetic sought a "fierce wild freedom" from the constraints of traditional respectability and class-bound privilege.[224] Embodied in Whitman's poetry and persona, this aesthetic has continued to define the American Bohemian.

"The Gypsies Are All Gone"

The coming of the Civil War scattered the Bohemians—Whitman went to Washington to nurse the wounded, Ada Clare and Adah Isaacs Menken went to San Francisco, O'Brien served as a soldier and was mortally wounded—and the *Saturday Press* folded after 1860.[225] Clapp briefly reestablished the paper in 1865, only to find that the bourgeois press was even more hostile toward Bohemianism than before. In an article entitled "About Bohemians," the *New York Leader* recapitulated the *Times*'s 1858 editorial, describing the remaining Pfaffians as "a peculiar mixture of the seedy, bloated, whiskey-sucking, kid-gloved, airish and pretentious" and even suggested that "the police should be vested with the power to arrest them as public nuisances." Similarly, the *Round Table* described Bohemianism as "the feculent product of Parisian low life."[226] Such antipathy toward the Bohemians seems even to have reunited the northern and southern press into a newfound bourgeois consensus: the *Herald* of Wilmington, North Carolina, echoed the *Leader*, declaring that the Pfaffians lived "idle, lazy, thriftless, imprudent" lives, doing "all the harm they [could] to reputable people."[227] Yet as newspapers further embroidered the mythos of Bohemia and perpetuated the Bohemian-Bourgeois antagonism, the Bohemians once again retaliated, reprinting Ada Clare's earlier defense of their creed. The dialectics of Bohemianism thus continued, and the phenomenon provided an ongoing impetus for both contesting and advancing dominant social, cultural, and political agendas.

Beyond their numerous editorial sallies, the Pfaffians of 1865 most fully reasserted their Bohemian commitments through their continued quest for a new literary aesthetic, one that might represent a more broadly democratic America. The Bohemians did find another writer who, along with Whitman, promised to do just that: the *Saturday Press* was the first eastern periodical to publish the irreverent writing of Mark Twain, the "Sagebrush Bohemian." In so doing, Clapp and his coterie once again rewrote, and respatialized, *la vie bohème*, bringing the romance of Bohemia to New York via San Francisco.

2

Bret Harte, Urban Spectatorship, and the Bohemian West

SHORTLY AFTER THE PFAFFIANS announced their version of *la vie bohème* in the *Saturday Press*, the mythos of Bohemia traveled to San Francisco. If the essence of Bohemia involves a constant interplay between the real and the imagined, then the "instant" city of San Francisco would seem to be among the locales most suited to realizing countercultural fantasy. Early San Franciscans represented their metropolis as such a proto-countercultural site; they extolled their city in terms analogous to the opposition between the Bohemian and the Bourgeois, frequently recasting the polarity as an opposition between the Western and Eastern states. To this end, the 1855 *Annals of San Francisco* celebrated the city's vitality and distance from a Puritan inheritance, and inhabitants proclaimed that their metropolis was "freed from the multitude of prejudices and embarrassments and exactions that control the Eastern cities."[1] And lest it be thought that the city departed from Eastern mores through a lack of cultural sophistication, newspapers further announced that as early as 1853 San Francisco was fast "becoming a second Paris."[2] The sense of being at a far remove from Eastern concerns only increased during the years of the Civil War, and California "boosters" were ever ready to promote settlement by advertising social difference.[3]

These sentiments suggest that the designation of a Bohemia in San Francisco may have been somewhat redundant—too close to most western self-representations to retain any oppositional power. Yet the pioneer of Bohemian San Francisco largely refused to identify his literary ideal with his city. For Bret Harte, San Francisco's first self-declared Bohemian, the metropolis remained intractably bourgeois. In contrast to the 1855 *An-*

nals of San Francisco, Harte characterized the "dominant tone" of the city as eminently "respectable"—the very quality that the Pfaffians had identified as their nemesis. His retrospective essay "Bohemian Days in San Francisco" strove to overturn popular perceptions about the city, arguing, "It was a singular fact that while the rest of California was swayed by an easy, careless unconventionalism, or swept over by waves of emotion and sentiment, San Francisco preserved an intensely material and practical attitude, and even a certain austere morality." Harte further insisted that "an unmistakable seriousness and respectability was the ruling sign of its governing class," even suggesting that under the brief reign of the Vigilance Committees in the mid-1850s, "the lawless and vicious class were more appalled by the moral spectacle of several thousand black-coated, serious-minded business men in embattled procession than by mere force of arms."[4] Against such a procession, Harte offered his own experience, which he defined as "Bohemian."

For Harte, the cultural work of the Bohemian-Bourgeois divide could not be displaced onto a geographic axis opposing San Francisco and the East. Instead, the act of calling himself a Bohemian, even in the San Francisco of the 1860s, positioned Harte to stage a productively adversarial relation to his surroundings; through "the Bohemian," he and other members of his coterie received and exploited a literary subjectivity dedicated to trenchant social observation, aesthetic achievement, and cosmopolitan aspiration. As Harte would have it, locating a Bohemia within (and without) the city was both a mode of cultural service and critique; it was a form of civic engagement that distanced itself from San Francisco. For the Bay City writers and performers who embraced a Bohemian identification (including, for a brief time, Mark Twain), the dichotomy between the Bohemian and the Bourgeois thus remained timely and relevant; in its developing mythology, Bohemia offered a locale west of the (west of the) West, a never-closing frontier.[5]

Like the Pfaffians, the early San Franciscan Bohemians fashioned an oppositional stance that belies the attempts of subsequent theorists to view the legacy of Bohemianism as mere "reaction and corruption," a form of decadent individualism antithetical to social engagement.[6] Countering those who interpret the phenomenon as a frivolous affectation incapable of substantive protest, the early writings of Bret Harte and other local journalists help document the extent to which a "Bohemian" subjectivity could enable social criticism and register the desire for social alternatives—albeit for the most part within the relatively circumscribed parameters defined by

American liberalism. On the pages of the San Franciscan newspaper, the *Golden Era*, the dialectic between the Bohemian and the Bourgeois translates into a series of tensions between and within a wide range of American bourgeois ideologies, whether "residual," "dominant," or "emergent."[7] Exposing (if also at times eliding) a range of ideological fissures, these columns amount to an immanent critique, one that, under the sign of "Bohemia," provides an alternative or supplement to that of "America." As such, Bohemia seeks to increase the social goods allegedly guaranteed by liberal freedoms.

In particular, many "Bohemian" columns, especially those of Bret Harte, generate conflicts between individualism and commodity culture, independent artisanship and mass production, populism and elite hegemony, civic culture and domesticity, pluralism and Manifest Destiny—as well as the proverbial Bohemian and Bourgeois conflicts between libertinism and self-denial, culture and society. Moreover, registering the many ways in which these conflicts were mediated by social divisions and arose as responses to contemporary urban developments, the columns further reveal Bohemia's role in recording and fomenting both ideological "dissensus" and "consensus."[8] This chapter seeks to recover such moments as they arose in San Francisco's *Golden Era*.

In so doing, the chapter focuses on Harte's early columns, tracing his efforts to articulate a Bohemian identity, to critically deploy the Bohemian-Bourgeois opposition, and to locate or create a Bohemian community. Quickly establishing himself as a central figure of San Francisco's "literary frontier," Harte was also the most invested in Bohemia, sharing the Pfaffians' desire to chart its boundaries and to explore its imaginative possibilities. That Harte identified himself with Bohemianism may seem surprising: to the extent that literary history remembers him, it does so under the "sentimental" rubrics of "regionalism" and "local color," genres seemingly antithetical to the cosmopolitan and critical values of Bohemia.[9] Even as canny a chronicler of Bohemianism as Albert Parry refused to take Harte's vision of Bohemia seriously, insisting, "He mistook the color, the aroma, and the bustle of the pioneering days for Bohemianism."[10] For Parry, Harte's very attempt to connect Bohemia with his own experience only provided further evidence of his provincialism. Yet an examination of his early journalism and fiction confirms that Harte understood both the history and metaphoric reach of the term, as well as its mobile, shape-shifting power.

This chapter begins with a brief analysis of Harte's early life, focusing on those elements that anticipated his later Bohemianism. It then examines how Harte constructed a discursive identity as a "Bohemian spectator" and how he used this subjectivity to register "Bohemian impressions" and to search for a Bohemian milieu. The chapter continues to follow Harte's Bohemian spectator through a variety of urban scenes, enclaves, and literary topographies as he implicitly measures each against the (sometimes more and sometimes less) subversive or utopian requirements of his mythic Bohemia. Unsurprisingly, the world that most approximates Harte's Bohemia turns out to exist primarily on paper, fashioned in and between the columns of the *Golden Era* itself. It is on the pages of this literary weekly that Bohemia begins to rematerialize and reassert its position within the larger social geography of early San Francisco.

Even before arriving in California, Harte was a likely enough candidate for a Bohemian identity. His early life was a continuous history of dislocation, economic insecurity, and conflicting ethnic and religious affiliations. Born on the East Coast, he inherited this sense of displacement from his father, Henry Harte, who was the son of a brief union between a Protestant woman and Bernard Hart, a wealthy Jew (and future secretary of the New York Stock Exchange). Once this marriage dissolved, Henry Harte had little contact with his father but was well aware that Bernard Hart had remarried and was living a life of luxury while his mother struggled to put him through school. To signify his resentment, and perhaps further to distance himself from a Jewish identity, Henry Harte eventually added an "e" to his surname and converted to Catholicism (though the rest of his family, including his son Bret, remained Episcopalian). Henry Harte continued to be dogged by economic difficulties, however, and during Bret's childhood he moved his family to seven different eastern cities as he tried to earn a living as a schoolmaster. In 1845, when Bret was nine years old, Henry Harte died. The family was left penniless and struggled to maintain a semblance of gentility.[11]

Yet for Harte, such struggle ultimately became the stuff of Bohemian romance, and, in a later interview, he interprets his father's struggles as an uncompromising dedication to a superior realm of literary pursuit: "He was true to his training and inspiration, for he would not give up a vocation which enabled him to cultivate the literary graces, even though by doing so he could have earned a little more money. . . . I had rather have my family cherish the memory of their grandfather than the traditions associated with five governors of Connecticut."[12] If within Bohemian mythology the "literary graces" justify economic struggle, they also promise a means of transcending the very difficulties they impose. Fusing familial and literary romance, the young Bret Harte had apparently yearned for such transcendence, grasping the essential Bohemian practice of seizing upon literature as an alternative reality, as an imaginary realm of pure possibility. The only adventure of his boyhood he would recall in later years neatly dramatizes his desire to realize a fictitious world, to use fiction (quite literally) as an escape from present circumstances. According to this reminiscence, after feeling himself "subjected to an act of grievous injustice," Harte briefly ran away from home, hoping to arrive at the "island where Captain Cook was killed."[13] As he matured, Harte increasingly immersed himself in his studies of Latin and Greek, and in the novels of Dickens and Cooper. If literature no longer provided the illusion of escape, it still provided Harte with a frame to offset and even redefine his own reality; he began to view his life through the contours of literary genre, noting: "My life is a mixture of broad caricature and farce when I think of others, it is a melodrama when I feel for myself."[14] Bohemianism eventually became another such defining frame.

When his mother remarried in 1853, Harte resumed a nomadic existence. The family sailed to Oakland in 1854, and for the next six years, he drifted through northern California as a schoolteacher, miner, Wells Fargo guard, printer, journalist, and editor. If such nomadism presaged a Bohemian self-identification, so did Harte's growing sense of himself as a social misfit, destined for a literary career because, as he noted in the winter of 1857, "The conviction forced on me by observation and not by vain enthusiasm [is] that I am fit for nothing else."[15] Harte's Bohemian tendencies also manifested themselves in his persistent desire to set himself apart. A friend from Union, Humboldt County, later recalled Harte's incongruously foppish appearance and the way it goaded the locals in the little frontier town of five hundred: "He was not especially popular, as he was thought to be fastidious, and to hold himself aloof from 'the general,' but he was simply a self-respecting, gentlemanly fellow."[16] Yet Harte also forecast his "Bohemian Days" by speaking out on behalf of those most socially marginalized and dispossessed. Most notably, Harte editorialized in Union's *Northern Californian* about an "indiscriminate massacre of Indians" in the neighboring town of Eureka, insisting that the butchering of sixty Native Americans (many of them women and children) by local whites was an unpardonable evil and that "a more shocking and revolting spectacle never was exhibited to the eyes of a Christian and civilized people."[17] Following this unpopular editorial, his life was allegedly "threatened and in no little danger," and Harte soon left for San Francisco.[18]

However ripe Harte may have been for a Bohemian identification, there is no evidence that he applied the term to himself before he returned to San Francisco on March 27, 1860. He took up the term, appropriately enough, as a discursive identity; as a signature for a column entitled "Town and Table Talk" in San Francisco's literary weekly, the *Golden Era*. Harte had started his work on the paper as a printer, and quickly began contributing sketches and stories. Fortuitously, the paper changed management and editorial policy around the time Harte arrived. "Colonel" Joseph E. Lawrence, the new editor and co-owner with James Brooks, hoped to retain the paper's popularity in the rural districts by continuing the departments on mining and agricultural news, as well as the informal "Correspondents' Column." Lawrence also wanted to give the paper a more sophisticated, polished dimension, however, one that would enable the paper to speak to (and elevate) the city's increasingly urbane readership.[19] Lawrence was able to articulate this objective through the writings of his local "Bohemian," Bret Harte.[20]

The Flâneur, the Spectator, and the Bohemian

As envisioned by Lawrence and fashioned by Harte, the "Town and Table Talk" column—later renamed "The Bohemian Feuilleton" and, finally, the "Bohemian Papers"— participated in an established and even outworn literary/journalistic genre: that of the strolling urban spectator. Bohemianism (and most particularly Harte's Bohemianism) was intricately tied to this genre—so much so that *la vie bohème* has sometimes been subsumed by it in critical discussions. Combining French and English traditions, the genre of urban spectatorship has a long, complex history that alternately prefigures, parallels, counters, and overlaps with that of the Bohemian. Such intersections create a kind of genealogical confusion—especially since most commentators see the spectatorial genre as working to uphold the very bourgeois manners and values that the Bohemian ostensibly attacks.

Within recent critical theory, the spectatorial genre has reached its apotheosis in the figure of Walter Benjamin's flâneur. The touchstone of Benjamin's writings on Charles Baudelaire and his unfinished "Paris

Arcades" project, "flâneur" was a term that originated in early-nineteenth-century Paris.[21] It described the writers and journalists who used the feuilletons (the serial sections of the Parisian press) to represent the city as a dramatic spectacle. This spectacle, the feuilletons implicitly argued, required the interpretive magic of the ideal spectator: the flâneur. With elegant detachment and ideal critical acumen, the flâneur operated as an acutely sensitive interpreter, capable of divining the essential workings of modern capitalistic society. Amidst the upheavals of the rapidly expanding, industrializing metropolis, the flâneur was allegedly able to penetrate the pasteboard mask of the spectacle, grasp the secret life of things, and categorize the exotic plethora of urban "types." Part magician, part scientist, a belletristic journalist who was simultaneously a "botanist on asphalt," the flâneur attempted, "unencumbered by any factual knowledge, . . . to make out the profession, the character, the background, and the life-style of passersby."[22]

Yet, for Benjamin, the flâneur ultimately had a conservative function and worked to support the developing bourgeois order. Though fragmentary, Benjamin's notes on the flâneur suggest that he viewed the figure (at least in most instantiations) as an agent of social control, as one who used the feuilletons to reassure the bourgeoisie that the urban crowd was "harmless and of perfect bonhomie" and that "life in the big city was not nearly so disquieting as it probably seemed to people."[23] Under his knowledgeable scrutiny, urban scenes and "types" became legible and categorizable. He helped to bring epistemological order to the dislocations of urban life. Beyond serving as an urban guide, Benjamin's flâneur also contributed to the more insidiously hegemonic and pervasive spectacle of commodity fetishism. The act of management and interpretation, according to Benjamin, ultimately served to dramatize the values of the marketplace: commodities in and of themselves, the feuilletons gleefully recommodified the pageant of urban life, celebrating such displays of consumer culture as trade fairs, arcades, department stores. As an integral part of this culture, the flâneur, in Benjamin's words, was thus "someone abandoned in the crowd. In this he share[d] the situation of the commodity. . . . The intoxication to which the *flâneur* surrender[ed] [was] the intoxication of the commodity around which surges the stream of customers."[24] The poet of consumer desire, the flâneur magnified this spectacle of commodity fetishism, appropriating and compounding it as he strove to sell his own perceptions.

A figure analogous to the flâneur emerged in the American periodical press during the 1830s. This figure derived not only from the French tradition but also from that of the flâneur's English cousin, the "spectator."[25] Arriving in London by the late sixteenth and early seventeenth centuries (before the flâneur ever strolled through Paris), the English spectator was attracted even then by the spectacle of commercial activity and an ever more diverse population. Yet the spectatorial genre did not mushroom until periodical publication expanded in the late seventeenth century. As a representational strategy, serial publication mimicked the episodic, fleeting movements of the wandering spectator, and it was at this time that the spectator began to develop his own characteristic consciousness. Regarding the city with a somewhat bemused detachment, if also with a subversive, carnivalesque edge, early spectators like the *English Lucian* incorporated the common seventeenth-century figure of the Cynic philosopher while describing, often with bawdy detail, the excesses of urban life. It was not until the *Spectator* and *Tatler* of Addison and Steele, however, that the genre reached its most definitive and influential expression.

As many have argued, the eighteenth-century spectator observed and helped to create a newfound "public sphere" within English culture.[26] An emerging sector of civil society, the public sphere arose out of the numerous clubs, journals, coffee houses, and periodicals that dedicated themselves to the diffusion of enlightened discourse. This sphere also mediated between the aristocracy and the increasingly powerful English bourgeoisie; in so doing, the public sphere worked, in Terry Eagleton's words, "to prise the definition of the gentleman free of any too rigidly genetic or class-specific determinants" and to link gentility to the practices of "polite discourse," taste, decorum, and reason.[27] The "Spectator," namesake of both a club and a periodical, became a widely imitated discursive posture, a model for the new ideal gentleman. In the hands of Addison and Steele, the *Spectator* exaggerated the detachment of its predecessors (their spectator was a bachelor with an independent income, one of the "Fraternity of Spectators who live in the world without having anything to do in it") but, unlike the *English Lucian*, the *Spectator* strictly avoided the illicit and the bawdy in the effort to elevate its readership and effect a kind of "social hygiene." Like Benjamin's flâneur, the spectator helped to sanitize and order civil society. As part of this agenda, the spectator also worked to annex the city's commercial spaces for the public sphere, lauding the "grand Scene of Business" found at the Royal Exchange; like the flâneur, Dana Brand argues, the spectator suggested the cosmopolitan, "benign benevolence of commercial activity" and its aesthetic satisfactions.[28]

By combining moral and philosophical instruction, positing social order, and extolling commerce, the spectator operated as an ideological force; indeed, as Brand maintains, the spectator "may have contributed to the process by means of which 'a successful bourgeois society' established itself in England."[29]

The spectator of nineteenth-century England and America continued to rely on many of the features that distinguished Addison and Steele's creation—though, perhaps through cross-pollination with the French flâneur or because of the demands of an ever-expanding readership, the spectator began to emphasize amusement over and against didacticism. Writing under the pseudonym of "Boz," Dickens advances this distinction, noting that it would be difficult for someone to walk through London "without deriving some amusement—we had almost said instruction, from his perambulation."[30] Dickens's early urban sketches were extremely popular in the United States and helped to inspire a host of journalists who constructed similar droll and urbane narratives of city life (though most avoided Boz's countervailing pathos).

Though the first American spectator/flâneurs were travel writers who extolled the sights of London and Paris, American urban journalists began to turn their spectatorial gazes toward New York by the late 1830s and 1840s, if only because of what noted travel correspondent Nathaniel Parker Willis described as that city's "imminent Parisification." "What makes Paris the world's golden centre, is positively coming here!" Willis exclaimed, defining the "golden centre" as "the point where money is spent most freely for pleasure."[31] Such sentiments began to abound in the New York press, most emphatically in the *Knickerbocker* magazine. The *Knickerbocker* dedicated many a serial to the observations of the detached man of leisure, including "Town and Country," "Loaferiana," "The Leisure Hunter," and "Odds and Ends—From the Port-Folio of the Penny-a-Liner." Titles like "Loaferiana" and "the Leisure Hunter" suggest a proto-Bohemian opposition to the demands of the bourgeois work ethic, but Dana Brand convincingly argues that these early American spectators became, like their European models, "the most representative spokesm[e]n for the pride of the bourgeoisie in the kind of world that they and the economic system associated with them were able to create."[32] They sought the leisure to consume the products of that system, and, as the Willis quote reveals, the American spectators often celebrated commercial culture as they made their rounds and mingled with the crowd. Indeed, despite the prominent American strain of antiurban and anti-European rhetoric, the spectator was particularly well suited to the American scene; as Brand maintains, the spectator's belief in the value of competitive trade and the harmonious nature of the urban crowd "would have placed him more definitely in the ideological mainstream than he would have been in Europe."[33]

This brief history of the genre of urban spectatorship demonstrates the extent to which the spectator/flâneur, at least within recent interpretations, is seen as a hegemonic construction, steadily working to celebrate a culture where social order intersects with the relentless commodification of existence. But if to write in the urban spectatorial mode implies such a strict adherence to dominant bourgeois values, how could the Bohemian emerge out of this discursive position? Was the Bohemian journalist merely the "Leisure Hunter" under a different name (and without an independent income), or did a "Bohemian Feuilleton" promise a critical difference, an (under)worldly approach to the urban spectacle?

Benjamin himself allows for a partial, temporary distinction between Bohemian and more consumerist flâneurs. His distinction is chronologically based: relying on French rather than English materials, Benjamin concludes that the Bohemian preceded rather than followed the commodity-driven flâneur into the crowd, and that, at least on first appearance, had not assumed all of the latter's characteristics. In other words, even though Benjamin ultimately aligns the flâneur with the consumer and the commodity, this alignment, his analysis suggests, was itself the product of a complex historical dialectic: the flâneur was not "always already" at one with the marketplace. It is within this dialectic that Benjamin locates *la bohème*: "As *flâneurs*, the intelligentsia came into the market-place. As they thought, to observe it—but in reality it was already to find a buyer. In this intermediary stage, in which they still had Maecenases, but were already beginning to familiarize themselves with the market, they took the form of the *bohème*."[34]

Just as Benjamin's flâneur belongs to the streets of early- and mid-nineteenth-century Paris, so the Bohemia of which he writes exists in a specific time and place. This is the original French Bohemia, the Bohemia that flourished in Murger's sketches and that often engaged in the political struggle over the policies of the post-Napoleonic "Bourgeois Monarchy" throughout the 1830s and 1840s. Within this particular historical context, Bohemia emerged as writers and intellectuals attempted to redefine their social roles and positions, as they made a transition from the culture of artistic patronage to one of marketplace commercialism, and as they (generally) attempted to maintain the connection between bourgeois rule and the most radical ideals of the French Revolution. For Benjamin, the flâneur as Bohemian thus existed in France during an "intermediary" stage before the conservative character of urban spectatorship had begun to solidify. To remove Bohemia from this historical dialectic is, of course, in some way to reify and essentialize it. Yet the writers who took up a Bohemian identity in different times and places (or, for that matter, the successive generations of Latin Quarter Bohemians) generally felt a lasting connection to the term's original social and political valences, however utopian that connection often became. Even within the genre of urban spectatorship, a Bohemian subjectivity could still register an oppositional posture, an ambivalence toward the very urban spectacle that the spectator admired and the flâneur came to celebrate.

Yet, though more ambivalent than the prototypical spectator, the Bohemian, Benjamin's analysis insists, could not finally evade the pull of an all-pervasive marketplace economy. By "beginning to familiarize themselves with the market," Benjamin's Bohemian flâneurs learned to operate within the very spectacle they first sought merely to observe and critique. Most Bohemians learned to operate in the marketplace *by* protesting its implacable workings, often attempting—through a combination of pragmatism and sheer bravado—to subvert it from within its own logical coordinates. "Finding a buyer" thus meant learning to promote their own alienated personae, using the market's predilection for novelty to gain an audience for their alternative social visions.

Accordingly, the "Bohemian" signature at the end of his "Town and Table Talk" column enabled Bret Harte to declare his independence from the urban spectacle—and in so publicly doing, to claim a distinctive position within it. As a young writer struggling to establish himself on San Francisco's literary frontier, Harte understood the roguish allure of his pseudonym and how conjuring the still novel but evocative term enabled him to assert his vocation as a literary artist and social critic. Even when writing "Town and Table Talk," the "Bohemian" could distance himself from the spectator's bourgeois spectacle and market his own literary persona. Of course, it could be argued that Harte's "Bohemian" signature was merely an unexamined afterthought, a little-understood sign of cosmopolitan sophistication intended to give "Town and Table Talk" added resonance and credibility. If *Golden Era* editor Joseph E. Lawrence suggested the signature to Harte, it may well have been to such an end. Though the editorial section occasionally lauds the "Bohemians in New

York," specifically the "patriarch Walt Whitman, the genial Clapp, the brilliant O'Brien, [and] the poetic Winter," Lawrence blandly (and reductively) defines them as "a band of pleasant gentlemen of literary pursuits and fond of lager and gossip."[35] For Lawrence, the New York Bohemians primarily represented a metropolitan literary identity and not a substantive antibourgeois animus. As we will see, Harte shared Lawrence's interest in achieving a metropolitan literary identity. His columns attempt to showcase his sophistication, frequently alluding to his extensive reading and embracing many of the standard conventions of spectatorial writing. "The Bohemian" might thus have been largely like other common spectatorial signatures such as the lounger, the idler, the man-about-town, etc., and may not have conveyed any oppositional commitments (beyond signaling urbanity in a largely frontier society).[36] The columns belie such a reading, however. As Harte makes the urban rounds, surveying such common subjects of spectatorial interest as trade shows, fairs, restaurants, and disparate neighborhoods, his "Bohemian" refuses the complacency of the archetypal spectator/flâneur, even as he seeks that figure's social influence and legitimacy.

"The Bohemian at the Fair"

In fall 1860, the *Golden Era* sent Harte to the San Francisco Mechanics' Fair, a monthlong tribute to commodities and their producers. Such scenes had been a staple of spectatorial literature ever since Addison and Steele frequented the Royal Exchange and enthused over "such a Body of Men thriving in their own private Fortunes, and at the same time promoting the Publick Stock."[37] An official press release from the San Francisco Mechanics' Institute (circa 1864) itself voices the optimism of the bourgeois spectator, and further reveals the hegemonic function of the industrial fair: the fair acts, according to this release, "to foster the Mechanic Arts, elevate the character of the workman, and stimulate ingenuity, invention, skill, and industry in all their branches, in the hope of exercising a wholesome influence upon the general prosperity of the country."[38] In his own "Town and Table Talk," Harte avoids such encomiums, however, and explicitly separates himself from the proceedings by accentuating his Bohemianism. Instead of upholding the bourgeois industrial community, Harte offers his own Bohemian persona to his readers as a kind of alternative spectacle, as a more remunerative commodity than any his employers would have had him describe.

At the beginning of the first of three columns he devotes to the fair, Harte's "Bohemian" quotes from the popular operetta *The Bohemian Girl* (then playing in the city at Maguire's Opera House): "Come with the Gipsy bride/And repair/To the fair."[39] Harte searches for the gypsies represented in the operetta, and in so doing reenacts the primary identification underlying an artistic Bohemian identity; moreover, he expresses the essential Bohemian desire to live a romantic fiction and create a heightened, even histrionic reality, one that he connects, much like the Pfaffians, with German festive culture. He longs for "the gaily painted booths and tents, and gipsy fortune-tellers, and Bavarian beer, and painted flagons, and picturesque groups . . . of my Bohemian friends." But he does not find such exuberant festivities at the Mechanics' Fair: "Oh, no! but THINGS! practical, substantial, unromantic useful things—and PEOPLE! in black coats and crinoline—every-day PEOPLE—Chacun a son gout—Allons!"[40] The final French flourish seals his identification with the original Parisian prototype and emphasizes his own superior distance from the surrounding spectacle.

By contrasting Bohemian romance with the intractable realism of "THINGS," Harte also refuses the spectator/flaneur's role as an incipient advertising agent. Material goods remain largely inert in his account and resist signification. His refusal to act as an advertiser is in fact quite self-conscious—apparently the *Golden Era* wanted him to be just that. As Harte describes it, he walks around the fair, willfully "forgetting that the 'Golden Area,' [the pun is Harte's] who has an immense advertising interest, has coached me up to the attractive qualities of the 'Patent Toothpick,' the 'magic Mouse Trap,' and supplied me with pencil and note book."[41] To publicize his aversion to commodity culture and the interests of capital is of course to assert his Bohemianism: it is to brave a contradiction, uneasily entering the marketplace by promoting resistance to commercial imperatives, and attempting to use the mechanisms of publicity for his own literary and critical purposes.

When Harte does manifest the anthropomorphizing tendencies of the would-be advertiser or commodity fetishist, it is with satiric intent. His target was already ubiquitous: largely a product of the mid-nineteenth century, the animated commodity had become, as Thomas Richards notes, "the living letter of the law of supply and demand."[42] Seven years after Harte's column, Marx would famously describe this quasi-mystical, "fetishistic" process by which "the productions of the human brain appear as independent beings endowed with life, and entering into relation both with one another and with the human race."[43] Yet Harte undermines such mysticism by conjuring a parodic version. Describing the sewing machine he discovers in the "gorgeous palace of Wheeler & Wilson," Harte writes:

> The sewing machine is an old maid. It has a stridulous mechanical voice, and a glittering, incisive ophidian tongue. . . . But when you get the right side of the "old girl" and wheedle her and oil her, she turns out her work splendidly. . . . Therefore, *pater familias*, standing doubtingly by, note her idiosyncrasies, and when "you come to know her well and love her," you'll be sure to *buy*.

Here, the patriarchal stereotype of the old maid (reinforced by Harte) compromises the glamour of personification and capitalist seduction. A disturbing combination of sex, love, and consumption, the machine suggests an unholy trinity that vulgarizes the techniques of the advertiser. If the commodity is animate, Harte implies, it is only because of a lurid, even satanic (or "ophidian") illusion.[44]

The fetishization of commodities demands that they appear as independent beings endowed with life, and Harte further deflates such mythologizing by reconnecting products with their producers or operators. At one point in his literary perambulation, Harte comes upon "THE GREAT STEAM CYLINDERS." Just as Henry Adams would regard the Dynamo some forty years later, Harte first views the steam engine as a quasi-religious force; it is the "genius of the Mechanics' Fair" around which "the worshippers stand as at a heathen ungodly shrine," in awe of its "awful but mute suggestiveness of power." The Corliss steam engine had similarly fueled the popular imagination at exhibits beginning with London's Great Exhibition of 1851, and it later functioned as the piece de resistance at the Philadelphia Centennial Exposition in 1876. John F. Kasson has indicated the intensity of many fairgoers' descriptions of the steam engine, noting that they "frequently became incipient narratives in which, like some mythological creature, the Corliss engine was endowed with life and all its movements construed as gestures. The machine emerged as a kind of fabulous automaton—part animal, part machine, part god."[45] Harte does not record such wonder before the "sublime machine," however.[46] He subverts the awesome power of the engine by observing it at a time when the cylinders were quiet and "pulseless," further noting, "delicate ladies may lay their dainty gloved fingers upon them." Whatever phallic power might be ascribed to the engine has, presumably, ceased to be potent. Instead, Harte invests omnipotence in "any of these mechanical fellows" that could "choose to endow it with the moist, warm breath of life and say unto it 'do this.'" Thus animated by human agency, "'it doeth it,' and drives the big paddles, and so, the great steamer, over the rolling Pacific." For Harte, the machine remains in the province of a godlike, but thoroughly human control. (By 1876, however, William Dean Howells, for one, did not share this benign sense of human power in relation to the Corliss. He recognized that this "prodigious Afreet" could crush its attendant engineer "past all resemblance of humanity.")[47]

Harte further attempts to reassert human power and to disrupt the independence of the commodity when he asks: "Have you not seen some earnest figure go up to a trifling article and handle it almost caressingly, and set it up so that it might show to advantage?" He identifies this figure as the exhibitor, as one who has infused the article with his own labor-value and for whom the commodity is thus "the record of laborious and hopeful days, months or it may be years." Most likely a local artisan attempting to compete with larger companies, this figure moves Harte away from his customary urbane irony to the sentimental pathos his later tales often hold out for the outsider: "I say, if you mourn in spirit over those who are elected to be the GREAT UNREWARDED AND UNDIPLOMATIZED, you shall take this Bohemian's hand and he will walk with you again at the *Mechanics' Fair*." For Harte, it is the unalienated labor of the exhibitor—combined with his apparent marginality—that resonates with the Bohemian sensibility and receives his approbation. Writing in the tradition of social criticism that includes Carlyle and extends to Ruskin and Morris, Harte promotes a labor-oriented aesthetic. For Harte, this aesthetic is also implicitly tied to his culture's most cherished ideals of self-possessive individualism. This aesthetic thus becomes a form of immanent critique, one that calls attention to the ideological distance between republican rhetoric and the emerging commercial structures that this rhetoric also, if somewhat perversely, worked to guarantee.

With his purported independence from the advertising interests of the *Golden Era*, Harte's Bohemian implies that his own writing was similarly unalienated (if also unprofitable). To be sure, much like the flâneur Benjamin identifies with *la vie bohème*, Harte went to the marketplace—and the fair—looking for a buyer for his prose and to publicize his own Bohemian persona. But the estrangement such commodification involved was mitigated; like the artisan, he retained a close connection to the products of his labor. As Harte suggests in another *Golden Era* piece, to write was, in and of itself, in some sense to own the means, and results, of production; it was to have property in words.[48] Significantly, Harte develops alienated artistry by the implied contrast he establishes and typesetting, the latter a job he performed for his first :. It was likely through this job that he best came to un- ıning of capitalist alienation.

perhaps so resistant to endowing commodities with life ed that, as a printer, the reverse process had happened to made into a thing. " 'Wanted—a printer,' " Harte writes, nical curiosity, with brain and fingers—a thing that will in a day—a machine that will think and act but still a ıcks the correspondents, editors, and authors who, like s, "scorn the simple medium of [their] fame." Resuming entimental tones he reserves for the oppressed and rte charges: "think not that the printer is altogether a ot he is indifferent to the gem to which he is but the ı subtle ray may penetrate the recesses of his brain, or ers may leave some of their fragrance on his toil-worn to rehumanize the printer, Harte challenges the divi- vould separate the manual from the intellectual, and pears as the medium of a possible reconciliation. For vord at least momentarily breaks down the divisions thought, collaborative labor, and the "second nature" gy. Typesetting rematerializes the social character of

ause of such hopes for reconciliation though print, l his anger at being denied all rights to the prose he forfeited except when he was able to set or "copy- mself written). Other prominent nineteenth-century ıding Mark Twain and William Dean Howells— careers as printers, but Harte was unusual in the ex- the job as a proletarian endeavor; such estrangement and deepened his Bohemianism, confirming his gen- ıe bourgeois economy and his desire for the relative au- he production of (one's own) art, even in a widely circu- nalistic weekly.

trangement, I would argue, was qualitatively different onventional detachment of the prototypical urban/urbane cially by the mid-nineteenth century, the potential radical- orial detachment had diminished, generally appearing as ement. Yet, where the spectator/flâneur's aloofness often signified self-sufficiency, control, and abstract appreciation, the Bohe an's alienation involved social unrest and critique; where spectatorial tance could translate into benign approval, Bohemian marginality manded persistent protest; and where the spectator passively glori commerce, the Bohemian flamboyantly co-opted the commercial spe cle. In the second column he devotes to the Mechanics' Fair, Harte h self implies such distinctions as he mockingly appropriates the traditi spectatorial gaze. After a long passage interpreting the gestures and gla of the crowd, Harte addresses his assumed spectatorial persona in second person:

> Conscious of all this and priding yourself on your superior knowledge and dis ment, and happily oblivious of your being at all ridiculous to any body else's pe tion, suppose you turn your penetrating glance to this microscope and discov round globules of gold visible in that impalpable yellow dust on the glass belov lected from the chimney of a smelting furnace. The microscope is a great inve but then you and I know old SPONDULIX, who has a couple of convex lenses in both eyes, and a quarter of a dollar sometimes assumes proportions that bl the blessed sun itself.[51]

Harte thus turns his probing gaze upon himself, disrupting any illus spectatorial detachment and superiority as he implicates himself i urban spectacle. He critiques the arrogance of the urban spectator l ening his "penetrating glance" to a distorting, dehumanizing len that exaggerates material worth to the exclusion of other values. Th ticipating a Benjaminian analysis, Harte implicitly connects the st spectator to the workings of the marketplace, to a blinding fixation currency of wealth. As this column reveals, Harte recognizes his ov to spectatorial journalism, yet he questions its conventions as he fa his own Bohemian identity. Revisiting the scene of so many sketches, he insists upon his critical difference, rendering his own s performance a diversion from, or partial alternative to, the many "T he refuses to animate.

Bohemia and "the Mingling of Public and Domestic Economy"

On August 11, 1862, Harte further undermined his spectato tachment by getting married, and, more importantly, by describ conjugal status in print. Whereas the "perfect flâneur," accor

Baudelaire, scrupulously avoided the domestic (instead finding it "an immense joy to set up house in the heart of the multitude, amid the ebb and flow of movement, in the midst of the fugitive and infinite"),[52] Harte's Bohemian spectator admits to a more grounded, traditional existence. Though his estrangement from the spectacle of the Mechanics' Fair bolstered Harte's claims to a Bohemian identity, this departure from the typical spectatorial mold threatened to invalidate his nom de plume. Indeed, biographer Richard O'Connor himself dismisses Harte's Bohemian pretensions as "sheer romanticizing" (though, I would counter, Bohemianism always involves a measure of just such romance), maintaining that "he was a husband and father who came home for dinner every evening, a thoroughly domesticated man who preferred the seclusion of his study and the coziness of his hearth to the wildest revels and headiest talk of his more feckless associates."[53] Charles Webb, a former Pfaffian who began contributing to the *Golden Era* in 1864, and who soon after started a new literary monthly entitled the *Californian* with Harte, also mocked Harte's chosen subjectivity; he ironically protested that all of the *Golden Era*'s regular contributors were sober and respectable, with the exception of "Bret," whose debauchery was legendary.[54] Yet if Harte did not, for the most part, live the archetypal *vie de bohème*, he remained committed to his Bohemian signature, perhaps more than ever. Far from being "thoroughly domesticated," Harte quickly became an unhappily married man and often used his Bohemian columns to register his discomfort with the domestic "private sphere"—which was, after all, one of the most central institutions of mid-Victorian bourgeois life. Understanding that Bohemianism could signify more than artistic libertinism, Harte used his literary identity to unsettle the boundaries between the public and the private in his search for a more utopian, and Bohemian, social space. Though often limited by his difficulty envisioning alternative gender relations, Harte's search looked forward to a more communal public sphere, one that would reverse the increasing privatization of the city's economic, social, and political life.

To be sure, the first of Harte's Bohemian columns were written before his marriage and detail a more typical *vie de bohème*. Still a bachelor during the first year of his Bohemian column, Harte lived (and publicized) the roguish male camaraderie of the archetypal Bohemian life. Harte celebrates this bachelor culture in many of his early columns, and positions it as the requisite Bohemian affront to conventional pieties. For instance, one "Town and Table Talk" column entitled "A la Bohemian" specifically connects Harte's Bohemian with a rowdy, working-class mining camp culture over and against that of a genteel, feminized religious establishment. Describing a service at the "church of St. Craesus, the Wealthy," Harte ironically maintains that, "in common with other Bohemians, we have a great respect for St. Craesus." Such respect manifests itself in a profane comparison, however:

So . . . we glided into a velvet seat, and listened to the round-toned organ, and to the refined modulations of the exaltant hymning choir, and tried to feel as devotional as we used to in that log-built "meetin'us" up at Nigger Bar, with the sepulchral spicery of pine logs about it, and the tappings of the Wood-pecker over head. Thinking of this and having a dreamy consciousness of somebody saying something in a monotonous voice, like the "big blue bottles" in the aforesaid old church, we were startled by the whispered voice of "the Peerless" [elsewhere identified as "Constantina, the Peerless"] who wanted to know how we liked the sermon, and if we "were ready."[55]

Aligning his Bohemian with the mining camp roughs he would later commemorate in his tales, Harte commits the self-conscious sacrilege of comparing a church and a bar—all the while suggesting, more seriously, that the camaraderie and natural setting of the mining camps afforded a greater spirituality than that provided by formalized religious worship. Such spirituality is represented as exclusively male, however, subject to disruption by a bourgeois Protestant culture identified with one of its female adherents.[56] This Bohemia thus emerges as a society of bachelors, one that affiliated itself with mining-camp, working-class elements in opposition to "effeminate" urban gentility. Alternately opposing and likening the masculinized barroom and the feminized church, Harte reinforces existing gender divides even as he hopes to broaden class affiliations.

Just two years after this celebration of male bachelorhood, however, Harte had married a contralto in the church choir of the Reverend Thomas Starr King. Many of Harte's friends retrospectively claimed not to have understood this marriage, one that now seems to have been, at least in part, the by-product of Civil War fervor. After the outbreak of war, Harte became close to King, a much-admired orator from Boston who had taken over the pulpit of the First Unitarian Church in 1860. Harte attended rallies at which King organized the citizenry to support the Union cause, and even became, under the guidance of King, a poet-propagandist whose work was read at patriotic meetings all over the state. For a time, the war effort seems to have assuaged Harte's sense of marginality: the conflict between the North and the South displaced that of the Bohemian and the Bourgeois, and Harte identified himself with King's vision of a unified national culture. He took on the public role of a Civil War poet—even jumping onstage at one rally, brandishing an American flag—and discontinued his Bohemian column for almost a year.[57] The one Bohemian column to mention the war displays King-inspired rhetoric, imagining a "fierce west wind" on a godly mission to "greet our Eastern brothers" and "steal into the hearts of the rebellious crew."[58] It was during his year away from the *Golden Era* that Harte married one of King's protégées.

The marriage was not successful, however, and ultimately resulted in separation. Harte married one Anna Griswald, by all accounts a woman more interested in maintaining a stable, middle-class family life than in her husband's literary ambitions. By the time of his marriage, Harte had obtained, in the tradition of Hawthorne and Melville, a government sinecure that provided a more stable income and enabled him to avoid the pitfalls of literary hackwork. His wife apparently hoped he would stop writing: according to one of Harte's later sketches, she preferred that he repair their home himself rather than hire a carpenter, arguing, "You might do it yourself after office hours instead of writing and you'd save money by it."[59] Harte's *Golden Era* columns are less explicit about his domestic discord, but they repeatedly address the relation between Bohemianism and domestic conditions, often viewing Bohemian subversion as a means of countering middle-class feminine influence—at least insofar as that influence constituted a "separate sphere" of social life. If his courtship had been conducted as an extension of his public role as a poet-propagandist, his Bohemian columns suggest that Harte had come to feel trapped by the privatized world of the home. Using many of his columns to renegotiate a "mingling of public and domestic economy," Harte's "Bohemian" looked beyond his earlier, more conventional representations of *la vie bohème*, implicitly asking how Bohemia could manifest itself outside the precinct of the saloon and within the larger social geography of bourgeois San Francisco.[60]

Immersion in the domestic called into question his self-definition as a Bohemian spectator. Whereas the typical flâneur was only at home in the crowd, Harte often describes himself at his desk, focusing his "Bohemian eyes" on the surrounding bric-a-brac of his home. True to the tradition of Bohemian-Bourgeois opposition, however, such views invariably highlight the tension between literary pursuits and the demands of bourgeois domesticity—a tension that many male versions of American Bohemianism (including Harte's) have all too frequently rewritten as gender conflict. At one point, Harte's bay window itself becomes the locus for this conflict. Affording a view of the city's most dramatic vistas—"Alcatraz, Lime Point, Fort Point, and Saucelito were plainly visible over a restless expanse of water that changed continually, glittering in the sunlight, darkening in rocky shadow, or sweeping in mimic waves on a miniature beach below"—and opening "invitingly from a popular thoroughfare," Harte's bay window appears to be the ideal lens through which to register the dynamism of the landscape and the passing spectacle of urban life. Indeed, the bay window metonymizes the act of literary spectatorship: at once public and private, the window promises both engagement and contemplation, immersion and distance, and thus, Harte claims, "the bay-window was supposed to be sacred to myself and my writing materials." Disrespectfully enough, however, the domestic—with all of its telltale materiality—begins to impinge upon this scene of writing: "A rocking-chair and crotchet basket one day found their way there. Then the baby invaded its recesses, fortifying himself behind intrenchments of colored worsteds and spools of cotton, from which he was only dislodged by concerted assault, and carried into captivity. . . . To apply one's self to serious work there was an absurdity."[61]

The mock heroics of this battle with dry goods invite the reader to sympathize with the plight of an imaginative, masculine writer rudely grounded to the stuff of the home, to the details of feminine occupation; ostentatiously transfiguring the experience of domestic distraction, the metaphors plead for Harte's right to transcend such nuisances, for his right to include this column among his "Bohemian Papers."

Yet, precariously dividing the public and the private (or, as Harte suggests, the Bohemian and the Bourgeois) the bay window ultimately serves a more transformative (and Bohemian) function: "The opening of the bay-window," Harte observes, "produced a current of wholesome air which effectually removed all noxious exhalations."[62] Opposing, however playfully, the "wholesome air" to the suffocating, "noxious exhalations" of domestic space, Harte reverses "the mid-century axiom of separate spheres ideology that the world of commerce and industry is poison, and its only antidote, the home."[63] In so doing, Harte anticipates the late Victorian concern that sentimental, domestic excesses—"the feminization of American culture"—had eviscerated the individual and the nation at large.[64] (And this at a time when the *Golden Era* routinely published articles applauding,

"Home is women's sphere. There is much sentiment about home.")[65] Beyond simply reversing the terms of the opposition between the two spheres, however, Harte uses the open window as a figure for the undoing of public-private boundaries. As other "Bohemian Papers" imply, it is this moment of displacement that is more fully Bohemian than the effort to enforce the boundary between the public and the private, even in the name of Bohemian and Bourgeois, or male and female, antagonism.

With the public sphere saturated by the values of the marketplace and the home idealized as a purified, decorous, and hypermoral retreat, neither sphere could unproblematically serve as the locus for Bohemian revolt. Further, with commodification extending into the home and private interests increasingly dominating the "public," neither sphere protected the would-be Bohemian from the encroachment of the other. Not only complementary but mutually implicated, the two spheres each placed restrictions on communal life.[66] As many of Harte's columns suggest, a "Bohemian" mingling of the private and the public would have to involve a more thorough restructuring of both realms: it would have to counter privatization both within and without the home. Harte never arrived at a socialist politics—instead he mourned a perceived betrayal of the nation's republican past and democratic promise—yet his writings do adumbrate later, more radical Bohemian visions of collectivity.

Harte's Bohemian columns were written at a time when delineations between public and private spaces were becoming increasingly formalized. As Burton Bledstein has observed, "in the ideological world of the eighteenth-century republican, all desirable things were public." Benjamin Rush insisted that all republican men were "public property" and, as late as 1829, *Webster's Dictionary* defined "private" as an essentially negative quality, meaning "separate, unconnected with others, secret, secluded, isolated, closed."[67] The mid-Victorian bourgeoisie enshrined the ideology of separate spheres, however, and it was the public-private split that most goaded the "Bohemian." Again and again, Harte's columns uphold instances of proto-Bohemian displacement between the two "separate" spheres. One scene occurs when Harte describes "Seeing the Steamer Off" for one of his "Bohemian Papers." This sketch also reveals that the goal of this Bohemian displacement was less a scorn of the feminine as such—though it is often compromised by just that—than a critique of the class interests supported by the ideology of separate spheres. As he describes the personal "farewells" he witnesses before a steamship departs for the East Coast, Harte observes that the scene appeals to him precisely for the "democratic," even (in class terms) antibourgeois way in which it melds the public and the private: "This system of delaying our parting sentiments until the last moment—this removal of domestic scenery and incident to a public theatre . . . is a return to that classic out-of-door experience and mingling of public and domestic economy which so ennobled the straight-nosed Athenian."[68]

This scene suggests that Bohemianism resides in this moment of "mingling" between "public and domestic economies"; the column, like much American Bohemian writing, also elides the Bohemian and the democratic, locating both within this "removal of domestic scenery and incident to a public theatre." If Harte's democratic Bohemianism reveals a certain condescension—noting that in such gatherings we may share "our lives" with "humblest coal-passer or itinerant vender of oranges," Harte simultaneously excludes the coal-passer and vendor from actually *having* one of "our lives"—this Bohemianism nevertheless hopes to foster a more broadly collective existence; by lessening the boundaries between the public and the private, Harte aspires to demystify class divisions, to expose and create common feeling. The "Bohemian," in effect, hopes to bring about a more populist version of the English spectator's bourgeois public sphere.

Elsewhere in his journalism, Harte suggests that the public-private divide not only functioned to mystify class divisions, but was itself the expression of middle-class prerogatives and attempts at social control. Harte's urbane irony partly lays claim to such privilege as he describes the living conditions at a lower-class apartment building; still, Harte's irony conveys more fascination than superiority. "The gentility of our neighborhood suffered a blight from the unwholesome vicinity of McGinnis's Court," Harte announces in one of his "Bohemian Papers": "This court was a kind of cul do sac, that, on being penetrated, discovered a primitive people living in a state of barbarous freedom, and apparently spending the greater portion of their lives on their own doorsteps. Many of those details of the toilet which a popular prejudice restricts to the dressing-room in other localities were here performed in the open court without fear and without reproach."[69] This mock ethnography uses the mythos of noble savagery (with its suggestions of racialized Otherness) to endow the inhabitants of McGinnis's Court with a kind of Bohemian exoticism, a "freedom" from bourgeois "prejudice." Other "Bohemian Papers" further demonstrate how Harte's Bohemianism was enhanced by the court—it was not only that the court inspired Harte with an object upon which to wax ironic, but, more importantly, it offered a trope for a democratic Bohemia: "McGinnis's Court was a democratic expression of some obstinate and radical property holder. Occupying a limited space between two fashionable thoroughfares, it refused to conform to circumstances, but sturdily paraded its unkept glories, and frequently asserted itself in ungrammatical language. My window—a rear room on the ground floor—in this way derived blended light and shadow from the court."[70]

The parade of "unkept glories" refuses the gentility of privacy, and, in so doing, resists the dominance of the surrounding bourgeois ethos. The combination of light and shadow Harte receives from the court also manifests the building's Bohemian indifference to middle- and upper-class norms: at a time when popular novels and guidebooks to city life frequently used the terms "light and shadow" as euphemisms for class divisions between the well-to-do and the poor, Harte, an able parodist of such literature, enjoys a "blended" mixture.[71] In effect, Harte's Bohemian becomes the representative of the unfixed, liminal "middle-class" position ideally occupied by all Americans in the nation's ideological imaginary. Eschewing the front-facing bay window for the rear window's access to an even more blended fusion of the public and the private, Harte respatializes and reclaims a democratic perspective.

In keeping with his desire for a public sphere containing multiple, fluid classes, Harte also fulminates against emerging restrictions on audience behavior in such venues as the opera house. As Lawrence Levine has described, the mid-nineteenth century witnessed increasing attempts to discipline audiences and to effect a further division of the public and the private (and the "people" and the bourgeoisie) at the level of spectatorship. Though the opera at mid-century continued to unite working-class and elite audiences, opera houses, as well as many other cultural venues, began to insist on strict bourgeois standards of conduct; in effect, to demand that opera and playgoers become privatized receptors, resisting attempts at raucous, public response.[72] Such class-specific expectations led more and more to class-specific audiences, and Harte protested the new "genteel" restrictions: "In place of refreshing and amusing, the opera would be an intolerable bore if one had to sit it through night after night in silence, only speaking or moving at given signals like children at school. . . . The silence of a funeral service [is not] appropriate in a light-hearted company."[73] The public-private division, Harte once again implies, prevents a vibrant and democratic public sphere from coalescing.

Lamenting San Francisco's lack of inviting, hospitable public space, Harte proposes to "give a Bohemian's view of [urban] improvements," derisively noting the "identity of interest" between "Front Street," the business community, and "the City." If corporations are "soul[l]ess bodies," Harte reasons, then he is "skeptical of any improvements that are solely for the profit" of their business interests, and that take as their credo: do not spend "more than you'll ever get out of it."[74] One such "improvement," a new urban square, particularly goads Harte with the irony of its reference to revolutionary political culture: "The square of the Father of his Country! It was approachable by a slough on the south side, and occupied an equilateral space, with the same remote reference to building lots as the Plaza. . . . I am told that reviews are often held there—why I cannot say, except perhaps, that it's generally deserted."[75] Instead of promoting the "mingling of public and domestic economy" that Harte found essential to the maintenance of a democratic public sphere—one that would do honor to Washington's memory—Harte finds a desolate square whose only meaning derives from its "remote" relation to real estate values. Washington Square here functions as a type of "American jeremiad,"[76] as a painful reminder of the distance between foundational republican ideals (which Harte implicitly sanctifies) and contemporary realities. Harte even misses the clotheslines of McGinnis Court, which at least suggested a life lived in open-air camaraderie, and thus decries a developing trend within the urban geography.

As Mary Ryan has demonstrated, in postbellum cities like New York and San Francisco, "the former arrangement of quadrants of marketplaces and squares, linked by prominent thoroughfares and anchored in public landmarks, was becoming obscured and bypassed by the sweeping contours of new business districts, rapid transport lines, apartment buildings, office towers, and great parks"; alternatively, "only on the margins of the dense and poorly differentiated streets could one find a space set aside by public mandate for public sociability."[77] According to Harte, the new Washington Square was such a marginal space, one that refused to open into a truly public space. In the essential mode of Bohemian opposition, Harte concludes his jeremiad ironically, thus highlighting the painful gap between the real and the ideal America as well as that between the strength of his criticism and its (most likely) negligible social effect: "But as I walked sadly homeward," Harte writes, "I thought I would relate my vision, and like Front street, give my individual experience to the public benefit."[78] In this incisive statement, Harte's irony not only underscores the imperiled value of civic participation, but also suggests that "individual experience," now in the form of economic self-interest rather than republican citizenship, had become the guiding spirit of the business community. For Harte, the "residual" civic humanism allegedly found in the early republic thus serves as ideological purchase against the increasing privatization of bourgeois life.[79]

Nor did public-spiritedness inform the city's transportation system, according to Harte. The feuilleton "A Rail at the Rail" suggests that in San Francisco, the very notion of "public transportation" was as an oxymoron. Harte decries the corrupt city legislature that gave one company (a "company that had but one idea, and that to make money") a monopoly on city rail service. He protests: "the conductors and drivers are miserably underpaid and overworked. . . . The charge of six and a quarter cents is an extortion unwarranted by law." Here, once again, Harte uses his "Bohemian" persona to investigate the essential structures of urban life and to reveal the extent to which a commercial calculus prevented a sustaining civic culture from emerging.[80] While the English Spectator had assumed that a "Body of Men thriving in their own private Fortunes" would at the same time promote the "Publick Stock," Harte questions the reciprocity of private and public interests.

The public-private divide goaded Harte because of its antidemocratic implications. It also disturbed him by exaggerating what the New York Bohemians had seen as a particularly grievous offense to their sensibilities: bourgeois humbuggery. Not only did the opposition between the public and the private represent bourgeois class interests, but in so doing it expressed and formed bourgeois character; it created an urban geography that encouraged hypocrisy. The critique of hypocrisy—a preoccupation of bourgeois culture itself in the antebellum period—was becoming less self-propelled in the gaudy, hoodwinking "Age of Barnum" and more the province of Bohemian dissent.[81] Indeed, for Harte, the desire to circumvent such dreaded hypocrisy is another reason why his "Bohemian eyes" gravitate to moments that publicize the private; why, in yet another column, he again privileges the view "From a Back Window":

> Show me the back windows of a man's dwelling, and I will tell you his character. The rear of a house only is sincere. The attitude of deception kept up at the front windows leaves the back area defenseless. The world enters at the front door, but nature comes out at the back passage. That glossy, well-brushed individual, who lets himself in

with a latchkey at the front door at night, is a very different being from the slipshod wretch who growls of mornings for hot water at the door of the kitchen. . . .

I am writing at a back window.[82]

"Bohemian eyes" here have the power to penetrate shams, to see the inner "character" disguised by calculated self-display; in effect, to expose the more "natural," more "slipshod" Bohemian within the Bourgeois. It is at such times that Harte's irony characteristically gives way to sentimentality, and distancing becomes identification: "In front of his own palatial residence I know him to be a quiet and respectable middle-aged businessman, but it is from my back window that my heart warms toward him in his shirt-sleeved simplicity." This "disgraceful habit" of sitting (semi-)publicly in shirtsleeves signals just the lapse from perfect decorum and bourgeois pretension that appeals to the Bohemian in Harte, and that seems to provide a more "sincere" portrait. Indeed, Harte fancies that this bourgeois businessman so thoroughly escapes his class status at his back window that the businessman is returned to an earlier historical moment—he is psychically transported into a bygone agrarian or Arcadian existence and can almost hear the "tinkling of bells as the cows come home" instead of the sounds of urban traffic. For Harte, the Bohemian was never far from the pastoral—or, more precisely, from the "residual" ideology of the yeoman farmer (or, as the next section will demonstrate, the culture of the Mexican *californios*).

Though Harte often critiqued emerging divisions between the "separate spheres," patriarchal ideologies mark the limit of his deconstruction of the public and the private in such columns as "The Bohemian on Balls." In this feuilleton, Harte, much like any paternalistic bourgeois moralist, complains that public balls erode feminine modesty, and he even suggests that a public ball takes democracy itself to an untenable extreme:

Suppose I see that pretty school girl-daughter of my democratic friend, who believes that all men are born free and equal and endowed with certain inalienable rights, among which is the Public Ball. Suppose I shall see her graduate there. That I shall see her first blush wear off as she grows accustomed to the ardent gaze of the gallant strangers around her. That I shall notice, though she shall not, that her lady *vis-a-vis* talks rather loud and laughs rather boisterously and is rather overdressed, to be in her company.[83]

As this column reveals, Harte's "Bohemian" displacement of the public-private split and desire for cross-class affiliations did not always allow female participation. Though many of his later stories display a willingness to undo traditional gender roles, this and other related columns suggest that his Bohemianism, at least at this stage, remained tied to conventional male privileges.

Perhaps as a result of his ongoing ambivalence about eradicating a separate domestic sphere (for women), and also as a result of his desire for a public sphere untainted by private commercial interests, Harte looked askance at two of the institutions that most visibly mingled commercial and domestic economies: restaurants and hotels. Prototypical stages for *la vie bohème*, these institutions were generally viewed—by bourgeois moralists and Bohemians alike—as sites of subversive social transformation. One unsigned *Golden Era* article, threatened by such radical potential, offers a moralistic critique of hotel and restaurant life. Explicitly connecting hotel habitation with a gypsylike existence, the article ("The Nomads of San Francisco") maintains that the nomads' "tents are only pitched for refreshment and repose. Lodging in those vast beehives in the central portion of our city, they seek their cells only to slumber a few hours. . . . 'They live' from restaurant to restaurant, and from lodging to lodging. . . . The general education of this out-door life, with the young, is not apt to inculcate habits of refreshment or taste."[84] A later article raises further bourgeois objections. In "Hotel Ethics," the *Era*'s New York correspondent maintains that hotels "engendered bad habits for the wife, rendering her lazy and capricious, and unfitting her for the real sober duties of her position as a wife and mother."[85] Unsurprisingly, most Bohemians celebrated the nomadism of hotel and restaurant life for exactly the reasons that the bourgeois moralists critiqued it. Such a typical "Bohemian" view is found later in the decade in the *Overland Monthly* (the journal Harte himself edited in the late 1860s). In "What Is Bohemianism?" George F. Parsons broadly defines the movement as the triumph over "formulas" and "conventional restraints," and he approvingly cites the influence of hotels in breaking with tradition (defined here as an un-American past): "Thousands of our [Western] citizens know no other homes than [hotels], and being thus deprived of one of the strongest links in the European social systems, they are by so much advanced towards Bohemianism."[86]

Yet, for Harte's Bohemian spectator, these institutions were not liberatory social spaces. "If there is a spot where life acquires the superlative condition of deadly-liveliness, it's at a hotel," Harte writes, contending that these commercial establishments fail to provide a sustaining fusion of the public and the private.[87] Unlike McGinnis's Court, the hotel cannot foster a sense of shared community; instead it imparts a sense of transience, an "ever conscious presence of a changing tense." Reinforced by a constantly changing clientele, such hyperawareness of time, further punctuated by the commodification of its passage, creates a "dreadful vacuity of soul"—a condition echoing that of Baudelaire's own alienated, phantasmagoric Bohemian. Harte also anticipates Henry James's critique, in *The American Scene*, of the American "hotel civilization," especially of the vacuous "publicity" that threatened to vulgarize (and reify) human relations and the individual consciousness.[88] If the mingling of public and private requires an increased displacement onto the commercial, Harte suggests, then a certain degree of separation between the two spheres might still be preferable.[89] Reflecting upon his large experience with restaurants, or what he derisively refers to as "an economic arrangement for human exigencies," he affirms the appeal of more "respectable" habits:

> When the pervading sloppiness has entered your soul, and small tabs of butter have adhered to your elbows; when you are tired of the skeleton at the feast—the pecuniary reminder, expressed on the ticket prematurely thrust upon you—then you will . . . see the hollowness of this way of living, and its thin, unsubstantial economy. You will look back regretfully at the family board and its certain and sincerer comforts.[90]

The transparent commodification of human pleasure and necessity, this "unsubstantial economy," appalls Harte, all the more so because it is endemic to Bohemian experience. Restaurants, Harte insists, belong to the "depths of vagabondage," and, with regard to hotel life, Harte admits, "A Bohemian knows something of the institution. It is his natural resting place. His tent is pitched in its extensive Sahara with other nomads." These institutions were quite literally the price one had to pay for Bohemian "free agency."[91] Symbolized by the "skeleton at the feast," the phantasmagoria of consumption provided little solace and only the most spectral of alternatives to the "family board." In the logic of Harte's sketch, a restaurant meal functions as a symbol of monetary value, and so abstracted, it ceases to signify sustenance and nurture. The repudiation of domestic life for commercial "services" provides only the most dubious of liberations.

Thus, according to Harte, Bohemia did not offer any simple transcendence of the bourgeois economy of the public and the private. "The Bohemian" could hold up proto-utopian instances in which the public-private divide broke down into a more liberatory fusion, but in his own life, he had difficulty finding such a space for his Bohemia, at least outside of his columns or the *Golden Era* offices. (Harte himself acknowledged in one column, "Bohemia has never been located geographically.")[92] While he was a bachelor, Harte's Bohemianism eschewed bourgeois domesticity only to accommodate itself more fully to the imperatives of the bourgeois marketplace, to a debased mingling of the public and the private; once married, Harte felt that his private life threatened his journalism, the very basis for his public role as a Bohemian. Rather than blunting the edge of his criticism, however, the very precariousness of his Bohemian standpoint challenged him to use his columns as a way of continually negotiating between the public and the private (even if always under the auspices of a commercial journalistic enterprise). This precariousness also challenged Harte's displaced Bohemian to inhabit ever more foreign social spaces within the urban geography as he sought an actual embodiment for his mythic realm.

Bohemia, the Mexican Quarter, and Chinatown

Describing the ethnic communities of the "Mexican Quarter" and "Chinatown," Harte further constitutes himself as a "Bohemian" spectator. Whereas the traditional flâneur generally devotes his attention to the most centralized, and bourgeois, of social spaces, Harte's "Bohemian" redefines the parameters of urban spectatorship, ever seeking an alternative to the city's dominant ethos. The Pfaffians had already established the American Bohemian pattern of gravitating toward ethnic locales. Yet, however nativists may have railed against German immigration, the German immigrants were generally not seen as racial Others and quickly received the American citizenship they sought.[93] The status of the Chinese and Mexicans in the United States was far more uncertain, however, and their social marginalization both complicated and incited Harte's desire to identify Bohemia with their ethnic quarters. Though the Treaty of Guadelupe Hildago (1848) had stipulated that Mexicans already living in California could become American citizens, the imperial violence of Manifest Destiny, combined with sustained social and economic exploitation, made such citizenship largely untenable. The Chinese also had a precarious foothold in San Francisco. Since existing naturalization laws required prospective citizens to be "white," and since many Chinese came in search of the small fortune that would enable them to return home to China, the Chinese in the San Francisco of the 1860s often considered themselves, and were treated as, temporary "sojourners."[94] For both communities, racial violence and legislative maneuvers continually reinforced this sense of separation.

The uncertain position of Mexican Americans and Chinese in San Francisco structures Harte's own responses. Whereas the Pfaffians had clearly identified with and located their Bohemia amongst German immigrants, Harte admits a much more tentative affinity: his "Bohemian eyes" regard the Mexicans and Chinese as exotics and register an ambivalent combination of attraction and repulsion. Alternately signaling urbane superiority and disdain, sympathy and admiration, such spectatorship nonetheless includes these communities (however imperially and partially) in the topography of a Bohemian San Francisco. Indeed, although Harte recycles dominant racial ideologies, he refashions and (partly) revalues them by implicitly connecting the marginality of the Mexican and Chinese communities with that of his own Bohemian subjectivity.

When Harte first begins his discussion of "The Mission Dolores" in one of his Bohemian Papers, he parrots the jingoism of Manifest Destiny:

> The Mission Dolores is destined to be "Last Sigh" of the native Californian. When the last Greaser shall indolently give way to the bustling Yankee, I can imagine he will, like the Moorish king, ascend one of the mission hills to take his last lingering look at the hilled city. For a long time he will cling tenaciously to Pacific Street. He will delve in the rocky fastnesses of Telegraph Hill until progress shall remove it. He will haunt Vallejo Street, and those back slums which so vividly typify the degradation of a people; but he will eventually make way for improvement. The mission will be last to drop from his nerveless fingers.[95]

By the time of the Mexican War, expansionists increasingly employed the racial discourse of Anglo-Saxonism in the effort to justify U.S. aggression. In this discourse, progress, liberty, thrift, and industry emerged as part of a superior Anglo-Saxon racial inheritance, while the qualities of idleness, effeminacy, weakness, and imbecility were consigned to the "degraded mongrel race" that inhabited the desired Mexican territories. Harte's statement clearly voices such racial beliefs; further, written after the U.S. conquest of California, Harte's ominous notion that the Mexicans must still inevitably "give way" to the Yankees echoes some of the most virulent Anglo-Saxonists who foresaw not only conquest but ultimate elimination.[96]

Yet, if Harte insists upon the inevitability of this "giving way," his attitude is more elegiac than celebratory, more ironic than reverently jingoistic. With what has been theorized as "Romantic irony"—an artistic process by which, in Anne K. Mellor's words, a literary "world must be both sincerely presented and sincerely undermined, either by showing its falsities or limitations or, at the very least, by suggesting ways of responding to it with other than whole-hearted assent"[97]—Harte both voices the central tenets of Manifest Destiny and turns many of its corresponding values and assumptions inside out. As employed by Harte, the discourse of Manifest Destiny doubles back upon itself. For instance, despite his claim in the passage quoted above that the Mexicans must "eventually make way for improvement," much of the essay questions the extent to which "progress" actually improves.[98] Harte furthers this ironic questioning with recourse to the pastoral mode, and as he problematizes the effects of Yankee "civic encroachment," his description of the scene surrounding the Mission Dolores becomes an example of the "distinctively American, post-romantic, industrial version of the pastoral design":[99] "The shriek of the locomotive discords with the Angelus bell. An Episcopal church, of a green gothic type, with massive buttresses of Oregon pine, even now mocks its hoary age with imitation and supplants it with a sham. Vain alas! were those rural accessories, the nurseries and market-gardens, that once gathered about its walls and resisted civic encroachment. They, too, are passing away."

Among the most primal of scenes in mid-nineteenth-century American literature, the shriek of the locomotive—in Hawthorne's words "the long shriek, harsh, above all other harshness"—entering into a bucolic or wilderness setting repeatedly functions as a metonym for industrial expansion.[100] The shriek typically disrupts a moment of harmony between the human and natural worlds, signaling the passing of a simpler, more integrated way of life. However, Harte departs from Anglo literary convention (up to this point) in applying this complex pastoral mode to the Mexican community.[101] In doing so, nonetheless, he perpetuates many of the racial assumptions of Manifest Destiny, identifying the Mexican community with the past (as opposed to the Anglo-Saxon present) and with nature (as opposed to Anglo-Saxon "civilization.")

In Harte's "Mission Dolores," a "pastoral" economy of nurseries and market gardens accommodates itself to both the spiritual and natural worlds, creating a quasi-Arcadian wholeness and self-sufficiency. An elegiac sense of the past ever impinges upon the moment, however, and the pastoral mode grounds change in time and space. As in Virgil's first eclogue (sometimes called "The Dispossessed"), this pastoral landscape is threatened by the encroachment of a complex, implacable civilization.[102] Rather than unambiguously spreading "the steady triumphs of commerce, art, civilization, and religion," the "tide of Anglo-Saxon blood" introduces a disturbing dissonance:[103] the "shriek of the locomotive discords with the Angelus bell" and a new Episcopal church supplants the mission with a "sham" (and unaesthetic) religiosity. In another "Bohemian Paper" devoted to the Mission, Harte further complains that modern capitalism has so far obtruded into this pastoral haunt that a motherly cow walking down the street looks "as if she were hired to give a rural effect to the locality."[104]

Written around the same time as his "Mission Dolores," Harte's "The Legend of Monte del Diablo" expresses a similar, though far more dramatic, reversal of the standard teleology of Anglo-Saxonism.[105] The story, his first published in the *Atlantic Monthly*, recounts the pilgrimage of a Spanish priest to a mountain in the Sierras where he foresees "all that vast expanse gathered under the mild sway of the holy faith and peopled with zealous converts." The devil himself then appears to the priest and describes the eventual fall of this new Spain at the hands of "pushing, bustling, panting, and swaggering" Saxons lured west by gold. According to the logic of the tale, the "Saxons" thus emerge as part of a Satanic design to destroy "the Christian grace of holy Spain" with the "vagrant keels of prying Commerce."

This nightmarish vision of a dispossessed population giving way to a swaggering, materialistic civilization resonated with Harte's own Bohemian alienation from what he saw as the "dominant tone" of San Francisco. Eulogizing the Mission Dolores in his "Bohemian Papers," Harte implicitly asserts such a connection: the Mission emerges as an outpost of Bohemian romance imperiled by the crassness of modern bourgeois society. Harte signals his identification in smaller ways as well: indeed, somewhat compensating for his introductory account of Mexican indolence, Harte observes that his own presence at the Mission was itself part of a "purposeless ramble" (though the publication of this ramble might belie such a claim) in a city where, as another of his "Bohemian Papers" wryly notes, "Business habits, and a deference to the custom, even with those who have no business, give an air of restless anxiety to every pedestrian."[106]

The retrospective essay "Bohemian Days in San Francisco" (1900) further reveals the importance of the Mexican or "Spanish Quarter" to Harte's Bohemian self-fashioning. Insisting upon the "vagrant" and "Bohemian" quality of his early spectatorial writings, Harte describes the extent to which his interests wandered from the "sober, materialistic, practical" calculus controlling the city and toward, among other sites, the Spanish Quarter. Signifying, for Harte, a world at odds with the city's dominant ethos, the Quarter provides the material and the impetus for "Bohemian impressions."[107] The doubleness of this phrase—does it refer to the impressions of a Bohemian or to impressions of a Bohemian scene?—insists on the simultaneity of both possibilities. The self-reflexive process of acquiring "Bohemian impressions" thus constitutes and performs Bohemian identity; the spectator is implicated in (and appropriates) the cultural differences he records.

Further, using the term "Spanish Quarter" in his latter-day Bohemian romance, Harte anticipates such turn-of-the-century figures as Charles Fletcher Lummis, one of the leaders in the movement for the preservation of California's Spanish missions. As Victor M. Valle and Rodolfo D. Torres demonstrate, Lummis "provided the narratives and symbols with which [California, and specifically] Mexican Los Angeles could be revalorized as a fantasy landscape of Spanish romance," one that might "claim Southern California as a homeland for a displaced and alienated Anglo middle class." Accordingly, Valle and Torres argue, "the blatantly anti-Mexican discourse of the mid-nineteenth century" was exchanged by Lummis for a "more subtle Hispanic fantasy [that] appropriated those Mexican cultural images that could be interpreted as 'Spanish' (read white and European) or dependent on Anglo leadership and protection while excluding others."[108] Constructing this Spanish "fantasy heritage" (and appropriating it for his own Bohemianism), Harte remembers his own "wanderings through the Spanish Quarter, where three centuries of quaint customs, speech, and dress were still preserved; where the proverbs of Sancho Panza were still spoken in the language of Cervantes, and the high-flown illusions of the La Manchian knight still a part of the Spanish Californian hidalgo's dream." Positing a clear racial hierarchy, Harte then recalls "the more modern 'Greaser,' or Mexican—his index finger steeped in cigarette stains."[109] Using this derogatory image and term, Harte establishes a racial/national/class-based hierarchy that he makes even more explicit in a later essay: "The Spaniard," Harte writes, "was called a 'Greaser,' an unctuous reminiscence of the Mexican war, and applied erroneously to the Spanish Californian, who was not a Mexican. The pure blood of Castile ran in his veins."[110]

In the Mexican or "Spanish Quarter," Harte thus glimpses the value of a multiethnic culture. At the same time, however, he subjects that culture to rigid distinctions of race, class, and nationality. Seeking to transcend the racial ideology of Anglo-Saxonism, and to identify a counterdiscourse within its controlling terms, Harte nonetheless reestablishes the very conditions of dominance that he had sought to undo. He creates a nostalgic romance of the "Spanish Quarter," but it is one that largely subordinates and effaces the "Mexican Quarter."

According to Harte, there was a still "more remarkable and picturesque contrast to the bustling, breathless, and brand-new life of San Francisco than the Spaniard." This "contrast" was provided by the city's Chinese population and also did much toward elaborating Harte's own Bohemianism: "They brought an atmosphere of the Arabian Nights into the hard, modern civilization; their shops—not always confined at that time to a Chinese quarter—were replicas of the bazaars of Canton and Peking, with their quaint display of little dishes on which tidbits of food delicacies were exposed for sale, all of the dimensions and unreality of a doll's kitchen or a child's housekeeping."[111]

Simulating foreign travel, Harte's "vagrant" wanderings through the Chinese quarter approximate the cosmopolitan ideals of the Bohemian spectator.[112] Literature further enhances his experience of Chinatown; just as the Mexican Quarter makes Harte hear "the language of Cervantes," so Chinatown dramatizes literary romance.[113] By transporting him ever closer to his most romantic imaginings, both ethnic quarters also bring "Bohemia" closer to reality. However, as Harte would have it, Chinatown's claims on Bohemian romance go beyond the quarter's uncanny ability to connect the literary with the real. Chinatown offers—using Hawthorne's definition of the romance—an "available foothold between fiction and reality" insofar as it allows its "inhabitants have a propriety of their own":[114] they continue to follow their own cultural traditions and to create their own social geography within the confines of a predominantly Anglo-American San Francisco. These cultural differences, this "daring fidelity to their own customs," thus translate, for Harte, into a certain "unreality":[115] as such, they enter the realm of the romance. And because this romance provides an elaborate contrast to a reality constructed by American bourgeois aspirations, it becomes, more specifically, a Bohemian romance. Representing an alternative culture, Chinatown thus provided (for the white Bohemian spectator) a suggestion of the exotic possibilities derailed by "the hard, modern civilization."[116]

Contemporary theories of racial and cultural difference allowed Harte to further his contrast between Chinatown and bourgeois San Francisco. The pervasive tropes of Orientalism repeatedly enunciated such a contrast, constructing the Chinese as backward, despotic, childlike, sensual, and feminine in relation to a progressive, democratic, adult, moral, and masculine America. To this end, the nineteenth-century American press promoted rhetorical visions of China as an "emasculate Mammoth,"[117] and the Chinese as "semi-barbarians and a half-civilized race, who have been stationary for twenty centuries or more."[118] In short, their static condition rendered them "infantile," "childish," or "adolescent"; their development never attained the level of "white" adults.

Harte accepted the basic premises of Orientalist discourse, but often questioned their negative connotations along with the racial and cultural hierarchies they supported. Such a revaluation of existing stereotypes involved many of the same distortions and projections that obtained in more negative versions; nonetheless, Harte's representations of the Chinese valuably temper their stereotyping with sympathy and calls for justice, particularly at a time when the *Golden Era* reported that "Strong Anti-Coolie Resolutions are before the Mechanics' Institute [where] they declare uncompromising opposition 'to the continued and increasing importation of barbarians incapable of becoming citizens.'"[119] Harte used his columns to protest such oppression, even questioning the central Orientalist opposition between Western superiority and Eastern inferiority. In the "Bohemian Paper" titled "John Chinaman," Harte expresses the hope "that poor John in his persecution is still able to detect the conscious hate and fear with which inferiority regards the possibility of even-handed justice, and which is the keynote to the vulgar clamor about servile and degraded races." Though his desire to promote the contrast between Chinatown and bourgeois San Francisco leads Harte at other times to embrace racist dichotomies, these oppositions—especially when used in service of the central Bohemian versus Bourgeois conflict—also attempt (however inadequately and crudely) to compel a reconciliation between self and Other under the aegis of Bohemia.[120]

For Harte, the mediating term between his Bohemian and "John Chinaman" was the child. The Orientalist conception that the Chinese existed in a state of arrested development was frequently articulated by Harte: "All were singularly infantine in their natural simplicity. The living representatives of the oldest civilization in the world, they seemed like children"; "it was generally impossible to judge of a Chinaman's age between the limits of seventeen and forty years";[121] and so on. The appeal of such racial ideologies for Harte becomes apparent when these passages are placed alongside his many romantic evocations of childhood. Indeed, throughout his Bohemian columns, Harte endows children with his ultimate term of approbation: he refers to them as Bohemians. "I meet those dear little Bohemians—the school children—here of an afternoon. We know each other at once—there is a magnetic attraction of the vagabond principle . . . and such ridiculous things as parents, and schoolmasters, and books, and lessons are speedily forgotten."[122] Similarly, Harte celebrates "his Bohemian friends," the "artful and designing boys" who inhabit "an area of freedom" in which they play truant, conduct pranks, and roam "to distant and remote localities."[123] Though Harte's Chinese generally appear far more simpleminded than his children, their "childlike" traits nevertheless enable them to approach the condition of the "Bohemian."[124]

Harte never refers to the Chinese as Bohemians, however. Like the Mexican Americans, they facilitate his "Bohemian impressions" of cultural difference, but he does not explicitly grant them a Bohemian identity. That he does not may mark the limits of Harte's Bohemian subversion: his general sense of alienation (no doubt compounded by racial stereotyping) precludes a full identification with ethnic Others, who remain largely separate, part of the urban scene that the Bohemian spectator surveys without embracing. At the same time, however, the failure to include San Francisco's ethnic quarters fully within the precinct of Bohemia also respects their cultural autonomy, allowing that they were not coextensive with any imported romantic construct. Broadening his vision of cultural possibilities and further estranging the dominant order of the city, the Mexican Quarter and Chinatown helped Harte to define his *own* Bohemian identity, but he does not fully identify these communities with Bohemia.

Bohemia and the Literary West

As a Bohemian flâneur, Bret Harte investigated a range of social spaces, implicitly measuring each against the requirements of an ideal Bohemia. From the Mechanics' Fair, a quintessential bourgeois spectacle, to the Mexican Quarter and Chinatown, ethnic communities that conjured Bohemian romance yet remained fundamentally Other for Harte, San Francisco resisted a full identification with his mythic realm. He recognized this incommensurability, and, even as his "Bohemian eyes" continued to survey the urban landscape, he acknowledged the distance between his literary romance and metropolitan reality. If such distance often translated into social critique, it also put added pressure on the "literary" itself: Harte began writing fiction alongside his feuilletons, and his tales partially supplied the romantic, countercultural community (or "pastoral happiness") that his spectatorship had, for the most part, failed to discover within the urban scene. Yet, even Harte's fiction betrayed a similar tension between the Bohemian (broadly defined) and the Bourgeois, suggesting once again that the two "require and attract one another." Indeed, as a working out of this central opposition, his tales increasingly become the province of a "perverse romanticism," one that represents a series of paradoxical, marginalized characters, exposes social conflicts even as it attempts to displace them, constantly unsettles narrative perspective, and ultimately enters the very marketplace from which it holds itself apart (and negatively defines itself).[125] Much like his spectatorship, Harte's tales discover that if it exists at all, Bohemia primarily resides in the discursive interplay between the romantic and the real, the conventional and the subversive.

Harte's most extended effort to define "a Bohemian's idea of Bohemia" recognizes that the mythic realm inheres largely within the artistic imagination itself. Yet rather than provoking rhapsodies over the autonomy of art, this recognition is coupled with another: the Bohemian must still attempt to achieve social recognition. Harte thus describes the vexed relation between Bohemia and bourgeois realities:

> [Bohemia is] a fairy land, full of flowers, with a clear, unclouded sky. All day long the people go up and down the walks and pick boquets [*sic*]. Flowers don't cost anything in Bohemia, and the only trouble the people have is in selecting and arranging their boquets. Then they travel away from Bohemia, and rove about trying to sell their flowers. Sometimes people don't like flowers, and then the poor Bohemians are in a bad way. Then again, perhaps, there's a taste for roses, and the poor Bohemian only has a few violets. Or people want Leaves of Grass, dirt and all.[126]

Replete with a broadside against Walt Whitman (presumably too sexually graphic and even self-promoting for the more Victorian of the two Bohemians), this "perverse" fairy tale laments the need to commercialize the products of Bohemia. According to Harte, "poor Bohemians" depend upon a fickle and wayward literary marketplace, and must subject the natural flowering of their imaginations to a cheapening economic calculus. "So the life of a Bohemian is, after all, rather precarious," he concludes: "it's no wonder if he sometimes gets ragged and offers such a surprising contrast between his flowers and himself that people get distrustful of him." Harte himself was allegedly in constant debt (one of the more definitive characteristics of the typical Bohemian), in part to maintain the dandified level of sartorial elegance that would enable him to avoid such a contrast between his own personal appearance and his aesthetic sensibility. Yet if Harte depended on fashion as a template for bringing together the aesthetic and the real, he maintained, as we have seen, that Bohemia itself had "never been located geographically." His "Bohemian's idea of Bohemia" qualifies this claim with one final romantic vision, however, promising that on "any clear day when the sun is going down, if you mount Telegraph Hill, you shall see its pleasant valleys and cloud-capped hills glittering in the West like the Spanish Castles of Titbottom. That's Bohemia." Bohemia thus inheres in a Romantic correspondence between individual perspective and the natural sublime.

Beyond identifying *la vie bohème* with the artistic imagination, this early feuilleton also provides a more specific indication of how Bohemia would later enter Harte's writing. Allegedly a response to a query from "a young person, who calls herself 'Coralie,'" his "Bohemian's idea of Bohemia" is brought forward at the expense of this Coralie—a figure who soon returns as "Clytemnestra Morpher," Harte's fictional embodiment of bourgeois correctness in "The Work on Red Mountain" (later retitled "M'Liss" in an expanded version). Bohemia, Harte's column implicitly acknowledges, only has meaning in relation to bourgeois practice. Within Harte's feuilleton, Coralie "wishes to know what a Bohemian is," but, before Harte answers, he makes it abundantly clear that this girl is not, and could not be, a Bohemian herself. He describes the "physical peculiarities of [the] letter" and its writer:

> Subject confined to six rigid parallels written over pencil marks to carry along the text. Begins and ends exactly in the centre of the line. Mechanical construction always the paramount idea. Written on small note-paper, pink, with insertion edging. . . . Deduction from the foregoing: —Coralie is a short High-school girl, with curls, of 14, —Looks more like Jane than Coralie—but that don't matter. Has small hazel eyes and round mild face. Double chin. Receives good marks for "ORDER," "DEPORTMENT" and "PUNCTUALITY." . . . Has a geranium leaf in her Reader and two pressed flowers (Rosebuds smashed in their sepals) in her Arithmetic. Also two worsted book-marks: "Friendship's Gift" and "Affection's Offering." . . . Carries on housekeeping, to a small extent, in her desk, and has a little bit of everything in its place. Is pointed out by her teachers as a model scholar. Is beloved by trustees. Is generally an EXAMPLE.[127]

Represented as the definitive antithesis of the Bohemian, "Coralie" and her letter conjure the feminized, sentimental middle-class culture that

Harte claims to resist. Known through tell-tale keepsakes, the product of a bourgeois system of rote education that emphasizes manners over independent thought, and, as a final insult, lacking physical attractiveness, Coralie becomes the representative of a culture allegedly dominated by material artifacts, hackneyed emotion and conformist expectation. Reminiscent of similar figures in Twain, Coralie is everything that the Bohemian strives not to be.

A version of Coralie returned just a week later when the *Golden Era* published Harte's "The Work on Red Mountain," directly alongside one of his Bohemian feuilletons. One of the best of Harte's early Western tales, this story opposes a vagabondish child of the mining camps against a Coralielike figure of official deportment. The vagabondish child is also female (in this case, the opposition between Bohemian and Bourgeois does not bolster the division between the masculine and the feminine). Instead of relying on gender, the contrast between the "lawless" M'liss and "neat, orderly, and dull" Clytemnestra is marked by the archetypal light versus dark iconography of historical romance: M'liss is a brunette, Clytie is a blonde, and they both vie for the attention of the town schoolmaster. Though the story never explicitly states that M'liss has a mixed racial heritage, the "motherless" child at times croons the "negro melodies of her younger life" and disparagingly refers to Clytie as "the white girl." Thus implying, however tenuously, a racialized division, the contrast between light and dark ultimately accrues to M'liss's advantage, enabling her to inhabit the region (later colonized by Huck Finn)[128] beyond "respect and civilization": the exoticizing stereotypes and marginal social position associated with racial darkness further her intriguing separateness. Her "quick, restless and vigorous perception" and unrestrained "gipsy life" even inspire the schoolmaster to look beyond bourgeois commonplaces: when he first meets M'liss, the schoolmaster is "carefully making those bold and full characters inculcating such bromides as 'Knowledge is power,' or 'Riches are Deceitful,'" but, through M'liss's example, he is finally able to resist the charms of Clytemnestra Morpher's blonde correctness. And even though the schoolmaster embarks upon the "reclamation" of M'liss, she leads him on a journey into a new social world, one similar to the "sporting" areas of early San Francisco that Harte later claimed "represented a certain Bohemianism—if such it could be called—less innocent than my later experiences."[129] M'liss is no stranger to this realm and, "in out of the way places, low groggeries, restaurants and saloons; in gambling hells and dance houses," the schoolmaster follows his young pupil into Harte's fictional Bohemia of combined freedom and abjection.[130] By the end of the story, the twelve-year-old, orphaned M'liss and the schoolmaster determine to leave town together (Harte interestingly elides the question of just what their relationship will be) and the tale refuses to resolve whether the schoolmaster will succeed in taming his rebellious ward or she will further unleash his own more wayward instincts.

Harte wrote an expanded version in 1863, republishing the tale in the *Golden Era* as "The Story of M'liss." The later version concludes with an unequivocally civilized M'liss, even dispatching a genteel mother to reclaim her and noting the results of her final reformation: "There is a more strict attention to the conventionalities of life; her speech is more careful and guarded; her walk, literally, more womanly and graceful."[131] Containing the story of M'liss's gypsy life within a narrative of bourgeois socialization, the later version proves that even in the fictional realm, conventional expectation could derail Harte's projected Bohemia. Harte himself appears to have recognized the extent to which the second version compromised his narrative, later informing his eastern publisher, James R. Osgood, that he had "wound [the story] up in disgust" and that he "always preferred the first conception."[132] The final version had tamed the perverse romanticism of the first, neutralizing its "Bohemian" content.

"The Work on Red Mountain" and "M'liss" are the only two of Harte's well-known tales to appear in the *Golden Era*. They anticipate the direction of the *Overland Monthly* stories that would garner Harte his literary reputation. In the *Overland* tales, Harte again eschews the contemporary urban landscape of the Bohemian spectator, instead focusing on the already receding world of Gold Rush–era mining-camps. Like the earlier stories, many of these tales depict the tension between genteel values and Western liberties. Yet if Harte essentially transposes the opposition between the Bohemian and the Bourgeois to the fictional arena of historical romance, many commentators maintain that he resolves the conflict in favor of the status quo. Expressing this view, Lee Mitchell reads the tales as proclaiming "that a set of rough-hewn western characters need no . . . personal transformation to become upright, middle-class Americans. They already are what they have yet supposedly to become, essentially civilized beings under the wild and wooly costumes."[133] In effect, Mitchell sees the tales as accomplishing the function of much traditional spectatorial literature: they reassure the genteel reader that even the most threatening "type" is really a good bourgeois at heart. This is allegedly the result of Harte's paradoxical characters—the whore with the heart of gold, the noble gambler, the family-oriented miner, and so on.

Other recent interpretations offer a more radical Harte, one more in keeping with the "Bohemian" spectator. J. David Stevens recovers such a Harte, arguing that "what critics have labeled sentimental excess is actually Harte's method of exploring certain hegemonic cultural paradigms taken for granted in other Western narratives."[134] For Stevens, "The Luck of Roaring Camp" is such an exploration. This story—one that, we should remember, was originally deemed "immoral and indecent" by *Overland Monthly*'s proofreader and printer[135]—has subsequently been read as a highly moral tale, even a modern parable of the Nativity; as such, a Christ child renamed "the Luck" redeems a dissolute mining camp full of unsavory gamblers, causing them to emit their "first spasm of propriety." This synopsis would seem to support the notion that Harte's "reckless" miners are essentially exemplars of middle-class behavior and "sentimental" piety.[136] For Stevens, however, the miners of "The Luck" are only normatively bourgeois in a perverse sense: they subscribe to feminine rather than masculine gender roles. According to Stevens, the tale thus questions "the usefulness of a patriarchal order in which domestic roles are assigned strictly according to sex"; the men of the mining camp "assume the roles of father and mother, defender and nurturer; in so doing, they find their lives made remarkably more complete."[137] In keeping with the Bohemian spectator's desire to loosen the boundary between the public and the private, such gender trouble complicates attempts to define what is and is not conventional. Further, I would add that beyond calling into question dominant gender norms, "The Luck" offers what is perhaps an even more radical alternative to traditional nuclear or even extended family structures, and instead projects a communal world of collective nurture.

Harte underscores the essentially utopian nature of Roaring Camp by its ultimate destruction: the camp occupies an idyllic moment so outside the purview of the dominant culture that it cannot be sustained. Following a "golden summer" (one that is literal and figurative, given that "the claims had yielded enormously"), the miners' "luck" turns against them and the camp and its inhabitants are destroyed in a great flood. Part random chance, such destruction is also represented as a kind of wish fulfillment, occurring just after the camp had itself decided to capitulate to bourgeois expectation and "to invite one or two decent families to reside there for the sake of 'The Luck,' –who might profit by female companionship." Yet according to the narrative, the "sacrifice that this concession to the sex [i.e., to women] cost these men, who were fiercely skeptical in regard to its general virtue and usefulness, can only be accounted for by their affection for Tommy" and the miners continued to "hope that something might turn up to prevent [the arrival of women]." That "something" materializes in the form of the flood: women and the conventional civilization they metonymize never obtrude upon this pastoral idyll (unless in the elemental, "return of the repressed" form of an angry feminized Nature—an entity identified in the tale by the female pronoun). Along with other instances of "Bohemian" escapism, including the all-male clubs that flourished at the fin-de-siècle (described in Chapter 4), the Roaring Camp and its alternative social vision are both structured and compromised by gender conflict and anxiety. Yet rather than seeking the freedom to become more normatively masculine, the Roaring Camp seeks the opportunity for men to perform the traditionally female role of primary caregiving. It is as though only the absence of women allows men to become less rigidly masculinized; only the abeyance of sexual dualism prepares for its dissolution. Both sentimentalizing and ironizing the camp's fate, the narrative recognizes the poignancy and limits of the miners' pastoral. Much like "Bohemia" itself, the Roaring Camp glimpses social transformation without fully transcending its social context.

Harte never identified the Western world of his mining-camp stories and sketches as "Bohemia," perhaps recognizing that Bohemia was, by definition, an urban variant of the Arcadian pastoral that the tales so romantically glimpsed. Still, his first book, *The Luck of Roaring Camp and Other Sketches* (1870), republishes four of his "Bohemian Papers" (so identified in the text), including "The Mission Dolores," "John Chinaman," and "From a Back Window," and thus implicitly connects "Bohemia" with his mythic West. Published by Boston's eminent Ticknor, Osgood and Co., this well-received collection may have helped ignite the late-nineteenth-century fascination with all things "Bohemian," even as it fueled the rage for Western tales. An 1878 sketch in *Scribner's Monthly*, Margaret B. Wright's "Bohemian Days," suggests the extent to which Harte's writing memorably linked the world of Bohemia with the world of the mining camps in the popular imagination. The tale of a "Queen of Bohemia" who holds court among a group of artists and writers, "Bohemian Days" finds the Queen reminiscing about her "wild life among the Nevada mines . . . where Colonel Starbottle was her devoted admirer and Jack Hamlin told his love."[138] Invoking two of Harte's best-known characters, this sketch assimilates Harte's Western topography to his Bohemian romance, perhaps more fully than Harte himself did. Yet such a move was implied by his tales themselves; together with the "Bohemian Papers," the best of Harte's *Overland Monthly* tales illustrate the need for more liberatory social relations even as they register the tenuousness of their subversion.

Alongside such fictional projections, Harte also sought another means of establishing a Bohemia within San Francisco's literary world. His Bohemian spectator could not identify an authentic *vie bohème* in the city at large, but Harte and other local writers resolved to create their own Bohemia at the *Golden Era*, and later at the publishing ventures Harte organized and spearheaded. *La vie bohème* could finally materialize through the medium of print culture: through publicized camaraderie and flamboyant self-promotion, collective literary accomplishment and social criticism, this San Franciscan Bohemia strove to rewrite the romance of the Parisian Latin Quarter and provide an antidote to the alienation of the individual Bohemian spectator. In so doing, this Bohemia shared Harte's desire to "fill the void in the Literature of the Pacific Coast" and to help San Francisco transcend its immersion in the purely practical and material.[139] Poised within and without the metropolis, this Bohemia would also act as a cultural bridge between the city and the nation.

The *Golden Era* set the foundation for this Bohemia, and, to a large extent, Harte's vision of a print-culture Bohemia built upon Colonel Lawrence's earlier plans for his own literary weekly. As mentioned, Lawrence may well have been the one who proposed Harte's "Bohemian" signature, and a variety of editorial notices later began directly and indirectly to link the *Golden Era* with the glamorous notoriety, literary prestige, and enviable camaraderie of Bohemia (as embodied in the New York *Saturday Press*). Lawrence promoted this connection to New York whenever possible. Closely following the New York literary scene, and most particularly the various writers identified with the Bohemia at Pfaff's, Lawrence even republished a slew of articles from the New York press under the burlesqued headlines "The Siege of Bohemia!," "A Monster Shell Thrown into Pfaff's," "Brilliant Sallies of the Heroic Besieged." The "monster shell" in question was launched from the *Round Table* (whose anti-Bohemianism was discussed in Chapter 1), and took the form of an indictment of Bohemian drama critics that accused them of the usual evils: they were "shiftless, lazy, moneyless, glorying in a condition of poverty"; they were corrupt minions of the marketplace whose opinions were for sale; they were "moral and social lepers"; and so on. The *Golden Era* excerpted this critique, along with numerous defenses of the Bohemians. Throughout these republished articles, various *Golden Era* editorial interjections display a collegial familiarity with the players in question, and thus project a sophisticated, bicoastal, cliqueish literary culture: a national Bohemia united in self-defense against a traitorous journalist. The burlesqued allusions to war—and this during the Civil War—also reinforced the sense of a patriotic esprit de corps within the imagined community of Bohemia, while aligning it with the larger national agenda. As part of this defense, the *Golden Era* even offered one of the more apt descriptions of mid-nineteenth-century American Bohemianism: "For the benefit of such of our readers as may not be *au fait* in literary technology, it may be as well to state, that 'Bohemia' is a name used to designate collectively those free and easy knights of the quill who are banded together in the bonds of good fellowship and minor journalism, and may be characterized as the 'unterrified Democracy' of the Republic of Letters." Playfully literalizing and repoliticizing the standard phrase "Republic of Letters," the *Golden Era* thus identified itself with the cooperative, democratic impetus of Bohemia, here seen as a purified version of the larger nation. At the same time, the phrase "knights of the quill" also unites the Bohemians with a Southern ethos of neochivalric honor, thus bringing together Northern "democracy" and Southern "aristocracy" within the realm of Bohemia. By rhetorical fiat, the Bohemians would become prototypes for national reconciliation.[140]

Making Bohemia a national agenda combated the *Golden Era*'s provincialism, and as part of this effort the paper also did its best to attract visiting writers, especially those who had once frequented Pfaff's. Among the former Pfaffians to relocate, however briefly, to San Francisco and the pages of the *Golden Era* were Charles Webb (who joined the staff in 1863 and who may well have helped Lawrence with his references to Pfaff's), Fitz-Hugh Ludlow (the "Hasheesh-Eater"), Adah Isaacs Menken, and Ada Clare. The *Golden Era* was especially jubilant upon announcing Clare's arrival: "Ada Clare has justly acquired an intellectual renown far surpassing any heretofore awarded to a lady journalist, either at home or abroad. . . . As regards to what is popularly and eccentrically known as the 'Bohemia' of newspaperdom, she is unquestionably a Queen."[141]

Harte also used the pages of the *Golden Era* as a staging ground for literary good-fellowship: engaging in bantering dialogue with other writers, Harte enabled the paper to perform as well as to describe a collaborative Bohemian life. Harte's chief partner in this endeavor was the former

Pfaffian, Charles Webb. As Franklin Walker has noted, Webb was "a bona fide representative of the Bohemianism which had created such a furor in the East." Even before joining the Bohemia at Pfaff's, Webb had had the requisite romantic past: he had spent four years whaling in the South Seas and in the Arctic, he was a notorious womanizer, and in San Francisco he lived at the Occidental Hotel among the "fast set" of urban bachelors.[142] More importantly, his weekly column, "Things," exhibited much of the *Saturday Press*'s incisive irreverence and bursts of moral indignation, and Webb and Harte quickly determined to start a new magazine together. For all its Bohemian pretensions, the *Golden Era* was finally not Bohemian enough for Webb and Harte. Webb was most explicit in this view, complaining that the "virtuous and reverent editors" had suppressed part of his columns "through fear that [they] might offend the prejudices of their readers, and interfere seriously with the interests of their paper."[143] (Nonetheless, the *Golden Era* published this and other attacks on its editorial practices.) Envisioning a less restrictive journal, Harte and Webb used their respective columns to play at negotiation, Bohemian rebellion, and repartee.

"Bret and I laid our heads together over a Mint julep the other day, and have determined to start a paper," Webb announced (using the pseudonym "Inigo"): "Bret is to write all the clever things for it, I am to get credit for it."[144] In his own response to Webb's proposal, Harte continued the literary banter, recounting that Webb had confided, with "an exaltation in his manner, as of one drunken with wine" that "I have chosen you, my dear Bret, as a contributor, for although you have the reputation of a moral English writer, I can detect a latent skepticism which would flourish vigorously in this new expression. I am not certain but as a writer of morality—French morality, you understand—you would equal if not excel George Sand."[145] Invoking drunken musings, lighthearted good-fellowship, and the requisite French scandalousness, Harte and Webb replayed the winning formula of *la vie bohème* and helped to advertise their future magazine (ultimately *The Californian*, a short-lived but well-respected literary periodical). Even—or especially—in the Far West, their columns insist, an audacious yet sophisticated and cosmopolitan Bohemia could flourish. By producing "The Best Journal on the Pacific Coast, and the Equal of any on the Continent," they resolved to put their city on the national cultural map.[146]

Webb and Harte proposed to include another sometime *Golden Era* writer in their Bohemian endeavor. "Any author expecting pay for anything which he contributes, is to be kicked down stairs in an ignominious manner by the Washoe Giant, whom we intend to employ specially for that purpose," Webb announced.[147] The "Washoe Giant" was none other than Mark Twain. Twain had begun contributing to the *Golden Era* in the fall of 1863, while he was still living in Virginia City (though often passing through the Bay City), and after moving to San Francisco he contributed to Harte and Webb's *Californian*. Though less demonstrably attached to the ethos of Bohemia than Harte, Twain did conceive of himself as an inhabitant of that literary region during his years in California—and his rivals in the local press promoted, and perhaps even initiated, Twain's characterization as the "Bohemian of the Sagebrush." This identity—that of a "lazy, idle, good-for-nothing vagabond"[148]—underscored Twain's local "literary celebrity," and as represented in such sketches as "Those Blasted Children" (first published in the *New York Sunday Mercury*) and "The Jumping Frog of Calaveras County" (first published in none other than the briefly revived *Saturday Press*), this Bohemian-Western persona no doubt helped him to gain a national audience. Wielding this persona, his early *Golden Era* sketches derive much of their humor from the tension between bourgeois expectation and Bohemian subversion; like Webb's columns, they often represent "Bohemia" as a carnivalesque inversion (or more truthful mirror) of the official culture, and they endow Twain with a transgressive mystique redolent of the mining-camps and Virginia City. Indeed, with "Sage-brush" modifying "Bohemian," Twain's epithet both conflated the terms and compounded their separate meanings. Together with Harte and Webb, Twain enabled the *Golden Era* to define the Bohemian West.

By all accounts, the epithet "Sagebrush Bohemian" had first been foisted upon Twain by one Albert S. Evans (referred to by Twain as "Fitz-Smythe"), a moralistic writer for the *Alta California* and a correspondent for the *Gold Hill Daily News*. Their journalistic feud rearticulated the Bohemian-Bourgeois divide, reinforcing Twain's status as an unrestrained humorist existing beyond the pale of propriety. As Evans would have it, Twain was thoroughly dissipated, unprincipled, even venal; his Bohemianism chiefly consisted of disturbing the peace. For example, by way of countering Twain's exposure of police corruption and brutality, Evans not only insists that the city jail was one "of the best managed public institutions in the United States," but also claims that Twain's anger at the institution was merely sour grapes, the outrage of a wastrel frequently arrested for public drunkenness: "By-the-by, speaking of Mark Twain reminds me of the fact that he is seriously down on the police," Evans recounts, proposing that "a great deal of ill feeling might be avoided by sage-brush Bohemians if they would remember to adhere to the following simple rules." These rules include: "When getting drunk, seek the company of gentlemen, not that of Pacific street jayhawkers" and "go quietly into the cell and lay down on your blankets, instead of standing at the grating, cursing and indulging in obscene language until they lock you up."[149] On another occasion, Evans writes that the stench of the slaughterhouses "is only second in horrible density to that which prevails in the Police courtroom when the Bohemian of the Sage-Brush is in the dock for being drunk over night."[150]

With somewhat different emphases, the young Twain appears to have embraced his identity as the "Bohemian of the Sage-Brush." He prided himself on his participation in a raucous, sporting subculture of bachelors and literary men; as Justin Kaplan notes, "he was to become a prominent part of the Pacific Slope's gaudy subculture of writers, reporters and entertainers, traveling actors, and short-term promoters, and he was to look back on such times as these with nostalgia."[151] Well before nostalgia had set in, however, Twain had boasted of his sporting lifestyle, even taking the quintessentially Bohemian step of publicizing it in print: the life of literature and the stuff of literature began to merge, further preparing the way for the literary celebrity Twain epitomized. Indeed, a *Golden Era* piece written by Twain's one-time roommate, fellow humorist Dan De-Quille, exposes this nexus between celebrity, Bohemian escapades, and print culture, promising to reveal the misadventures "that have befallen two of the literary celebrities of the Silver Land."[152] Twain himself wrote similar sketches, and while staying at the Lick House in San Francisco (a hotel "occupied by sociable bachelors"). Twain also recorded his antics for the *Golden Era*: "Home again to San Francisco, drunk, perhaps, but not disorderly. Dinner at six, with ladies and gentlemen, dressed with faultless taste and elegance, and all drunk, apparently, but very quiet and well-bred—unaccountably so, under the circumstances, it seemed to my cloudy brain. Many things happened after that, I remember, —such as visiting some of their haunts with those dissipated *Golden Era* fellows."[153] These words function as a performative, both announcing and thus ensuring his membership in the *Golden Era's* Bohemian coterie.

Many of Twain's other *Golden Era* sketches also implicitly proclaim his membership in Bohemia and revel in his status as a "Sage-Brush Bohemian." These sketches derive much of their humor and even, at times, their sense of moral outrage from the thematics of Bohemian and Bourgeois opposition. For Twain, "Bohemian" burlesque resides in a constant interplay between conventional meanings and subversive understandings. For example, one early sketch, "Early Rising: As Regards Excursions to the Cliff House," provides a disingenuous application of Ben Franklin's quintessential bourgeois dictum: "Early to bed, early to rise / Makes a man healthy, wealthy and wise." Brandishing the dissolute behavior that led Evans to call him the "Sage-Brush Bohemian," Twain writes: "I have tried getting up early, and I have tried getting up late—and the latter agrees with me best. As for a man's growing any wiser, or any richer, or any healthier, by getting up early, I know it is not so; because I have got up early in the station-house many and many a time, and got poorer and poorer for the next half a day, in consequence, instead of richer and richer."[154]

Other sketches complicate the interplay of Bohemian and Bourgeois, revealing the extent to which these putative opposites coincide with one another. Consider "The Great Prize Fight Between His Excellency Gov. Stanford and Hon. F. F. Low, Governor Elect of California." Styling itself as a faithful report of a boxing match between Stanford and Low, this sketch suggests that the hierarchical distinction between the bourgeois politics of "refined and educated gentlemen" and the "loathsome and degrading pastime of prize-fighting" is a sham—or "humbug," to use one of Twain and other Bohemians' favorite derogations. Yet by the end of the piece, Twain acknowledges that he himself has humbugged his readers, inadvertently relying on the false testimony of a supposed friend: "I had believed him so implicitly as to sit down and write it out (as other reporters have done before me) in language calculated to deceive the public into the conviction that I was present at it myself." And of course, Twain wants us to recognize that his confession of humbuggery is an instance of further humbuggery. The Bohemian journalist, Twain suggests, is no better—and no worse—than the bourgeois humbug. If anything, his critical difference from the bourgeois lies in calling attention to his own deception: he ironically fulfills the bourgeois ideal of "sincerity" by emptying its meaning.[155]

Conversely, other sketches suggest that the "Sage-Brush Bohemian" occupies (a truer version of) the moral high ground claimed by the bourgeois. The same Twain who "sought surcease of sorrow in soothing blasphemy" during his early morning Cliff House outing could also generate a moral frenzy. Describing the "virtuous" police who had let a petty thief die in his cell after they had broken his head with a club, Twain writes:

> And why shouldn't they shove that half senseless wounded man into a cell without getting a doctor to examine and see how badly he was hurt. . . . And why shouldn't the jailer let him alone . . . because he couldn't wake him—couldn't wake a man who was sleeping and with that calm serenity which is peculiar to men whose heads have been caved in with a club? . . . Why certainly—why shouldn't he?—the man was an infernal stranger. He had no vote.

As such sketches indicate, the Bohemian could recuperate the very values of "Christian sympathy" that the official culture allegedly supported but too often denied unless goaded by political exigencies. The "Sage-Brush Bohemian" could, in the estimation of the *Californian*, be "surnamed the Moral Phenomenon" (the irony being the absence of irony).[156] Whether playfully contesting or angrily denouncing dominant protocols, the Sage-Brush Bohemian registered both his dissent from and ties to a bourgeois value structure.[157]

In a later reminiscence, the elder Twain (much like his younger counterpart) acknowledged that Bohemia operated within and without the dominant culture. He refers to his time in San Francisco as "that old day when Bohemianism was respectable—ah, more than respectable, heroic."[158] The notion that Bohemianism was respectable (Twain had perhaps forgotten Evans's diatribes) acknowledges that Bohemia dwelt within the accepted borders of bourgeois life, yet his qualification that it was "more than respectable" nonetheless insists that *la vie bohème* somehow exceeded the quotidian, that it could not be reduced to an existing (or even emerging) status quo. For Twain, the permeable line between heroism and respectability implicitly corresponded to one between the Bohemian and the Bourgeois, a divide that enabled the ironic excess of the early sketches. Much like Huck's romantic "territories," Bohemia existed at the imagined limit of contemporary civilization.[159]

For both Twain and Harte, Bohemia also transcended "respectability" by creating a like-minded, mutually supportive community. Bohemia ennobled the difficult life of letters, defining its social position within the literary marketplace. Twain appreciated his membership in the Bohemian coterie of San Francisco, even viewing it as the sort of "Bohemian's Protective Union" that Webb had envisioned. "We of Bohemia keep away from Carleton's," Twain announced in a letter, thus implying that the

Bohemians had set up an informal boycott of that publisher (a "Son of a Bitch" who would "swindle" his clients).[160] Being part of a Bohemian's Protective Union also ensured that the *Golden Era*'s most prominent writers helped one another to develop their craft. Though Twain and Harte became estranged later in life, Twain finally acknowledged the literary debt he owed his former friend: "He trimmed and trained and schooled me patiently until he changed me from an awkward utterer of coarse grotesqueness to a writer of paragraphs and chapters that have found a certain favor."[161]

As Twain indicates, Harte had perhaps found his Bohemia in cooperative literary labor. Indeed, for Harte, the *vie de bohème* that had largely eluded his Bohemian spectator appears most fully realized in his own literary and editorial practice. Generally considered the creative high point of his career, Harte's years in San Francisco suggest just how galvanizing the sense of being part of a Bohemian literary circle could be. Part media spectacle, part critical framework and part cooperative community, the world created in and around the pages of the *Golden Era* revitalized the mythos of Bohemia. Though Harte claimed that the best view of "Bohemia" came at sunset on Telegraph Hill, his columns—especially when joined with those of Webb and Twain—suggest that Bohemia achieved its fullest local expression on the printed page.

Throughout the 1860s, new writers and publications (particularly the *Californian* and the *Overland Monthly*) renewed the literary world that the *Golden Era* had initiated. Yet though Harte's own *Overland Monthly* tales can be seen as a respatialization of Bohemia, the *Overland Monthly* itself sought the bourgeois audience that the "Bohemian" Harte and Webb had tried to disavow when they founded the *Californian*. The journal viewed itself as a West Coast *Atlantic Monthly*, and its prototypical reader (according to one of Harte's editorials) was "a respectable citizen, having good social connections, a seat at the opera, [and] a pew at the church."[162] Whether or not Harte meant to satirize such a reader in the guise of praise (and I imagine that he did), the *Overland Monthly* eschewed Bohemian marginality in favor of a broader circulation and prestige.

Such history has a poetic logic: Bohemia is often seen as a developmental stage, a realm of youthful aspiration—even a prelude to a more settled bourgeois existence. Murger called it "the verdant slope of youth," and San Francisco's *Golden Era*, along with its young writers, embraced this ground as the basis for a local literary culture that looked toward national recognition.[163] The cosmopolitan associations of Bohemia transported the literary weekly beyond its provincial origins and endowed it with cultural legitimacy; once San Francisco had a more established literary culture, Bohemia had (for a time) lost some of its usefulness. Harte himself showed a similar trajectory; he used his "Bohemian" signature throughout his tenure at the *Golden Era*, but dropped his nom de plume after he left that paper and began to achieve a wider fame (though, as noted, he did republish some of his early sketches under the title of "Bohemian Papers" in his collected works). Still (like Murger himself) Harte never fully achieved a settled bourgeois existence, and spent most of his life dogged by debts and the vicissitudes of a fluctuating literary reputation. He left California in 1871, lured East by an unprecedented offer from the *Atlantic Monthly*. By most critical assessments, however, Harte never again achieved the greatness of the *Overland* tales, and instead rehashed his best stories, generally without recreating their narrative complexity and critical drive. His mythic West became increasingly disconnected from the "Bohemia" and oppositional perspective that he had so productively cultivated.

As the early careers of both Harte and Twain reveal, a self-conscious Bohemia has existed in San Francisco ever since the early 1860s. Alternately asserting cosmopolitan sophistication and proverbial western liberties, the Bohemia of the *Golden Era* sought to fuse the polish of a literary high culture with the coarse freedoms of the mining camps, thus creating a new countercultural hybrid; in so doing, the periodical ultimately produced two of the writers most responsible for defining the West for the nation. Both as a critical stance toward bourgeois San Francisco (and, by extension, America) and as a vibrant community of young writers, the Bohemia Bret Harte superintended proved the relevance of the romantic French ethos to its members' own social explorations and literary subjectivities. Bret Harte, Mark Twain, and the *Golden Era* opened the "Bohemian" West, styling it—however contradictorily—as a democratic, oppositional realm of thought and practice that challenged the city, region, and nation to maintain and expand the freedoms that they each claimed to embody.

Part II "I'd Rather Live in Bohemia Than Any Other Land": The Bohemian Vogue, 1870–1920

"And the last rose dropped from her hand." From Robert W. Chambers, *The Common Law,* illustrated by Charles Dana Gibson (New York: D. Appleton and Company, 1911).

3

"A Plot to Live Around": *La Vie Bohème* in Fiction, City Sketches, and Memoir

THE BOHEMIAN LIFE THAT Bret Harte and the Pfaffians had sought to import to the United States in the 1850s and 1860s gained considerable traction throughout the last decades of the century. In 1885, John Boyle O'Reilly declared, "I'd rather live in Bohemia than in any other land, / For only there are the values true."[1] Others pledged allegiance: the poem became a favorite recitation piece in club and drawing rooms across the nation, and the refrain "I'd rather live in Bohemia" appeared on the mastheads of numerous self-titled "Bohemian" periodicals from Buffalo to Cincinnati, New York City to Fort Worth.

Appleton's Journal provides an index to changing attitudes toward Bohemianism. At the beginning of the 1870s, *Appleton's* still patronizingly described the "many persons who, while having a sort of recognition in the editorial rooms of the New York press, are commonly described as adventurers—a class, known as Bohemians, who live loosely, and precariously, spend their uncertain and irregular earnings lavishly, and who usually are more fond of the convivial glass and the merry song than of labor."[2] The "Bohemian" remained the obverse of the disciplined, well-regulated bourgeois. *Appleton's* further elaborates upon this definition in 1877, praising "the French, with their witty habit of seizing delicate shades of character," for having successfully "embalmed in a name the resemblance between the ethnographical gypsy [whom the French then believed had originated in the country of Bohemia] and a social class." Crediting the felicity of the name and the popularity of Murger's "Vie de Bohème," *Appleton's* declares, "the term [Bohemian] has come to have a pretty definite meaning":

In the broader sense it takes in all restless, unsettled, unthrifty people, who live from hand to mouth, with no definite source of income or place in society. Taken more specifically, it betokens the large class of minor scribblers, musicians, artists, actors, and other young professional men of a somewhat irregular kind, who get their daily bread by their wits, with a large though desultory outlay of the latter to a meager return of the former. It excludes in general, all idea of official position, church-membership, recognized social status, and—most essential of all—landed estate or bank-credit. The very name is redolent with associations of adventure and precarious existence, of midnight jollity, tobacco and whiskey; of clever but fitful exertion with pen or pencil; of greenroom intimacies and box-office intrigues; of long credits, duns, and unpaid bills; of brilliant thinking and anxious living; of shabbiness within and assumption without—in short, all the elements which inhere in the lives of those facile people, who, albeit wittier and perhaps sometimes wiser, than their neighbors, lack the two great elements of a well-organized community—practical tact and thrift.[3]

Bohemia thus remained the land of the artistic wastrel who resided on the fringes of respectable society. In essence, *Appleton's* defines the Bohemian as one who lives on credit—but never "bank-credit." Yet with this definition in mind—the very definition that had bedeviled the Pfaffians and Harte—the anonymous writer of the article recalls being struck "with a tingle of surprise, one day, to overhear a new reading of the term":

It was a clever woman who used it, learned in histories and schools, well known to platforms and pressrooms, but equally so to fashionable dinner-tables and salons; with a social place equal to the best, and a fine culture superior to most. Yet, talking with a clever man of the world of equally good position, she wound up something she had said with the phrase, "For such Bohemians as you and me, my dear fellow"—and then, seeing his look of surprise, she added, smiling, "For we are Bohemians, aren't we?—*good* Bohemians, of course![4]

Impressed by the possibility of "Good Bohemians," the article enjoins us to "read the term in its more imaginative sense, get at its essential characteristics, and not its mere exterior traits. If we are to make a metaphor of a name let us at least manufacture it on finer principles and not on the cheapest points of resemblance." For the gypsy, the article insists, had other qualities that might recast the analogy: He was not merely "vagrant, lawless, idle, and often dishonest," but was "independent, brave, adroit, with a wild poetry and elasticity in his personal habits, and hints at least of an imaginative mysticism in his traditions or his religion." This last set of qualities defined the "Good Bohemian." Embracing this positive reading of the "Bohemian," the writer waxes romantic:

> The real, the better Bohemia is neither geographical nor local, it is bounded by no line of fortune or caste, it lies in the temper and intelligence of its children. It is not to be sought only in Grub Street or Printing-House Row, in the Quartier Latin, or the Studio Building, or Leicester Square. Its real bounds lie far beyond, wide as human nature, and no class or neighborhood but can show some scrap of its territory.[5]

Both Harte and the Pfaffians had pioneered this romantic definition, but by 1877 it gained a wider currency. Critics continued to inveigh against the "bad" Bohemian, but more and more defenders identified themselves with the "good" Bohemian (often while savoring the scandalous allure of the "bad"). A cultural shift had taken place: Bohemia had arrived.

Not incidentally, the "Good Bohemian" was much more compatible with the Bourgeois. "To justify their title of good," *Appleton's* stipulates, "they may pay their debts, wear clean linen, use good grammar, keep a penny for a rainy day, and altogether behave like the respectable citizens they are."[6] Still, though the good Bohemian gave "due observance to all fair limits, ethical, political, or social," he "left his moral elbows free" enough to resist whatever limitations he deemed unjust. In particular, the good Bohemian disavowed the narrow-mindedness of "Mrs. Grundy" and all petty bourgeois restrictions (though, as we will see, even good Bohemians could not always determine the line between "fair limits" and petty conventions). The good Bohemian also continued to defy the bourgeois insofar as he could "never quite unlearn his pestiferous habit of looking at the higher result of his activity rather than at its mere material results."[7] This tendency might limit the Bohemian's potential for worldly success, but it rendered Bohemianism a socially acceptable antidote to commercialism.

Appleton's "Good Bohemians" reflected and contributed to the growing fascination with genteel variants of *la vie bohème*. Whether perched in literal garrets or in the elevated precincts of the imagination, more and more Americans sought to occupy the "higher" ground of Bohemia. Part Two of this study seeks to understand the causes and effects of the late-nineteenth- through early-twentieth-century Bohemian vogue, charting the advent of Bohemia as a compelling "plot to live around" (Chapter 3), a bourgeois retreat (Chapter 4), a regional outpost of modern sophistication (Chapter 5), a cosmopolitan locus for a more multicultural America (Chapter 6), and, finally, a "spiritual geography" centered in the Greenwich

Village of the second decade of the twentieth century (Chapter 7). Taken together, the chapters explore what it meant to live in Bohemia while living in the United States at the turn of the century.

This Was Bohemia!

This chapter introduces the stock Bohemian settings and plots that American writers and artists sought to dramatize and experience. In ever greater numbers, novels, dramas, and city sketches recycled and recontextualized Murger's *Scenes*; this popular vogue culminated in the "Trilbymania" of the 1890s and the revival of Murger in Puccini's *La Bohème* (first performed in New York in 1898). These narratives all convey a consistent message: to live with the utmost intensity and spirit, one must live in Bohemia. When the title character in *Phyllis in Bohemia* demands "a plot to live around," she knows where she must go.[8]

Most travels to Bohemia first occurred through the medium of print. The life dedicated to the aesthetic inevitably began in an imitation of art. In his memoirs, Theodore Dreiser recalled his excitement on first entering an artist's studio as a young newspaper reporter in St. Louis: "Yes! This was Bohemia!" he declares, rejoicing that he had finally entered a world of which he had "long heard and dreamed."[9] Dreiser realized his Bohemian ideal, yet Mary Heaton Vorse suggested that Bohemia "was a kingdom that has existed more between the covers of books than anywhere else." Indeed, Vorse speculated that the many books written about Bohemia "have a little wistful note which implies, 'Here you have an account of what I hoped to find' "—mostly on the basis of their author's previous reading. "Youth hates defeat," she explains, "so he calls what he has found 'Bohemia,' and unless he has a very honest mind, he reads that which he has read into what he sees, and then, perhaps, writes another book."[10] The cycle necessarily continued, since so many who sought a literary Bohemia were, of course, aspiring writers themselves.

It is unsurprising that Dreiser identified his Bohemia with an artist's studio. In most Bohemian plots, artists' studios provide a variant of what Philip Fisher has termed "privileged settings": "They are ideal and simplified vanishing points toward which lines of sight and projects of every kind converge. From these vanishing points, the many approximate or bungled, actual states of affairs draw order and position."[11] The studio as a privileged setting appears at its most glorified in *Art Journal*'s 1879 guide to "Studio Life in New York":

> This is the republic composed of the artistic fraternity, and it presents many phases prolific in interest to those who love to wander from the high-road and seek the lanes and byways of Bohemian or quasi-Bohemian life for scenes and suggestions which "respectability with its thousand gigs" cannot furnish. Those who know the way to them, and the ways of them, find the studios "roadside dells of rest." . . . One gets tired of the dusty tramp and dreary round of the monotony of his social surroundings and daily prosaic life, with its formal gatherings and stereotyped appointments, or it may be one hardly realizes the sameness of scene and stagnation of temperature which surround him, until he climbs the stairs of some colony of artists and enjoys a quiet smoke with new relish in a rarefied aesthetic atmosphere, and in the presence of "such stuff as dreams are made of."[12]

Self-consciously drawing upon the language of pastoralism (much like Bret Harte in his own Bohemian reveries), the article removes the phrase "roadside dells of rest" from its usual context and imports it into an urban environment. Positioning this "rarefied aesthetic atmosphere" both within and without the city, this locution suggests that the privileged setting of the studio offered a modern version of an "ideal pasture" (as defined by Leo Marx): it occupied a "middle ground somewhere 'between,' yet in a transcendent relation to, the opposing forces of civilization and nature."[13] Eschewing the regimented tedium and restraint of bourgeois civility while offering cultivated leisure and aesthetic experience, the studios provided "the best of both worlds—the sophisticated order of art and the simple spontaneity of nature."[14] As one commentator wrote in 1905, the "bohemia of fiction" provided a racier, urbanized version of pastoral equilibrium: a "neutral ground between propriety and license."[15]

Interest in Bohemia and "the life of the studios" mounted alongside the aesthetic movement of the 1870s, 1880s, and early 1890s. In 1878, *Scribner's* announced that the nation was in the midst of an "intellectual awakening" in "matters aesthetic." Whereas ten years earlier, the "general public has had its attention very thoroughly occupied hitherto about matters quite foreign and indeed quite hostile to aesthetic matters—the election of presidents and selectmen, the settlement of the slavery question, settlement of the Genesis and geology question," now "aesthetic things" had evolved into "the subjects of a craze."[16] Historians have concurred with *Scribner's*, noting that the 1870s marked the beginning of the aesthetic movement in the United States. "In the aftermath of the country's splintering, bloody Civil War and its almost equally divisive Reconstruction, Americans were eager for a new truth," Mary Warner Blanchard writes. "The Gilded Age would become quite simply the golden age of American aestheticism."[17] The 1876 Philadelphia Centennial Exposition acted as a clarion call for the arts, helping to inspire a generation to appreciate, collect, and create a wide variety of aesthetic forms: according to *Lippincott's*, the Centennial was a cultural watershed, a "renaissance in American art."[18] By 1882, so pronounced were the effects of the aesthetic movement that the *New York Times* observed: "That we are rapidly developing into an art-loving people goes without saying."[19] All things "artistic" had developed a quasi-fetishistic power, promising to transport the nation into a loftier sphere, easing and redressing the cultural conflicts that arose in a period of massive cultural changes. Rapid industrial growth and urbanization, monopoly capitalism and the threat of oligarchy, new networks of transportation and communication, the closing of the frontier and ongoing sectional tensions, alternating boom and bust cycles, widening class divisions, the rise of the new immigration and the intransigence of the color line, the challenges of secularization and "the woman question": all produced the sense of dislocation and turmoil that the ideality of "art-life" helped to manage.

As a neopastoral "roadside dell of rest," the Bohemian studio was well positioned to rise above the fray. "I like to step from the noise and bustle of a busy thorough-fare into the studio of an artist, where the contrast of the world without and that within is as marked as that of light and darkness," attested one visitor: "All within the artistic precincts is found at once tranquilizing, soothing, ideal."[20] For contemporary urbanites, "art" increasingly assimilated the functions of "Nature." As Roger B. Stein notes, " 'Nature' . . . had been an emblem of national geographic destiny, a spiritual resource and a sign of innocence, as well as the place for the family farm and the source of economic well-being," and, for many late-nineteenth-century Americans, "the aesthetic movement adapted the cultural language of natural forms to new purposes, more in keeping with the urban and industrial society of which it was a part."[21] The idea of Bohemia as a liberatory space removed from conventional restrictions was one part of this process of adaptation.

And though the studio provided a "roadside" retreat, the open road always beckoned. Bohemian artists could employ more traditional forms of pastoralism, leaving the studio to range across the countryside for subjects and inspiration. Once transferred to the canvas, such expanses would then reopen inside the studio. Artists easily justified their Bohemian nomadism. *The Book of the Tile Club* (members of the club included William Merritt Chase and Stanford White) says of the artist: "The vacations of other people being his working time, he steps hither and thither with a busy eye, making the world his workroom."[22] The space of the "studio" was potentially infinite.

The artist used the "vacations of other people" as the occasion for productive work; conversely, most fin-de-siècle accounts of Bohemia emphasize that aesthetic labor was also a form of play. This happy union of work and play further enhanced the neopastoralism of *la vie bohème*. As Daniel Rodgers observes, the postbellum economy had made it increasingly difficult to maintain some of the central tenants of the Northern bourgeois work ethic: "as jobs were divided, simplified, and routinized in the quest for efficiency, as outlets for individuality narrowed and skills disappeared, a wedge was driven between art and work, creativity and labor, self and job."[23] The Good Bohemian arose to bring those elements together again in a period when more and more Americans felt that economic conditions were militating against such a fusion. At a time when leisure pursuits were increasingly called upon to express the creative self that the workaday world suppressed, the happy middle world of Bohemia reconciled the personal and the professional.[24] In 1858, the *New York Times* had insisted that Bohemians threatened the integrity of work, but by the end of the century Bohemians enshrined the ideal of rewarding, unalienated labor. Thus, in answer to the question, "But as a man . . . what do you do when you are not the artist," Albert Sterner (in a publication titled *The Bohemian*) answered: "The man and the artist are never separated. I neither play billiards nor golf; I love my work and it follows me wherever I go."[25]

Escaping the discipline of the time clock, the rhythm of Bohemian work/play followed the dictates of individual whim and inspiration. Sterner emphasized his all-encompassing delight in his work (suggesting continuous diligence), yet others stressed the flexibility of the Bohemian schedule and its ability to accommodate spontaneous impulse. In many Bohemian plots, the idealized Bohemians are always "carefree," avoiding the plague of American Nervousness by living completely in the moment. For the Bohemian, work ceased to be a dispiriting obligation: "His whole life appears to be a holiday, as free from constraint and convention as the happy days spent afield in summertime"—or so the *Chautauquan* remarked of "life in Bohemia."[26] By reconciling work and play, the middle ground of Bohemia also dispensed with past and future, resolving into a continuous present tense. In Margaret Stirling's "The Artist's Last Picture," for example, the titular artist exemplifies the Bohemian modus operandi:

> The artist was young, and had, undeniably, talent. But he was wholly without ambition. Sometimes for weeks, he would work steadily, dashing off clever, little sketches, with astonishing rapidity; and then weeks would go by, without his touching a canvas. . . . He and his wife had lived carelessly and happily, in true Bohemian fashion, from day to day, thoroughly enjoying the present, and very literally obeying the Bible in "taking no thought for the morrow."[27]

Joyously adhering to his own inner creative economy, the painter resembles *Appleton's* "Bad Bohemian" in that he lives by "clever but fitful exertion" and lacks the "thrift" that would require regular cycles of productivity. Unlike *Appleton's* anatomy of bad Bohemian habits, Sterling's description eschews moral disapproval (her Bohemians even live in compliance with at least one Biblical rule), though the story portentously raises questions about what might befall these enviably happy Bohemians some tomorrow.[28] Yet as changing business patterns demanded increased efficiency and routine, such Bohemian conjunctions of work and play offered an appealing fantasy of pastoral innocence and relaxation.

The Bohemian balance of work and play might not result in wealth, but (in romanticized versions) it always provided for basic needs. Whether ancient or modern, the ideal pastoral "middle ground" promised "economic sufficiency": "nature supplies most of the herdsman's needs and, even better, nature does virtually all of the work."[29] So too in idealized depictions of Bohemian life: Art (equated with natural reserves of inspiration) feeds the artist, financing a hand-to-mouth existence (Stirling's artist, for example, "was entirely dependent on his brush; but, fortunately, his pictures always commanded a ready sale, so that he never came to want"). Bohemians could even circumvent bourgeois economics with a return to the barter system ("pictures [were] made a medium of exchange with the butcher and the tailor").[30] Better yet, art offered the Bohemian aesthetic sustenance (in the case of the self-consuming starving artist who "often stints his stomach and feeds his eye").[31] In the ideal Bohemia, a communal esprit de corps also maintained economic sufficiency. Frances Hodgson Burnett described one such Bohemian economy amongst the occupants of a house in "one of the shabbiest corners of the Latin Quarter" in Paris:

> They were a gay, good-natured lot and made a point of regarding life as airily as possible and taking each day as it came with fantastic good cheer. The house . . . was full of them from floor to garret—artists, students, models, French, English, Americans, living all of them merrily, by no means the most regular of lives. But there were good friends among them; their world was their own and they found plenty of sympathy in their loves and quarrels, their luck and ill-luck. Upon the whole there was more ill-luck than luck. . . . And yet, as I've said, they lived gaily. They painted, and admired or critiqued each other's pictures; they lent and borrowed with equal freedom; they bemoaned their wrongs loudly, and sang and laughed more loudly still as the mood seized them.[32]

One Bohemian's good fortune, readily shared, offsets others' "ill-luck," thus sustaining a basic economic equilibrium.

This Bohemian balancing act continually oscillated between the economic extremes of wealth and poverty. For Dreiser, this was the essence of Bohemia: "This was Bohemia! This was that middle world which was better than wealth and more heavenly than simple poverty!"[33] "Simple" poverty might embody ascetic virtue, but Bohemian poverty compounded the "heavenly" qualities of this economic condition because (we might infer) it entailed a quasi-spiritual commitment to art, as well as a willful sacrifice of, or indifference to, bourgeois comforts. At the same time, the aesthetic riches of Bohemia implicitly surpassed other forms of "wealth." The "middle world" of Bohemia thus mediated between wealth and poverty—but it was not normatively middle class: Dreiser's Bohemia disavowed the thrift, propriety, and traditional piety associated with a conservative middle-class orientation. Dreiser's "Bohemian Creed" involved becoming so committed to art as to gain an "absolute immunity from thought or want of money"; "a fine liberty as to personal conduct"; and the knowledge that "religion as preached in the churches had already lost its significance."[34]

Indeed, in the orbit of this pastoral middle world, all class distinctions dissolved—and this during a period that witnessed a rapidly widening gap between the rich and poor. Here was the true classless society long upheld in the American ideological imaginary. According to *Scribner's Monthly*, "social distinctions are not rigidly drawn in this little artistic world. Nothing is so leveling as a community in a great idea. . . . There are ornaments of fashionable circles who come down to the schools and studios and form friendships with a cordiality which must be attributed by their more conventional acquaintances to quite a hopeless bohemianism."[35] True equality, freedom, and fraternity could be found in Bohemia, if not in the nation at large. For the *Art Journal*, at a time when "not a few artists would insist that they live under a veritable oligarchy," Bohemia remained a shining "republic."[36] Bohemia also countered one of the unfortunate results of this "oligarchy": the emergence of a neo-aristocracy in New York. "Yes, gentlemen . . . caste covers the face of New York society with a loathsome, crawling, fungoid growth. That is why I am so happy to escape from those social trammels, to which, alas, I was born, and breathe at times the free air of Bohemia," declares Harpalion Bagger, a character in one of the first novels about Bohemia written in the United States, Charles De Kay's *The Bohemian: A Tragedy of Modern Life*.[37] The Cincinnati *New Bohemian* was even more effusive about the egalitarian possibilities of Bohemia: "The Tramp by the wayside may warm his heart, chilled by the Philistine world, in the warm glow of Bohemia's kindly atmosphere, without money and without price, if he have but a touch of the divine afflatus—either the creative or appreciative side of it; and the millionaire may hold the key to its golden dream-portals despite his hoarded wealth."[38] The dissolution of "social trammels" also facilitated a truly romantic love that defied practical considerations. In the ideal Bohemia, love as well as art and "good-fellowship" triumphed over the economic—as the Bohemian protagonists in Ellen Glasgow's *Phases of an Inferior Planet* insist, "love is a self-sustaining force, independent of material conditions."[39]

A "neutral ground between propriety and license," Bohemia could also temper differences of gender. According to Henry James's "Collaboration," Bohemia destabilized conventional masculinity and femininity; with "propriety" and "license" normatively gendered as female and male respectively, *la vie bohème* prompts each gender to exchange qualities (or at least to imagine that they are exchanging qualities). In the story, James describes a studio gathering filled with women who come "because they fancy they are doing something Bohemian"; conversely, "just as many of the men come because they suppose they are doing something correct." Under the aegis of the Bohemian studio world, each gender assumes characteristics associated with the other sex. The women experience the titillation of greater license, and the men feel themselves properly cultured (at a time when "culture" appeared to be a feminine prerogative). A

Bohemian "middle world" thus supplements both genders, though in opposing ways; in the process, Bohemia briefly produces a more fluid, heterosocial space.[40]

Whether imagined as a "neutral ground" or a resplendent "middle world," Bohemia quickly emerged as an ideal setting, capable of reconciling or transcending a spectrum of opposing forces. In Bohemian narratives, however, such equilibrium is rarely sustained. The social and economic exigencies from which Bohemia provides refuge inevitably impinge upon *la vie bohème*; the forces that Bohemia seeks to oppose or resolve create the conflicts that structure the typical Bohemian plot. Economic uncertainty, conventional morality, bourgeois Philistines, worldly socialites, adult conservatism, and traditional gender roles: all of the normative parameters of bourgeois life unsettle the Bohemia that was to be their vanishing point. Indeed, the very article that upholds Bohemian studios as "roadside dells of rest" acknowledges, "Prosaic needs and petty cares and galling troubles intrude here as elsewhere, and there is none to drive out the moneychangers even from the high Places of Art." Still, the *Art Journal* also maintains that the intrusion of the "workaday world" into *la vie bohème* does less to dispel its romance than to open it to tragic intensities: "Perhaps by reason of the very prominence and altitude which the artistic temperament involves, 'the slings and arrows of outrageous Fortune' have a better target, and are all the more keenly felt."[41] Contemporary chroniclers and readers agreed: the genteel and popular monthlies serialized novels and ran stories and sketches about life in Bohemia, all of which explore just how far this romantic terrain could extend beyond conventional bourgeois limits.

These many narratives demonstrate the wide range of social conflicts that "Bohemia" continued to chart and negotiate as it challenged the norms of bourgeois life: in plots and tableaux derived from Murger, scenes of Bohemian life routinely involve overlapping tensions between artists and "Philistines," art and commerce, wealth and poverty, women and men, propriety and license, work and play, youth and age, America and Europe, art and life. These tensions intersect with, and intensify, the conflicts explored in the rest of Part II: conflicts between work and leisure ethics, the regional and the national, the national and the cosmopolitan. In all cases, Bohemia is either identified with one of these binary terms or it functions as a third term, capable of mediating (if only temporarily) between these conflicting forces.

Wealth and Poverty

In "The Social Side of Artist Life" (1891), the *Chautauquan* posits a specific location for the Bohemian "middle world between wealth and poverty." As it notes:

> The so-called "Latin Quarter" is on the boundary line in a double sense. . . . It includes a region about Washington Square, . . . the northern side of which is as aristocratic as any part of New York, and the southern side of which has been hardly redeemed from the slums. It is peculiarly a neighborhood where one need have no care for appearances, and where artists and artists' models come and go without exciting question as to their relations or affairs.[42]

This double boundary line exists in most Bohemian narratives, whether or not they are set in Greenwich Village.

As we have seen, in idealized accounts, Bohemia occupies a middle space that balances and transcends the wealth and poverty of its environs. In many Bohemian plots, however, this balance is ultimately destabilized, tipping in the direction of either the penury of the slums or the luxurious world of the neo-aristocracy. At the opening of "A Bohemian," which appeared in *Lippincott's* in 1882, we meet the handsome young artist Paul Goldbeck, who is then living in the happy middle world. In good Bohemian fashion, he attempts to borrow ten dollars for dinner from his friend Stern, insisting that he will then invite Stern to dine with him. Neither Bohemian has money, but they go out to dine anyway—in answer to the question, "How are you going to pay for it?" Goldbeck tells Stern: "Don't intrude those sordid practical considerations upon me. The man who cannot control his destiny to the point of compelling it to give him a good dinner when he needs it is unfitted to live."[43] In this Bohemian pastoral, the two artists trust that their needs will be satisfied (perhaps through the pawning of a watch or the exchange of a painting). Destiny then intervenes in the form of a rich gentleman named Mr. Litchfield, who not only wants to buy the Bohemians dinner, but also hopes to purchase one of Goldbeck's paintings. Goldbeck is reluctant to part with the painting, however, and charges such a large price that he feels Litchfield is certain to decline; Litchfield accepts, however, and Goldbeck, despite his financial windfall, feels that "its loss impoverished him." As a "good Bohemian," he values "the higher result of his activity" over any financial return.[44]

Yet with the sale of the painting, the forces of wealth and poverty start to assail his Bohemian middle world. Embodied in two love interests, these opposing forces vie for Goldbeck's affections. On the one hand there is the "irresistibly pretty" Sibyl, the subject of the painting purchased by Litchfield. She lives in a "dingy, disorderly room" with her grandfather (himself an impoverished Bohemian musician), and Goldbeck admires her picturesque simplicity and youthful spirit. He frowns upon a new hat she has purchased, telling her "it is pretty and stylish . . . but I have idealized you a little. I want to keep you out of the world, and that is of the world, worldly." On the other hand, there is the consummately worldly daughter of Litchfield, a gracious socialite. Goldbeck notes that with her, "I felt that I might become whatever I desired, that I could get out of the world just what I wanted." Despite his idealization of Sibyl, the choice appears simple. Goldbeck admits that marrying Sibyl would be tantamount to throwing himself "into the abyss with her": "If I were married to Sibyl, poor as poverty, with a baby coming every year, and all my senses crazed by the din and disorder and discomfort, I should blow out my brains." With Miss Litchfield, however, he would never be "bound down to common necessities." Goldbeck is grateful for her offer of romantic patronage, but, complicating his decision, he wonders if "it were in him to do good work without heavy pressure, the sting of necessity and ambition." This uncertainty, combined with his desire to be Sibyl's manly protector rather than the feminized "husband of a rich woman," ultimately determines his choice. The story does not reveal whether this choice will open the abyss, or whether Goldbeck and Sibyl will reconstitute the Bohemian middle world.[45]

Conversely, in Stephen Crane's *The Third Violet* (1897), the impressionist painter Hawker finds himself more attracted to the haute bourgeois heiress, Miss Fanhall, than to the Bohemian artist model, Florinda, who also adores him. A study of Bohemian and Bourgeois attraction, the novella demonstrates that Hawker and Miss Fanhall are each drawn to the other's apparent difference, and both long to cross the socioeconomic boundary that separates them. The problem is that Hawker wants to cross into the world of her bourgeois brownstone and she wants to enter *la vie Bohème*. Hawker and Miss Fanhall each embody distinct social types, but more to the point, each wants to hold the other to that type. As in such better-known works as his *Maggie: A Girl of the Streets* (1893), Crane takes aim at the erroneous and limiting constructions that his protagonists place on each other and their separate worlds.

For his part, Hawker imagines that Miss Fanhall has "everything" that she wishes for, declaring her "unreasonable" when she implies that her resistance to this notion has something to do with the limitations of her gender role.[46] For her part, Miss Fanhall similarly romanticizes the life she imagines Hawker lives. The two meet while on holiday in the country: she is staying at a local inn, and Hawker is visiting his family on their modest farm. One bucolic afternoon, Miss Fanhall "stare[s] dreamily" and reflects,

"It must be fine to have something to think of beyond just living," said the girl. . . .

"I suppose you mean art?" said Hawker.

"Yes, of course. It must be finer, at any rate, than the ordinary thing."

He mused for a time. "Yes. It is—it must be," he said. "But then—I'd rather just lie here."

The girl seemed aggrieved. "Oh no, you wouldn't. You couldn't stop. It's dreadful to talk like that isn't it? I always thought that painters were—"

"Of course. They should be. Maybe they are. I don't know. Sometimes I am. But not to-day." (31–32)

Miss Fanhall seeks in Hawker the romantic figure of the artist who lives life at a greater intensity, and with a greater purpose, than members of the prosaic bourgeoisie. Hawker can approximate that figure, but only at certain times. He tries to represent himself as a Realist character instead of as her Romantic ideal, but Miss Fanhall refuses to let him puncture her fantasy. In another conversation, she adds:

"It must be a fine thing," said the girl dreamily. "I always feel envious of that sort of life."

"What sort of life?"

"Why—I don't know exactly; but there must be a great deal of freedom about it. I went to a studio tea once and—"

"A studio tea! Merciful heavens—Go on." . . .

"Well, he had the dearest little Japanese servants, and some of the cups came from Algiers, and some from Turkey, and some from—What's the matter?"

"Go on. I'm not interrupting you."

"Well, that's all; excepting that everything was charming in colour, and I thought what a lazy, beautiful life the man must lead, lounging in such a studio, smoking monogrammed cigarettes, and remarking how badly all the other men painted" . . .

"I was on the verge of telling you something about artist life, but if you have seen a lot of draperies and drunk from a cup of Algiers, you know all about it." (179–180)

Her view derives from the carefully orchestrated spectacles of artistic life found in such famous studios as that of William Merritt Chase. Hawker tries to emphasize the difficult realities that comprise so much of "art-life," but everything he says only makes her see him in rosier terms:

> "But still, the life of the studios—" began the girl . . .
>
> Hawker scoffed . . . "There were six of us. Fate ordained that only one in the crowd could have money at one time. The other five lived off him and despised themselves. We despised ourselves five times as long as we had admiration" . . .
>
> "In a case like that one's own people must be such a blessing. The sympathy—"
>
> "One's own people!" said Hawker.
>
> "Yes," she said, "one's own people and more intimate friends. The appreciation—" (44)

Hawker tries to deflate her sentimental notions of Bohemia in their dialogues, but she remains committed to her romantic construction. And—seemingly at cross purposes with his protagonist—Crane goes on to celebrate the Bohemian life that Hawker disavows.

In the manner of Murger's *Scenes of Bohemian Life*, Crane highlights both the poverty and the charm of the Bohemian middle world, so much so that his own scenes of life in the studios would have satisfied Miss Fanhall's ideals. The Bohemian scenes that appear in the novel are adaptations of Crane's own earlier sketches of his experiences with painters and illustrators, his closest companions during his early years in New York. With palpable nostalgia, Crane recalls in one sketch spending the night at the Art Students League on East Twenty-Third Street, a building that "contained all that was real in the Bohemian quality of New York":

> Everyone was gay, joyous and youthful in those blithe days and the very atmosphere of the old place cut the austere and decorous elements out of a man's heart and made him rejoice when he could divide his lunch of sandwiches with the model. . . . Who does not remember the incomparable "soap slides" of those days when the whole class in the hour of rest slid whooping across the floor one after another.[47]

In the novel itself, as in Murger and *Trilby* (1894), George Du Maurier's immensely popular romance of the Latin Quarter, the Bohemians live a life of intimate camaraderie, signified by such affectionate nicknames as "Wrinkles" and "Great Grief." They are starving artists, but their mutual plight is the occasion for comic self-dramatization (in which Crane, as narrator, also participates). When they do have funds, Crane's painters create an impromptu party, dining in the studio on spaghetti, claret, potato salad, and Welsh rarebit, all staples of the Bohemian diet. Alternately, they splurge on a table d'hôte at one of the local Bohemian haunts, a restaurant in which "Latin" emotions have free reign (168–169).

Hawker had once delighted in this ambiance, declaring this café "the one natural, the one truly Bohemian, resort in the city" (171). But now, under the sway of Miss Fanhall's world, he complains of "the blooming din!" His companion, the writer Hollanden, then predicts, "You are about to achieve a respectability that will make a stone saint blush for himself. . . . It is the fact that there are indications that some other citizen was fortunate enough to possess your napkin before you; and, moreover, you are sure that you would hate to be caught by your correct friends with any such consommé in front of you as we had to-night" (172). Instead of the freedom of *la vie bohème*, Hawker now longs for Miss Fanhall's sepulchral brownstone, "about which there was the poetry of a prison" (163). Whether Hawker will succeed in exchanging *la vie Bohème* for the bourgeois brownstone (or whether Miss Fanhall can exchange such entombment for "the life of the studios!") remains unclear at the end of the novel. Crane leaves the sexual tension between Hawker and Miss Fanhall, Bohemian and Bourgeois, forever unresolved by implying, but not confirming, their engagement.

Dreiser celebrated the Bohemian "middle world" between wealth and poverty, but he still recalled longing for his own "Miss Litchfield" or "Miss Fanhall." With regard to his friend Dick Wood—he of the prototypical Bohemian studio—Dreiser enthuses:

> What airs! What shades of manner! He, like myself, was forever dreaming of some gorgeous maiden, rich, beautiful, socially elect, who was to solve all his troubles for him. But there was this difference between us, or so I imagined at the time, Dick being an artist, rather remote and disdainful in manner and handsome as well as poetic and better-positioned than myself, as I fancied, was certain to achieve this gilded and crystal state.[48]

Bohemianism might thus function as a lure for romance and patronage. Paradoxically enough, it would appear that one of the reasons Bohemia was "better than wealth," in Dreiser's estimation, was that it kept the prospect of future wealth alive (and in Dreiser, wealth in fantasy is always better than reality). Better than poverty and wealth (and partaking literally or figuratively of both states), Bohemia was also a middle ground between the two because it was, potentially, a way station from the former to the latter.

Yet, along with *The Third Violet* and "A Bohemian," many Bohemian narratives express anxiety over the achievement of such a "gilded and crystal state." As the title suggests, Edgar Fawcett's "The Gilded Cage" views wealth as a form of entrapment. The story involves an unusually promising young poet, Clarence Chetwynde, who wishes he had more time for his art instead of having to profane his gift: "I scribble for a newspaper that wishes me to gossip about the shape of our new celebrity's nose and the density or thinness of his eyebrows," he complains. Yet such commercialization of his prose has not damaged the poetry he has managed to write; he only values his poetic, noninstrumentalized use of language all the more, and retains a bracing work ethic. Astounded by Clarence's gifts, a patron from "upper Bohemia" decides to endow the poet with a yearly income of $7,000. ("Upper Bohemia," in this tale, is an undefined realm; it would appear to consist of wealthy, socially respectable dilettantes who locate themselves somewhere between the haute bourgeoisie and the struggling Bohemians.) Clarence travels alone to England, begins dressing like a "swell" and affects a "new, lazy, drawling voice." Upon his return, his patron reads Clarence's new poems, but the moral of the story is readily apparent: "prosperity has killed the poet!"[49]

Scribner's echoes this moral, warning the artist that "the tempting solicitation of society" might result in a "vain scattering of his forces, and a frittering away of his honesty."[50] Most accounts seek to preserve Bohemia from this temptation, resisting the Cinderella-like narrative Dreiser had envisioned for Dick Wood. The self-styled "Bohemian" Tile Club, for example, proudly guarded itself against social interlopers.[51] The club formed in 1877, and, as member F. Hopkinson Smith notes, "it's a singularly interesting thing that, although none of us had any particular reputation at the time, every man who ever belonged to the Tile Club ultimately met with success," and several of its members became some of the most prominent artists of the era.[52] Original members included Elihu Vedder and Napoleon Sarony; by the early 1880s, Augustus St. Gaudens, J. Alden Weir, Stanford White, and the aforementioned William Merritt Chase also belonged; membership remained limited to a small group of artists, writers, and architects. When the club published its limited edition *A Book of the Tile Club* in 1886, it boasted that it had managed "to keep the flood-gates of the Club against Society, which beat at the barriers demanding admission," because "not a few of the members had a demoniac talent for telling an after-dinner story, for improvising a monologue in dialect, for delivering society-verses with point and distinction." Unlike the Bohemian Club of San Francisco (the subject of the next chapter), the Tilers refused to allow members of "Society" to participate in or subsidize their activities. It was only through its *Book* and a series of self-promoting articles in *Scribner's* that the Club allowed outsiders to listen in on "the talk of artists among themselves, so studiously slangy and Bohemian" (and all the identities of the members were veiled by nicknames).[53] The very exclusivity of a club at once within and without "Society" most likely enhanced the market value of individual members.

As part of its recorded "shop-talk," the club distinguishes itself from a "mediocre society painter" who, in its estimation, pandered to potential patrons by establishing himself in Newport: "In thirty days he knew everybody worth knowing. He dressed well, talked well, played tennis, drove tandem (his brother-in-laws), and dined out every night." What really launched this "Linseed," however, was his refusal "to paint a real estate man's two hundred pound wife"; this act guaranteed his "exclusiveness, good taste, and artistic instincts" and he became all the rage. He sealed the deal when he "rented a suite of rooms, carted in a lot of old tapestries, brass, Venetian chests, lamps and hangings . . . [and] gave a five o'clock tea."[54] The Club then debates the merits of this apparent sacrifice of art to commerce. The Owl (F. Hopkinson Smith, a painter, author, and engineer who built the foundations of the Statue of Liberty) plays devil's advocate and defends Linseed: "I call it the act of making the most of your opportunities. . . . You want to shuffle around in carpet slippers, live in a garret, and wait until some Dives of a Diogenes climbs up your rickety staircase with a connoisseur's lantern and discovers you. . . . Merchants, Lawyers, physicians, and scientists, when they have anything to sell, go where there is somebody to buy; why not the artist?" The "Saint" (sculptor Augustus St. Gaudens) retaliates by articulating the aesthetic ideology, tinged with anti-Semitism, that they all seemingly shared:

> Just like a Jew peddling suspenders. . . . Owl, I am ashamed of you. . . . You have too fine a perception of what is true and beautiful to believe any such bosh. The pursuit of the ideal in art absorbs a man's entire life. . . . I am poor, and suppose I always will be. I love my work for the good it does me. It is three fourths of my existence, nine tenths of my happiness, and all of my ambition: and, I would see your chuckleheaded money-bags in Hades before I would move out of my studio six inches to get from him a commission for a monument a mile high, unless I got something else out of it besides the sum of money set down in the contract.

In elevating his own artistry beyond material considerations, the appropriately named "Saint" defines himself against an easy target.[55] As Sarah

Burns observes, "the figure of the society painter" had become a "popular caricature": "Painters who circulated in the realm of society and fashion were corrupt almost by definition, because success depended on the mastery of slick sales techniques, practiced on those who lived only for pleasure and for the assertion of status through commodity display."[56] Instead of savoring the ideality of art, the society painter was a purveyor of conspicuous consumption, memorializing the wealth that financed his endeavor.

The Owl has the last word in the debate, however, facetiously noting, "I don't expect you fellows to agree with me. You all occupy garrets, carry up your own coal . . . and live on one pound of bologna sausage and quarter of a pound of tea a week. You Briareus haven't got any bric-a-brac, or dress coats, or palms or brother-in-laws or things. You just starve all the time, and like it."[57] The irony, of course, was that most club members had long ceased to live the prototypical *vie de bohème* of the starving artist. Moreover, as Hopkinson Smith insinuates, "Briareus" (William Merritt Chase) was himself quite famous for his "bric-a-brac"–filled studio on West Tenth Street; his Bohemia had become an elaborate collection of exotic artifacts acquired from around the world. Many journalists, including the *Art Journal*'s John Moran, guided readers through the studio, detailing hundreds of objects (by 1896, Chase had amassed 1800 pieces), including: stuffed cockatoos, Renaissance velvets and tapestries, Japanese umbrellas and bronzes, "a unique collection of woman's foot-gear," piles of "quaint old books," "strange little wood carvings of saints, Virgins, and Crucifixes," "the weatherbeaten sail of a Venetian fishing-boat, with its reefing-cords attached," rococo brocades, a Nuremberg chair, "a crucifixion by Piazetta, master of Tiepolo," and "many other articles too varied to specify." As his collection grew, Chase's purchases increasingly reflected the fin-de-siècle "mania" for Orientalist art, and he could be found reposing in the studio under a Moroccan tent.[58]

Contemporaries had varying theories about the purpose of such a studio: for some, it was the very embodiment of a transcendent "art atmosphere," and, for others, it was a practical investment solidly rooted in commercial designs akin to those of the artistically dubious "society painter." Of course, Chase himself stressed the former, claiming that the studio was part and parcel of his art.[59] In 1906, he noted that he had long believed that "the secret of the success of the old masters in the good times when they left their great works was their environments—and it was this influence that helped to produce their great works." Chase highlighted this inchoate influence by representing his studio in a series of paintings, literalizing the notion of the studio as a space of "art for art's sake."[60] Other artists were reportedly inspired by the atmosphere; after the pianist Paderewski performed in Chase's studio, *Godey's Magazine* raved, "one could not conceive of a place more suitable to the highest artistic sense or more capable of drawing out all that was poetic in this great pianist."[61] Equally enthralled, Arthur Hoeber recollected that Chase's studio was "a veritable glimpse of heaven" for the young art student, "a shrine into which he entered with bated breath and deep humility."[62] By contrast, writing of a "successful artist" modeled on Chase in his novel *The Golden House*, Charles Dudley Warner deflates such romantic responses, viewing the "studied litter" of the studio less as the expression of the "highest artistic sense" than as a spectacular advertisement: the site of frequent receptions and performances for the wealthy, his are "surroundings which contribute to the popular conception of his genius."[63] For Warner, the aesthetic objects were reduced to the redundant materiality of "litter," catapulting their owner to popular success but failing to cultivate the rarefied atmosphere of the eternal. Still, whatever his reasons for collecting so assiduously, Chase continued to spend more than he earned, and his vast collection of aesthetic objects ultimately had to be sacrificed to the demands of "vulgar materialism": all were sold in 1896 to help pay off Chase's creditors.[64]

The society painter pandered to the wealthy, disrupting the precarious balance of the Bohemian middle world. So too might the wealthy and upwardly mobile seek to appropriate Bohemia's "rarefied aesthetic atmosphere" or "invade" its territory. The definition of the "good Bohemian" invited such crossings of Bohemian and Bourgeois, and some commentators celebrated the extension of Bohemia into bourgeois interiors and leisure itineraries. Yet, for others, such appropriations called into question the very existence of an authentic Bohemia. Many novels, stories, and journalistic accounts from the period record (and participate in) the bourgeois "invasion" of Bohemia. They alternately explore the attempts of Bohemians to reclaim their homeland, satirize Bourgeois-Bohemian posturing, or capitalize on the popular fascination with *la vie bohème*. All attest to the increasing role of Bohemia in bourgeois life.

In his sketch "Bohemia Invaded," James L. Ford describes what happens when he foolishly introduces "young Etchley" to the Garibaldi table d'hôte in a "snug little basement below Washington Square." Etchley is an artist, but Ford characterizes him as a "poseur" who gives "studio teas" which "are admitted by all whose privilege it is to attend them to be 'most delightful affairs and so thoroughly Bohemian, you know.' " Etchley is the consummate society painter, and he has many profitable connections with the "Philistines" who seek to explore Bohemia. Ford notes with alarm that "before the week was out Etchley appeared again on the scene [at Garibaldi's], accompanied by two stock-brokers" and that "a few days later other gentlemen of unmistakably commercial aspect bore down upon us, . . . forced themselves upon us under every possible pretext, but also whispered to one another about us, pointing us out as if we had been so many animals in a cage." Resenting their positions as de facto entertainers, the Bohemians devise a plan to turn the tables (quite literally) on the bourgeois interlopers. They decide to treat the bourgeoisie as part of the local color, exclaiming loudly:

> Why this place is fairly alive with commercial talent to-night. . . . If you want to get the kings of finance and the merchant princes together just set out a free feed, and they'll come all the way from Yonkers for it. Do you see that man with the mayonnaise whiskers? You'd never think to look at him that he holds a very responsible position in one of our largest retail emporiums.

The plan works, and the Bohemians once again have Garibaldi's all to themselves.[65]

By 1906, Ford recognized that the "invasion" could not be so easily foiled. In "Seeing the Real New York: Trip No. 4—Bohemia," Ford writes of a touristic excursion into "Bohemia." The tour guide pulls up to a doorway marked "Bohemian Hall: Table d'hôte with wine, fifty cents" and recites O'Reilly's verses through a megaphone, bellowing: "I'd rather live in bohemia than any other land." According to Ford, Bohemia had now been thoroughly appropriated by bourgeois interests: "This delightful country was discovered in the late forties by Henri Murger, but it is only in recent years that it has been developed and put on a strictly business basis." Moreover, the "Bohemians" within the restaurant all pursue the most bourgeois of occupations. The proprietor boasts that "most of our clientele are bohemians," and he points to several "Bridgeport, Waterbury, and New Haven bohemians, chiefly from the watch and brass trades." Next the tour stops "in the fashionable preserves of bohemia," at "one of the delightfully bohemian studio-parties" given by "Horace Drypoint, a famous society artist." There "a committee of typical bohemians, consisting of a reckless insurance adjuster, an improvident cotton broker, an open-handed subway contractor and a large-hearted public accountant" sing a "merry chorus of 'He's a Jolly Good Fellow.'" High spirits and social effervescence ostensibly qualify these guests as good Bohemians; moreover, in the words of one "Bohemian," while "there are plenty of people that can *paint* pictures," only the wealthy "can *buy* them."[66] The relationship between contemporary constructions of Bohemianism and bourgeois "good-fellowship" will be further explored in Chapter 4 of this study; Chapter 6, in turn, takes up the commercialization of ethnic restaurants under the auspices of *la vie bohème.* As both chapters will reveal, Ford's satire was only slightly exaggerated, and by 1906, almost thirty years after *Appleton's* announced the advent of the "Good Bohemian," the bourgeois annexation of Bohemia was well under way.

Of course, Ford's sketches were themselves responsible for many a bourgeois discovery of Bohemia. Indeed, in the aforementioned *Phyllis in Bohemia*, "the frank observations of Mr. Ford" are credited with enticing Phyllis to a Bohemian table d'hôte of "dyspepsia-attracting foods." *Phyllis* gently mocks its heroine's Bohemian pretensions; hers is such a tame version of *la vie bohème* that her fiancé confides, "Between you and me . . . I don't really believe that we ever were in Bohemia."[67] Indeed, in the wake of the turn-of-the-century vogue, many commentators wondered whether a genuine Bohemia was still possible. To the extent that Bohemianism meant the defiance of the philistine, then its very popularity spelled its demise.

H. C. Bunner recognized his own part in popularizing *la vie bohème.* In his 1886 novel *The Midge*, Bunner had publicized the Bohemian charms of the "French Quarter."[68] Writing in the passive voice and without explicitly holding himself accountable for the rise of the "posing Bohemian," Bunner nonetheless alludes to his own role in his later sketch "The Bowery and Bohemia" (1896):

> Ten or fifteen years ago the "French Quarter" got its literary introduction to New York, and the fact was revealed that it was the resort of real Bohemians—young men who actually lived by their wit and their wits, and who talked brilliantly over fifty-cent table-d'hote dinners. This was the signal for the would-be Bohemian to emerge from his dainty flat or his oak-panelled studio in Washington Square, hasten down to Bleecker or Houston Street, there to eat chicken badly braisé, fried chucksteak, and soggy spaghetti, and to drink thin blue wine and chicory-coffee that he might listen to the feast of witticism and flow of soul that he expected to find at the next table. If he found it at all, he lost it at once. If he made the acquaintance of the young

men at the next table, he found them to be young men of his own sort—agreeable young boys just from Columbia and Harvard, who were painting impressionless pictures for the love of Art for Art's sake, and living very comfortably on their paternal allowances.[69]

Bunner retained a distinction between "real" and Bourgeois-Bohemians, but O. Henry was not so certain that such a distinction was tenable. In his story "A Philistine in Bohemia," O. Henry reveals, " 'Tonio's restaurant is in Bohemia. The very location of it is secret. If you wish to know where it is ask the first person you meet. He will tell you in a whisper." An effective marketing ploy, the veneer of secrecy guarantees a crowd of "Bohemia-hunters." Yet, along with the tourists, 'Tonio's also welcomed "a sprinkling of real Bohemians . . . who came for a change because they were tired of the real Bohemia." The difference between the "real" and the sham Bohemian is thus partially obliterated: both go to 'Tonio's to escape the tedium of their respective realities.[70]

Like the sketches of Ford and Bunner, William Dean Howells's *The Coast of Bohemia* also documents the absurdity of Bourgeois-Bohemian affectations.[71] Always eager to dispel hackneyed literary conventions from fiction—and to prevent those conventions from being imitated in real life—Howells unsurprisingly took aim at the contemporary phenomenon of *la vie bohème*. His polemics on behalf of literary realism sought an art that imitates life instead of prior artistic models, but the representation of *la vie bohème* presented a particular problem for the realist writer: Bohemianism explicitly sought to emulate the literary romances of Murger and his followers, all in the name of creating a life devoted to artistic production. How then could realist fiction hope to represent Bohemianism without falling prey to literary conventions, when those conventions were the very essence of the life? Howells concluded that a realist treatment of Bohemianism must try to satirize the literary clichés that existed in both the telling and living of the Bohemian life. As we have seen, Stephen Crane's *The Third Violet* attempted a realist debunking of the mythos of Bohemia, but ended up largely succumbing to the conventions of Bohemian romance. Howells's novel, on the other hand, never becomes an example of the very phenomenon it seeks to undercut, but the satire is gentle, recognizing the charms of the pretensions it exposes.

The character that hovers along *The Coast of Bohemia* is Charmian Maybough, a New Yorker from a newly rich family who nonetheless aspires to be a "perfect Bohemian" (202). Her family home asserts its occupants' position within the haute bourgeoisie: it is "tasteful and refined, with the taste and refinement of the decorator who had wished to produce the effect of long establishment and well-bred permanency" (127). Charmian, however, announces that she "simply endure[s] it because it's in the bargain," and tells her friend Cornelia, "This is where I *stay*, when I'm with mamma, but I'm going to show you where I *live*, where I *dream*" (127). She leads Cornelia into her studio, which she has designed to approximate her "Bohemian ideal" (207):

> She invited Cornelia to a study of the place by turning about and looking at it herself. "It seemed as if it never would come together, at one time. Everything was in it, just as it should be; and then I found it was the ridiculous ceiling that was the trouble. It came to me like a flash, what to do, and I got this canvas painted the color of the walls, and sloped so as to cut off half the height of the room; and now it's a perfect symphony. You wouldn't have thought it wasn't a real ceiling?" (129)

Charmian also vows to possess the other accoutrements found in studios such as Chase's showroom: a wolfhound, a suit of armor, and "then two or three of those queer-looking, old, long, faded trunks, you know, with eastern stuffs gaping out of them" (131). "You can imagine what a relief it is to steal away here from all that unreality of mamma's, down there, and give yourself up to the truth of art; I just draw a long breath when I get in here, and leave the world behind me," Charmian confides in Cornelia, adding: "Why, when I get off here alone, for a minute, I unlace!" (129). For the realist Howells, the notion that Charmian's carefully staged Bohemian lair is more authentic, more real than "all that unreality of mamma's" is obviously absurd. The irony is compounded by the fact that her mother insists upon bourgeois standards of cleanliness, enforced by a maid who in turn reveals the socioeconomic hierarchy that structures Charmian's Bohemia: though Charmian "might and did keep things strewn all about in her studio, . . . every morning the housemaid was sent in to sweep and dust it" (202–203). Charmian thinks that she has managed to keep her studio "free from pose" (130), and the joke is at her expense. Nonetheless, for all her apparent obtuseness, Howells does allow Charmian a partial understanding of Wildean paradox: she implicitly argues for the "truth of lying" when she announces that she hopes to perform in a theatrical, because "then I could be *natural*" (133). Yet Howells's point does not seem to be that she has arrived at an important truth about the social construction of identity, but rather that she is a poseur who can parrot aesthetic jargon: in its context, her assertion does more to uphold than to deconstruct the opposition between the natural and the theatrical.

However amusing, Charmian, the Bourgeois-Bohemian, is not the heroine of the novel. Her friend Cornelia, a fellow art student, is the protagonist, and Charmian's affectations function in the narrative primarily to offset Cornelia's "straightforward and downright" nature (239). Cornelia is a talented artist—and not incidentally a much more gifted artist than Charmian—and she has no desire to cultivate a Bohemian identity. When Charmian organizes a Bohemian masquerade at their art school, Cornelia comes "simply as herself"; in Charmian's words, "Cornelia is so perfectly truthful, you know, so sincere, that any sort of disguise would have been out of character with her" (323). Cornelia embodies the principle of Howellsian Realism, and Charmian represents the literary Romanticism against which Howells repeatedly inveighed. Yet if Howells hoped that Realism would appear more compelling than Romanticism through the respective examples of these two young women, he was mistaken. Cornelia remains blandly virtuous, while Charmian is the more engaging character. Indeed, in an "introductory sketch" to the second edition of the novel, published in 1899, Howells imagines the book speaking back to him: "You gave me two heroines, and you know very well that before you were done you did not know but you preferred Charmian to Cornelia."[72]

Charmian attempts to carve out an alternative Bohemian space in the interstices of her haute bourgeois residence, but others sought to bring the trappings of Bohemia into their very living-rooms. Clarence Cook, a leading authority on interior design, offered "Studio Suggestions for Decoration," encouraging readers to "try for some of that freedom from conventionalities and old-time preciseness that is at least shadowed forth in the best of our artists' studios." In his earlier tome, *The House Beautiful* (1881), Cook had stipulated that his "purpose is not to recommend eccentricity, nor even a modified Bohemianism" in home décor.[73] Yet at the apex of the Bohemian vogue, Cook maintained that Chase's studio was exemplary as "a not unfit type of what might in many ways be desirable in our homes" as part of a "revolt against formality and a too strict insistence upon uniformity of manners and ways of living": "It is a good example of what, to the taste of some of us, at least, a living-room ought to be. All the decoration consists of pictures and casts, and these are set off by abundant light and space, so that all the members of an ordinary family group could pursue their domesticities at ease without interference, and yet with a sense of companionship and facility of communication."[74] For many Bourgeois-Bohemians, the studio could be introduced into the home in the form of a "cozy corner." As M. H. Dunlop notes, "in its basic form, the cozy corner consisted of a low divan set diagonally across one corner of the living room; the divan was draped with an Oriental rug, and heaped with pillows. Suspended above it were 'Baghdad curtains,' which could be looped back on either side." Thus, Dunlop concludes, "the path to the East—first glimpsed at the 1876 Centennial Exposition—tangled itself in the long American fascination with Paris studio life, passed through French Orientalist art, . . . flowered in Chase's studio and dozens like it . . . and ended in a draped and cushioned segment of anyone's living-room called a cozy corner."[75] The "cozy corner" might be an opulent, haute bourgeois affair; alternatively, the *Ladies Home Journal* provided tips on how to fashion an affordable version on a tighter budget.[76] In many a tale involving a would-be Bohemian, a "cozy corner" can be found in his or her abode, ever mediating between Bohemian and Bourgeois sensibilities.[77]

Most turn-of-the-century accounts of Bohemia emphasized, in James L. Ford's words, the many "points that the fields of Bohemianism and society come into contact." Whether such contact was facilitated by wealthy patrons, studio teas, society painters, cozy corners, or Philistine "invasions," the boundary line that separated Bohemia from the bourgeoisie remained extremely porous. Conversely, Ford notes that the field of "low life is entirely cut off from both by a chasm which is temporarily bridged now and then for the benefit of 'slumming parties,' or writers in search of 'local color.' "[78] Yet, if most contemporary narratives tended to tip the balance of the "middle world between wealth and poverty" in the direction of "high life," others destabilized the Bohemian pastoral by emphasizing the ravaging, though at times ennobling, effects of Bohemian poverty.

Popular versions of *la vie bohème* often stressed that Bohemianism involved "living by one's wits" in a hand-to-mouth-existence. But, as we have seen, this existence usually remained "merry" and "jolly," the occasion for playful expedients and good-natured guile. At times, however, Bohemian narratives looked into the "abyss" glimpsed in "A Bohemian." In Bunner's *The Midge*, for example, the parents of the title character began their life together "with the picturesque, easy-going poverty of Bohemia." After the birth of their daughter, however, "it was poverty out and out, hard, shabby, degrading, worrying, toilsome, troubled, ugly poverty"

(21). Even plots that highlight Bohemian poverty of the most "worrying" variety generally reassure readers that such dire straits are temporary aberrations that breed character and foster love. In "A Bohemian Love Story," for example, two struggling writers, one Clayton Gibbs and Miss Savannah Moore, live in "genteel" poverty and share their misfortunes in a San Diego rooming house; but just as they have exhausted their resources ("My comrade! My comrade! I have eaten your bread and condemned you to starvation," moans Clayton), he receives an offer to edit a small-town paper and promptly offers her a job. They are fortuitously rescued from starvation, and recognize that poverty and the communal good-fellowship of *la vie bohème* have nurtured their burgeoning love story.[79]

But when did Bohemian poverty become a hackneyed affectation or pathetic spectacle? Contemporary chroniclers tried to ascertain the point at which Bohemian poverty lost the moderation of the happy middle world and entered the realm of sheer excess. This is the question that underlies many descriptions of *la vie bohème*. In "Young Artist's Life in New York," for example, *Scribner's* describes the impoverished conditions of many beginning painters:

> The studio of the poorer class is a sleeping room, and generally more or less kitchen as well. Disregard of conventional forms sometimes reaches the point of actual squalor. Here in one costing fifteen dollars a month, three persons are sleeping, two on a lounge—which also serves as a coal box—and one on a shelf conveniently placed at night on trestles. Coffee is drunk from a tomato can. . . . It is a veritable vie de Bohème that goes on. . . . Landlords are regarded in an odious light, and if possible locked out. One, who would be put off no longer, was paid his rent in busts of Evangeline, which even the amiable Longfellow had repudiated. . . . If fortune be propitious the bohemian luxuriates at boarding-houses and restaurants, whose walls he becomingly adorns. At other times he takes but a single meal or only mush and milk.[80]

Scribner's isn't entirely convinced that the "veritable vie de Bohème" is strictly necessary. The article suggests that, in their own modest ways, the Bohemians enact cycles of boom and bust in their everyday life, always at the mercy of the market, and without the more moderate habits that would, it is implied, allow them to avoid such shifting swings of fortune. Though *Scribner's* notes that "such straits are often the result of an aversion to regular labor, or of such an improvidence that it amounts to a choice," the magazine also admits that "often enough the pinching is a genuine necessity." *Scribner's* mentions "an artist of known standing, [who] found himself reduced by the failure of the Sixpenny Savings Bank during the absence of his friends in the country, to a summer of scarcely more than bread and water." Even a "Good Bohemian" might thus find himself in financial trouble. But however desperate the situation, *Scribner's* commends the self-reliant American artists who—in implicit contrast to the French Bohemians—"have never been encouraged to feel that it is the business of any government or princely patron to take care of him" (359). Self-reliance must not shade into self-delusion, however, and in the case of the "tribe of incapables" (those who ignore "the most glaring evidence of incapacity"), *Scribner's* insists that they are simply "pathetic martyrs to mediocrity"—they do not even obtain the dignity of being pathetic martyrs to Art (364). Only significant talent, in other words, could justify the squalor of the young artists, and only for a limited amount of time.

Of the Bohemian poverty described in another essay, "The Social Side of Artist's Life," the *Chautauquan* focuses on only one melodramatic example. It is the sad tale of a student returning from Munich who "set out to compel the success that he felt was his due," only to find himself "locked out of his studio for arrears for rent, and turned overcoatless into the street on a cold night." He then bought "a pistol with his last money" and "achieved more distinction for a passing hour, by killing himself somewhat dramatically, than he had ever won with his brush." The *Chautauquan* deflates the dark romanticism of this gesture, however, by attributing this act to "the morbid dictates of a foolish and wounded pride." And, in this conventional urban sketch of sunshine and shadow, the *Chautauquan* then reintroduces the light: "But I did not mean to introduce a tragedy into this story of life in Bohemia. It is but a shadow across which the sunshine and glint of color may show more brightly, and its only lesson is that life in the dreamland of the artist is not less real and earnest than in the work-a-day world in which the rest of mankind plod."[81] Though still more glamorous than the plodding "work-a-day-world," the Bohemian "dreamland" is, in other words, not as otherworldly as readers may have supposed: Bohemians must face economic realities as surely as other citizens. Indeed, the article notes that some of the older, more successful artists have left the "Latin Quarter" of Washington Square and moved uptown. There they cease to parade their Bohemian difference from the Bourgeois:

> The Bohemianism of the "Latin Quarter" is being outgrown. The conventions of polite society are in greater respect than formerly. It is a long time since long locks swept the coat collar, and loosely knotted neck scarves of brilliant hue and velvet

jackets were the recognized uniform of the professional painter. Now but for the pointed Parisian beard (a la Vandyke), and not always by this sign, the artist of New York is not to be distinguished in appearance and manner from any other gentleman. (748)

The balance of the Bohemian middle world once again tipped in favor of the bourgeois establishment.

Some retained the antibourgeois animus of Bohemia, however. The painter John Sloan spoke in favor of the Bohemian who forsook bourgeois conventions—most especially the tendency to make money "an end in itself." For Sloan, Bohemian poverty was "nothing more than [one of] the outward, visible manifestations of the spirit of liberty within":

Money, being neither his god nor his aim, is usually scarce with him, so that it comes about that he lives mostly in cheap, crowded quarters, cooking nearly all his meals in his own room, since he can seldom afford to patronize a restaurant, and showing in his often prematurely haggard face the marks of the conflict which he wages. . . . It does not apply to the lives of all Bohemians . . . because persons in almost any walk of life or of any income may elect to live freely; but I think that it is a fair statement of the portion which society allots the great majority of Bohemians. Bohemia's message to the world, however, lies behind all this—behind any externals. It is summed up in that state of mind which makes it possible for people to endure such conditions in order that they may continue to live their own lives in their own way. It seems to me that the message is: "Let there be real life; let there be real liberty."[82]

As a member of Robert Henri's "Ashcan School" of painters, a model for Theodore Dreiser's titular character in *The "Genius,"* and a future artist for the socialist magazine *The Masses* (see Chapter 7), John Sloan voiced a more explicitly antibourgeois version of Bohemianism than most of his contemporaries. Indeed, the same article that quotes Sloan while trying to ascertain "The Message of Bohemia" immediately contrasts Sloan's "low" vision with that of the painter F. Luis Mora, who found "no place [in Bohemia] for the grim accompaniments which so insistently occupy the other": "Mr. Sloan looks upon a Bohemia at war with society, retiring loweringly unto itself; Mr. Mora's Bohemia, on the other hand, rests upon a superstructure of exalted sympathy." This Bohemia readily lent itself to "studio gatherings whereat polite young ladies sip tea and nibble almond-studded cakes with polite young men, discussing Nietzsche and tentatively playing at being 'artistic' and 'unconventional.' "[83]

Propriety and License

As this image of the "polite" studio gathering suggests, idealized versions of Bohemia offered a "neutral ground between propriety and license."[84] Just as the ideal Bohemia provided a "happy middle world" between wealth and poverty, so did Bohemia mediate between social restriction and individual freedom. This balance might occur within specific Bohemian locales and social situations (and sometimes only for an evening), or it might be achieved in the lives and psyches of particular Bohemians. Along with the "Good Bohemian" who paid his bills but left his "moral elbows free," many Bohemians of the era purportedly integrated conventional and (somewhat) unconventional manners and mores. For instance, describing the artists' gatherings that took place at "Mack's" in "Mid-Town," the *Chautauquan* insisted that, though "there is an atmosphere of art and smoke there that is simply delightful . . . it is withal most decorous revelry and presents no suggestion of excess."[85] Similarly, of the Authors Club of New York City, first formed in 1882, George Cary Eggleston declared that the club embodied "the better kind of Bohemianism—the Bohemianism of liberty, not license; the Bohemianism which disregards all meaningless formalities, but respects the decencies and courtesies of social intercourse."[86] A novel titled *A Conventional Bohemian* appeared in 1886, maintaining that, with respect to its title character, this phrase was not a contradiction in terms.[87] Indeed, so many narratives featured "decorous revelry" and "conventional Bohemians" that James L. Ford marveled at the "exalted moral tone that pervades the Bohemia which our story-tellers have created for us."[88] Nonetheless, though many narratives figure Bohemia as an ideal "neutral territory," the threat of the dissolute "Bad Bohemian" also pervades them, and the balance between propriety and license is often a precarious one. Many Bohemian plots feature attempts to negotiate between the competing demands of social restraint and personal liberty; the "neutral ground" upon which they meet is not always stable or secure. Faultlines rooted in gender, class, and national or ethnic divisions frequently erupt, and Bohemia quickly devolves into a "dangerous land" or a decorous sham.

Of course, in many Bohemian plots, *la vie bohème* is desirable precisely because it provides the antithesis to a stifling bourgeois propriety. Henry James's early story "The Sweetheart of M. Briseux," for example, concerns a young English woman who becomes disillusioned with her eminently proper fiancé, Harold Staines.[89] Though Harold was an aspiring artist, his fiancé notes, "I was not surprised that he shouldn't care to fraternize with the common herd of art-students. They had long, untidy hair, and smoked bad tobacco; they lay no one knew where, and borrowed money and took liberties" (191). At first, she sees Harold as a faultless "embodiment of the serene amenities of life" (191), but she increasingly comes to share the assessment of a young man who refers to him as a "confounded prig." She ceases to believe in his talent, and as a final challenge, asks him to paint her portrait. Harold struggles with the painting until one day, an "impudent little Bohemian" arrives at the studio before Harold has arrived, dismisses Harold's work, and begs the narrator for a chance to finish the painting. The choice between the two painters is stark: "Poor little Briseux, ugly, shabby, disreputable, seemed to me some appealing messenger from the mysterious immensity of life; and Harold, beside him, comely, elegant, imposing, justly indignant, seemed to me simply his narrow, personal, ineffectual self" (208). She chooses Briseux, even though it means forfeiting her engagement, and the two share a moment of sexualized consummation as he finishes her portrait, "flushed and disheveled, consuming [her] almost with his ardent stare, daubing, murmuring, panting" (205). This is as far as their relationship goes; once she is transferred to the canvas, Briseux has no use for her. But understanding the greatness of Briseux's talent, she has no regrets, explaining: "We women are so habitually condemned by fate to act simply in what is called the domestic sphere, that there is something intoxicating in the opportunity to exert a far-reaching influence outside of it" (209). Her role as a model might have been largely passive, but it was predicated on a more defiant act, a rejection of the bourgeois life she had always assumed she wanted.

Most contemporary narratives, however, question how much license a female Bohemian could legitimately afford to take. Indeed, for many commentators, it was the very engrafting of bourgeois "prudery" into Bohemia that made it an agreeably "neutral ground between propriety and license." Describing the writer Jonna E. Wood, author of *The Untempered Wind*, the periodical *Current Literature* proposes her as the prototypical "good" female Bohemian:

> She is never commonplace. Unconventional in the most charming way—that is, unconsciously—she would be a favorite in Bohemia. Indeed, she is a Bohemian of the modern type. She would not vote if she could, she can actually sew, always dresses well and with no taste but the best, and can see no reason why a woman can't be literary and wear good boots, too. Woman characterizes every thing she says and does.[90]

Despite the example of Jonna Wood and other "good" Bohemians, many continued to feel that Bohemia posed a notable threat to traditional womanhood. Howells, for one, was glad that he had only allowed his heroines to venture to *The Coast of Bohemia* in his novel; in the introductory sketch to the second edition, he imagines the book itself telling him:

> You know you were vexed when some people said I did not go far enough, and insisted that the coast of Bohemia ought to have been the whole kingdom. As if I should have cared to be that! There are shady places inland where I should not have liked to my girls to be, and where I think my young men would not have liked to meet them; and I am glad you kept me within the sweet, pure breath of the sea.[91]

As Howells's fear of the "shady places inland" suggests, Bohemia often represented a constellation of urban threats that hovered around "the girl who is employed." This last phrase derives from an article written by the *Ladies' Home Journal*'s Ruth Ashmore (Isabel Mallon). Like her boss, the *Journal*'s editor, Edward Bok, Ashmore believed in maintaining traditional gender roles, arguing that such roles were based in religious truth. In "The Restlessness of the Age," she writes, "When the good God was arranging the human pegs into their abiding places, He did not put the round ones in the square holes, but when a woman rushes away from the work that is laid out for her, she finds that she is wrongly situated, and she wears herself out worrying over this."[92] Bok himself minced no words on the issue of women in the workforce: "I am an ardent believer in woman's progress, in her advancement toward the highest position in life which she is capable of adorning. . . . But sometimes I begin to wonder if woman is not progressing in the wrong direction, if she is not drifting away from that home anchorage for which God intended her."[93] Both Bok and Ashmore, however, recognized that economic need compelled some women to work (though, as Helen Damon-Moore notes in her study of the *Journal*, Bok was "worried that the image of the working woman had begun to entice those who did not have to work"),[94] and the periodical did feature a regular column on "Women's Chances as Bread Winners," instructing women on how to enter such fields as nursing, fashion, and office work. While upholding the virtues of domesticity, Ashmore also announced herself the "dearest friend" to the "girl who must, perforce, earn her living" (following "must" with "perforce," Ashmore makes doubly sure her readers understand that her support of working women extended only those who work due to economic necessity). To the "girl who is employed," Ashmore offered advice, counseling her to be punctual, avoid gossip, eat nourishing food, dress appropriately, and rebuff familiarities from male coworkers. But some of her most pointed warnings revolved around the "dangerous land," namely "that one of Bohemia which seems to you so attractive":

> In reality it is a country of which you should not become a citizen. No matter whether your friends call you a prude or not, do not permit the social side of your life to degenerate into a free and easy condition where no respect is shown to you as a woman. In Bohemia there may be some laughter, but be sure there are many tears. In that land you would probably spend all your wages in one day of festivity, and be a beggar, or worse still, a borrower for the rest of the week. In that land a woman buys one fine frock, too fine for her position in life, and during the working hours she looks untidy and always suggestive, by her shabby finery, of a gay girl rather than a well-bred woman, which is what the busy girl should aim to be. In Bohemia it is claimed there is a jolly good-fellowship, and nothing else, between men and women. You don't want to be a jolly good fellow. You want to be a woman who is respected.[95]

Just where this "Bohemia" existed, Ashmore does not say; her "dangerous land" appears to encompass the rooming houses, inexpensive table d'hôte restaurants, and dance halls that were emerging as sites of heterosocial flirtation and increasingly attracting members of all classes.[96] Exceeding the bounds of propriety, Ashmore's Bohemia was a land of inordinate license that might forever compromise the working woman.

On the pages of the *Journal*, other advice columns, fiction, and memoirs reiterated Ashmore's warnings about *la vie bohème*. Alice Preston, for example, counsels women who "will have to take care of themselves" to "be careful how you go into Bohemia."[97] Similarly, Katherine Ferguson's "The Autobiography of a Girl," provides a cautionary tale of life in Bohemia that echoes the message of the other advice givers.[98] As an aspiring young writer, Ferguson records being initiated into Bohemia by her roommate, Eunice, who was in love with an unnamed "Artist" and who insisted that the two women travel together to this new terrain. Ferguson provides a stock image of racy Bohemianism (most likely set in the famed Bohemian haunt "Little Hungary," discussed in Chapter 6 of this study):

> Eunice was quite delighted with my first enjoyment, for I acknowledge that Bohemia seemed to me enchantingly full of color, warmth, and laughter. One does not recognize at first that the color is glaring, the warmth sickening, the laughter oftenest harsh or pitiful.

> "Here are plots for stories galore," the Artist said. "For instance, that young fellow over there with the girl in black spangles was starving once. I happened to find it out and saved him. It is a question, though, whether one ought to save a fellow like that. The girl in spangles helped me with him. I want you to meet her."
>
> "I'd love to meet her. She must be fine and good."
>
> The artist smiled cynically. "Not good, exactly, nor fine," he replied.
>
> The girl in spangles put out her hand frankly enough.
>
> "Hope you'll like Bohemia. We're just a happy-go-lucky lot, and we do as we please; that is the first and last law in Bohemia. We're not half as bad as we're painted, though."
>
> "And you're not painted bad at all," said the young fellow opposite her, with a laugh. "By Jove, I call it well done—couldn't tell it from genuine, you know."
>
> A general laugh, in which the Artist joined, went up. . . . The music, which had been tuning noisily its fifths, began now with a rough crash and hurled into a wild Hungarian measure.
>
> "It makes one feel like a gypsy," Eunice said dreamily, strumming with one pretty, ungloved hand on the table. (6)

Replete with "painted" women, cynical "brilliant" wits, and "wild" music, this was the heterosocial Bohemia that contemporary commentators feared. As the narrative continues, the women return to their rooms, and while Eunice enthuses about their "glorious" experience, our heroine demurs and contemplates a photograph of her sister: "Polly, who lived still in the sweet home atmosphere. I had always thought Polly's idea of a girl's sphere such a narrow one; but now I seemed to realize suddenly, almost without reason as one often does with the great truths of life, that the best life for a girl, the broadest, best, fullest—fullest of opportunity, of usefulness, of happiness—is the home life" (6). Given this moral, it is unsurprising that the *Journal* was the periodical that serialized Howells's *The Coast of Bohemia*; as we have seen, that Bohemia was comprised of genteel play-acting (primarily *within* the space of the parental home) instead of the racy intrigues of the urban nightlife.

Like the *Journal* writers, many others looked askance at the ways in which Bohemianism had altered sexual relationships and destabilized moral parameters. The male Artist in Ferguson's narrative ultimately concludes that Bohemia was no place for a woman with any "womanliness in her"—certainly no place for a matrimonial prospect—and a male writer in *Cosmopolitan* vehemently endorsed this point of view:

> The most eagerly sought of all the privileges of Mock Bohemia [for women] is the privilege of "comradeship," of having numerous male friends with whom may be put aside ostentatiously the reserves by which social usage has recognized the difference of sex. To go where you please with whom you please; to say what you like to any one you like,—these things belong to 'comradeship' as Mock Bohemia understands the word. . . . Their pretence is that they are merely exercising a natural freedom which emancipates them from the fetters of sex. Actually, they are forever seeking the salacious, and exciting in themselves by its discussion with their "comrades" the vulgar sensations which are imperfect, to be sure, but wholly safe.[99]

According to this writer, Rafford Pyke, the "mock" female Bohemian is merely a vulgar tease while the refined traditional woman—"the woman who carries her external daintiness into her thought" and accepts that the "normal woman differs from a man in mind, precisely as she differs from him in body"—actually makes the best comrade (611-612). Without holding women exclusively responsible, still another commentator complained about how Bohemianism was interfering with traditional courtship patterns. Writing in *Life*, Harold Van Santvoord editorialized against "an impending evil," namely the fact that the number of marriages was allegedly decreasing every year. To explain this evil, he claimed that youth no longer felt like "sacrificing the frolic and fun of Bohemia" for the "domestic circle," in part because the "idle flirtations" that occurred within this brave new world had "destroyed the confidence of young people of romantic temperament in one another."[100]

Such views spurred Emilie Ruck de Schell to ask, "Is Feminine Bohemianism a Failure?" Writing in *The Arena*, she answers this question largely in the affirmative, maintaining that male Bohemians would ultimately forsake their female comrades, wanting to marry only the most womanly of women. "The average man is a Bohemian by nature until his deeper being is awakened by the touch of a woman's hand. The loose, irresponsible life of the college chapter-house or the club-room possesses a fascination for him that is irresistible until he becomes satiated with its shams and its follies"; at this point, "the man who has drunk the last dregs of Bohemianism is the man who will select the purest woman for his wife and the most sequestered nook for his home." He has passed through this youthful phase, but "What is to become of his Bohemian sister when she is 'sick unto death' of struggling alone with this awful problem of living?" According to de Schell, "she would scorn the advances of an unsophisticated man, and for the man of the world she has been divested of her charm." She is thus unable to find a congenial mate, and is doomed to a life of lonely toil. But, worse still, de Schell warns, was the possibility of being seduced and abandoned in Bohemia. Though "city-bred girls" were comparatively safe in the hands of even the most unprincipled of men, the unsuspecting country girl was an easy target: after "the usual elegant supper, finished off with a glass of champagne, . . . [t]he door is shut, and she is told that she is in a private assignation-house. To resist were folly; to cry out, worse than vain, for there is no one to hear."[101]

The threat Bohemianism posed to women had apparently been confirmed a few years before de Schell's essay, exemplified by the infamous "Pie Girl Dinner." In 1895, Wall Street broker Henry W. Poor organized an all-male party at the studio of James L. Breese, a society photographer, and guests included the famous architect Stanford White and such prominent painters as J. Alden Weir and J. Carroll Beckwith. The dinner was named for one Susie Johnson, the model who appeared from within an enormous pie at the end of the evening. She mysteriously disappeared several months later, and the New York *World* used the affair to warn against the dangers of haute Bohemia, especially for working-class young women:

> Somewhere in the big studio buildings of New York's Bohemia the girl is hidden. Perhaps this article will bring Susie Johnson home to her parents and put a stop to the bacchanalian revels in New York's fashionable studios. These amusements of wealthy young men-about-town are beyond the reach of police or municipal reformers. Safely screened in the luxurious studios of artist friends, the shocking scenes of dissipation are carefully kept from the knowledge of the public. But the contamination reaches into the little flats and big tenements of the east and west sides and works sorrow and misery in these humble homes.[102]

As Sarah Burns has noted, the Pie Girl Dinner "became a sign for the decadence of art and high society, fatally twinned in the pursuit of erotic sensation and in the ruin of innocence."[103] Inequalities of class and gender combined to make the working-class woman particularly vulnerable to Bohemian hijinks, and to the relaxation of manners and mores that would help to legitimize her exploitation.

The linkages between Bohemianism and the "ruin" of innocence only became more deeply soldered during the later "trial of the century." Harry Kendall Thaw murdered Stanford White on June 25, 1906 in the rooftop theatre of Madison Square Garden (which White had designed), and the trial revealed that Thaw sought to avenge White's 1901 seduction of Evelyn Nesbit (who was married to Thaw at the time of the murder). The seduction occurred when the artist's model and chorus girl was sixteen years old. In her 1914 memoirs, Nesbit herself, who famously modeled for Charles Dana Gibson's "Gibson Girl" illustrations, insisted that the Bohemian ambiance of White's studio facilitated the seduction:

> Think of this cozy room, with its shaded lights, its thick carpets, its divans, its rare objects of art. There was no jarring note in the composition, no picture that offended or any touch of color that irritated. Nor to my eyes was there any note of decadence that might cause the slightest uneasiness; a pleasant meal with a pleasant man, a sense of security and well-being—that is my memory of that night.

Nesbit then recalled drinking "bitter and funny-tasting" champagne, at which point "the whole room began to go around and everything went black."[104]

Raising the possibility that "Feminine Bohemianism is a Failure," de Schell warns against the peril of such ruined innocence. But her description of feminine Bohemianism is more nuanced than it first appears. She empathizes with the "bachelor girl" who chooses her "liberty" over the "simple delights of a home" (which de Schell characterizes as "ministering to the wants of an often ungrateful, always self-centered husband") and speculates that, difficult as it is for women, passing "the perilous boundary of Bohemia" might ultimately help them to become better wives and mothers:

> The girl who has had a glimpse of the seamy side of human nature can never become a simple, trusting wife; but she may be a more enlightened companion and a wiser helpmeet because of her own experience. Surely she will be a wiser mother than her own mother was. Her children will be few, for she will marry when her prolific period is past; but they will be all the world to her. (75)

The feminine Bohemian is thus recovered for the domestic, but with the hope that she will have acquired sufficient knowledge of the world and herself to help improve her "sphere" and her relationships within it. She would not be the type of "comrade" envisioned by the traditional Rafford Pyke, but she would be an "enlightened companion" to a more progressive man (75).

But did men want the worldly wise companion envisioned by de Schell? Some stories answer affirmatively. In F. H. Lancaster's "Out of Bohemia," young Maxwell lounges in the studio of a woman writer whom he calls

"Frank." She is serious about her writing, and abuses herself when she feels her work is "mawkish—damnably mawkish" (28). Yet when she denigrates the institution of marriage and rebuffs his invitation to lunch, Maxwell calls on another woman, a "sweet, dainty, pure" woman that "any man would be proud to win" (32). As they talk, however, Maxwell cannot help but compare this womanly paragon to "Frank." While the dainty woman begins rehearsing "the things that all the best morning papers had said," Maxwell realizes that "SHE would have had something original to say or else she would have remembered her quotation marks." And, despite Frank's crude language and constant cigarette smoking, he comes to realize that she is "pure," though in a more desirable sense than the woman before him: "Good Lord, she was the purest thing this side of heaven. . . . Not the innocence of ignorance, but a resolute cleanliness that had been tried and not found wanting." He returns to Frank, and announces, "I am going to share your life" (34). This declaration hopefully implies that Maxwell will share her life in Bohemia (though the story is titled "Out of Bohemia.") In any event, at least Maxwell values her Bohemian spirit—in large part, of course, because the "pure" Frank has essentially stayed within the parameters of that refined Bohemia, that "neutral territory between propriety and license." As to whether a man or a woman imagined this story, that information may be irrecoverable. We might infer, however, that a woman wrote the story, given that the heroine goes by the name of Frank, and the author's first name is indicated simply by the initial "F."[105]

In other narratives—written by men and women—a brief but chaste foray into Bohemia can lend the heroine an additional depth and charm, but the workings of the plot are designed to rescue her from the potential corruption of *la vie bohème* and to deliver her into the safety of traditional marriage, usually through the agency of an upstanding bourgeois suitor. For example, L. H. Bickford (Ralph Henry Barbour) and Richard Stillman Powell's *Phyllis in Bohemia* (1897) removes its heroine from Bohemia and installs her in the apparent comfort of bourgeois matrimony. A comic narrative, *Phyllis* never subjects its titular heroine to the dangers of Bohemian seduction (unlike many contemporary narratives), but the novel does give voice to many of the yearnings that attracted many of Phyllis's real-life counterparts to Bohemia. And though Phyllis ultimately repudiates Bohemia, the narrative does admit the value of (a modest variant of) *la vie bohème* within a female developmental narrative.

At the beginning of the novel, we meet Phyllis, a plucky woman from an "Arcadian" small town who, we quickly gather, has recently become engaged to the narrator of the tale, a well-heeled man from one of the "first families" of New York. Phyllis pronounces that she has become "particularly tired of being 'eminently respectable' " (6). Her fiancé immediately promises Phyllis that he will buy her whatever her heart desires; yet for Phyllis, such a response is part of the problem: "That is what most men say they will do for women they intend to marry—buy things. Well, you cannot buy me experience—knowledge of life, of the unusual incidents of which life is formed. . . . I want to do the things 'eminently respectable' young women do not do. I want a plot to live around." (10). And the plot that Phyllis has her heart set on is that of *la vie bohème*. She wishes to go to Bohemia—which her ever-bourgeois fiancé first takes to mean that she wishes to go to the central European country as part of the grand tour they will undertake for their honeymoon. "Can you understand nothing?" Phyllis sneers, "Bohemia—art, letters, poverty, struggling genius, people that make the world, people on the verge of great careers, people toiling to make themselves powers—such is the Bohemia I ask for" (13).

Despite her references to "plots," and despite the fact that her knowledge of Bohemia is derived from contemporary poetry, Phyllis maintains that her Bohemian narrative will follow a strictly realist trajectory that will fill her with "true knowledge of humanity":

> We [women] sit in dairy kitchens, or perhaps in back parlors, illustrating what you call the "domestic virtues," and all the time, out on the broad stage, there is being enacted a drama which we must not witness because some of its incidents are too realistic to be thought "proper." . . . You call experience—a brushing against this same "improper" part of life—something that every man should undergo before he settles down to the hearthstone. It is, I have heard you say, a part of the education of man. But what of woman? (10–11).

The narrator's mother endorses this argument; like de Schell, she also imagines that having a little experience beyond the traditional bounds of the "proper" will ultimately make women better wives and mothers, if only because they would be less likely to crave an additional, extramarital "plot" of the "Sarah Grande" variety (29).

Equating Bohemia and the real, Phyllis echoes the sentiments of the polite company that finds itself "in bohemia" in Warner's *The Golden*

House (1894). In a flutter of expectation at seeing something on the borderline of propriety, the guests "gathered in a famous city studio" enjoy a "titillating feeling of adventure, of a moral hazard bravely incurred in the duty of knowing life, penetrating it to its core" (1). Yet for all of her would-be realism, Phyllis is content with a tame version of Bohemia that scarcely ruffles convention. She moves to New York with a female chaperone in tow ("an elderly lady with gray hair and bowed spectacle" [51]), and into a boardinghouse that has "an air of New England respectability" (41). Nonetheless, the house does contain many aspiring artists, writers, and musicians, and Phyllis makes her way into "Maria's basement of unconventional late suppers" (91). She finally has enough of Bohemia, however, after an elderly playwright dies on the very night that his play has become a critical success. Thus fortified with "experience," Phyllis is ready to "legally become a part of man" (29).[106]

Like Phyllis, many contemporary heroines are ultimately "Extradited from Bohemia," in the words of the title of one of O. Henry's stories. In this story, the hometown suitor of the would-be female Bohemian brings her back to her New England roots: "Did you think you could fool me? How could you be run away to that Bohemia country like you said when your letter was postmarked New York plain as day?" (1348). This Yankee literalism in itself destroys the romantic license of *la vie bohème*.[107] Yet not all female Bohemians were "extradited" from Bohemia by male protectors.

In "Female Bohemian Life in Boston," Mellie A. Hopkins describes her life with "M—," another female Bohemian. Hopkins emphasizes that they live within the bounds of propriety, though they covet their freedom from the surveillance of the "everlasting 'muck-rakers' of the village." The two women live in a "respectable but obscure lodging house," and sometimes go to the theatre, "for, in Boston, wherever it is proper for women to go at all, they can go unattended by gentlemen." Of their "life in Bohemia," Hopkins insists: "We are happy, perfectly happy, because we are free to do as we like. We find pleasure in small things, and happiness in being busy. M— is devoted to her art, and I to my singing, and each to the other, and so runs our world away." When they pass small children, Hopkins does "wonder if M— thinks as I do, of what might have been once for us, in our younger days, before the crows' feet came to our eyes and the gray hairs to show faintly on our brows, but for our own folly." Still, the two women had what became known as a devoted "Boston marriage." Hopkins writes that M— is "so little and pretty, and I so large and gaunt and awkward, that I feel as though she were some pretty kitten put under my protecting care." It is difficult to determine if this is a coded reference to lesbian eroticism;[108] what is clear is Hopkins's commitment to M— and to their shared "Bohemia."

Most Bohemian plots, however, revolve around heterosexual melodrama. Several such novels written by Robert W. Chambers involve narratives in which virtuous males protect the purity of Bohemian heroines. Relatively conservative, these novels nonetheless mount an increasingly pointed critique of the ways in which sexual double standards inform the dichotomy between propriety and license (within and without Bohemia). Like de Schell, Chambers represents as a problem what other writers accepted as a given: the fact that the very definition of license and propriety varied according to gender.

In Chambers's *Outsiders: An Outline* (1899), our protagonists, novelist Oliver Lock and artist model Dulcie Wyvern, cohabit in a rooming house "fairly crawling with Bohemians," known ironically as The Monastery (99).[109] At first, Dulcie thrives in Bohemia:

> "Did you hear me singing—the air, I mean—while they all were carrying on the serenade—and the blue-eyed girl and the harp—"
>
> "Was that your voice?" he exclaimed.
>
> "Yes, my voice. I had never until then heard that serenade. What a strange, strange evening—not like a dream, but like something that ought to be always, but never is."
>
> She went on, opening one hand for emphasis;
>
> "I care for all that; I want what I had there, freedom!" (81)

Flirting with Oliver, finding her voice in a public gathering, Dulcie experiences a moment of exhilaration unlike anything she had ever known. She finds a glimmer of utopian freedom beyond the bounds of traditional propriety, the "something that ought to be always, but never is," and yet the narrative ultimately resolves into a cautionary tale.

Dulcie's tale, Chambers tells us, was the familiar "story of an outsider among outsiders—a chapter in the stale story of the unclassed" (143). Even though she has "more innate purity of character than you'll find in some entire congregations" (173), Dulcie exists in a liminal demimonde because her mother is a kept mistress of a wealthy publisher; Dulcie herself left home when it became clear that she was expected to "entertain" the publisher's brother. Dulcie then moves into a boardinghouse with several female Bohemians, all aspiring writers and actresses, and yet, each time she attempts to earn an independent livelihood, she experiences more sexual harassment: at the "celebrated cloak and mantle makers, Beetle Brothers," Dulcie "stayed until the Beetles became intrusive"; next, the director of a chorus line "offered her a role beyond her ambition" (144–45). She confides in young Oliver, who warns her about the ever-present dangers of heterosociability, particularly her new habit of attending parties and restaurants with Bohemian men: "Try to hold out, Dulcie; they're liars—everyone . . . And—the danger is everywhere—*everywhere*" (146). After saving Dulcie from yet another attempted seduction, Oliver decides to offer her a room in his apartment till he could "place her in more suitable quarters" (193). They live chastely as Bohemian comrades, but rumors soon swirl. Dulcie voices concern for Oliver's own reputation, though Oliver, well aware of the double standard that governs sexual morality, thinks to himself, "there was no use in telling her that it is never the man in such cases who suffers from slander" (218). He realizes too late that he wants to marry Dulcie: after returning to her mother, she is mortally wounded in a train crash.

According to Christine Stansell, *Outsiders* and other stories of turn-of-the-century Bohemian life "invite young men of sophistication to believe that enlightened solutions—a shared urbanity rather than separate spheres, mixed company at cheap restaurants rather than same-sex jollity at gentlemen's clubs—might reconcile men's customary dominance over women with a belief in women's right to a wider sphere of action."[110] Chambers, however, is not certain that such sociability is an "enlightened solution"; in *Outsiders* and his later novel, *The Common Law* (1911), Chambers sympathizes with "women's right to a wider sphere of action," but fears that this "shared urbanity" will lead to increased "dominance over women," especially in the form of sexual violence and harassment. While he does feature several enlightened "New Men" who seek friendships or respectful courtships with Bohemian New Women, he emphasizes the risks—for women—of Bohemian heterosociability.

In *The Common Law*, the heroine, Valerie West, has even greater exposure to the joys of *la vie bohème*.[111] A graceful and expressive artist's model, Valerie exalts in the life of the studios. After a sheltered childhood, Valerie marvels at how Bohemia has instilled in her "this quickened interest in life, this happy development of intelligence so long starved, this unfolding of youth in the atmosphere of youth" (53). For a time, she experiences Bohemia as the ideal "neutral ground between propriety and license"; she relishes the joy of subverting certain conventions, all the while recognizing the essential harmlessness of her transgressions. But the comfortable balance between propriety and license begins to shift once Valerie and the painter, Louis Neville, fall in love. Neville is a young artist from an elite old New York family, and Valerie, who grew up in genteel poverty, is a paragon of beauty, "nobility" of character, and an ever-questioning intellect that is attracted to free-love ideologies. He wants to marry her, but she wants to consummate her love for Neville "without asking benefit of clergy and the bureau of licenses," boldly reasoning: "You once said that love comes unasked and goes unbidden. Do vows at an altar help matters? Is divorce more decent because lawful?" (217). When Neville counters, "I'm respectable enough to want you for my wife," she vows to resist becoming "a selfish, dependent, conventional nonentity" (263). More dialogic than Chambers' other Bohemian novels, *The Common Law* allows the female heroine space to debate the virtues of "the arbitrary laws of a false civilization" (225). Weighing sexual license in the balance against traditional propriety, the novel ultimately endorses the "common law" of marriage over and against the doctrine of free love espoused by Valerie; and yet, even more insistently than *Outsiders*, the later novel acknowledges that unequal standards of sexual propriety are the outgrowths of an unjust patriarchal society.

Neville does succeed in convincing Valerie to marry him. Despite her purported desire for "individuality and independence," one of the principal reasons Valerie initially resists marriage is that she knows that Neville's family will not approve of her, and she refuses to be the occasion for his estrangement from his Old New York world (225). It is thus her selfless love that motivates her resistance (paradoxically revealing her eminent suitability as a wife), and, though she defends her decision with recourse to emancipated rhetoric, Neville attempts to reduce her modern thought to adolescent posturing and secondhand rhetoric, asking, "What rotten books have you been reading?" and whether "she expected to overturn, with the squab-logic of twenty years, the formalisms of a civilization several thousand years old?" (225). Far from being one of the "arbitrary laws of a false civilization," Neville reasons that marriage is the evolved manifestation of instinct, natural law (225–26), and "divine convention" (311). Valerie does not immediately accept this logic, yet she ultimately concurs.

In truth, the flirtatious yet ever chaste Valerie had never advocated promiscuity, and even after she initially refuses Neville's proposal in favor of a more informal arrangement, she is deeply offended when he attempts to seduce her: "Why did you offer our love such an insult? . . . To me, the giving of myself to you is to be, in my heart, a ceremony more solemn than any in the world." (267, 269). She had always wanted to initiate their sexual relationship through a rite of passage of her own design, yet she finally realizes that this right must have an official legal sanction for two principal reasons. First, she recognizes that sex might produce children, and that consequently, "each for the other's sake is not enough" (525). Valerie's second reason for reassessing the necessity of marriage implies an ongoing critique of current conditions, specifically of double standards and sexual violence. She knows the difference between "what is thought about a girl's unwisdom and the same unwisdom in a man" (339). After a harrowing night in which she is almost raped by another painter, she reluctantly concludes:

> Do what she may to maintain her freedom, her integrity, there is always—sometimes impalpable, sometimes not—a steady, remorseless pressure on her, forcing her unwillingly to take frightened cognisance of men;—take into account their inexorable desire for domination; the subtle cohesion existent among them which, at moments, becomes like a wall of adamant barring, limiting, inclosing and forcing women toward the deep-worn grooves which women have trodden through the sad centuries;—and which they tread still—and will tread perhaps for years to come before the real enfranchisement of mankind begins. (474)

She now believes that she needs the protection of a man who "understands his man's world well enough to fight it with its own weapons." For Valerie, this masculine "desire for domination" may or may not be rooted in natural instinct; she hopes for eventual female "enfranchisement" but insists "no woman can—yet" change the laws of a patriarchal society (485).

Such reflections place a darker cast on her final acceptance of matrimony. Since this is an unjust, patriarchal man's world (and this, as we have seen, is one of the stated premises of Valerie's defense of marriage), both novels reason that it is best for women to avail themselves of whatever protections patriarchy affords them. The novels offer the beginnings of a feminist critique, but each narrative imagines that marriage (to the right man) will enable the protagonists to achieve a happy ending. What happens to the heroines after marriage is not part of the story.

Representing the liberatory excitements of heterosociability while highlighting the dangers of sexual victimization, Chambers's Bohemian novels rely upon two competing discourses. Both discourses centered on the young working women who resided in urban rooming houses. As Joanne Meyerowitz has demonstrated, the first discourse drew upon Victorian conceptions of womanhood, and was employed by turn-of-the-century reformers and "working girl" romance novelists alike; it "portrayed women lodgers as passive, passionless, and imperiled," always threatened by unscrupulous men. By the early twentieth century, however, Meyerowitz notes, "sociologists, moviemakers, and pulp magazine writers depicted them as active, pleasure-seeking, and opportunistic." Both discourses had potential advantages and disadvantages for actual women (who no doubt embodied aspects of both stereotypes in their own individual ways). The earlier discourse denied female agency and sexuality, but it drew attention to the realities of sexual harassment and female economic dependence. The second downplayed the latter realities in order to emphasize the former, while sometimes announcing the "sexually 'emancipated' woman as a potential threat to men."[112] Mediating between propriety and license, Chambers's novels negotiated between both discourses. He permitted his female Bohemians to experience the modern joys of heterosociability (in their own chaste fashion) and, especially in the case of Valerie, he emphasized the strength of her individual will and desire for autonomy (even when contemplating becoming Neville's lover, Valerie "modestly requested non-interference in her business affairs and the liberty to support herself" [Chambers, 223]). Though Chambers continued to uphold the virtues of sexual purity, his novels relied less on the metaphysical dangers of sexual corruption and more on the concrete pragmatics of sexual and economic vulnerability.

Like Valerie West, Rachel Gavin, the heroine of Ellen Glasgow's first novel, *The Descendant* (1897), seizes upon the "license" afforded by Bohemia to test the boundaries between convention and personal freedom, traditional gender roles and individual autonomy.[113] Rachel experiments with the type of informal sexual relationship that Valerie only contemplated, but she ultimately arrives at a similar conclusion; after much suffering, she admits the value of the traditions she had renounced. This awareness comes too late for the happy ending that Chambers afforded Valerie. Still, it is not simply the heroine's late awareness that impedes her happiness: Glasgow raises the question whether traditional marriage could possibly have provided Rachel with the happiness that eluded her.

At the beginning of *The Descendant* (1897), Rachel Gavin is a promising painter at the Art Students League in New York. At first, Rachel views Bohemia as the site of her emancipation, the place where she might utterly devote herself to her art and cast off the conventions of her Southern girlhood. Determining that "success and society are contradictions with me" (71), Rachel chooses to lead an independent Bohemian life in the "most advanced flank of the New Woman's Crusade" (83). Self-reliant Rachel scoffs at the prediction of Madame Laroque, a neighbor who warns,

> I had quite a talent for painting. . . . But I gave up my ambition for marriage; it's the way with women. You'll do it some day. . . . I suppose the Lord intended it. I guess He knew if he made women any smarter the race would come to a stop. I guess He knows best—at least, He ought to; but it does seem strange to me that He couldn't have found a better way to arrange things." (114)

Within the novel, Madame Laroque's warnings prove justified. Whether women's self "abnegation" (132) was the result of divine intention or the Darwinian product of the struggle for existence, Glasgow suggests that female emancipation, for better and for worse, defies the dictates of human nature; of her heroine, she announces: "Rachel thought herself emancipated, and was as strong in her conviction as the most of us, before Time has shown us our error" (84).

As Susan A. Glenn has argued, the feminism that emerged in the early twentieth century involved a set of principles and goals that included the "idea that although men and women were biologically different, gender roles and identities were not 'predestined by God or nature' but shaped by socialization."[114] It is this idea that Glasgow both anticipates and calls into question. Though attracted to new womanhood and the license it gave women to explore new possibilities, she was deeply influenced by contemporary evolutionary thought, so much so that it was difficult for her to imagine human behavior as anything but the result of biological determinism.[115] Even if God or nature "should have found a better way to arrange things" for women, Glasgow suggests, those Bohemians who rebel against convention will inevitably find themselves thwarted by their own desires as much as by any external societal force. Like Chambers's Valerie, Glasgow wonders if female emancipation defies both social convention and natural order.

Rachel remains committed to finishing her great work, a painting of the Magdalen, wrought with "the hand of genius, a hand whose strokes are powerful and falter not." Yet Rachel's Magdalen, painted "with traces of sinful passion and sinful suffering upon her face" (82), ominously mirrors her creator, and Rachel realizes that she herself is harboring a passion that, whether "sinful" or not, might yet provoke suffering: she has fallen in love with Michael Akershem. This passion infuses the painting but also stalls its completion. " 'Let me finish it, O God!' she prayed. 'Let me make of it a great, great thing. Give me this, and I will ask nothing else my whole life long.' "(92).

Akershem is the illegitimate son of a farmer's daughter and a rakish "scoundrel." In his apotheosis as the "iconoclast" (the name of the magazine he edits and whose ethos he embodies), Akershem advocates a radical combination of socialism and individualism, one that leads him to conclude that the institution of marriage has become an archaic "fetich" (75). When he falls in love with Rachel, he vows to renounce his principles and marry her. But Rachel instead wants to become his "comrade," and to live with him out of wedlock (122). In this instance, her defiance of traditional propriety is motivated by her all-encompassing love for Akershem. Just as Valerie's free love ideology was designed to serve Neville (so as not to estrange him from his family), so too is Rachel's sexual radicalism the paradoxical result of her traditional gender role. Both Valerie and Rachel aspire to put the needs of their male lovers above their own, and, despite their modern ideologies, they fulfill traditional feminine ideals of selfless devotion.

Rachel and Akershem are happy, at first: "Many a merry evening they had, dining first at one place, then at another; always finding something to laugh over. . . . A jolly little Bohemian she was, and much of the Bohemian world had she known" (148). Yet Rachel's experimental new "Bohemian world" now consists of love, not art; as Madame Laroque had predicted, Rachel finds that all her passion is now directed toward love. Soon, love destroys Rachel's very ability to paint, and Glasgow editorializes: "To a woman the mental toil of an eternity may sink to nothingness before one heart-throb" (118). Such is Rachel's womanly fate, even though Michael is himself able to "balance" work and love. Rachel thus reflects, "Do you think that a man's love can extinguish ambition? Only a woman's love can do that" (120). She mourns her art, but tells herself that she has traded representations of life for the thing itself. She passes a woman who had been a fellow-student at the Art League and feels "a contemptuous pity for that other woman, and for the art students, and for their teachers, and for all who painted with cold brushes upon cold canvas," assuring herself, "They have not lived" (217).

But Glasgow makes sure that her readers know this Bohemian idyll will not last. We know that Rachel never really understands Akershem and the "inconsistency of his life," his own internal split between the Bohemian and the Bourgeois. Rachel, Glasgow tells us, "did not see . . . that though he opposed marriage, yet he blushed because he himself had been born without the pale" (81). He is Bohemian because he cannot be Bourgeois. Rachel is a Bohemian in part because "the buoyancy of her belief in him had exalted her above conventions," yet Glasgow portentously reminds us: "despised conventions avenge themselves as inevitably as despised truths. It may be that we have never clearly defined wherein lies the difference between them" (209). Far from being an outmoded social "fetich," Glasgow suggests, marriage is a convention that continues to express—or at least to codify and regulate—the truth of the human heart. If marriage and domesticity are the objective correlatives of female devotion and commitment, Glasgow suggests, they are also the forms that prevent men from acting in accordance with their own wayward sexual impulses. Akershem's friend Driscoll, ever the voice of reason, warns: "Men aren't so good that they should be allowed full liberty to do evil; it would be pretty sure to end in their doing it. . . . Marry her if she will marry you" (142). To his own detriment, Akershem does not heed this warning.

For Akershem and Rachel, convention first reasserts itself in the form of Anna Allard: she represents bourgeois rectitude, all of the "proprieties of life" (204) that are threatened by Bohemian love; she is "healthy, untainted by the degeneration of the day" (170). Desiring bourgeois legitimacy while proclaiming Bohemian ideals, Akershem is attracted to Anna and the respectability she represents. "Would a good woman have loved him as Rachel loved him?" he asks himself (189). As de Schell and Pyke might have predicted, Akershem finds himself drawn to the traditional woman instead of to his Bohemian "comrade."

Rachel in turn renounces her claim to Michael and is able to achieve success as an artist after the end of their relationship. Her art teachers congratulate themselves that they have "won [her] back to art" (267), yet she still longs for Michael, and takes him back in the end as he dies of consumption. " 'He is mine,' she thought, exultingly—'mine for all time' " (275). Yet Glasgow doesn't let the reader share Rachel's exultation, specifying just what it is that Rachel possesses in Michael: "The broken and wasted remains of a great vitality, the decay of a towering ambition, querulous complaints in place of an impassioned reserve, death in place of life—these were hers" (275). This is the result of their Bohemian romance. No ideology (at least not yet?) can emancipate "woman" from "her own heart," from the impulses that cause her to put love, however tainted, above and beyond all else. Bohemian experimentation cannot undo woman's naturalistic determinism.

Yet in *Phases of an Inferior Planet* (1898), Glasgow's follow-up to *The Descendant*, marriage is not the answer for the Bohemian heroine, Mariana Musin (at least not in the initial "phases" of the novel). For Mariana, it is her husband, and not "her own heart," that blocks her artistic ambitions and Bohemian exuberance. The love story involves the starving scientist, Anthony Algarclife, and Mariana, an aspiring singer. Their Gotham boardinghouse represents the familiar world of *la vie bohème*. For these Bohemians, the life of the studios is ever "delightful," marked by tea parties that punctuate moments of artistic creation. On a typical afternoon, the artist Nevins invites Mariana in to "have a look" at his current painting in progress and to delight in their mutual Bohemianism:

> "A good Bohemian conscience is the only variety worth possessing," observed Mr. Nevins. "It changes color with every change of scene and revolves upon an axis. Hurrah for Bohemia!" . . . "Hear! Hear"! cried Mariana, gaily. She lifted a glass of sherry, and, lighting a cigarette, sprang upon the music stool. Mr. Ponsonby drew up a chair and seated himself at the piano, and, blowing a cloud of smoke about her head, Mariana sang a rollicking song of the street. (84)

Mariana is in her element, but Algarclife remains sufficiently bourgeois to disapprove of her Bohemian revelry, viewing it as "an orgy of abandon" (84). Just what it is that Algarclife disapproves of remains unclear; what is clear is that he wants Mariana all to himself, and he quickly seeks to assert his proprietary claim and to isolate her from the communal atmosphere of *la vie bohème*.

Passionate Mariana tries to redirect her energies toward Algarclife alone: "She had given up her music, and she even went so far as to declare that she would give up her acquaintances, that they might be sufficient unto each other" (102). But they cannot be so self-sufficient (and the double standard is such that it is only Mariana who is expected to give up outside interests), and Glasgow reflects that it was a "fallacy" to believe, as her protagonists once maintained, that "love is a self-sustaining force, independent of material conditions" (112). Algarclife attempts to fulfill his patriarchal role, reserving for himself the responsibility for financing these conditions, but they can only eke out a hand-to-mouth existence from his scientific journalism. When Mariana gives birth to a child, their poverty begins to take its toll. Algarclife forbids Mariana from accepting a part in a comic opera, one that would enable her to take their sick baby out of the city; the baby subsequently dies, and Mariana decides to leave Algarclife in order to heed "the artistic genius of her nature" (175).

The Second Phase of the novel begins eight years later. While the First Phase documented the extent to which her marriage had extinguished Mariana's Bohemian *joie de vivre*, the Second Phase returns to a more conventional romantic plot, suggesting that Mariana and Algarclife were star-crossed lovers after all, still married in spirit despite their divorce. Art is no substitute for love. In the intervening years, Mariana has concluded that she "had the artistic temperament, but not the art" (236), and she longs for nothing more than to reunite with Algarclife. On the verge of their elopement, however, she dies, in his arms, of pneumonia. Glasgow ends the relationship on a note of high melodrama, implicitly endorsing the very romantic ideology that the first half of the novel had worked to critique. Once again, the heroine cannot have both love and an artistic career, and love emerges as woman's true calling.

More nuanced than many contemporary treatments of "feminine Bohemianism," Glasgow's early novels nonetheless question whether *la vie bohème* could compensate for the loss of a traditional bourgeois marriage. Expressing yearnings for artistic creation, self-determination, and a collaborative communal existence, Glasgow's early heroines also experience a contradictory urge to devote themselves to their male lovers. Still, by revealing the delights of Bohemia and refusing to idealize her heroines' romantic relationships, Glasgow highlights the conflicts that most contemporary commentators were eager to contain in the many narratives that safely "extradited" women from Bohemia.

Like Glasgow's early novels, Theodore Dreiser's semiautobiographical novel *The "Genius"* explores the tensions between Bohemian love and marital convention, feminine Bohemianism and traditional womanhood.[116] Dreiser details what happens when Eugene Witlaw marries the proper Angela Blue, a relationship modeled on Dreiser's own difficult marriage to Sara White. Before meeting Angela, the adolescent Eugene had longed for the license afforded the Bohemian: "to assume the character and habiliments of the artistic temperament as they were then supposed to be; to have a refined, semi-languorous, semi-indifferent manner; to live in a studio, to have a certain freedom in morals and temperament not accorded to the ordinary person" (50–51). Eugene attends art school in Chicago, and commits himself to painting, and to associating with other "Bohemians after dark" (94).

But as with so many Bohemian protagonists, Eugene plays out his ambivalence about bourgeois propriety in his romantic relationships. He has a romance with an artist's model, and yet he also courts the traditional Angela, and it is to Angela that he engages himself before leaving Chicago to seek his fortune as an artist in New York. Angela's beauty and sensuality thrill Eugene, but he is also drawn to her because of her conventionality, imagining that she would be "the keeper of an ideal middle class home" (64). He fancies himself committed to Angela, but he keeps delaying their marriage, promising to send for her when he has established himself. In the meantime, he has another relationship with a talented opera singer, Christina Channing, whose Bohemianism is underscored by her lead role in *La Bohème*. The independent Christina spurs Eugene to consider whether or not his Bohemianism could extend to a disavowal of traditional gender roles—and even to the overthrow of marriage and domesticity. Shocked "to hear an artist of her power, a girl of her beauty, discussing calmly whether . . . marriage in the customary form was good for her art; whether she should take him now when they were young or bow to the conventions and let youth pass," a frightened Eugene opts to marry Angela.

And yet marriage to the conventional Angela drains the artistic power that had enabled Eugene to make a success of his first major gallery show. Unlike *La Bohème*'s prototypical Rudolpho, who buries his Bohemian youth along with his Mimi, Eugene seeks to prolong his youth by falling in love with a series of younger women. As an integral part of his Bohemian creed, he dedicates himself to "beauty," but not the "beauty of maturity": "No! The beauty of youth? Yes. The beauty of eighteen. No more and no less" (296). Without this nubile beauty as his inspiration, Eugene cannot paint. Indeed, Eugene remains so fixated on this vision of youthful perfection that, even after he has achieved haute bourgeois success, first as the artistic director of an advertising agency and then as director of a major publishing house, he is willing to give it all up to pursue the fashionable society girl Suzanne Dale, another beautiful eighteen-year-old who shares his romantic visions of Bohemian life. She fancies that "she and Eugene would meet in some lovely studio" and that their love could transcend all practical exigencies (672).

Dreiser based Eugene's relationship with Suzanne on his own relationship with Thelma Cudlipp, an affair he began while married to Sara and editing the illustrious Butterick trio[117]—*The Delineator*, *The Designer*, and *New Idea Women's Magazine*, all periodicals dedicated to selling Butterick dress patterns, and—in Dreiser's words—to "strengthening" women's "moral fight for righteousness in the world" (a "righteousness" that, for the most part, remained based in traditional moral tenets and gender roles). Yet just before his ill-fated affair with Thelma began, Dreiser had initiated another rebellion against the Butterick ethos: he purchased a magazine entitled *The Bohemian* in the spring of 1909. Just as Suzanne/Thelma represented a liberatory alternative to the conventionality of Angela/Sara, so did Dreiser begin to enact the conflict between propriety and license on the pages of his two magazines. While keeping his involvement with the new periodical a secret from Butterick, he hoped *The Bohemian* would become the "broadest, most genial little publication in the field"; as he wrote H. L. Mencken in August 1909, "I don't want any tainted fiction or cheap sex-struck articles but I do want a big catholic point of view, a sense of humor, grim or gay, and an apt realistic perception of things as they are."[118] By contrast, that same month he announced that *The Delineator* "buys [fiction] of an idealistic turn. We like sentiment, we like humor, we like realism, but it must be tinged with sufficient idealism to make it all of a truly uplifting character. Our field in this respect is limited by the same limitations which govern the well regulated home."[119] In conception, the two magazines embodied the split between genteel bourgeois and iconoclastic Bohemian sensibilities, between the "True Woman" and—as we will see—the emerging "New Woman."

Dreiser only kept *The Bohemian* alive for four issues. In those issues, however, he put his own stamp on the periodical. His editorial page announced: "*The Bohemian Magazine* has gone into new hands. . . . New people, new ideas, a NEW DEAL in magazine making—these are the ingredients of THE NEW BOHEMIAN."[120] And many of the "new ideas" consisted of explicit endorsements of "New Womanhood" (in a series of unsigned editorials, most of which were written by Dreiser and Mencken). An editorial titled "The Superior Sex," for example, ridiculed a state senator from Brooklyn for telling male graduates of public school that "nature has made you mentally superior to the opposite sex": "It is fortunate that the senator should have found it necessary to inform the boys of this important truth. . . . Nothing in their school experience would have led them to appreciate it—provided there were girls in the school."[121] The editorial explicitly posits that "any point in which either sex is superior or inferior will be found due to some [social cause]; not to any essential quality of maleness or femaleness." And while Dreiser, in his role as editor of *The Delineator*, relished his sense of power ("the famous Butterick fashions will, as ever, charm the feminine heart . . . Never forget that it is *The Delineator* that decides how they shall appear to you and me"), his *Bohemian* magazine critiqued the sexual politics and economics of fashion and their role in policing female behavior:

> Although it is men who criticize women for their excessively funny hats, it is nevertheless men who design them and force them upon women with all the resources of great capital, advertising and business skill. . . . A considerable contingent of men, in fact, make their living by pushing arbitrary changes of style in women's clothes. If women adopted one rational and uniform style of dress, these worthy persons would go into bankruptcy. . . . And there [are] not wanting animadversions in the press upon the "new woman," who thus abandoned posies. . . . In fact, woman may console herself with the reflection that whatever she does, man will find her worthy of criticism, and that at no time can he forbear talking and writing about her. It may be pertinent, also, to offer the suggestion that when woman needs a head-covering, she has to take what the stores offer. She cannot make her hat. Men took that industry out of the home a long time ago.[122]

The magazine also touted the accomplishments of numerous women. Dreiser added photographs of various notables, male and female, who contributed to the "new thought" that characterized his Bohemia. Such honorary Bohemians range from Mrs. J. Borden Harriman, "a type of the present day society woman who takes an interest in sociology" to Emma Goldman, who, according to the caption "wants to revolutionize the institutions of this and every other country."[123] By featuring the politically radical Goldman (who would remain a key figure in the Greenwich Village of the second decade of the twentieth century), *The Bohemian* indicated its willingness to imagine women in roles that militated against traditional feminine proprieties.

The best-represented group of women in the magazine were actresses—women whose profession had long placed them in an uncertain relationship to genteel proprieties. Even before Dreiser took over the *Bohemian*, the magazine had devoted considerable attention to the theatre. In and out of the periodical, the term "Bohemian" was frequently used as a synonym for "thespian," and, when used to describe actors and actresses, the term only intensified ongoing bourgeois suspicions of the theatrical life. In 1888, an article in *The Theatre* complained of the indecency of the theatrical profession, arguing, "The greater number of the women of our stage are proved integrants of the blazing cauldron called Bohemia."[124]

Though some tried to distance themselves from notions of Bohemianism, other turn-of-the-century actresses proudly laid claim to this "blazing cauldron." In her 1907 autobiography, for example, the leading actress of the era, Sarah Bernhardt, referred to herself as a transgressive "little Bohemian."[125] Her contemporary, the American actress Belle Livingstone, also embraced the term in her memoirs, *Belle of Bohemia* (1927). By employing the very term that had been used to discredit the theatrical profession (and most especially its female performers), both women welcomed the Bohemian license that the stage afforded them. As Susan A. Glenn has argued, the theatre provided a notable venue for protofeminism in the late nineteenth century. "On the critical demand for women's right to sexual expressiveness and personality or self-development," Glenn observes, "female performers clearly constituted a protofeminist vanguard. The creativity with which female performers put these cultural blasphemies into practice in the years between 1880 and 1910 laid some of the groundwork for feminism even before that term was coined."[126] Livingstone's memoirs paid tribute to the ability of Bohemia to affront traditional expectations and enable female self-expression. For Livingstone, such defiance and self-assertion began at home in her early "stage-struck" years:

> I went right on doing pirouettes before mirrors, looking straight in at myself, none of my conceit dampened by the presence in Chicago at that time of either Lilian Russell or Lily Langtry. But although I was for ever telling my mother of [the actress] Jessie Bartlett Davis's kindness and goodness to everyone, she only saw in the stage a sink of iniquity and I had to content myself slipping off secretly to visit my idol, who lives in my mind as the most wonderful, great-hearted, talented Bohemian I ever knew.[127]

When her parents refused to let her travel with the chorus "without being married," Belle records that she promptly proposed to a male passerby, with the stipulation that they would part company immediately after the marriage and the promise that she would soon give him back his name: "I'll buy you your liberty when I become a star, which I am certain of doing" (50–51). Thus mocking the propriety (and dependence) that her wedding was supposed to guarantee, Belle of Bohemia claims that she used her marriage license as a passport out of the domestic sphere and into *la vie bohème*. Belle was never featured in Dreiser's *Bohe-*

mian, but she was brash, ambitious, and opportunistic enough to have been a character in one of his novels.

Europe and America

In many Bohemian plots, the conflict between propriety and license is echoed and intensified by a closely related tension between American and European manners and mores. Once again, Bohemia alternately polarizes or reconciles these apparent binaries; it is either a middle ground between (European) license and (American) propriety, or it appears as one of the pivotal forces that convey the seductions of the former over and against the more restrained charms of the latter. Insofar as Bohemia was itself a European import, it appears, even in American contexts, as the portal to cosmopolitan sophistication or decadence; unsurprisingly, contemporary commentators felt that the potential risks and benefits of Bohemia were both compounded when the young American sought Bohemia in its original homeland, Paris, and most especially the Parisian Latin Quarter.

In 1895, featuring an article "written by an American girl after two years of Parisian art study," *The Arena* poses the question, "Shall Our Young Men Study In Paris?" To answer this question, the article employs a simplified version of the Jamesian "international theme": that plot in which innocent Americans "encounter a Europe that seemed both endowed with cultural wonders and suffused with a sinister, often sexual, knowledge of the world."[128] The writer answers the titular question in the negative by challenging popular conceptions that Bohemia could provide "the royal road to knowledge" and vital experience:

> I say openly that I know the majority of the leading studios for men in Paris to be hotbeds of immorality. That this Old World has much to battle against in overthrowing the effects of climate, of inheritance, and of established custom we must not forget; but do we dare imperil our future by too close an intimacy with this frightful quality of Parisian life? . . . Young men, do not be in too much haste to leave the comparatively pure atmosphere of our American schools. What more do you really need for your growth than a model, a wholesome work-room, industry, and observation?[129]

The standard oppositions established in this essay inform many contemporary plots: America versus Europe, hotbeds of immorality versus wholesome purity. One such narrative, Gertrude Christian Fosdick's *Out of Bohemia: A Story of Paris Student Life* is yet another tale of feminine propriety threatened by Bohemian decadence, but the threat is all the more pointed because it occurs on a European stage.[130] The novel focuses on the romantic adventures of Miss Beryl Carrington, an American art student in the Parisian Latin Quarter. A latter-day Daisy Miller, "her manner had all the careless freedom of an American girl" (22). Her compatriot, the honorable Clay Sargent, admires her "childlike innocence" and regrets that "she was not as securely situated as one would wish a young, pure girl to be." Clay warily watches over Beryl, reflecting upon the folly of female Bohemianism, "[It was] another instance of what I was constantly encountering in Paris, but never without a stunned amazement at the almost criminal credulity of my own countrypeople, who will confidently send their young girls to Paris alone, or improperly chaperoned, to study art, when they would not think of leaving them alone in New York" (22).

The story contrasts Clay with another American art-student, Georges Latour. Though both hail from the United States, Clay's features are "distinctly Anglo-Saxon": he is the "genuine American, masquerading for a time in the Bohemian Latin Quarter, but losing none of the principles instilled in a country that recognizes freedom apart from license" (5). Georges, on the other hand, is of "French extraction" and his physiognomy betrays what the novel constructs as a national weakness: "his is a face which is described as beautiful rather than noble. Not a face to inspire trust, but one that it would be difficult not to admire" (4). The upstanding Clay is "more charitable than some" to his friend's "many weaknesses" because he remembers Georges in their "native land" before "Paris had too speedily developed the lower side of his nature" (20). Even in Bohemia, and among two "American" art students in Paris, the Bohemian and Bourgeois divide thus breaks according to latent national essences.

Both men reveal their respective characters when they observe Beryl for the first time at a masquerade party at the Academie Colarrossi, an "ultra-Bohemian art school" (7). She is dancing in a "Spanish costume of black and gold lace," moving her body "first this way, then that, in the graceful movements of that most abandon [*sic*] of all dances, the Spanish cachucha" (10). Georges imagines that she is a genuine Spanish dancer, and likens her to Carmencita, who famously danced in Chase's New York studio. However, Clay insists that the dancer has none of Carmecita's "sensuality": "this is the dancing of a merry, innocent child." It turns out that

Clay is correct; when Georges whispers to her, "*Ah, ma petite Espagnole, que vous êtes charmante*," Beryl, with her "eyes flashing indignantly," reveals her presumably more respectable national origin: "I am not your little Spaniard; I am an American, whom you will do well to respect" (13). Yet Beryl succumbs to Georges's charms, and the two embark upon a Bohemian romance. They are in love, but Beryl remains "pure," enjoying Bohemia as long as it indeed remains a "neutral territory between propriety and license." Her fall from untroubled innocence into experience does indeed occur, but not at the expense of her virginity; it instead happens when Georges is unable to stand up to the "worldly-wise" Madame Dubray, who pointedly characterizes Beryl and Georges as "les amants" rather than as "les fiancés" (35). George does not immediately contradict her (Madame Dubray turns out to have been his mistress), and a disillusioned Beryl leaves the Latin Quarter.

Beryl quickly reclaims her threatened respectability. She tells herself "Beryl dear . . . you are to drop the Bohemian and play the grande dame now" (42). She moves to an "institution for unchaperoned English-speaking girls studying in Paris" that is "matronized" by "good English ladies" (44). She formulates the moral of the story, highlighting the difference between Anglo-American and French standards in favor of the former:

> She acknowledged that in adopting Bohemia as her home and allowing herself a free enjoyment of its privileges she had not calculated as to how those privileges might be misinterpreted by others, and she had tried to continue to live in Paris under the same rules of freedom which her own country commends. . . . American girls in Paris forget too often that the French do not measure them from an American, but from a French, standard of excellence." (47)

It is at the respectable English-run pension, where guests "never descended below the upper-middle class," that Beryl finally meets a more appropriate love interest than the French-extracted Georges. She develops a close friendship with Harold Bertram, the essence of American bourgeois rectitude: "He was not only American, but intensely Bostonian. Nurtured in the purity of a New England home, there still remained in him something of the Puritan" (69). He too is an artist, "out of tune with the commercial element" (205) in his nation, but he is more genteel than Bohemian (in this narrative, the two concepts are decidedly *not* interchangeable), and "it was well-known that he studied art for art's sake, having already an enviable bank-account" (60). Beryl doesn't immediately recognize that she loves Harold, because "Love to her had meant something so different from this sense of rest and sympathy, this sweet companionship, in which all her better senses were satisfied. . . . To have likened that mad, childish, passionate adoration for one whom she had now learned to despise bitterly, to this pure, elevated friendship which she felt for her friend Harold would have been to desecrate it" (66).

Still, as in many Bohemian plots, Fosdick replays the attractions of the Bohemia her heroine has renounced. Beryl is haunted by memories, filled with regret and shame, but these narrative flashbacks repeatedly refocus the story on the passion of Bohemian love. For instance, one evening Beryl observes a "distant fete" and remembers:

> A cold, clear night, a great wondrous moon overhead, the glitter, the music, the innocent amusements. She saw the dark shadows of the dancers flit before her in that mad, merry street-dance in which all who wished might join. Then a voice had tempted her; she had caught the infection of music gone mad with frolic, and her willing feet had joined the dancers. She felt again the support of those strong arms; then the pause for breath in the black shadow of the great statue in the center of the Place Clichy, and the arms are thrown about her again, the eyes are burning into her soul, hot lips pressed to her ear are murmuring, 'Beryl! Beryl! I love you!' She trembled at the mere recollection, and the warm blood rushed into her cheeks. (88–89)

Whether the flush connotes shame or sexual arousal, Beryl remains in the thrall of the past. The inevitable return of Georges does delay the (anti) climax of the narrative, but Beryl soon regains her bourgeois bearings. She and Harold reunite, become engaged, and return to the United States. Beryl is presumably once and forever "out of Bohemia."

The Parisian Latin Quarter represents a similarly alluring yet corruptive influence in Robert W. Chambers's first Bohemian novel, *In the Quarter*.[131] It is there that Gethryn, a brilliant young American painter, succumbs to the charms of Yvonne, a beautiful French grisette. The two initiate a sexual relationship, yet the narrator ominously muses, "the mists of passion rise thickly, heavily, and blot out all else forever" (162). Yvonne has already learned just what passion can "blot out"; before meeting Gethryn, she had been seduced and abandoned in Paris at seventeen by a dashing military officer, and her status as a fallen woman forever exiles her from conventional respectability. Gethryn remains, at first, sufficiently mindful of his *own* respectability (he comes from upstanding New England stock) to warn Yvonne, "We can't always be together," but he still proclaims, "I love you—once and forever" (126, 123).

Lest Gethryn start to view the relationship as more than a fleeting indulgence, his fellow painter, Braith, repeatedly warns: "Damn this 'Bohemian love' rot! I've been here longer than you have, Clifford, . . . I've seen all that shabby romance turn into such reality as you wouldn't like to face. . . . It is my solemn belief that an affair of that kind would be your ruin as an artist; as a man" (55, 59). Gethryn tries to discount such moralizing in favor of a more relativistic standard, noting "the Quarter doesn't regard things in that light" (59), but moral corruption has already infected his painting, validating Braith's dire predictions: "It was certain that the old, simple honesty, the subtle purity, the almost pathetic effort to tell the truth with paint and brush had nearly disappeared from Gethryn's canvases during the last eight months, and had given place to a fierce and almost startling brilliancy, never perhaps, hitting, but always threatening some brutal note of discord" (135). Such is the inevitable fall from innocence to experience wrought by Bohemian love and sexuality. In the cultural logic that equates truth with morality, and morality with sexual "purity," the experienced Gethryn must now exchange an aesthetic of honesty for one of decadence.

When fate conspires to separate the two lovers, Gethryn becomes interested in Ruth Dean, the very incarnation of his lost innocence and propriety: she is both upper middle class *and* American (in the logic of most Bohemian plots, she is thus doubly bourgeois), and reminds Gethryn of the cultural inheritance against which he has rebelled but for which he still feels an ongoing attraction. "She is a stunning girl, possessing manners, and morals, and dignity, and character, and religion and all that you and I have not," reflects one of Gethryn's Bohemian compatriots (301). Yet, unlike Fosdick, Chambers does not allow his paragon of bourgeois propriety the opportunity to rescue his protagonist—Gethryn continues to love Yvonne, and he meets his melodramatic demise when the novel's Svengali figure (as in *Trilby*, he is another scheming Jew) has Gethryn murdered in the hopes of securing Yvonne as a courtesan.

Both Fosdick and Chambers rely upon a relatively crude version of Henry James's international theme, but James himself drew Bohemia into some of his own fictional encounters between Americans and Europe. Whereas Fosdick's and Chambers's versions of the international theme emphasize the "sinister, often sexualized" aspects of European "experience," James himself never loses sight of the other side of his European dialectic: his Americans always encounter a Europe "endowed with cultural wonders" and enough storied romance to withstand the disillusionment that accompanies increased knowledge.[132] In *The Ambassadors*, this romance is explicitly associated with *la vie bohème*.[133]

The "ambassador" Lambert Strether arrives in Paris as the representative of the American rectitude seemingly concentrated in Woollett, Massachusetts's own Mrs. Newsome and her "Woollett categories." He must convince her prodigal son Chad to leave behind the seductions of Paris (which the Newsomes assume are embodied in the person of a "bad" woman) and return to America: to family, business, sexual propriety, profit, and property. Explaining his mission to his friend Maria Gostrey, Strether insists that he is ultimately *Chad's* ambassador: "I'm acting with a sense for him of other things too. Consideration and comfort and security—the general safety of being anchored by a strong chain. He wants, as I see him, to be protected. Protected I mean from life" (105). The figure of the "strong chain" evokes the consummate Jamesian tension: the cable that connects "the balloon of experience" to the earth, and that tethers the romantic to the real in James' "Preface to *The American*" (1907). As Strether first sees it, Chad must regain his anchorage in the real—what James defines in the "Preface" as a grounding in "a *related*, a measurable state." This anchorage—in the form of the family business and national affiliations—will protect Chad from the uncertainties of (European) "life." But the "strong chain" suggests the countervailing pull toward free-floating romance, toward what the "Preface" identifies as "experience liberated, so to speak; experience disengaged, disembroiled, disencumbered, exempt from the conditions that we usually know to attach to it, and, if we wish so to put the matter, drag upon it" (10).[134] Such is the buoyant "license" of the romantic condition.

For Strether, notions of liberated experience had long been infused with his own fantasy of the Parisian *vie bohème*, the literary romance that had initially given him "an almost envious vision of the boy's romantic privilege" (119). Once Strether returns to the Left Bank, he finds himself "float[ing]" on a "current of association" (119):

> Old imaginations of the Latin Quarter had played their part for him, and he had duly recalled its having been with this scene of rather ominous legend that, like so many young men in fiction as well as in fact, Chad had begun. . . . Melancholy Murger, with Francine and Musette and Rodolphe, at home, in the company of the tattered was one—if not in his single self two or three—of the unbound, the paper-covered dozen on the shelf; and when Chad had written, five years ago, after a so-

journ then already prolonged to six months, that he had decided to go in for economy and the real thing, Strether's fancy had quite fondly accompanied him in this migration, which was to convey him, as they somewhat confusedly learned at Woollett, across the bridges and up the Montagne Sainte-Genevieve. This was the region—Chad had been quite distinct about it . . . in which all sorts of clever fellows, compatriots there for a purpose, formed an awfully pleasant set. The clever fellows, the friendly countrymen were mainly young painters, sculptors, architects, medical students; . . . Chad had thrown out, in communications following this one—for at that time he did once in a while communicate—that several members of a band of earnest workers under one of the great artists had taken him right in, making him dine every night, almost for nothing, at their place, and even pressing him not to neglect the hypothesis of there being as much 'in him' as in any of them. (119–20)

Chad had seemed on the verge of living the romantic life that Strether had indulged only in "unbound" volumes.

Chad's Bohemian romance had even appeared, at first, as though it might satisfy some of the moral requirements of Woollett. The "cable" that tied Chad to his American locality might be stretched, but it was not yet in danger of severance:

The season had been one at which Mrs. Newsome was moved to gratitude for small mercies; it had broken on them all as a blessing that their absentee had perhaps a conscience—that he was sated in fine with idleness, was ambitious of variety. . . . There had been three months—he had sufficiently figured it out—in which Chad had wanted to try. He had tried, though not very hard—he had had his little hour of good faith. (121)

Had Chad shown evidence of an artistic calling, and had he been able to realize that calling through diligent effort, Bohemia would have been a legitimate outpost of the Puritan work ethic (according to "Woollett categories"). But his "little hour of good faith" passed and, so Woollett imagined, his Bohemian romance had taken on a darker cast. Chad's Bohemia was evidently the stuff of cheap French sensationalism. It was:

all of Musette and Francine, but Musette and Francine vulgarized by the larger evolution of the type—irresistibly sharp: he had "taken up," by what was at the time to be shrinkingly gathered, as it was scantly mentioned, with one ferociously "interested" little person after another. . . . They had all morally wounded, the last had morally killed. The last had been longest in possession—in possession, that is, of whatever was left of the poor boy's finer mortality. (121)

Woollett thus completes the plot of Chad's Bohemian romance. He had been seduced by a grisette and then, most likely, by ever more vulgar representatives of the French demimonde. Strether and the Newsomes imagine that Chad occupied the structural position of "Trilby" (the titular heroine of Du Maurier's romance). Like Chad, Trilby was once a happy, innocent child of the Latin Quarter (where she worked as an artist's model), but just as the evil Svengali ultimately possessed Trilby (through mesmeric influence), so did an unknown femme fatale "possess" Chad and destroy his moral substance. Such is the plot Woollett imagines for Chad. Scandalous European excess had seemingly overtaken virtuous American restraint.

Yet, all the while assuming this dire outcome for Chad, Strether finds himself once again moved by the possibilities of *la vie bohème*. As Strether strolls through the Latin Quarter, delighting in the scene and passing "a charming open-air array of literature classic and casual," he realizes that he hopes to "brush" against the youthful spirit of Bohemia:

> He was there on some chance of feeling the brush of the wing of the stray spirit of youth. He felt it in fact, he had it beside him; the old arcade indeed, as his inner sense listened, gave out the faint sound, as from far off, of the wild waving of wings. They were folded now over the breasts of buried generations; but a flutter or two lived again in the turned page of shock-headed slouch-hatted loiterers whose young intensity of type, in direction of pale acuteness, deepened his vision, and even his appreciation, of racial differences, and whose manipulation of the uncut volume was too often, however, but a listening at closed doors. He reconstructed a possible groping Chad of three or four years before, a Chad who had, after all, simply—for that was the only way to see it—been too vulgar for the privilege. Surely it was a privilege to have been young and happy just there. Well, the best thing Strether knew of him was that he had had such a dream. (122)

For Strether, "the stray spirit of youth" inheres in *la vie bohème*, the elusive literary romance that haunts the Latin Quarter and that momentarily "live[s] again in the turned page of shock-headed slouch-hatted loiterers." So inspirited are these youth by the romance of Bohemia that their evocation of a "turned page" is less metaphor than metonym: emulating Murger's characters, they are the fleeting embodiments of Rodolphe et al. As yet, their young lives are essentially an "uncut volume," though Strether doubts that even they will so "manipulate" their respective texts as to penetrate the "closed door" of the romance and release the full spirit of youth. Chad had evidently been "too vulgar" to have achieved anything but a tawdry, second-rate version of *la vie bohème*, but he is ennobled for Strether by virtue of simply having "had such a dream."

The dream further materializes when Chad's friend Little Bilham brings Strether to his own studio. There, Little Bilham (who in good Bohemian fashion swears that he would "simply rather die" than return to America and enter business) gathers with several "ingenious compatriot[s]" for tea, and Strether experiences

> the faraway makeshift life, with its jokes and its gaps, its delicate daubs and its three or four chairs, its overflow of taste and conviction and its lack of nearly all else—these things wove round the occasion a spell to which our hero unreservedly surrendered. . . . He liked the delicate daubs and the free discriminations—involving references indeed, involving enthusiasms and execrations that made him, as they said, sit up; he liked above all the legend of good humoured poverty, of mutual accommodation fairly raised to the romantic, that he soon read into the scene. The ingenious compatriots showed a candour, he thought, surpassing even the candour of Woollett; they were red-haired and long-legged, they were quaint and dear and droll; they made the place resound with the vernacular, which he had never known so marked as when figuring for the chosen language, he must suppose, of contemporary art. They twanged with a vengeance the esthetic lyre—they drew from it wonderful airs. This aspect of their life had an admirable innocence. (147)

In this midst of their Bohemia, Strether's compatriots exhibit the "innocence" that—from the Woollett perspective—they supposedly left behind in America. Strether thus experiences one of the many reversals of expectation that characterize his European sojourn. Instead of threatening American morals with licentious temptation, Bohemia fosters the very purity of mind that conventional propriety strove to protect but often sabotaged. It is perhaps this "admirable innocence" that allows the expatriated Little Bilham to appear "more American than anybody" else, despite (or because of) his renunciation of "business" and what James elsewhere termed the "religion of doing."[135]

Paradoxically enough, the Parisian *vie bohème* thus fosters Americanness, here defined as romantic potentiality. Though Waymarsh doubts that Little Bilham represents the "good American," Maria Gostrey objects: "The name of the good American is as easily given as taken away! What *is* it, to begin with, to *be* one, and what's the extraordinary hurry? Surely nothing that's so pressing was ever so little defined" (150). Maria objects to the notion that there is as yet a stable American identity; Little Bilham represents the "good American" precisely because he refuses to congeal or assume a preexisting "mould" (215). Instead, residing in Bohemia, he retains a "state of faith" and "sense of beauty" (150): the idealism that is the apparent hallmark of the good American. In the person of the Bohemian Little Bilham, the "good American" remains a positive term, but only insofar as this identity defies closure and restriction.[136]

La vie bohème contributes to Strether's idealization of Paris *and* America. Peopled by American expatriates in Paris, this Bohemia suspends more rigid definitions of national identity. Strether's perception of the "innocence" of this condition helps set the stage for his acceptance of Little Bilham's description of Chad and Madame de Vionnet's international alliance: it is, according to Little Bilham, a "virtuous attachment" (187). For Strether, this seemingly innocent attachment belongs to the realm of the romantic, exempt from the usual conditions and clichéd narratives that would compromise its purity. Like the Bohemians, Chad and Madame de Vionnet play "the esthetic lyre" (here the pun on lie becomes crucial) and "they dr[aw] from it wonderful airs." Strether is seduced by their "anti-realist" text, one that, Kevin Kohan notes, "release[s] its characters from the burden of knowing and into a world of desire."[137] Significantly, the new Chad is first revealed to Strether in a theatre box, and he enacts what Kohan describes as a "performance of performance"; that is, he "stag[es] the superiority of the stage, the aesthetic life" (380). Madame de Vionnet, herself an expert at creating artful Old World surfaces, captures Strether's imagination most completely when he encounters her in Notre Dame. Having just purchased the collected works of Victor Hugo in what was, for him, an expression of extravagant license (he had given "the rein for once in a way to the joy of life" in this transaction), Strether is primed to find Madame de Vionnet at this moment, and in this space, "romantic for him far beyond what she could have guessed" (275).

Strether also plays the "esthetic lyre" when he departs for the French countryside. He experiences what "had been as yet for the most part but a land of fancy for him—the background of fiction, the medium of art, the nursery of letters"; these are the "elements" of "Romance" (452). And so when he spies "a boat advancing round the bend and containing a man who held the paddles and a lady at the stern, with a pink parasol," the vision seems "exactly the right thing" to accord with his picturesque composition (461). With the "slow current," the vessel moves "slowly, floating down" toward the shore, and it is at this moment that Strether identifies Chad and Madame de Vionnet in the boat and must finally recognize the illicit nature of their "virtuous attachment." The downward flotation recalls what implicitly happens to the "balloon of experience" when it leaves the realm of the romantic and is regrounded in the real. Previously, it had been his "theory" that "the facts were specifically none of his business, and were, over and above, so far as one had to do with them, intrinsically beautiful"; yet, as this theory is deflated, Strether "knew he had been, at bottom, neither prepared nor proof." It is at this point that Strether reconjures *la vie bohème*, this time as a way of cushioning the fall of his own "balloon of experience":

He then knew more or less how he had been affected—he but half knew at the time. There had been plenty to affect him even after, as has been said, they had shaken down; for his consciousness, though muffled, had its sharpest moments during this passage, a marked drop into innocent friendly Bohemia. They then put their moral elbows on the table, deploring the premature end of their two or three dishes; which they had tried to make up with another bottle while Chad joked a little spasmodically, perhaps even a little irrelevantly, with the hostess. What it all came to had been that fiction and fable were, inevitably, in the air, and not as a simple term of comparison, but as a result of things said. (465)

Bohemia now registers a "marked drop" instead of a free-floating state of "romantic privilege." Fiction, fable, and *la vie bohème* remain "in the air," but they are now anchored to the facts they would obscure.

"Things must have a basis," Maria Gostrey reminds Strether when they discuss the "virtuous attachment" after the river scene. Strether recognizes that he had previously taken "flights" of fancy based on a relatively shaky "foundation":

> "If you mean," she went on, "that she was from the first for you the most charming woman in the world, nothing's more simple. Only that was an odd foundation."
>
> "For what I reared on it?"
>
> "For what you didn't!"
>
> "Well, it was all not a fixed quantity. And it had for me—it has still—such elements of strangeness. Her greater age than his, her different world, traditions, association; her other opportunities, liabilities, standards. . . . Of course I moved among miracles. It was all phantasmagoric. But the great fact was that so much of it was none of my business—as I saw my business. It isn't even now." (493–94)

From the Woollettian foundation of moral propriety, the scandalous "fact" of illicit sexual intimacy demanded Chad's return. But even in view of his greater knowledge, Strether still resists subjecting this fact to such a "fixed" construction. With regard to Little Bilham's characterization of Chad and Madame de Vionnet's relationship, Strether concludes: "It was but a technical lie—he classed the attachment as virtuous. That was a view for which there was much to be said—and the virtue came out for me hugely. There was of course a great deal of it. I got it full in the face, and I haven't, you see, done with it yet" (493). Strether must find his own way of negotiating between knowledge and desire, America and Europe, propriety and license: "Then there we are!" he declares in the final line of the novel, locating himself, in transit, between Paris and America: in a liminal space between the moral common sense of the traditional realist narrative that had "booked" his mission (449) and the free-floating romantic liberation he glimpsed in *la vie bohème.*

Art and Life

Strether comes fully alive to the possibilities of *la vie bohème* in Paris, but he'd been there before: as we have seen, he had inhabited Bohemia via the text of "melancholy Murger" (120). When Little Bilham brings him to his studio, it is thus unsurprising that Strether would "read into the scene" the very "legend" he had hoped to find: there he locates the devotion to art, tolerance of poverty, homosocial camaraderie, and youthful enthusiasm that typified *la vie bohème* (147). His guide to this world is appropriately named Little Bilham, whose name and small stature suggests Du Maurier's own Bohemian hero, the Little Billee of the phenomenally popular *Trilby* (1894). Interestingly, in a now-famous gesture of the sort of aesthetic fraternalism that so inspires Strether, George Du Maurier had offered James the plot of *Trilby* some years before writing the novel;[138] James declined but paid homage to his friend's romance through the observations of the mature Strether. Strether's own experience of the "makeshift" studio world is tellingly mediated by literary romance: explicitly by Murger and implicitly by Du Maurier.

Strether famously advises Little Bilham, "Live all you can; it's a mistake not to"; noting that he is "too old for what I see," Strether offers himself as an object lesson, as an instance of someone who made the very mistake he urges his young friend to avoid. Yet, the Parisian *vie bohème* provides just one of the impressions through which Strether begins to experience "the youth he had long ago missed," and it emerges as "queer concrete presence, full of mystery, yet full of reality, which he could handle, taste, smell, the deep breathing of which he could positively hear" (426). Though not the thing itself, "the youth he had long ago missed" returns in an externalized yet vital shape; indeed, the figure of the "queer concrete presence" suggests the material form of a book, and we are reminded of "the unbound, the paper-covered dozen on the shelf" that contained Strether's romances of Bohemian life and the promise of what it meant to be "young and happy." As Ross Posnock notes, "Strether's sense of lost youth is not represented as the loss of a prior plenitude. Rather, his responsiveness converts loss into plenitude. To oppose the actual to the vicarious, life to art, and active to passive is antithetical to the libidinal sublimation of James's psychic economy."[139] As part of his "libidinal sublimation," Strether's ongoing attachment to Bohemianism suggests that *la vie bohème* had a special ability to destabilize such oppositions.

Literary representations of *la vie bohème* routinely inspired actual imitations, which in turn inspired new representations in an endless cycle. Some Bohemian plots were so compelling that they effectively reduced the element of the vicarious, thus bridging the gap between representation and reality; of the best-selling *Trilby*, *Outlook* magazine noted: "Mr. Du Maurier not only bids us welcome [into Bohemia] but actually installs us; we do not look on, we participate. It is the secret of the extraordinary charm of this story that it does not appear to be a story."[140] Many readers yearned for still more direct participation.

Theodore Dreiser, for one, tied his own desire to marry Sara White to his quest for the Bohemia of *Trilby*. The novel that had the nation yearning for *la vie bohème* ultimately had Dreiser yearning for Sara:

> There was another thing which had a strange psychologic effect on me at the time, as indeed it appeared to have on most of the intelligentsia of America. That was the publication in Harper's magazine this spring and summer of George Du Maurier's *Trilby*, a romance the effect of which was, in my case at least, electric—one of profound emotional perturbation, leaving me as sadly craving and seeking in my spirit as any other event ever in my life. I have often doubted the import of novel-writing in general, but viewing the effect of that particular work on me as well as on others, one might as well doubt the import of power or fame or emotion of any kind. . . . I was lost in the beauty of Paris, the delight of studio life, and resented more than ever, as one might a great deprivation, the need of living in a land where there was nothing but work.[141]

Trilby transported Dreiser, along with so many of his contemporaries, to a Bohemia that seemed the quintessence of youthful spirit and desire; as

Murger's *Scenes* had decades earlier, *Trilby* once again enshrined the Latin Quarter as the place where one might experience an ideal blend of work and play, life and art. Dreiser also responded to the nostalgic mood of the novel, describing it as a "perfume of memory and romance conveyed by some one who is in love with that memory and improvising upon it as musicians do upon a theme." Dreiser maintained that this novel played a fateful role in his life, compelling him to return for a visit to his "Western sweetheart" at her childhood home: "I decided before I went farther away, possibly never to return, I should retrace my steps and see her. The sense of an irrecoverable past which had pervaded *Trilby* had, I think, something to do with this—so interfused and interfusing are all thoughts and moods."[142] Tellingly, Dreiser only managed to delay the very loss that the novel prefigured: this interlude with Sara White, the woman who became his wife several years later, thereafter became part of a romantic past that Dreiser could never again recover.[143]

Though Dreiser's attachment to the novel appears to have had a particularly dramatic effect on his life, the cultural phenomenon known as "Trilbymania" was replete with numerous and quite variegated attempts to engage with the text beyond the confines of the written page. The tale concerns Trilby, a young artist's model who fraternized with a merry (but thoroughly respectable) band of English painters in the Parisian Latin Quarter. She falls in love with the painter Little Billee, only to leave him for fear of damaging his reputation and denying him his bourgeois birthright (though in actuality she dooms him to a life of despair). At this point, she is pursued by the "mad genius" Svengali, a Jewish musician from the Latin Quarter, who places her under his hypnotic influence. While under his mesmeric control, she becomes his wife and transforms into a world-class opera singer. This is the outline of the melodramatic plot that so intensified the fin-de-siècle Bohemian vogue. Even more popular in America than in Du Maurier's own England, *Trilby* topped the first bestseller list (published in *The Bookman*), and went on to sell over two million copies in two years; libraries, too, found themselves besieged by readers—a librarian at the Chicago Public Library noted that "every one of our 54,000 card-holders seems determined to read the book."[144] But such numbers do not begin to measure the intensity of reader responses to the novel. Jonathan Freedman has described the distinctive form that reaction to the novel took as one of "mimetic enthusiasm": the "response assumed a thoroughly imitative guise; readers took to re-enacting scenes from the novel, singing the songs contained in it, modeling ice sculptures on its characters, and buying clothes and other accouterments based on its artist-author's designs."[145] Such mimetic enthusiasm suggests that the story (in all its many forms) provided a means of living *la vie bohème* and dissolving the boundaries between art and life.

In 1895, a year after the publication of the novel, *The Critic* published a special edition to record and commemorate the multifarious phenomenon it termed "Trilbyana." Tracing the "rise and progress" of the novel, *The Critic* marshaled reports of the various "Trilby Entertainments," all of which demonstrate the mimetic desire generated by the book. "The most pretentious" event, according to the editors, was a philanthropic affair featuring a "series of 'Scenes and Songs from Trilby,' given at Sherry's . . . for the benefit of that admirable institution, the New York Kindergarten Association."[146] Less genteel venues also participated in Trilbyana: "The Greatest Show on Earth" featured one Miss Marie Meers, riding bareback in Trilby costume "to the snapping of ringmaster Svengali's whip" (21). And though admittedly it was "a pretty far distance from Paris to Omaha" (in the words of an item republished from *Harper's Weekly*), "Trilby's voice . . . carried that distance without the least trouble," taking the form of an "Evening with Trilby," a protoacademic conference in which various "gentlemen" read papers titled: " 'The Story of Trilby,' 'Du Maurier, his Life and Work,' 'The French of Trilby,' 'The Identity of the Artists in Trilby,' 'Trilby's Voice and Method,' 'Trilby as a Hypnotic Subject,' and 'Could Trilby Be Successfully Dramatized?' " To enliven the atmosphere, the evening also featured "Trilby Music" between each paper (20). And, unsurprisingly, Trilby was in fact "successfully dramatized." Paul M. Potter's theatrical adaptation further extended "Trilbyana"—otherwise known as "Trilbymania"—throughout the United States (in 1896, twenty-four separate touring companies performed Potter's play).[147]

Trilbymania, and the Bohemia it metonymized, also enabled other intersections between "art" and "life": it spawned a host of what we might anachronistically term "commercial tie-ins."[148] On March 30, 1895, *The Critic* noted, "A Broadway Caterer now 'molds his ice-cream in the shape of a model of Trilby's ever-famous foot,' " and admonished, "That there is not a 'Trilby' shoe on the market reflects little credit upon the enterprise of our bootmakers" (25). But on April 13, the magazine published this correction:

Mr. C. W. Coleman, Librarian of William and Mary College, writes from Williamsburg, Va., to say that I am in error in supposing that the bootmakers of this wide-awake

> country have not yet seized the name of du Maurier's heroine for advertising purposes. In his note of correction, he encloses a clipping from the catalogue of a Chicago house, containing a picture of a high-heeled ladies' shoe, flanked by an advertisement of " 'The Trilby,' price $3, postage 15 cts.—'an ornament to any foot,' " etc. And I hear that the shop-windows of Norfolk, Va., fairly bristle with shoes of this brand. Moreover, a bootmaker's advertisement in the Pittsburg *Post* shows (as a punning Pennsylvania correspondent writes to me) that "Trilby has obtained a foothold even in the Iron City." (25–26)

Other correspondents offered still more outrageous examples of Trilby-inspired merchandising campaigns: "G.A.D. writes from Philadelphia to deplore the Quaker City's vulgarization of the name and fame of Trilby; and in justification of his plaint encloses a Chestnut Street dealer's advertisement of the 'Trilby Sausage'! This, it is claimed, 'is something new, and fills a long-felt want'; 'they melt in your mouth.' They don't melt in G.A.D.'s mouth, but they rankle in his aesthetic soul" (26). This "vulgarization" might well have "rankled" the rarified "aesthetic soul," but such was the synthesis between art and life that modern commodity culture demanded.

Indeed, the advent of Trilby-inspired commodities promoted the very synthesis of the aesthetic and the economic that Chad appears poised to advance at the end of *The Ambassadors* through his newfound interest in "advertising scientifically." Chad tells Strether: "It's an art like another, and infinite like all the arts . . . in the hands, naturally, of a master. The right man must take hold. With the right man to work it *c'est un monde*" (504–5). And it is thus, as Kevin Kohan notes, that Chad "turns the highly aestheticized Parisian epistemology to the tasks of commerce, the principle lure of Woollett's claim that Chad should 'return.' He will indeed return with more potent skills, uniquely suited to exploit the modern world of the image-market . . . where the primary goal is to manipulate desire."[149] The unnamable, "vulgar," and "rather ridiculous object of the commonest domestic use"[150] that is the source of the Newsomes' wealth thus seems well positioned to follow in the footsteps of the "Trilby sausage": through Chad's mediation, the novel suggests, the vulgar object produced in Woollett may yet achieve an aesthetic apotheosis.[151]

Though speaking specifically about literary illustrations, James reflected:

> That one should, as an author, reduce one's reader, "artistically" inclined, to such a state of hallucination by the images one has evoked as doesn't permit him to rest till

he has noted or recorded them, set up some semblance of them in his own other medium, by his own other art—nothing could better consort than that, I naturally allow, with the desire or pretension to cast a literary spell.[152]

The "state of hallucination" inspired by *Trilby* resulted in Trilby entertainments, commercial tie-ins, and, perhaps most preposterously, the creation of a new town: Trilby, Florida.

The cultural geography of American Bohemianism reveals many attempts to map the fictive territory of *La Bohème* and to render it coextensive with the real. One notable attempt occurred when Henry B. Plant, a "millionaire railroader" and "President of the Plant system of railways, steamship lines, and hotels" decided to develop a town at the crossing point of two of his railroads. According to the *New York Times* in an article published in 1897:

President Plant was just at the time deeply interested in a second reading of Du Maurier's book the popularity at that time amounted to a craze with the American people. The character as drawn by the author and given to the little waif about the streets of Paris had touched the railroad magnate with all its weird and grewsome phases, and when one of his officials came to him and asked what the new station should be named Mr. Plant looked up with his accustomed bright twinkle about the eye . . . and said: "We will name it Trilby"—and Trilby it is to-day. . . . Ever-alert real estate agents took hold; winter tourists on the west coast of Florida craned their necks out of Pullman car windows to see Trilby, and went home to talk about it among their fellow capitalists of the North; newspaper writers wrote about it; the map of Florida held it out the most conspicuous of all names of towns and cities. Under such environment the little town of Trilby bids fair to become an important point some day. The streets have been named after the characters of the famed book; there is a Svengali Square, with the network of railroad tracks in the centre, presenting the fanciful spider web which was the emblem of the book; there is a Little Billee Street, a Taffy Street and a Laird Lane.[153]

It is fitting that the town of Trilby was located at a railroad crossing: marking the mobility inscribed within the romance of *la vie bohème*, the town further signified the Bohemian conjunction between the imaginative and the geographical.

The following chapters explore many other Bohemian intersections between the romantic and the real. Moving fluidly between art and life, the Bohemian "plot to live around" inhabited a wide range of social spaces within the cultural geography of turn-of-the-century

America. Continuing to register conflicts between wealth and poverty, propriety and license, and Europe and America, Bohemian plots entered into leisure retreats (Chapter 4), regional cultures (Chapter 5), the American "cosmopolis" (Chapter 6), and the "spiritual geography" of Greenwich Village (Chapter 7). From within these geographic spaces, the romance of Bohemia performed its cultural work, revealing social tensions, cultural fault lines, and modern possibilities.

4

The Bohemian Grove and the Making of the Bourgeois-Bohemian

Bohemia triumphs, for grim Care is dead!

Annals of the San Francisco Bohemian Club, 1880

AT THE BEGINNING OF 2000, a spate of books heralded the advent of the "Bourgeois-Bohemian"—or, in social commentator David Brooks's reduction, the "Bobo." This figure, Brooks and others argue, represents a new American upper/middle class ethic, one that forges a synthesis between Bohemian and traditional bourgeois values. Alongside Brooks's bestseller, *Bobos in Paradise: The New Upper Class and How They Got There* (2000), Ann Powers's *Weird Like Us: My Bohemian America* (2000) celebrates and ironizes the ever more rapid embourgeoisment of Bohemian mores. Christine Stansell's *American Moderns: Bohemian New York and the Creation of a New Century* (2000) similarly maintains that post–World War I versions of Bohemianism have mainly served as "a reserve of inspiration for renovating middle-class life in the great shift from a nineteenth-century work-oriented ethic to a consumerist, leisured society."[1] With different emphases, all three books suggest that these historical antagonists have become more and more indistinguishable.

Rife with paradox, the Bourgeois-Bohemian of today allegedly reconciles such bourgeois values as thrift, diligence, sobriety, and self-restraint (the "culture of production") and prototypical bohemian desires for rebellion, personal liberation, play, and self-indulgence (the "culture of consumption"). Though each of these books recognizes that the well-known dichotomy between the Bohemian and the Bourgeois has always involved dialectical convergences and divergences, many recent analysts suggest that the current "Bobo" (or "boho-bourgie")[2] effects a more complete reconciliation, self-consciously integrating countercultural urges with conventional bourgeois virtues: accordingly, the late-twentieth- through early-twenty-first-century bourgeoisie has "revived itself by absorbing (and being absorbed by) the energy of bohemianism."[3] In an orgy of mutual cooptation, the Bourgeois and the Bohemian thus redefine the dominant culture.

Yet, well over one hundred years ago, members of San Francisco's bourgeoisie and artistic community had already sought to mingle the Bohemian and the Bourgeois, uniting these apparent foes in an elite organization. This group, the Bohemian Club, represents one of the first American attempts to "synthesize" *la vie bohème* and clubbable capitalism. The club became an increasingly prestigious site for connecting the rich and powerful with the artistic and the intellectual. Though ever unstable, this late-nineteenth-century Bourgeois-Bohemian identity enables us to historicize today's "Bobo," exposing the contradictory ideals and desires that the "Bobo" contraction apparently elides. If the Bobos (in Jackson Lears's words) "celebrate . . . the assimilation of bohemian ideals to capitalist realities," the Bourgeois-Bohemians of the past register the cultural conflicts that the Bobo purports to resolve or overcome.[4]

The present chapter examines the genesis of the Bohemian Club, analyzing its rhetoric, rituals, and ideologies to discover how and why this group yearned for "Bohemia." Promising the leisure that bourgeois life often precluded (or tinged with guilt), "Bohemia" became an unlikely, and frequently divisive, focal point for both the social elite and artistic community; here, Bohemia irrevocably compromised itself through its systematic social exclusions, and yet here, Bohemia also evoked many of the ideals and desires that the "Bourgeois-Bohemian" of today still hopes to fulfill.

Bohemian Versus Bourgeois

During the summer of 1881, in the midst of the fin-de-siècle Bohemian vogue, the "Sire" of the all-male San Francisco Bohemian Club issued this "Invocation to His Children":

> 'Tis Nature's myriad voice invites—'tis Nature's self that sues
> Then let us turn from toils that wear, and thoughts that craze the brain,
> Let us for one bright, blissful day be careless boys again![5]

An invitation to the fourth annual midsummer encampment of the club, this invocation offered "Brother Bohemians" the opportunity to "shake the dust of the city from their feet" and join in "Club merrymaking, beneath the trees" of the resplendent redwood forest bordering the Russian River.[6] "We are such stuff as dreams are made of, and I dreamed that with one accord we arose and followed the Sire, long time our President, into the wilderness," another member wrote, eagerly anticipating the "mysterious ceremonies" and "Rites of Bohemia" that would be performed in a small amphitheatre surrounded by giant redwoods and a cascading brook.[7]

An unlikely assortment of self-declared "Bohemians" hailed this latter-day errand into the wilderness. There were the usual suspects—writers, journalists, painters, actors, and musicians. As historian Kevin Starr has observed, the Bohemian Club's roster of writers and artists during this time period "might function as a Who's Who of local creativity." Ambrose Bierce, Joaquin Miller, and Charles Warren Stoddard were members; by the turn of the century, the list boasted Jack London, Frank Norris, Henry George, John Muir, Will Irwin, George Sterling, and Gelett Burgess. Painter-members included Jules Tavernier, Maynard Dixon, and Xavier Martinez. Stanford and University of California professors also joined the club, including Joseph Le Conte, the noted evolutionary theist. Yet alongside such artists and intellectuals was another, somewhat larger contingent drawn from what club historians classified as the "bourgeoisie." Prominent lawyers, judges, doctors, bankers, merchants, tradesmen, naval officers and government officials, even senators and congressmen joined; by 1880, the club annals note that the "Brotherhood contained not a few senators, congressmen, and other office-holding magnates."[8] "Bohemians" all, each of these men embraced and identified himself with the evolving mythos of Bohemia; each, at least ostensibly, dedicated himself to establishing "an ideal Bohemia in which art, fancy, and literature dwelt."[9]

Almost from its beginnings, the Bohemian Club welcomed members who, even at the time, would not otherwise have been considered "Bohemians." The club was originally founded in 1872 as a retreat designed for local journalists committed to the goals of earlier American Bohemians, including "good fellowship," the defiance of "the ogre Respectability," and "the elevation of journalism to that place in the popular estimation to which it is entitled." Just a month later, however, the club revised its constitution, broadening its scope and announcing more genteel objectives: "The object of the Club shall be the promotion of social and intellectual intercourse between journalists and other writers, artists, actors and musicians, professional or amateur, and such others not included in this list as may by reason of knowledge and appreciation of polite literature and the fine arts be deemed worthy of membership."[10] Those deemed worthy increasingly came from eminent bourgeois backgrounds: by 1879, the club was listed in the *Elite Directory* and quickly made its way onto subsequent social registers.[11] Surveying the club during his American tour in 1882, Oscar Wilde allegedly quipped that he had never seen "so many well-dressed, well-fed business-like looking Bohemians."[12]

Commentators on this phase of American Bohemianism never fail to note the irony of a club of largely bourgeois Bohemians. For many, the club has much of the absurdity of Babbitt's later (and brief) involvement with Bohemians, and the hypocrisy of socioeconomic elites identifying with, yet patronizing (in both senses of the word) the struggling artists in their midst. Such irony was not lost on many of the club's earliest artist-members and, as even the official *Annals of the Bohemian Club* reveal, the club itself often became an especially focused and intense staging ground for Bohemian and Bourgeois opposition. One recorded incident from 1879 involved a conflict between those allegedly most deserving of the name "Bohemian" and "a certain other set," one described in the *Annals* as "men who entered the Club through the broad gateway of 'lovers of art, literature, etc,' not caring a rag about the sentiment involved, but because it was the proper thing to belong to this new and unusual organization." Such men, the "Bohemian" opposition claimed, were only passive consumers of a rarefied spectacle; they "could not and did not add to the general entertainment, but sat themselves down in the choice seats of the synagogue and waited with an air which insolently said, 'Now, amuse us.'" Yet perhaps protesting too much, the club historiographer insists that "this friction was not from a class antagonism"; that "some of the very best Bohemians have been capitalists"; and that the majority of those who were known as "silent members" were actually "hearty, whole-souled comrades, quick to see a point, ever ready with their laughter and prodigal of applause." Such members thus represented the true spirit of Bohemia. It was only the "empty-headed man of fashion," the historiographer claims, who incurred the wrath of club artists and performers.[13] And, for the most part, the club continued to thrive: whatever Bohemian-Bourgeois opposition erupted within the confines of this "Bohemia" generally resolved itself in recognition of mutual need or benefit.

The Bohemian Club of San Francisco exemplifies Jerrold Seigel's argument that the "Bohemian and the bourgeois were—and are—parts of a single field: they imply, require, and attract each other." That "single field" was, in this instance, demarked by the club: oscillating between Bohemian and Bourgeois identifications, members both collectively and individually traversed between these two "magnetic poles."[14] Indeed, with its haute bourgeois membership, the San Francisco Bohemian Club has proven especially susceptible to one of the most common critiques of Bohemianism: whether his habitat was the Parisian Latin Quarter or the Bohemian Club, the Bohemian was little more than "the bourgeois playing at being bourgeois," and thus only reproduced, in a somewhat playful or exaggerated fashion, the central tenants of bourgeois ideology, particularly its emphasis on individualistic liberties.[15] According to this view, Bohemianism was ideological complicity masquerading as dissent and, as such, merely bolstered the dominant culture's own liberal self-representation. And yet, an examination of the Bohemian Club suggests that, as the bourgeois played at being the bourgeois, this tautological action did not simply re-create a static, self-identical bourgeois subject. Passing through Bohemia, the bourgeois initiated a ritual process that helped to distinguish him from his social predecessors.

In playing at being the bourgeois, the members of the Bohemian Club identified themselves as Bohemians. To do so, the "capitalists" needed to associate themselves with a group of artistic and intellectual men who, at the time, would have been seen as more authentically Bohemian outside the confines of the club. The benefits of club membership for artists and writers were clear: the club facilitated a partial resurgence of patronage over and against the uncertainties of the market. Indeed, the larger socioeconomic history of Bohemia further explains the logic of this development. As César Graña has demonstrated, the beginnings of the Bohemian-Bourgeois dichotomy can be traced to the decline of the aristocratic patronage system in France. By the mid-nineteenth century, "Bohemia" had became the name of an artistic subculture, one that alternately viewed itself as liberated from conventional restraints and as stranded without support under the new commercial dispensation. Thus, while the club attempted to *bridge* the Bohemian-Bourgeois opposition, it is fitting that it reinstated a form of elite patronage.[16] The club itself often commissioned paintings and more generally, provided the setting for artists, writers, and performers to cultivate lucrative connections. Creative members also enjoyed the luxuries of a well-appointed (and fully solvent) men's club. Periodic protests against the increasing respectability and grandeur of the club only highlighted Bohemian and Bourgeois interdependency. In what became known as the "Pandemonium Secession" of 1880, a group of painters and newspaper men undertook to form a new Bohemian club, complaining that commercialism had corrupted the original spirit. Yet when they hired their own rooms, the members of the new Pandemonium ultimately had to borrow the rent from "certain capitalist friends of the Bohemian Club." Though the new club supposedly had several nights "brilliant with song and story and oratory, and was surcharged with wit and sarcasm, directed principally against the parent institution and its capitalist members," within a few days, according to the Bohemian Club historiographer, "the latter-day Bohemians began sidling back to the flesh-pots of Pine Street" and relinquished what remained of their independence.[17] The "Secession" thus demonstrated that creative Bohemians in a commercial culture require the bourgeois; the "capitalist" not only provided much of the financial support for their achievement, but also served as their self-defining opposite, as part of their very justification for being. In the family romance of Bohemia, rebellion against the "parent institution" was both limited and fraught.

Yet if it is apparent why artists would rely upon the Bohemian-Bourgeois interplay as a condition for their membership, why would so many of the representatives of San Francisco's haute bourgeoisie want to associate with and (temporarily) recreate themselves as questionable Bohemians? This composite membership, sociologist William Domhoff notes, made the Bohemian Club "unique among high-status clubs in America. . . . Only a few, such as the Century in New York and Tavern in Boston, [were] like the Bohemian Club in bringing together authors and artists with bankers and businessmen." And, Domhoff adds, "No other club . . . attempt[ed] to put on a program of entertainments and encampments."[18] As we have seen, the pre–Civil War bourgeoisie had largely recoiled at the spectacle of Bohemian "uselessness" and "affectation." Even as late as 1876, a local guidebook referred to Bohemians as "that class of unfortunates."[19] Now many prominent San Franciscans sought to immerse themselves in just this social element.

No doubt these "bourgeois" members had multiple reasons for affiliating with Bohemia. Just as the earliest defenders of "Old Bohemia" had maintained, the "Swallow-Tails of Fashion" probably did seek amusement, diversion, and the chance to bask in an exclusive setting; others most likely hoped to acquire greater "cultivation" at a time when Arnoldian versions of high culture (often approximated in the genteel productions of the club) helped to define and legitimate the position of new social elites; and many must have joined simply because other prominent people had already joined. But none of these reasons adequately explains the insistent rhetorical address of numerous club circulars, reminiscences, and rituals. The rhetoric of Bohemia suggests that something else was at stake besides status and entertainment, and that that something was well within the bounds of Bohemian opposition, however partially and contradictorily (or indeed because it was so partial and contradictory).

A product of the turn-of-the-century Bohemian vogue, the *Annals of the Bohemian Club* attests to the appeal that the mythic Bohemia came to have for a specific, and quite prominent, group of San Franciscans. Club rhetoric incorporated a number of intersecting neo-Romantic tropes and categories. Appeals to such reified entities as Nature, Childhood, Dreams, Art, Regeneration, Individuality, and Brotherhood pervade club literature and all fall under the rubric of "Bohemia." That these terms also recur through many of the period's nascent therapeutic discourses suggests the extent to which Bohemia, mythical land of freedom and imagination, responded to many of the common yearnings, dissatisfactions, and social upheavals of fin-de-siècle bourgeois life. Indeed, the type of "antimodern" sentiment identified by Jackson Lears receives both eloquent and absurd testimony in the records of the club.[20] During an era when the "feeling that there is something wrong with us" spurred a rethinking of the proper roles of work and play, collectivity and autonomy, leisure and self-culture, the mythos of "Bohemia" emerged as an increasingly popular source of protest, rejuvenation, and diversion. This ever-permeable romance often operated in tandem with such therapies as mind cure, cults of the wilderness, and the strenuous life; it also helped to renew interest in romanticism, aesthetic experience, "primitive" identities, and the mythological or evolutionary past. Concentrating multiple, largely inchoate aspirations, the "Bohemia" of the club became a focus of bourgeois desire.

Of course, the *Annals of the Bohemian Club* should not be confused with a direct reflection of what any of these men "really" felt. The rhetoric of Bohemia was a symbolic reformulation of ideals and social concerns (written by the most literary of club members), not a transparent window into the past. But especially in the context of an ongoing, voluntary association, such rhetoric is an important measure of what this group wanted (or wanted to want) to believe in and experience. This club may well have functioned as an instrument of "professional-managerial" class consolidation and hegemony; it likely provided a means for members of San Francisco's bourgeoisie to compensate for, and thus accommodate themselves to, the demands of modern capitalism; it certainly promoted white male exclusivity and "corporate" bonding; and yet, club records also reveal such an emphatic yearning for a different life that it is hard to deny its members their utopian urges and to dismiss the group as being entirely complicit in dominant ideologies (existing or even emergent). This chapter reveals how this club, in the name of Bohemia, proposed to supplement or transcend bourgeois work, gender roles, family relations, racial identities, and spiritual life. Revealing the cultural conflicts that helped to redefine late-nineteenth-century bourgeois (masculine) identities, this Bohemia staged a complex negotiation between accommodation and dissent, the Bohemian and the Bourgeois.

Bohemian Nervousness

The formal invitations to the midsummer encampments (at what would soon become known as Bohemian Grove) all proffer hope of a personal and collective transformation. The emphasis and imagery shift over the years, yet each invitation promises that the annual encampment will ease psychic distress and ultimately answer longings for a world elsewhere, both within and without the self. The club promoted numerous answers to modern malaise, ranging from the transcendental to the more strictly practical. At the more practical end, club idioms represent the therapeutic world of Bohemia as a variation on S. Weir Mitchell's well-known "rest cure," as a palliative for the nervous depletion or "wear and tear" that Mitchell found in "overworked" men (and "overeducated" women). Apparently addressing such a body of overtaxed men, one General W. H. L. Barnes, the club-appointed Sire for the 1880 encampment, issued this exordium:

> Bohemian!
>
> Midsummer is upon us; before us an annual expedition to the country-side. The Sire implores your presence, not for the Club or himself, but for your own sake. Whatever your cares, your anxieties, your sorrows, here are rest and forgetfulness . . . Your whole being will be renovated.[21]

Just one year after this invitation, the need for rest and self-renovation would appear even more acute with the publication of George M. Beard's *American Nervousness: Its Causes and Consequences*, a work that popularized the term "neurasthenia" as the diagnosis for a host of "nervous" complaints, including headaches, exhaustion, melancholy, dyspepsia, and insomnia.[22] Much like Mitchell's, Beard's work identified neurasthenia as a specifically bourgeois malady, as the disease of the "brain-working, indoor-living classes."[23] A popularizer of Beard made the socioeconomic—and racial—assumptions about the disease even more visible, maintaining, "Anglo-Saxon Americans . . . especially those in the higher walks of life" were particularly susceptible.[24] The constituency of the Bohemian Club could thus count themselves among those most neurasthenically prone. Beyond the supposed prevalence of the disease among the white middle and upper-middle classes, its very symptomology became a sign of an elite constitution; rather than implying any inherent moral or physical deficiency (or dreaded "degeneration"), the disease suggested the plight of the most advanced, refined individuals—or sensitive, complex "Bohemians"—in an ever-accelerating, ever-changing modernity.

And yet, though allegedly a product of modern civilization and social privilege, the disease could nevertheless be construed as the body's revolt against economic rationalization. Especially when combined with the mythos of Bohemia, the need for therapy could appear at one with the need for dissent. As Tom Lutz argues in his "anecdotal history" of turn-of-the-century "American Nervousness," neurasthenia is a "multi-accented story, a story necessarily read differently from different social positions." For Lutz, neurasthenic discourse is "polysemic" and "accommodated both processes of cooptation and processes of contention, as well as processes that were not clearly either." Bohemian Club rhetoric supports Lutz's contention that "neurasthenia plays a central, active, but far from unitary role in the reconstruction of social norms"; the club's therapeutic dissent further reveals both the conservative and oppositional uses to which neurasthenic discourse was put.[25]

In particular, within and without Bohemian Club rhetoric, neurasthenic discourse pleaded for a modification of existing attitudes toward work. Along with treatises such as Mitchell's and Beard's, the Bohemian Club suggested that little or no stigma should be attached to the need for rest and rejuvenation—a need none other than an exhausted Herbert Spencer would famously describe as the "Gospel of Relaxation" in 1882 (a gospel Spencer specifically directed at bourgeois America). On the contrary, such relaxation increasingly emerged as a requirement for mental and social well-being—if also as the just reward for long, sustained work or an intrinsically "higher nature." Reinforced by the neurasthenia epidemic, the developing cultural emphasis on rest, leisure, and recreation implied a critical rethinking of the dominant "work ethic" on behalf of the upper and middle classes. To be sure, this reassessment had already begun among Protestant ministers, those who had traditionally been the staunchest proponents of the work ethic. In 1848, Horace Bushnell encouraged a moderate alternation between "work and play," and even Henry Ward Beecher, he of the direst warnings against idleness, also came to promote the value of leisure time. (Such a shift may well have occurred in part because ministers felt themselves to be increasingly disaffected from—and disempowered by—a bourgeois economy driven by material profit.)[26] As the century progressed, summer vacations, previously only for the most wealthy, became more and more standard for the middle class. Yet, if representative of a general middle-class longing to "lessen the strain of modern life" and seek alternatives to work, the Bohemian club's prescription for rest, forgetfulness, and renovation went well beyond the activities of a typical summer outing.[27]

"The aim of these little festivals was to make one forget the cares of everyday life and reanimate the soul while the body relaxes," the club historiographer offers by way of explanation for the "wild and weird" ceremony that has ritualized the quest for renovation at Bohemian Grove ever since 1880.[28] Every year, following a musical and dramatic performance known as the "High Jinks," the assembled Bohemians (roughly 300 in the early 1880s and 600 by the 1890s) witnessed and participated in this collective rite. Though recreated each year, the ritual has remained essentially intact from the time of its inception. While gathered in the grove, the audience would first hear a distant martial strain heralding an approaching band of musicians. Next, the High Priest of Bohemia emerged in his robes of office, accompanied by a group of men similarly dressed in long red gowns, their faces concealed by hoods. Each carried a torch illuminating an otherwise darkened forest. Following these men, another company appeared, bearing a large coffin containing the body of "that enemy of mankind, the sworn foe of Bohemia, Dull Care" (in what form the *Annals* do not specify). Also in train was another group, variously arrayed as tree nymphs, "Red Men," devilish imps, druids, monks, gypsies, and similar personages. As the funeral procession neared, the seated club members arose and followed the coffin, "soberly and with decorum," locking arms two by two. The procession continued through the darkness, "while the solemn music pulsate[d] and throb[bed] among the walls of verdure." Finally the Bohemians reached a clearing, in the center of which was a funeral pyre, and the High Priest announced that he had come to cremate Care.[29]

Once the High Priest issued his command, the imps lowered the coffin into the pyre and ignited the blaze. The Bohemians joined hands, danced around the flames, and chanted:

Up through the night's soft haze
Let the pyre's joyous blaze,
Tell to Bohemia that Care's life has sped.
Long live this grand design,
Quaff deep this bubbling wine,
Bohemia triumphs, for grim Care is dead![30]

The stanza's sprightly rhymes marked the end of Care and the rebirth of Joy, a transition further punctuated by the explosion of firecrackers ascending "gloriously into the midnight sky."[31] Now that they had passed through this ceremony, the Bohemians could release themselves from their responsibilities and let the festivities commence. An example par excellence of Victor Turner's "antistructure"—a term used to describe any liminal ritual process that reacts against dominant social realities and creates a temporary suspension or inversion of governing norms—the Cremation of Care prepared the way for the "Spirit of Bohemia" to refresh its affiliates.[32] Beyond rest and relaxation, however, the Bohemian spirit promised members something else: a world not only antithetical to their everyday life, but replete with no less than transcendent possibility. Only in Bohemia, the club rhetoric implies, could members suspend the requirements of bourgeois life and cultivate better and more joyous selves.

Such an implication provided a more radical counterpoint to ideologies of work than the typical rest cure. It was one thing to advocate relaxation and a husbanding of individual energies, and quite another to revamp the aristocratic belief that true self-development required leisure. Even as that idea gained increasing currency at the end of the century, moralists still insisted in middle-class periodicals that "work is sacred . . . not only because it is the fruit of self-denial, patience, and toil, but because it uncovers the soul of the worker."[33] A part of the Protestant doctrine of the calling, the moral truism that work promoted godly virtue, the public good, and individual well-being remained vital. Yet contradictorily enough, while making worldly achievement a precondition for membership, the Bohemian Club often privileged the values of leisure over and against those of work. One "Sire's Announcement" offers the encampment

"For your brief respite from the ways of toil / At tasks depressing to your better selves."[34] Many other such announcements repeat the term "toil," even though the ranks of this Bohemia comprised many affluent and powerful "brain-workers": again and again, these circulars refer to the "chains" of "daily occupations."[35] Conversely, the *Annals* state that the serving of luncheon each day at the club "by the side of Bohemian 'Halcion harmonious springs'" was a chance for members to refresh their souls "between the sordid intervals of day."[36] In effect, the Bohemian Club rewrote and redramatized a traditional romantic narrative to meet the requirements of its own determinate social and historical situation. This "socially symbolic act" thus replayed some of the basic polarities of the romance form: the conflict between a "humdrum workaday world" and an "enchanted space" derived from a (neo)aristocratic realm of leisure.[37] For many members of San Francisco's bourgeoisie and artistic community, this enchanted space had become known as Bohemia.

Of course, much of this Bohemian Club rhetoric was most likely written by the more artistically inclined members, whether amateur or professional, and thus by those most prone to Romantic anti-utilitarianism and the exaltation of Art as a humanistic critique of mechanized, bureaucratic, commercialized work. (For the professional artists in the club, "care" was generally associated more with debt than with toil.) Still, the cremation ceremony, a ritual central to club identity, expresses such violence toward the dictates of necessity and the everyday that it cannot but suggest a more general discontent among the members. The "Spirit of Bohemia" may well have struck the broader membership as a key to revamping—or at least supplementing—traditional bourgeois culture. The club presupposes that its members still "toil" in some capacity, yet privileging "respite," it acts to legitimate an emerging "leisure ethic" and even a bourgeois "leisure class."[38] In effect, the club conjured Bohemia in order to turn against more traditional bourgeois manners and mores; in the process, it helped to create a new bourgeois identity.

The extent to which American culture in the late nineteenth and early twentieth centuries exchanged a "work" for a "leisure" ethic should not be overstated, though the Bohemian Club participated in some such change. Historians of American life have usefully related this shift to a movement from a "culture of production" to one of "consumption," thus positing a set of interrelated changes that responded to the developing needs of the capitalist economy. Unsurprisingly, within the Bohemian Club, the pursuit of "freedom from care" entailed elaborate rituals of consumption—even the cremation ceremony became increasingly costly, a reality that spurred several attempts within the club to return to what they termed "patriarchal simplicity."[39] As their clubhouse (denigrated by some as an "idol of brick and stone")[40] became more and more opulent, there were "misgivings in some Bohemian minds that these rich furnishings betokened a spirit of Philistinism that threatened the very foundations of [their] order," and yet, according to the club historiographer, "these forebodings did not deter them from playing the Sybarite just the same."[41] As members recognized, the club's conspicuous consumption functioned both as agent of and antidote to the workings of the capitalist economy: the "Sybarite" only partially opposed the "Philistine." Nevertheless, the Bohemians continued to embrace capitalism's own preferred answer to the malaise it generated. Furthered by consumption, the "Spirit of Bohemia" insisted on its ability to meet a care-defying agenda: Bohemian luxury and leisure would counteract the "nervousness" of bourgeois alienation.

The Children of Bohemia

Beyond the cremation ceremony and its increasingly extravagant clubhouse, the Bohemians had other means of defying work and proposing a more rewarding existence. One method lay in an insistent, nostalgic appeal to childhood. Club rhetoric repeatedly addresses members as the "Children of Bohemia" and beckons them to "come to the fountain of youth" and "be careless boys again."[42] As an offshoot of the Romantic Movement, Bohemianism easily accommodated nineteenth-century cults of childhood. Yet despite our familiarity with connections between Bohemianism and Romantic childhood (as we have seen, Bret Harte had previously stressed this linkage), it is still difficult to imagine a group of socially prominent late-nineteenth-century men (including judges and military officers) wanting to be directly referred to as "children." Nevertheless, the epithet recurs throughout numerous "Sire Announcements" in the first decades of the club.[43] Precisely because of its oddity, such an address underscores the power of "the child" as a metonymic figure; even solidly bourgeois, nineteenth-century men were openly susceptible to its appeal.

Bohemia is most often associated with young adults, but the San Francisco Bohemian Club's identification with children is also a likely motif.[44] Throughout the century, childhood emerged as an increasingly distinct stage of life (especially among the middle and upper classes); as a time of innocence rather than Original Sin; and as the emblem of Romantic freedom, imagination, and spontaneity. As such, childhood appeared to oppose the mandates of bourgeois adulthood. Still, the image of the child as Bohemian becomes even more plausible and specific when linked to contemporary bourgeois family structure, as well as to developing conceptions of the unconscious, "mental therapeutics," the natural world, racial identities, and artistic life. It was central to the club's effort at therapeutic dissent.

Though Romanticism had exalted the child from its beginnings, most early-nineteenth-century American men would probably have recoiled at the suggestion that they were childlike, much less sought to identify themselves with an inner child. Even in Romantic texts like *The Last of the Mohicans*, "self-disapprobation" results when Natty Bumppo analogizes "his own momentary weakness" to "the act of a boy." The divide between boyhood and manhood was carefully guarded. Though one young Massachusetts lawyer acknowledges in 1838 that "I can almost wish to throw aside the energies of man, the soul stirring scenes of later years, the hope, the cares, the joys, the realities of manhood, again to pass into the sweet dreamy times of boyhood's romance," he quickly counters such reflections by insisting, "Man is made for action, and the bustling scenes of moving life, and not the poetry or romance of existence. I am willing, I am earnest, to launch forth into the world."[45] Explicitly rationalizing his doubts, this young lawyer thus willed himself to leave behind "romance" and to enter the "manhood" of professional success.

As the rhetoric of the Bohemian Club reveals, however, "boyhood's romance" had become a more common and acceptable form of nostalgic fantasy by the last decades of the century. This fantasy was nurtured by many fictionalized representations. Formed by such works as Thomas Bailey Aldrich's *Story of a Bad Boy* (1870), Charles Dudley Warner's *Being a Boy* (1878), William Dean Howells's *A Boy's Town* (1890), not to mention Mark Twain's *Tom Sawyer* (1876) and *Huckleberry Finn* (1885), the genre of the "Boy's Book" became one of the most popular forms of literary romance, attracting both adult and child readers.[46] The appeal of "Boyville" for a Bohemia dedicated to unconventional freedoms is easily derived from Howells's description: "Everywhere and always the world of boys is outside of the laws that govern grown-up communities."[47] Despite Howells's insistence on the atemporality of Boyville, however, many of these retrospective accounts represent boyhood as a bygone era, both of personal and national development. Just as the child gave way to the man, so did the small-town world of antebellum America "grow-up" into an increasingly urban and rationalized society.[48] The prototypical "Boy's Book" thus offers boyhood as a time of relative freedom and unrestricted play. Still, such representations strictly cordoned off childhood from the world of contemporary men and their adult responsibilities. Howells's young males "grew up into the toils and cares that can alone make men of boys"—though this boyhood could still be revisited at leisure on the pages of both "realism" and "romance."[49] More radically, however, the equally genteel men of the Bohemian Club declared that childhood, in all its "immeasurable remoteness from the sphere of men," could be reincorporated into their everyday social lives and personal identities. In the rhetoric of Bohemia, club therapy could ensure that "Between the 'old boy' and the young small difference shall there be / For Age shall know the pulse of Youth, and Care give up the ghost."[50]

At the turn of the century, numerous self-help works echoed Bohemian Club sentiments, upholding the "child as ideal"—that is, as a therapeutic ideal. According to the popular mind-cure treatise *Power Through Repose*, the behavior of "a little child is another opportunity for us to learn what we need . . . for both work and rest." In club rhetoric and self-help treatises, "what we need" was defined as an "exquisite responsiveness to the spiritual truths" and a childlike freedom from self-consciousness.[51] But just *how* did the "children of Bohemia" learn what they needed both to defy and integrate themselves into the world of men? How did their regressive pursuits promote freedom from self-conscious inhibitions? Contemporary gender roles complicated any return to the putative "mental and bodily freedom[s]" of boyhood. The late-nineteenth-century binarism between boys and men corresponded to, and was mediated by, another between men and women. For the males of the Bohemian Club, to reimagine themselves as children thus most likely served, in part, as a therapeutic means of reconnecting with maternal nurture and the values of the domestic sphere. At a time when the doctrine of separate spheres represented the bourgeois home as the redemptive opposite of the marketplace, mothers often assumed the responsibility for inculcating nonmaterial, noncompetitive, nonexploitative values—the very values sanctioned by genteel versions of Bohemia. Entrusted with cultivating "sweetness and light," morality and culture, many women attempted, like Harriet Beecher Stowe, to instill a home "economy of the beautiful."[52] An integral part of "Christian Nurture," this economy created an affective nexus between art, spirituality, maternal love, and childhood, one that boys needed to detach themselves from (or put more psychoanalytically, had to repress), as they moved toward a normative masculine gender identification. Though mothers also taught and "cradled" values conducive to the needs of capitalism[53]—especially temperance, industriousness, and even aestheticized consumption—the polarization of masculinity and femininity in bourgeois life suggests that many boys ultimately needed to undergo the sort of disassociation from their mothers that psychoanalysis (itself an interpretation and product of the late-nineteenth- and early-twentieth-century family) has described as Oedipal crisis.

Yet with fathers largely absent at "work," further distanced by pursuits often ideologically at odds with the values of domesticity, it is possible that many boys experienced a degree of confusion or "gender anxiety." As Mark Carnes has argued, this anxiety may help to explain the prevalence of mid- to late-nineteenth-century fraternal organizations, particularly those groups that reconfigured father-son relations through ritual. Fraternities such as the Freemasons enabled men to identify with a world of fathers that nonetheless incorporated some of the emotional ties associated with the mother-son bond.[54] The Bohemian Club, however, did not represent surrogate fatherhood as it apotheosized many of the ideals associated with the bourgeois private sphere. Members could imaginatively reexperience "childhood" without ultimately undergoing an initiation ceremony into the world of men; quite the contrary, they were exhorted to achieve a kind of arrested development within the bounds of Bohemia. More fully in keeping with domestic values than most contemporary fraternities, and without the Oedipal intrusion of father figures, the club implicitly encouraged members to retrieve a feminized self and undo the repressions of masculine adulthood.

Club rhetoric often conflates Bohemia and domesticity, though at times with enough irony to promote simultaneous distance from, and identification with, a feminine role. In one invitation to a "Jinks" at the club, the Sire Captain Edward Field writes:

> Brother Bohemians:
>
> We will, for the good of our souls, on Saturday, May 29th, gather around the family hearth (which will be swept and garnished) and crack some conundrums of life. We will revive the earliest period we can distinctly remember and recall how our sponsors looked when they renounced for us
>
> THE WORLD, THE FLESH, AND THE DEVIL.[55]

This (at least partly) ironic renunciation of "the world, the flesh, and the devil" suggests more fire and brimstone than the liberal Protestantism of "Christian Nurture" was wont to imagine, thus mocking the feminized "family hearth" that the invitation conjures, and implicitly aligning Bohemia with a more "manly" religious past *and* the worldly pleasures of male vice. Still, this attempt at sophisticated parody does not fully obscure the invitation's appeal to domestic virtues. Morally, materially, and spiritually, the club repeatedly promised to approximate domestic life as it constructs a world apart from "fretful streets" and "tedious marts of trade."[56] The "earliest period" cited above may refer to the founding of the club, but this stage also metonymizes childhood in an ideally purified private sphere. Bohemia duplicates the mandate of a sacrosanct domesticity, but, significantly, locates this imperative within an exclusively male organization. Irony further masculinizes such an endeavor, all the while enabling an imaginative reconstruction of domestic bliss.

Of course, as E. Anthony Rotundo reminds us, boyhood was not conducted solely in the private sphere and under a mother's watchful influence; rather, nineteenth-century "Boy's Culture" generally involved an active peer group (of the sort represented in the "Bad Boy" novels), one that permitted a "masculine" rebellion against the strictures and values of the domestic. According to Rotundo, "Where women's sphere offered kindness, morality, nurture, and a gentle spirit, the boys' world countered with energy, self-assertion, noise, and a frequent resort to violence." Sometimes the boy's culture described by Rotundo combined nurture and competition, however, and even "affection joined with combat." In one boys' club, communal meals would routinely end up in bloody boxing matches. After boyhood, the many young men's associations that sprang up in the late eighteenth and nineteenth centuries (fraternities, debating and literary societies, sailing clubs, and similar groups, organizations that existed both within and without college settings) also fused a quasi-domestic nurturing with opportunities for masculine self-assertion—though such self-assertion often took the form of debates, theatrical displays, and verbal jousting rather than physical competitions.[57] The Bohemian Club was not just for the young, but it provided a liminal realm between the masculine and the feminine, the public and the private. As in other male societies, this club both parodied and affirmed domestic nurture, as well as "feminized" religious values. (For example, one club invitation flirts with sacrilege as it urges "regeneration in the Baptismal Font of Beer.")[58] Perhaps in part because of its artistic emphases, however, the Bohemian Club generally celebrated feminized values more than other contemporary male organizations.

Yet, however aligned with feminized values, the club strictly excluded women.[59] As with most fraternal groups, "brotherhood" functioned as the dominant familial motif. Though many if not most of the clubmen had wives and families, it is likely that they retained strict gender differentiations within their own homes. Among "brothers," however, they were perhaps freer to express the sentimental feelings the nineteenth century increasingly reserved for women. Brotherhood reinforced masculine identifications while also ostensibly permitting more emotional, less competitive and hierarchical bonds than those encouraged in the public sphere or even, to a certain extent, within the paternal and spousal relationships; it provided socially sanctioned ties akin to those cultivated among women.[60] A poem written on the occasion of the club's relocation to more commodious rooms manifests such feminized sentiment and quasi-domestic longings:

> Let us still have our Brothers' love,
> Still heed the tired heart's appealing;
> Still live in love the olden life,
> The life where heart to heart lay open,
> Traversing midst this world's strife,
> Our golden bond unstained, unbroken.[61]

In Bohemian brotherhood (and poetic discourse), male sentimentality or "human connectedness" found an acceptable form.[62] With the "world's strife" temporarily in abeyance, the male clubmen could enshrine a "religion of Bohemia," one "based on the divine injunction, 'Love one another!' "[63] For members who sought a less rigid version of masculinity, the club may well have provided therapeutic release, enabling members briefly to reconcile the contradictory demands of bourgeois masculinity and femininity. Describing the world of Victorian bachelor novels, Eve Kosofsky Sedgwick has argued that the young male protagonists of these texts approach "the flux of bohemia" as a "developmental stage" on their way toward the "more repressive, self-ignorant, and apparently consolidated status of the mature bourgeois paterfamilias." The Bohemian Club, however, relocated this "temporal space" within the everyday lives of many a mature bourgeois paterfamilias, raising the question of just how "consolidated" their gendered identities really were.[64]

Sedgwick further identifies the "temporal space" of Bohemia as the site in which "the young, male bourgeois literary subject was required to navigate his way through his 'homosexual panic.'"[65] From the *Annals of the Bohemian Club*, however, it is difficult to conclude whether or not club members' apparent ambivalence about gendered identities also spoke to ambivalence about sexual desires and orientations. However affectionate its talk of brotherhood, the official rhetoric of the club generally avoids suggestions of homoeroticism or even romantic friendship. Charles Warren Stoddard, best known for his homoerotic *South-Sea Idyls*, provides the most erotic poem included in the *Annals*, one he delivered at the "Devil Jinks" in 1880. Apostrophizing "Lucifer, Star of the Morning," Stoddard writes of the "elysium of forbidden bliss" and represents his Faustian pact with the devil (whom he identifies with the masculine pronoun) as a sexualized encounter: "When at thy hands I taste the loving-cup; / When at thy feet in amorous dreams I play; / When on thy breast my soul I render up / And am consumed away."[66] The poem does not include the Brother Bohemians within this erotic commerce but Stoddard's novel, *For the Pleasure of His Company,* describes a series of homoerotic relationships between the hero, Paul Clitheroe, and other "Bohemians." Stoddard quickly establishes that Bohemia is a realm in which conventional restrictions are in abeyance: "In Bohemia, everything and anything is in season" (30). The term *Bohemian* is also used ambiguously in the novel—in his correspondence, one male friend writes to another, "In a Bohemian sense, yours to command" (38). The very term *Bohemian* might thus have operated for Stoddard and others as a homoerotic code word.[67]

In their personal correspondence, a few of the most prominent "literary men" of the club did express both homoeroticism and homophobia. After Stoddard composed a romantic ode "To George Sterling," Sterling wrote to Ambrose Bierce that Stoddard had a "case of inversion of sex," one that this gave him [Sterling] the "jims." On the other hand, Jack London wrote to Sterling (whom he called the "Greek") that he wished he could attend Sterling's beach party at Carmel and that he would "like to be out with you one day for a muscle-feed." Since London, a self-professed "lover of women," nevertheless openly enjoyed observing the physiques of well-muscled men, it is likely that London was referring to the potential for voyeurism as much as he was punning on "mussels."[68]

Whether or not such clubs as the Bohemian were seen as encouraging homosexuality, they were at times viewed as a threat to normative domesticity. A guidebook to San Francisco from 1876 insists, without particular reference to the Bohemians, that "the influence the club exerts on society is perhaps disastrous. Any rival of home, whatever may be its objects, is an encroachment that should be challenged." The guidebook does partially exempt the Bohemians from this critique, however, noting that the Bohemian Club "is very pleasant and instructive."[69]

The Bohemian Artist

Enhancing the therapeutic closeness of brotherly love, the rhetoric of childhood also worked to define Bohemia through several other intersecting tropes. In particular, the figure of the artist (whether a writer, poet, painter, actor, or musician) mediated between the adult male "Bohemian" and a childlike, feminized self, thereby promoting a reassuring difference from everyday masculinity. The Romantic notion that artists possessed a childlike sensibility was, of course, a nineteenth-century commonplace: "The artist is always a child in the eagerness of his spirit and the freshness of his feeling; he retains the magical power of seeing things habitually and still seeing them freshly," *The Outlook* insisted in 1896. This popular belief itself explains why it would be desirable to become a "child of Bohemia." Not incidentally, the metaphor of the artist as child provides another means for domestic values to reassert themselves. Perpetuating the domestic "economy of the beautiful," the childlike artist could offer a relatively unthreatening way for a man to reidentify with the world of his mother and perhaps even to embrace his "feminine half." Though the effeminate aesthete often became an object of ridicule (most famously in Du Maurier's cartoons for *Punch*), many would nevertheless have endorsed the notion that the true artist synthesized, in Sarah Burns's words, the "best of both genders." *Forum* magazine describes such an ideal artist (while maintaining a strict gender hierarchy): "Coupled of course with high masculine qualities—knowledge, application, logical power, hard work—that gives the masterpieces of the world's progress. . . . There is, indeed, in all genius, however virile, a certain undercurrent of the best feminine characteristics."[70] The figure of the artist, well represented among club members, permitted all would-be Bohemians to return to childhood and feminine identifications with impunity.

Whatever its metaphoric and possible psychological coincidence with "the child," the figure of the artist provided the club with a central touchstone for Bohemian freedom. After all, the creation and appreciation of the arts were the stated purposes of this club, and the Bohemians exalted "Art" and "Culture" as means of approaching an alternative or higher reality. Developed at a time when the Victorian sages Ruskin and Arnold exerted much influence within the American middle classes, the Bohemian Club promised to make the privileges of culture and artistic endeavor available to its membership.[71] To this end, there were nights devoted to the appreciation of Shakespeare, Tennyson, Longfellow, and "German and Hebrew poets"; dinners for "various dignitaries" of culture, including Oscar Wilde and Henry James; musical and theatrical performances, as well as opportunities to deliver original papers on such varied subjects as "Things We Do Not Understand," "Misfits," and "Our Ancestors." Most of these performances took place under the rubric of the monthly "High Jinks," the club's term for their "intellectual, artistic and musical revel[s]." A Scottish term signifying a "frolic" (or, more specifically, a drinking game), the phase "High Jinks" was itself replete with literary reference: it was borrowed from Scott's *Guy Mannering*, and, the club historiographer hastened to add, the jinks therein were "of a rather more elevated character than the drinking bouts referred to."[72] Facilitated by literary and artistic romance, such "elevation" was what the club offered its members.

Within and without the Bohemian Club, this elevation of "Art" no doubt had multiple social motivations and effects. As several historians have argued, cultural commitments often helped old and new elites solidify their class positions. In Richard Brodhead's words: "The point about the postbellum upper class is that it was not an already-integrated 'group' but a group in the process of self-grouping, a coming together of elements with a common need to identify themselves as superior. And in this process of self-definition Culture played a crucial role. . . . A now segregated high culture became a chief sign of elite status and chief weapon of elite social sway." Expressed through support of such high cultural institutions as art museums, symphony orchestras, and the opera, the "parallel stratification[s]" of the cultural realm and the social realm worked in "complicated interaction" to produce a "new-style 'high' social class."[73]

High cultural pursuits helped to denote this elevated social status. What the rhetoric of the club suggests is that high culture accomplished this work in part because it was readily connected to the therapeutic imperative known in the club as "the spirit of Bohemia." With the childlike, playful artist as its exemplar, the Bohemian spirit suggested that members could experience, directly or indirectly, a more gratifying and complete mode of being. If "toil" generally circumscribed the self, Bohemia could substantiate the Arnoldian belief that "the true value of culture" lay in its ability to promote "the general harmonious expansion of those gifts and thought and feeling, which make the peculiar dignity, wealth, and happiness of human nature." With such a mandate, the spirit of Bohemia could provide a cultural therapeutics and produce a genuinely "dignified" human nature—the very foundation for bourgeois distinction and identity.[74]

Describing one midsummer encampment, the *Annals* note that "the artists sketched, the poets dreamed, philosophers meditated" and "smokers smoked and were actors, artists, philosophers and poets in turn."[75] The assumption is that the occupations of artists and intellectuals are so satisfying that they need no others; the further assumption is that such cultural pursuits are the fruits of leisure. Within the official rhetoric of the Bohemian Club, this division of labor and leisure approximates the assumptions voiced by "the banker" (identified only by his occupation) in Howells's *A Traveller from Altruria*:

> Of course, we all recognize a difference in the qualities, as well as in the kinds, of work. The work of the laborer may be roughly defined as the necessity of his life; the work of the business man as the means, and the work of the artist and scientist as the end. We might refine these definitions and make them closer, but they will serve for illustration as they are. I don't think there can be any question as to which is the highest kind of work; some truths are self-evident. He is a fortunate man whose work is an end, and every business man sees this, and owns it to himself at least when he meets some man of an aesthetic or scientific occupation.[76]

Rewriting the Declaration of Independence, Howells's "banker" insists on this "self-evident" truth: only artists and scientists are fully independent; theirs is the only work that forestalls an alienation of self. Spurred by the Altrurian, however, the banker quickly acknowledges the contradiction inherent in this social hierarchy: "On one side, the artist is kept to the level of the workingman, of the animal, of the creature whose sole affair is to get something to eat and somewhere to sleep. This is through necessity. On the other side, he is exalted to the height of beings who have no concern but with the excellence of their work, which they were born and divinely authorized to do."[77] It is just this contradiction that has made it so difficult to identify the class position of Bohemian artists; it is just this contradiction that the Bohemian Club and its Bourgeois-Bohemians alternately redressed and highlighted by providing artists with patronage and bourgeois members with a vicarious sense of themselves as unalienated creators.

Much like the Bohemian Club, numerous contemporary pundits endorsed the notion that culture and artistic expression provided relief from modern malaise and the chance for personal transcendence (and thus, implicitly, for social "distinction").[78] Aesthetic theory and self-help often merged. For instance, in addition to promoting the child as a therapeutic "ideal," Annie Payson Call's mind-cure manual, *Power Through Repose*, maintained, "Art is freedom, equilibrium, rhythm,—anything and everything that means wholesome life and growth toward all that is really the good, the true, and the beautiful."[79] Beard himself theorized that the "true psychology of happiness" involved intimations of a "nobler order," one in which "art, literature, travel, social life, and solitude, pour out their selected treasures." Indeed, according to Beard, the neurasthenic was particularly conditioned to receive such intimations: "their delicately-strung nerves make music to the slightest breeze" and their all too insistent physicality thus transcended its own limitations.[80] Though positing more tension between artistic release and the neurasthenic body, another Bohemian Club invitation, addressed to the "weary Bohemian," promises similar freedoms under the aegis of art:

> A cultivated mind can revel in celestial delights at any time and without expense, if dyspepsia does not intervene. The Elysian Field is peculiarly the province of the poet, and, as we are all poets, in addition to Charlie Elliot, we can do as he does, exercise the ideality and feast the mind with glorious and sublime visions. We can wander through the woods, o'er hill and dale, in the sweet ecstasy of rural bliss.[81]

With "Charlie Elliot" as their in-house representative, all members could (more or less vicariously) experience the poetic imagination and aspire to what Beard called an "exquisiteness of enjoyment."

However exquisite, such enjoyment might also have been a source of ambivalence for many of the Bourgeois-Bohemians. As Jonathan Freedman reminds us, a "complex affective dynamics" most likely accompanied what Lawrence Levine refers to as the late-nineteenth-century "sacralization of culture." According to Freedman, in the realm of the "middlebrow" (a notoriously slippery term that might be an appropriate adjective for some of the Bohemian Club members), there is "an uneasy combination of reverence for and insecurity in the face of the high cultural, a mingling of overestimation of the virtues of traditional high culture and a self-deprecation of the reader's own abilities to encompass it, and odd refluxes of resentment that follow upon this set of feelings and give further resonance to them."[82] The reference to "dyspepsia" (itself a sign of neurasthenia) in the Bohemian Club invitation quoted above might just signal such "middlebrow" ambivalence. This comic reminder of "low" bodily processes deflates high-cultural posturings, even while celebrating poetic flight.

The Bohemian Grove

Club rhetoric located the ultimate playgrounds in the unconscious mind and the primeval redwood forest. These relatively uncharted, nonrationalized terrains served fantasies of release from inner and outer compulsions, especially from economic imperatives. Seen as mutually corresponding, these realms both offered neo-Transcendental experience in a therapeutic idiom. The club represented "Bohemian Grove" as a territory within and without the self, as a source of revitalization and even communion; it combined the subliminal self, evolutionary history, and the proverbial wilderness into a cure for the careworn bourgeois. The ancient redwoods of "Bohemian Grove" promised to further a neo-Transcendental, unconscious merging of self and romantic "Nature," even leading to something like an Emersonian influx of spirit from the Over-Soul. Whether the club represented the grove as containing the spirits of ancient Buddhists, "gentle forest-folk," or classical "hamadryads," the redwood forest served as the ultimate source of therapeutic dissent.

Near the small town of Guerneville, seventy-five miles north of San Francisco, the grove (owned by the club ever since 1899) consists of 240 acres of forest land. Prior to 1899, the club rented the site every summer, and periodically attempted to purchase it. According to the poet and club member Will Irwin, the majesty of the scene was astonishing: "You come upon it suddenly. One step and its glory is over you. There is no perspective; you cannot get far enough away from one of these trees to see it as a whole. There they stand, a world of height above you, their pinnacles hidden by their topmost fringes of branches or lost in the sky."[83] Club painters tried to figure this glory: Ferdinand Burgdorff's "Bohemian Celebration" from the 1890s, much like Jules Tavernier's earlier "The Cremation of Care," represents the towering trees on a rectangular canvas (30" x 12") without exposing their tops; at the extreme base of the redwoods, and the painting, the tiny silhouette of a Bohemian playing the violin provides scale and suggests the ability of the scene to challenge the individual to answer its beauty—a challenge taken up by the painting itself. Extending to the heavens, the trees seem to provide a direct conduit for spiritual or priapic energy (if also to dwarf the individual). In its written documents, the club further insists that it was amid the giant redwoods that the aesthetic, the spiritual, and the therapeutic could best join forces to revitalize the bourgeois.

"Brother Bohemians," the Sire of 1891 (one Dr. J. D. Arnold) once again begins:

Ye that are worn and weary from the toil of towns
Come hither all, and cast each care aside;
Beneath the redwood shade no sorrow can abide.
Protected here from fickle fortune's frowns,
  The time beguile,
Afar from suffering, in nature's soft retreat.
Too soon ye must return to mart and busy street,
Where Mammon rules—where, prostrate at his feet,
Lie joy and hope, and all that makes life sweet.
  Rest here awhile![84]

If the redwood forest offered the ultimate rest cure and escape from "Mammon," the invitation goes on to reveal that this was largely because the grove furthered the club's recuperation of maternal nurture—which, as I have argued, itself represented the therapeutic/aesthetic/spiritual force associated with the "spirit of Bohemia." In a "Siren Song" attributed to "Rig Veda" (even as the title pun credits the "Sire"), Arnold bids members to "Approach thou now the lap of Earth—thy mother, / The ever wide extending earth—the ever kindly."[85] According to the invitation, this earthen mother could provide members with the freedom from care and the transcendence of the everyday that they so purposefully sought.

As other invitations specify, Mother Nature was herself a consummate aesthetician (or purveyor of a maternal economy of the beautiful):

For those with ears she will sing—
To those with hearts she will speak—
for those with eyes she'll paint the sky
With purest azure tone, the trees
With softest green; and hill-tops golden smite
With magic brush at morn and eve.

The invitation further specifies that such aesthetics were a form of therapeutics: "The forest harps, so deften smote by wafts / Of scented air, await to lure thee—dreamwise— / by their matchless strains to isles of fairy form, / Where Care dwells not, and the hour-glass needs no turning."[86] Purple phrases like "deften smote" and "golden smite" (quite common in turn-of-the-century magazine verse) themselves proclaim the ability of the forest to re-create the poetic experience associated with bygone eras and the therapeutic, mythopoetic unconscious of "fairy form." The ultimate nineteenth-century "Good Mother," the Bohemian Grove promised a fusion of art, therapy, brotherly bonding, and even spiritual satisfaction.

Many club invitations and productions emphasize the spiritual properties of the forest. According to the "Sire's Announcement" for the "Sons of Baldur," the midsummer encampment (with the reinforcement of Norse myth) provides a triumphant vehicle for that "old quest for healing grace." To this end, the Sire invites the club to approach the encampment with "such singing in your souls as draws / Some holy pilgrimage to ancient shrines"—and, as the Bohemian Sons of Baldur discover, the analogy ultimately translates into a metonymic substitution: healing grace turns out to "dwell / In Nature solely." The encampment thus becomes a means of transcendental worship. Further, the club insists that such worship could also serve what we might now call a Durkheimian end: it could become a source of group solidarity. Enjoining members to "behold . . . our own selves, our rare, high brotherhood" in "Baldur's holy forest-fanes," the invitation represents this hybrid genre, the "Forest Music-Drama," as a form of "prayer," one that binds Bohemian brother to brother.[87] Countering secularization and competitive individualism, the Bohemian faith offers a personal and collective balm, one that aligns itself with the oppositionality signified by "Bohemia" in the effort to create a more spiritual and communal mode of being.

In this effort to apotheosize the Bohemian Grove, the club once again helped to circulate romantic ideology—an ideology that, in relatively limited forms, may well have had more bourgeois adherents at the end of the century than at the time of its earlier instantiations. Indeed, as a "refuge of the weary heart," repository of "lasting happiness," and locus of spiritual and aesthetic fulfillment, the club's vision of "Great Nature" participated in emerging "cults of the wilderness." In effect, the traditional hierarchy between the wilderness and civilization (immortalized in the Puritan errand) became partially reversed and, thus reconfigured, worked to bolster Bohemian and Bourgeois opposition.[88] Nature thus emerged as a life-enhancing—and specifically Bohemian—antithesis to capitalist rationalization and urban development.

In 1858, in an article first published in the *Atlantic Monthly*, Thoreau had called for the formation of national wilderness preserves "not for idle sport or food, but for inspiration and our own true recreation."[89] For Thoreau, "true recreation" insisted on transcendence (re-creation) and not just on relaxation and agreeable pastimes. Later advocates for wilderness preserves and forest protection often emphasized one or both of these meanings of the recreational. Though many early proponents of wilderness protection recurred to more directly utilitarian motives ("forests protect a country against drought, and keep its streams constantly flowing and its wells constantly full"),[90] neoromantic and therapeutic designs had an impact on governmental policy as early as 1864, when a federal grant entrusted Yosemite Valley to the State of California as a park "for public use, resort and recreation." In his 1865 advisory report on the park for the California Legislature, Frederick Law Olmsted, on the verge of becoming the nation's most influential landscape architect, further highlighted the sublimely therapeutic effects of preserves like Yosemite: "the enjoyment of scenery employs the mind without fatigue and yet exercises it; tranquilizes it and yet enlivens it; and thus, through the influence of the mind over the body, gives the effect of refreshing rest and reinvigoration to the whole system." By 1881, Olmsted had borrowed the more technical vocabulary of American nervousness, insisting that the park movement in and out of cities could counter "vital exhaustion," "nervous irritation," and "constitutional depression."[91] Soon, wilderness protectionists would increasingly invoke such a vocabulary. This medicalized discourse extended "practical" forestry's concern with the economics of preservation—only now the natural resources that needed cultivation and protection existed within the self (and thus within the workforce at large). Yet, however subject to the instrumentalization it sought to escape, the wilderness preservation movement was one of the more effective and politically influential expressions of therapeutic dissent.

Rapid urbanization and changes in work patterns guaranteed that the therapeutic approach to the wilderness would become still more influential at the turn of the century. Bohemian Club member John Muir, the most neo-Transcendental and best known of the popular nature writers, insisted that "God's Trees" could comfort "thousands of tired, nerve-shaken, over-civilized people," and his essays, books and political activism helped propel measures to protect national forests and parks.[92] In 1891, the

New York Forest Commission sought to legislate Muir's therapeutic ideals, recommending that the state preserve the Adirondacks as a park, as "a place where rest, recuperation and vigor may be gained by our highly nervous and overworked people" (the measure passed in 1894).[93] Partly through Muir's efforts, the 1890s also saw the largest attempt at preservation to date: several national parks and many national forests were created; a number of them served to protect California's redwoods.

Both as an antidote to American nervousness and an antithesis to urban life (at least in fin-de-siècle rhetoric), wilderness parks represented an important locus of therapeutic dissent. Translated into the terms of Bohemian opposition, the wilderness protection movement also admitted a more direct challenge to the capitalist economy. The Bohemian Club invitation cited above regards "nature's soft retreat" as a restful alternative to the rapacious "Mammon," one that provides a welcome suspension of his influence. However, a later jinks suggests that the dichotomy between Mammon and the Bohemian Grove could result in a more conflictive form of opposition. Much like other wilderness protectionists, the club acknowledged that the (seemingly complementary) separate spheres of Mother Nature and Father Mammon could clash, resulting in "interminable forest wars" instead of promoting economic, psychological, and geographic equilibrium.

George Sterling's midsummer jinks "The Triumph of Bohemia"(1907) is a conservationist parable. In this jinks, the "Spirit of Bohemia" battles "Mammon, Spirit of Care," thus saving the "tree spirits" and his "forest children" from "the threatened depredations of the woodmen." Though Mammon tries to seduce the woodmen with visions of "my city lights" and the offer to "purchase for you each his dearest wish," the Spirit of Bohemia "arraigns the foresters for their lust to destroy" and counters the false promise of material gain with the hope of a truer happiness:

> For lasting happiness we turn our eyes
> To one alone, and she surrounds you now—
> Great Nature, refuge of the weary heart,
> And only balm of breasts that have been bruised!
> . . . So must ye come
> As children, little children that believe . . .

The Spirit of Bohemia convinces the woodmen to abjure their occupation and, in desperation, Mammon challenges Bohemia to mortal combat. Before Bohemia can take up arms, the "great owl," national bird of Bohemia, swoops down upon Mammon: he "dies at its touch." Together, the children of Bohemia, tree spirits, and former woodmen then cremate Mammon, who is, of course, none other than Care in disguise.[94] Just as Bohemia could ostensibly save the gypsy and Native American spirits, so could it rescue the Nature such "primitive" freedoms required.

A new metonym for Bohemian and Bourgeois conflict, the trope of the Forest versus Mammon was itself a common refrain within conservationist discourse. The trope operated within Thomas Cole's early "Lament of the Forest," a poem that pleaded with the nation to protect its landscape from becoming "an altar unto Mammon."[95] Later, this figure of speech defined a New Jersey congressman's insistence that the integrity of Yellowstone not be sacrificed to railroad and mining interests, what he termed "heartless Mammon and the greed of capital."[96] And it circulated in the newly formed Sierra Club's protests against those "selfish seekers of immediate Mammon" who feel "no exaltation of soul, no supreme delight in the conscious exercise or stirring of that something within us which we call the aesthetic." The trope readily lent itself to the Bohemian club's self-charted mission to foster the nonmaterialistic.[97]

The club echoed conservationists in their desire to preserve their "Bohemian Grove" from destruction and in their commitment to an "aesthetic" meeting of man (in this case, the appropriate noun) and nature. However, many wilderness protectionists probably would have looked askance at the club's model of a *private* wilderness park. "Mammon" enabled the club to purchase their extensive and exclusive retreat, one that has subsequently attracted many more wealthy investors in Bohemia.[98] This exclusivity reminds us that the turn-of-the-century recreation movement aided in the consolidation of new bourgeois identities and distinctions, as well as in those of the bourgeois' putative opposites: the Bohemians. The recreation movement not only promised to manage an unruly working class through its elevating influences—thus facilitating bourgeois cultural dominance—but it was itself a badge of bourgeois identity, a way for the bourgeoisie to "verify" their social difference through their enjoyment of distinct, often exclusive, social spaces. For example, in an article ("The Adirondacks Verified") written for the genteel *Atlantic Monthly*, Charles Dudley Warner writes: "The instinct of barbarism that leads people periodically to throw aside the habits of civilization and seek the freedom and discomfort of the woods is explicable enough. But it is not so easy to understand why this passion should be strongest in those who are most refined and most trained in social and intellectual fastidiousness.

Philistinism and shoddy do not like the woods."[99] Though alive to the apparent paradox, Warner reinforces the association between bourgeois refinement and the rustic vacation.

Of course, the trope of the wilderness against Mammon has proven susceptible to cooptation by the commercial interests that it has so often been used to counter. For instance, "the magic beckoning of old Mother Nature to rise up from the thralldom of business . . . and to betake ourselves to the woods," became an advertising slogan for the Bangor and Aroostook Railroad Company, as well as for a proliferating industry of recreational and lodging facilities.[100] Similarly, the Bohemian Club could hardly be said to have maintained a pure opposition between Mammon and the Spirit of Bohemia. Their world elsewhere came at a price, and no cremation ceremony can obscure the partnership between capital and this Bohemia. Yet, as a geographic locale and summer destination, "Bohemian Grove" offered both the space and time for utopian dreams.

The Bohemian Unconscious

In club rhetoric, the neo-Transcendental "Bohemian Grove" had its analogue in the unconscious mind. Building upon the romance of the childlike, playful poetic imagination, "Jinks" invitations adumbrated a new therapeutic language, one that conceptualized the unconscious itself as a source of mental and spiritual "renovation." Children, artists, and wilderness enthusiasts were perhaps most attuned to their inner, subliminal selves, but potentially everyone could reach this internal wellspring of creativity, energy, hope, and "higher life." Though club rhetoric never elaborates a full-scale theory of the unconscious, it glimpses the psychotherapeutic potential of the "hidden self."

"Brother Bohemian," one invitation exhorts:

> Life is an ever-changing drama of realities and fiction, in which rugged facts are softened by hope, and past miseries almost turned to pleasures when half hidden, half disclosed, behind the chameleon network of memory. Sleeping or waking, the brain finds rest by turning from what is to what may be; from stern facts to golden possibilities.
>
> Recognizing the mental and physical benefits which mankind owes to these unrealities of life, I entreat you to join me on saturday evening next in drinking a hearty toast to dreams.[101]

Revealing itself in dreams, operating whether one sleeps or wakes, mediating between realities of stern fact and fictions of golden possibility, and supplying "rest" and "mental and physical benefits," this "chameleon network of memory" resonates with emerging theories of the unconscious. Along with other club circulars, this invitation looks back toward the "dream-culture" that Henry Ward Beecher and other Protestant ministers had begun to advocate as a respite from the demands of work and excessive materialism, and toward new secularized practices and beliefs.[102] At a time when the medical and psychological professions were only just beginning to introduce the unconscious into their prescriptions for mental well-being, the club offered privileged access into this inner sanctum.

As a strictly therapeutic entity, the unconscious had first achieved popular recognition in America through the staged exhibitions of the mesmerists in the late 1830s and 1840s. The "mesmerized," sleeplike state of consciousness induced by these self-declared "professors of animal magnetism" revealed a wondrous state of mental life only dreamt of in the wildest gothic imaginings or most enraptured transcendental visions. Mind-cure practitioners similarly championed the restorative potential of the inner self, and by the 1880s and 1890s, the "New Psychology" began (tentatively) to view the "subliminal consciousness" as an important source of mental and physical health.[103] Reaching its apotheosis in the writings of William James, the New Psychology offered the "subconscious self" as a "mediating term" between physical science and religious faith: it was the "wider self through which saving experiences come."[104] Not only the repository of memory fragments, dreams, habit, passion, and "non-rational operations," the Jamesian subconscious also constituted the "higher faculties of our own hidden mind" and introduced "an altogether other dimension of existence from the sensible and merely 'understandable' world."[105] This other dimension could effect a "transition from tenseness, self-responsibility, and worry, to equanimity, receptivity, and peace"; it could promote "regenerative effects" and turn one into a new man.[106]

Though moving from James back to the Bohemian Club risks going from the sublime to the ridiculous, the broad parallels between the many contemporary theories of the unconscious and the rhetoric of Bohemia help us further understand how the club could represent itself as a therapeutic experience and a higher reality. One club poem recited at a Christmas Jinks describes "A Bohemian Vision" as a trancelike consciousness, "A lambent, radiant light—a light divine": "Into Bohemia had my waking mind / Wandered, the while my grosser body slept. / Under our roof-tree had Bohemia come, / The true Bohemia, that which knows not time."[107] Available to all members through the lulling effects of heavy alliteration, this "vision" acts as a performative, attempting to transport the Bohemians into the subliminal reaches of their minds and to provide a sanctuary from temporalities of "care." Further, much like other then-current theories of the unconscious, the poem interprets the visionary state as a variety of religious experience, as one that connects the therapeutic imperative with efforts to establish an alternative faith and source of ideal being. The "light divine," elsewhere described as the "religion of Bohemia," was what the club pledged itself to cultivate.[108]

Club performances also seem to have been geared toward activating the "chameleon network of memory" and releasing a hidden self. At the annual midsummer jinks that led into the "Cremation of Care" (and thus ultimately required the participation of all members), the club sought to revive a mythopoetic past, to enact a series of "primitive" racial identities and to link them with that of the Bohemian. Though never explicitly theorizing something like G. Stanley Hall's recapitulationist schema of human development or a proto-Jungian "collective unconscious," the club connected the restorative, "dreamwise" movement of Bohemia with the recovery of fairy tale, legend, myth, and orientalized mysticism. To this end, the club used performance to journey to that "purely mythical portion of the country" and move beyond the "territory" of "the real."[109] Club dramatizations, or "Jinks," included "The Man in the Forest, a Legend of the Tribe" (in which the Bohemians performed "Indian tradition"); the "Druid," "Buddha," "Hamadryad" and "Gypsy Jinks"; "The Sons of Baldur"; and "The Quest of the Gorgon."[110] In each of these jinks, Bohemia tries to recuperate a premodern sensibility and offers a romance that promises to bring the most enchanting of dreams to consciousness and, at least temporarily, to reanimate the real. According to Porter Garnett, club member and author of *The Bohemian Jinks: A Treatise* (1908), these jinks are "poetic in treatment and conception . . . likened to nothing so fitly as to a mysterious, inspiring, and unforgettable dream," one capable of helping members become "better spiritually and physically."[111] Indeed, at a time when "a web of connections joined childhood, the unconscious, and the childhood of the race in the late-Victorian imagination,"[112] all of these associations met in Bohemia; while performing archaic myths, the "Children of Bohemia" sought to translate fantasy and "primitive" experience into a usable past.

Many club productions centered on the desire to embody ethnic, cultural, or racial Others, implicitly connecting these groups with the freedoms of "unconscious" life. Several of these dramatizations involved a Bohemian coming to the rescue of an imperiled group, thereafter inheriting its traditions and absorbing its spirit. In "The Man in the Forest," an "Evil Spirit" (likened to Care) threatens a Native American tribe. Much as in the myth of the Fisher King, the land had become barren and unfruitful, incapable of sustaining life. Deliverance comes when a foraging party brings forth a "pale-face" captive who "announces himself as from the country of Bohemia" and promises to protect the forest. According to the stage directions, the Bohemian then lifts his hand to the hillside and "the forest becomes illuminated while down the hill pours a company of garlanded harvesters laden with corn and fruit"; and, as the jinks would have it, "the beauty of his presence / There remained to bless the forest / And the Indian ever after."[113] Though the narrative of the jinks imagines that the Bohemian saves the Native Americans from destruction, the lines quoted above betray the real story: in the Bohemian Club version of Manifest Destiny, the Bohemians and not the Native Americans are the ones who remain in the forest, ever blessing those who retain title to the grove only as ancestral presences conjured to help the club cremate care.

Similarly, "Gypsy Camp" retrieves the original identification underlying "Bohemian" identity, representing the club as the inheritors of gypsy traditions. This jinks includes poems, addresses, dance, and songs celebrating the incomparable "freedom and happiness of Gypsy life" before introducing dissonance: an aged sibyl delivers a "wild harangue," declaring that she foretold "the hosts of money-getters who chose to live in cities, passing their lives in cramped boxes of wood and stone and breathing a tainted atmosphere pursued from morning till night by grim care, ever growing vaster and vaster, crowding the gypsy from mountain to plain and from plain to forest until they were sore beset." There was "but one hope for the salvation of their free life," and this was that "in this sordid crew of slaves there was a brotherhood of men, who, like the gypsy, treasured good fellowship more than gold, cared more for music, song and story than bills of lading and stock reports, and once a year hied them to the forest to purify their hearts from the grime of care." Hope for the gypsy and gypsy life resided "in these people and their teachings." At this moment in the performance, the lights went out, and high up among the redwoods fireworks spelled the word "Bohemia." The cremation ceremony directly followed. Bohemia would continue the gypsy spirit, at least for the remainder of the encampment.[114] Even more preposterously, the "Buddha Jinks" imagines that the ancient redwoods contained the spirit of priests from a "fabled Eastern land" who had come to the grove to build the "temple of their fate in Buddha's name." Yet, long ago, the "Spirit of the New World" had transformed the priests into "forest monarchs" and "wrought the spell, / That ages after one should find and claim / Her [Buddhism's?] glories in a greater prophet's name."[115] The poem does not specify whether that greater prophet was Christ, Columbus, or a Bohemian. Implicitly, the Bohemians of the grove become the latter-day Buddhists. They thus enact a romance that continues unabated today with New Age movements and the "virtual Tibet" of recent Hollywood mythologies.[116]

The twentieth-century philosopher Johan Huizinga has argued that ritual acts promote effects that are "not so much *shown figuratively as actually reproduced* in the action." Such acts are performative, convincing "participants in the rite that the action actualizes and effects a definite beatification, brings about an order of things higher than that in which they customarily live."[117] Regardless of how solemnly the club members experienced their rituals (surely these jinks must have been somewhat camp?), the cremation and preceding performances all attempted such an "imaginative actualization," one that would psychologically unburden the Bohemians and allow them to enter another state of consciousness. With "Bohemia" itself represented in most of the jinks, and with all members becoming participants by the time of the cremation, the transformative, therapeutic possibilities of the club's version of *la vie bohème* could become available for the whole group: the Bohemian's "world-blind eyes" would be touched with "fairy unguents" and they would thus "open their eyes of fancy."[118] As the Pragmatists (including James) might have observed, the therapeutic unconscious or ritual processes had only to produce actual effects in order to constitute their own reality. What we might now call a "placebo effect" would thus be as real as any positivistic panacea.

Of course, the Bohemians were not the only club composed of white men to "play Indian" or to appropriate mystical traditions. Their attempts at mythopoesis occurred at a time when numerous scholars, popular romancers, poets, psychologists, and individual seekers similarly sought to recover "primitive," medieval, and Eastern lore. From the "Red Men" to the *Golden Bough* (1890), Theosophy to Mind-Cure, the American Folk-Lore Society (1888) to *When Knighthood Was in Flower* (1898), the widespread interest in myth, legend, folk beliefs, and mysticism assumed a variety of expressions and no doubt met many different wants. In a generalized explanation that seems to encompass the Bohemian Jinks, one author of medieval romances maintained that these fantasies provided a "vacation" from materialism and "self-consciousness."[119]

But *why* were these fantasies seemingly so effective at meeting this therapeutic agenda and releasing (or producing) the unconscious? Late-nineteenth-century psychologists and philosophers began to theorize possible explanations. Following the romancers' lead, they speculated about how myth and fantasy could help unlock the newly heralded, revitalizing unconscious—the very prescription the Bohemians seem to have followed. In particular, the psychological theories of G. Stanley Hall (encapsulated in the famous phrase, "ontogeny recapitulates phylogeny") argued that the child and the adolescent were most in touch with the mystical mythic past; they recapitulated the psychic, evolutionary development of the "race" as they developed into their own adulthood. Yet Hall argued that the progressive development of the human and individual consciousness should not mean the sacrifice of the unconscious "substratum" of mental life. Instead, the "larger self . . . with which we are continuous" would continue to provide a "wisdom beneath us we cannot escape if we would, and on which, when conscious purpose and endeavor droop, we can rest back, with trust, as on 'everlasting arms.' " The conscious person, according to Hall, could retrieve this wisdom by "brooding and incubation," and medieval legends, folk tales, and the spirit of play could aid the effort of recovery.[120] In Hall's and other "New Psychological" schemas, Bohemia and its attempts at mythopoesis might thus have been seen as incubators of the healing, self-transcending unconscious.

Similarly, William James, whose vision of the unconscious resembled Hall's, had earlier marveled at the similarities between the "trance-utterances" of different individuals. Part of an elaborate fantasy though not strictly a "trance," the "utterances" of San Francisco's Bohemian Club provide an interesting correspondence to James' uncanny speakers. In *The Principles of Psychology*, James notes that entranced Americans would often change their voices, mannerisms and languages, and generally be transformed either into a mystic who "abounds in a curiously vague optimistic philosophy-and-water, in which phrases about spirit, harmony, beauty, law, progression, development, etc., keep recurring," or what James calls a "slangy" personage. According to James, this latter personage often represented himself or herself as a Native American: the "calling [of] the ladies 'squaws,' the men 'braves,' the house a 'wigwam,' etc., etc., [was] excessively common." Such commonalties led James to wonder "whether all sub-conscious selves are peculiarly susceptible to a certain stratum of the *Zeitgeist*, and get their inspiration from it."[121] Of course, insofar as it existed, this late-nineteenth-century "zeitgeist" was also endlessly expressed in fiction, essays, song, painting, and other media, and the susceptibilities of these subconscious selves could thus be reduced to the cultural omnipresence of romantic fancy (a possibility that James's phrasing does not exclude). This would have created a self-perpetuating cycle as subconscious fantasy once again sought expression—though such an explanation does not answer the question why these common fantasies first became so popular and why they continued to appeal both to the conscious and the subconscious alike. Yet, whatever the causal relations between fantasy, the subconscious, and popular representations, James's observations further indicate the extent to which the mythologies and ritual enactments of the Bohemian Club resonated with contemporary understandings of unconscious life. Their rhetoric and rites of passage attempted to foster the alternative identities (including that of the Native American and the spiritual philosopher) from which, to paraphrase James, help might come.

More recent theories of the unconscious still seek to explain why the performance of such identities, particularly those of marginalized groups, might have been (or are) experienced as therapeutic. Further, they seek to reveal how such performances might manifest or at least anticipate dissent. From a Marxist perspective, the notion that help might come from our psychic reserves is suggested by Frederick Jameson's well-known conception of a "political unconscious." Influenced by Lacan's antiorganicist "Imaginary," this political unconscious is that which symbolically figures "the ultimate concrete collective life of an achieved Utopian or classless society."[122] As such, it can never simply mirror a mythical "zeitgeist," but is forged in and through the dialectics of history and class conflict. Peter Stallybrass and Allon White's *Politics and Poetics of Transgression* combines this conception with Bakhtin's "carnivalesque," and the resulting analysis indicates how a political unconscious could produce the sort of "slangy" personages noted by James and enacted, however genteelly, by the Bohemian Club. (James also refers to such personages as "grotesque" and "flippant," derogatory terms that are revalued in the study of the carnivalesque.)[123] Stallybrass and White even briefly relate their version of the "political unconscious" to late-nineteenth-century Bohemianism; their provocative analysis further illuminates how ritual, therapy, and dissent might have functioned in Bohemia.[124]

Stallybrass and White theorize the relation between the bourgeois suppression of carnivals and the presence of "carnivalesque" imagery within both "hysterical discourse" and aesthetic forms. Focusing on eighteenth- and nineteenth-century Europe, they hypothesize that the process of bourgeois suppressions on the social level helped to produce similar suppressions on the psychic level. As these critics observe, the "contents" of the unconscious corresponded to the "forms, symbols, rituals" that had structured (or antistructured) popular festivities both in Europe and in colonized cultures abroad. Whether revealed through neurotic, artistic, or other forms of discourse, this unconscious could be called "a political unconscious" in so far as "the exclusion of other social groups and classes in the struggle to achieve categorical self-identity" simultaneously produced "unconscious heterogeneity, with its variety of hybrid figures, competing sovereignties and exorbitant demands."[125] In this theory, pleas for a less rigid, hierarchical, and divided world thus clambered within the self even as that self was shaped by attempts to exile the "Other."

This emphasis on unconscious heterogeneity might seem to depart from Jameson's original formulation. For Jameson, the unconscious can be "political" and yet consolidate rather than disperse bourgeois identity. Thus, Jameson argues that "even hegemonic or ruling-class culture and ideology are Utopian, not in spite of their instrumental function to secure and perpetuate class privilege and power, but rather precisely because that function is also in and of itself the affirmation of collective solidarity."[126] In other words, this Utopian dimension holds even when "collective solidarity" confines itself to the ruling classes. In Jameson's model, it then follows that the Bohemian Club could both reinforce a bourgeois class consciousness and provide an allegory of a future, classless form of collectivity: to wit, a political unconscious. But such consolidation does not preclude hybridity, either in Jameson's model or in Bohemian Club practice. Like Stallybrass and White, Jameson also recognizes that threats of the "Other" dialectically produce the class consciousnesses of dominant groups. However, Stallybrass and White allow that "unconscious heterogeneity" never takes the unmediated, undistorted form of a return of the oppressed—the "repressed" is, in their reading, always a "complex hybrid fantasy," much as it is informed by the "contents" of the popular carnivalesque. As I have argued, such hybrid fantasy also informs most Bohemian Club productions while bolstering "class privilege and power."

The concept of a "political unconscious" underscores how ritual, therapy, and dissent could have met in the arcana of Bohemian Club "High Jinks." The relative availability of Bohemian lifestyles for men might even help to explain why turn-of-the-century hysteria was, or seemed to be, a predominantly female affliction. The *Politics and Poetics of Transgression* speculates that, having greater opportunities for "Bohemian" expression, men might, in fact, have been less susceptible to the disease: "in this same period bourgeois culture produced a compensatory range of peripheral [male] 'bohemias' which afforded 'liminoid' symbolic repertoires of a kind approximating to those of earlier carnival forms." Stallybrass and White cite the Bohemian, avant-garde movements of surrealism and expressionism as their analogies to the "discursive material of the [female] analysand."[127] With its own symbolic repertoire, however, the genteel Bohemian Club of San Francisco also staged the compensatory rituals and neocarnivalesque inversions that could promote release for its male constituents. Indeed, under pressure of the political unconscious, the very term "Bohemian" (as defined by the club) functioned as an antithetical word in the "primal," Freudian sense: it acknowledged the uncanniness of bourgeois identity itself.

In its myriad forms, Romanticism had long provided the bourgeoisie with a variant of the carnivalesque. What is most interesting about this Bohemian Club is how explicitly it represented its romance quest as therapy, as the answer to bourgeois neurasthenia and psychic distress. In effect transhistoricizing the Bohemian Club's equation between romance and therapy, Northrop Frye formalized the genre of "quest-romance" under the Freudian rubric of "wish-fulfillment," as "the search of the libido or desiring self for a fulfillment that will deliver it from the anxieties of reality but will still contain that reality."[128] It was just this quest for deliverance and containment that led so many of San Francisco's rich and famous to the lush woodlands of the Bohemian Grove, every summer, to cremate care. Wanting both to accommodate and transcend the dictates of "care," the club found its Bohemia in the interstices of bourgeois life.

The duality of the Bohemian quest-romance offers a complicated, contradictory legacy. To the extent that the Bohemia of the club fostered psychosocial equilibrium, it may well have prevented hystericization or cured less extreme forms of neurasthenic upset, supporting bourgeois hegemony in the process. Accordingly, this club may have "managed" or "contained" the Bohemian unconscious, thus reinforcing bourgeois self-identity, within and without the individual. Further, with its collective fantasy life, this club may have (both directly and indirectly) prepared a bridge from an individualist to a corporatist economy, one that used "fraternal" bonds to solidify the pseudotranscendental bodies of corporations. As the following section will explore (by way of Frank Norris), the club's escapist fantasies (and accumulation of finance capital) may even have nurtured early forms of the "society of the spectacle," that hallmark of late-twentieth-century capitalism. The Bohemian Club of San Francisco may have fulfilled its therapeutic imperative all too well.

Still, this very success should give us pause. Just as psychologists were discovering the unconscious, the club promised that divisions between the ego and the hidden self could be resocialized in the separation between everyday life and Bohemia. Even in its limited, class-bound framework, this quest-romance suggested that personal revitalization needed a social context, that each individual could experience multiple identities, and that neurasthenic symptoms could be something other than signs of personal inadequacy. A "Bohemian unconscious" might even have promoted those "ideal extensions of the self" that intimate a more broadly collective existence. The club failed to transcend social divisions (to put it mildly) and often amounted to little more than a glorified corporate retreat. And yet, in their own contradiction-riddled ways, the early Bourgeois-Bohemians tried to fashion new, more gratifying selves. The rhetoric and rituals of the Bourgeois-Bohemians reveal psychic fractures that the club may not have been able to accommodate or fully contain.

The Bohemian *Octopus*

Thus far, I have adhered fairly closely to the official rhetoric of the Bohemian Club, analyzing its tropes to understand how the group imagined and negotiated between the Bohemian and the Bourgeois. Yet, what happens when we make a lateral move away from the club and its rhetoric and toward the related world of the turn-of-the-century naturalist novel? The Bohemian Club figures briefly, yet importantly, in the works of several of the best-known literary naturalists, particularly in Norris's *The Octopus*. As mentioned, Jack London and Frank Norris were both members of the club, and Norris's semi-autobiographical *Blix* notes that its protagonist had "joined a certain San Francisco club of artists, journalists, musicians, and professional men that is one of the institutions of the city, and, in fact, famous throughout the United States."[129] London's Martin Eden is a member of the club, as is Norris's Vandover. It is in *The Octopus*, however, that Norris most fully critiques Bourgeois-Bohemianism, highlighting its contradictory ideologies of masculinity and femininity, aesthetics and economics, production and consumption, the natural and the unnatural, the romantic and the real.

For Norris, the naturalistic "Romance" was "an instrument with which we may go straight through clothes and tissues and wrappings of flesh down deep into the red living heart of things."[130] As represented in *The Octopus*, Bourgeois-Bohemianism cannot adequately accomplish this objective. Quite the contrary, the Bohemia of the novel thwarts naturalistic efforts to recover "real life" and instead promotes a "sham of tinsel and pasteboard."[131] Toward the middle of the novel, Presley (poet and frequent authorial surrogate) accompanies the Derricks (gentlemen-ranchers from Tulare County) to "the club" in San Francisco. Once there, the wealthy industrialist Cedarquist condescends to Presley: "Hello, Pres, my boy. How is the great, the very great Poem getting on?" Presley, who has not worked on his projected epic poem of the West for several months, answers, "I've just about given up the idea. There's so much interest in what you might call 'living issues' down there at Los Muertos now, that I'm getting further and further from it every day." At this moment, the artist Hartrath joins the group "uninvited" (816). As the novel would have it, Hartrath is the quintessential Bohemian Club member, one of the "fakirs" who conspire to estrange the aesthetic from the real, thus justifying Presley's renunciation of art for living issues. On display at the club and supposedly representing the natural world, Hartrath's painting, "A Study of the Contra Costa Foothills," is instead an absurd simulacrum; "set in a frame of natural redwood, the bark still adhering," the painting nonetheless betrays the natural, adhering to hackneyed principles of formal composition and eliciting from onlookers "remembered phrases" about "mild technicalities" (823). Hartrath is not a true naturalist.

More than the painting itself, however, the outrage of Hartrath's "Study of the Contra Costa Foothills" is that it is being raffled at the club in service of a "projected Million-Dollar Fair and Flower Festival." Beyond its satirical portrait of Hartrath, the novel also joins Cedarquist (whose big Atlas Iron Works had just "ceased to be a paying investment") in ridiculing this Festival:

> When you get your Eastern capitalists out here with your Million-Dollar Fair . . . you don't propose, do you, to let them see a Million-Dollar Iron Foundry standing

> idle, because of the indifference of San Francisco businessmen? They might ask pertinent questions, your capitalists, and we should have to answer that our business men preferred to invest their money in corner lots and government bonds, rather than to back up a legitimate, industrial enterprise. We don't want fairs, we want active furnaces. We don't want public statues, and fountains, and park extensions and gingerbread fetes. . . . What a melancholy comment! San Francisco! It is not a city—it is a Midway Plaisance. California likes to be fooled. (817)

Cedarquist does not accept that cultural production—and the cultivation of the sort of public spaces that Bret Harte's "Bohemian" had earlier championed—might be a "legitimate" form of investment. Though Cedarquist recognizes that "Production," what he calls "the great word of this nineteenth century," is being replaced by "Markets," he remains dismissive of the emerging culture industry that increasingly supported the activity of *marketing* (819). Cedarquist and Derrick regard the fair as a feminized sham, an investment in culture at the expense of masculine industry and production. Conversely, the Bourgeois-Bohemians who promote the Million-Dollar Fair recognize that "the million we spend on the fair will be money in our pockets," attracting "Eastern visitors here by the thousands—capitalists—men with money to invest" (816).

The Octopus explores the interplay between the "two world-forces, the elemental Male and Female" (680). Not surprisingly, these two rival sexual forces or genders also come into conflict within the Bohemian Club of the novel. As Mark Seltzer has demonstrated, in the act of naturalizing male generativity, Norris often *de*naturalizes female (re)productive power.[132] One of the ways he does so, I argue, is by identifying the feminine (if not exactly the "elemental female") with what he regards as the therapeutic artificiality of fin-de-siècle aestheticism. Though exclusively male, the Bohemian Club is finally not masculine enough for naturalism. Norris underscores the club's effeminacy by making the day of the raffle of Hartrath's painting a "double occasion"; it is one of the rare "Ladies Days" at the club—as Presley notes, on all other days "the presence of women within [the club] was not tolerated (821). While Mr. Cedarquist scoffs at Hartrath and the Million-Dollar Fair, Mrs. Cedarquist champions the artist and promotes the "gingerbread fete." Hartrath is himself feminized, speaking the idioms of the aesthetic movement (or, more precisely, Gilbert and Sullivan–esque satires of the aesthetic movement): "Beauty," he closed his sore eyes with a little expression of pain, "beauty unmans me" (827). The all-male Bohemian Club may have paradoxically worked to legitimize male identifications with a "feminine" role; the "emphatically 'male' genre of naturalism,"[133] however, disassociates itself from such feminized versions of the Bourgeois-Bohemian.

Yet in the particular battle between "the elemental Male and Female" that takes place at the Bohemian Club of the novel, feminized (re) production, in all its apparent artificiality, triumphs. At the end of Book II, Chapter I, it is Magnus Derrick, the virile patriarch, who is "unmanned" when he learns of the court's decision in the case of the League versus the Railroad. Unable to withstand the power of the railroad monopoly, his potent vision of his "wheat, like the crest of an advancing billow, crossing the Pacific, bursting upon Asia, flooding the Orient in a golden torrent" (831) is exposed as "only the flimsiest mockery." During the same narrative moment, the winning number in the raffle for Hartrath's picture is being drawn. "I've won. I've won," Mrs. Cedarquist cries, while her husband reiterates: "Not a city, Presley, not a city, but a Midway Plaisance" (832–33).

Mr. Cedarquist thus ruefully acknowledges that the "feminine" principle of cultural reproduction has, at least momentarily, overtaken his own imperial quest for markets. By invoking the "Midway Plaisance," however, Mr. Cedarquist implicitly acknowledges that the feminized "separate sphere" of cultural reproduction duplicates and even exceeds the masculine imperial mandate. As exemplified by the World's Columbian Exposition in Chicago (1893), the "Midway Plaisance" provided a form of imperialist spectacle; the neoclassical White City of the Exposition strove (in Alan Trachtenberg's words) to "represent America" while "the outlying exotic Midway stood for the rest of the world in subordinate relation."[134] According to the contemporary Rand McNally *Handbook*, the exoticized Midways offered an "unusual collection of almost every type of architecture known to man—oriental villages, Chinese bazaars, tropical settlements, ice railways, the ponderous Ferris wheel, and reproductions of ancient cities."[135] The spatialization of the World's Fair thus reproduced and promoted visions of U.S. empire building. In so doing, as Robert W. Rydell has further demonstrated, the Midway rendered "the commodity fetish . . . an imperial fetish as well": the Midways "gave millions of Americans firsthand experience with treating nonwhites from around the world as commodities."[136]

In the context of the scene at the Bohemian Club, this reference to the Midway is even more precise than it might at first seem. The feminized Bourgeois-Bohemianism of Hartrath and Mrs. Cedarquist thrives on just the kind of spectacular, hierarchically ordered, and globalized eclecticism that characterized the expositions. In therapeutic, neocarnivalesque fashion, such spectacles provide a highly mediated form of access to the social groups and practices that the normative bourgeois subject traditionally subordinates or excludes. Indeed, as described by Norris, the many spectacles and reified identities staged both at the club and within the Cedarquists' drawing rooms anticipate a postmodern landscape in which, as David Harvey observes, "spaces of very different worlds seem to collapse upon each other, much as the world's commodities are assembled in the supermarket and all manner of sub-cultures get juxtaposed in the contemporary city."[137]

Through such flattened juxtapositions, the Midways and Bohemian Club spectacles partially duplicated naturalist visions of empire building, all the while staging the conventional naturalist antinomy between a privileged spectator and social populations defined as part of "brute" nature.[138] At the World's Fairs, the juxtaposition of different worlds generally did more to reinforce than to displace social and cultural hierarchies; yet in so doing these spectacles also disrupted the (always tenuous) naturalist binary between the natural and the unnatural, and even the masculine and the feminine. *Not a city, but a Midway Plaisance*, the San Francisco colonized by the Bourgeois-Bohemians of the novel provides a never-ending parade of "fakirs" and "shams." To quote Harvey again, this (proto)postmodern space brought "together different worlds (of commodities) in the same space and time. But it [did] so in such a way as to conceal almost perfectly any trace of origin, of the labour processes that produced them, or of the social relations implicated in their production."[139] Norris recognizes "Bohemia" as the stage for this globalized, "sham" commodity culture:

> The Russian Countess gave talks on the prisons of Siberia, wearing the headdress and pinchbeck ornaments of a Slav bride; the Aesthete, in his white cassock, gave readings on obscure questions of art and ethics. . . . The bearded poet, perspiring in furs and boots of reindeer skin, declaimed verses of his own composition about the wild life of the Alaskan mining camps. . . . The Cherokee, arrayed in fringed buckskin and blue beads, rented from a costumer, intoned folk songs of his people in the vernacular. . . . The Armenian, in fez and baggy trousers, spoke of the Unspeakable Turk . . . all in the name of the Million-Dollar Fair. Money to the extent of hundreds of thousands was set in motion. (82–27)

Such circulation is one of the many abstracted "forces" that the Bohemian *Octopus* represents. Though Norris's own naturalism relies upon social

"Others" (a term Norris employs in *The Octopus*) to effect a return to "brute" nature, this scene recognizes that there may well be nothing natural in such reified constructions. Norris's romantic fiction wants to return to the "masculine" real world and to renounce the seemingly autonomous, "feminine" space of art, yet the scene at the Bohemian Club demonstrates the extent to which the two realms—and genders—interpenetrated one another.

Famously, *The Octopus* ends its naturalistic explorations with recourse to the concept of the "invisible hand" of supply and demand, a trope that tries to reconcile the natural and the abstract, the embodied and the disembodied. Yet throughout the novel and in this scene at "the club," Norris implicitly recognizes that the danger of trying to strike through the pasteboard mask to the red living heart of "things" is the potential discovery that these "things" no longer have a heart. For Norris, the scandal of Bohemia was its failure to embrace the naturalist imperative. In representing the artificial world of the Bohemian Club, however, Norris begs the question whether his own naturalism can overcome the antinomy between escapist aesthetic production and "living issues." As Norris recognizes, the very premise of the club was to achieve just what he hoped to counter in his own art: an autonomous space that would transcend the real. Ironically enough, however, Norris suggests that even at the moment when Bohemian aesthetics claimed to separate "art" from "society," the Bohemian and the Bourgeois were in fact forging socioeconomic partnerships. In effect, "the club" *does* accomplish the naturalist objective, but from the reverse direction: art reanimates the real—not because it penetrates beneath the pasteboard mask, but because capitalist aesthetics overtakes reality itself. *The Octopus* underwrites critical narratives that identify Bohemia with an emerging therapeutic ethos based on consumption. Yet, in the spaces between official Bohemian Club rhetoric and Norris's naturalism, we can piece together a more complicated story, one in which Bohemia exists both within and without the dominant culture, both within and without the romantic and the real. While the club's rhetoric of therapeutic dissent promotes a withdrawal from the real world into a seemingly autonomous space of art, Norris's version of the club and its "Million-Dollar Fair" looks (critically) toward postmodern fusions of art and life, the aesthetic and the commercial. In the official club narrative, culture transcends basic realities; in Norris's account, culture insidiously superimposes itself back upon the real in the form of a capitalist-manufactured "Second Nature."[140] Underscoring the paradox of the

Bourgeois-Bohemian, these two narratives create an unstable series of oscillations between both alternatives: they highlight the many contradictions seemingly elided by the integrated identity "Bourgeois-Bohemian."

In the first decades of the Bohemian Club, members attempted to discover a world beyond that of their everyday lives. The club brought together the Bohemian and the Bourgeois, but it also insisted upon certain spatial and temporal separations between the two identities—even, or especially, when they met within the same individual. With a typical nineteenth-century zest for binarism, these early Bourgeois-Bohemians sought to compartmentalize work and play, the child and the adult, the artist and the professional, and the rational and unconscious psyche. According to club rhetoric, such reciprocal pairings not only encouraged equilibrium but also upheld the possibility of transcendence: this potential existed so long as the pairings did not become self-identical. For these men, "Bohemia" was valuable precisely because of its distance from bourgeois adulthood, whiteness, masculinity, and commercialism. Alternately a quasi-utopian mirage and ground zero for white male exclusivity, this Bohemia, at its best, kept alive hopes for a more collective, noninstrumentalized, multifaceted existence. At its worst, the club increased separations between rich and poor, men and women, Anglo-Americans and racial and ethnic minorities.

Among contemporary "Bobos," however, the melding of the Bohemian and the Bourgeois has compromised potentially enabling tensions between the two categories, while failing adequately to redress socioeconomic divides. Boboism relentlessly obscures or collapses the once-standard oppositions of bourgeois life—leisure versus labor, freedom versus systemization, culture versus society, art versus commodification, irony versus truth, the Bohemian versus the Bourgeois. But these alleged collapses have taken place even as income gaps have widened, raising the question whether we are really ready to surrender contradiction to advertising executives, management gurus, and the glittering surfaces of "capitalist realism."

Highway 101, the main thoroughfare of Silicon Valley, is a stretch of freeway where billboard after billboard proclaims a host of businesses, each offering new ways of consuming, investing, and socializing without ever having to leave one's own computer work/play station. Yet with some twists and turns, this same information superhighway still leads to the original Bohemian Grove and its pristine redwood forest. The first generations of Bohemian Club members wanted to believe that "Bohemia" was a rarefied realm apart from "busy marts of trade"; hopefully their successors will not suffer from the opposite illusion.[141] It is—and then again it isn't—reassuring to know that many of the most successful representatives of the corporate world still convene in this retreat, every summer, to cremate care.

5

Regional Bohemias

DURING THE HEYDAY of the fin-de-siècle Bohemian vogue, the desire to "live in Bohemia" extended throughout the nation. For many, this quest led to New York, San Francisco, or Paris. "I wish to go to Bohemia!" insists the titular heroine of L. H. Bickford and Richard Stillman Powell's *Phyllis in Bohemia* (1897), and, along with many U.S. writers and their fictional avatars, Phyllis leaves behind her "pastoral" life in an unspecified rural "Arcadia," searching for "a plot to live around" in the "American Bohemia" of New York City.[1] In this recurrent plot, Bohemia beckons the rural American, concentrating the romantic allure of urban culture and attracting promising youth away from their small-town communities and into national cultural centers. Commentators often figured this spatial and temporal shift as the displacement of an earlier pastoral "Arcadia" by its poetic successor, the mobile and metropolitan "Bohemia." A nation within the nation, the floating territory of Bohemia thus paralleled, and often abetted, the ongoing "incorporation of America."[2] According to one observer, "It is part of the fairyland of it that it refuses to be limited by the mere boundary lines of townships and municipalities."[3]

Throughout this same period, however, Bohemia also acted to forestall such cultural incorporation and to preserve regional autonomy. Many self-professed Bohemians located this mythical terrain within their own regional cultures; periodicals and clubs named the *Bohemian* appeared all over the country, and all extolled local versions of Bohemia. By claiming "Bohemia" for themselves, many of these clubs and magazines had an explicit agenda: to resist the centripetal pull of a national culture based in the Northeast, increasingly in Manhattan. Whether in the form of a periodical or a club, the mythos of Bohemia provided a portable buffer zone: *la vie bohème* mediated between the national and the regional, refusing the centrality of the one and the limits of the other.

Bohemia and Arcadia

For the earliest American Bohemians, the poetic landscapes of "Bohemia" and "Arcadia" had been essentially interchangeable. Bret Harte, for example, saw little competition between Bohemia and the Arcadia of pastoral romance. As Harte attempted to establish a Bohemia in the far West, these two mythic properties merge in his writings and provide the topos of antibourgeois ideality. Following Harte's lead, many late-nineteenth-century writers continued to align Bohemia and Arcadia. Some described the relation as a transhistorical—and transnational—poetic impulse. According to Mary Heaton Vorse, "Bohemia has had many incarnations in the world's history. It used to be called 'Arcadia,' and court ladies dressed themselves up as Shepherdesses, and had many pastoral emotions. Dreamers speak of it as the Golden Age, and Idealists look forward to it as the Millennium, and in all these various dreams, even in smoke-laden Bohemia, the ideal of youth and gaiety reigns."[4]

The stage props differ over the generations but the impulse is universal: as Vorse would have it, Bohemia and Arcadia both provide analogous archetypes for youthful dreams. Vorse thus reduces these historical vicissitudes to a matter of superficial fashion. Edmund Clarence Stedman, one of the early Pfaffians, also maintained that the two realms were continuous with one another in an article from 1892: "A dividing line has been drawn from time immemorial betwixt the conventional and the natural worshippers, betwixt the stately kingdom of Philistia and the wilding vales and copses of that Arcadia which some geographers have named Bohemia." Despite the fact that Stedman had become a Wall Street banker after his days at Pfaff's, the genteel poet insisted upon his ongoing place in Arcadia/Bohemia: "This is the way in Arcadia, and it has its pains and charms—as I well know, having journeyed many seasons in that happy-go-lucky land of sun and shower, and still holding a key to one of its entrance-gates."[5]

Yet by the end of the century, most accounts posited a more pronounced separation between the two poetic realms, increasingly identifying "Arcadia" with the rural and "Bohemia" with the urban. For example, in his *Airs from Arcady and Elsewhere* (1888), H. C. Bunner, a writer best known for his urban sketches, begins this short book of verse with a section called "Arcady" before entering into another called "Bohemia." The distance between the two locations figures a personal evolution from innocence to experience, a move from the pastoral to the urban. "Arcady" yearns for lost loves and springs, and "Bohemia" sighs over past lovers and debauches. Bohemia is the less wholesome, yet still poetic, successor to Arcady. Bunner does not locate these developmental stages within a specific historical time or social geography; nonetheless, his poetic self stands in for those many other contemporary selves whose personal histories involved a move from rural "Arcady" to urban "Bohemia."

Gelett Burgess, a San Franciscan (and member of the Bohemian Club), mapped the territories of Bohemia and Arcadia in his fin-de-siècle little magazine, *The Lark*. Burgess's fanciful "Map of Bohemia (from the Explorations of Gelett Burgess)" charts a land that bears no topographical similarity to the United States or the Bay Area. Its referents seem purely literary and map a self-contained world of poetic imagination and *l'art pour l'art*. For Burgess, pastoral "Arcady" is a province of the larger country of "Bohemia"—along with such regions as "Pays de La Jeunesse," "The Hills of Fame," "The Forest of Arden," and "Vagabondia." The hostile country of "Philistia," with its "Great Philistine Desert," borders this nation and defines its boundaries. The governing opposition is between the Bohemian and the Philistine and not, apparently, between the Bohemian and the Arcadian. Still, though Burgess places "Arcady" within the borders of "Bohemia," it is but a region within the larger Bohemian nation. The map thus indicates the relative power of these mythic domains. Drawn at a time when agricultural enterprises were themselves entering a national commodities market and coming under corporate control, Burgess's Bohemian geography tellingly relegates the pastoral to the margins.[6]

Mapping the temporal and spatial distance between "Arcadia" and "Bohemia," many fin-de-siècle fictions locate Bohemia in New York. William Dean Howells's *The Coast of Bohemia* (also discussed in Chapter 3) is no exception, and the novel explicitly juxtaposes Bohemia with the "Arcadia" that existed in Pymantoning, Ohio, in the recent past. Ever ambivalent about what Bohemia meant for American literature and culture, Howells represents *la vie bohème* both as a potential threat to an Arcadian America and a means for its ongoing preservation.

The Coast of Bohemia begins in Pymantoning and the town's would-be "Arcadian" status is quickly at issue. "Oh, nobody's very poor in

Pymantoning . . . You can't imagine how Arcadian we are out here," the local, Mrs. Burton, tells the visiting cosmopolitan artist, Ludlow. "Oh, yes, I can; I've lived in a village," Ludlow replies, thus inviting this qualification from Mrs. Burton:

"A New England village, yes; but the lines are drawn just as hard and fast there as they are in a city. You have to live in the West to understand what equality is, and in a purely American population, like this. You've got plenty of independence, in New England, but you haven't got equality, and we have,—or used to have." Mrs. Burton added the final words with apparent conscience.

"Just saved your distance, Polly," said her husband. "We haven't got equality now, any more than we've got buffalo."[7]

Mrs. Burton here defines the "Arcadian" as a condition of "equality," and she associates it with living in the West and existing within a "purely American population." Whether or not, by circular logic, the "purely American" also depends on the Western environment, a sociopolitical state of equality, or some other, unnamed variable remains somewhat unclear. Insofar as she equates the "American" and the "Western," however, she could be said to offer her own "frontier thesis"—and this during the same year in which Frederick Jackson Turner himself delivered his famous speech.[8]

For Turner, the hallmark of this American character was "dominant individualism"; yet for Mrs. Burton it is equality, a condition once fostered but now presumably undermined by Turner's aggressive American self.[9] Turner's ideal American culminated in the ultracivilized White City of the World's Columbian Exposition in Chicago, the place where Turner first announced his "frontier thesis." Embodied in Chicago, the imperial American self had developed "a complex nervous system for the originally simple, inert continent" and created "the complex mazes of modern commercial lines."[10] In Turner's vision, the American thus displaced earlier ideals of agrarian equality in the drive toward plutocratic hierarchy. Nonetheless, Turner insisted that earlier American ideological values endured, at least within the sanctuary of American character. Howells's Mrs. Burton, however, mourns the passing of an Arcadian moment. The destruction of the buffalo, alluded to by Mr. Burton, in itself revealed the drastic limits of freedom and equality in the "American" West. Their destruction had been linked to the genocide of Native Americans—"Every buffalo dead is an Indian gone," functioned as an unofficial governmental mantra in the years following the Civil War[11]—and the decimation of the great buffalo herds also signified the commercial greed that Howells saw as anathema to Arcadian equality. Indeed, written the same year as *The Coast of Bohemia*, Howells's third "Letter of an Altrurian Traveller" explicitly connects the loss of the buffalo with the loss of republican promise: "for all the forces of the plutocratic conditions, so few are conservative that the American buffalo is as rare as the old-fashioned American mechanic, proud of his independence, and glorying in his citizenship."[12] The absence of the buffalo figures the "distance" (Mr. Burton's word) between Arcadia and the Ohio of the novel.

Alternatively, Bohemia, or at least the "Coast of Bohemia," looms as a more contemporary destination. It is, first of all, largely an "aesthetic state," one capable of transposing imperiled ideological values into modern artistic and literary practice. As a missionary of Howellsian realism, the Bohemian painter Ludlow first appears in Pymantoning to distill and preserve the essence of the town and its people before its Arcadian promise entirely departs: "He thought, so far as he thought ethically about it, that the Americans needed to be shown the festive and joyous aspects of their common life. To discover and to represent these was his pleasure as an artist, and his duty as a citizen" (6). Ludlow adopts the central imperative of the realist creed, as defined by Howells; he dedicates himself to representing the "common life" of his nation at a time when (as Howells himself acknowledges by way of the Burtons) the common was increasingly fractured by social and economic inequality.

It is perhaps for precisely this ironic effect that Howells depicts a realist as flawed and elitist as Ludlow; as an artistic representative, Ludlow exposes the potential inadequacy of realism itself:

> He suspected, though, that the trotting-match was the only fact of the Pymantoning County Fair that could be persuaded to lend itself to his purpose [of representing a joyous common life]. Certainly, there was nothing in the fair-house, with those poor, dreary old people straggling through it, to gladden an artistic conception. Agricultural implements do not group effectively, or pose singly with much picturesqueness; . . . and heaps of grapes cannot assert themselves in a very bacchanal profusion against the ignominy of being spread upon long tables and ticketed with the names of their varieties and exhibitors. (6–7)

Ludlow can only view the scene through prior artistic categories that mediate and undermine his efforts to capture the "common." Howells himself had hoped to distinguish the realist from the more elitist aesthete, insisting that the "realist feels in every nerve the equality of things and the unity of men," while the aesthete functions as a latter-day aristocrat: "The pride of caste is becoming the pride of taste; but as before, it is averse to the mass of men; it consents to know them only in some conventionalized and artificial guise."[13] A would-be realist, Ludlow nonetheless embraces such aestheticism, reasserting distinction where he would find equality. He seeks the "picturesque" or a mythological bacchanal instead of regarding Pymantoning on its own terms; instead of representing the poor, or allowing the "ignominy" of market realities to intrude upon his Bohemian Arcadia, Ludlow retreats into the "Fine Arts Department" of the fair. The Bohemian thus doubles back upon himself, seeking art as a refuge from the real.

This strategy is more successful in New York than Pymantoning, and Ludlow quickly returns to his cosmopolitan residence. It is here that the mythos of Bohemia best flourishes. Indeed, for Howells, Bohemia often functions as the locus of the urban-"modern" par excellence. *The Coast of Bohemia* is more tolerant than many of Howells's earlier representations of *la vie bohème*, and the shifts in his various depictions help to chart his changing view of the American scene in its urban and regional coordinates. Before returning to the novel, it is worth reviewing how Howells had previously represented the cultural zone of "Bohemia."

In his earlier work, Howells had been suspicious of Bohemia, viewing it as a dangerous site of cosmopolitan excess and an open affront to the values of a more Arcadian America. A symptom of a more generalized condition of urban anonymity, Howells's Bohemia often fosters irresponsibility and individualism, helping to erode communal ethics. For example, in a retrospective account of his pre–Civil War visit to the Bohemians at Pfaff's, Howells questioned their attachment to the "freedom" of non-recognition (see Chapter 1).[14] Still a relatively knowable community, Howells's Boston discouraged the individualistic alienation so often associated with Bohemianism. Yet, as Howells elsewhere recognized, even genteel Boston contained a threatening element of the "Bohemian." While charting the breakdown of traditional cultural authorities (family, religion, community), Howells's *A Modern Instance* identifies the moral lapses of modernity with *la vie bohème*, a generalized version of which characterizes the early married life of the protagonists after they first settle in Boston. Throughout the novel, the doomed marriage of Bartley and Marcia Hubbard resists proper domestication and fails to emulate the social norms that Howells himself sought to fortify and reconstitute through his realism. After eloping, the couple moves to Boston from the small town of Equity, Maine; there, Bartley foregoes his ambition to become a lawyer, a profession of "dignity," and instead remains a journalist, a pursuit still tinged with the "degradation" that many early applications of the term "Bohemian" sought to convey. Indeed, as we have seen, in American parlance, "Bohemian" first referred almost exclusively to newspapermen or literary hacks who had not attained the status of prominent men of letters. *A Modern Instance* encompasses this narrow definition of Bohemianism, but also conceives of the phenomenon more generally, using it to refer to a "modern" existence of "relaxation and uncertainty."[15] It is this metropolitan lifestyle that helps to erode the Hubbard marriage; it is part of the consumerist romance that competes with older, presumably more stable definitions of the "real":

> Although [Marcia] willingly lived this irregular life with him, she was at heart not at all a Bohemian. She did not like being in lodgings or dining at restaurants; on their horse-car excursions into the suburbs, when the spring opened, she was always choosing this or that little house as the place where she would like to live, and wondering if it were in their means. She said she would gladly do all the work herself; she hated to be idle so much as she now must. The city's novelty wore off for her sooner than for him: the concerts, the lectures, the theatres, had already lost their zest for her, and she went because he wished her to go, or in order to be able to help him with what he was always writing about such things.[16]

Equated with urban amusements, extradomestic accommodations, and the sensational vicariousness of newspaper culture, this Bohemian life subverts marital stability. It is the essence of the modern: an urban mode of being based on hyperconsumption and ephemeral contacts. Still bound to more a more traditional work ethic and what Howells elsewhere calls the "moral effect of housekeeping," Marcia hopes for a more settled existence.[17] By contrast, Bartley thrives on the stimulus of diversion and indulges his citified tastes. His is the consummate urban self: "elusive, facile, adaptable."[18] Whereas Bret Harte's "Bohemian" spectator still had scruples about dissolving the private sphere into the realm of commodified "publicity," Bartley has no such qualms. For Bartley, the enchanting "phantasmagoria" of the city and its commercial entertainments replaces the would-be realism of a more self-contained private sphere (115). Bohemia, that fictive territory, is the appropriate domain for an urban economy based on the fleeting illusions afforded by seductive commodities, aesthetic or otherwise. Just as literary romance (in both genteel and mass market varieties) famously threatens Howellsian realism, so Bohemia affronts traditional cultural authorities.

A Modern Instance admits Bohemia into the purview of Boston, yet for the most part Howells identifies *la vie bohème* with New York. *A Modern Instance* itself distinguishes Boston from more contemporary urban domains; as one character insists, "Boston is more authentic and individual, after the old pattern. Cosmopolitanism is a modern vice, and we're antique, we're classic" (169). Relative to cities like New York, Boston remained, for Howells, a remnant of an older, morally superior dispensation. Howells himself moved from Boston to New York in 1888, and, by the time he wrote *A Hazard of New Fortunes* (1890), he had begun to reconcile himself to the cosmopolis in general and to Bohemian life in particular. In this novel, Howells's fictional surrogates, the Marches, also move from Boston to New York, reluctantly renouncing what Mrs. March views as her "provincial narrowness" (22). They lament the "literary peace, the intellectual refinement of the life they had left behind them," yet they also recognize that that life had become calcified: it had ceased to be vital. As Basil March observes, Boston was "very pretty," but it was "not life—it was death in life" (265). Rather than denying the modern and living a dated "realism," the Marches resolve to enter modernity as metonymized by New York City.

To this end, the Marches go "bohemianizing" within the cosmopolis, along with their children, Tom and Bella. Used as a verb, "to bohemianize" signifies, for Howells, the stuff of metropolitan living, the act of engagement with the city: "They really enjoyed bohemianizing in that harmless way: though Tom had his doubt of its respectability; he was very punctilious about his sister and went round from his own school every day to fetch her home from hers. The whole family went to the theater a good deal and enjoyed themselves together in their desultory explorations of the city" (258). In *A Modern Instance*, Bohemian life is clouded by moral uncertainty; in *A Hazard of New Fortunes*, it is potentially benign, "harmless," and even a source of familial togetherness instead of dispersal. Like many other writers at this time, Howells seeks to domesticate the antidomestic, to tame Bohemia and recover it for the social values it was once thought to destroy. While the Marches attempt to adjust their family life to the conditions of metropolitan life, Howells analogously hopes to colonize the city for realism. Such earlier realist protagonists as Silas Lapham and Marcia Hubbard flee the city and return to their small-town origins, but the Marches remain in New York. Mediating between realism and romance, Bohemia now provides Howells with an acceptable trope for urban existence.

In making Bohemia safe for realism, Howells even goes so far as to reimport Arcadia. Perhaps, Howells suggests in both *Hazard* and *The Coast of Bohemia*, the two territories were not really so far apart, and, once combined, could provide a template for a rejuvenated America. To this end, Howells turns to the literary and artistic communities of New York. As we have seen, Howells's Bohemia was part of the general tenor of urban life (especially insofar as that life was increasingly constructed out of the materials of "romance," such as the theatre, department store windows, bucolic Central Park), yet he recognized that Bohemia's realm was also more specifically that of the cosmopolitan artistic community. To be sure, just as Howells remained suspicious of the influence of romance (as opposed to realism) in everyday life, so too was he skeptical of any aestheticized lifestyle that would mediate and distort the "real." Jonathan Freedman has shown the extent to which Howells demonizes aesthetes within his novels (particularly Beaton in *A Hazard of New Fortunes*), thus implicitly distinguishing realist practice from their elitist, aristocratic affectations. These aesthetes only highlight the solidly bourgeois character of other literary and artistic figures within the novels, and *Hazard* and *Coast* both counter aesthetes with neo-Arcadian Bohemians. Indeed, in his own version of American exceptionalism, Howells represents New York Bohemias that are as "wholesome" and egalitarian as their European counterparts are supposedly degenerate and effete.

If *A Hazard of New Fortunes* has a utopian moment, it is the "common ground" encountered at one New York reception for "clever literary, artistic, clerical, even theatrical people." So refreshingly decorous and unpretentious is this reception that Howells wonders if it was "Arcadia rather than Bohemia." This gathering adumbrates the kind of "American," democratic (and Mugwumpish) public sphere to which Howells hoped to contribute through his own literary practice, and, as such, is worth quoting at length:

> The house was one where people might chat a long time together without publicly committing themselves to an interest in each other except such as grew out of each other's ideas. Miss Vance was there because she united in her catholic sympathies or ambitions the objects of the fashionable people and of the aesthetic people who met there on common ground. It was almost the only house in New York where this happened often, and it did not happen very often there. It was a literary house primarily, with artistic qualifications, and the frequenters of it were mostly authors and artists. . . . There was great ease there, and simplicity; and if there was not distinction, it

> was not for want of distinguished people, but because there seems to be some solvent in New York life that reduces all men to a common level, that touches everybody with its potent magic and brings to the surface the deeply underlying nobody. . . . It is the spirit of the street transferred to the drawing room; indiscriminating, leveling, but doubtless finally wholesome, and witnessing the immensity of the place, if not consenting to the grandeur of reputations or presences. (209–10)

This passage is part of Howells's ongoing response to Matthew Arnold's contention that America lacked "distinction." In an earlier essay, Howells had made a democratic virtue of this ostensible absence, insisting, "somehow, the idea that we call America has realized itself so far that we already have identification rather than distinction."[19] As an "idea" (or ideal), Howells's "America" promotes "solidarity" and the "common" rather than social hierarchies. Throughout his career, Howells tried to maintain and variously embody this "American idea" in his fiction and criticism; yet increasingly, he recognized that such "realist" representations did not correspond to mimetic truth. As we have seen, *The Coast of Bohemia* admits that "American" (there used synonymously with "Arcadian") equality had departed, even from its supposed former element, the small midwestern town of Pymantoning. In both that novel and *Hazard*, however, Howells (improbably enough) relocates Arcadia in New York, particularly among its "aesthetic inhabitants." As the passage quoted above would have us believe, "the spirit of the street" is both leveling and wholesome, and readily transfers itself into the cultivated drawing-room (where "simplicity" and enlightened discourse reign). *Hazard* elsewhere attests to many of the brutalities of urban life, yet in this instance, Howells cannot resist trying to enshrine "the street" as the realization of the American democratic ideal.

In representing an Arcadian Bohemia, Howells voices the romance that animated the Bohemian Club and many a "travel sketch" of the mythic land published in the leading genteel monthlies beginning in the late 1870s. Just as these periodicals guided the upper-middle-class reader through exotic locales around the world, so did they introduce their readers to the outlandish yet paradoxically familiar world of American Bohemia, a terrain they generally located in New York. As we have seen, in such sketches as *Scribner's* "Young Artist's Life in New York," Bohemia emerges as an oasis within the plutocratic desert of the city (see Chapter 3). According to the sketch, Bohemia serves as a purified version of America itself, as a "republic within the republic" in which "social distinctions are not rigidly drawn in this little artistic world" and "nothing is so leveling as community in a great idea."[20] Anticipating Howells (and extending the representations of such Bohemian pioneers as the Pfaffians and Bret Harte), this sketch sees Bohemia as an outpost of democratic community, one capable of "leveling" class-based inequalities.

In *The Coast of Bohemia*, the neo-Arcadian sites are the studio, the art school, and, once again, the Bourgeois-Bohemian reception. Charmian Maybourgh's studio is described as "a kind of Arcadia," and, like Howellsian realism, "innocent" enough for "the apprehension of an American girl" (216–17). Similarly, the art school is a "little republic," and a "natural condition" (108). Arcadia also reconstitutes itself at the Bourgeois-Bohemian dinner table. When the painter Ludlow returns from Ohio to New York (after failing to represent the small-town "common life"), he re-enters his proper element, one that resists the effete yet is still removed from "the Pymantoning point of view." Back in New York, among his peers, Ludlow dines with "painters . . . literary men, lawyers, doctors and their several wives," appreciating all the while "that the time had been with them when they lived closer to the ground, in the simple country towns, as most prosperous and eminent Americans have done" (77). Providing a metonymic link between an earlier, rural existence based on regional identities and a more contemporary, centralized, and metropolitan culture, this dinner party projects a synthesis of past and present Americas, thus enabling the national "idea" to enter modernity. As such, the gathering represents spatial, economic, and cultural mobility as a "common" American inheritance. Bohemia serves as a point of mediation between the old and the new and circumvents the pitfalls of each: neither provincial nor materialistic, it is cultivated without being vicious, simple but not narrow-minded. If Ludlow had failed to represent Pymantoning, it was, so the novel implies, because America (and, by extension, realism itself) now largely belonged to New York.

This, anyway, is how Fulkerson, the publisher and "advertising genius" of *A Hazard of New Fortunes*, expresses the cultural significance of New York. As he tells Basil March: "The great cities draw the mental activity of the country to them, sir. Necessarily New York is the metropolis" (150). And again: "There's only one city that belongs to the whole country, and that's New York" (12). And still again, "There's no subject so fascinating to the general average of people throughout the country as life in New York" (128). Fulkerson also states that "the great mass of the readers are outside of New York" and that "the rural districts are what we have got to go for" (89), but these recognitions only enhance the cultural power of the metropolis. (*Cosmopolitan*, which Howells briefly coedited, served up features detailing the "Wonders of New York"; similarly, *Munsey's* of 1899 gave its readers access to articles like "Broadway's Grenadiers" and "Behind the Scenes in the Big Stores.")[21] Paradoxically enough, though identified with the city, Fulkerson and March's periodical, *Every Other Week*, offered its dispersed audience participation in a mainstream of national culture: New York, as embodied in the periodical form and emanating from its Bohemia, provided a synecdoche for the nation and a solvent for regional difference "from ocean to ocean."[22]

"The metropolis, as such, will always allure writers, and be a stimulus to them." These words are not Fulkerson's but those of Richard Watson Gilder, editor for the *Century*, the most widely circulated among the "traditional" genteel monthlies in the 1880s.[23] In 1886, *Lippincott's Magazine* (published in Philadelphia) concurred:

> That New York . . . is now the center of literary activity can hardly be gainsaid. More than half the solidly established publishing houses are permanently fixed in New York. Nearly all the weekly papers of any weight, and all the foremost monthly magazines, with two or three exceptions only, are issued from New York. . . . There are now more literary men living in and around New York than in or near any other city in America.[24]

Similarly, citing Howells's move from Boston to New York, the *Journalist* asks the rhetorical question: "Why not give the city in which three-fourths of the magazines are published credit for being the literary center?"[25] At a time when periodicals were "the only medium that reached a national audience on a regular basis," New York's status as the literary center endowed it with the capacity to "represent 'America' itself."[26] In many accounts, "Bohemia" was the name of this New York artistic and literary center, and, as such, it appeared to concentrate and control America's rhetorical power. In the words of George Alfred Townsend: "As London stands to the provinces, so stands the empire city to America. . . . It is the end of every young American's aspiration, and the New Bohemia for the restless, the brilliant, and the industrious."[27]

Designated as an artistic center, Bohemia exerted a strong attraction on the rural "margins," both within and without literary narrative. "I wish to go to Bohemia!" announces the titular "pastoral maiden" of Bickford and Powell's *Phyllis in Bohemia* (also discussed in Chapter 3). Phyllis follows Howells's Cornelia Saunders of *A Coast of Bohemia* in her move to the city from "Arcadia" (with the important difference being that Howells's Pymantoning, as we have seen, is a fallen Arcadia). She yearns for *la vie bohème*: "Bohemia—art, letters, poverty, struggling genius, people that make the world, people on the verge of great careers, people toiling to make themselves powers—such is the Bohemia I ask for," Phyllis tells her bemused fiancé, informing him that she must have a sojourn in Bohemian New York before their nuptials (13). And so Phyllis and her fiancé "leave Arcadia," even though he warns her:

> It has no laws, Phyllis, and there are no April days, like this, nor purling, contented brooks, like that yonder, nor skies so blue as that which it seems we may almost touch. And it is a land of dreams—not the dreams that you enjoy when you retire, with the consciousness of a day well spent, not the dreams that take one in fancy over the peaceful valleys and the sublime hills; but dreams, Phyllis, that come from contact with the whirring machinery of humanity, from crowded streets and thronged boulevards, from dens as impure to look upon as is the impure air breathed within them—dreams of a fame that seldom comes, but that seems always nearer and that is finally grasped at only to take wings and fly away. (15–16)

According to Phyllis's fiancé, Bohemia cannot approximate the peace and contentment of Arcadia. The former is phantasmagoric while the latter is the essence of wholesome existence; where Bohemia is a fabrication, Arcadia is the life lived according to the rhythms of nature. Nevertheless, they "leave the pastoral land behind" and move to the "Bohemia" of a New York boardinghouse filled with struggling artists, writers, and musicians. Here, Phyllis and her fiancé encounter representatives from the nation's various regions—New England, the South, and the West—all of whom have also experienced the centripetal force of *la vie bohème* and relocated to New York. The Southerner hails from an aristocratic family, the Westerner writes "cowboy verses," and the New Englander is "thin, pale and earnest." Despite all of their stereotypic regional attributes, this assortment of would-be Bohemians has arrived in New York to pursue their dreams and many of them will "contribute 'space' matter to the newspapers" and the magazines that attempt to suture the nation (56). Phyllis ultimately tires of Bohemia and returns to "Arcadia," but, whereas Bickford and Powell set their "Bohemia" in New York, the Arcadia of the novel does not have any specific location. Phyllis returns, but Arcadia necessarily recedes into the realm of pure myth; it is a place where "from the fields came the music of the evening, and the kine, properly Arcadian, were lowing in gracious accord with all the precedents of poesy" (232).

Howells himself found Bohemia to be an inadequate substitute for Arcadia, and, in the same year that he published *The Coast of Bohemia*, he also produced his first utopian romance of "Altruria." In Howells's socialistic Altruria, cities virtually disappear, though "capitals" remain for "the transaction of public affairs" and as "centers of all the arts." Trains operating at 150 miles per hour permit frequent travel to and from these "centers." Further, each "Region" has its own capital and retains its own integrity (while still upholding national affiliation) so that "now a man is born and lives and dies among his own kindred, and the sweet sense of neighborhood, or brotherhood, which blessed the golden age of the first Christian republic is ours again."[28] As Howells finally recognizes, romance must construct what his realism had hoped to identify and fleetingly had found along the "coast of Bohemia."

Regional *Bohemian*s

Represented by Howells and in features in leading magazines, Bohemia in America had become an artistic and literary center located primarily in New York. It absorbed regional talent and disseminated a nationalized culture through the medium of print. To be sure, magazines like the *Atlantic* and the *Century* embraced literary "regionalism," hoping more adequately to represent each part of the nation. Still, they saw regionalism largely as a means of encouraging cultural reconciliation—in Gilder's words, the "sentiment of nationality."[29] Accordingly, Howells also celebrated "our decentered literature"—particularly when that literature was brought together in Northeastern periodicals. The genteel monthlies thus aspired to do nothing less than help bind each region into a national whole. As Richard Brodhead has observed, regionalism "has as its social background the draining of life from an old agrarian culture to the new cities, and the suppression of local cultures by the new national culture modern transportation and marketing opened up"; according to Brodhead, this culture was also opened by the genteel monthlies, and "in terms of its cultural production the literature of regionalism is a product . . . of the high-cultural establishment" based in the urban Northeast.[30] Regionalism thus enacted the very cultural centralization it seemed to oppose. Similarly, Nancy Glazener has described regionalism (particularly its "writing of the rural") as "the depiction of more 'primitive' or 'simple' subcultures at the periphery of national life for the benefit (and from the vantage point) of the supposedly more modern and sophisticated metropolitan center."[31] As Glazener argues, "regionalism" paradoxically bolstered the national center.

Yet, as Glazener argues, not all regionalisms were superintended by such a center. Alternatively, Glazener suggests, "periodicals that were themselves 'regional'—i.e. not based in northeastern cities—might have provided a better forum for the elaboration of a counterethic and a counteraesthetic of regionalist writing: a regionalist reading of regionalist writing."[32] Given Bohemia's association with New York and its artistic culture, one would not expect *la vie bohème* to be a recurring part of this "counterethic"—at least outside of San Francisco or perhaps Chicago and New Orleans. Surprisingly enough, however, periodicals entitled *The Bohemian* appeared all over the country at the end of the century, and all of them elaborate regional versions of Bohemia, thus claiming for themselves one of the cultural forces that appeared to threaten their identities. Cities such as Richmond, Fort Worth, and Cincinnati all had *Bohemian*s, as did several Eastern cities (also marginalized in relation to the literary center, New York), including Buffalo and Philadelphia. These regional Bohemians did not seek to reconstitute a rural, Arcadian past (though the Buffalo *Bohemian* partakes of Arcadian imagery) but they all resist the centripetal pull of a national culture based in and disseminated from New York.

Connections between Bohemia and the South were particularly strong, and Bohemian-Bourgeois opposition often served to reinforce, if ultimately to displace, the divide between the South and the North. As early as 1863, a Southern periodical named itself *The Bohemian*, and exiled Southern "Bohemians" appear in several postbellum depictions of the American *vie de bohème* (several of which were written by Northerners). Thomas Nelson Page, the foremost plantation mythologizer, dedicated a book of verse to *The Coast of Bohemia*, and a self-professed "Southern" periodical from fin-de-siècle Fort Worth, Texas, seized upon Bohemia to mount its own challenge to Northeastern print-culture. In all of these texts, Bohemia is identified with the South, and works to express and negotiate sectional conflict.

The first American periodical titled *The Bohemian* originated in the South. In 1863, at the height of the Civil War, an issue of this Richmond, Virginia, periodical was published, optimistically declaring itself the first of many to come. No other issue ever appeared. At the same time that Bret Harte was writing his pro-Union Bohemian columns and a group of Northern war correspondents named themselves "the Bohemian Brigade," this Richmond periodical sought to annex the mythos of Bohemia for itself.[33]

A section called "Bohemiana" offers a Southern version of the Bohemian spectator, insisting: "He does not profess to be wiser than the rest of the world, but he does claim to be more observant than most men." This observant Bohemian bemoans the presence in the Confederate capital of a merchant by the name of "Mr. Grindem" (of the house of "Grindem and Squeeze"), a Southern representative of an allegedly Northern commercial ethos. In the Southern context, the magazine implies, the opposition between the Bohemian and the Bourgeois became especially acute, even appearing to underscore the Confederate cause.

Another story in the Richmond *Bohemian* adds a further parallel to the Bohemian-Bourgeois polarity. Entitled "Burnt at the Stake: A Tale of 1692," this story implicitly analogizes Bohemian-Bourgeois opposition to earlier conflicts between the Cavaliers and the Puritans. Describing the Salem witchcraft trials, the story insists that "cruelty, the chief characteristic of the Puritan, reigned supreme"; in contrast, the narrative offers an appealing martyr, a "merry young girl, whose proud aristocratic features at once betokened that she came from a different race—that grand Old Cavalier stock so hateful to the Puritan." Rigid bourgeois Puritans oppress the playful proto-Bohemian Cavaliers, and history repeats itself in the outbreak of the Civil War. Allegedly conducted by the descendents of these different "stocks," the war became newly racialized (in all-white terms) and emerged as just "retribution" for Puritan evil. Thus claiming the Cavalier race and the Confederate cause for Bohemia, the Richmond *Bohemian* further demonstrates how adaptable the romance of Bohemia could be in nineteenth-century America.[34]

During and after the war, several Northern writers elaborated connections between "Bohemia" and the fallen Confederacy. In a satiric account, George Alfred Townsend represents the "Bohemian Days" of a group of Southern "exiles" who resided in the Parisian Latin Quarter throughout the conflict. Their assets frozen, Townsend's exiles had "reached the catastrophe of their decline." Used to a life of expatriate decadence, these plantation heirs became "Bohemians" by default; sudden insolvency reduced their aristocratic excess to Bohemian "dissipation and incontinence." Lamenting his fate, one of Townsend's Confederates cries:

> When I see these nobel spih-its dwelling obscu' and penniless; when I remembah that two short years ago, they waih of independent fohtunes—one with his sugah,

anotha with his cotton, a third with his tobacco, in short, all the blessings of heaven bestowed upon a free people—niggars, plantations, pleasures!—I can but lay my pooah hand upon the manes of my ancestry, and ask in the name of ou-ah cause, is there justice above or retribution upon the earth!

Too cowardly to return home to fight, the "rebel colony" festers in Paris, living a destitute *vie bohème* on dwindling credit and the proceeds of roulette. Crippling debt is the final price of their expropriative "freedom" and antibourgeois animus.[35]

While Townsend associated Bohemia with Confederate shiftlessness and debauchery, Charles De Kay offered a far more romantic linkage. The first American novel to thematize *la vie bohème*, De Kay's *The Bohemian: A Tragedy of Modern Life* (1878) takes place in New York City; however its titular "Bohemian" is a former Southerner, and the novel views his descent as part of his pathos rather than his shame.[36] The young protagonist, De Courcy Plantagenet Lee, refuses Lost Cause bitterness; nonetheless, his Southernness and Bohemianism commingle, spelling his alienation from the "modern life" of New York. He ultimately commits suicide.

Much like Balzac's original "Prince of Bohemia," De Courcy is a dispossessed, displaced aristocrat. A Virginian, he "thought himself of excellent birth" and, according to the novel, "was one of those rare characters in which the word chivalry still appears something more than a hollow word" (6). Nevertheless, De Courcy is condemned to a petit-bourgeois existence: he lives in a "vulgar boarding-house" (8) and works as a "cashier in a large dry-goods house on Broadway," earning his "meagre salary by close attention to work which was neither interesting to him nor recognized as particularly honorable by some people with whom he might otherwise have associated" (6). His father, the "Major," laments "that a son of mine, a member of as fine a family as exists on the face of this globe, should become a counter-jumper!" (19) and De Courcy himself admits that "he was not in his right sphere" (9). With his aristocratic inclinations, De Courcy gravitates toward the one realm available to the superior, disaffected soul: he becomes a Bohemian.

Living in a city in which it was "hard to find . . . any one class of people more than another, upon whom the odious term *bourgeois* could fasten" (27), De Courcy seeks relief from this apparent socioeconomic homogeneity by joining a group called the "Expressionists." The members of this group "claimed to be Bohemians," and they met "in the back-room of a well-known restaurant," a place that "owed its fame to its dinginess and dirt" (22). The novel does not specify the restaurant, though it may well have been modeled on Pfaff's itself, the famous eatery that remained a mecca for would-be Bohemians throughout the 1870s. It is in this "frowsy den" that De Courcy enters the rarified world of "art and literature" (23). Here he seeks "to breathe at times the free air of Bohemia" and identify with "the social band which knows no distinctions save those naturally created by intellect" (34).

Despite De Courcy's own endorsement of these meritocratic sentiments, the novel is not sure about whether a "caste" system is more or less likely to breed the "natural" intellect (35). De Courcy, the "last of a family of slave aristocrats," is also the most authentic Bohemian of the group (64). Though the novel satirizes some of the Bohemians, De Courcy himself is represented as a true poetic soul (even if his work at the dry goods store rarely allows him the time to write poetry). Unlike the pretentious leader of the Expressionists, Harpalion Bagger, De Courcy eschews foppish postures and self-aggrandizing rhetoric; he steadfastly refuses to compromise his honor or chivalric spirit. De Courcy remains a modest clerk only because "he found that to be successful meant to lie," and "he would not lie for his own interest" (99). Even when he is discovered by the beautiful Adelaide Bryce, a member of the "upper or wealthy strata of population of New York," this Southern Bohemian retains his superiority (30). Both as a poet and as "a Lee of Lynchburg," he is "not apt to consider the dollars of New York people . . . of any real importance," and he cannot understand those who "worship material possessions" (59). Only love, the most poetic of emotions, impels De Courcy's courtship of Adelaide. The novel upholds the relative worth of its "Bohemian" in relation to New York high society. Succumbing to the seductions of a stockbroker, Adelaide, the New York haute bourgeoise, finally betrays their love. Her betrayal devastates De Courcy, and he takes his own life by throwing himself in front of the consummate symbol of a relentless modernity: a train. According to the novel, Bohemia is finally too marginalized to absorb the displaced Southerner and integrate him into bourgeois America. Only a textual region can accommodate *The Bohemian.*

From the Richmond *Bohemian* to the fictions of George Alfred Townsend and Charles De Kay, the opposition of the Bourgeois and the Bohemian echoed and restated the divide between the North and South. As these various texts reveal, Bohemia readily mapped itself onto sectional conflicts. Within each account, Southern "Bohemians" hold themselves apart from sordid bourgeois "mudshills," disavowing a wage-based economy. Alternately represented as feckless degenerates and as natural aristocrats, these Bohemians all tried to secede from bourgeois life. Bohemian alienation thus extended Southern exile.

De Kay himself was not a Southerner, however. Indeed, he was professionally and personally connected to several of the most powerful representatives of Northern genteel culture—the very culture that many regional writers and editors would explicitly define themselves against. De Kay parlayed his own Bohemian sympathies into a famed high-society salon, and he became an art critic for the *New York Times*. The salon met in "The Studio," a building De Kay inherited from his brother-in-law, Richard Watson Gilder, the first editor of *The Century* and a noted "genteel" poet. Designed by Stanford White, "The Studio" was a remodeled old stable just off Union Square. First under Gilder, and after 1888 under De Kay, the salon became a staple of literary and artistic gossip columns (favored by the new mass monthlies that ultimately displaced *The Century*) and even society pages. De Kay became a leading representative of New York cosmopolitanism.[37]

The tradition of the Southern Bohemian lived on, however, and at the end of the century, a new periodical revamped the romance of Bohemia for a New South. Insisting that it was "in touch with the French litterateurs who gave [Bohemia] a name,"[38] but situating itself "in the sunny land of Dixie, as it borders on the West,"[39] the Fort Worth *Bohemian* embodied regional aspirations to counteract the cultural dominance of *The Century* and other New York periodicals. The regional press hailed the magazine: "It is well enough to read the writers of cosmopolitan literature if we wish to be informed in regard to the affairs of the world," the *Texas Guide* declared in 1900, "but it is somewhat like a sin to forget the aspirations of those with whom we come in contact every day." In the interest of eradicating this "sin," the *Texas Guide* recommended the new publication, which it described as "an earnest effort for the development of native talent."[40]

This quarterly periodical began in 1899, started by Henrie C. L. Gorman, a tenacious woman who referred to herself as "the little woman in a big hat." Gorman originally hailed from Georgia, and she claimed that her life had been "typical of the Southron who came to maturity during the awful period of the Civil War." As a biographical sketch published in her periodical describes, this awful period compelled the young Gorman to confront the vicissitudes of the literary marketplace and thus to enter Bohemia: "From affluence and a life of ease in her youth, she had to face bereavement of parents and orphanage and wealth swept away, with younger members of her family dependent alone on her exertions as a teacher in the schools of her beloved South-land, and on her ever-busy pen." For Gorman, "Bohemia" first became a practical necessity and then a romance that could vie with postbellum plantation mythology—Confederate-inspired myths Gorman herself helped to circulate by writing "home idyl[s] of long ago in the patriarchal age of the South, when the two races lived in amity."[41]

Gorman's *Bohemian* occasionally featured plantation romances, but it also promised to eschew nostalgia and bring the "South" into modernity. "You are happy in a selection of a name," a Mrs. Tobin-Montague writes from Allendale, South Carolina, recognizing the title's ability to signify the "up-to-date" and cultural "advance."[42] What the trope of Bohemia did *not* signify in the context of the periodical was a conflict with the local bourgeoisie: in fact, they were endorsed by the Fort Worth Board of Trade. In their effort to synthesize the modern and the local within the New South, these self-professed "Bohemians" projected the standard opposition between the Bohemian and the Bourgeois beyond the confines of their city, state, and region. Conversely, in Fort Worth itself, the Bohemian and the Bourgeois existed in strict symbiosis, and were often one and the same. The Fort Worth *Bohemian* strove to become an integral part of the bourgeois New South, and the various responses it garnered (and republished) further elaborate its own self-conception and marketing strategy. For example, the *Texas Guide* applauded the commercial potential of the periodical, concluding (in one of the many promotional blurbs republished in the "Jottings" section of *The Bohemian*) that "there are cogent reasons why 'The Bohemian' should be sustained, foremost among which is the fact that the publication of such a serial in Fort Worth must eventually be of inestimable advantage to the city in affecting its material prosperity."[43] Many editorials called for intensified localism, urging: "Let us begin in the present to use Fort Worth flour, beef, and hams; Fort Worth sauces, catsups, pickles, and preserves; Fort Worth candy, crackers and cakes; Fort Worth beer and cigars, if they must be used at all, let them be Fort Worth made."[44]

The magazine also embraced the prototypical virtues of the nineteenth-century American middle class and its local representatives. True to the goals of such definitive bourgeois movements as Chautauqua, as well as the numerous Browning and Ruskin Societies, the Fort Worth Bohemians define their "object" as "self-improvement."[45] Bohemianism itself could be improved upon, and rendered safe for the bourgeoisie. Leon Mead's essay, "In Bohemia," for example, disavows the "late hours, irregular diet, bad luck, dissipation, spasms of nerve-wrenching toil" associated with earlier Bohemians, insisting, such "may be a satisfactory life for the erratic and homeless, but it is not elevating, much less profitable to a man who has any serious purpose." Mead projects a new, more refined Bohemian: "a man of sterling character."[46] "Our Literary Club in Bohemia" attests to the sterling character of its own local Bourgeois-Bohemians in its "Portrait Gallery." Therein one Dr. J. L. Cooper is touted as a "gentleman of high literary attainments" (in particular, "he is well known as a writer on sanitation"). Another Bohemian, Judge B. R. Webb, is described as a successful legal author, having published works on the criminal law of Texas and record titles; despite his authorship of "prosy legal works," he is also, apparently, a "literateur of the 'airy, fairy Lillian' order." And "though behind the drug counter twelve to sixteen hours a day," the local pharmacist J. P. Brashear nevertheless managed to become a "Bohemian laureate."[47] For "Our Literary Club," The "Bohemian" was experienced as a necessary supplement to the bourgeois.

As in the case of the San Francisco Bohemian Club, such Bohemian-Bourgeois integration might appear to violate the very essence of the "Bohemian" concept. Accordingly, Albert Parry dismissed the Fort Worth *Bohemian* as pure humbug, claiming that it was "neither rakish nor ritzy, but busybody provincial."[48] True enough—and yet, Gorman's Southern Bohemia did not eschew Bohemian-Bourgeois opposition altogether. The periodical defined itself in relation to a still more formidable bourgeois antagonist-competitor: the Northeastern bourgeoisie and its cultural establishment. As Gorman would have it, a Texan-Southern Bohemia would ideally extend *and* overcome sectional conflict, providing a locus for literary competition and potential parity with the North. Far less combative than the Richmond *Bohemian* of 1863, Gorman's turn-of-the-century *Bohemian* encouraged national reconciliation—albeit on Southern terms. In its loftiest imaginings, this Fort Worth magazine would travel throughout the nation, resisting narrow regionalism even as it remained faithful to Southern constituencies. "We can produce the Magazine, will our friends furnish the patronage to cause us to grow and reach out until our name—The Bohemian—becomes a household word in every home in this broad, Heaven-favored land."[49] The "name—The Bohemian" promised to provide a buffer zone between the national and the regional: "There is a kind of 'Free Masonry' between all writers, and especially those of the 'Bohemian' order—and they feel a pride and pleasure in lending their willing assistance in the building of a magazine of which all sections will be proud; —for although this will be, without question, a Southern magazine, we welcome to our pages writers from every clime and nation."[50]

Always "without question, a Southern magazine," the *Bohemian* sought to fortify Fort Worth and the New South against Northeastern cultural supremacy. In particular, it represented itself as a local alternative to both the genteel and popular monthlies of the Northeast, the magazines that were increasingly underwriting the class consciousness of both the established bourgeoisie and the newly minted "professional-managerial class" (PMC).[51] As Jonathan Freedman has argued, "the upwardly mobile, professional, or managerial classes . . . living outside the great cultural centers of the East . . . increasingly sought the social respectability that they associated with the established, early-nineteenth-century 'gentry' elite who dominated the organs of high-cultural expression—the 'genteel' magazines like *Scribner's*, *The Atlantic*, and *The Nation*; the (largely Bostonian) prestige publishing houses; the universities, especially, of course, Harvard." Consequently, "the new elites . . . devot[ed] themselves to the task of cultural improvement with an extraordinary avidity," and "culture [was] experienced as a site of intense competition."[52] The newer popular monthlies, notably *Munsey's* and *McClure's*, had also played important roles in defining the new elites. According to Richard Ohmann, popular magazines in the 1890s "constituted a figurative yet very real cultural space homologous to the literal spaces that came more and more to define the PMC's understanding of itself and its world."[53]

The Fort Worth *Bohemian* laid claim to this cultural space. On a mostly regional scale, the *Bohemian* projected a similar view of progressive development, of the mastery of social, technological, scientific, political and even cultural machineries. Just as *Munsey's* and its ilk functioned as cultural guides for the middle class and its upwardly mobile, professional-managerial elites, so too did the Fort Worth *Bohemian* cultivate "cultural capital," that valuable commodity capable of strengthening fledgling class positions. "We live in a progressive age," Gorman writes, "and we are anxious that our city of over 40,000 souls may not be behind the rest of the world in this age of progress."[54] Bohemia would implicitly serve as an agent of such aspirations, both safeguarding the local and giving it greater visibility.

Gorman's appeal to local contributors, subscribers, and advertisers made explicit the connection between her magazine and her regional politics: "We are proud of our Magazine, we are proud of our Contributors, who have so nobly taken their stand by our side, assisting us in our efforts to make this, 'The Bohemian,' the Magazine of the South, the Magazine of the Future. . . . All are cordially invited to lend a willing hand in this glorious work."[55] Such zealous rhetoric seems somewhat absurd in relation to a magazine that Frank Luther Mott quite rightly describes as "well printed but undistinguished in content" (at least by most formalist criteria).[56] Yet however attributable to Gorman's own idiosyncratic enthusiasms or delusions of grandeur, the urgency of her "Bohemian" crusade was widely embraced throughout the region by correspondents anxious for a Southern answer to East Coast periodicals. "*Harper's*, *Century*, *Munsey's* and others, will soon have to look to their laurels," writes a correspondent from Byran, Texas, expressing many a reader's apparent hope.[57] Gorman's "Jottings" section constantly reiterates this regional will to publication. It is the sheer volume of such testimonials that best reveals the cultural work of Gorman's Bohemia. A republished blurb from the *New Albany Gazette*, New Albany, Mississippi, describes it as "an oasis in the desert of literary matter, furnished by New England"; Texas's *The Vehicle Fashion* calls it "a complete refutation of the idea that a magazine of merit cannot be produced outside of the Eastern cities"; Atlanta's *Saturday Review* insists that it "reflects great credit upon the South"; the *Texas Guide* proudly declares that "*The Bohemian* is fully up to the average magazine published a thousand miles from home and far ahead of anything in its kind in Texas"; and the *Labor Journal* compares it "favorably with the older magazines of the country," even concluding that it "is far ahead of most of them" and that "our people should be proud of such a high grade publication as *The Bohemian*."[58]

Such comments all betray the cultural anxiety that *The Bohemian* proposed to redress. Implicitly, each of these "Jottings" recognizes that the "magazine revolution" of the late nineteenth century exerted a powerful hegemonic pressure, both responding to and redefining the interests and desires of the American bourgeoisie.[59] For the South to participate in this new cultural hegemony, it had to have a "first-class" magazine. Gorman spoke to such desires, and regardless of the quality of her magazine, it seems to have became something of a minor regional cause. Its glossy pages and numerous half-tone engravings signify its determinedly "high grade" status, bearing witness to the Southern quest to establish its own version of the Northern "PMC" elite.

However concerned with becoming first-class and thus metonymizing the aspirations of the local and regional bourgeoisie, the Fort Worth

Bohemian also extolled the virtues of amateurdom—which it implicitly connected to the ethos of the struggling Bohemian writers of the French tradition. This was partly from necessity. As Gorman acknowledges, "our many friends in the literary world 'donate' their contributions" and "we have no 'usual rates' to 'remit.'"[60] Gorman represents such "donations" as a charitable contribution, as part of the "Strenuous Efforts of Magazine Building in the South."[61] Yet it was precisely its amateurdom that gave the magazine one of its self-professed advantages over the Northeastern behemoths. Much as Gorman and her "Bohemians" fantasized about competing with the likes of *Munsey's* and *The Century*, they also recognized that the virtue of their magazine depended on the fact that it was *not* commercially viable. When a correspondent writes "*The Bohemian* fills a long felt want—that of a good 'home-made' periodical" capable of standing amongst the "first-class magazines," she reveals the often contradictory yearnings of Gorman's Bohemia.[62] The phrase "long felt want" was quickly becoming an advertising cliché, one used in the national marketing campaigns of the mass-manufactured goods featured in the popular monthlies; such commodified "wants" increasingly militated against the "home-made," a phrase that the correspondent herself destabilizes between quotation marks. Much like Gorman herself, this correspondent alternately wants to protect the amateur and the regional and to enter the national marketplace.

The odd conjunction between Bohemia and regional politics should not be understood as the idiosyncratic whim of one Henrie C. L. Gorman. Remarkably enough, the Fort Worth *Bohemian* had several predecessors, all of which used the word *Bohemian* in their titles. These periodicals also sought to perform similar cultural work, and in regions other than the South. One of the Fort Worth periodical's more ambitious counterparts hailed from the Midwest, and it too fashioned itself as a cultural bulwark against the Northeast. This magazine, *The New Bohemian: A Modern Monthly*, was published in Cincinnati, Ohio, by the Bohemian Publishing Company, and it posed the question:

> "Does the West really need a magazine?" To this we will answer most emphatically, yes! Genius knows no geographical limitations. Literature and art are universal. While the center of population is moving swiftly Westward, the center of culture, of literature and art is as rapidly changing its frontiers. Why should the West receive its literature only from publishers of the Eastern seaboard? Does not the West need

> within its own borders a publication that will creditably represent its literature and art, its social interests and industrial progress—a fresh and vigorous magazine breathing the ozone of its vast plains, stamped with the individuality of its people, and strong with the local color of its soil? Why should the mighty West, unmindful of its strength, forever bow its head in the lap of the Delilah of the East?[63]

According to *The New Bohemian*, the West not only needed a magazine, it needed a "high-class home magazine." It needed *The New Bohemian*. So set against the "publishers of the Eastern seaboard" was this periodical that the contemporary *New York Press* marveled at the "frank ferocity of its attitude toward the effete East in literature." The *Press* concluded that such "Occidental profanations of Oriental etiquette needs explanation or demands investigation sociologically."[64]

Like the Fort Worth *Bohemian*, this literary periodical self-consciously embraced "Bohemia," connecting the mythic terrain to its editorial goal of combining the regional and the modern. For this magazine, the "Bohemian" (not to mention the "New Bohemian") and the "modern" were synonymous, and the subtitle, "A Modern Monthly" thus restated the title. However tautological, the publication constantly reiterated this equation. As a representative of Bohemian modernity, the periodical claimed to break with tradition and outworn cultural conventions. Self-referentiality also governed the contents of the magazine, and many of the stories, poems, and articles represent Bohemia itself: "The Woman Bohemian," "A Night in Bohemia," "Bohemian Simplicity: A Scene," "In Bohemia," "Bohemia and Her Herald," "Bohemia's Land," "The Old and New Bohemia," "The Borders of Bohemia," "The Prince of Bohemians," "Charles Hote, Bohemian," "Bohemia and Its People," and so on. Still, though the periodical aspired to the modern "sparkle of Bohemia," *la vie bohème* of *The New Bohemian* was relatively tame—"A Night in Bohemia," for example, eschews the Bohemia of "long hair and soiled finger-nails and vulgar grisettes" in favor of "a cozy, home-like Bohemia with the Little Woman to do propriety."[65] Nonetheless, the periodical passed over "Bible and Temperance Stories" (a mainstay of the Fort Worth *Bohemian*); instead, such fin-de-siècle, "decadent" topics as extramarital desire, independent women, anarchism, the occult, and eastern mysticism made their way into its contents. In such pieces, the magazine sought to be "up-to-date," to transcend the provincial, and align itself with the Bohemians, that "tribe of young rebels who are making the welkin ring in these end-of-century days."[66]

Yet the periodical did not seek to dissolve the regional into the modern. Far racier than the Fort Worth *Bohemian*, *The New Bohemian* nevertheless derived most of its oppositional energy from the same source: an aggressive regionalism. Substitute the "West" for the "South," and many of the editorial pronouncements and published correspondence in the two magazines are interchangeable. "Boston is no longer the Mecca of thought or New York the Jerusalem of Journalism," *The New Bohemian* insisted. "The mighty West, where genius so long has slumbered, has at last awakened and with the vigor of a giant refreshed."[67] Taking the form of *The New Bohemian*, this vigorous giant portended no less than "a movement for the literary emancipation of the West."[68] As in the case of Fort Worth, the regional press endorsed this editorial mission, and *The New Bohemian* republished a series of hyperbolic tributes in every issue. "Does the reader of the *Review* know that our own Cincinnati is the home of a first-class magazine?" asked the Cleveland *Review*, thus uniting the causes of *The New Bohemian* and the region:

> *The New Bohemian* is not quite a year old yet, but it has come to be recognized as at least equal to the old "standards." There is a Western freedom and dash about it . . . while its strength and refinement commend it to all truly cultured people. It is the duty of our good people to support this excellent publication, not merely because it is published outside of New York and Boston, but because it is not hampered by the close-corporation spirit of the Eastern press, and particularly because it is one of the very best of the many purely literary publications.[69]

Both Western and refined, cultivated and inclusive, *The New Bohemian* (according to the *Cleveland Review*) challenged the cultural hegemony of Eastern publishing. Many contributors, correspondents, and, we might imagine, the editor himself, had been wounded by this "closed-corporation," thus making the identification with Bohemia and its struggling artists all the more apt. (In the words of one: "I then wrote another serial—spent all my leisure time for a year upon it: sent it to the *Century*; it was returned unread.")[70] When fused with regional politics, such individual disappointments translated into the mighty indignation voiced on the pages of *The New Bohemian*. The divides between the amateur and the professional, the regional and the national, the modern and the traditional, and the Bohemian and the Bourgeois all echoed and reinforced each other.

Within and without the Midwest, many a magazine in the 1890s employed a similar rhetoric of the "New," even as they (much like *The New Bohemian*) adhered to some of the old genteel "standards." For example, such periodicals as *Munsey's*, *McClure's*, and *Cosmopolitan*, those most frequently cited as the vanguard of the "magazine revolution," initially pitched themselves as popular versions of the traditional genteel monthlies or "quality magazines"; increasingly, however, they distinguished both their form and contents from those of their predecessors and emphasized up-to-the-minute journalism. "Dead subjects are good enough for dead people, but not for the wide awake American," Frank Munsey declared from his "Publisher's Desk."[71] Although located on the East Coast, *Munsey's* "Publisher's Desk" often bolstered its claim to timeliness with recourse to the opposition between East and West, professing to convey the "unconventional spirit" of the latter (located, presumably, in the mythic frontier rather than in Cincinnati). A contemporary critic thus summed up many of the claims of the new popular magazines when he wrote that *Cosmopolitan* (also located in New York) had "a true Western adaptability, fertility of resource and quickness in seizing a point, all of which tend to dismay the more staid eastern mind."[72] *The New Bohemian* echoed such rhetoric and of course, its "Westernness" was more than metaphoric.[73] Nonetheless, the fact that *Munsey's* and others used regional tropes in this way must have provoked the Western Bohemians, both enhancing their confidence and confirming their desire to claim their own cultural territory.

Still, though embracing the "thoroughly up-to-date" (and also costing only ten cents an issue), *The New Bohemian* did not set out to become a Western version of *Munsey's*, any more than it modeled itself on the *Atlantic*. (Indeed, it editorialized that "*Munsey's* has come to be a periodical insult to intelligence and good taste.")[74] *The New Bohemian* combined elements of these far more illustrious periodicals, yet it also set its sights upon another trend in 1890s magazine publishing: the "little magazine." Little magazines first burst onto the American scene in 1894, inspired in large part by *The Yellow Book*, a self-consciously Bohemian and decadent periodical launched by Henry Harland, an American expatriate in Paris. Defying both genteel censorship and commercial dictates, *The Yellow Book* sought a third path. In the United States, notable successors included *The Chap-Book*, *The Philistine*, *The Lark*, and *M'lle New York*, and similar imitations abounded (*Every Other Week*, the fictitious periodical of *A Hazard of New Fortunes*, anticipated such aesthetic magazines). In the words of Larzer Ziff, "*The Yellow Book* galvanized bored illustrators, ambitious story-writers, defeated poets, cynical subeditors, and alert literary jokesters, and overnight every American city had its magazine."[75] To varying extents, such magazines courted rebelliousness and eccentricity, reveling in arcane diction and "aesthetic" design, extolling scandalous European writers, and searching for young native talents. Not all of these publications defined themselves as "decadent" (some even shunned the term) but all, as *The New Bohemian* decreed, hoped to challenge "the accepted canons of staid magazinedom."[76] Accordingly, Gelett Burgess of *The Lark* (whose "Map of Bohemia" is discussed above) characterized the movement as a "revolt against the commonplace," one that "aimed to overthrow the staid respectability of the larger magazines and to open to younger writers opportunities to be heard before they had obtained recognition from the autocratic editors."[77]

The New Bohemian drew upon the example of both the popular and avant-garde periodicals in its own challenge to the established literary tribunals. "Between the jejune inanity of Bokish exploitation [Edward Bok was then the editor of the popular *Ladies' Home Journal*] and the hectic apex of decadent ribaldry there is a mean, native to rectilinear thought," the magazine insisted.[78] This healthy "mean," of course, emanated from the Midwest, taking the form of none other than the *New Bohemian*, a "fresh and vigorous magazine breathing the ozone of [the West's] vast plains, . . . drawn from the fecund mind of gifted unknowns."[79] In its own view of little magazine "decadence," decay resided in the East and freshness in the West.[80]

Fusing regional politics and an aestheticized "revolt against the commonplace," *The New Bohemian* made explicit many of the cultural dynamics that structured American responses to late-nineteenth-century British aestheticism. One of the more remarkable aspects of American aestheticism, Jonathan Freedman notes, was its "extraordinary proliferation . . . in wholly unexpected areas of the country." According to Freedman, aestheticism thrived in such places, in part because of the role it played in the social competition between traditional Northeastern gentry elites and the emerging professional managerial classes. At a time when the gentry elite remained suspicious of such British aesthetes as Walter Pater and Oscar Wilde, many upwardly mobile middle Americans responded favorably to aestheticism. While Charles Eliot Norton and other influential genteel figures objected to the lack of moral content in the doctrine of "art for art's sake," emerging elites seized upon aestheticism as a more or less subversive affront to, or version of, gentry high culture. Since British aestheticism both developed out of and partially radicalized the same Romantic-Victorian literary tradition that informed American gentry culture, regional elites could use aesthetic doctrines both to challenge and to lay claim to status-bound cultural authority. This is how Freedman accounts for the spread of little magazines in the Midwest and West; for the fact that Oscar Wilde, during his 1882 tour of the United States, had been more enthusiastically received outside of Eastern cultural centers; and for none other than Cincinnati having the most prominent center for "aesthetic" ceramic design.[81] Particularly among young, often college-educated Midwesterners (this period saw the opening of land-grant universities throughout the West and Midwest), aestheticism promised both to redress the cultural limitations of the region and to question entrenched authorities.[82] As we have seen, the Fort Worth *Bohemian* also embraced regional competition and identified itself with PMC progress, but it lacked the tinge of aestheticism that made *The New Bohemian* and other little magazines more distinct and challenging cultural agents.

Still, Freedman complicates the East-West, old elite–new elite dichotomies, recognizing that, to somewhat different degrees, both regions and groups sought to "normalize aestheticism, to admit it into the canon of the 'cultural' by stripping it of its subversive power."[83] *The New Bohemian* also, at times, tamed or "normalized" the related phenomenon of *la vie bohème*, and, once again, the "Bohemian" often capitulated to the Bourgeois. Like many previous Bohemians, *The New Bohemian* tried to justify the movement by muting its threat, and by representing Bohemianism as an extension of dominant bourgeois mores—if also a privileged, "higher" expression of those values and one more tailored to the particular needs of the professional-managerial bourgeois. Thus, Bohemians were "unconventional," but "not as crude minds seem to think . . . for they would not break down one single good convention, or one of the delicate barriers which guard the real proprieties or help to protect society from the license of the uncouth." Upholding the construction of the "Good Bohemian" (see Chapter 3), the periodical claimed that because the Bohemians "have arrived at a higher stage of evolution, where, being sure of refined instincts, they feel that they can safely dispense with some of the outer forms, so essential for the unformed, uncultured soul, and can live and act by the higher law of the spirit."[84] This definition of Bohemianism left room for rebellion (exactly what counted as a "good convention" or "real propriety" remained vague) while placating moralistic critics.

By and large, this strategy of purifying, even spiritualizing, Bohemia seems to have satisfied "Bohemian" and "Bourgeois" readers alike, as well as those who did not see the two categories as mutually exclusive. For example, *Watson's Illuminator* (from Boston, no less) noted that the periodical was "tinged with a mild Bohemian flavor not unpleasant even to the Philistines," and the *Sioux City* (Iowa) *Journal* claimed that "the contributions are all unconventional, all bright and breezy, all written with evident freedom from all restraint, and the effect on the reader is wholesome." And, despite this wholesome mildness, this sanitary modernism, self-professed Bohemian artists such as this correspondent from West Virginia continued to write glowing affirmations: "I admire *The New Bohemian* very much. An artist, my life devoted to art, believe me, *The New Bohemian* is the magazine for that wonderful borderland where the artist loves to live, to strive and dream."[85]

Other correspondents made similar connections between the modern, the Bohemian, the unconventional, and the wholesome, suggesting that such equations had become commonsensical by the 1890s. The editors strengthened this chain of meaning by expunging more decadent or "vulgar" correlatives, including those that suggested East Coast ethnic and working-class quarters or mass cultural entertainments: "Out upon the pretender who would drag Bohemia's banner through the mire of the beer cellar, or flaunt its colors amid the foul smoke of cheap tobacco! Shame to him who would place an indecent word or a blasphemous oath upon the lips of the true Bohemian!" And addressing a critical correspondent, the editors railed, "What does he imagine Bohemia is anyway—a Bowery ball?"[86] Perhaps protesting too much, the periodical also spoke out against the "Decadent School" in art and poetry, claiming that the former was headed by Aubrey Beardsley, "who corrupts the excellent influence of the Japanese," and the latter by Verlaine, "who, in his larger hours of life, set an example that is like to ruin half the fledgling poets of the world."[87] The *New Bohemian* thus exorcised more radical versions of its own modernity.

Beyond its distance from more decadent Bohemias (and the East Coast), much of the perceived wholesomeness of the periodical inhered in its ability to accommodate modern PMC lifestyles and aspirations. As a periodical called the *Medical Gleaner* attested, *The New Bohemian* could contribute, most concretely, to PMC success: "One of the neatest things on earth a doctor or any other professional man can do, is to keep one or two good magazines lying on the table of his waiting room. It is notable that the more catchy and attractive the periodicals thus exposed are, the better it is all around, and the *Bohemian* is catchier than fly-paper."[88] Flaunting its ungenteel colloquialisms, the *Medical Gleaner* thus claimed

Bohemia as a business strategy for upwardly mobile middle-class Americans and their professional commerce. Similarly, some praised the magazine for its modern, efficient use of time and money. Unlike the traditional monthlies, The *New Bohemian*, they implied, did not require genteel leisure or independent wealth: it is "worth the time and money expended on it"; and "the casual reader gets a full return for his investment and not a collection of incomplete rot that can have little or no interest for one seeking an hour's pleasure or respite from everyday cares."[89] The phrase "incomplete rot" seems to refer to serialized fiction, once a mainstay of the genteel monthlies and a practice that the more popular monthlies eschewed in favor of readily digestible short stories. A notice from the Memphis *Commercial Appeal* makes the comparison even more explicit, declaring, "The crisp, pithy articles of this monthly are refreshing in comparison with the padded stuff one often comes across in the older magazines."[90]

Unsurprisingly, in keeping with its timely appeal to professional-managerial values, *The New Bohemian* sought to circumvent both the meandering "indirection" of genteel prose and the decadence of art for art: "As the chief characteristic of the Old Bohemia was indirection, so is 'Purpose' the watchword of the New Bohemia. . . . To strive, to achieve, to uplift is his constant thought,"[91] the periodical announced, using the very idiom of PMC success. *The New Bohemian* recognized that some still objected to its "morals," but it did its best to assuage such critics and accommodate itself to emerging professional-managerial ideologies. Such accommodation might seem to conflict with the magazine's interest in "amateur" Midwestern writers, but it is congruent with the PMC's interest in opening and expanding (if also formalizing) positions of professional status.[92] Championing "fledgling" writers over and against the "closed-corporation" of established talents, the periodical did not object to professionalized authorship as such, but instead sought to open the profession to more aspirants. In this way, the magazine supported a central tenet of PMC ideology: it would help to structure bourgeois social mobility—though without succumbing to geographic rootlessness.

Dedicated to the overlapping causes of regional development and the upward mobility of the PMC, *The New Bohemian* nonetheless had a mixed response to Cincinnati, its urban base, as well as to Chicago, the Midwestern metropolis par excellence. Whereas the Fort Worth *Bohemian* unequivocally endorsed local boosterism, *The New Bohemian* occasionally lashed out against both its own city and Chicago. Its regional rewriting of the Bohemian-Bourgeois dichotomy was thus more complex than the Fort Worth *Bohemian*'s: it did not entirely displace Bohemian and Bourgeois opposition onto the divide between region and nation. Instead, Cincinnati and Chicago often appear in the magazine as the very embodiments of the dreaded bourgeois. While celebrating PMC "purpose," *The New Bohemian* also raged against the usual bourgeois suspects: materialism, conformity, and conservatism. Its periodic outbursts against these Midwestern cities seem to correlate with the reception of the magazine and its wavering financial fortunes (this narrative must be inferred, though we do know that the periodical only existed for roughly one year). In February of 1896, the periodical complained:

> The Cincinnati hog is as much in evidence as is the Chicago porcine, but he is of the biped variety. The bristles of this ungodly beast stood angrily erect upon the appearance of the initial number of *The New Bohemian*, and ever since he has unceasingly grunted his disapproval. . . . Cincinnati would not welcome a literary venture emanating from Chicago or any other Western city. She worships forever at the altar of the East.

As a result, "The prophet who would gather the fragrant nosegays of well-won honor should take a vacation. To wear the plug hat of popular approval he must get an exodus on himself."[93]

According to *The New Bohemian*, the divide between the East and the Midwest had severed the material and the cultural, segmenting them into discrete locations on the national grid. Anticipating such chroniclers of Midwestern alienation as Sinclair Lewis, Floyd Dell, and Sherwood Anderson, *The New Bohemian* set itself against what it perceived as the materialistic, provincial, and conservative elements of its regional culture. It is in relation to the idea of "getting an exodus" from one's society that the cultural work of *The New Bohemian* became most urgent. Bohemia, that mythic land of exile, presented itself as a possible solution, a means of healing social ruptures. Only Bohemia could mediate between culture and society, art and commerce, the alienated individual and the Midwest, the region and the nation. Only Bohemia could transcend "geographical limitations" while retaining local allegiances. Opposing both the cultural dominance of the East and "all that is mean and narrow" in Cincinnati and Chicago, the magazine aspired to the "higher culture" of Bohemia.[94]

Thus, with respect to Chicago, a city of "cowardly and provincial conformity," one Eva Katherine Clapp (who claimed to be a distant relative of none other than Henry Clapp, the "King of Bohemia" during the reign of the Pfaffians) wrote of her hopes for a Bohemian Chicago. "We believe that our 'New Bohemia' means the ushering in of a better day, a time when Chicago shall have so thoroughly cast off her swaddling clothes as to be able to take her place intelligently among the great cities of the world," Clapp declared. She admitted that this was "very far from being the state of affairs now," and she charged Bohemia with the role of instigating this cultural transformation. If Chicago ever achieved true sophistication, she specified, it would be "due to the efforts of no man's or woman's club, no matter how great the wealth of its individual members; not to any church, no matter how eloquent its pastor; but to those terrible people, the Iconoclasts, the Bohemians, who tear down idols, think for themselves, speak the truth about a badly painted picture, no matter how much its owner may have paid for it."[95] With respect to Cincinnati, *The New Bohemian* expressed a similar hope: "We have received the encouragement and support, necessarily limited, of [Cincinnati's] best and brainiest people. And though the swine may trample our pearls, we shall remain steadfastly loyal to the Queen City and shall ever seek to advance her loftier interests and vindicate her claim as a centre of culture, of literature and art."[96]

Further, unlike the Fort Worth *Bohemian*, *The New Bohemian* resisted the regional coupling of Bohemian and Bourgeois. At times endorsing PMC values and taming *la vie bohème*, the periodical nonetheless alternated between local boosterism and condemnation. One editorial praised Cincinnati as an emerging art center, noting that "her splendid schools and magnificent Museum are enduring monuments to the city's culture, the priceless private collections of her citizens are eloquent testimonials to the same, while her artists have found the shores of every land and their brushes have laid the colors of a fadeless fame."[97] Yet, just two months later, in its final issue, the editors issued this bitter response to a correspondent: "Replying to your query: 'Is there a Bohemia in Cincinnati?' we will say that there is not. The very meaning of the word 'Bohemia' has been lost here—if, in fact, it was ever known. This is the most cursedly conservative and cowardly conventional community on all God's verdant footstool."[98] On the verge of extinction, *The New Bohemian* attributed its failure to the provincialism it had tried to mitigate. Instead of healing the divide between region and nation, the periodical finally surrendered to it.

New Women and the "Borders of Bohemia"

In both the Fort Worth and Cincinnati *Bohemians*, the "borders of Bohemia" also helped to mediate between "old" and "new" definitions of womanhood, enabling the modernity of the "New Woman" to enter regional cultures. Many women contributors seized upon the mythos of Bohemia to articulate a progressive feminist politics, and their writings help to revise our existing conceptions of "regionalism" and women's writing. Focusing on such figures as Jewett and Freeman, some feminist readings of late-nineteenth- and early-twentieth-century women regionalists have located these writers within a transhistorical women's culture. Yet, as Nancy Glazener has observed, "feminist readings shaped by the politics of the 1970s tended to overemphasize and universalize the utopian possibilities of the female-dominated spaces, benevolent matriarchs, and domestic expertise that they found in regionalist works, isolating these features from the historical circumstances in which they functioned."[99] The women's writing found in the Bohemian periodicals helps to supply another perspective on regional women writers, demonstrating the extent to which many sought to embrace the modernity of the "New Woman" and to move outside of traditional women's spheres—precisely the spaces that have often been conflated with regional identities.[100]

For many correspondents, the very existence of the Fort Worth *Bohemian* represented the triumph of New Womanhood. Spearheaded by Gorman, the periodical embodied a "grand triumph for women in journalism," according to Miss Fannie May Gibbs from Wortham, Texas.[101] From Omaha, another correspondent noted, "Here is another example of a woman showing her ability to manage business enterprises when given an opportunity."[102] From Humphreys, Louisiana, still another applauded, "Your work proves you to be one of the great women of the country, an independent, brave, self-respecting woman of brains, living your own life."[103] And all the way from England, another woman wrote, "Though compelled for the present to live in this slow-moving country, I am as one with the American woman [Gorman] whose motto is 'to dare and to dare and to dare again.' "[104] The *El Paso News* commended the periodical as the "only magazine in the South or West published by a woman; and, insisting that "women's worth in the field of modern literature is not fully appreciated," the *American Home Journal* declared Gorman "a star in the galaxy of women who love literature and have been successful in the paths of literary endeavor. She possesses in a marked degree those rare essentials to literary success—i.e. knowledge, talent, and a capacity for hard labor."[105]

For her part, Gorman celebrated other women who managed to navigate between "old" and "new" conceptions of womanhood. Describing a Mrs. William King, the president of the Georgia Press Club and a writer of a regional newspaper's "women's and juvenile page," Gorman declared that "in her are combined the best elements of the old as well as the 'new woman.' " Even with all her "multifarious duties," Gorman writes, "she is an ideal wife, mother, grandmother and great-grandmother. She thoroughly disproves that antique, but rapidly growing extinct, masculine theory that a business woman cannot be a womanly woman." Gorman also describes a Mrs. Julia Iverson Patton who

> is essentially feminine and a refined and gracious lady, but she is advanced in her views and believes that when a woman must work she should have the entrée to any of the professions or occupations for which she is fitted by nature or training. She believes in the justice of women's suffrage, is an ardent socialist and is interested in all the subjects that promise to make the twentieth century the turning point in the history of the human race.[106]

Bridging traditional and modern definitions of femininity even as it negotiated between region and nation, Gorman's *Bohemian* insisted upon the simultaneity of the "womanly woman" and the "business woman." In this regard, Gorman was "in advance" of many of the national magazines: during this period, the *Ladies' Home Journal* published editorials warning that New Women sought to "repudiate their womanhood, become sexless" and that the "over-discussion of the woman in business" had a "disastrous effect" on the female psyche.[107] As noted in Chapter 3, the *Journal* specifically warned women about the "dangerous land" of Bohemia. Indeed, several *Journal* articles focus on the specific threat that Bohemia posed to "The Girl Who Lives in a Small Town," insisting that enticing tales about "the delightful Bohemian atmosphere of den and studio" compel the small town girl to long "to be there in the art centres"; and yet she leaves her "comfortable home" at her own peril, "for her pure, white soul does not realize or know that even the outer coast of that Bohemia is filled with quicksands out of which many women never step on to the strong rock of perfect womanhood again."[108]

The Cincinnati *New Bohemian*, however, encouraged the longings that the *Ladies' Home Journal* sought to suppress. In one issue, Eva Katherine Clapp proclaims:

> There is something sacred to me in that word Bohemia—something that makes my cheek flush, my heart beat quicker and my hand tremble. It seems to me that I can claim a little corner in the dear realm as my very birthright, for the mother who bore

me was one of the noblest and truest Bohemians I have ever known. Artist and poet, she broke her heart beating against the bars of petty conventionality in the little ignorant frontier community, where it was deemed a more fitting thing that a woman should be able to swing the mop or manipulate the rolling-pin than to appreciate the glorious prairie sunsets or read Shakespeare's plays.

Clapp claimed Bohemia as an alternative cultural space, one that existed apart from the overlapping constraints of gender and provinciality. She ends her essay by affirming John Boyle O'Reilly's popular recitation piece, "In Bohemia": "And I'd rather live in Bohemia / Than any other land."[109] Celebrating *la vie bohème*, another female contributor identifies "Bohemia's Land" as the place where she might move, in Eve Sedgwick's phrase, "across gender and across sexuality":

> Oh! sing of a saffron-scented pipe
> That a man may smoke at his ease,
> In a dingy den where the dust lies ripe
> And the spiders do as they please!
> Let others shorten in dull home lives
> Their hair and their liberty,
> And be constrained at the word of their wives—
> Bohemia's land for me!
>
> . . .
>
> Oh, sing of the pretty girls we've kissed
> And the jolly days when we dined,
> With only a laugh for the dinners missed
> And the girls to our loves unkind;
> With hearts as light as our pocket's freight,
> We scorn all satiety,
> And laugh in the face of fickle fate—
> Bohemia's land for me!"[110]

Taking on a male persona, and with it female sexual objects, Eve Brodlique imagines "Bohemia's land" as the site where she might transcend the expectations of normative femininity. In a period just before many female modernists would adopt male dress as a deliberate act of political provocation, this writer performed her own act of literary cross-dressing.[111]

Yet it was in the regular feature "The Borders of Bohemia," written by "the Woman Bohemian," that the periodical most committed itself to the redefinition of womanhood. In this section, Elizabeth Cherry Haire appeals to Bohemia as the ground for the "emancipation of woman from the mountain of custom and conventional rubbish that has been piled upon her":[112]

> Hark! what is it the world waits to hear? It is the laugh of the woman who dwells on the Borders of Bohemia,—she, the Free Thinker, the world's daring one. Is there not a thrill in it that is even as the thrust of a keen lance used playfully? It is bright and tantalizing and it rouses opposition even in lazy minds—opposition, censure, anything but peace and calm, which in these days must be looked for only in convent gardens. The Woman Bohemian cares not, for she is walking on the borders of that enchanted land—the true Bohemia—and has naught to do with that gnarly wood with many and devious paths called the world.[113]

With the archaic "hark" signaling the realm of the aesthetic, a high-cultural sphere above and beyond convention, Haire invokes Bohemia as the "enchanted" place wherein she might wield a priapic "lance" or pen. In "The Borders of Bohemia," she also applauds concrete advances in women's rights: "The women are fairly besieging the higher institutions of learning." Further, in another essay, Haire apparently endorses women's suffrage: "Enfranchisement may be the one step forward, O ye of yearning, which will bring to a yearning heart the sight of the promised land from the Delectable Mountains."[114] Though she does not specify what form the great abstraction "Enfranchisement" must take, her words resonate with those of contemporary suffragettes. Combining feminism and aestheticism (an ever unstable mixture, as I discuss below), Haire uses the trope of Bohemia to imagine a space of female liberation—though the title and content of her column emphasize the extent to which the adjacent territory impinged upon "The Borders of Bohemia."

Several months after Haire joined the staff of the periodical, the editors issued a statement about her column. Previously, the editors had not identified her apart from her pseudonym "The Woman Bohemian," yet they claimed that they had been "so besieged with letters of inquiry from persons desirous of learning the identity of the 'Woman Bohemian' that [they were] forced to make a statement in self-protection." The editors do not say if any of the letters they received were critical of the column—the only letter they quote is from someone who gushes about the "onward sweep of [Haire's] vervy, compelling pen"—yet the overall gist of the editorial is defensive, seeking to contract and patrol "The Borders of Bohemia." While ostensibly affirming the column and declaring it a resounding success, the editors nonetheless establish Bohemia as an inviolate "separate sphere," one in which "broad-minded, high-thinking, progressive and liberal women" might still subscribe to many of the Victorian norms of the "cult of true womanhood."[115]

First, the editors somewhat mute the radicalism of the column by revealing that it was they who had first approached Haire with the idea "that she adopt the pen name of 'The Woman Bohemian' and conduct for *The New Bohemian* a department that would prove of special interest to . . . liberal women." In so doing, the editors suggest that, as the "Woman Bohemian," Haire merely fulfilled male editorial requirements. Still, they insist that "the suggestion received her instant approval" and that "the results have demonstrated alike the value of the idea and the ability of Mrs. Haire to lead her sisters into the fields of untrammeled freedom—freedom of Thought, Speech and Conscience." But they give and then they take away:

> In the short space of four months she has achieved a leadership among her sex to which the foremost agitators of Equal Rights may aspire in vain. She has maintained and proved that Bohemia is the only place in all the world where woman may claim her truest rights—where the sexes can meet on a real equality. Not in the fierce strife of political contention nor within the contaminating circle of the polling-place shall womanhood come to her own; but in the rare realm of Bohemia, where alone is lofty courage, where high honor rules and chivalry still survives—there may the fair anadem of Equal Rights replace the thorny circlet of subjection with which she was crowned in Eden.[116]

Safely confined to this honorable Bohemia, women's "untrammeled freedom" no longer sounds like much of a threat. The "sexes can meet on a real equality," but, paradoxically, "chivalry still survives." Moreover, the editors reassure readers, "In Bohemia woman may be natural and still be chaste." With Bohemia so conservatively defined, the editors pose the rhetorical question: "who doubts that in Bohemia there is a place for woman?"[117]

As constructed by this editorial, "Bohemia" largely reconstitutes the ideology of a separate woman's sphere, one in which women diffuse "culture and refinement" and thus redeem the stultifying effects of the "male" marketplace. Explicitly aligning this sphere with the Aesthetic Movement, the editors credit "the Woman Bohemian" with "lift[ing] Bohemia to a loftier plane" and offering "the pleasures of aesthetic Bohemia, a Bohemia of culture and refinement—the direct antithesis of the popular conception of what constitutes Bohemianism, born of the teachings of Murger and his school of brilliant debauchees."[118] While upholding the value of this feminized "aesthetic Bohemia," the editors nonetheless curb its challenge to traditional male hegemony. As Roger B. Stein has argued, aesthetic ideology often posited women's skills in the arts to be "an expression of their 'natural' abilities, their female instincts." Stein admits that aestheticism "offered opportunities for work—new creative outlets for social and aesthetic productivity—to middle-class women," yet he also recognizes the extent to which it reified existing views of female "nature." Succinctly stated by a male faculty member of the Art Academy of Cincinnati, this ideology maintained that: "The nature endowed aptitude of most women makes them the ready exponents of the creed-beautiful, placing their loving labor upon [a] high plane."[119] Such was the plane on which the editors of the *New Bohemian* sought to place the "Woman Bohemian," simultaneously elevating her and containing her more radical energies.

Haire never openly contradicted this editorial. She had in fact resigned herself to the limitations of Bohemia in an earlier essay: "I will strive, though a woman, to be a partner in my own uplifting. If in Bohemia, so be it."[120] Recognizing the limitations of Bohemia (at least as it was defined by her editors), she nonetheless claimed this space as her own.

Region and "the Significance of the Term Bohemian"

As the examples of Fort Worth and Cincinnati attest, these regional *Bohemians* bore considerable symbolic baggage. Alternately representing women's emancipation, cultural uplift, geographic mobility, modern lifestyles, and regional difference, Bohemia functioned as a mythic topography, existing both within and without the nation and its regions. As such, Bohemia offered an escape from provincialism, all the while protecting the regional "margins" from the national "center" (and even, in some versions, elevating the margins to that center). From Cincinnati to Fort Worth, the naming of a club or periodical "the Bohemian" signified a complex act of self-positioning, one that negotiated between the local and the cosmopolitan, the traditional and the modern, the regional and the national. In the end, of course, these periodicals could not compete with the national popular culture embodied in *Munsey's* and its ilk. While they lasted, however, they looked to Bohemia to mediate temporal and geographic conflicts, and to provide a sense of cultural self-determination. As David Hollinger notes, there is "a field of concrete possibilities" between the abstractions of provincialism and cosmopolitanism; thus "somewhere amid these real options most of us try to have it both ways, avoiding at once the constraints of a province too narrowly defined and the discomforting instability of a universe too vast and varied for us to make our own."[121] The ever-permeable "Borders of Bohemia" functioned as just such a middle space. Though not always a strictly "neutral ground," Bohemia both intensified local feeling and pointed to a larger horizon.[122] It helped to negotiate what Anthony Giddens has described as one of the constitutive features of modernity: "the complex relations between *local involvements* (circumstances of co-presence) and *interaction across distance* (the connections of presence and absence)."[123]

On the East Coast itself, small to mid-sized cities also invoked "Bohemia" to bolster their cultural positions and deflect charges of provincialism. Even traditional cultural centers such as Boston and Philadelphia boasted periodicals dedicated to *la vie bohème*, ones that tried to fashion a more modern and cosmopolitan framework and to keep abreast of New York. For example, beginning in 1900, Boston's *The Bohemian*, a "monthly magazine of unique stories," strove to free itself from what Howells had described as "the Puritan mask, the cast of a dead civilization."[124] Instead of the staid respectability associated with Boston, the periodical appealed to "those who love pleasure without regard to conventionalities," and most issues featured melodramatic tales of illicit love and villainy in the Parisian Latin Quarter. Still, perhaps hoping not to alienate more traditional Bostonians, the magazine insisted that "the significance of the term Bohemian has been somewhat enlarged within a few years" and that even those "good-fellows" who remained "within the pale of convention" could now safely enjoy the Bohemian lifestyle (at least in the form of the periodical).[125] Further, even in Bohemia, villains ultimately reaped the wages of sin, and domesticity beckoned as the ultimate good. As in the other "regional" Bohemias, cosmopolitan modernity thus accommodated traditional restrictions: the Bohemian continued to overlap with the Bourgeois.

Unlike their Southern and Midwestern counterparts, the Eastern *Bohemian*s did not rage against the hegemony of New York publishing. Nonetheless, even as mild a publication as the Buffalo *Bohemian* seized upon the topos of Bohemia to negotiate cultural conflicts and combat geographic limitations. Once again, Bohemia offered itself as the harbinger of a higher and more modern culture. Alongside the Fort Worth and Cincinnati periodicals, the Buffalo *Bohemian* of 1893 sought to foster artistic and literary development and to compensate for a perceived cultural lack. It too felt that its own city had not yet "reached the era when the homage due literature and which culture demands, can be proffered." The

Bohemian apologized for this state of affairs, noting that Buffalo was "in a state of transition; all is hurly burly, nor can the majority sit down to digest the contents of a book, still less become book-lovers in the full measure of the term. The stimulant of the money-hustlers is anything but books."[126] In conjunction with the local Bohemian Sketch Club, the periodical proposed to ease the transition by publishing monthly art and book notes (with many notices about the Sketch Club and the Buffalo Society of Artists), as well as stories and articles from both amateur and "trained pens," many of them members of the club. (The writing of these pens ranged from bland accounts of Niagara Falls to a bizarre story called "My Occult Wife," one that provided melodramatic speculation on "art, nature and the aesthetics of the soul.")[127]

A temperate Bohemia, more inclined to encourage cultural activity than to decry provincialism, the Buffalo periodical was of the genteel variety. Apart from "My Occult Wife," it published little that suggested decadence. Instead, it represented itself as a kind of "Central Park of the imagination," as a wholesome means of integrating the pastoral into the urban, of uniting Bohemia and Arcadia: "THE BOHEMIAN! The title itself is suggestive. It whispers of babbling brooks, stray zephyrs, the songs of birds in dim woodlands green, of tender pathos, of sentiment, of all that comprises the sum of human enjoyment that fond fancy imagines to lie embosomed in the classic vales of Bohemia."[128] True to its genteel imperatives, the periodical complained that the city housed an estimated 2,500 barrooms (traditional haunts of *la vie bohème*) but only six bookstores.[129] Further establishing its genteel credentials, it announced that it was "read by the best society," and specified that it carried "no objectionable advertisements." Yet the periodical did not represent Buffalo as a static outpost of gentility. Instead, it stressed that it was "sold on all outgoing and incoming trains," thus insisting upon its place within a larger cultural and commercial network, one highlighted by the nomadism of Bohemia.[130] Like Fort Worth and Cincinnati, this Bohemia hoped simultaneously to support local industry, cultivate the bourgeoisie, and enter the national marketplace (though on its own terms).

During this period, local boosterism also brought Bohemia to the Northwest. In Cottage Grove, Oregon, a publication called *Bohemia Nugget* offered itself as a means of helping the town "enter the front rank of prosperity." Still, in keeping with its pioneer locality, the publication admitted more modest objectives than those of the other regional *Bohemians*: "We do not come to you with a view of turning the world upside down by way of great literary productions. . . . We have taken up our abode among you with the view of making a decent living." The periodical never accounted for its title, and instead, a more suggestive usage of "Bohemia" appeared on its advertising page. There, a local hotel named "Bohemia" promoted itself as a "strictly first-class headquarters for traveling men," one that "meets all trains." As a travel headquarters, the Bohemia Hotel promised to accommodate the commercial mobility that, increasingly, bound each region into a larger nation. Through such structures as print and hotels, the romance of Bohemia thus traversed the open spaces of modernity itself.[131]

The name of the proprietor of "Bohemia Hotel" further reminds us that *la vie bohème* escaped both regional *and* national boundaries. At the bottom of the ad, the words "Fong Sing, Proprietor" open Bohemia to still a larger cultural and geographic compass, aligning it with the transnationality of immigrant life. It is to Bohemia's role in expressing and mediating tensions between the national and the transnational that this study will now turn.

6

Cosmopolitan Bohemias

I'd rather live in Bohemia than in any other land,
For only there are the values true . . .
Here, pilgrims stream with a faith sublime
From every class and clime and time.

John Boyle O'Reilly, "In Bohemia," 1885

WHITMAN ENVISIONED "OUR LAND, America, her literature, esthetics, etc., as, substantially, the getting in form . . . of deepest basic elements and loftiest final meanings."[1] Emerson located "America" at a transcendental intersection between literature and geography: "America is a poem in our eyes; its ample geography dazzles the imagination and it will not wait long for metres."[2] By the turn of the century, however, the "dazzling world" that captured the imaginations of many U.S. writers, artists, urbanites, and clubmen and clubwomen belonged not to "America" but to the fabulous land of "Bohemia."[3] "I'd rather live in Bohemia than in any other land, / For only there are the values true," declared John Boyle O'Reilly in a poem so popular that contemporaries described it as "the national anthem of the boundless realm of Bohemia."[4] In Philadelphia, a former mayor went so far as to proclaim, "Dynasties and nations may rise and fall, empires decay and pass away, but Bohemia is always. It is the only true democracy in the world—the safest, merriest, jolliest state in all Chistendom."[5]

Literary history teaches us that American writers have lacked "a sense of a world elsewhere, this indeed being the world elsewhere."[6] Displacing the gap between the real and the ideal, the present and the future, the symbol of "America" has encouraged U.S. authors to commit themselves, with

Emerson, to the "Spirit of America."[7] And yet, by the mid-nineteenth century, a number of U.S. writers were insisting that they would rather live in Bohemia. Flirting with expatriation, these Bohemians pledged their allegiance to a state that defied national boundaries. Upheld as "the only true democracy," replete with its own "pilgrims of sublime faith," Bohemia absorbed foundational American mythologies and supplemented its ideals.[8]

At the turn into the twentieth century, Bohemia provided a liminal territory between the regional and the national. Throughout the same period, this expansive cultural terrain also acted both to map and to displace the divide between the national and the global. From its very beginnings af Pfaff's, American Bohemianism had promoted a cosmopolitan blend of cultural forms. Allied with the gypsies (via the Parisian Latin Quarter), Bohemia represented both the exotic and the sophisticated (for proponents) and cultural degeneration (for critics). The passions that fueled these opposing views of *la vie bohème* only escalated at the turn of the century, an era in which twenty million "new immigrants" entered the nation and Jim Crow laws further entrenched the color line. At this cultural moment, the familiar opposition between the Bohemian and the Bourgeois often highlighted a tension between more restrictive and more multicultural conceptions of national identity. To varying extents, self-declared Bohemians aligned themselves with the latter and their opponents adhered to the former. Accordingly, when viewed as a social negative, Bohemia and its putative danger underwrote efforts to prevent the "old world" from contaminating the "new"; when seen as a social positive, Bohemia became a traveling contact zone, enabling cultural interaction between diverse constituencies and facilitating the commercial circulation of exotic commodities.

The Old World in the New

One of the best ways of measuring the cultural significance of this multicultural and cosmopolitan "Bohemia" is to listen to its critics and to record the rhetorical processes by which they strove to limit the scope of this expansive territory. Such critical efforts reveal the extent to which the threat (and allure) of Bohemia lay in its ability to metonymize the foreign. In 1895, for example, in an article "written by an American girl after two years of Parisian art study," *The Arena* poses the question, "Shall Our

Young Men Study in Paris?" To answer this question, the article juxtaposes American innocence and European experience in a simplified version of the Jamesian "international theme." According to *The Arena's* "American girl," the danger of Old World decadence was intensified by *la vie bohème.* Once young male art students traveled to Paris, itself a city of dubiously "pleasure-loving people," they reoriented their "dreams and fancies" toward Bohemia: "Arrived in Paris their Mecca is soon converted into the no less fascinating Bohemia, that strange country which lies here, there, and everywhere." As the reference to Mecca implies, Bohemia allegedly compounded the danger of Paris by introducing an orientalized "unrestraint"—and, since Bohemia existed "here, there, and everywhere," it threatened to override moral, geographic, psychic, and even temporal boundaries.[9]

To control the spread of Bohemianism, the article urges, "Mothers and fathers, think more than twice before you let your boy enter this Bohemian life." Only such supervisory vigilance could prevent the Old World from impinging upon the New:

> That this Old World has much to battle against in overthrowing the effects of climate, of inheritance, and of established custom we must not forget; but do we dare imperil our future by too close an intimacy with this frightful quality of Parisian life?
>
> Young men, do not be in too much haste to leave the comparatively pure atmosphere of our American schools. What more do you really need for your growth than a model, a wholesome work-room, industry, and observation? There is no royal road to knowledge; you must make yourselves. . . . Come and study in the galleries and churches of Europe when the time is ripe for it, but keep in yourselves the purity which I pray it may be America's province to further for the world.[10]

The "American girl" thus rehearses many of the axioms of nineteenth-century American nationalism. America versus Europe, the wholesome versus the decadent, the New versus the Old: such were the standard antinomies that articulated America's "exceptional" status. Interestingly, however, the article envisions America less as a moral preserve than as an incubator of imperial righteousness. Signifying both national self-enclosure and a more amorphous breadth of moral authority, the very doubleness of the phrase "America's province" suggests how readily exceptionalism could translate into imperialism. By remaining "provincial"—by rejecting urbane, continental sophistication and Bohemian immorality—the young American art student and the nation might both possess the world.

Written in 1894, Robert W. Chambers's novel *In the Quarter* juxtaposes the Bohemian and the virtuous American girl (and, implicitly, the nation she metonymizes). According to Chambers, the young American art students who live in the Parisian Latin Quarter quickly fall prey to the seductions of the Old World. Even within the bounds of Bohemia's so-called "American colony," the art students soon lose their personal and national integrity; no longer separated from Europe through the buffers of space and time, this fledgling colony cannot withstand the weight of history or uphold the boundary between the Old and the New. And no one is more vulnerable to Old World corruption than the "American girl." Figuring both the comparative freedom and purity of her nation—as well as its susceptibility to degenerative influence—the American woman owes it to her female compatriots to abjure *la vie bohème*. Bohemia, in other words, cannot be colonized without exerting a reciprocal power over its American settlers in turn, and especially over its female inhabitants. The novel thus endorses the warnings of a beleaguered Parisian grisette, cautioning the would-be Bohemian:

> American women, brought up to think clean thoughts, and see with innocent eyes, to exact a respectful homage from men and enjoy a personal dignity and independence unknown to women anywhere else—why do you want to come here? Do you not know that the foundations of that liberty which makes you envied in the Old World are laid in the respect and confidence of men? Undermine that, become wise and cynical, learn the meaning of doubtful words and gestures whose significance you never need have suspected, meet men on the same ground where they may any day meet fast women of the continent, and fix at that moment on your free limbs the same chains which corrupt society has forged for the women of Europe.[11]

Rhetorically embodying New World independence, the American woman thus provides Chambers with a justification for a renewed cultural isolationism. For Chambers, the American Colony could not transform (or reform) Bohemia; rather, Bohemia invaded the naive American psyche, introducing a postlapsarian knowingness.

Yet if the notion of young Americans abroad in the Latin Quarter threatened many cultural commentators, the idea of a Bohemia *in* the United States provoked even more unease. Observing New York's Bohemia, Charles Sears Baldwin, a writer for the *Atlantic Monthly*, insisted in 1903 that *la vie bohème* promoted Old World decadence: "They that dwell in Bohemia because they have unlearned the way forth suffer dreary and repulsive decline." For Baldwin, the degenerative qualities of Bohemianism derived from its racial inheritance:

> An old gypsy is tolerable only if he be a real gypsy, not in choice or lapse of will, but in the blood. This is the race whose journey has no end, for whom life and all the world is Bohemia, only a space for travel. . . . For any but the blood to spend a lifetime on the road is as unnatural as for this blood to keep house. The real gypsies are happy, doubtless, as the nomads of the world's childhood. Perpetual youth is perpetual limitation; once the limitation is seen, intolerable to any zeal for manhood.

According to Baldwin, Bohemia functioned as a "time of passage" between Anglo-American adolescence and adulthood, one that enhanced the organic, yet fleeting, connection between the Anglo-Saxon youth and other "childlike" races. Implicitly drawing on the belief that ontogeny recapitulated phylogeny, Baldwin acknowledged that Bohemia might well act as a normative developmental stage. If prolonged, however, Bohemianism could also lead to arrested development and even degeneration (that is, to "dreary and repulsive decline"). The opposition between the true and the false Bohemian could relax only during adolescence; after that, Baldwin insists, it had to be vigilantly guarded.[12]

Baldwin implicitly hoped to contain the spread of "Bohemia" by arguing for its hereditary basis. Written at a time of unprecedented immigration (particularly of the "new" immigrants from Southern and Eastern Europe) his phrase "the nomads of the world's childhood" registers the combined threats of the Old World encroaching upon the New, of "childlike" races compromising Anglo-American "manhood," and of the national "home" dissolving into a space of endless transnational movement. Asserting the irreducible difference between the true gypsies and "us others, not of the blood," Baldwin also attempts to distance Bohemia by describing it as a separate nation, as "a country of inns—inns for the poor adventurous young, responsive to the freedom in others which they must have in themselves." For Baldwin, Bohemia was (or should be) a foreign port, a touristic destination outside the borders of the United States: "Like the actual Switzerland," Baldwin asserts, "it is only for our summer." Though the "real gypsy" might believe that "all the world is Bohemia," the "false gypsy" should recognize that Bohemia belonged within a discrete (and discreet) time and place—even if that mythic place could not actually be located.

Baldwin posits an unbridgeable divide between the "real" and the "false gypsy," between those "of the blood" and unconventional poseurs. Yet, in the turn-of-the-century United States, this dichotomy was mediated by the presence of Bohemian immigrants—that is, by immigrants from the central European country of Bohemia (who may or may not have also had gypsy ancestry). The immigrant *from* Bohemia brought together the (already analogous) figures of the new immigrant and the metaphoric Bohemian, prototypes that allegedly posed related threats to traditional gentility: both departed from Anglo-American norms, migrated between the Old World and the New, espoused a "looser" morality, and resided in unsanitary urban environments (sometimes in the very same neighborhoods and tenement buildings). Bohemian immigrants highlighted these connections, especially since they often excelled in the arts and yet supposedly lacked more practical abilities. Edward Ross's xenophobic *The Old World in the New* (1913), an influential argument against the new immigration, maintains that "a Bohemian leader puts his people above the Americans in music and the fine arts, but concedes the superiority of the Americans in constructive imagination, organizing ability, and tenacity of purpose."[13] In other words, the genetic stock of Bohemian immigrants (and that of many other new immigrants) condemned them to an erstwhile *vie de bohème*, a lifestyle that would ultimately vitiate American initiative unless contained through immigration restriction.

The connections between Bohemian immigrants and metaphoric Bohemians are highlighted in Willa Cather's story "The Bohemian Girl" (1912). For Cather, the figure of the Bohemian immigrant negotiates between true and false gypsies, and between Old and New World identities. Posing the question whether or not *la vie bohème* inheres within "the blood," the story alternately conceptualizes Bohemianism as a distinctive racial inheritance and as a catalyst for more cosmopolitan lifestyles. And yet, in the final analysis, Cather's "Bohemian girl" is not the "American girl"; at the end of the story, Clara Vivrika leaves the United States and returns to her Old World origins. Freed from her uncanny Bohemianism, her midwestern town reconstitutes its insular community.

Cather's title "The Bohemian Girl" echoes the title of a popular mid-nineteenth-century operetta about gypsy life. Published in 1912, the title would have also conjured *la vie bohème* and the contemporary women who sought to defy convention in such locales as Greenwich Village and Chicago. Yet the title character does not live in a gypsy camp or the Village; rather, Cather's Bohemian Girl is the inhabitant of a small town in rural Nebraska. Nevertheless, as her lover, Nils Ericson, reminds her, she is the real thing, the "real Bohemian Girl."[14]

What enables Clara Vavrika to achieve such authenticity? She is first and foremost a Bohemian because she and her family immigrated to the United States from the region of the Austrian Empire called Bohemia, the country then thought to be the point of origin for gypsy migrations. She is also the "Bohemian Girl" because she herself has something of the gypsy about her. The story repeatedly grounds Clara's character in racialized traits. Cather notes, "Her eyes slanted a little, as if she had a strain of Tartar or gypsy blood, and were sometimes full of fiery determination and sometimes dull and opaque" (101). Revealed through her eyes, Clara's gypsy spirit sets her apart from the other townspeople. As Nils appreciatively tells Clara, "race" is "everything that makes you yourself"; it is the "Bohemian" essence that, according to Nils, determines Clara's "love of life, [her] capacity for delight" (126). Distinguishing Clara from the more austere Scandinavian immigrants, this Bohemian vibrancy becomes, for Nils, the basis for her allure.

At the beginning of the story, Nils Ericson returns to Nebraska after a twelve-year absence in order to seek out the Bohemian Girl. He returns via the transcontinental express and wears clothes with a "foreign cut," sports a "blue silk necktie with loose ends," and carries a flute case (89). As such, we recognize Nils as a (metaphoric) "Bohemian," as a nomadic figure who represents the foreign and the artistic as a matter of style. And yet, we quickly learn, his Bohemianism might be encoded in his own genetic makeup; as Nils's mother implies, his own nature has something of the gypsy in it, and she even suggests that this inheritance might be attributed to a racial impurity (on his father's side, of course), saying: "You'd never be contented tied down to the land. There was roving blood in your father's family, and it's come out in you. I expect your own way of life suits you best" (96). As the prodigal son, Nils bears the dreaded hereditary taint that might yet return to threaten the integrity of the family. His continued passion for Clara portends just such destabilization.

We first see her, through Nils's eyes, out riding at a gallop:

> She sat lightly in the saddle, with her chin high, and seemed to be looking into the distance. As she passed the plum thicket her horse snuffed the air and shied. She struck him, pulling him in sharply, with an angry exclamation, "Blazne!" in Bohemian. . . . The horse and rider, with their free, rhythmical gallop, were the only moving things to be seen on the face of the flat country. (93)

Just as this description defines Clara against "the face of the flat country," so the story foregrounds her Bohemianism against the provincial bourgeois values of the rest of the town. Clara has had ample opportunity to exercise this defiance. During Nils's absence, she has married his brother, Olaf, an Ericson who does not bear any sign of "roving blood." Though continually surveyed by her mother-in-law, the matriarchal Mrs. Ericson, Clara maintains many of her "Bohemian" habits and tastes—she rises late, much to the chagrin of the Ericsons, and she dresses in a "tight-fitting black dress" that the "people thereabouts thought very plain." More threatening, however, is Clara's sexuality, and, as the real Bohemian Girl, her artistry and passion triumphantly fuse: after seeing Nils again for the first time in twelve years, Clara Vavrika sits down at the piano and plays "as if the house were burning over her head" (106). Clara is the antidomestic, and, as this image suggests, her very passion portends the destruction of the home. Taking due measure of Clara's disruptive sexuality, Mrs. Ericson warns Nils, "If I were you, I wouldn't see too much of Olaf's wife while you are here. She's the kind of woman who can't see much of men without getting herself talked about. She was a good deal talked about before he married her" (106).

Though still provocative, Clara has nonetheless attempted to make some concessions to respectability after her marriage to Olaf. Clara tries to avoid her father's saloon, but Nils, hoping to return Clara more fully to her Bohemian "race," lures her back to the beer hall. There, the two indulge their former practice of drinking beer and singing Bohemian songs. Once they enter the Bohemia of Vavrika's saloon, they wax nostalgic about the "fun" they used to have together: "None of the other kids ever had so much fun. We knew how to play" (116). The content of their "play" is especially revealing; reunited in the saloon, Clara and Nils sing their favorite song together. It is from the operetta "The Bohemian Girl," and if this were not enough to return Clara to her putative self-identity, the lyrics of the song also suggest a more intricate racialism:

> I dreamt that I dwelt in ma-a-arble halls,
> With vassals and serfs at my knee . . .

Conjuring fantasies of feudal opulence, these lines have a cultural logic that begins to make sense once we remember the prevalent turn-of-the-century associations that linked feudalism, adolescence, and non-Anglo-Saxon races. In the recapitulationist evolutionary schema embraced by the psychologist G. Stanley Hall in his 1904 construction of "the adolescent," the development of the individual corresponded to the development of the race. This conception became a popular truism—for example, the 1914 Boy Scout *Handbook for Scout Masters* tells us, "The early Adolescent or Chivalry period is racially parallel to the Feudal or Absolute Monarchical period with its chivalric virtues, vices and actions."[15] According to such paradigms, each race also occupied different positions on this evolutionary continuum (as noted, Charles Sears Baldwin connected the present-day Gypsies with the "nomads of the world's childhood"). Thus, when Nils tries to reacquaint Clara with their courtly fantasies, he implicitly seeks to restore Clara to their youth *and* to her racial identity—and thus to their past love). After renewing their courtship, Nils tries to convince Clara to run away to Europe with him: "Where's your old dash, Clara Vavrika? What's become of your Bohemian blood?" (128).

Clara responds to these pleas, yet she does not fully endorse his romantic racialism. Though Nils threatens Clara with the loss of self if she remains in Nebraska, Clara meditates on the loss of self involved in flight. For Clara, it is geography, not blood, that bears the map of her own desires: "The ground seemed to hold her as if by roots. Her knees were soft under her. She felt as if she could not bear separation from her old sorrows, from her old discontent. They were dear to her, they had kept her alive, they were a part of her. There would be nothing left of her if she were wrenched away from them" (128). Clara's Bohemianism is defined against (and thus constituted by) the provincialism of the town; and, as this passage more romantically suggests, her identity is intimately bound up with the land, perhaps even more than with her "roving blood." Like Hester Prynne and Isabel Archer (American heroines whose national identities are similarly conflicted), Clara has become attached to the place where she has, in James's phrase, "dropped her secret sadness"; unlike Isabel, however, Clara does not recover a sense of her own will after the climactic onslaught of male passion-aggression.[16] Whereas Isabel finally breaks "free" from Caspar Goodwood, Clara allows Nils to lift her into her saddle and to command her horse to the train station. She appears drained of volition; her last registered thought is that quoted above. Nils' insistence that she retain the boldness of her racial self paradoxically achieves the opposite effect.

Yet, in the end, her roving blood overcomes the pull of geographic roots. We learn from her letters to her father that Clara is finally happy; the narrator even confirms this happiness, writing: "Clara had always been fond of her father, and happiness made her kinder" (129). Nils appears to have been correct: Clara belongs to (and in) the Old World. Not so the other Ericsons. Nils sends his younger brother money to join them in Europe, and Eric Ericson runs away from home only to find himself plagued by homesickness. He gets off at the next train station and turns around. He returns to his mother, at which point she reveals that she had always meant to leave him the family farm:

> The boy started and slid closer. "Oh Mother," he faltered, "I don't care about the farm. I came back because I thought you might be needing me, maybe." He hung his head and got no farther.
>
> "Very well," said Mrs. Ericson. Her hand went out from her suddenly and rested on his head. Her fingers twined themselves in his soft, pale hair. His tears splashed down on the boards; happiness filled his heart. (132)

This then is the happiness that is most directly represented in the text; bowed down before the mother, shedding sentimental tears, Eric Ericson has come home. Defying representation, Nils's Bohemian romance has none of the solidity, or pathos, of "keeping house." Nature and nurture, custom and habit conjoin to displace the exotic Clara Vivrika and to bring Eric Ericson home. The New World domesticates the blond Scandinavian, but the dark Bohemian must seek life, liberty, and happiness outside the United States.[17] Even the bonds of marriage cannot restrict Clara and her roving blood. The story thus comes to a conclusion much like Baldwin's: "For any but the blood to spend a lifetime on the road is as unnatural as for this blood to keep house." Cather eschews the moralism of Baldwin, Chambers, and "the American Girl," but she tells a similar story: Bohemianism underscores the discrepancy between immigrants and "Americans," between Old and New World identities.

"The Cosmopolitan Bohemian Democracy" and *The American Scene*

If for some Bohemia represented all that must be excluded from the United States, for others, *la vie bohème* suggested a middle ground, one that brought the "Old" and the "New" into a diverting, even mutually transformative relation. According to a guidebook entitled *Bohemia: The East Side Cafes of New York* (1903), "'Bohemia' takes up a most interesting phase of life in the metropolis—that section of the great city of New York, which is neither strictly native nor wholly foreign—which resembles more closely an enlargement and improvement of Murger's 'Bohème' than perhaps any other spot on the globe." More specifically, this Bohemia resides in "that section of the east side of New York where are found cafes and eating houses of all nations, making it a dazzling world peculiar to itself."[18] *Everybody's Magazine*'s "Hunt for Bohemia" (1905) also provides a guided tour through the "*table d'hôte* bohemia" of New York, noting that "in the broader use of this word [Bohemia], which has become the most elastic in our language, there is more bohemia in New York to-day than ever, if one knows where to find it, but it is cosmopolitan in character and divided into very many provinces."[19] And Charles F. Peters's "When New York Dines a la Bohème" specifies: "There is the French, Italian, Spanish, German, Hungarian, and Armenian Bohemia."[20]

Within such accounts, Bohemia annexes the foreign for the "delectation" of the United States. Yet, while providing a quasi-imperial stage for cosmopolitan consumption, Bohemia also constituted a liminal space, a "world peculiar to itself" where national boundaries and identities might become less entrenched. Embodied in international cuisine and imported "atmosphere," Bohemia was the place where the foreign and the domestic met and, to varying extents, consumed one another's time, food, money, or labor. Imaginatively positioned within and without the United States, Bohemia acted as a buffer zone between the nation and its new immigrants. By definition a romantic "world elsewhere," Bohemia both glamorized such cross-cultural spaces and, to a certain extent, neutralized their perceived threat by suspending the question whether immigrant cultures were or were not properly "American." Such a suspension may have ultimately facilitated the incorporation of these cultures into the nation and its commercial marketplace; in the process, the mythos of *la vie bohème* also helped to inaugurate a more cosmopolitan nationality, all the while gesturing toward a larger geographic and imaginative terrain.

According to guidebooks, city sketches, and contemporary novels, "Bohemian" restaurants provided an exotic "atmosphere," an ambiance born in large part through proximity to "foreign" bodies.[21] In *Bohemia: The East-Side Cafes of New York*, the author, William Reimer, invites the readers to "Come along with me to 'Little Hungary!' There you will find solace for your wounded heart." In Little Hungary, Reimer not only enjoys wine of "exquisite foreign vintage," but partakes of a rejuvenating cultural spectacle: "In a dim corner the Gypsy band are tuning their instruments. Soon the swarthy, dazzling uniformed musicians are drawing their bows tenderly across the strings, and we hear a mellow dolce that sounds like an allegory of a gentle zephyr softly sighing through the pines on a balmy

Summer's night." The wine and the music produce a moment of "ecstasy" in which Reimer longs to transgress ethnic boundaries through even closer physical contact: "I am tempted to take the vivacious Jewish maiden near by in my arms and whirl her dancing around till exhaustion stops us both."[22] In this erotic reverie, Reimer projects another form of consumerist desire, a yearning to "exhaust" the vitality of the vivacious Jewish woman and, in so doing, to soothe his own "wounded heart."

In his series of sketches, *Types from City Streets*, Hutchins Hapgood describes a similar experience at a Hungarian resort, emphasizing the imaginative transport enabled by the foreign atmosphere and the sight of "dark faces." Hapgood even goes so far as to propose the foreign restaurant as a cure for "American nervousness," as a means of introducing the repose necessary for modifying the national character. Like other former students of William James, Hapgood dedicated himself to exploring plural forms of identity, even as he tried to delimit identity into a variety of urban "types." For example, entering into the first person in a chapter entitled "An American Bohemian," Hapgood contemplates "with vague joy" a "*table d'hôte* Hungarian dinner":

> I turned to the east and soon reached my Hungarian resort, where they played vigorous foreign music. I sat down with an inward sound unpleasant in itself, but indicative of internal satisfaction. I looked around for a moment at a lot of faces, mainly dark and foreign, but most of them smiling or talking with animation. . . . I became aware, too, of the deeper meaning in the dark faces about me. . . . They seemed pleased not at any little trivial circumstance that was amusing, but because they were feeling, in physical content, the satisfaction of their own deeper needs and the beauty and interest of their companions. Trivial in its origin, of food, drink, and leisure, the feeling nevertheless had something of the religious depth which is impossible without thoroughgoing happiness.

Hapgood's table d'hôte dinner is a bargain: seventy cents affords him "an unusually good wine" and the pleasure of observing the dark and foreign patrons. Like Reimer, visual pleasure leads to an ecstatic moment, though Hapgood's experience is less erotic than "religious." Hapgood's consumption of the foreign brings about the desired transformation, endowing him with a vicarious happiness and a "keener insight."[23]

According to Hapgood, foreign restaurants provide an oasis of leisurely, contemplative Bohemianism in an otherwise un-Bohemian city. "There is very little Bohemian atmosphere in New York, for it is a very 'swift' town," Hapgood maintains. He echoes George M. Beard's diagnosis, insisting that "nervousness" was a peculiarly "American" condition: thus, for the "New Yorker who is thoroughly saturated with the most American spirit of the town," contemplation is the one thing completely shut out." Consequently, "thought" had became a thoroughly "nervous impulse, quickly over, having no genial, philosophic fringe, looking not before nor after, but pinned to the exciting moment" (114). To combat this "unmeaning activity" (114) and to cultivate "genuine Bohemian charm" (118), Hapgood prescribes: "The only practicable means of subjecting the typical city American to the contemplative is therefore through some influence which is connected with his daily, practical life and amusements. Now, this element is partly found in what is contributed to our metropolitan existence by the foreigners" (115).

Hence, the value of the foreign restaurant to Bohemianism: involving "practical life" (eating) and entertainment (music, dancing, and dark faces), such restaurants as "Little Hungary"—much like Pfaff's several decades earlier—suspended the "nervous haste of the metropolis," inviting patrons to linger and reflect, to wax poetic and philosophic: in short, to become Bohemians. "The fearful Anglo-Saxon habit of standing at a bar and draining off whisky, as an indication of good-fellowship, has been much modified by the foreign café, and particularly by the German type of family beer-hall," Hapgood records. In these "foreign" haunts, time lost its nervous imperative, and "a couple of friends, or a man, his wife, and family, sit down comfortably, drink light beer or wine moderately, and talk in a rational and pleasant way, sometimes for hours" (117). The foreign restaurant, Hapgood proposes, must even replace reading as the dominant means of gaining access to "the contemplative, the eternal, the artistic." Because the "nervous New Yorker is too busy to read" books, he or she must ingest philosophy and art by means of café culture—that is, by the "reading" of the dark exotic face and the experience of exotic tastes (115).

Turn-of-the-century novels also upheld the cosmopolitan delights of the Bohemian table d'hôte. "Ah, this is *nice*!" declares Fulkerson in William Dean Howells's *A Hazard of New Fortunes* (1890) after he sits down to eat at Maroni's, "a restaurant of the Latin ideal" (69). Fulkerson brings the former Bostonian, Basil March, to the restaurant in order to soak up the ambiance of "young literary men and artists" and diners "of all nationalities and religions." March and his family learn to relish such New York establishments as part of their "bohemianizing" (270); for them, "Italian *table d'hôtes* formed the adventure of the week" (267).

Stephen Crane's *The Third Violet* (1897) also attests to the inspiriting effects of the "truly Bohemian" cafes that were "thoroughly Parisian in spirit" (171, 175). Crane notes that at one such resort, "the long, sweeping, mad melody of a Spanish waltz . . . seemed to go tingling to the hearts of many of the diners. Their eyes glittered with enthusiasm, with abandon, with deviltry" (169).[24]

Unlike the authors of such rhapsodic accounts, Henry James was not so certain that the ethnic restaurant would have a salutary effect on the American character. Provocatively raising questions of "possession and dispossession," of the mutual transformation of self and Other, the ethnic restaurant struck James as one of the most notable features of *The American Scene*, and he too sought to understand the meaning of these cultural locations.[25] He explores a variety of ethnic restaurants in his American travel writings, asking how these sites transform "American" and "ethnic" identity (terms he himself destabilizes through quotation marks). As James experiences the cafés of New York's Lower East Side—that region Reimer and other guidebooks identify as "Bohemia"—he also ponders the "question of intercourse and contact" between the immigrant and the "native" American (457). In so doing, he recurs to images of eating and being eaten, wondering who will ultimately consume or "devour" whom (469). In answering this question, James subjects it to a series of dialectical reversals. On the one hand, the ethnic restaurant provides James with a trope for the immigrant's "possession" of the Anglo-American sensibility. With respect to the "alien," James asks, "Is not the universal sauce essentially *his* sauce, and do we not feel ourselves feeding, half the time, from the ladle, as greasy as he chooses to leave it for us, that he holds out?" (453). As James suggests, the Anglo-American consumes ethnic cuisine, but, in so doing, he does not master the alien; instead, he relinquishes part of his cultural dominance and his ability to signify the "universal" (though the disgust registered by the image of the "greasy ladle" attempts to reassert the normative power of genteel tastes). According to James, the East Side cafés even demanded the sacrifice of the English language, becoming "torture chambers of the living idiom." James grants that "the accent of the very ultimate future, in the States, may be destined to become the most beautiful on the globe and the very music of humanity," yet he insists that "we shall not know it for English—in any sense for which there is an existing literary measure" (33).

On the other hand, James predicts that ethnic identities will also be possessed and consumed by the American scene. Putting it "at the worst,"

James writes, "they were but the more certainly to fatten into food for the Ogres" (469). As such, they were at the mercy of a powerful "assimilative force," one that "immediately glazed them over as with some mixture, of indescribable hue and consistency, the wholesale varnish of consecration, that might have been applied, out of a bottomless receptacle, by a huge whitewashing brush" (461). This assimilative force, according to James, converts the ethnic into part of the "formidable foreground" of New York, a conversion that raises the question of what happens to the "various positive properties" of the ethnic or racial self. "Do they burrow underground," asks James, "to await their day again?" (463).

In the most utopian moment of James' travels on the Lower East Side, he uses one café as an image for this underground world of inviolate ethnic identity. He experiences this café as a "tiny temple" of "Germanic peace," and, while retaining the metaphor of surfaces and depths (though he switches the metaphoric vehicle from ground to water), James discovers

> a happy generalization—the bold truth that even when apparently done to death by that property of the American air which reduces so many aspects to a common denominator, certain finer shades of saliency and consistency do often, by means known to themselves, recover their rights. They are like swimmers who have had to plunge, to come round and under water, but who pop out a panting head and shine for a moment in the sun. My image is perhaps extravagant, for the question is only of the kept recollection of a café pure and simple. (522)

In this its "moment in the sun," the café withstands the "formidable foreground" of New York life by "making publicity itself delicate, making your barrier against vulgarity consist but in a few tables and chairs, a few coffee-cups and boxes of dominoes" (522–23).[26]

Yet, such delicate publicity is not characteristic of the next ethnic restaurant that James visits. Instead, this restaurant conforms to what James famously refers to as "the amazing hotel-world," a glittering realm of "unmitigated publicity" so strident that "one is verily tempted to ask if the hotel-spirit may not just *be* the American spirit most seeking and most finding itself" (440). According to James, it is this hotel-spirit that relentlessly works to "convert" the immigrant into the "American," rendering ethnicity itself a theatrical form and an exchangeable commodity. Functioning "to gild the temporary," this hotel-spirit introduces a "perpetual passionate pecuniary purpose which plays with all forms, which derides and devours them" (447). James's description of this hotel-world resonates with his account of his visit to a popular Hungarian restaurant—perhaps one and the same as Reimer's beloved "Little Hungary" or Hapgood's "Hungarian resort," and most likely the same haunt that contemporary journalist James Huneker described as a "tinsel Bohemia":

> This establishment had learned to lay on local colour with malice prepense—the local colour of its "Slav" origin—and was the haunt, on certain evenings of the week, of yearning groups from Fifth Avenue sated with familiar horizons. . . . The flourishing establishment of my present reference offered distinctly its outland picture, but showed it in an American frame, and the features of the frame and picture arranged themselves shrewdly together. (524–25)

Though "the indication, for the moment, might have been of some evening note of Dantzig or of Buda-Pesth," the scene quickly loses its authenticity, becoming a simulacrum of its former self, a self-conscious performance for the uptown public. Even with its exotic props, the scene submerges the ethnic self, reducing it to the dimensions of the formidable foreground. Alienated and commodified, ethnic identity appears to lose its depth, becoming only a surface phenomenon, a "phantasmagoric" manifestation of history within the all-consuming American present (466). Ethnicity thus evaporates even as it is most self-consciously paraded. Radically decontextualized, it threatens to become little more than a marketable artifact; once "launched," James argues, the "foreign personality" becomes one of the "heaped spoils of the sea," a remnant of a racial unconscious that climbs "higher and higher . . . into the very light of publicity" (459, 464, 470).

In his analysis of ethnic cuisine and the "performance of group identity," Roger Abrahams observes a similar contradiction: "in going public" and entering the commercial marketplace, "the very act of food preparation and cooking may simultaneously proclaim and undermine ethnicity."[27] For the Hungarian restaurant's perversion of its own "local colour," James partly blames the scrutiny of the "up-town public." (Reimer himself admits that his Bohemia had "become 'the thing' among New York's social leaders," noting that the majority of the patrons appeared to be "Americans or Americanized.")[28] Still, James does not see the proprietor—whom he refers to as the "ethnic boss"—as a passive victim of the assimilative force; rather, he sees him as a "possibly far-reaching master-spirit," implicitly one of the "master-spirits of management" who orchestrate the American "hotel civilization" at large (444, 525). Indeed, the very phrase "ethnic boss" alludes to ethnic machine politics, whose overriding power other members of the contemporary, postgenteel bourgeoisie sought to counter through Progressivist reform. Thus, reversing the dialectic of possession and dispossession once again, James imagines for the moment that it is this "ethnic boss" who, with "malice prepense," has consumed the bourgeois Anglo-American; for James, the "fluent East-Side New Yorkese" of the proprietor provides a metonym for "*his* inward assimilation of our heritage and point of view, matched as these were, on our own side, by such signs of large and comparatively witless concession" (524–26).

The malign ethnic purveyor of Bohemianism—one who simultaneously "proclaims and undermines ethnicity"—also appears in a contemporary story by Onoto Watanna. In "The Wife of Shimadzu," Watanna writes of a Japanese restaurant that was first "known only to the initiated and the elite of Manhattan Japanese society. Within . . . everything was Japanese." Upon entering the restaurant, the Japanese artist Narbara experiences the relief of a "traveler returning home." He returns every night until the owner, Shimadzu, marries Madame Kiku, formerly of San Francisco:

> Within a comparatively few hours the entire policy and management of the house of Shimadzu were altered. The day following the advent of the wife of Shimadzu a glaring advertisement appeared in the newspapers soliciting the trade of American patrons. . . . From that time forward the hospitable Japanese precincts hitherto reserved exclusively for the sons of Nippon became the stamping ground of that class which, drinking unknown wines in foreign show restaurants, calls itself "bohemian." Writers who had gained a certain short vogue, accompanied by actresses, were to be found in profusion. . . . Before this peroxide invasion, the guests of Shimadzu—the Japanese guests—melted away.[29]

In James L. Ford's "Bohemia Invaded" (1895), the invaders are the bourgeois "Philistines" who seek to gawk at the artistic Bohemians who frequent "the Garbaldi table d'hôte" in a "snug little basement below Washington Square."[30] For Watanna, however, the invaders are the Anglo-American "bohemians" who seek commodified versions of cultural otherness (with or without the help of Reimer's guidebook). They drive away the Japanese guests, destroying their private sanctuary, and the restaurant becomes an inauthentic sham.[31]

The irony, of course, is that Watanna played fast and loose with her own ethnic identity for commercial purposes; though the daughter of an English father and Chinese mother, she created a highly marketable persona as the best-selling novelist "Onoto Watanna," the biracial daughter of a Japanese noblewoman. As Amy Ling notes, Watanna had "a keen marketing instinct and sense of timing," capitalizing on the turn-of-the-century fascination with Japan and Japonica at a time of rampant anti-Chinese sentiment. Like the "Bohemian" restaurants, her fiction offered an escape into an exotic locale; "when one reads her book," declared the *American Illustrator*, "he seems to be enveloped in an atmosphere sweet with the mellow, fruity, lulling odor of opium."[32] "The Wife of Shimadzu," however, suggests her own discomfort with her role as a purveyor of ethnic exotica, and unlike the contemporary guidebooks, the story does not represent the "Bohemian" experience as a liberatory relaxation of cultural boundaries.[33] Instead, Watanna satirizes the Bohemian invaders (her own *Smart Set* readers?) in order to uphold the lines between the ethnic and the native, the authentic and the commercial, the immigrant and the Bohemian—the very lines she herself traversed in her life and work.[34]

From the perspective of the would-be tourist, other commentators also bemoaned the commodification of all things "Bohemian." Frustrated by his encounter with a "pasteboard Bohemia" in the Parisian Latin Quarter, the self-declared "new cosmopolitan" James Huneker had hoped to find the real thing on the Lower East Side, a place where he could drink "Pilsner beer served across genuine Bohemian tables!" For Huneker, the figure of the Bohemian immigrant promised to provide the authenticity that was lacking even in Paris. Yet a disappointed Huneker ultimately concluded that the Lower East Side had also become "fabulous": once again, Bohemia had been reduced to a commercial enterprise. He writes (perhaps singling out none other than "Little Hungary"): "We ate paprika-seasoned food to the clangour of the usual gipsy band that never saw the Hungarian Putzta. It was at one of the tinsel Bohemias so plentifully scattered along the avenue."[35] Robert Haven Schauffler also bemoaned the inauthenticity of what he terms "small b" bohemianism. In his travelogue, he embarks upon an exploration of the putative Old World in the New (after vowing to "cut out the Princeton Club and the gang"). Hoping for cultural authenticity, he instead finds *la vie bohème*. Unlike most commentators, he distinguishes between "small b" bohemianism and capital B Bohemianism—for Schauffler, the latter refers to the culture of Czech immigrants, the former to the Parisian-inspired realm of commodified pleasure. When he discovers, amidst the "din and foul tawdriness of the new Italy," what he judges to be an authentic Italian experience at "Azure

Grotto of Capri" (which, he slyly notes, "is not its real name. It would never do to have it Americanized"), he is thrilled: "In the New World this was the first Italian restaurant I had found that had apparently discovered neither America nor bohemia with a small b." Better yet, Schauffler then arrives at the "famous Bohemian Peasant Ball" (given by Czech immigrants) and waxes ecstatic:

> I was rapt away into the very heart of Bohemia among its strange, proud, stolid, gloomy people, apparently so cold and dull and sullen, yet full in the depths of them of color and fire, or music and passionate poetry—people that blossom out so touchingly in response to a little human tenderness. . . . I began to feel almost like a stranger in some forgotten corner of the Old World.[36]

Allegedly exchanging a "tawdry" bohemia for an authentic slice of the real Bohemia, Schauffler thus demonstrates the "fantasized dissociation from . . . the rituals of tourism" that, as John Frow notes, "is built into almost every discourse and practice of tourism."[37] Seeking authenticity, the Princetonian in effect denies that the Old World is part of the New. The Lower East Side is, instead, a place where he can go to satisfy his own "wanderlust."[38] Much like Cather's "The Bohemian Girl"—but unlike Reimer's guidebook—Schauffler upholds the separation between the foreign and the domestic.

Others represented the Bohemian contact zone of the "Old World in the New" far more positively. Along with many other "foreign" eateries, Gonfarone's (one of the restaurants noted in "New York Dines a la Bohème") capitalized on its connection to Bohemianism in order to cultivate a cross-cultural appetite. In her memoirs, Maria Sermolino, daughter of the proprietor, distinguishes the restaurant from other "pseudo-bohemian retreats," but she admits that her father attracted those "impecunious American artists and writers in the neighborhood" by helping to "propagate among Americans a simple, Latin variety of hedonism" (15).[39] The busboy played harmonica, the waiter juggled, the "smells, noises, and commotion of the kitchen" pervaded the dining-room; in this Bohemian atmosphere, the restaurant, Sermolino claims, "opened up new approaches to sensory and spiritual pleasures. . . . [It] brought new tastes, new sounds, new scents, new form, new colors, but above all, new feelings to America" (15). Such "immigrant gifts" also redounded on the giver. The "Bohemian" cross-cultural encounter enabled Sermolino to appreciate her own ethnicity; of the artists who patronized the restaurant, she writes: "They never tried to make us feel ashamed of our Italian descent but rather gave us reason to glory in it. We did not know why they thought it was wonderful to be 'Italian' but since they said so we believed it" (14).

Though concerned about who would ultimately assimilate whom, in *The American Scene* James also saw the ethnic restaurant as a site of mutual transformation. "A pavilion of light and sound and savoury science" (526), the East Side restaurant offered a dazzling stage, a place where the " 'ethnic' synthesis" of the future might begin to materialize (471). It was thus part of the "New York phantasmagoria," a constantly changing scene in which all identities entered into a radical flux, and in which ethnicity itself loomed as a spectral presence over and against an indeterminate future (466). Defying the stolidity of realism, the scene belonged within the realm of romance:

> Who were all the people, and whence and whither and why, in the good New York small hours? Where *was* the place after all? . . . Was it "on" Third Avenue, on Second, on fabulous unattempted First? Nothing would induce me to cut down the romance of it, in remembrance, to a mere address, least of all to an awful New York one; New York addresses falling so below the grace of a city where the very restaurants may on occasion, under restless analysis, flash back the likeness of Venetian palaces flaring with the old carnival. The ambiguity is the element in which the whole thing swims for me—so nocturnal, so bacchanal, so hugely hatted and feathered and flounced. (526–27)

Still submerged in the "element" of "ambiguity," the scene "swims" before James—it is not yet grounded, not yet fully assimilated into the "formidable foreground." The ethnic restaurant, "neither strictly native nor wholly foreign," holds the question of what is or is not "American" in abeyance.[40]

James does not go as far as Reimer in touting the East Side cafés of New York as a site of "BRILLIANCY AND COSMOPOLITAN BOHEMIAN DEMOCRACY."[41] James marvels at the scene, yet its meaning is still unclear—it is ultimately part of "Remarkable, unspeakable New York!" For Reimer, however, this Bohemia provides nothing less than a "genuine democracy" (in implicit contrast to that of the United States), one in which "high" and "low," rich and poor, "native" and "foreigner" might meet on more or less equal footing. Reimer's Bohemia thus offered a utopian space that accommodated the "entire heterogeneous multitude." Its position within the social geography was itself telling: "Little would any stranger suspect, indeed, that he could strike among these quarters of the poor such a well appointed place."[42]

The romance of Bohemia commodified the Lower East Side and its ethnic restaurants, but, as Reimer's account suggests, the very commercial self-consciousness that James derided in the "ethnic boss" helped to popularize more progressive ideals of cosmopolitan interchange. At a time when Americanization programs often operated under the assumption that "the horde of foreign born" had "dietary habits . . . maladjusted to American life," these restaurants promoted the appreciation of ethnic foodways and the group identities they represented.[43] However imperial and self-serving (on the part of would-be Anglo-American Bohemians or ethnic proprietors), these constructions of Bohemia still performed important cultural work beyond soothing the nervous American and enriching Bohemian restaurateurs. As John Higham has demonstrated, it was only around 1900 that the doctrine of "immigrant gifts . . . turned into a defense of the foreign-born from nativist attack": "The traditional theory of America's cosmopolitan nationality emphasized the triumph of unity over diversity. Although the country was supposed somehow to gain from the blending process, no one had pointed proudly to the immigrants' concrete contributions to the final amalgam."[44] Bohemia, at once within and without the United States, was a place that encouraged and legitimated this diversity. Without the paternalism that informed the Progressive Settlement Movement (the main proponent of the doctrine of "immigrant gifts"), Bohemia helped to foster new versions of "cosmopolitan nationality," or even what Reimer called the "COSMOPOLITAN BOHEMIAN DEMOCRACY."[45]

Of course, as Roger Abrahams has argued, "it would be too easy to say that a culturally pluralistic and egalitarian ethic is taking over" simply because of the widespread popularity of ethnic cuisines; moreover, Abrahams notes, "eating other people's foods has often been a sign of their having been subjugated."[46] Indeed, even Reimer reintroduces an imperial Americanism into the core of his Bohemian Democracy. Along with Hapgood, Reimer maintains that the foreign café can "remedy" the "defects" of the national character. In so doing, however, his language calls into question the equality figured by the scene: "It is said of us by foreigners, that we as a nation know how to make money, but that we don't know how to live. If this be true, we surely can remedy the latter defect by invading the East Side cafés and enjoying 'ad libitum' their inviting aspects and picturesque attractions."[47] Like Watanna, Reimer uses the trope of "invasion," and, in so doing, annexes Bohemia for the United States, reasserting the very divide between "us" and "them" that Bohemia ostensibly erased. The phantasmagoria of "possession and dispossession"—that relentless Jamesian dialectic—thus overtakes the Bohemian Democracy.

Frank Norris and Imperial Bohemianism

In his account of "Bohemian" San Francisco, Frank Norris also uses the site of the ethnic restaurant to explore the dialectics of self and Other, Bohemian and Bourgeois, the national and the cosmopolitan. For the literary Naturalist, however, Bohemia does not so much presage a future "ethnic synthesis" as it reveals the primitive identity buried within all civilized selves; the racial and ethnic Other might have more immediate access to this primitive essence (supposedly never having evolved beyond it) but it is always already part of the white bourgeois American. In both *Blix* (1899) and "The Third Circle," ethnic restaurants lead to the recovery of this more natural or primitive self, but in each, the consequences of Bohemian "slumming" vary enormously. Still, neither story suggests that primitivism ultimately breeds equality (or "Bohemian Democracy"); rather, Bohemia restages the internal and external colonization of the "primitive," one that consolidates (or attempts to consolidate) a bourgeois American identity.

As in New York, fin-de-siècle guidebooks to San Francisco also identify Bohemia with "foreign" restaurants—or rather, with the "American" experience of the "queer little restaurants, where rare dishes are served, and where one feels that he is in a foreign land, even though he be in the center of a high representative American city." Elaborating such encounters with culinary Otherness, *Bohemian San Francisco: Its Restaurants and Their Most Famous Recipes; The Elegant Art of Dining* asserts:

> San Francisco's Latin quarter is appealing, enticing and hypnotizing. Go there and you will learn why San Francisco is a Bohemian city. You will find out that so many things you have thought important are really not at all worth while. Go there and you will find the root of Bohemian restaurants. These people have studied gastronomy as a science, and they have imparted their knowledge to San Francisco, with the result that the Bohemian spirit enters into our very lives, and our minds are broadened, and our views of life and our ideas have a wider scope.[48]

The guidebook thus advances a familiar equation: the consumption of foreign culture helps produce the American Bohemian. Reminiscing about turn-of-the-century San Francisco, Arnold Genthe (a member of the Bohemian Club and noted photographer) makes a similar observation, fondly recalling the "gay Bohemian element, a group of writers and artists, whose playgrounds were the many French, Italian, and Spanish restaurants" of the city's own "Latin Quarter."[49]

In his loosely autobiographical *Blix*, Norris uses the city's ethnic restaurants as Bohemian "playgrounds." He describes the courtship of Condy Rivers and his girlfriend, Travis Bessemer, a relationship based on Norris's own romance with his future wife, Jeanette Black. Condy is a young San Franciscan journalist, a member of none other than the "Bohemian Club," and a gallant man-about-town.[50] Despite (or because of) his club affiliation, Condy leads a fairly typical life, sporting with the city's "Younger Set," and courting the eminently respectable Travis. Their courtship also follows normative patterns: "They had known each other in the conventional way (as conventionality goes in San Francisco); during the season Rivers took her to the theatres Monday nights, and called regularly Wednesdays and Sundays" (17). But in its very typicality, the romance becomes stale, and the two vow to become "chums," foreswearing the "time-worn, time-honored customs" of courtship in favor of a "sincere" camaraderie, one unburdened by the pretense of romantic love. As Travis announces, "I'm done with conventionality for good. I am going to try, from this time on, to be just as true to myself as I can be" (20). They decide to embark upon adventures together, to become more unconventional and Bohemian by exploring the city's ethnic quarters, and, more specifically, by frequenting its ethnic restaurants.

On their first adventure, Travis urges Condy to take the somewhat outré step of drinking tea with her in a Chinese restaurant. Condy loves the idea, "fun! It is—by Jove—it would be *heavenly*!" They dine amidst "enormous screens of gilded ebony" and alongside "divans with mattings and head-rests for opium smokers" (34). After this initial encounter, they continue to "go round to queer little, interesting places" (51), including the famed Mexican restaurant, Luna's (also mentioned in the guidebook *Bohemian San Francisco*). By consuming ethnic and racial Otherness, Condy and Travis become naturalists: Travis realizes her resolve to become "just as true to myself as I can be," abjuring conventionality (and thus the dreaded habitat of "realism"). Instead, both she and Condy discover the naturalism of Romance (which for Norris had less to do with Jamesian phantasmagoria than with capturing a more authentic realism or truth). Condy gets in touch with his "virile, masculine energy," Travis radiates "sweet strong womanliness," and they realize, finally, that "*they were for each other*" (128–29). What is striking is that the apparent contradiction—that of finding themselves by means of experiencing Otherness—does not strike the characters, or the novella, as a paradox. *Blix* upholds a naturalist (and Bohemian) logic whereby the racial or socioeconomic Other functions as a more authentic version of the Anglo-American self, an inner essence only loosely obscured by evolutionary development or stale conventions.[51]

That is to say, the Other is an apt version of the *youthful* Anglo-American self. By the conclusion of the novella, even a Charles Sears Baldwin might have approved of these protagonists. Condy and Travis accept that their Bohemian idyl must come to an end, that it is a temporal stage confined to their youth. The two declare their love while overlooking the western sunset, but then: "With one last look, they turned about and set their faces from it to the new life, to the East, where lay the Nation. . . . Their little gayeties were done. . . . Now for the future. The sterner note had struck—work was to be done" (130). Bohemianism must end with the onset of adulthood; moreover, Norris implies that *la vie bohème* belongs only to the far-flung frontier, that it is not fully part of "the Nation." And yet, Condy and Travis can only become mature national subjects by way of Bohemia: to achieve self-mastery and become adult Americans, they must first consume the Other.

Blix does not highlight the inequity or potential violence of this dynamic. Elsewhere, however, Norris acknowledges that the consumption of ethnic, cultural, and racial difference was often itself a form of domination; the Anglo-American self sought transformation by incorporating the foreign and exotic, yet was not necessarily prepared to relinquish its own privileged status in the process. Much like *Blix*, Norris's "The Third Circle" represents a young couple abroad in San Francisco's Chinatown; this time, their "slumming" more explicitly thematizes the tension between entitlement and vulnerability, possession and dispossession. "Of unmixed American stock," the Easterners Miss Ten Eyck and Tom Hillegas decide to explore the exotic terrain on their own, stumbling upon the restaurant of the Seventy Moons. There, they delight in all "the grotesque jimcrackery of the Orient" and declare their adventure "queer and original." Yet, their would-be Bohemianism is compromised by their need to claim ownership of the scene:

> "This is the way one ought to see places," said Hillegas, as he lit a cigarette; "just nose around by yourself and discover things. Now, the guides never brought us here."
>
> "No, they never did. I wonder why? Why, we just found it out by ourselves. It's ours, isn't it, Tom, dear, by right of discovery?"

Posing as imperial explorers, Hillegas and Miss Ten Eyck assert proprietary privilege. Norris underscores their arrogance when Hillegas tries to speed the service: "I say, John . . . I want some tea. You sabe?—upstairs—restaurant. Give China boy order—he no come. Get plenty much move on. Hey?" In perfect English, "John" responds: "I regret that you have been detained. You will, no doubt, be attended to presently." The Chinese merchant's elegant diction instantly disrupts Hillegas's sense of control and superiority, foreshadowing the next power reversal: while Hillegas has been demanding service, Miss Ten Eyck has been abducted.[52]

By conducting their own exploration of Chinatown, Hillegas and Miss Ten Eyck behave like good Bohemians. After all, the guidebook *Bohemian San Francisco* encourages potential Bohemians to circumvent the divide between the touristic Chinatown and the thing itself. "A number of places have been opened to cater to Americans, and on every hand one sees 'chop suey' signs, and 'Chinese noodles,'" the guidebook observes, adding, "It goes without saying that one seldom sees a Chinaman eating in the restaurants that are most attractive to Americans." To be a "brave Bohemian," one must foray beyond "the ordinary Chinese restaurants frequented by Americans," though with regard to the more exotic Chinese restaurants, *Bohemian San Francisco* offers this caveat: "The ingredients are so numerous and so varied with occasion that one is tempted to imagine them made of the table leavings, and that is not at all pleasant to contemplate." And so Chinatown presents the Bohemian with a conundrum: "there is nothing except superficiality in the ordinary Chinese restaurant frequented by Americans, and those not so frequented are impossible because of the average Chinaman's disregard for dirt and the usual niceties of food preparation." Danger inheres within the food itself, the ingestion of which potentially damages the "American" body.[53]

At a time when neo-Darwinian accounts posited biology as destiny, eating loomed as one of the most viable ways of taking in, and literally embodying, another culture; it was as though the ingestion of these foreign foods obviated the divide between the "true" and the "false gypsy," enabling the would-be Bohemian to become "of the blood." In effect, gastronomy nullified the opposition between biology and culture. Consuming "the Other," most directly through food or sex, invited the promise, and the threat, of self-transformation. As bell hooks argues:

> The point is to be changed by this convergence of pleasure and Otherness. One dares—acts—on the assumption that the exploration into the world of difference, into the

body of the Other, will provide a greater, more intense pleasure than any that exists in the ordinary world of one's familiar racial group. And even though the conviction is that the familiar world will remain intact even as one ventures outside it, the hope is that they will reenter that world no longer the same.[54]

When the guidebook *Bohemian San Francisco* maintains that the cuisines of the Latin Quarter enable the "Bohemian spirit" to enter "into our very lives" and to broaden our ideas and perspectives, it urges just such a transubstantiation of self into Other.

Yet in "The Third Circle" it is not primarily the food that threatens to transform the "unmixed" American self. To a point, the tale resolves into a conventional example of "city mysteries" sensationalism: a story of white bourgeois innocence lost within a corrupting urban quagmire. Chinatown functions as the ultimate labyrinth; it is a place where (according to Will Irwin's introduction to "The Third Circle") a "surface gentility and grace in life greater than anything our masses know" gives way to "something deep below the surface." In Norris's Chinatown, literal tunnels penetrate below the civilized surface, and (quoting Irwin again), such was their gothic perfection that it was "as if Mrs. Radcliffe had imagined them." Indeed, the story itself offers the type of Chinatown promised by *Bohemian San Francisco*, providing a "trip through its mysterious alleys, peering into the fearsome dark doorways, listening to the ominous slamming doors of the 'clubs,' and shuddering in a delightful horror at the recumbent opium smokers."[55] The abduction of Miss Ten Eyck—and her reappearance some twenty years later in a Chinese opium den, as primitive as her former self was refined—confirms the dangerous allure of Chinatown.

Given Hillegas and Miss Ten Eyck's presumptuous behavior at the restaurant, however, the tale seems more ironic than sensational, more a satire of Bohemian consumption than a straightforward account of Orientalized mystery and menace. "The Third Circle" asks what it means to lay claim to ethnic restaurants, to incorporate them within a "Bohemian San Francisco" or "New York Bohemia." *Whose* restaurants are these? Hillegas and Miss Ten Eyck feel that they own the Chinese restaurant "by right of discovery" and yet their hubris leads irresistibly to Miss Ten Eyck's degeneration. However exacting, the irony of their fate thus has a certain poetic justice, and it signals the potential hypocrisy of *la vie bohème*. Bohemianism requires a disregard of conventional boundaries and the penetration of unknown "depths," particularly of ethnic quarters, but few would-be Bohemians want to give up their traditional entitlements. The narrative enacts this Bohemian logic, but implicitly critiques it by dramatizing the arrogance of "slumming." Alongside his protagonists, Norris gravitates toward Chinatown's "Third Circle," announcing: "There are three parts of Chinatown—the part the guides show you, the part the guides don't show you, and the part no one ever hears of. It is with the latter part that this story has to do."[56] Much like the Bohemian tourist, the Bohemian story must explore this unfamiliar territory. If Chinatown is a duality of "Show Place and Forbidden Things," then the brave Bohemian has to travel from facade to essence—or, as Norris would have it, from realism to romance.[57] The outcome of Hillegas and Miss Ten Eyck's tourism problematizes this narrative trajectory, however, raising the question whether the Bohemian tale also seeks to appropriate and misread the exotic setting, all in the effort to appear "queer and original" (4).

In *Blix*, Condy and Travis are allowed their Bohemian adventures on their way toward consolidating an adult, bourgeois American identity. In "The Third Circle," however, the restaurant of the Seventy Moons resists "discovery" by would-be Bohemians, and instead of enabling the tourists to consume the Other, the Other consumes *them*. This possibility is always part of the appeal of Bohemian consumption; in hooks's words, "even though the conviction is that the familiar world will remain intact even as one ventures outside it [by consuming Otherness], the hope is that one will reenter that world no longer the same." Yet Miss Ten Eyck's fate undoes this contradictory structure, revealing its fundamental instability. She is indeed transformed—but transformed beyond recognition; she can no longer reenter her past world. Condy and Travis simply become more "sincere," but Miss Ten Eyck becomes the ultimate degenerate. She is now a "dreadful looking beast of a woman" (8), identified only by the small tattoo that she had had done just before her abduction, one she had intended to be a subtle, "chic" reminder of her naturalistic Bohemian adventure (and one that she had planned to cover with her marquise ring). Thus, like James, Norris recognizes that the dialectic of possession and dispossession could go both ways, and that the ethnic Other could exert a controlling influence over the "American" self. Still, according to Norris, such a reversal is entirely negative, producing only degeneration and not a new ethnic synthesis.

For Norris, degeneration is the final consequence of penetrating what Sartre called the "antinature" of bourgeois identity. Yet in the context of the Bohemian Club (if not of the ethnic "Bohemian" restaurant), Norris admits that there might not be anything so natural about the identities staged under the sign of Bohemia—though, here too, the staging of ethnic identities displays an explicitly imperial impetus. In *The Octopus*, the Bohemian Club's cultural work is likened to a "Midway Plaisance" (for a fuller discussion, see Chapter 4). In neocarnivalesque fashion, the Bohemian Club of *The Octopus* provides a highly mediated form of access to the social groups and practices that the normative bourgeois subject traditionally subordinates or excludes: "The Cherokee, arrayed in fringed buckskin and blue beads, rented from a costumer, intoned folk songs of his people in the vernacular. . . . The Armenian, in fez and baggy trousers, spoke of the Unspeakable Turk . . ." (826–27). Performing for the market, these social "Others" defy the very authenticity that naturalism hoped to uncover.

The East Side Bohème

As Norris suggests, *la vie bohème* contributed to the commodification of ethnic identity, imbuing the ethnic Other with added romance and market value. Under the auspices of Bohemia, race and ethnicity signified the pleasures of alterity; as "Bohemia," the "foreign" café became a vacation spot, one that relaxed the discipline of bourgeois whiteness. Signaling both cultural appreciation *and* appropriation (in ever-varying proportions), the mapping of Bohemia onto ethnic neighborhoods worked to collapse the boundary between the Old World and the New, turning both into what one commentator described as a mobile "commercial geography."[58]

Yet the extent to which the likes of a Hutchins Hapgood, William Reimer, or "Condy Rivers" did or did not impose the concept of Bohemia on ethnic restaurants remains somewhat unclear. Some restaurant proprietors probably recoiled at the notion that their establishments were part of "Bohemia." Still, the evidence suggests that, like the Sermolinos and Charlie Pfaff (in the late 1850s), other "ethnic" proprietors embraced the designation, even going so far as to market their restaurants as such. Several developed symbiotic relationships with local artists and writers: such haunts as New York's Maria's and San Francisco's Coppa's extended ample credit to these often "impecunious" patrons, and, in return, they gained a reputation for being epicenters of *la vie bohème*, thus attracting even more fame and business.[59]

But the strongest indication that Bohemia was not simply the imperial projection of the Anglo-American tourist is found in two early-twentieth-century novels: James Weldon Johnson's *The Autobiography of an Ex-Colored Man* and Abraham Cahan's *The Rise of David Levinsky*.[60] Both Cahan and Johnson take up the term "Bohemia," using it to identify cafés and clubs within the Jewish American and African American communities of New York. Existing within and without literary narrative—and though part of Bohemia's mobile commercial geography—these sites do not appear to have become cultural spectacles along the lines of "Little Hungary," and they represent a much more complex engagement with the figures of the slummer and the literary tourist. Without suspending the dialectics of possession and dispossession, Johnson's "black Bohemia" and Cahan's "East Side Bohème" worked to renegotiate the contract between these communities and the dominant culture—including its commercial imperatives. Moreover, these cultural locations mediated tensions *within* these particular communities, revealing the extent to which issues of sexuality and class also cut across ethnic and racial divides.

Cahan was a well-known public intellectual who represented Jewish life in mainstream U.S. publications and who also edited the socialist Yiddish newspaper, the *Jewish Daily Forward*. He frequented the Jewish cafés of the Lower East Side, and his very use of the term "East Side Bohème" reclaimed Bohemia from the domain of Anglo-American literary tourists.[61] To understand the power of such semantics, we have only to examine Hutchins Hapgood's usage of the term "Bohemia." Hapgood was the literary tourist who was perhaps the most fascinated by the world of the Jewish Lower East Side. Nonetheless, in *Types from the City Streets*, Hapgood identifies *himself* as an "American Bohemian," but he excludes Jews from this category: "There are, to be sure, very interesting Jews who lead, in New York's Ghetto, an artistic, intellectual, poverty-stricken existence. They are, however, intellectual debauchees rather than Bohemians; for they are full of passion, of storm, and stress: expelled from Russia, and belligerent with ideas about politics, literature, and life, they lack the repose and balance which is an essential of the true Bohemian."[62] Hapgood's earlier *Spirit of the Ghetto: Studies of the Jewish Quarter in New York*, a generally sympathetic portrait, also hesitates over applying the term "Bohemia" to the cultural milieu of Jewish poets, dramatists, musicians, and writers on the Lower East Side. He refers to "what might roughly be called the literary 'Bohemia' of the quarter," withholding the term even as he bestows it.[63] Thus, when Cahan describes the "East Side Bohème" of the Jewish quarter (without surrounding the term with quotation marks), he implicitly challenges Hapgood's assessment. Reterritorializing *la vie bohème*, Cahan locates it outside the phenomenology of literary tourism.

Still, *The Spirit of the Ghetto* was largely the product of Hapgood's friendship with Cahan. Both Cahan and Hapgood became writers for Lincoln Steffens's *Commercial Advertiser* in 1897, and Cahan was the one who introduced Hapgood to the world of the Jewish Lower East Side. However "roughly" or pointedly construed, Bohemia was a terrain that both men valued and shared. Located within and without the dominant culture, the East Side Bohème suggested cultural possibilities beyond assimilation or hyphenated Americanism, and as such attracted both Hapgood, a disaffected Anglo-American patrician, and Cahan, a Russian-Jewish immigrant. That Hapgood and Cahan could differ over the applicability of the very term "Bohemia" reminds us of the difficulties of overriding cultural boundaries, even in the name of what was, by definition, a mobile cultural territory. Still, both found in the East Side Bohème an alternative to what Hapgood called the "stupid Philistinism of content," an alternative that brought together Anglo-American aestheticism and Jewish socialism in an unstable alliance against the American "bourgeois."[64]

What were the grounds for this alliance? Answering this question reveals the complicated ways in which class intersected with questions of ethnicity and nationality. As Jonathan Freedman has argued, there was an intricate and deeply contradictory nexus between Jews, ideas of Jewishness, the Anglo-American gentry elite, and the delineation of "such enduring figures as the marginalized artist and the alienated intellectual."[65] It is just such a nexus that the world of the East Side Bohème helped to produce, both within and without *The Spirit of the Ghetto* and *The Rise of David Levinsky*.

To a large extent, this nexus depended on a shared disavowal of "the bourgeois," a disavowal that became all the more intense at a time when contemporary cultural discourses posited "the bourgeois" as a function of American or Jewish character (and, of course, some Jewish and Anglo-American intellectuals wanted to separate themselves from the bourgeois by putting the onus on the other group).[66] As we have seen, James's own reading of the Lower East Side oscillates between these conceptions of American and Jewish character, combining both within the dialectic of possession and dispossession. For James, this dialectic often appears rigged in favor of a bourgeois commercial ethos, one that overwhelms the national "foreground," regardless of whether it is predominantly "ethnic" or "American." By contrast, both Hapgood and Cahan imagine that a synthesis of the "American" and the "Hebraic" could undermine rather than uphold this bourgeois ethos, thus transforming the national culture in the process. As an expatriated high-cultural observer, James largely exempts himself from the dialectic of possession and dispossession, but Cahan and Hapgood hope to reincorporate such an alienated perspective and thus to lay claim to what Waldo Frank (another alienated intellectual) would polemically refer to as "Our America."[67]

For both Hapgood and Cahan, such a synthesis depended on a cross-class and cross-ethnic alliance of the sort staged within the East Side Bohème (however differently the two men sought to configure these alliances). Hapgood's class analysis is largely a matter of literary aesthetics, yet it is a pervasive feature of his criticism, and the "literature" he advocates acts as a metonym for the larger national culture he hopes to realize:

> There is an esthetic relationship between the highest and the lowest. The imagination of an intensely cultivated man plays about the common and necessary elements of his being; and the tough remains eloquently embedded in these same elements. They are both unhesitating and authoritative in matters of relative value; for the aristocrat has learned that the simple things are the best and most significant; while the tough has known no other. They both, therefore, express only the best. The middle-class person, on the other hand, striving constantly to rise, to get where he is not, is comparatively vulgar, graceless, and unformed. He is admirable in a moral sense, but his words lack literature, for they are confused and pointless, overabundant and reveal a lack of conviction as to what is the "real thing." How can he know, in his Cook's tour-like voyage through life, what the necessary and fundamental things are?[68]

According to Hapgood, it is on the plane of the "real"—both within and without literature—that the "highest" and the "lowest" properly connect. This meeting does not undo the hierarchy of the classes, and Hapgood is careful to distinguish between the ways in which each class arrives at the "necessary and fundamental things"; what is necessity for one is cultivation for the other, a distinction Hapgood never elides. Yet to the extent that he does align the highest and the lowest, his logic works to isolate the middle classes and to challenge the ground on which they would claim to represent a national consensus. Hapgood seeks to detach realism from the "formidable foreground"—and the commercial middle-class world it spatialized. Much like Norris (though without ironizing his own pretensions), Hapgood seeks to penetrate beneath a middle-class "realism" he sees as occupying a "geometric place, without dimensions of depth, a mere outside."[69]

For Hapgood, aligning the "highest" and the "lowest" against the bourgeois required a corresponding synthesis of the "American" and the "foreign." Searching for both "low life" and foreignness, Hapgood was drawn to the Lower East Side, imagining that here, the literary tourist could find something of value that was lacking in the larger national culture. If the Hungarian café helped the nervous American to develop contemplative repose, the Jewish ghetto provided an influx of "moral earnestness and native idealism." Whether in the form of the "old traditions" or the "new socialism," this idealism fulfilled an aesthetic agenda: it helped "detach the soul from the sordid business of life." Thus reduced to aestheticized forms, the "old traditions" and the "new socialism" were largely interchangeable for Hapgood, and both represented the type of "spiritual unity" that America needed to incorporate into its own national culture as a counterweight to the "vulgar, graceless, and unformed" bourgeois.[70]

Hapgood rhapsodizes about this Lower East Side world (even though he questions whether it is properly "Bohemian"):

> Enthusiastic young men gather every evening in cafés of the quarter and become habitually intoxicated with the excitement of ideas. In their restless and feverish eyes shines the intense idealism of the combined Jew and Russian—the moral earnestness of the Hebrew united with the passionate, rebellious mental activity of the modern Muscovite. In these cafés they meet after the theatre or an evening lecture and talk into the morning hours. The ideal, indeed, is alive within them.[71]

According to Hapgood, these cafés not only synthesize the Jew and the Russian, but also help "supply the demand for a serious life which at the same time shall be American." Hapgood delights in the Jewish cafés, maintaining that the exchange of ideas, creeds, nationalities, and identities produces a "veritable intellectual fermentation," one that is "not primarily interested in the dollar."[72] The East Side Bohème does not preserve and market an ethnic past to upscale "American" consumers, nor does it constitute a closed ethnic enclave. According to Hapgood, it is instead a place where a future "ideal" could be imagined and debated. Existing between Old World orthodoxy and New World "Philistinism," the East Side Bohème instead offers a third term, one that displaces the hyphen between "Jewish" and "American"—the very hyphen that emerging theories of cultural pluralism sought to install. In the process, "American life as a whole" could be infused with this (largely departicularized and deracinated) idealism.[73]

To varying extents throughout his long career, Cahan also upheld an intellectual culture that negotiated between the "highest and the lowest" and the Jewish and the American. For Cahan, these negotiations took place both through the genre of literary realism and in the literary-social world of the East Side Bohème; and more specifically, these negotiations also took place in the East Side Bohème of Cahan's great realist novel, *The Rise of David Levinsky*. Though Cahan shared Hapgood's desire for synthesis of Jewish and American, intellectual and working-class cultures, he did not want to sacrifice socialism or Jewish nationalism to the demands of "Our America." *Levinsky*'s East Side Bohème suggests some of the ways in which Cahan's and Hapgood's projected syntheses do and do not align.

Complicating this comparison is the matter of Levinsky's narration. The East Side Bohème was Cahan's own social milieu, but it is not that of Levinsky. Though written in the first person, Cahan's novel is, as Werner Sollors has argued, an "ironically antithetical construction": Levinsky is Cahan's double, an "antiself" whose life story stands in implicit contrast to that of his creator.[74] Whereas Cahan became a socialist, Levinsky is an archcapitalist; whereas Cahan realized his intellectual ambitions, Levinsky relinquishes his dream of attending college; and whereas Cahan was at home in Bohemia, Levinsky feels like a "rank outsider."[75] By this process of inversion, the East Side Bohème represents many of the cultural possibilities that Levinsky's rise threatens to forestall.

As a member of the Jewish bourgeoisie, Levinsky admits that the East Side Bohème is "the last place in the world for me to visit." But visit he does, entering Bohemia in search of Tevkin, the father of Anna, the latest woman he dreams of marrying. Once a Hebrew poet in Russia, Tevkin is now "a passionate frequenter of Yampolsky's café, a well-known gathering-place of the East Side Bohème." In this café, most of the patrons are "socialists or anarchists or some other kind of 'ists' " (454). Levinsky knows that, if recognized in this Bohemia, he will be seen as a class enemy. He is himself acutely aware of his own class difference; he not only worries about how he will be perceived, but he is repelled by the customers and their lack of bourgeois niceties:

> I sat at the end of one of the tables, a glass of Russian tea before me. There were two other customers at that table, both poorly clad and, as it seemed to me, ill-fed. . . . A

man with curly dark hair who was eating soup at the table directly in front of me was satirizing somebody between spoonfuls, relishing his acrimony as if it were spice to his soup. . . . I was wretchedly ill at ease at first. I loathed myself for being here. I felt like one who had strayed into a disreputable den. In addition, I was in dread of being recognized. The man who sat by my side had the hair and the complexion of a gipsy. He looked exhausted and morose. Presently he had a fried steak served him. It was heavily laden with onions. As he fell to cutting and eating it hungrily the odor of the fried onions and the sound of his lips sickened me. (455)

On first glance, the patrons of the café strike Levinsky as politically threatening and socially repulsive. Levinsky's very bourgeois disgust establishes the café as a Bohemian locale.

In this first impression, Levinsky views the café as a repository of what Hapgood refers to as "low life" (without the positive inflection). Yet Levinsky begins to change his mind about Bohemia, and, however ironized, his perspective seems increasingly to merge with that of Cahan. Levinsky is, after all, a frustrated intellectual, and his sense of what he should have been in life confirms Cahan's own choices. Thus, while in the East Side Bohème, Levinsky's sense of superiority quickly dissipates, and he begins to intuit that Bohemia provides the stage for something like Hapgood's "esthetic relationship between the highest and the lowest"; in other words, he recognizes that it provides the cultural capital that (from the standpoint of the "highest") could catapult one into an "intellectual aristocracy" (169). Also, much like Hapgood, Levinsky imagines that this aristocracy could further a (specifically classed) synthesis of the Jewish and the American, a synthesis that his own bourgeois life has been unable to bring about.

Levinsky begins to reevaluate Bohemia when "an intellectual-looking Gentile" (perhaps modeled on Hapgood) appears on the scene:

"Either a journalist in search of material," Tevkin explained to me in answer to a question, "or simply a man of literary tastes who is drawn to the atmosphere of this place."

The café rose in my estimation. (461)

Levinsky further reevaluates the café when Tevkin points out a "literary liquor dealer" who "would be a celebrated writer if he were not worth half a million." Levinsky reflects, "The last piece of information was a most agreeable surprise to me. It made me feel safe in the place. I regarded the liquor-dealer with some contempt, however. 'Pshaw! half a million. He's probably worth a good deal less. Anyhow, I could buy and sell him." But Levinsky quickly qualifies this "vulgar" assessment, and Levinsky/Cahan makes it clear that he shares the values of the (possibly "Gentile," presumably educated) reader:

> At the same time, I said to myself, "He's well-to-do and yet he chums around with people in whom intellectual Gentiles take an interest." I envied him. I felt cheap.
>
> I felt still cheaper when I heard that the literary liquor-dealer generously contributed to the maintenance of *The Pen*, the Hebrew weekly with which Tevkin was connected, and that he, the liquor-dealer, wrote for that publication. (46–62)

Levinsky thus acknowledges that social status comprises something besides net worth. Still, Levinsky can only assess such values by relying on a monetary scale. Even when he professes to weigh intellectual accomplishment above and beyond his own fortune, he cannot escape the idiom of the marketplace; he feels "cheap" in relation to the literary liquor-dealer, implicitly calculating the value of the latter's cultural capital, a sum which compounds the putative "half a million."[76] Yet though his observation "I felt cheap" undercuts Levinsky's desire for transcendence, the narrative as a whole endorses his sense that literary and intellectual pursuits have a higher value than his own financial gains. Further, written in English instead of Yiddish, the narrative itself acknowledges that cultural capital is enhanced by being "one in whom intellectual Gentiles take an interest." As for Cahan, he valued being part of a cosmopolitan intelligentsia, and, in particular, he himself helped to facilitate the explorations of two prominent "intellectual Gentiles" when he introduced Hapgood and William Dean Howells to the Lower East Side.

In coming to America, it had been Levinsky's intention to receive a college education and to become part of such a cosmopolitan intelligentsia, and at the end of the novel he maintains, "I should probably have made a much better college professor than a cloak-manufacturer" (529). Though he had lost his old religion, he had hoped that its place could be "taken by something else," namely by the university. "University-bred people were the real nobility of the world," Levinsky concludes, insisting, "a college diploma was a certificate of moral as well as intellectual aristocracy" (169). As part of this aristocracy, Levinsky had hoped to achieve a synthesis between Orthodox Jewish culture, with its reverence for spiritual education, and patrician Americanism, with its neoaristocratic exaltation of "Culture" over and against the business of moneymaking. Yet, while dreaming of City College, Levinsky became increasingly involved in business, spurred by necessity and ultimately by that "passionate pecuniary interest," that devotion to financial gain that Henry James and other members of the older gentry elite complained had become the dominant obsession of bourgeois America. The presence of the intellectual-looking gentile reminds Levinsky of his earlier ambitions, and he becomes even less secure in his own class position. Suddenly, this café, which had first struck him as entirely "disreputable" and déclassé, seems to represent a higher status than that attained by David Levinsky, the wealthy cloak manufacturer. As the "University of the Ghetto" (in the words of one contemporary observer), the East Side Bohème helped to cultivate the "intellectual aristocracy."[77] This is the class that Levinsky wants to join. It is not simply that he wishes to associate with Gentiles so as to achieve a more Americanized identity. Indeed, however "Americanized" and elite, the identity that Levinsky covets is also, paradoxically, a quite self-consciously marginalized one.

Yet Cahan was also skeptical about the alliance between the Jewish and Anglo-American intelligentsia, particularly when the "intellectual aristocracy" threatened to fold back into the bourgeoisie and the world of its commercial entertainments. Moreover, he did not believe that the relation between "the highest and the lowest" (to the extent that he accepted these terms) should be merely "esthetic." He recognized that, for the slummer and the literary tourist, the dreaded "bourgeois" was primarily an aesthetic and social category rather than an economic designation. As a socialist organizer, Cahan recoiled against such diluted versions of class analysis. In *The Rise of David Levinsky*, he ironically recounts how it was that a cloakmakers' strike had united uptown slummers and the Jewish working class:

> The press supported the strikers. It did so, not because they were working-people, but because they were East-Siders. Their district was the great field of activity for the American University Settlement worker and fashionable slummer. The East Side was a place upon which one descended in quest of esoteric types and "local color," as well as for the purposes of philanthropy and "uplift" work. To spend an evening in some East Side café was regarded as something like spending a few hours at the Louvre; so much so that one such café, in the depth of East Houston Street, was making a fortune by purveying expensive wine dinners to people from up-town who came there ostensibly to see "how the other half lived," but who only saw one another eat and drink in freedom from the restraint of manners. Accordingly, to show sympathy for the East Side strikers was within the bounds of the highest propriety. (284–85)

Replete with a broadside against one of the fashionable East Side cafés (perhaps "Little Hungary," but not "Yampolsky's"), Levinsky/Cahan questions whether a revolt against bourgeois manners and mores constitutes an appropriate basis upon which to sympathize with Jewish workers. Cahan himself did not necessarily see the revolt against bourgeois manners as a desirable corollary to a socialist politics; describing his editorial agenda at the *Jewish Daily Forward*, Cahan elsewhere claimed that it was as "important to teach the reader to carry a handkerchief in his pocket as it is to teach him to carry a union card."[78] Still, Cahan recognized that the alliance between the Jewish cloakmakers and the Anglo-American tourists was effective; the support of the press helped to bolster the power of the union. The allure of Bohemia could thus have important political benefits for the workers—at this moment (which Cahan based on the cloakmakers' strike of 1890), the commodification of Otherness paradoxically helped the garment workers to gain greater control over their own labor power. Carrie Tirado Bramen has argued that the contemporary interest in urban local color—what she calls the "urban picturesque"—acted "to switch the focus from concern about the growing economic chasm to celebration of ethnic diversity."[79] Yet, as Cahan suggests in *Levinsky*, this switched focus might, in this instance at least, have done less to divert attention away from the economic divide than to renew and intensify such concerns.[80]

To be sure, the café that Cahan identifies with the East Side Bohème is a much less spectacular venue than "Little Hungary," and it seeks to oppose bourgeois life through literary culture, Jewish nationalism, and socialist doctrine instead of through a commodified "freedom of manners." Still, pivotal as the East Side Bohème was in Cahan's own life, the novel only provides a brief glimpse of this world. As Susan K. Harris has argued, Cahan never fully realizes "the potential socialist community in his work: it exists either as a dark window onto an unspecified, unexplored territory, as at the end of 'The Imported Bridegroom,' or, at its best, in the evocation of family solidarity in the socialist Tevkin home in *The Rise of David Levinsky*."[81] In the context of *Levinsky*, the East Side Bohème also remains largely "unexplored," illuminated by a fictional surrogate who remains an outsider, unable to understand the "jargon of nicknames, catchphrases, and allusions that was apparently peculiar to the East Side Bohème" (456). It is likely that Cahan more fully explicates the world of the East Side Bohème in his own Yiddish-language autobiography *Bletter fun Mein Leben* (most of which remains untranslated); in his English-language fiction, however, he limits the access of the would-be slummer. Located within and without the dominant national culture, between the foreign and the domestic, the East Side Bohème ultimately eludes realist representation and the "consuming vision" of the literary tourist/reader.[82]

Black Bohemia

Published in 1912, the year before Cahan's "Autobiography of an American Jew," James Weldon Johnson's *The Autobiography of an Ex-Colored Man* represents another version of *la vie bohème*, the "black Bohemia" that flourished around the turn of the century in the Tenderloin and San Juan Hill districts of midtown Manhattan. Prior to the development of Harlem, this earlier black Bohemia provided a space for the development of African American artistic culture. A compound term, "black Bohemia" denoted a new cosmopolitan mixture, one that sought to retain the specificity of African American expressive culture while redefining the "American" culture industry and its musical productions. Along with the "East Side Bohème," this Bohemia located itself within and without the "American Scene," and through a process of immanent critique, sought to transform the larger national culture.[83]

The term "black Bohemia" invites the question how race structured *la vie bohème*. The term appears in the title of Will Marion Cook and Alex Rogers's musical drama *Black Bohemia: An Act Depicting Life as Seen in the Negro Cafes and Rathskellers Around New York City* (1911), and it figures prominently in Johnson's writings, from *The Autobiography of an Ex-Colored Man* to his own autobiography, *Along This Way* (1933).[84] Members of black Bohemia, Johnson, Cook, and Rogers all sought to represent the milieu they frequented in their life and art.

Black Manhattan, Johnson's nonfictional history, also devotes several chapters to this turn-of-the-century Bohemia, analyzing its position within dominant social and cultural geographies:

> New York's black Bohemia constituted a part of the famous old Tenderloin; and, naturally, it nourished a number of the ever present vices; chief among them, gambling and prostitution. But it nourished other things; and one of these things was artistic effort. It is in the growth of this artistic effort that we are here interested; the rest of the manifestations were commonplaces. This black Bohemia had its physical being in a number of clubs—a dozen or more of them well established and well known. . . . It was in such places as this that early Negro theatrical talent created for

itself a congenial atmosphere, an atmosphere of emulation and guildship. It was also an atmosphere in which new artistic ideas were born and developed.[85]

Insisting that gambling and prostitution were "ever present" and "commonplace" elements of Bohemia, Johnson emphasizes that these "vices" were in no way specific to a black artistic milieu.[86] Still, as Johnson's clarification suggests, invoking Bohemia together with blackness was a risky proposition, and the color line significantly complicated the Bohemian and Bourgeois dichotomy. On one level, the whiff of Bohemianism compounded the pernicious racial stereotypes of the period. As James H. Dormon notes, popular "coon songs" at the turn of the century (the very songs that the musicians in black Bohemia were expected to write and perform) represented African Americans as "indolent and unambitious, devoid of the work ethnic or internalized bourgeois values"[87]—a description that matches negative characterizations of the Bohemian. The "black Bohemian" might thus be seen as doubly shiftless.

On the other hand, Bohemia's absence of "bourgeois values" also helped African American leaders like Johnson to articulate how black culture offered a valuable difference from the norms of white America. They did so, in part, by appealing to the more genteel versions of Bohemia that, as we have seen, had become popular by the turn of the century. Merging with Arnoldian versions of "Culture," Bohemia helped inspire a struggle against "the common tide of men's thoughts in a wealthy and industrial community" through the development of "a general *humane* spirit."[88] This view of Culture was often used as a way of legitimizing the dominant national cultures that produced it, and later generations have doubted whether the "genteel traditions" of England and the United States were at all oppositional. Still, in many cases, these more genteel versions of Bohemia challenged the status quo, especially when embraced by a constituency already marginalized by race, class, gender, or sexual orientation. For example, Paul Laurence Dunbar, who was at times part of the social milieu Johnson describes as "black Bohemia," suggests the oppositional uses of "purity" when he writes to his future wife:

I never sent you a copy of the "*New Bohemian*" [the little magazine published in Cincinnati] which I mentioned a long while ago because its contents grew entirely too erotic. I am a Bohemian, but not of that type,—there is as much purity of thought, motive and action in Bohemia as elsewhere—perhaps more. In this world it isn't so much among what people one lives or where one lives,—it is more *how* one lives."[89]

This genteel interpretation of Bohemia allows Dunbar to claim the "purity" that the racial stereotypes of white America sought to deny African Americans. Similarly, though granting that *la vie bohème* was still connected with "the ever present vices" of gambling and prostitution, Johnson refuses to pander to voyeuristic interest in such vices; he announces that his own account will focus instead on "the growth of . . . artistic effort" that Bohemia—specifically his "black Bohemia"—worked to produce.[90]

In the context of this "artistic effort," however, Johnson did connect black Bohemia with cultural forms that were well outside the province of the genteel tradition and its version of *la vie bohème*. For Johnson, black Bohemia represented a "new world—an alluring world, a tempting world, a world of greatly lessened restraints, a world of fascinating perils; but, above all, a world of tremendous artistic potentialities."[91] Part of this artistic potentiality derived from the "taste of primitive joy in life and living" that Johnson identified with black Bohemia. Johnson thus linked his Bohemia to emerging (and highly controversial) notions of cultural "primitivism." The allure of Bohemianism helped such African American leaders as Johnson to articulate how black culture might offer an enabling difference from the norms of bourgeois whiteness. In one of the most frequently cited scenes in *The Autobiography*, Johnson's Ex-Colored Man explains how his first experience of ragtime released what Johnson elsewhere describes as "a taste of primitive joy in life and living":

> It was music of a kind I had never heard before. It was music that demanded a physical response, patting of the feet, drumming of the fingers or nodding of the head in time with the beat. The barbaric harmonies, the audacious resolutions, often consisting of an abrupt jump from one key to another, the intricate rhythms in which the accents fell in the most unexpected places, but in which the beat was never lost, produced a most curious effect.[92]

Figured as "barbaric," the demand of a bodily response elicits the "primitive" vitality that many contemporary blacks and whites alike sought (often quite ambivalently) in African American music. This music, Johnson suggests, was what all Bohemians had long been waiting for in their efforts to cast off bourgeois restriction. However double-edged, the term "Bohemia" helped to emphasize the extent to which African American expressive forms might challenge what Du Bois referred to as the "mad, money-getting plutocracy."[93] More pragmatically, black Bohemia also enabled African American writers and performers to resist commercialism from within: to challenge the entertainment industry by claiming ownership of their own cultural productions.

Both a fictional and an actual location, Johnson's black Bohemia delineates, in Robert Stepto's words, new "spatial configurations of music, interracial liaison, and intemperance such as the Negro cabaret." Indeed, according to Stepto, "'the Club' . . . inaugurates all such spatial configurations in modern Afro-American letters" and serves as the "most remarkable symbolic space in the *Autobiography*."[94] As one of the sites in which, as Johnson writes, "black Bohemia had its physical being," the Club enacts a spatial politics that recognizes the simultaneity of the abstract and the material, of cultural representations and lived experiences, the past and the present, the individual and the collective.[95] In so doing, it achieves what Sara Blair describes as the "desideratum of cultural geography as a mode of social critique": it begins to imagine how "practices of location, reterritorialization, and boundary making can be differently situated, and thus reinvested with social agency."[96] The Club performs such reterritorialization within the larger social geographies of the "new cosmopolis" and African American narrative; even within its own interior, the club respatializes social relationships between the "colored Bohemians and sports" and the members of "the Talented Tenth"—as well as between "the white and colored people of certain classes." Describing the Club, Johnson notes:

> On the main floor there were two large rooms: a parlor about thirty feet in length, and a large, square back room into which the parlor opened. The floor of the parlor was carpeted; small tables and chairs were arranged about the room; the windows were draped with lace curtains, and the walls were literally covered with photographs or lithographs of every colored man in America who had ever "done anything." There were pictures of Frederick Douglass and of Peter Jackson, of all the lesser lights of the prize-fighting ring, of all the famous jockeys and the stage celebrities, down to the newest song and dance team. . . . In the back room there was a piano, and tables were placed around the wall. The floor was bare and the center was left vacant for singers, dancers, and others who entertained the patrons. (76)

Connecting the parlor with its photographs and the back room with its piano, the very layout of the Club bridges the worlds of black Bohemia and the black bourgeoisie. Though Du Bois disparaged the black Bohemian nightclubs—particularly as represented in the work of such later Harlem Renaissance writers as Claude McKay and Langston Hughes—the topography of the Club suggests that the "parlor" (the space of Du

Bois's Talented Tenth) and the "backroom" (the space of popular entertainment) were in fact coterminous: occupying much the same cultural plane, both worked in tandem to challenge the color line. In Stepto's words, "the communion between the two rooms is but a spatial expression of the bond between artful acts in the present and a sense of tradition shaping past, present, and future into a single continuum."[97]

By locating popular entertainment within a larger tradition of African American expressive culture, the Club helped performers resist the expropriation of their talents. Offering "an atmosphere of guildship," black Bohemia enabled performers to question the axiom that no "audiences would pay to see Negro performers in any other role than that of Mississippi River roustabouts." Of the "visiting stage professionals" who performed at the club, the Ex-Colored Man remarks:

> There was one man, a minstrel, who, whenever he responded to a request to "do something," never essayed anything below a reading from Shakespeare. How well he read I do not know, but he greatly impressed me; and I can say that at least he had a voice which strangely stirred those who heard it. Here was a man who made people laugh at the size of his mouth, while he carried in his heart a burning ambition to be a tragedian; and so after all he did play a part in a tragedy. (77)

Performing in black Bohemia thus gives this actor the space in which to cast off minstrel stereotypes and to become a tragedian on his own terms. According to Johnson, the atmosphere of guildship within black Bohemia also encouraged "the younger and brighter men" to discuss "the time when they would compel the public to recognize that they could do something more than grin and cut pigeon-wings"; in black Bohemia, African American performers could free their talents from the bonds of racial caricature and direct their own cultural productions (77). Itself an example of such imaginative freedom, Cook and Rogers's *Black Bohemia* involves a "singer in a big white café" who stops in at the black "rathskeller," and delights in singing and dancing spontaneously with other black musicians on stage and in the audience.[98] It was just such community and guildship that helped to produce what Johnson elsewhere calls the "second phase" of African American musical and theatrical development, a phase that sought to reconstruct popular minstrelsy and the white-dominated culture industry it supported.[99]

Like the Ex-Colored Man, Johnson himself had hoped to use popular music to help achieve such cultural reconstruction, upholding black Bohemia as the site from which progressive change could take place.

Though black Bohemia afforded an enabling distance from exploitative social structures, Johnson did not position it as a marginal location; rather, it was the internal "centre" from which the larger national culture might be transformed.[100] Between 1900 and 1906, Johnson was part of the songwriting team "Cole and Johnson Brothers," and together with his brother, J. Rosamond Johnson, and Bob Cole, he became one of the leading black songwriters in Broadway musical theatre. As a member of this songwriting team, Johnson became a major influence in "the making of popular songs for the American people."[101] Johnson recognized that African American folk songs had long been an essential part of American musical theatre; the difference was that, during this second phase, black composers were able to copyright and market their own songs. As Johnson records, blackface minstrelsy had "depended for its songs almost entirely on the Negro plantation jingles," yet such performances had consisted of "merely slavish imitation or outright appropriation of this folk-material."[102] In this context, the phrase "slavish imitation" not only reclaims ownership of the music, but also challenges contemporary racial discourses that imputed "imitativeness" (not to mention servility) to African Americans.[103] Johnson's history thus extends the efforts of the many turn-of-the-century black musicians—including Johnson himself—who strove to counter such appropriations and to make Broadway theatre more equitably cross-cultural.

During this second phase, there were several popular Broadway musicals written by black composers and lyricists and performed by all-black casts—though the producers and publishers of the sheet music were generally white.[104] One of the first was *Clorindy—The Origin of the Cake-Walk* (1898), with lyrics by the African American poet Paul Laurence Dunbar, and with music by the African American composer Will Marion Cook. It was staged with an all-black cast by the white producer, George Lederer, and, according to Johnson, "It was the talk of New York. It was the first demonstration of the possibilities of syncopated Negro music. Cook was the first competent composer to take what was then known as rag-time and work it out in a musicianly way. His choruses and finales in *Clorindy*, complete novelties as they were, sung by a lusty chorus, were simply breath-taking. Broadway had something entirely new."[105]

It was the challenge of taking ragtime music and "working it out in a musicianly way" that most appealed to Johnson and his peers. Helping to bridge the "front" and "back" rooms of black Bohemia, this challenge also appeared to herald a new "American" popular culture, one that would more fairly include African American writers and performers, and one that would displace the color line through the very hybridity of its musical and theatrical forms. Johnson records that it was at this time that he "began to grope toward a realization of the importance of the American Negro's cultural background and his creative folk-art, and to speculate on the superstructure of conscious art that might be reared upon them."[106]

Black Bohemia provided a space where such a "superstructure" could be erected. As Johnson records in *The Autobiography*, ragtime had first

> originated in the questionable resorts about Memphis and St. Louis by Negro piano players who knew no more of the theory of music than they did of the theory of the universe, but were guided by natural musical instinct and talent. It made its way to Chicago, where it was popular some time before it reached New York. These players often improvised crude and, at times, vulgar words to fit the melodies. This was the beginning of the ragtime song. Several of these improvisations were taken down by white men, the words slightly altered, and published under the names of the arrangers. They sprang into immediate popularity and earned small fortunes, of which the Negro originators got only a few dollars. (72–73)

In the hands of the white "arrangers," the ragtime song often became a latter-day version of the minstrel "coon song." As such, most popular rag songs consisted of syncopated rhythms, combined with lyrics that represented black characters in dialect. In its very form, production, and reception, ragtime had as its structuring tension the "problem of the color line." As Cristina Ruotolo argues, the music itself combined the "rhythms and harmonies of African American expressive culture with the Euro-American march form"; thus, "the 'line' between white and black might have been heard within the music as an implied tension between downbeats and syncopated offbeats." Ruotolo also notes that this tension "persisted quite dramatically among musicians as a difference between 'trained' musicians who wrote down their songs, marketing them as sheet music, and those for whom music remained an oral practice, inseparable from performance."[107] The black Bohemians sought to renegotiate this color line, both by developing (in Johnson's words) a "style that displaced the old 'coon songs'" and by gaining increased economic control over their own creations. In black Bohemia, Johnson writes, "a number of colored men, of not only musical talent, but training, [were] writing out their own melodies and words and reaping the reward of their work."[108] Composers like Rosamond Johnson and Will Cook were able to do so in large part because of their "mastery of and mobility across different musical traditions":[109] Rosamond Johnson had been trained at the New England Conservatory of Music and Will Cook studied at the Hochschule in Berlin. They notated their own music, thus deterring would-be pirates and demonstrating their ability to excel in a "white" print medium. Challenging the racialized divide between notation and performance, these musicians also sought to create more hybrid musical forms, ones that would transform the already hybrid "coon songs" by bringing "a higher degree of artistry, especially with regard to the text."[110]

In this transitional moment, much of the minstrel structure of the "coon songs" remained, even as African American artists began to subvert the form from within. It was a difficult trade-off; the minstrel structure ensured a popular audience and an entrée into the music industry, yet it also imposed many denigrating stereotypes. Still, even though *Clorindy* featured songs with such titles as "Hottest Coon in Dixie" and "Who Dat Say Chicken in Dis Crowd," Cook recalled in 1944 that it had represented an advance for African American artists: "Negroes were at last on Broadway, and there to stay. Gone was the uff-dah of the minstrel! Gone the Massa Linkum stuff! We were artists and we had the world on a string tied to a runnin'red-geared wagon on a down-hill pull. Nothing could stop us, and nothing did for a decade." Ernest Hogan, the star of *Clorindy*, echoed Cook: "we came along in leaps and bounds after weighing the good with the abuse." Johnson himself sought to overcome the double bind of the "good with the abuse" by setting "the level of musical entertainment several degrees higher." Though this ambition would seem to endorse a racialized cultural hierarchy, one that would relegate African American expressive culture to a "lower" level than that of the Euro-American classical tradition, Johnson insisted that his project of "elevation" mainly applied to the "conscious imitations" of African American folk-songs—particularly, one would imagine, those of black-face minstrelsy—and not to the folk originals, which, Johnson emphasized, had "excellencies" that could not translate into mass cultural copies.[111]

It was in black Bohemia that many of the new "artistic potentialities" were explored. A liminal space between African American "folk" culture and the white-dominated entertainment industry, black Bohemia was where such musical transformations took place. Like other contemporary black Bohemians, Johnson's fictional "Ex-Colored Man" takes ragtime and "works it out in a musicianly way." Just as his light skin enables him to "pass" back and forth across the color line, so his musical training allows him to move between African American and Euro-American traditions, and even to develop new fusions of the two. Thus he reports:

> Through continually listening to the music at the "Club," and through my own previous training, my natural talent and perseverance, I developed into a remarkable player of ragtime; indeed, I had the name at that time of being the best ragtime-player in New York. I brought all my knowledge of classic music to bear and, in so doing, achieved some novelties which pleased and even astonished my listeners. It was I who first made ragtime transcriptions of familiar classic selections. I used to play Mendelssohn's "Wedding March" in a manner that never failed to arouse enthusiasm among the patrons of the "Club." Very few nights passed during which I was not asked to play it. It was no secret that the great increase in slumming visitors was due to my playing. (83–84)

The Ex-Colored Man is proud of this increase in "slumming visitors": even as he incorporates classical music into ragtime, his playing opens the space of black Bohemia to "interracial" sociability and commerce.

As the Ex-Colored Man demonstrates, however, such commerce often did more to reinforce than to displace the color line. Despite the "guildship" of black Bohemia, the slummers once again threatened to commodify racial Otherness in a relentless search for "novelty," one that provided new opportunities for African American entertainers but that also left many existing racial and economic power differentials mostly intact. Johnson notes the presence in black Bohemia of the many white "variety performers and others who delineated 'darky character'" and who "came to get their imitations first hand from the Negro entertainers they saw there" (78). Indeed, James L. Ford, a frequent chronicler of Bohemianism, never explored black Bohemia, but, tellingly enough, he does note the presence of ragtime in one of the Bohemian haunts on the Lower East Side: in his "Trip No. 4—Bohemia," Ford observes, "the Hungarian band struck up the favorite Bohemian tune, 'My Ragtime Liza Jane,' the entire company joining in the chorus." African American music thus helped to define the Bohemia of the Lower East Side, but African Americans were not present as performers.[112]

Black Bohemia was, as Stepto argues, "an ambiguous domain between America's black and white worlds."[113] Even the interracial sexual relationships formed within black Bohemia as described by Johnson involved economic and erotic power struggles. With respect to the relationship between the white "rich widow" and her "well-setup, very black" male companion, Johnson even invokes the ultimate figure of popular fin-de-siècle Bohemianism: Trilby. The widow, Johnson writes, has "eyes very much like Du Maurier's conception of Trilby's 'twin gray stars.' " In Du Maurier's melodrama, the Bohemian Trilby, mesmerized by the Jewish Svengali, is utterly possessed by him. In *The Autobiography*, the widow has the financial power, and yet she is enthralled by the "surly, black despot who held sway over her deepest emotions." Racial, sexual and economic difference conjoin to produce the violence that results in the widow's death (79, 89).[114]

Many of the "slummers" who came to black Bohemia, Johnson notes, hoped to find an antidote for the boredom and ennui of genteel whiteness. One of these slummers is the young millionaire who becomes the Ex-Colored Man's patron. First viewing the Ex-Colored Man in black Bohemia, the patron hires him to play at private parties. Thus removed from black Bohemia, the Ex-Colored Man is treated as an exotic commodity, catering to those "who were ever expecting to find happiness in novelty, each day restlessly exploring and exhausting every resource of this great city that might possibly furnish a new sensation or awaken a fresh emotion, and who were always grateful to anyone who aided them in their quest." The Ex-Colored Man and his ragtime music become a means to this end, and, following one of his performances, his patron gloats, "Well, I have given them something they never had before" (86–87). As a commodity, the Ex-Colored Man's music enters into a consumerist culture that thrives on the constant search for "newness" and that values ragtime precisely because of its Otherness; instead of displacing the color line through the combination of aural experience, hybrid musicality, and interracial commerce, the commodification of ragtime threatened to exaggerate racial difference and to enhance the economic privileges of whiteness. While providing the Ex-Colored Man with adequate financial compensation, the patron nonetheless exploits his artistry: at times, the patron so consumes the Ex-Colored Man that he becomes "oppressed with fatigue and sleepiness," even to the point that it "took almost superhuman effort to keep [his] fingers going" (88).

As Johnson suggests, black Bohemia could only hold the racialized cycle of possession and dispossession in partial abeyance. Even when the Ex-Colored Man's ragtime seems most to dissolve racial difference, the color line returns as quickly as it is erased. When the millionaire's "blasé" friends respond to the Ex-Colored Man's ragtime by "involuntarily and unconsciously" performing "an impromptu cake-walk," the astonishment and delight of the white audience seemingly confirms the ability of the music to cross racial divides; it even goes so far as to elicit a visceral, bodily response, one that "unconsciously" produces dance movements associated with African American expressive culture (87). Yet this unconscious movement, the novel suggests, had its basis in what Eric Sunquist describes as the "complicated cross-currents of expression, appropriation, and parody that go together to constitute the modern cake-walk."[115] The cakewalk was a dance that, in all of its manifold forms, exemplified the problem of the color line. On the white minstrel stage, the cakewalk was often reduced to an offensive caricature of slave culture—even though, ironically enough, the dance itself originated as a parody of "the high manners of the folks in the 'big house,'" one that further resisted white domination by incorporating ritual festivity and African cultural retentions into the cycle of plantation labor.[116] Appropriated by the white-minstrel stage, the dance was then reappropriated by African American performers, both in minstrel troupes and in other turn-of-the-century theatrical companies, often with an additional layer of parodic "signifying."[117] In this form, perhaps because of the success of *Clorindy*, the cakewalk, together with ragtime, became a national vogue, particularly within American high society, the class represented by the millionaire's blasé friends.

That this upper-class dance craze implied another appropriative "possession" of African American expressive culture is suggested by the well-known publicity stunt of Williams and Walker, a famous African American dance team. As Johnson recounts in *Black Manhattan*, "Cake-walking became such a society fad that on Sunday morning, January 16, 1898, Williams and Walker, dressed just a point or two above the height of fashion, dared, as a publicity stunt, to call at the home of William K. Vanderbilt." Thus signifying on high society fashion (much like the earliest cakewalk), the two left a note stating:

To Mr. William K. Vanderbilt
Corner of Fifty-second Street and Fifth Avenue
New York

Dear Sir:

In view of the fact that you have made a success as a cake-walker, having appeared in a semi-public exhibition and having posed as an expert in that capacity, we, the undersigned world-renowned cake-walkers, believing that the attention of the public has been distracted from us on account of the tremendous hit which you have made, hereby challenge you to compete with us in a cake-walking match, which will decide which of us shall deserve the title of champion cake-walker of the world.[118]

However facetious, this publicity stunt issued a challenge that attempted to take back an African American cultural form from none other than William Vanderbilt, one of the ultimate representatives of privileged whiteness and capitalist power. Further, from the standpoint of spatial politics, the prominently featured address, "Corner of Fifty-second Street and Fifth Avenue," itself reveals the extent to which the turn-of-the-century black Bohemians saw themselves as challenging dominant cultural geographies, seeking to enter the very citadel of power while stating their own conditions. Though Williams and Walker proposed a low "stake" of fifty dollars for the competition, the figurative stakes were clearly much higher. Johnson's fictional Ex-Colored Man ultimately "sells his birthright" (both his blackness and his musicality) and passes into bourgeois whiteness, but other black Bohemians—including Williams and Walker and Johnson himself—instead positioned themselves to reclaim African American cultural forms. At the same time, they hoped to build a new cosmopolitan musical culture, one that, like black Bohemia itself, existed both within and without national and racialized boundaries.

Indeed, Williams and Walker's note to Vanderbilt suggests that the "stakes" were nothing less than the ability to represent an increasingly globalized "American" popular culture both nationally and transnationally. As Johnson remarks, the "second period in the Negro's theatrical development" that centered in and around black Bohemia afforded African Americans "an important place among the makers of the nation's songs," particularly through the introduction of ragtime music. According to Johnson, black Bohemia functioned to bring about "revolutionary change in New York artistic life" and to restructure American popular culture as a whole.[119] The Ex-Colored Man comes to a similar conclusion when he travels abroad and recognizes the extent to which ragtime had come to represent the nation—the larger cosmopolitan context, combined with the workings of the emerging culture industry, acts to distill the "American" from its many disparate cultures and hybrid musical forms. As the Ex-Colored Man remarks, ragtime achieved tremendous success as a cultural export: "No one who has traveled can question the world-conquering influence of rag-time, and I do not think it would be an exaggeration to say that in Europe the United States is popularly known better by rag-time than anything else it has produced in a generation. In Paris they call it American music" (63). The irony is of course that the United States obtained commercial clout from the cultural productions of the people to whom it would deny anything close to the benefits of full citizenship. Underscoring this irony, the Ex-Colored Man later puts "American Music" in quotation marks (103). Yet, by highlighting the perverse gap between signifier and signified, the Ex-Colored Man also insists that the very meaning of "America" must be socially, politically, and culturally reconstructed from within a cosmopolitan framework.

With an implicit awareness of the extent to which U.S. "external" and "internal" imperialism overlapped, Johnson himself first arrived in black Bohemia, and the related worlds of Broadway and Tin Pan Alley, with the draft of a musical entitled *Toloso*, cowritten with his brother. According to Johnson, *Toloso* had a "capital" story:

> The United States had, the year before, annexed Hawaii, and was at the time engaged in the Spanish-American War. We decided to write a comic opera satirizing the new American imperialism. The setting was an island kingdom in the Pacific. The story was concerned with Tolsa, the beautiful princess; her prime minister, a crafty old politician; the entrance of an American man-of-war; the handsome, heroic American lieutenant; and finally annexation.[120]

Johnson does not indicate whether he saw any connection between this satire of the new American imperialism and the legacies of slavery and Jim Crow; nonetheless, it is striking that the Johnson brothers chose this plotline for their first musical. While seeking to market a musical that satirized U.S. imperial action, the Johnsons went to New York fully prepared to encounter would-be cultural imperialists, namely the white "arrangers" who gained cultural and economic power by expropriating African American intellectual property. The Johnsons recognized that they had "a valuable piece of work which was not copyrighted" and that they had to be extremely careful of the white "pirates just waiting for the chance to plunder."[121] Indeed, when they arrived at M. Witmark & Sons, the music publishing house that became one of the central institutions of Tin Pan Alley, they were greeted by two writers of light opera who said, "Well, let's hear it; we might be able to steal something from it." Johnson notes that "we didn't quite see the joke—if it was a joke—and . . . gathered up our precious manuscripts and made a quick exit." Though Johnson adds that they eventually did collaborate with these white composers and that they later laughed about their first meeting, it is worth noting that Johnson still questioned whether or not the original comment had been entirely a "joke."[122] The guildship afforded by black Bohemia helped provide a measure of protection against the power of the white publishers and producers, but most African American musicians were still exploited by the music industry, often needing to sell songs and future royalties to well-capitalized publishers for much less than their market value.

Johnson's reference to American imperialism highlights his ambivalence about the relation between the racial and the national. The African American press praised the Johnsons' songs, emphasizing their ability to "blend the music of the Negro enslaved" with the "intellectual strivings of a newer life, prompted by study of purely classical lore," and it even upheld this blend as exemplifying "a new spirit, peculiarly American."[123] Johnson himself advocated such musical syntheses, and claimed that African American music was the "touchstone . . . by which the Negro can bridge all chasms," yet he was wary of dissolving the racial into the national (at least until "America" had been more adequately reconstructed). Recent histories describe Johnson as an "integrationist" and a "pragmatist"; these descriptions are apt enough, but they should not obscure the extent to which Johnson, like Du Bois, sought to guard against any premature synthesis that would leave existing racial hierarchies largely intact while proclaiming a triumphant "melting pot" aesthetic.

In 1926, in his preface to *The Second Book of American Negro Spirituals*, Johnson reiterates the musical history he included in *The Autobiography*, and draws a clear distinction between the national and the racial in the process: "The first of the so-called Ragtime songs to be published were actually Negro secular folk songs that were set down by white men, who affixed their own names as the composers. In fact, before the Negro succeeded fully in establishing his title as creator of his secular music the form was taken away from him and made national instead of racial."[124] For Johnson, the nationalizing of ragtime was a form of cultural imperialism, an unjust annexation of a racial property. In his own autobiography, *Along This Way* (1931), Johnson deemphasizes this act of theft while evoking a national culture based on African American music, but he still does not fully "integrate" the racial into the national:

> It is . . . in his lighter music that the Negro has given America its best-known distinctive form of art. I would make no extravagant claims for this music, but I say "form of art" without apology. This lighter music has been fused and then developed, chiefly by Jewish musicians, until it has become our national medium for

expressing ourselves musically in popular form, and it bids fair to become a basic element in the future great American music. The part it plays in American life and its acceptance by the world at large cannot be ignored. It is to this music that America in general gives itself over in its leisure hours, when it is not engaged in the struggles imposed upon it by the exigencies of present-day American life. At these times, the Negro drags his captors captives.[125]

In Jeffrey Melnick's reading of this passage, Johnson "begins with an opposition between race and nation" and from there "he subtly weaves 'the Negro' into the fabric of 'American life.' " According to Melnick, Johnson accomplishes this maneuver in his third sentence, where, with the intervention of the "Jewish musicians," the opposition between "Negro" and "American" is supplanted by "*our* national medium."[126] For Melnick, this statement represents a pragmatic acknowledgment of the role of Jews in the turn-of-the-century music industry, one that (for whatever combination of motives) echoes the melting-pot discourse of Tin Pan Alley itself. This discourse centered on (and was perpetuated by) such figures as Irving Berlin, and it variously suggested that the "plastic racialness" of the Jews enabled them to take African American folk material and transform it into the stuff of "American" popular culture.[127] Still, much as Johnson seems to employ this discourse, I would argue that his final irony in many ways undoes it: even as Jewish musicians sought to orchestrate "our national medium," Johnson maintains that its basis in African American expressive culture remained undiminished. In the ongoing, ever racialized cycle of possession and dispossession, Johnson ultimately insists that "the Negro drags his captors captives" through the medium of popular music. Johnson thus complicates any facile celebration of cultural integration. African Americans must first have the opportunity to control and possess their own culture, he suggests, before that inheritance could ever be construed as "national instead of racial."

As these statements demonstrate, Johnson continued to posit a gap between the "racial" and the "national," and it was at this juncture that black Bohemia proved most crucial to his cultural geography. Of course, Johnson often expressed great pride in the fact that African American musicians were prominent "makers of the nation's songs" (he would never have endorsed the contemporary white music critic who insisted that African American music was "in no sense a national expression" and that it was "as foreign a music as any Tyrolean jodel or Hungarian czardas");[128] yet he also recognized how important it was for African American artists to be able to negotiate the future terms on which the "racial" would enter into the "national" popular culture. Not impervious to white "slummers" and "pirates," black Bohemia nonetheless provided the guildship necessary to combat wholesale appropriation and to forestall an imperial annexation of African American expressive culture.[129]

Coda: Living in Bohemia

In African American and other ethnic cultures, "Bohemia" offered an alternative cultural space, one that helped to shape experiences of exile, relocation, displacement, and in-betweenness. Bohemia also provided a name for the "contact zone" in which the dominant culture encountered ethnic and racial Otherness.[130] As such, the concept of Bohemia structured a wide range of intercultural connections, the multiplicity of which demands renewed critical attention. In calling for "an explicitly transnational and intercultural perspective," recent practitioners of literary and cultural studies have allied with cultural geographers in the effort to "rethink the production of locality and transnationality as lived structures of feeling" and experience.[131] Both a literary and a spatial concept (and one that demonstrates the interpenetration of the two), Bohemia constitutes an important locus for such analysis. Living in Bohemia meant inhabiting a realm that existed both within and without the United States. Part metaphor, part cultural nexus, and part socioeconomic reality, Bohemia was a historically specific construction that housed many different forms of traveling culture. Partially suspending (though at times facilitating) the demands of cultural "incorporation," *la vie bohème* alternately resisted and accommodated the conversion of race and ethnicity into national properties. From William Reimer's "Cosmopolitan Bohemian Democracy" to Abraham Cahan's "East Side Bohème" and James Weldon Johnson's "black Bohemia," turn-of-the-century Bohemias negotiated and redefined tensions between the "Bohemian" and the "Bourgeois," and—by extension—the local and the global, the racial and the national, the democratic and the commercial, the aesthetic and the instrumental.

This study now turns to the most famous American Bohemia, the Greenwich Village of the second decade of the twentieth century. Often represented as the culminating moment of American Bohemianism—indeed, as the only authentic American Bohemia—the Village must be restored to its proper context within a more expansive Bohemian geography. The concluding chapter looks ahead to the Village, and back again to the neglected American Bohemias that this book has sought to recover.

7

The Spiritual Geography of Greenwich Village, 1912–1920

AT THE BEGINNING OF the late-nineteenth-century Bohemian vogue, *Appleton's Journal* announced, "The real, the better Bohemia is neither geographical nor local, it is bounded by no line of fortune or caste, it lies in the temper and intelligence of its children."[1] In 1913, at the advent of what he called "the New Bohemia," Hutchins Hapgood situated his modern Bohemia in a similarly expansive terrain: "The New Bohemia, like the old, is a figure of speech. It is an attitude of temperament. Its geography is a spiritual geography." Though the New Bohemia had "nothing to do with any geographical area," it had "local names in various places." In New York City, Hapgood noted, that place was "Greenwich Village."[2] Though only one "local name" for a phenomenon that continued to defy geographic boundaries and conventional limits, "Greenwich Village" became increasingly synonymous with "Bohemia" throughout the decade 1910–1920. At once extending the nineteenth-century tradition and taking it in modern directions, the "New Bohemia" represented a constellation of energies that belonged to a specific time and place, though its influence could not be so contained.[3]

At the turn of the century, Hapgood had been eager to discover "Bohemian charm" in the foreign restaurants on the Lower East Side of New York. His New Bohemia in Greenwich Village bordered this East Side Bohème, the region known for bringing the "Old World" into the "New." Thus, when Hapgood wrote that the New Bohemia was "bounded . . . on the East by the Old World Bohemia, the classical example of which was the Paris Latin Quarter," his metaphor should also be taken more literally. The southern border of the New Bohemia was also familiar;

Hapgood identified this region as the zone of "the Artistic Temperament." But, according to Hapgood, the western and northern reaches of the New Bohemia promised something different, for the Greenwich Village Bohemia was "bounded on the North by the Feminist Movement . . . and on the West by the IWW."[4]

Feminist issues had already surfaced within of *la vie bohème*, yet Hapgood correctly sensed that feminism achieved a new centrality in his modern Bohemia. Bohemia had long represented an ideally "classless" realm, but, with the exception of individual Bohemians like Jack London, the New Bohemians were the first to connect their art, literature, and personal lifestyles to the cause of organized labor and the socialist movement. Accordingly, Hapgood insisted, "due in large part to the effect of the Feminist Movement and the IWW," the New Bohemians exhibited a "greater seriousness" than their predecessors. This increased solemnity even reshaped the "adjacent area" of the Artistic Temperament: "The Artistic Temperament which, in the Latin Quarter, lingers on the simple note of human pleasure and art for art's sake, becomes in the New Bohemia, the adoration of life for the sake of Causes, Reforms or Revolutions, and an adoration of art not for the sake of art but for the sake of Life." Since the purposeful "Life" was dedicated to "Causes," an art that existed "for the sake of Life" necessarily supported political and social commitments. The New Bohemia thus further obliterated the distinction between "art" and "life," the very boundary that Bohemian "art-life" had always sought to unsettle. Though Hapgood raised the question whether art had sacrificed too much of its autonomy or become too subservient to "Causes," he recognized that the "new" Village offered a particularly vital fusion of the aesthetic and the political.[5]

The Old World Bohemia, the Artistic Temperament, the IWW and the Feminist Movement: along these borders, the New Bohemia staked its various positions, negotiating between art and life, capital and labor, women and men, the modern and the genteel, the spiritual and commercial, the Bohemian and the Bourgeois. More than ever before, the mythic Bohemian "republic within the republic" became a palpable reality. Identified with Greenwich Village, this New Bohemia attempted to extend the democratic liberties that the nation ostensibly guaranteed. In this "spiritual geography," the Villagers pioneered experimental approaches to love, art, and political activism, hoping to expand the compass of human freedom and to bring about "more and always more consciousness, in both art and life."[6] Such pursuits promised to give free reign to the "human spirit."[7]

The story of the Greenwich Villagers has been justly celebrated. As Alfred Kazin noted in 1942:

> Who does not know the now routine legend in which the world of 1910–1917 is Washington Square turned Arcadia, in which the barriers are always down, the magazines always promising, the workers always marching, geniuses sprouting in every Village bedroom, Isadora Duncan always dancing. . . . No other generation in America ever seems to have so radiant a youth, or has remembered it in so many winsome autobiographies written at forty.[8]

Written by the likes of Max Eastman, Floyd Dell, and Mabel Dodge Luhan, these autobiographies helped to enshrine the "New Bohemia" as *the* American Bohemia. A number of histories have since assessed the cultural significance of the Villagers. While some view the New Bohemians as neo-adolescent "children of fantasy," others see them as vibrant "American moderns."[9] In most accounts, however, the Greenwich Village of the second decade of the twentieth century represents the culminating moment of American Bohemianism. It was here that those who shared a Bohemian "attitude of temperament" came together in a number of intersecting venues. These institutions extended the camaraderie that earlier generations of Bohemians had developed in particular rooming houses, artist-studio buildings, restaurants, clubs, and beer halls, and helped to channel the energies of the New Bohemians in important social, political, and artistic directions. Whether campaigning for the IWW, birth control, or free speech, the New Bohemians sought to create the more broadly democratic America that the Pfaffians had glimpsed from their basement beer cellar.

The Eastern and Southern Borders: The Old World Bohemia and Artistic Temperament

Commentators had long recognized the similarities between Greenwich Village and the Parisian Latin Quarter. "With the atmosphere of France in some of the streets," the Art Students League on Fourteenth Street, and the famous studio building on Tenth, the Village first emerged as a "kind of Bohemia" and preferred destination for young artists in the last decades of the nineteenth century.[10] Once the "New Bohemia" began to form, "Greenwich Villagism" emerged as a synonym for Bohemianism, and in 1914 *The Dial* reiterated, "Greenwich Village is the American parallel of the Latin Quarter."[11]

The winding streets and quaint, semidilapidated buildings invited the comparison, but *The Dial* insisted that the deepest connection between the Latin Quarter and the Greenwich Village of the period derived from a shared "communal spirit." Many New Bohemians fostered this "spirit" and acknowledged its Old World history. In 1912, for example, at the end of his first year in Greenwich Village, John Reed penned "The Day in Bohemia, or Life Among the Artists," an updated version of Murger's *Scenes de la Vie de Bohème*. The memory of Murger informs the poem, as it likely helped to structure the very experience it celebrates: at one point, after recounting the drunken revelry of his Bohemian compatriots, Reed notes, "Singing, the Four wend to the LAFAYETTE / Quite like a scene from Murger" (though he completes the rhyme with the self-deprecating observation—"*sans grisette*").

This poem about the latter-day Latin Quarter owed its genesis to a friendship cultivated in yet another Bohemia, the Bohemian Club of San Francisco. As Mabel Dodge remembered: "[Lincoln] Steffens had been a friend of Reed's father in Portland, Oregon, and they were both members of the old Bohemian Club in San Francisco. This father went to Steffens and said: 'I have a boy graduating at Harvard this year and going to New York afterwards. I think he's a poet; I don't know, though. I wish you'd keep your eye on him.' Steff did." And, according to Dodge, what "Steff" wanted for young Reed was *la vie bohème*:

> He was amused at the antics of the young, and he liked watching them. He put Reed on the *American Magazine* that he was editing at the time but he told Reed he didn't want him to really work. Reed didn't. Steff even went down to live with a group of boys of whom Reed was one, in that famous, ramshackle old house at 42 Washington Square South. It was kept by a couple of frowsy old landladies who cursed these young men when their rent was overdue and who nursed them when they were sick. . . . Reed wrote a long, gay poem while he was living there, and he dedicated it to Steff."[12]

The "long, gay poem" of close to fifteen hundred lines commemorated Reed's year living on the third floor of 42 Washington Square South with three roommates, just above the apartment of the famous "Muckraker" and Bohemian Club member, Lincoln Steffens (whose *Commercial Advertiser* had published Hapgood's earlier Bohemian sketches). All four roommates had just graduated from Harvard, and the lively apartment "became a kind of way-station for other Harvard men."[13] Here, "Bohemia" facilitated the transition from the college dormitory to the streets of Manhattan.

With its mock-heroic hubris, "The Day in Bohemia" at once satirizes and reanimates the prototypical *vie bohème*. The narrative poses the traditional Bohemian dilemma: "How can an artist create his Utopia / With his best eye on the World's cornucopia?" Though he had not yet developed the revolutionary convictions that would cause him to see the relationship between material conditions and artistic creation as a socialist issue, Reed explores tensions between art and life, the aesthetic and the commercial. In good Bohemian fashion, he laments the "commercial soulless age" that had relegated art and poetry to second-class status: "Bohemia! Where dwell the Sacred Nine, / Who landed, steerage, from the White Star Line." At a time when even the Nine Muses depended on commercial navigation and had to ride in "steerage," what hope had the "unknown men of genius" at 42 Washington Square South? Since "Art cannot flourish on infrequent rations," Reed thus records the usual Bohemian compromises:

> We condescend to work in humbler sort,
> For Art is long and money very short.
> Hence it is not so terribly surprising
> That ANDREWS deigns to scribble advertising;
> ROGERS, whose talent is of epic cast,
> At Sunday-paper stuff is unsurpassed.
> LEE teaches in an Art School he abhors,
> And LEWIS tries to please the editors;
> BOB EDWARDS, when he needs some other togs,
> Draws pictures for the clothing catalogues.
> And I, myself, when no one wants my rhymes,
> Yes, even I relax a bit at times.

But their Bohemia in Greenwich Village provided the spiritual antidote:

> Yet we are free who live in Washington Square,
> We dare to think as Uptown wouldn't dare,
> Blazing our nights with arguments uproarious;
> What care we for a dull old world censorious
> When each is sure he'll fashion something glorious?[14]

Like other American Bohemians before him, Reed uses the narrative frame of Murger's *la vie bohème* to endow the lives of these aspiring writers and artists with heightened importance, elevating the struggle of art versus materialism to heroic—if still comical—status.

As the poem suggests, there was one material condition in particular that propelled *la vie bohème* and shaped its social geography: the paying of rent, or more precisely, the need to circumvent that necessity. True to the spirit of Murger's Bohemians—who, in one scene, politely inform their landlord that they will not be able "to adhere to the custom of paying rent"[15]—Reed and his friends try to charm their way out of their financial obligations. They find themselves "in actual BOHEMIA" when their landlady enters and "her voice is ominous." But so hospitable to Bohemia is their landlady that she merely stipulates: "Those who have not PAID RENT for half a year / Must keep the peace—they cannot rough-house here."

Not all landlords were so forthcoming, but it was the low rents, quite as much as the foreign atmosphere, that made Greenwich Village the American answer to the Quartier Latin in the 1910s. "The rents were cheap because the rush of traffic could not make its way through the little twisted streets that crossed and recrossed each other and never seemed to get anywhere else," Floyd Dell later remembered. "That was before Seventh Avenue had been ruthlessly and efficiently cut through as the West Side subway extended southward; Greenwich Avenue still, like a barrier flung athwart the Village, protected it from the roaring town all about." Dell's couplet provides the coda to the Bohemian Village: "Here life went to a gentler pace, / And dreams and dreamers found a place."[16]

For Dell, as for Reed, Bohemia attracted its residents due to a combination of economic, social, and "temperamental" considerations. Of his own interest in Bohemia, he noted, "this was in part a matter of economics": "There were periods when I was out of a job and dependent on the irregular and uncertain gains of free-lancing. I barely managed to keep my head above water; I was one of the intellectual proletariat, sure enough." The inexpensive rent (eight dollars a month for a ground-floor apartment on Christopher Street), as well as the "Villager restaurateurs [who] made a point of keeping their patrons fed in their periods of hard luck," made Greenwich Village a desirable location for Bohemians, especially those who were "economically insecure with uncertain or unproved talents—or perhaps no real talents, but only artistic temperaments."[17] The "communal spirit" of the Village—embodied in the generosity of individual restaurateurs—helped the Bohemians to cope with economic exigencies. Economic need provided the occasion for this communal spirit to manifest itself; economic need also contributed to the development of this very spirit. In "The Rise of Greenwich Village," Dell explains the paradoxically enriching effects of poverty:

It was, for all of us, a life that was quaintly enriched by our poverty. How otherwise, except by being very poor, should we ever have learned to make the most of those joys that are so cheap, or that cost nothing at all, the joys of comradeship and play and mere childlike fun? When someone had sold something, we trailed across Washington Square to spend the money gorgeously in the basement of the Brevoort; but when there was no such luck, there was always the Staten Island ferry, or the Fifth Avenue bus—and always and always there was talk to keep us up till dawn.[18]

Of course, poverty was not the only force that sustained Village camaraderie. There was also the matter of a shared "artistic temperament"—the term Dell used and Hapgood also employed when establishing the borders of his "spiritual geography." Though low rent, found only in specific locations, supported this geography, Hapgood insisted that the Village was also shaped by "an attitude of temperament." In his published memoir *A Victorian in the Modern World* (1939), he elaborates: "Wherever a group of individuals—the men animated by a dislike of regular business or professional life, inclined toward the freedom of art and literature, the women of the same type, bored by some small place in the Middle West, the business office or domesticity, filled with restless ambition to lead their own lives—came together, there was the Village."[19] Once these individuals came together, Dell affirmed, "bohemia seemed a place where improbable and delightful things could happen."[20]

John Reed channeled Murger in his "Day in Bohemia." Another link between the Village and the "Old World Bohemia" came in the person of an immigrant from the Central European country of Bohemia: "a little puzzled-looking gypsy from the real Bohemia of the old world."[21] This "real" Bohemian was Hippolyte Havel, a Czech "anarchist philosopher, journalist, . . . bohemian," and sometime cook for Polly's Restaurant. Adjacent to The Liberal Club, this restaurant (founded by Havel's lover, Polly Holladay) existed in a little basement on the west side of Washington Square. Stoking Bohemian and Bourgeois antagonism, Havel loudly proclaimed his beliefs at the restaurant, grumbling about the "Bourgeois pigs!" Havel was "cook, waiter, dishwasher and chief conversationalist" at the new restaurant. "Without Hippolyte, the Village might have existed," Floyd Dell maintained, "but it would not have been what it was."[22]

Himself a link to the "old world Bohemia" of Central Europe, Havel also stressed the affinity between the Village and the Parisian Latin Quarter. In an essay written in 1915 for Guido Bruno's *Greenwich Village: A*

Fortnightly, one of the periodicals that helped to launch the Village as a self-conscious Bohemia, Havel reflects:

> There is a wonderful atmosphere in this part of Manhattan. In the squalid studios and garrets, ideals are forged into new forms. If your eyes are open and your heart sympathetic, you will see Francois Villon spending the borrowed dime in the 'Working-girl's Home.' . . . Van Gogh and Gauguin are formulating their ideas. And Verlaine is to be met, if you have the divine spark in your soul.[23]

Though he recognized that contemporary urban planning might compromise the integrity of this Bohemia—the "subterranean barbarians" were already "busy in reconstructing Seventh Avenue and building a subway for the men in a hurry"—Havel, like his friend Hapgood, felt confident that Greenwich Village defied any specific "geographical conception": "The term Greenwich Village is to me a spiritual zone of the mind." He put his own twist on this statement, however, adding, "If the Village did not exist, we would have to invent it." This spiritual zone of the mind produced its own objective correlative—and, at the same time, the Village was a material space that structured Bohemian lives and sensibilities. The "subway for the men in a hurry" might alter that space in the future (and Dell later confirmed that it had done just that); nonetheless, writing in 1915, Havel still held out hope for the "men and women in the attics and studios" who used their elevated positions to develop "enthusiasm for a higher form of life": "They try to forge their ideas, revolutionary ideas, mind you, into new rhythmic forms and this, to me, is the supreme effort. The knight errants of the social revolution, those fighters against capitalistic society are also to be met in Greenwich Village; they are the boon companions of the craftsmen of the chisel, the brush and the pen."[24]

Like Havel, Floyd Dell took it upon himself to cultivate the Bohemian "spirit" and temperament. "The wartime years turned Greenwich Village into a melting pot in which all group boundaries were dissolved [between] artists, writers, intellectuals, liberals, radicals, IWW's, bohemians, well-to-do patrons, onlookers," Dell reflected, highlighting his role in this process: "I helped in organizing a series of fancy-dress balls to which I gave the name 'Pagan Rout,' and I wrote and produced frivolous one-act plays."[25] First organized to raise money for the *Masses* and the Liberal Club in 1914, the "Pagan Routs" drew upon the tradition of the Quatre-Arts balls of the Latin Quarter. The balls reflected the double imperative of Bohemia: to make art-life economically feasible and spiritually gratifying. For Dell, the all-night costume balls were the quintessence of *la vie bohème*, "focusing in a mood of playfulness the passion for loveliness that was one of the things that had brought us to the Village."[26] At one ball, the "hobo-poet" Harry Camp appeared as an Assyrian king crowned by a tin washbasin; at the "Red Revel," Emma Goldman dressed as a nun and performed a step she termed "the Anarchist's Slide."[27]

Extending the dramatic exhibitionism of the balls, the "amateur theatricals" also forged a Bohemian synthesis of those often antagonistic forces: art and life. As part of her effort to foster community—to give "intelligent people to-day . . . the same chance to know each other that the church and the tavern gave their grandparents"—Henrietta Rodman promoted the new Liberal Club as the "social center of Greenwich Village." She asked Dell to write a play for the opening of the club, and he spun a "satire upon the earnest Bohemianism of our little world." The play starred Helen Westley and Sherwood Anderson, who was visiting the Village at the beginning of his literary career: "Every one invented his own lines, and forgot them, and made up new and better ones on the spur of the moment; and the play, because it made fun of our own earnest 'modernity,' was tremendously successful."[28] Henri Murger had defined Bohemia as the realm wherein "everyday existence is a work of genius," and the Village plays fashioned the daily life of the New Bohemia into the stuff of art—if not always of "genius."[29] And "where these productions fell short of dramatic art," Dell averred, "they did succeed in being gay communal ritual."[30] Blurring the boundary between art and life—in classic Bohemian fashion—the amateur theatricals invested the community with an intensified significance, even as they encouraged the Villagers to laugh at themselves. Like the Bohemian Grove plays before them, the amateur theatricals at once reflected and created a Bohemian community.

Hapgood insisted in 1913 that art in the New Bohemia existed "for the sake of Life." By 1915, the newly formed Provincetown Players helped to bolster that claim. Though a "more ambitious undertaking" (in Dell's words) than the amateur theatricals of the Liberal Club, the Provincetown Players first emerged during an evening of informal theatre.[31] That year, a number of Villagers were summering at Provincetown, lamenting the current state of American theatre while sitting around a campfire. Among the Villagers there that summer was a group that included Dell, Susan Glaspell and her husband George Cram Cook, Hapgood and his wife Neith Boyce, John Reed and his new love Louise Bryant, and Max Eastman and his wife Ida Rauh. The most acclaimed playwright associated with the group, Eugene O'Neill, joined the Players at the beginning of his career during the summer of 1916. It was Glaspell and Cook, however, who became the leaders of the Players and who served as the "group's ideologues."[32] For Glaspell, involvement with the Provincetown Players summed up the New Bohemian ethos and raison d'être: "Life was all of a piece, work not separated from play"; for Cook, the art-life of the Players embodied "The Will to Form the Beloved Community of Life-Givers."[33] Always one of the most articulate chroniclers of the New Bohemia, Hapgood concurred—of the Provincetown Players, he wrote: "They wanted to express the simple truth of their lives and experience by writing, staging, and acting their own plays. . . . At once we were expressing something sweetly personal and sweetly social.[34]

Still, Hapgood admitted, though only half-apologetically, "We Provincetowners were more successful in living our lives than in expressing them in our writings and pictures."[35] Questions about the ultimate quality of much of the art and writing produced in the New Bohemia quickly emerged. In 1917, for example, John Quinn wrote to Ezra Pound: "I don't know whether you know the pseudo-Bohemianism of Washington Square. . . . It is a vulgar, disgusting conglomerate of second and third-rate artists and would-be artists."[36] While the New Bohemians would have certainly objected to this characterization, many did not view the production of "first-rate" art as their primary objective. For many, the artistic process was more important than the final product: art was for the sake of life, not strictly for the sake of art. Instead of creating reified art-objects, the New Bohemians hoped to integrate artistic expression into their daily lives.

The Provincetown Players thus lived up to the "doctrine" of Bohemia, a "system of ideas" that, according to Malcolm Cowley, had "remained the same in spirit . . . since the days of Gautier and Murger." Two of those ideas were "The idea of self-expression.—Each man's, each woman's, purpose in life is to express himself, to realize his full individuality through creative work and beautiful living in beautiful surroundings" and "The idea of living for the moment.—It is stupid to pile up treasures that we can enjoy only in old age, when we have lost the capacity for enjoyment. Better to seize the moment as it comes, to dwell in it intensely, even at the cost of future suffering. Better to live extravagantly, gather June rosebuds, 'burn my candle at both ends. . . . It gives a lovely light.' "[37] Intensifying the moment and allowing for self-expression (and reflection), the plays enacted two important aspects of the Bohemian "doctrine." With respect to how the Provincetown Players reanimated "the Old World

Bohemia" and "the Artistic Temperament," it is worth quoting the words of Abraham Cahan (as remembered by Hapgood). Cahan accompanied Hapgood to Christine's Restaurant atop the Provincetown Theatre (after it had traveled from Provincetown and taken up residence in the "geographic" Village). It was here that the actors, playwrights, and other Villagers gathered after the shows, and Cahan, "much impressed," observed: "This is really a Russian atmosphere, this is the atmosphere of Dostoevsky, there is a tumultuous inner life here, externally expressed. It is not the classical Bohemia of Paris, but the more vital individual Bohemia of the Russians of the best period, not crystallized into the tradition of the Latin people." Whether or not this expression of a "tumultuous inner life" was more in keeping with French or Russian traditions, it was, Hapgood insisted, "bohemian in the best sense."[38]

As noted, the Provincetown Players emerged after Hapgood had already declared that art in the New Bohemia was not "for art's sake" but rather "for the sake of Life." When he first made this claim in 1913, he was likely referring, in part, to the influence Alfred Stieglitz had over the New Bohemians. It was at "291," a small fourth-floor art gallery on Fifth Avenue, a few blocks north of the Village, that Stieglitz promoted photography as a legitimate art form and first introduced modern art to American audiences. Stieglitz passionately believed, in his phrase, that "art and life are synonymous."[39] Indeed, according to Edward Abrahams, Stieglitz frequently employed the phrase "art—not for art's sake, but for life's sake."[40] Whether or not Hapgood got that actual phrase from Stieglitz, he amply testified to the galvanizing effects of Gallery 291:

> The "work of art" was never, I imagine, of much interest to Stieglitz, who was the soul of "291." . . . Stieglitz is of course an artist himself, but what makes his peculiar value is not his photographs, innovating and remarkable as they are, but his restless, life-breathing personality, his endless quest. Art is an intermediate process, the strongest of the propagandas for life, and for the deeper education, and Stieglitz has been an indefatigable propagandist. Apropos of a picture by Marin, a drawing by Rodin, or a painting by O'Keefe, Stieglitz would talk by the hour about "life," as it manifests, or should manifest, itself in all human relations—marriage, politics, morality.[41]

Already influenced by Gallery 291, Hapgood and Dodge approached the famous Armory Show of 1913 (which featured many of the modern artists first showcased in the United States by Stieglitz) with Stieglitz's aesthetic philosophy in mind. In 1913, Hapgood wrote of the Armory Show in his regular column for the *Globe*: "It makes us live more abundantly. And if this art has its logical effect it will help us all to understand more deeply what happens to us in life—to understand better our love and our work, our ambitions and our antipathies, and our ideas in politics and society."[42] Dodge herself was appointed an honorary vice president of the exhibition, and some lines she had written about the show ended up on the bottom of a small card that was distributed to visitors. There, she announced that the show was "the most important thing that ever happened in America, of its kind" and asserted, "what is needed is more, more and always more consciousness, in both art and life."[43] Though the promoters of the "new art" issued what might now seem like hyperbolic claims for the impact of modern art on "life," contemporary detractors do not seem to have viewed such arguments as far-fetched (though, of course, they saw this impact as negative rather than as positive). The *New York Times*, for example, opined that the exhibition could "disrupt, degrade, if not destroy, not only art but literature and society too."[44] For many critics, Marcel Duchamp's abstract *Nude Descending a Staircase*—described by one as an "explosion in a shingle factory" and by another as "Rude Descending a Staircase"—constituted an assault on the very foundations of the genteel tradition.[45]

The New Bohemians would have had it no other way. Rather than constituting a rarefied space above the fray, art was part of a larger struggle "for freedom of experience and justice in the fullest sense of the word."[46] And as Hapgood suggests in his "spiritual geography," many New Bohemians sought to use art to enter into this struggle for freedom and justice in very direct ways. For these Bohemians, "art was for Life," and "life was the sake of Causes"—in particular, such causes as socialism (especially in the form of the IWW), and feminist politics.

The Western Border: The IWW and the Class Struggle

In his memoirs, Max Eastman sets out to explain his unlikely personal trajectory: "how a poet and philosophic moralist, with a special distaste for economics, politics, and journalism, became known to the public as a journalist campaigning for a political idea based primarily on economics."[47] After earning his Ph.D. in philosophy at Columbia under the direction of the pragmatist philosopher John Dewey, Eastman determined that he would write poetry and works of aesthetic theory. "But I had that fixed heroic notion that I must earn my bread and do something for my fellow man before I could devote myself to the sacred play of writing," he later recorded. On behalf of the Suffrage Movement, Eastman had already organized a "Men's Suffrage League," and in the summer of 1912, he now wanted to find work in "service to socialism that might combine . . . a small income with a participation in the struggle." Eastman insisted that the "notion of a paid part-time job in the service of socialism was not fantastic in 1912": "The Socialist idea flourished to its highest bloom in America in that exciting year. Eugene V. Debs . . . got a million votes for President, and The Appeal to Reason, a socialist paper published in Girard, Kansas, attained a circulation of 761, 000."[48]

Opportunity presented itself in the form of a letter sent to Waterford, Connecticut, where Eastman and his family were summering. "Scrawled with a brush on a torn-off scrap of drawing paper, and signed by the artists John Sloan, Art Young, Charles A. Winter, Alice Beach Winter, Maurice Becker, and the writers Louis Untermeyer, Mary Heaton Vorse, Ellis O. Jones, Horatio Winslow, and Inez Haynes Gillmore," the letter stated: "You are elected editor of *The Masses*." The rub came in the second and final sentence of the note: "No pay." Though Eastman had had no intention of accepting an unpaid position, he was curious about the "whimsical bunch" and met with them when he returned to New York and took up residence in the Village at 27 West Eleventh Street. Delighted by the mood they cultivated—the "sense of universal revolt and regeneration, of the just-before-dawn of a new day in American art and literature and living-of-life as well as in politics"—Eastman discovered a new way of combining art and politics, Bohemianism and socialism.[49]

The revived *Masses* "made quite a splurge" when it appeared in December 1912. In this inaugural issue, Eastman advanced his editorial agenda, a more "revolutionary" version of socialism than that of his predecessor. Combining Deweyan Pragmatism and "red" socialism, Eastman committed himself to both "Knowledge and Revolution." The former was to be an "experimental knowledge—a free investigation of the developing facts and continuous retesting of the theories which pertain to the end we have in view"; the latter entailed "a radical democratization of industry and society, made possible by the growth of capitalism, but to be accomplished only when and if the spirit of liberty and rebellion is sufficiently awakened in the classes which are now oppressed." Eastman followed this declaration by announcing his support for Eugene V. Debs and "the rebels in every industrial or legal battle then in progress: the IWW in Lawrence; the anarchists in San Diego; the Structural Iron Workers in Indianapolis; the Timber Workers in Louisiana; [and] the miners waging a "civil war" in West Virginia."[50] Debs, in turn, wrote in support of the inaugural issue: "The current number of *The Masses* abounds with vital matter from the virile pens of some of the ablest writers in the movements. The clear cry of the revolution rings all through its pages, and the illustrations are such as could be produced only by artists animated by the militant spirit of Socialism."[51]

Indeed, it was "Art Young's double page cartoon portraying the 'capitalist press' as a whorehouse" (where Madame Editor and her writers cater to their client, Big Advertising) that Eastman credited with making the biggest impact on readers. Though not all were equally "animated by the militant spirit of Socialism" (as later events would demonstrate), the artists of *The Masses* all longed for the opportunity to create the kind of art that commercial periodicals shunned. In particular, the artists were united in their distaste for the commodified "cover girl." As art historian Rebecca Zurier notes, "to the artists of *The Masses*, the cover girl represented the forces of capitalism because it used art—and by implication sex—to sell a magazine filled with illustrated advertisements designed to sell goods."[52] Many of the artists of *The Masses* had studied with Robert Henri and belonged to what became known as the "Ashcan School"; it was to these artists that the magazine owed the "realist note" of its graphics. Equally committed to "real experience" and to the defiance of commodified ideality, Eastman approved of having "an outburst of dirt and dreariness in realms before consecrated to sweetness and light."[53] He shared enough of the artists' antipathy toward the "cover girl" to further their critique of this figure in his novel *Venture* (1927). In one scene, the protagonist Jo Hancock (based in large part on John Reed) goes to visit his friend Christine the "Cover-artist" at her studio:

> She was the greatest "Cover-artist" in the world, without rival and without challenge. This means that she could paint pictures of a pretty girl with different colored hair, with different colored eyes, with different noses, different lips, different hats, different shirt-waists, different absences of shirt-waists, different golf-clubs, or tennis-racquets, or bathing-suits, or surf-boards, or Russian wolf-hounds, but always with the same unerringly delineated, and dyed, and concentrated, and mercilessly flashed forth upon your defenseless nervous system, sexual appeal.

To visit Christine, Jo must travel to Fifty-Seventh Street, the realm of the "uptown Bohemians," most of whom he judges to be shallow "patterns" as opposed to the more substantive "real people" found downtown in Greenwich Village. It is because most of her friends are "patterns"—"people whose business is popularity and financial success"—that Jo believes she is so successful at painting "types instead of individuals." He opines: "Types never disturb anybody, and if you put a little sexual lure into them, everybody likes them. I like them myself. . . . But they don't stimulate me, they don't trouble me, they don't give me something I didn't have before. They are not life advancing into the future. They are just repetition."[54] It was both the cause and the effect of this repetition that *The Masses* hoped to counteract.

John Reed, the original Jo Hancock, first contacted Eastman because of his own frustration with the commercial press. Eastman recalled a forthright telephone call one morning from "a person named John Reed": "I work on the *American Magazine*, and I've got a story they won't print. I'd like to offer it to *The Masses*." This statement did not immediately endear Reed to Eastman, for Eastman "still suspected that a magazine that set out to publish what could not be sold in the market would probably be filled for the most part with claptrap," but he was pleasantly surprised: the tale, a "simple story of a New York prostitute" took on a "significant phase of American life that no other magazine would dare to mention unless sanctimoniously" and Reed had written it in "a style both vivid and restrained."[55] Here too, *The Masses* broke with the conventional restraints that had been imposed by the genteel tradition.

Still knowing little about socialism, but wanting to be part of *The Masses*, Reed came to see Eastman a second time carrying with him a "Statement" that he proposed running every month on the masthead of the magazine: "We refuse to commit ourselves to any course of action except this: to do with *The Masses* exactly what we please." Much as Eastman admired Reed's iconoclasm, he felt that the "Statement" smacked too much of the sort of revolt for revolt's sake that Reed's "The Day in Bohemia" had also enacted. Of his reaction, Eastman noted: "To a pupil of John Dewey, making an intellectual fuss without committing yourself to a course of action was anathema." Instead of adopting Reed's manifesto, Eastman incorporated a few of Reed's phrases into a new "Statement" for the masthead, one that would emphasize "the catholicity" of *The Masses* while simultaneously proclaiming its "revolutionary" agenda:

THIS MAGAZINE IS OWNED AND PUBLISHED COOPERATIVELY BY ITS EDITORS. IT HAS NO DIVIDENDS TO PAY, AND NOBODY IS TRYING TO MAKE MONEY OUT OF IT. A REVOLUTIONARY AND NOT A REFORM MAGAZINE; A MAGAZINE WITH A SENSE OF HUMOR

AND NO RESPECT FOR THE RESPECTABLE; FRANK, ARROGANT, IMPERTINENT, SEARCHING FOR TRUE CAUSES; A MAGAZINE DIRECTED AGAINST RIGIDITY AND DOGMA WHEREVER IT IS FOUND; PRINTING WHAT IS TOO NAKED OR TRUE FOR A MONEY-MAKING PRESS; A MAGAZINE WHOSE FINAL POLICY IS TO DO AS IT PLEASES AND CONCILIATE NOBODY, NOT EVEN ITS READERS—THERE IS A FIELD FOR THIS PUBLICATION IN AMERICA.[56]

This statement appeared on the masthead for the run of *The Masses*. Extending the Bohemian *Saturday Press*'s early defiance of bourgeois respectability, Eastman's *Masses* now pledged itself to socialist "revolution."

The statement stood, but for some, it did not fully clarify how the editors envisioned the relationship between art and politics, both within and without the magazine. A contemporary jingle articulated one skeptical view: "They draw nude women for the *Masses*, / Thick, fat, ungainly lasses— / How does that help the working classes?"[57] This jingle itself embodies the sexism that *The Masses* pledged to fight; with regard to women's rights and the struggle for racial equality, Eastman insisted that the periodical did not subscribe to the "socialist dogma [that] declared that all of these problems would be solved when the economy of capitalism was replaced by a co-operative commonwealth."[58] Still, the general question raised by the verse—how did the art featured in *The Masses* help the working classes?—was also addressed by other critics. In a letter to the magazine, E. Ralph Cheney declared that a devotion to art and the picturesque might be "an amiable weakness . . . in a mere Bohemian" but that it was "distinctly reprehensible in a revolutionist."[59] Eastman implicitly responded to such critiques in his memoirs, reflecting on the relationship between art and the class struggle. Never entirely repudiating the doctrine of "art for art's sake"—and clearly embracing the generalized dictum "art for life's sake," Eastman maintained that the art—whether explicitly political in content or not—still had a specific political function in the context of *The Masses*: it made the magazine's socialist "propaganda" more palatable. At the same time, Eastman insisted, "I hate and always did hate smart-alecky and irresponsible leftism."[60]

The words quoted above were written in Eastman's 1948 memoir, *Enjoyment of Living*. An article written by Eastman in 1934 casts light on why he felt the need to devote as much space as he did in his memoir toward defending himself, and the "old" *Masses*, from charges of political irresponsibility. In "Bunk About Bohemia," Eastman challenges more recent versions of old complaints about his mixture of Bohemianism and revolutionary politics. He argues that the pro-Stalinist *New Masses* sought to discredit him for his ongoing defense of "Trotsky's position" by characterizing him (and by extension Trotsky) as a Bohemian dilettante and "detached intellectual."[61] He sketches a complicated conspiracy theory, and even raises the possibility that Albert Parry's *Garrets and Pretenders: A History of Bohemianism in America* (1933) was written at the behest of *The New Masses* and their "drill masters in Moscow" as part of a plot to undermine him—a "mere tiny American corollary of the great international world-bewildering lie that Leon Trotsky is a bourgeois counter-revolutionist."[62] Just as Trotsky was smeared with the adjective "bourgeois," so too did Parry hurl that insult at *The Masses*. Eastman took particular umbrage at the following quote from Parry: "The Greenwich Village of *The Masses* period . . . waved the banner of revolt, but it did not really mean it. Being middle class, it revolted for revolt's sake, and not for the sake of reshaping the world."[63] That Joseph Freeman then reviewed *Garrets and Pretenders* in *The New Masses*, using it as the occasion to characterize Bohemians as "confused adolescents," led Eastman to suspect a plot of "dexterous forethought."[64]

Parry's book (which, in the interest of full disclosure, helped to inspire this book) is not uncritical of *The New Masses*, and, though Parry admits to knowing its editors, it is difficult to see him as an obedient agent in a plot to discredit Eastman.[65] Whatever the truth, Eastman offers an unintentional tribute to and continuation of Parry's study, responding to *Garrets and Pretenders* by writing what appears to be his most sustained commentary on Bohemianism. Here he elucidates the relationship between Bohemianism, art, and revolutionary politics:

> I must say that I think there is a great deal of strictly theological bunk in the Marxian talk about "Bohemia." . . . The resort to a free and candid mode of life upon the part of young rebels against bourgeois convention and respectability bears a relation to the scientific enterprise of social revolution similar to that of the efforts of utopian socialists of the type of Fourier and Robert Owen. They think to realize the aim of a "society of the free and equal" on a small scale within a capitalist regime. Their motive is entirely sincere and it is, so far as it goes, admirable. Moreover, practically all the revolutionary intellectuals, after they have generalized their ideal, or brought into it a thought for humanity at large, continue to live personally, in this good sense, a "Bohemian" life. A Bohemian life, in this good sense, is precisely the kind of life that they hope to make natural to the race of man after the artificialities that spring out of our money culture are removed.

> It is not Bohemianism, but mere Bohemianism against which the scientific revolutionist protests. And it is not mere Bohemianism, either, for that is permissible at most periods and not important, but mere Bohemianism donning the aspect and intruding into the place of serious social thought and effort. It is not pure poetry, either, that is to be condemned [but] the pretence of pure poetry to be a solution to the problem of life. The wish to live a free and real life, and to cherish and communicate its qualities in works of art, deserves the respect of every revolutionist.[66]

These reflections suggest that Eastman well remembered E. Ralph Cheney's letter to *The Masses*, quoted above, that had scoffed at the "mere Bohemian." Eastman finally answered this charge. Providing an intimation of the freedom and equality that would become more widely available at the end of the class struggle, Bohemianism, properly understood, should motivate political action. This is what Eastman hoped to convey in his novel *Venture*: "Taking Bohemianism at its very highest—as the desire, that is, to 'live,' to experience the 'reality' of life in our times—my novel . . . shows how that motive leads inescapably into the class struggle and the necessity of *making a political choice*."[67] "Live all you can; it is a mistake not to." Eastman politicizes this advice (which, as we have seen, Henry James offered by way of Lambert Strether) by associating "living" (much like James) with his own version of *la vie bohème*.

These comments were offered retrospectively, yet during the era of *The Masses*, the Villagers often debated the role of art—and the Bohemia that fostered it—in the class struggle. One such debate occurred at one of Mabel Dodge's famous "Evenings." Beginning in 1913, Dodge had offered her elegant apartment at 23 Fifth Avenue to the cause of an "experiment"; in the words of a contemporary headline: " 'THE PRINTED PAGE WILL SOON BE SUPERSEDED BY THE SPOKEN WORD,' DECLARES MRS. MABEL DODGE, WHO HAS BEEN HOLDING A NEW YORK 'SALON' FOR FREE SPEECH." As the headline suggested, Dodge envisioned the salon as a space that would encourage sociability (of an implicitly Bohemian variety). Such sociability—especially the mingling together of assorted groups ranging from IWWs to "Modern-Artists, Clubwomen, Woman's-place-is-in-the-home Women, Clergymen, and just plain men"—just might, she hoped, lead to important, if still unknown, political results (though interested in socialism, Dodge never shared the fixed goal of the "scientific revolutionaries"). At the very least, she hoped to unsettle the social boundaries that the genteel tradition had enforced. Dodge explained to a reporter at the time:

They were a kind of propaganda for free speech, but with my own views about *free* and about *speech.* I never discussed it with the grave members of the Free Speech League, nor did they know I was in league with them! I wanted to try and free more than speech—I wanted to try and loosen up thought by means of speech, to get at the truth at the bottom of people and let it out, so that there would be more understanding. . . . So many interesting people only meeting each other in print! So I thought I would try to get people together a little and see if it wouldn't increase understanding.

Hoping to substitute something like Cook's "Beloved Community" for the fractured "imagined community" of print culture, Dodge brought assorted groups together once a week to discuss particular topics. The evenings always featured guests that Dodge judged to be among the leading "Movers and Shakers" of American culture. One of the most memorable featured Bill Haywood, one of the leading organizers of the Industrial Workers of the World (IWW).[68]

About this evening, she recalled (in her Gertrude Stein–inspired note of casual sophistication): "the artists were there listening to 'Big Bill' Haywood tell them that he thought artists thought themselves too special and separate, and that some day there would be a Proletarian Art, and the State would see to it that everybody was an artist and that everybody would have time to be an artist." Eastman also recreates this same evening in his novel *Venture.* While Mabel Dodge becomes Mary Kittredge, Bill Haywood remains Bill Haywood. Describing the life of a worker in one of the Pittsburgh steel mills, Eastman's Haywood insists: "He does not live. He just works. He does the work that enables you to live. He does the work that enables you to enjoy art, and to make it, and to have a nice meeting like this and talk it over." As an alternative, Eastman's Haywood promotes a proletarian fusion of art and life:

There will be a social spirit in it. Not so much boasting about personality. . . . The highest ideal of an artist will be to write a song which the workers sing, to compose a drama which great throngs of the workers can perform out of doors. When we stop fighting each other—for wages of existence on one side, and for unnecessary luxury on the other—then perhaps we shall all become human beings and surprise ourselves with the beautiful things we do and make on earth.[69]

Dodge was taken enough by Haywood's vision of proletarian art to propose the event that became "The Paterson Pageant." In late April 1913, Dodge, Hapgood, Reed, and several others met with Bill Haywood in an apartment near Washington Square. He told them about the ongoing silk workers' strike in Paterson, New Jersey. Twenty-five thousand workers had closed down 300 mills that February, asking for an increase in their poverty-level wages and an eight-hour day. The year before, the IWW had successfully organized the wool workers of Lawrence, Massachusetts, and the union hoped that Paterson would confirm the viability of their revolutionary agenda. Formed in 1905, the IWW sought, in Haywood's words, "to confederate the workers of this country into a working-class movement in possession of the economic powers, the means of life, in control of the machinery of production and distribution without regard to capitalist masters."[70] The IWW offered itself as a revolutionary alternative to what it called "the American Separation of Labor," otherwise known as the American Federation of Labor, and its more conservative emphasis on craft unionism. By the time Haywood met with the Villagers, however, he was discouraged about the possibilities of the strike. According to Dodge, he "growled":

> But there's no way to tell our comrades here in NY about it. . . . The newspapers have determined to keep it from the workers in NY. Very few of them know what we've been through over there—the drama and the tragedy. The police have turned into organized gunmen. God! I wish I could show them a picture of the funeral of Modestino, who was shot by a cop. Every one of the silk mill hands followed his coffin to the grave and dropped a red flower on it. They cut their geraniums from the pot in the window—and those who hadn't any made a little flower of red tissue paper. . . . The grave looked like a mound of blood. As they marched they sang the "International." By God, if our people over here could have seen it, we could have raised a trunkful of money to help us go on. Our food is getting mighty scarce over there.

It was at that point that Dodge offered her suggestion: "Why don't you bring the strike to New York and show it to the workers?" Haywood liked the idea, and John Reed volunteered to organize the pageant.[71]

The pageant came together in a few weeks. This required dedicated effort on the part of Reed, Dolly Sloan, Dodge, and other Villagers. But the relative ease with which the scenes were transferred from Paterson to Madison Square Garden also spoke to the fact that the IWWs were themselves already well on their way toward realizing Haywood's vision of proletarian art. Like the Villagers, IWWs or "Wobblies" developed their own publications and promoted a vibrant culture of protest; they embodied their message in original articles, songs, poems, stories, cartoons, and skits. Reporting on the 1912 strike in Lawrence, the reporter for the *American Magazine* noted:

> It is the first strike I ever saw which sang. I shall not soon forget the curious lift, the strange sudden fire of the mingled nationalities at the strike meetings when they broke into the universal language of song. And not only at the meetings did they sing, but in the soup houses and in the streets. I saw one group of women strikers who were peeling potatoes at a relief station suddenly break into the swing of the "Internationale." They have a whole book of songs fitted to familiar tunes—"The Eight Hour Song," "The Banner of Labor," "Workers, Shall the Masters Rule Us?"[72]

Reed quickly entered into the spirit of Wobbly culture, and fitted one of their songs to a new tune—"Harvard, Old Harvard." Thus did Reed, a former cheerleader at Harvard, transfer a medium of elite cultural solidarity to the workers.

On June 7, more than a thousand workers took the ferry from Hoboken to the Lackawanna pier in the Village. They marched up Fifth Avenue to the old Madison Square Garden on East Twenty-Sixth Street. It was there that they reenacted a series of scenes from the strike in front of 15,000 spectators. Even outside of the Garden, the message was illuminated: red lights spelled out IWW on each of the four sides of the Madison Square Garden tower, a "Seditious Blaze," in Mabel Dodge's words. According to one reporter, the "scenes unrolled with a poignant realism that no man who saw them will ever forget. . . . That the Paterson Pageant was a tremendous dramatic success no one can doubt."[73] Hutchins Hapgood enthused in his *Globe* column: "This kind of thing makes us hope for a real democracy, where self-expression in industry and art among the masses may become a rich reality, spreading a human glow over the whole of humanity."[74]

A dramatic success, the Paterson Pageant nonetheless failed to produce the desired practical result. The expense of the production resulted in a financial deficit rather than the hoped-for "trunkful of money" that was to have fueled the strike. Elizabeth Gurley Flynn noted other negative effects: "Over a thousand of our best strikers were taken out of activity and their attention centered on a play. It was detrimental to our real picket line and meetings. Jealousies arose as to who could go to New York."[75] Many factors contributed to the ultimate failure of the strike, especially the fact that Paterson mill owners were able to shift production to newer mills in Pennsylvania. All told, the high hopes raised by the Village-IWW alliance were disappointed. Villagers continued to ally themselves with the IWW, however, and the two groups worked together later that year during the unemployment crisis.[76]

The effort to combine art and revolutionary politics remained fraught. In the wake of the Paterson Pageant, John Reed reassured his mother that he would not join the IWW: "I am not a socialist temperamentally any more than I'm an Episcopalian. I know now that my business is to interpret and live life, wherever it may be found—whether in the labor movement or out of it."[77] Yet, for Reed, that Bohemian raison d'être—to interpret and live life—was increasingly tied to the revolution, though he did admit, "this class struggle plays hell with your poetry."[78] In the context of *The Masses*, the tension between art and politics erupted in 1916 when a group of artists protested the "policy" of the magazine and objected to the political captions placed alongside some of their drawings by the editors. Retrospectively, Eastman characterized the conflict as "a war of the Bohemian art-rebels against the socialists who love art." At the time, Art Young, who allied with the latter group, told the New York *Sun*: "For my part, I do not care to be connected with a publication that does not try to point the way out of a sordid materialistic world. And it looks unreasonable to me for artists who delight in portraying sordid and bourgeois ugliness to object to a policy." The dissenting artists resigned. Speaking for the group, John Sloan told a reporter, "It just proves that real democracy doesn't work—yet."[79] Most of the owner-editors agreed with Eastman, affirming that the value of the enterprise lay in the very attempt to combine "art and propaganda, poetry and practical effort."[80]

The Masses was ultimately suppressed as a result of the Espionage Act of 1917. The act pledged that the United States would punish anyone who "willfully obstruct[ed] the recruiting or enlistment service of the United States." Under the terms of the act, Postmaster General Albert Burleson ordered the postmaster in New York City not to mail the August 1917 issue of the periodical because of three articles, four cartoons, and a poem; all told, these pieces either denounced World War I as imperialistic, opposed conscription, or advocated conscientious objection. The government also prosecuted the editors for violating the Espionage Act. This resulted in two trials. The first ended in a mistrial; the second occurred after the end of the war, and though the trial again failed to produce a verdict, the government decided not to continue the prosecution.[81] *The Masses* was partially revived in the form of *The Liberator*, but the altered political landscape (the rise of Bolshevism, the Red Scare) and changed personal circumstances of the editors (not to mention the death of John Reed in Russia) spelled the end of the Bohemian revolutionary moment.

From 1912 to 1917, however, *The Masses* had aggressively agitated on behalf of the class struggle and many other social causes. The most political of Bohemian periodicals, *The Masses* nonetheless had strong affinities with earlier organs of American Bohemianism. Just as the *New York Saturday Press* denounced religious hypocrisy, complaining of how "the rich and religious Corporation of Trinity Church" profited from the slum conditions and failed to aid the homeless, so too did *The Masses* attack the failure of the Christian church to rise to the occasion of the unemployment crisis of 1913. The "Special Christmas Number" of *The Masses* that year, for example, included a frontispiece titled "Their Last Supper," a "vicious drawing by Maurice Becker of a gang of gluttonous prelates dining extravagantly with Christ hanging on a cross above them."[82] Like the *Saturday Press*, *The Masses* hoped to release the "fierce wild freedom" that genteel restrictions contained—in art and politics alike. *The Masses* also extended the cosmopolitanism of that first American Bohemia, transforming it into a commitment to international socialism and the Industrial Workers of the World. The magazine looked askance at the increasing commodification of art and everyday life, much like Bret Harte's "Bohemian" flâneur, and railed against bourgeois complacency, in much the same spirit as *The New Bohemian* and a host of other Bohemian little magazines. By developing the feminist commitments of earlier American Bohemias, *The Masses* further solidified its prominent place in the annals of American Bohemianism.

The Northern Border: The Feminist Movement and "Sex Antagonism"

From the time of the first American Bohemia at Pfaff's, women embraced Bohemianism as a means of existing "above and beyond convention." At Pfaff's, unmarried women could enter a public space and partake of the heterosociability that "convention" had rendered taboo. Women were excluded from the elite, all-male Bohemian Club of San Francisco, but they were welcomed into such groups as Fort Worth's "Our Literary Club in Bohemia." On the pages of turn-of-the-century Bohemian little magazines, women writers and readers looked to "The Borders of Bohemia" as spaces for the "emancipation of women from the mountain of custom and conventional rubbish that has been piled upon her."[83] The

Ladies' Home Journal warned of the corruptive influence of Bohemia, but women continued to gravitate to *la vie bohème* in search of unchaperoned "experience" and independent livelihoods in journalism and the arts. Ellen Glasgow and other women writers explored the question whether Bohemian "comradeship" might positively transform heterosexual relationships; and, as early as Henry Clapp and the *Saturday Press*, male Bohemians questioned double standards of sexual morality.

Yet when Hapgood defined the borders of the "New Bohemia," he noted—with some trepidation—that feminism had become an increasingly pivotal part of modern Bohemianism. Throughout the decade, the New Bohemia did indeed encourage many forms of feminist expression. From Henrietta Rodman's "Feminist Alliance" to individual attempts to restructure marital relationships, Village feminism sought multiple ways of redefining women's lives. Whether in the form of designs for a "Feminist Apartment House" that would help working women manage their homes and child care or through agitation for maternity leaves for female teachers, many Villagers were in the vanguard of modern feminism.[84] "We are sick of being specialized to sex," Marie Jenney Howe announced. "We intend simply to be ourselves, not just our little female selves, but our whole, big, human selves."[85]

Many feminist goals intersected with anarchist and socialist agendas: birth control, for example, was promoted as a means of giving working-class women and their families greater control over their lives. Though a number of Village feminists were arrested under the Comstock laws while rallying for birth control, they refused to capitulate. When Emma Goldman was sentenced to fifteen days' imprisonment for delivering a lecture on birth control, an undaunted Goldman told the judge (in a statement reprinted in *The Masses*) that birth control was part of "the great modern social conflict, . . . a war of the oppressed and disinherited of the earth against their enemies, capitalism and the state, a war for a seat at the table of life, a war for well-being, for beauty, for liberty."[86] The Villagers also supported women's suffrage on the pages of *The Masses* and in massive franchise-for-women marches from Washington Square up Fifth Avenue in 1913 and 1914. Such groups as Heterodoxy, a Greenwich Village women's club founded by Marie Jenney Howe in the winter of 1912–13, also looked beyond suffrage and toward broader definitions of women's liberation. Seeking to define a range of new goals while publicizing the movement, Howe organized two "feminist mass meetings" at Cooper Union under the title "What Is Feminism?"

The first meeting, on February 17, featured six women and six men addressing the question, "What Feminism Means to Me." The *New York Times* covered both meetings and recorded the wide-ranging responses. Rose Young, for example, argued: "Feminism means that woman wants to develop her own womanhood. It means that she wants to push on to the finest, fullest, freest expression of herself. She wants to be an individual." Max Eastman, in turn, began by ironically noting: "Feminism is the name for the newly discovered and highly surprising fact that it is just as important for a woman to be happy as a man." He concluded: "And one woman will be happy by going out and seeking adventures of her own and another will be happy staying at home." A Mrs. Frank Cothren ("the only speaker who used her husband's name") insisted: "The basis of feminism, the basis of suffragism, the basis of all the modern movements making for progress lies in the labor movement."[87] Held on February 20, the second mass meeting spoke to the subject of "Breaking into the Human Race," and it featured seven women speaking out on "The Right to Work," "The Right of the Mother to Her Profession," "The Right to Her Convictions," "The Right to Her Name," "The Right to Organize," "The Right to Ignore Fashion," and "The Right to Specialize in Home Industries." All told, the agenda covered a host of issues that "second wave feminism" would repoliticize in the 1970s and 1980s, decades after Village feminists highlighted these issues. For example, according to the *Times*: "Rheta Childe Dorr spoke on 'The Right to Work.' She admitted that no one had ever questioned women's right to work—to drudge without pay. But she said it was conceded nowhere that woman had a right to work with equal pay for equal work with men, and with equal chances of promotion." Anticipating working-class challenges to the middle-class ethos of early second-wave feminism (and ongoing concerns about ageism, within and without the feminist movement), Rose Schneiderman, the garment industry strike leader, then called attention to the fact that

> among the women of the real working class there was not and never had been any question as to their right to work, which Mrs. Dorr had so insisted upon. Most of them, she said, had never been denied that privilege, and they wished they could stay at home a bit. "We are learning that as we must work the same as our brothers and sweethearts, it behooves us to organize the same as they for higher wages and better conditions," she said. "Last week there were women of the unemployed here. Some of them could not get work because they had grey hair. . . . These women were thrown on the scrap heap because of their grey hair. The working woman not only faces the

sex question but the question of exploitation as well. Only when industrial solidarity has been achieved can she gain industrial freedom and with it sex freedom."

Taken together, the two mass meetings announced the arrival of modern feminism in Greenwich Village and American culture at large.[88]

Both Eastman and Dell spoke in favor of feminism at the first mass meeting, and they published so many profeminist views in *The Masses* that five Village feminists placed an advertisement in the February 1916 issue calling on women readers to donate five dollars or more as a New Year's gift to the magazine. "Max Eastman, Floyd Dell, Art Young, and the rest are genuine warm-hearted Feminists. They like us and want us to win."[89] As Mari Jo Buhle has argued, *The Masses* did indeed make "woman and her liberation a major subject": "Never before had Socialist journalists so avidly depicted the slum woman as oppressed but nevertheless capable of a profound resistance, offered so much subjective evidence of an awakening female sensuality, and devoted [themselves] to the fondest expectation of woman's triumph, politically, economically, and sexually. Woman's situation became for these writers and artists a way of knowing and believing, a touchstone for revolution."[90]

The feminists who supported *The Masses* were no doubt thinking of such stories as Dell's "Confessions of a Feminist Man." In this story, Dell writes from the point of view of a middle-aged business man who had been on his way toward a full-fledged feminism before he suffers a temporary ideological setback:

I had . . . begun to feel that the one-sexed world in which I had been living was inadequate to human needs—that life ought to be lived and shared by men and women together. The reality of my feelings was soon tried by children and illness. I had the choice of assuming a perfunctory responsibility for the affairs of my home, while giving my real energies to my work, or—honestly sharing them. So I ceased to be simply a businessman. I became a woman's friend and helper. It wasn't until later, when the panic threw me out of a job, that I realized the heavy economic disadvantage of the transformation.

It is at that point that he comes to resent his wife for "soften[ing] his masculine will." Then one day he discovers his wife's old notebook. The earliest entries date two years before their wedding, when she records her desire to become an architect. The pages are blank after their wedding, save one, dated the year her husband lost his job. She wrote: "I did not deliberately decide to spend the rest of my life sitting in a house and taking care of children. It just happened to me." It is at this moment that her husband decides to embrace feminism. To the extent that having a family had been an obstacle to his career, he now realizes that his was not the only sacrifice.[91]

In another, more satirical piece titled "Adventures in Anti-Land," Dell observes the activities of a female antisuffrage activist whose mantra was "woman's place is in the home." He wryly muses: "Had she had to struggle with herself before she could come forward and sell anti-suffrage pamphlets? No doubt, no doubt. Like a Spartan mother, she concealed her agony. She did up my pamphlets without a trace of suffering and took my fifty cents with apparent cheerfulness. One would have thought she actually enjoyed being there in that public place and talking to casual strangers." After reading the pamphlets, Dell declares that he now finally understands "the true nature of woman." Whereas he had once believed "that they were persons just like myself" on the basis of his "experience of the sex, as a son, a brother, a husband, a lover" and coworker, he now realizes "the dark facts about women" as revealed by "the great scientific authorities" cited in the publications. But while these "facts" are the alleged basis of the male desire to protect and coddle women, Dell insists, "I can't get any consolation or delight out of that kind of creature. . . . I don't want to protect her, I don't want anything to do with her."[92]

Other male Villagers were more ambivalent about feminism, however. In his unpublished manuscript on the "New Bohemia," Hapgood quickly reveals his own anxiety about the movement:

> Through the adjacent . . . territory of the Feminist Movement, there is in the New Bohemia, a tendency among the women to dispise [*sic*] not only the men but the customs and sentimentalities and moralities which they think were made by men in order to keep women enslaved. Consequently, they wave aloft the banner of Sex-Antagonism. Hence there are many tragedies in the New Bohemia, and, as I have said, a peculiarly fierce and terrible jealousy. And the jealousy is made deeper by the belief of the men that they should be above jealousy. Their principles and their feelings are totally opposed, and so a new kind of suffering has come into the community. Over the still medieval nerves and ideas of the men the women stomp without sentimentality or sympathy for the men's inherited weaknesses.[93]

Hapgood apparently stopped writing the essay shortly after declaring, "the victims are men." Yet he expanded upon his conflicted ideas about "Sex Antagonism" that same year at one of Mabel Dodge's renowned evenings. According to Dodge, both she and Lincoln Steffens thought that

Hapgood would be so "eloquent" on the subject of Sex Antagonism that they devoted an evening to his talk; moreover, they assumed that "Hutch and the others would probably be so brilliant that [they'd] better try to record the conversation, so Steff secured a stenographer and put her, unbeknownst to Hutch, behind a screen." Dodge noted that "Hutch was a little drunk" and that the stenographer was not used to transcribing "his kind of mentality"; Hapgood himself, reading over the transcript apparently proclaimed it "quite Steinesque." The transcript includes several pages of a rambling, often incoherent monologue that returns to the points Hapgood also attempted to frame in his essay:

> "Man has now a deep, primordial pain, which he never had before, because not only has he a pain, but he has a pain in connection with jealousy. That is the first time man ever felt jealousy. They also have a feeling of the injustice of it, because they know that the woman's propaganda is all wrong in morality. They know that the feminist propaganda is wrong. They know they are right, and they also know that this feminist movement is barbaric, savage. They have a sentimental interest in history."

In response to this speech, Lincoln Steffens reportedly said, "I felt that Mr. Hapgood was talking from his heart," a line that drew laughter from the audience.[94]

It was not until his autobiography of 1939, *A Victorian in the Modern World*, that Hapgood clarified some of his views on feminism and *la vie bohème*. First, he claims that in the "traditional life of the Latin Quarter," the women were not viewed as equals to the men: "They were 'little' shop-girls, sweet creatures, intended by themselves and the men as playthings and tender conveniences; to satisfy instinct, supply amusement, or inspire poetry in the nobler male! They never dreamed of 'feminism,' not even of the relatively external aspect of it expressed by the suffrage movement. They were victimized, no matter how tenderly and delicately, by the men." He contrasts this "tender" victimization with the more brutal treatment of the modern male in the New Bohemia:

> In Greenwich Village, however, the women were not victimized in any way. . . . The woman was in full possession of what the man used to regard as his "rights," and the men, even the most advanced of them, suffered from the woman's full assumption of his old privileges. To be sure, man retained the same "freedom," or what was called freedom, that he had always had, but his "property" had been taken away from him, and no matter what his advanced ideas were, his deeply complex, instinctive,

and traditional nature often suffered, a suffering the woman was relatively spared. From the emotional point of view, the man, rather than the woman, was the victim. . . . She has the power and the primitiveness of the earth. Woe to the more artificial male, dependent on the unconsciously remembered past and on willful desire to maintain the impossible structure of civilization—woe to this delicate spiritual organization if he gets in her way![95]

This later commentary partially clarifies his drunken rambling decades earlier at Mabel Dodge's salon. The "barbaric" quality of the feminist movement can now be attributed to the earthy "primitiveness" of women, and the "genuine feeling about history" that the male cherishes is part of his dependence on the "unconsciously remembered past," what his unfinished manuscript had termed "medieval nerves." Men had apparently inherited acquired characteristics including civilized conventions over the centuries (according to Hapgood's neo-Lamarckian schema), but women remained powerful primitives.

By contrast, his wife, Neith Boyce, insisted that feminism was a boon for men: it released the male from "a role for which he is temperamentally unfitted—that of the careful, responsible provider." In a sly counterintuitive argument published in *Life* magazine in 1915, Boyce describes feminism as "a movement to free Man":

His dumb cry has reached her soul. She has stretched out her hands to lift his load. "Give us back our work!" cries Woman. She means to take her rightful share. She means to assume again her natural task, the responsible practical drudgery of the world, the larger housekeeping, politics included—and to set free the [male] Poet, the Philosopher, the Lover—the bright errant flame that our modern world has lost.

Thus feminism benefited men, and ultimately rebounded upon woman by giving her back her "Lover," the "singer, the dreamer, the splendid romantic adventurer of the past."[96]

Boyce articulated a similar view in her short story, "The Wife of a Genius." Adela, the wife in question, had supported her family for years by painting miniatures; she "earned a good living" while her husband, Richard, painted in his studio and never sold a painting. "The little colony of literary and artistic people where they lived" remained skeptical: "Adela was aware, of course, of the general attitude toward Richard and his painting. Every now and then some idle woman, who perhaps envied her, would say something sharp. And the men—they generally admired Adela, and, having to work pretty hard to support *their* families, they all felt superior to Richard." Adela, however, was satisfied with their arrangement. When a new acquaintance, a "railroad man" frets about "a little delicate creature like you having to work, to make money," she pronounces him "Victorian," and insists, "I like being obliged to paint." Soon afterwards, however, Richard is discovered and becomes a celebrated painter. The colony now admits that Adela's faith had been justified, but she knows that her willingness to finance him had never been a calculated investment in his future success. Just before Richard becomes a recognized "genius," she tells herself: "I don't know whether Richard's work has any value, apart from himself. All I know is, that he wants to do it, and I want him to do what he wants. He does it, and is happy, and I am happy." Equally happy before and after Richard becomes a celebrity, Adela sees no reason why the role of provider should fall to the man. What she enjoys is her work and her husband's happiness.[97]

Though Hapgood remained ambivalent about feminism, other male Bohemians rallied around the vision of a feminist politics that promised to reward men as well as women. In his aptly titled essay, "Feminism for Men," Floyd Dell enthused, "Feminism is going to make it possible for the first time for men to be free."[98] As Boyce had forecasted, Dell welcomed a movement that would release men from the obligation to provide for economically dependent women. Female autonomy, Dell predicted, would also enable men to enjoy greater sexual satisfaction in the context of a committed relationship:

> The home is a little dull. When you have got a woman in a box, and you pay the rent on the box, her relationship to you insensibly changes character. . . . It is in the great world that a man finds his sweetheart, and in that narrow little box outside of the world that he loses her. When she has left that box and gone back into the great world, a citizen and a worker, then with surprise and delight he will discover her again and never let her go.[99]

Eastman shared Dell's hope that feminism would fuel male sexual passion and commitment. Hoping to save his troubled relationship with his wife Ida Rauh, Eastman was encouraged when she became involved with the Washington Square Players: "The easement of spirit produced in me by this outward flow of her interest was enormous. Love in me is so largely composed of admiration that, if we are to be happy, the woman I live with *must* go somewhere and do something in which I am not involved."[100]

Many Villagers hoped that feminism would enable them to pioneer new approaches to love, sexuality, and marriage. Influenced by the writings of European intellectuals, the Villagers sought to "combine mutual sexual fulfillment with interpersonal intimacy."[101] In particular, they embraced the ideal voiced by Edward Carpenter, an English socialist, in his influential *Love's Coming of Age*: "marriage shall mean friendship as well as passion . . . a comradelike equality shall be included in the word love."[102] Yet the attempt to realize the "free" and egalitarian ideal often led to painful results; what many couples agreed to in theory they could not tolerate in practice. As Ellen Kay Trimberger has demonstrated, the relationship between Neith Boyce and Hutchins Hapgood provides an illuminating case study; copiously documented in their letters and semiautobiographical fictions, the difficulties of their marriage underscore Hapgood's various rants about "Sex Antagonism."[103]

Hapgood and Boyce met in 1898 when they were colleagues at Lincoln Steffens's *Commercial Advertiser*. That year, he wrote to his mother: "There is a girl in N.Y. who has been much more to me than any other girl I ever knew. . . . She is a 'new woman,' ambitious and energetic, a hard worker, more or less disliked by all my friends that know her, and she has no idea of getting married, at any rate to me."[104] For Boyce, the attraction was based on "the warm, life-quality in him, the capacity for enjoyment, the desire to enjoy and to have others enjoy," and it proved strong enough to overcome her objections to marriage. They wed in 1899, with the understanding the Boyce would keep her own name and continue to pursue her writing career.[105]

They attempted to fashion what would be described in the 1970s as an "open marriage." During Boyce's first pregnancy, Hapgood began a series of so-called conventional affairs. What was unconventional for the time was his desire to tell his wife about his various dalliances. In his semiautobiographical novel *The Story of a Lover* he explains: "I wanted my relations to her to be of that inner truth which was independent of all external manifestations and of all conventions."[106] More unconventional still was his insistence that his wife *also* experiment with extramarital relationships: "To have her know other men intimately, was with me a genuine desire. I saw in this one of the conditions of greater social relations between her and me, of a richer material for conversation and for a common life together."[107] Though her "reason" approved of such an arrangement, Boyce never fully reconciled herself to Hapgood's affairs. In 1907 she wrote to him: "I assure you that I can never think of your physical passions for other women without pain—even though my reason doesn't find fault with you. But it's instinct and it hurts. The whole thing is sad and terrible, yet we all joke about it every day."[108]

Still, she tried to experiment with the infidelity that, for Hapgood, was to spell the end of the sexual double standard and become the basis for a higher form of intimacy. In 1908, Hapgood encouraged her to begin a flirtation with his college friend Arthur Bentley while they were abroad in Europe. In *The Story of a Lover*, he notes: "I in the first stages of their affair played the part of an encourager, of an abettor and promoter of their friendship. Then, as always, I longed for her the fullest life, rejoiced in all that heightened her feeling and caused a warmer glow in her physical and moral nature."[109] At first, Hapgood records, the experiment brought them all great pleasure. The affair operated in the structure of "triangular desire"—the desire that, in René Girard's words, "transfigures its object" through the influence of a mediator.[110] Accordingly, the initial stages of the affair worked to intensify the relationships between all three participants, involving them in baroque patterns of imitative yearning:

> I had loved him for his sensibility and his one-time nervous need of me, and now after long years of separation he came to us, abroad, nervously needing rest. . . . And he loved Her, my Her, of course! And I loved him all the more! . . . I loved to have him so perfectly appreciate her.[111]

But Hapgood's delight in the love triangle quickly changed once he saw how close his wife and friend had become: "They understood one another at once; of course I was therefore on the outside, an interested spectator of a relation I did not understand, but longed for." The triangle continued to fuel *his* desire, but he no longer felt that this desire was returned. When he had to admit to himself that he was jealous, he lamented: "Oh, how may we be broad-minded, tolerant and civilized and yet keep our feet firmly on the basic reality of our natures. . . . In me the deeper jealousy was threatening to overcome my assumed and superficial civilization." His modern ideals succumbed to his emotion, though he continued to hope that "others in the remoter future" would be better equipped to "accept the light of the higher reason."[112]

For Boyce, the triangle ultimately resulted in "a destructive inner conflict" and a period of "nervous" illness. According to Hapgood, she rejected the idea of having another lover, and he too tried to be faithful, for a time—but when Boyce saw him "sinking into the reserve and timidity of old age," he maintains that she soon "felt that she had invaded my personality and thereby weakened it, and in about a year she withdrew from her position and tacitly gave me to understand that she would be well content to have me go my ways" (what he modestly defined as "metaphysical needs, my sexual straining toward the universe's oblivion").[113]

Mabel Dodge also struggled with her desire for a monogamous relationship, an arrangement that many Villagers believed was stifling, backward, and not consistent with their efforts to "live" life to its fullest. During her relationship with John Reed, she wrote a searching, thoughtful, and anguished letter to Boyce:

> What is this deep down necessity in women that makes them—drives them—for their own peace to ask of men that they shall be what is called "faithful"—and which, without it, tortures love? . . . Reed and I are at separation's point because of this. . . . Before I loved him I talked logically enough about "invading other people's" personalities—about how wrong it was to want anyone to be different from what they are— . . . but now it is all different. . . . I tell him that it's his "freedom" and happiness against mine because I can't be happy if I love him and he has other women and that *It's not good enough*: it's not worth it. . . . Women have *always* asked men to be faithful—will men change and become so if women *won't take less*? Or are women to get over asking it? To whom is this victory to go? *To whom is it meant to go*? . . . Are we both right and both wrong—and how do such things end? Either way it kills love—it seems to me. This is so fundamental—is it what feminism is all about?[114]

With the virtue of fidelity in doubt, and the prevalence of the "free love" belief that affairs might supplement rather than undermine committed relationships, the experience of jealousy became both emotionally painful and intellectually confusing. Still, Dodge holds out hope that feminism will ultimately address the many questions she poses, helping to negotiate between the rights of men and women in intimate relationships.

The question of fidelity revealed a central tension in the Village ideology of modern love. On the one hand, love had to provide true intimacy, but on the other hand, it also had to respect the individual autonomy of both partners (and in so doing, dispel residual patriarchal attitudes). In many Village relationships, this proved to be a delicate balancing act; many of the stories and plays written by the Villagers speak directly to the difficulty of achieving the desired balance between intimacy and autonomy. Published in *The Masses*, Mabel Dodge's story "A Quarrel" focuses on how the assertion of independence on the part of the woman simultaneously compromises that of her male partner. "Listen, dear," the woman tells him, "I have been thinking it over in the night. I have made a mistake by trying to satisfy myself by devoting myself to you. It hasn't been fair to you or to myself. I must find something to do besides loving you. . . . I don't want to bother you anymore." Yet far from reestablishing a comfortable equilibrium between intimacy and autonomy, this announcement is tantamount to a declaration of war. "Must she forever pierce him and draw his life from him?" her lover reflects: "He guessed her meaning, her innate cruelty, her instinct for picking the raw nerve in his male nature. He knew he could not live with her if she chose other interests than himself." Imagining his lover as a vampiric parasite, he concludes that any gain of individual strength on her part will be at his own expense. His interpretation is confirmed by the woman's reaction: "She saw his pain and exulted. She had done it to him. Now she thrilled at her life within. She felt life in her, nearly filling her, nearly fulfilling her."[115] Recognizing that his "male nature" depended on her female support, she deliberately upsets the balance that had given him his own false sense of autonomy.

In many of his plays and short stories, Floyd Dell also devoted himself to telling tales of *Love in Greenwich Village* (the title of a collection of his stories). These plays and stories frequently hinge on the conflict between love and the work of artistic creation—a variant on the tension between intimacy and autonomy, insofar as the latter was seen as a necessary precondition for creative work. In a play titled *Sweet-and-Twenty*, for example, a young man and woman arrive at the same time to look at a house they both want to buy. They have never met before, but they decide that they are in love and should think about getting married and living there together. At that moment, the agent enters and warns them about the marital relation: "Marriage is the nest-building instinct, turned by the Devil himself into an institution to hold the human soul in chains." Somewhat shaken, George, the young man, nonetheless insists, "Of course we'll get married. You have your work and I mine." Helen, the young woman, responds, "Well, if we do, then you can't have that sunny south room for a study. I want it for a nursery." The play ends with George crying, "Good heavens!"[116]

The woman Dell cast in his play was Edna St. Vincent Millay, the young poet who had recently arrived in the Village. As Ross Wetzsteon notes, "*Sweet-and-Twenty* delighted the Players' subscribers as 'a satire on marriage,' and the playwright and his leading lady soon found themselves enacting its scenario."[117] But, in life, it was Millay who balked at the idea of marriage and domesticity. Dell fictionalized this scenario in his story, "The

Kitten and the Masterpiece." In the story, the young writer, Paul, first resolves to hold out against the attractions of the young female poet: "He might all too easily fall in love with such a girl, and that would be absurd. With a novel to write, he had no time for being in love." Yet fall in love he does, so much so that he is willing to give up his novel and take a regular editorial position. He proposes, but it is she who says, "But—but I can't. . . . I don't want to be your wife. I don't want to be anybody's wife. I want to write poetry."[118] Dell's story, "Why Mona Smiled," explains why marriage—at least for a woman in a still patriarchal society—might interfere with a woman's artistic production. Mona, the title character, dedicates herself to her husband's work, to the detriment of her own. "There's nothing like having a wife to make a man do his best," her husband raves: "And a woman loves nothing so much as to help some man do what he wants to do. She will give up her own plans any time, to carry burdens for him."[119] Just like Ellen Glasgow's female Bohemians before her, Mona's experience of love results in a loss of autonomy and an inability to concentrate on her own work. Rarely did Village relationships achieve the sort of balance that Louise Bryant claimed to have found in her relationship with John Reed in 1916: "We don't interfere with each other at all, we just sort of supplement, and life is very lovely to us—we feel like children who will never grow up."[120]

The tensions in the personal lives of the Villagers frequently became the stuff of drama on the Provincetown stage. In his memoirs, Hapgood discusses the play he cowrote and acted in with Neith Boyce:

> It was at Provincetown in the summer of 1915 that Neith and I wrote *Enemies*, a dialogue between a man and a woman. Neith wrote the woman's part and I the man's, and we acted it together in the fish-house theatre. . . . This play had significance leading into the lives of many of my acquaintances and still further into a general situation between men and women. Neith and I, like many another couple who on the whole were good fathers and mothers, were conscious of the latent feminism urging men to give up the ascendancy which women thought they had, and women to demand from men that which they didn't really want, namely so-called freedom from the ideal of monogamy. In many of these couples this passionate attempt, which often went to the limit, resulted in separation. . . . But . . . there was still healthy vigor and moral idealism underlying the effort. So that the total result was a working-out of the situation into a more conscious companionship, greater self-knowledge, and a broader understanding of the relations between the sexes.[121]

There is much to quibble with in this summary of the "general situation between men and women" at the time. At least in the case of Hapgood and Boyce, it appears that Boyce did not "demand" freedom from "the ideal of monogamy"—quite the contrary, Hapgood imposed that "freedom" on her, and recoiled at the results. But the play is a fascinating cultural document. Performed for a small group of friends that summer, the play offered itself as a new communal ritual. Just as a traditional marriage ceremony gives the community the opportunity to witness and sanction the new union, so did this play bring a fifteen-year-old marriage back to the public in the form of a new spectacle. Indeed, for much of the play, it seems that the two are acting out their reasons for an impending separation, that they are explaining the dissolution of their relationship to their community of friends. The central conflict between the two has less to do with the question of fidelity than with her ongoing desire for autonomy and his countervailing need for romantic communion (and control). He tells her: "You have harassed and destroyed me. I am no good because of you. You have made me work over you to the degree that I have no real life. You have enslaved me, and your method is cool aloofness. . . . Let us separate—you are my only enemy!" She returns: "You, on account of your love for me, have tyrannized over me, bothered me, badgered me, nagged me, for fifteen years. You have interfered with me, taken my time and strength, and prevented me from accomplishing great works for the good of humanity. You have crushed my soul, which longs for serenity and peace, with your perpetual complaining." But instead of proclaiming their upcoming divorce, the play then turns into a type of recommitment ceremony after the two recognize that they have infuriated—but never, ever bored—one another:

> HE: You have harassed, plagued, maddened, tortured me! Bored me? No, never you bewitching devil! (*Moving toward her.*)
>
> SHE: I've always adored the poet and mystic in you, though you've almost driven me crazy, you Man of God!

And so they declare an "armed truce" and literally fall into each other's arms.[122] The restaging of conflict—in this and other plays—often proved therapeutic for the Villagers. The plays acted as a form of transference, recontextualizing and ultimately diffusing some of their own personal difficulties as they attempted to fashion more modern relationships.

Whatever the conflicts in individual relationships, the feminism of the New Bohemia was remarkable for its reconstruction of female sexuality. As Nancy F. Cott has argued, the feminists of the early twentieth century "assigned more liberatory meaning and value to passionate heterosexual attachment than did any woman's rights advocates before them. Seeing sexual desire as healthy and joyful, they assumed that free women could meet men as equals on the terrain of sexual desire just as on the terrain of political representation or professional expertise."[123] At a time when Villagers looked to psychoanalysis for ways of undoing their own sexual repressions, liberated sexuality—for women and men alike—promised to be part and parcel of a freer society. By publishing sexually suggestive verse by women poets ("A mad, wild essence is her blood, / She hears the storm when winds are still, / And all the rushing torrent flood / Is in her will"[124]), *The Masses* and its successor, *The Liberator*, helped to convey "the awakening experience of woman as sufficient to herself, no mere object of man's feckless passion but subject of her own" (whatever Freud himself might have suggested about the relative sexual passivity of women); this, in Mari Jo Buhle's words, announced a new "cultural breakthrough."[125] Whereas the belief in female "passionlessness" had underscored earlier feminist agendas, Village feminism claimed for women the "mad, wild essence" of desire as part of a larger quest for sexual equality.

Spiritual and Commercial Geographies

The Feminist Movement, the IWW, the Artistic Temperament, and the Old World Bohemia: the borders of Hapgood's "New Bohemia" created a legendary "spiritual geography." Whether inflected with nostalgia or written during the moment, numerous accounts emphasize the vitality of this "spirit." For Heterodoxy club member Bernadine Keilty Scherman: "New York's Bohemia before World War I was a spiritual haven. I doubt if ever in America there has been a spot where art and living, intertwined for a short time, brought forth such earnestness of such good companionship. . . . We were young and free, and our values were singularly true." But, like youth itself, this spiritual haven did not last; according to Scherman's retrospective account: "its span of idyllic life was short—1912 to 1915. By 1916 it was already becoming self-conscious."[126]

This rising self-consciousness coincided with the advent of the New Bohemia as a tourist destination, its "spirit" a marketable commodity. "Are you looking for the Real Spirit of Bohemia?" asked an advertisement for Charley Reed's Purple Pup, one of the Village restaurants that began to entice outsiders with the promise of *la vie bohème*.[127] A guidebook by Anna Alice Chapin titled *Greenwich Village* also located "the quintessence of the Spirit of the Village" in particular restaurants—indeed, in all the "typical Greenwich restaurants," she advised, "you will find the same elusive something, the spirit of the picturesque, the untrammeled, the quaint and charming—in short, the *different*!"[128] Such establishments as the Trilby Waffle Shop, La Bohème, and the Garret dispelled any remaining doubt that the Village was the American answer to the Latin Quarter.[129] Thus "did the serpent enter Eden," wrote Floyd Dell of the many restaurants that contributed to "The Fall of Greenwich Village."

For Dell, this development demonstrated "again the dear old doctrine of economic determinism":

> Little restaurants, of which Polly's had been the first, sprang up to minister to our comforts, tucked away in basements and garrets, gay with varicolored furniture, named with odd, childish, playful names. . . . Restaurants can scarcely cater exclusively to the impecunious elite—though an honorable few bravely did so, till overtaken by the Day of Reckoning; a quixotic example that was not widely imitated. These little restaurants served to advertise the Village to the people from uptown, who presently began to come on sightseeing tours, with their pockets full of money and their hearts full of a pathetic eagerness to participate in the celebrated joys of Bohemian life.[130]

James L. Ford first commented on the bourgeois "invasion" of Bohemia in 1895; in 1906, he imagined a sightseeing tour of New York's "Bohemia": at a doorway marked "Bohemian Hall: Table d'Hote with wine, fifty cents," the tour would stop while the guide recited John Boyle O'Reilly's verses through a megaphone, proclaiming, "I'd rather live in bohemia than any other land" (see Chapter 3).[131] Whether organized tours of "Bohemia" actually existed in 1906, by the late teens, interested customers could in fact sign up for special sightseeing tours of "Manhattan's Montmartre." The tours were advertised through local publications dedicated to publicizing the Village, like *The Quill*, *The Ink-Pot*, and *The Spectator*, and they featured such guides as Adele Kennedy, who would appear in "her uniform of smudged artist's smock, tam-o'-shanter, and open-toed sandals, weather permitting." In 1918, the Fifth Avenue Coach Company, known for its quaint double-decker buses, began to run a regular column titled "Bohemian Excursions" in the complimentary magazine that the line distributed to over one million riders a year. "Presumably for a small fee, the magazine endorsed and gave directions to a selection of Village establishments of bohemian persuasion, including some tearooms it touted as 'mad dens of iniquitous vice.'"[132]

In 1914–16, before the Fifth Avenue Coach line armed passengers with copies of "Bohemian Excursions," those exiting the coach in the Village were instead welcomed by "Bruno's Garret," strategically located across from the bus stop on the southeast corner of Thompson Street and Washington Square. Guido Bruno (aka Curt Josef Kisch) arrived in the Village in 1913 and quickly discovered his mission: "All at once it came to me! . . . Of course, this is the Quartier Latin of America. And I thought of the curious people that I knew lived in the neighborhood. How they worked: how they spent their lives in the happy solitude of creating. I made up my mind to tell the world about this strange spot in the most commercial business city on earth."[133] In his three-roomed "garret" atop a two-story wooden shack at 58 Washington Square, he published several publications, including *Greenwich Village* (the periodical that published Hippolyte Havel's "The Spirit of the Village"), *Bruno's Weekly*, and *Bruno's Bohemia*. He sponsored art exhibits, poetry readings, and lectures. A "First Aid Station for Struggling Genius," Bruno's Garret announced its purpose in a boldly lettered sign on the front of the building: "To get it written / to get it spoken / to get it down at any cost / at any hazard / it is for this only / that we are here." The P. T. Barnum of Washington Square, he proclaimed, "I, Bruno, have given birth to myself," in an indefinable foreign accent whenever anyone pressed him about his origins. Though critics dubbed him the "Czar of Charlatanism," Jan Seidler Ramirez notes that "he was actually born and raised in a village north of Prague"; and thus, ironically enough, "by curious accident of nationality, 'Bruno' was a *genuine* Bohemian." Moreover, Ramirez adds, "hindsight shows Guido Bruno to have been an astute talent broker who provided formative opportunities for expression to a number of struggling Village artists and writers—Djuna Barnes, Alfred Kreymborg, and Hart Crane among them."[134] For better and for worse, Bruno fulfilled his mission: he told the world about Greenwich Village. Purporting to capture the vitality of the scene, the exuberant statement printed on the cover of *Greenwich Village* initiated a rigorous program of local boosterism of a sort not to be found on the pages of *The Masses*:

GREENWICH VILLAGE! A republic in the air! A gathering of constantly changing men and women that have a past or have a future and live in both. A gathering of people that worship the highest ideals, constantly building bridges from one illusion to another, not noticing the mud that covers their roads and that is thrown after them from all sides. GREENWICH VILLAGE! Refuge of saints condemned to life in the crude hard realistic world, you playground of sensation—thirsty women with a yellow streak and of men that mistake the desire to sow wild oats for artistic inclination. GREENWICH VILLAGE! Where genius starved and gave the world the best it had, where fortunes were squandered and fortunes made, where heavens of earthly bliss prevail and tortures of hell are suffered, where night and day cease to be the regulating element of the world, where new ideas are developed into systems, into systems that will be overthrown tomorrow and substituted by others that will live longer.[135]

Eminently quotable, Bruno was featured in many newspaper stories, and requests for his periodicals came from around the country. And lest anyone doubt that the Village provided opportunities for *la vie bohème*, Bruno also staged "Greenwich Village," a comedy with music in three acts at the Little Thimble Theater, which he started with Charles Edison, son of Thomas Edison. The play (described in his magazine) featured a young college woman who "knows instinctively that there must be more in life than just figures and society and the same things over and over again . . . and so she walks out into life." Life appears in the form of:

A studio, on the south side of the Square, and the man who lives in it, and his friends. He is a real Greenwich Village dweller. He will remain so, no matter where he lives. Every place under the sun means to him a Quartier Latin. . . . He is a painter or he is a writer or he is a sculptor. . . . It is he who 'creates atmosphere.' And then, there are the other elements, the sons of rich parents, who are sowing wild oats and mistake their desire to drink life to the full for artistic inclination. There are women who desire to make the world better after realizing that they have tried in vain to better their own lives. And above all hovers that happy element of youth, of ambition, and of the desire to do something, to be somebody, to live.

Bruno assured the would-be spectator that the people featured on stage were representative copies of the "originals . . . around the corner, on the Square."[136] Like Henri Murger before him, Bruno literally turned *la vie bohème* into a dramatic performance. Yet, unlike the productions of the Liberal Club and the Provincetown Players, Bruno's play seems to have lacked the personal or satirical dimensions that made the other "amateur theatricals" a more provocative, though still amusing, part of the very life they strove to represent.

The emerging "self-consciousness" of the Village troubled Max Eastman. Noting that "the birth of *The Masses* coincided with the birth of 'Greenwich Village' as a self-conscious entity, an American Bohemia or gipsy-minded Latin Quarter," he insisted that the periodical's "relations with that entity were not simple":

I lived in Greenwich Village, and believed in the life that flowed there so brimmingly, and I moved *The Masses* office up there from Nassau Street as soon as I could.

But I disliked the developing self-consciousness. I took tacit exception when people first began to say "the Village," and fastidiously refrained from using the term myself. To me it all only meant being alive, and this complacent self-labeling was the beginning of a new death.[137]

Djuna Barnes agreed—writing of "what we call our Bohemia," she noted: "localities and atmospheres should be let alone. There are so many restaurants that have been spoiled by a line or two in a paper. What can we do? Nothing. The damage has been done, we find, and the wing of the butterfly is already crumbling into dust." Still, the irony could not have been lost on her that she was herself inflicting this "damage." Her observations were written in a 1916 essay in *Pearson's Magazine* titled, "Greenwich Village as It Is." There she publicized many Village restaurants and again advertised the spirit of the neighborhood: "The greater part of New York is as soulless as a department store; but Greenwich Village has recollections like ears filled with muted music and hopes like sightless eyes straining to catch a glimpse of the Beatific Vision" (and this a few decades before Jack Kerouac would find haunts for his Beat Generation in the Village).[138]

Dell, however, openly admitted his own culpability. He noted that "with the best of intentions," he had "assisted in the betrayal" by organizing the first Greenwich Village ball: "Those balls finished the process which the restaurants had begun. Yes, and it was I who furnished, out of my Roget's 'Thesaurus,' that name, 'Pagan Rout,' so potent in its appeal to the fevered imaginations of the bourgeoisie!" And though "the first of these Village balls . . . were spontaneously joyous and deliberately beautiful," the later balls, in Dell's estimation, "were likely to be dreadful, being merely given to make money." In sum, he realized that he had "shown the more commercially enterprising among us another way to make money out of the bourgeoisie."[139]

Dell also acknowledged a still more troubling complicity with the "professional 'Villager' " who played "his antics in public for pay or profit." He describes one in particular, a thinly disguised version of a Villager called Tiny Tim who went from restaurant to restaurant, selling the spirit of the Village in the form of "soul candies." (Dell calls him Willy the Wisp and has him selling psychic candies). These candies featured his psychological verses on the wrapper, and, according to Jan Ramirez and Rick Beard, "when his candies failed to sell at five cents a bag, Tim quadrupled the price and decreased the amount on a marketing tip from a

Philistine friend."[140] Though realizing that "it is necessary for people to make a living" and that "this method was as honest as most others," Dell recoiled at Tiny Tim because he presented a disturbing mirror image: "It was a bitter thing to have to look at these professionals, and realize that this was the sort of person oneself was supposed to be! Perhaps the imitation, like a malicious caricature, was too close for comfort; and the foundations of a future settled respectability may have been laid in the heart of many a careless inhabitant of the Village by seeing just some such mawkish counterfeit."[141] But this did not fully explain Dell's horror at Tiny Tim / Willy the Wisp; there was a still more troubling level of identity:

> But why did I suffer when I saw Willy the Wisp come into a restaurant?—why did I writhe in my chair as he delivered his pretty little speeches?—why did I turn away, and wish I wasn't there, and try not to hear or see him? Was it, indeed, as some cynical person might say, that he was too much a symbolic figure nakedly revealing the state of all the arts today, of all the artists, and even of my haughty and scornful self?—offering the bourgeoisie, in our poems and pictures and plays and stories, "psychic candies," and saying gently, "Yes, dear lady, I have looked into your subconscious, and seen its secret need, and these are especially for you!"—then pocketing the reward with a shameless smirk. Oh, I have no doubt that Willy the Wisp despised the bourgeoisie as much as ever I did![142]

"Cette bohème-la, c'est mon tout," wrote Baudelaire in an early poem, acknowledging his own proximity to the prostitutes of the Latin Quarter: "Je trenchais du tartufe et singeais las hauteur, / Moi qui vends ma pensée et qui veaux être auteur."[143] Willy the Wisp prompted a similar recognition in Dell.

Yet much as Dell deplored the commodification of the Village, he also admitted that "it was rather pitiful, this anxious desire, on the part of people who had worked respectably all their lives, to be shown how to play." They too wanted "freedom and happiness," and were enervated by the "machine-made efficiency and scared respectability" of "bourgeois America."[144] Their very "desire to buy their way into Village companionship" and learn how to "play" attested to the alienation that *The Masses* had hoped socialism would one day redress. At once pathetic and poignant, the advent of the Village as a "playground" for the bourgeoisie fueled the Village economy in the late teens and into the twenties. Like the Bohemian Club of San Francisco, the Village attested to the bourgeois yearning to inhabit a world elsewhere, if only for the duration of a designated evening.

As early as 1917, Anna Alice Chapin felt the need to defend the Village from charges of fakery and frivolity in her guidebook, *Greenwich Village*:

"But such an amount of play-acting and pose!" I hear someone complain, referring to the Village with contemptuous irritation. "They pretend to be seeking after truth and liberty of thought, and that sort of thing, and yet they are steeped in artificiality."

Yes, to a certain extent that is true—true of a portion of the Village, at any rate, and a certain percentage of the Villagers. But even if it is true, it is the sort of truth that needs only a bit of understanding to make us tender and tolerant instead of scornful and hard. My dear lady, you who complained of the "play-acting," and you other who . . . see in the whimsies and pretenses in our Village only a spectacle of cheap affectation and artifice, have you lived so long and yet do not know that the play-acting instinct is one of the most universal of all instincts?[145]

Unlike the Progressive reformers or Village socialists who theorized about the social functions of "art" and "play," Chapin does not worry about the larger consequences of what she calls the "play-acting instinct"—as a universal human compulsion, "play" was simply an important part of life. The Village was the place where that instinct might have free rein, and such venues as the "Mad-Hatter" and "Aladdin Shop" provided magical stage sets and props, enabling the release of the latent "play-acting spirit." At the latter location, after climbing "a rickety, but enchanted staircase outside the old building," patrons could encounter "a riot of strange and beautiful colour—vivid and Eastern and utterly intoxicating." Chapin enthuses: "While you are there you are in the East. If it isn't the East to you, you can go away—back to Philistia." Offering the sort of Orientalist fantasy associated with Bohemia since the fin de siècle, the Aladdin Shop was only one of the establishments that, according to Chapin, served as "monument[s] to the make-believe capabilities of the Village."[146] Here one could exchange Philistine rigidity for Bohemian transport.

Yet, Bohemian transport no longer required the patronage of local ethnic restaurants. "It is not many years since Bohemia ate chiefly in the side streets, at restaurants such as Enrico's, Baroni's—there are a dozen such places," Chapin records: "They still exist, but the Village is dropping away from them. They are very good and very cheap, but the tourist—that is, the uptowner—thinks he is seeing Bohemia when he eats in them, but not many of them remain at all characteristic." She cites Bertolotti's as the exception, "a survival of the days when all Bohemian restaurants were

Italian."[147] As early as 1915, the *New York Tribune* confirmed that writers and artists had oriented themselves away from the restaurants that had defined Bohemian sociability just a few years earlier: "If Greenwich Village ever did gaze entranced upon the surroundings of Americanized Italy, its eyes are turned away now. For Greenwich Village is eating all to itself in little cubby holes."[148] While their political involvements continued to involve Villagers with immigrant cultures, particularly through the IWW, they no longer appear to have used restaurants as a means of experiencing the "COSMOPOLITAN BOHEMIAN DEMOCRACY" that William Reimer touted in his guidebook of 1903 (see Chapter 6). Many of the tearooms promised access to the exotic, but they often substituted an atmosphere of fantasy for the experience of local ethnic cultures.

Like Chapin, *The Ink-Pot* magazine also upheld the tearooms as important conduits of the Village "spirit" in an essay titled, "Greenwich Village—Its Spirit and Significance." Instead of associating this spirit with play, however, *The Ink-Pot* identified it with soulful camaraderie. The tearooms facilitated such sociability by encouraging guests to linger and reflect, to converse and soak up the atmosphere without needing to "crank up the phonograph or rush madly into a moving-picture melodrama."[149] Instead of the manic "rush" of the emerging mass culture, the tearooms enabled contemplative thought and discussion. In the postwar Village, however, café-cabarets and "cellar dump" speakeasies soon outpaced the tearooms as purveyors of Bohemia. "No longer is the typical Village café kept by a girl who came from Iowa to sing in the Metropolitan Opera, or paint pictures for the Metropolitan Museum, and who found that, whatever the flop she might be as an artist, she was still a good enough cook to attract customers," noted the *New York Times* in 1923; instead, "the typical café keeper is [now] a person from uptown, probably an ex-waiter who found himself far down the waiting list for a place in the prohibition enforcement service. . . . Patrons and customers, too, are mostly from outside; and people come down to do the Village as they used to do Chinatown." Though such urban tourism was nothing new:

> Add to it the complex problems introduced by prohibition, and that other familiar phenomenon, the revolt of the younger generation, and you do have something new. The complaint against some of these newer Village cafes is that they rob the cradle. They advertise the lure of Bohemia in school and college papers; and it has an awful pull for collegians and schoolboys, and youths in their teens who would like to be mistaken for collegians and schoolboys, and girls in their teens who think it would

be merry sport to tell mother that they're going to the movie around the corner, and then beat it down to West Fourth Street to meet college youths in a romantic and Bohemian way.[150]

As the *Times* suggests, Prohibition helped to transform Greenwich Village into a party zone, and the promise of Bohemian revelry became its most marketable attraction. Lewis Erenberg confirms that the Village proved a desirable place for Broadway cabaret owners to relocate in the wake of the Volstead Act. First, it was relatively "out-of-the-way"; second, "as an Italian neighborhood, the Village had access to a ready supply of homemade red wine," and thus "it quickly became known as a good place to get a drink"; and third, "with its bohemian background, the Village was the perfect spot to merchandise the concept of free expression of personal desires" and the defiance of bourgeois authority.[151] The "revolt of the younger generation" may well have been a "familiar phenomenon," as the *Times* insisted, but the impact of this revolt on changing manners and mores was as yet unprecedented. According to Nathan Miller: "For the first time—and in a prelude to the Sixties—the nation's youth rather than their elders set the standards for American society."[152] Bohemia helped to shape, popularize, and market this revolt.

An overdetermined phenomenon, the revolt "would have occurred if the Village never existed," Malcolm Cowley insisted; nonetheless, Cowley maintained that "it would not have followed the same course" without the example of Bohemia:

> The Greenwich Village standards, with the help of business, had spread through the country. Young women east and west had bobbed their hair, let it grow and bobbed it again. . . . They were not very self-conscious when they talked abut taking a lover; and the conversations ran from mother fixations to birth control while they smoked cigarettes between the courses of luncheons eaten in black-and-orange tea shops just like those in the Village. People of forty had been affected by the younger generation: they spent too much money, drank too much gin, made love to one another's wives and talked about their neuroses. Houses were furnished to look like studios. . . . The "party," conceived as a gathering together of men and women to drink gin cocktails, flirt, dance to the phonograph or radio and gossip about their absent friends, had in fact become one of the most popular American institutions; nobody stopped to think how short its history had been in this country.[153]

Even the conformist Babbitt, Sinclair Lewis's proverbial bourgeois, soon "wanted—Oh, he wanted to be one of these Bohemians you read about.

Studio parties. Wild lovely girls who were independent. Not necessarily bad. Certainly not! But not tame, like Floral Heights."[154] As Lewis attested, it was during this period that Bohemia decisively readjusted the "boundaries of bourgeois life," forever loosening the strictures of the genteel tradition and the limits it had placed on heterosociability.[155]

In the Village itself, many commentators failed to find any trace of the deeper "spirit" that had once animated its Bohemia. "Bohemia has, indeed, a commercial geography; but it has none other," declared Charles Sears Baldwin in *The Dial*. For Baldwin, Bohemia promoted a debased form of consumerist escapism: "Imagination, though stirred more by Bohemia than by moving pictures or fat clubs or board walks, is not released."[156] The sellers of soul who still plied their trade in the Village often failed to deliver the promised spiritual uplift. For a quarter, visitors could enter Merton Clivette's "Soul Light Shrine," and view a mural designed in an early version of Day-Glo paint in his pitch-black cellar. But a reporter for the *Ladies' Home Journal* (always a critic of Bohemia) wrote of the Shrine: "my own soul was strangely unaffected." In 1927, *Vogue* advocated the (once antifashionable) "Soulful Artist's Look" of Bohemian smocks, shawls, and peasant costumes; whether this now-fashionable look promised to penetrate the very soul of the wearer, *Vogue* did not say.[157]

Still, as George Chauncey has argued, "the condescension of contemporary observers toward the newcomers should not be allowed to obscure the fact that the Village's reputation as a center of unconventional behavior—particularly of unconventional sexual behavior—had made it a beacon not only for rich slummers but also for increasing numbers of disaffected youths." In particular, Chauncey notes that "the Village took on special significance for lesbians and gay men around the country," and he quotes one gay man who wrote in 1924: "I have for the longest time tr[ied] so hard to make people understand me, and [it] was so very hard; my friends that I know don't care for people of that kind and I left them because I always thought they would find [me] out, then I went down the Village and [met] plenty [of gay people]." Homosexuality had both a private and public presence in the Village before the 1920s (lesbian couples were part of the Heterodoxy Club, and vice reports from the era comment on the male "Homosexualists" who attended Village balls); yet, "by the mid-twenties [gay men and lesbians] were organizing their own balls at Webster Hall, and had appropriated as their own many of the other social spaces created by the bohemians of the teens. Chief among these were the cheap Italian restaurants, cafeterias, and tearooms that crowded the Village." The spaces of Bohemia still provided important sites for the shaping of personal and collective identity.[158]

As one of the most vocal critics of the postwar scene, Dell had announced "The Fall of Greenwich Village" in 1926. He later admitted: "For this I was bitterly reproached by a Village friend whose real-estate business was, he thought, threatened by my sinister utterances; and I was laughed at by other Village friends, who asked: 'Doest think, because thou has turned Puritan, there shall be no more cakes and ale?"[159] Though claiming that he would never want to belittle the importance of "cakes and ale," Dell still maintained that the Village could no longer claim to be a legitimate Bohemia: its steadily escalating rents made the cost of living prohibitively expensive for struggling writers and artists. If Dell's realtor friend was none other than Vincent Pepe, then he had much to do with this development. Pepe amassed blocks of ramshackle dwellings and remodeled the homes into stylishly "Bohemian" apartments and studios with all the latest amenities.[160] In the words of one commentator, "the Village changed from the irresponsible Bohemian community, where men and women starved for a dream, to a realtor's plot to make money by commercializing its romantic reputation."[161] The extension of Sixth and Seventh avenues south through the Village also conspired to drive up rents. According to the *New York Times*, the average rent went up 40 percent between 1920 and 1922, and in 1920, the rents were "already double or triple the rents of 1915."[162] "Bohemias must be based on low rents in a blighted residential area of a large city which is a cultural center; at least, the old-time kind of bohemia was so based," Dell insisted, asking rhetorically: "And how can American literature flourish without low rents?"[163]

Just as low rent had once enabled the "spiritual geography" of Greenwich Village to materialize, so did high rent finally curtail this most famous of American Bohemias. Between the repressions of the Red Scare, the rising rents, and "tawdry" commercialism, the constellation of energies that had created the legendary Bohemian "spirit" in the Village soon dissipated. Yet many of the trends the Village had pioneered—widely available in diluted and commodified forms—continued to redefine the contours of bourgeois life and to generate hopes for a more fulfilling and meaningful world elsewhere.

Coda: Bohemian and Bourgeois

More decisively than ever before, Bohemia became a recognized part of bourgeois life in the wake of the Greenwich Village of the second decade of the twentieth century. As party playground and zone of sexual adventure (within and without "the Village"), Bohemia helped to loosen the remaining grip of Victorian restraint. As such, it provided a useful supplement to the bourgeois routine; alternating cycles of work and play went hand in hand, just as a "producer ethic" demanded a countervailing "consumption ethic" in a culture of abundance.[164] Bohemian and Bourgeois: variously allied and opposed throughout the history of Bohemia, the two putative foes arrived at the usual compromise. Bohemia was the "permitted diversion," the safety valve that released the pressures of the workaday world on any given Saturday night or as part of a transition from adolescence to adult responsibility.[165] For some, Bohemia continued to presage more radical alternatives; for others, it compensated for the absence of such alternatives.

Those who *had* imagined more radical alternatives—those who had hoped that the Bohemian society of "the free and equal" would become more widely available through the advent of a socialist republic—coped with the end of their Bohemia in variety of ways. For John Reed, the Soviet Union replaced Bohemia as the privileged locus of cultural possibility. Like the mythic Bohemia before it, the USSR became a repository of transnational aspiration; it was perceived as a liberatory state "capable of extension through space" and functioned as an increasingly "tangible part of intellectual life in New York."[166] *Ten Days That Shook the World* (1918), Reed's account of the October Revolution, went on to inspire many other Bohemians and radicals; in Christine Stansell's words, "many poured their considerable faculties into endowing the new Soviet Union with an imaginative democracy that stretched across the world to include them."[167] After Reed died of typhus in Moscow in the fall of 1920, his example inspired fellow travelers to form "John Reed Clubs," a network of writers' organizations that served as the vanguard of the American Communist Party's cultural front.

For Floyd Dell, however, Bohemianism was not the forerunner of Communist Internationalism; on the contrary, it represented the last gasp of Victorian idealism (however anti-Victorian its sexual morality might have appeared). Comparing himself to the "new Greenwich Villagers" of the 1920s, Dell wrote:

They did not mind the changes, because they had never seen our Village. And perhaps they had a healthy insensitiveness to all this uglification and pretense. Under the aegis of our legendary gayety, they were enjoying themselves, in their fashion. Perhaps they were more robust than we had been. Doubtless they knew already all the things we had so painfully learned. For them the world would never suddenly go blank of meaning. They were accustomed to its not having any meaning. I saw ourselves, in retrospect, as touched with a miraculous naïveté, a Late-Victorian credulousness, a faith, happy and absurd, in the goodness and beauty of this chaotic universe. These young people knew better. Well, it was their Village now; let them have it, and make of it what they chose![168]

No longer believing in the teleological narrative that was to transform Bohemia into the future utopia of socialist democracy, Dell instead reconciled himself to a more stable bourgeois life. This shift was motivated in part by disillusionment and in part by the discovery, as middle age approached, that he himself harbored "certain bourgeois traits—the desire for, say, a house in the country, and children, and a settled life."[169] No longer advocating "feminism for men" (or for women), Dell decided by 1919: "I felt quite sure now that I did not want to be married to a girl artist; I wanted to be married to a girl who would not put her career before children—or even before me, hideously reactionary as the thought would have seemed a few years ago."[170] In 1930, in *Love in the Machine Age*, he articulated the influential ideal of the companionate marriage. This ideal still involved the integration of sex, love, and intimacy in romantic unions—but, as Ellen Kay Trimberger demonstrates, for Dell, "sex, love, and intimacy could now be effectively integrated only in monogamous marriage—one centered on a full-time wife and mother. Single women, he argued, should work only as a means to find a mate and develop maturity. . . . Young married women might also need to work temporarily to provide an adequate economic base for the marriage. Married women with children, however, should never work."[171] Consequently, Dell may well have been happy with the sort of Bohemianism that William Barrett found in the Village of 1954:

On its most domesticated and bourgeois level, the Village has become a popular haven for young marrieds who prefer its informal—they still call it "Bohemian"—atmosphere to the featureless neighborhoods uptown. In the typical couple, both husband and wife have their separate careers, or just plain jobs, at least until the babies come. She may be in something like publishing, got to know the Village during leaves from Bennington or Vassar. . . . The young husband is probably a "Bohemian" because he is in publicity rather than advertising, but when the babies come and he wants more security, it will be advertising and our young couple will disappear into a suburb. In the meantime, home may be a whitewashed basement apartment with a couple of African masks on the wall, . . . an elaborate hi-fi set ("Bohemian" because its mechanism is unhoused by a cabinet).[172]

Thus, for Dell and Barrett's "young marrieds" of the 1950s, Bohemianism belonged to a particular developmental phase, one that passed once the responsibility of children completed the transition to bourgeois adulthood.

Less willing to renounce his Bohemian-revolutionary aspirations, Max Eastman in the 1920s went back in time to the preceding decade, writing a bildungsroman about Jo Hancock, a Reed-like poet in the Village. In *Venture* (1927), he imagines a few alternative fates for his hero. First is the possibility that Jo will become what Dell called a "professional Bohemian." With the help of a reporter named Rodney Kemp and the Dodge-like Mary Kittredge, Jo launches a career as a "Portrait-Poet." Rodney acts as publicist in a Sunday edition story with the headlines: "GREENWICH VILLAGE PRODUCES A NEW FREAK—NEW YORK SOCIETY WOMEN FLOCK SOUTH TO HAVE THEIR PORTRAIT POEMS DONE BY JO HANCOCK, GENIUS." In effect, this first career imagines Jo as a latter-day version of the Society Painter, the man-about-town with the artful fin-de-siècle studio. He is a Bohemian, but a canny Bohemian who knows how best to manipulate and profit from the bourgeoisie.[173]

The second possible fate that Eastman sketches for his Reed/Hancock is perhaps even more in line with Bourgeois-Bohemianism (in our own contemporary sense of the term). As previously noted, cultural commentator David Brooks sees Bourgeois-Bohemians or "Bobos" as products of the 1990s, a "cultural consequence of the information age": "Bobos" are the new elites, "the ones who can turn ideas and emotions into products. They are highly educated folk who have one foot in the bohemian world of creativity and another foot in the bourgeois realm of ambition and worldly success."[174] For the fictional Hancock, the product that makes him a proto-Bobo is gourmet coffee. After developing a friendship with a wealthy financier (whom Eastman based on Archer Huntington, the "son of California's famous railroad 'buccaneer'"),[175] Hancock becomes involved in the java trade. Jo takes the opportunity to learn about coffee, and arrives at an idea of his own. He learns that coffee is far richer in flavor if brewed immediately after the beans are roasted, and he tells his friend, "I believe there's a fortune to be made right here in New York distributing it fresh. . . . I bet there are two hundred thousand people in this town who would pay extra for a real cup of coffee" (155). Once they decide to rely on the milk distribution network, the business becomes a practical reality. For Jo, the business is, at first, the happy medium between pleasure and practicality:

> It pleased him . . . that his was to be the business of distributing pleasure. . . . He thought that maybe his coffee business would prove a beginning of something very great. The dream of a celestially smooth-running New Yorker's utopia began to grow up around it in his imagination. . . . This dream gave Jo some very fine and grandiose moments of emotion, and helped him to be as practical about freshly-roasted coffee as though it were a lyric poem. (158–59)

Fresh-roasted coffee thus promised to be the fluid medium that united Bohemian and Bourgeois in a fusion of "private wealth and the public utopia." Jo does not imagine a Starbucks-like network of coffee shops as part of this new coffee-based utopia, but he does distribute his coffee to "a firm that [runs] a chain of restaurants" (164). (And Brooks in fact names Starbucks as one of the "new establishment institutions" that best exemplify the Bobo ethos.)[176]

It is at this point that Jo discovers the IWW, and his fate is sealed. Before this, as much as he enjoyed socializing with his factory workers, he "was quite aware that he was having most of the fun, as well as most of the profit. . . . There was not equality in essentials—wealth, power, liberty, opportunity to live" (176). His workers strike, and though advised to fight them "if they try to get IWW" (180), Jo gravitates toward Big Bill Haywood at Mary Kittredge's salon, and soon the IWW begins to replace coffee in "the large space in his cerebrum reserved for the proliferation of ideal dreams" (296). He heads to Paterson, hoping to find in the strike a "real life" (398).

When *Venture* appeared in 1927, F. Scott Fitzgerald praised the novel: "It is beautifully written and it tells me so much about what are to me the dim days of 1910–1917 that formed so many people of the liberal side in the generation just ahead of me and mine. You make it all very real and vivid—nothing so sane on that terribly difficult subject—for it was after all a creed, a faith, in the purest and most helpless sense." Much as Eastman valued the praise, he was disappointed that the novel struck readers as a period piece. And yet the Red Scare had significantly weakened the Wobblies, and in 1927, the union no longer seemed poised to triumph over "plutocracy." Nor did Eastman hold out hope that a Stalinist Soviet Union would realize the dream of a worker's democracy.[177]

Almost one hundred years have passed since 1910. A revitalized IWW has recently targeted Starbucks, our own modern "Distribution System" for gourmet coffee—a campaign that seems to have raised wages in New York and Chicago (no doubt benefiting some of the many aspiring artists, writers, and performers who work in the service industry while pursuing their respective crafts).[178] The radical hopes of the Greenwich Village of the years following 1910 might be difficult to recapture, but still American Bohemianism survives (and not only in the form of the "Bobo" synthesis that Eastman envisioned, and rejected, for his Bohemian hero).

The Bohemian tag remains a meaningful rubric for many groups, organizations, businesses, neighborhoods, and individuals. Appropriately enough, "Bohemia" has taken up residence on the World Wide Web. As a mobile cultural geography, Bohemia has always defied geographic boundaries (even as it has become identified with specific spaces and places), and its existence on the Web figures the simultaneous presence and absence, embodiment and disembodiment of this romantic territory. Like their predecessors during the heyday of the nineteenth and early-twentieth-century Bohemian vogue, these self-described Bohemias appear in a variety of forms, and all define themselves through the mythos of *la vie bohème.* Much like the Fort Worth *Bohemian* of an earlier era, some turn to Bohemia as a mode of local boosterism. Echoing earlier Bohemian manifestos like Hippolyte Havel's "The Spirit of Greenwich Village," a posting on "bohemian.org" advertises a locale in the San Fernando Valley as a "Bohemian Paradise": "True and imagined, both a physical space and a state of mind, 'North Van Nuys' can be your neighborhood!" Numerous "Bohemias" seek to showcase and support local artists. In Tucson, Arizona, "Bohemia" is an "artisan's emporium" that works with "over 200 different local and regional artists and craftspeople to create a diverse inventory that will inspire your senses and color your soul." In Florida, the Bohemian Society of the Arts and Sciences publicizes itself on its website as "a non-profit, non-political, cultural organization helping communities develop and solidify their own cultural identity." Others hope to create a community of like-minded individuals under the aegis of Bohemia. A group calling itself the "New Bohemia" in Cincinnati (over one hundred years after the *New Bohemian* of Cincinnati) recently declared itself a "haven for artists, poets, writers, novelists, punks, anarchists, goths, ravers, bis, lesbians, gays and unique people." And in the virtual community of "myspace.com," the Bohemian tag helps individuals identify one another as "friends."[179]

As this book goes to press, Jonathan Larson's *Rent*, the phenomenally successful retelling of Murger and Puccini's *La Bohème*, is about to end its twelve-year run on Broadway (1996–2008). Yet its recreation of the early 1990s East Village—of artistic passion, defiance, and camaraderie in the face of poverty, gentrification, and AIDS—will no doubt be restaged by touring companies and in high school auditoriums throughout the nation and for years to come.[180] Still negotiating a variety of pathways between art and life, the local and the cosmopolitan, the Bohemian and the Bourgeois, the cultural geography of Bohemia continues to make its spiritual imprint on the American scene. When and where Bohemia no longer exists, we will have to invent it.

Reference Matter

Notes

Introduction

1. Henri Murger, "The Bohemians of the Latin Quarter: Original Preface, 1850," in *On Bohemia: The Code of the Self-Exiled*, ed. César Graña and Marigay Graña (New Brunswick, NJ: Transaction Publishers, 1990), 45. Self-proclaimed British Bohemians also grappled with Murger's statement and attempted (somewhat defensively) to locate a Bohemian geography within their own nation. For example, in 1907, Arthur Ransome championed "this London Bohemia of ours, whose existence is denied by the ignorant." He admitted: "Our Villons do not perhaps kill people, but they are not without their tavern brawls. They still live and write poetry in the slums." Ransome, *Bohemia in London* (New York: Dodd, Mead, and Co.,1907), 10.

2. William Dean Howells, *Literary Friends and Acquaintance: A Personal Retrospect of American Authorship* (1900; repr., New York: Harper and Brothers, 1901), 68.

3. James Jeffrey Roche, *Life of John Boyle O'Reilly: Together with His Complete Poems and Speeches* (New York: Cassell Publishing Co., 1891), 10.

4. Harry T. Levin, "The Discovery of Bohemia," in *Literary History of the United States*, ed. Robert E. Spiller (New York: Macmillan, 1948), 1066.

5. Richard H. Brodhead, "The American Literary Field, 1860–1890," in *The Cambridge History of American Literature*, vol. 3. *Prose Writing 1860–1920*, ed. Sacvan Bercovitch (Cambridge: Cambridge University Press, 2005), 41. David Weir has recovered a similarly neglected tradition of self-defined American "Decadents" in turn-of-the-century America. Though at times the concepts of the "Bohemian" and the "Decadent" converged (as both Weir and this study discuss), Weir quite rightly recognizes that the two terms were not simply interchangeable. See David Weir, *Decadent Culture in the United States: Art and Literature in the American Grain, 1890–1926* (Albany: State University of New York Press, 2008).

6. Jerrold Seigel, *Bohemian Paris: Culture, Politics, and the Boundaries of Bourgeois Life, 1830–1930* (New York: Penguin Books, 1986), 5.

7. As Mary Gluck has argued in *Popular Bohemia: Modernism and Urban Culture in Nineteenth-Century Paris* (Cambridge, MA: Harvard University Press, 2005), Murger himself authorized two somewhat contradictory views of Bohemia. On one level, he dramatized the extent to which the artist's life and calling "stood for enjoyment and spontaneity in opposition to puritanical self-restraint and a rigid work ethic" (16). On another level, he

often "reduced [Bohemia] to a form of apprenticeship in the artist's life," viewing it as a prelude to bourgeois professionalism (19). The view of Bohemia as a deeply subversive phenomenon has had many adherents, in life and in scholarship. For example, the historian Elizabeth Wilson argues that Bohemia was "the 'Other' of bourgeois society, that is to say it expressed everything the bourgeois order buried and suppressed. In that sense it was an image of utopia." *Bohemians: The Glamorous Outcasts* (New Brunswick, NJ: Rutgers University Press, 2000), 241. As we will also see, many other participants and scholars have deemphasized the oppositional potential of Bohemia, either viewing it (critically) as complicit with bourgeois values and practices or (positively) as a safe and fleeting lark.

8. Seigel, *Bohemian Paris*, 12.

9. Albert Parry, *Garrets and Pretenders: A History of Bohemianism in America* (1933; repr., New York: Dover Publications, 1960), xxiv.

10. Ibid., xxiii.

11. Akhil Gupta and James Ferguson, "Culture, Power, Place: Ethnography at the End of an Era," in *Culture, Power, and Place: Explorations in Critical Anthropology*, ed. Akhil Gupta and James Ferguson (Durham, NC: Duke University Press, 1998), 13.

12. Shakespeare's *The Winter's Tale* mysteriously invokes the "seacoast of Bohemia." Since the country of Bohemia in what is now the Czech Republic does not have a seacoast, self-declared "Bohemians" have felt even more free to claim that "Bohemia" existed most fully within the imagination—or in any location that they might choose to realize their mythic territory.

13. James L. Ford, "Seeing the Real New York: Trip No. 4—Bohemia," *Cosmopolitan* 40, no. 6 (1906): 712.

14. Daniel H. Borus, "The Strange Career of American Bohemia," *American Literary History* 14, no. 2 (2002): 376. The phrase "lanes and byways" occurs in John Moran, "Studio Life in New York," *Art Journal* (1879): 343.

15. William Reimer, *Bohemia: The East Side Cafes of New York* (New York: Caterer Publishing Co., 1903), 3.

16. Edward W. Soja, *Thirdspace: Journeys to Los Angeles and Other Real-and-Imagined Places* (Oxford: Blackwell Publishers, 1996), 6.

17. Sara Blair, "Cultural Geography and the Place of the Literary," *American Literary History* 10, no. 3 (1998): 546. Blair's review essay draws on the work of such cultural geographers as David Harvey, Arjun Appadurai, Saskia Sassen, and Soja.

18. Ibid., 550.

19. Sacvan Bercovitch, *Rites of Assent: Transformations in the Symbolic Construction of America* (New York: Routledge, 1993), 59.

Chapter 1

1. Immanuel Wallerstein, "The Bourgeois(ie) as Concept and Reality," in Étienne Balibar and Immanuel Wallerstein, *Race, Nation, Class: Ambiguous Identities* (London: Verso Books, 1991), 136.

2. Louis Hartz, *The Liberal Tradition in America: An Interpretation of American Political Thought Since the Revolution* (New York: Harcourt, Brace, 1955), 51–52.

3. Bercovitch, *The Rites of Assent*, 48 (see Introduction, note 19).

4. Stuart M. Blumin, *The Emergence of the Middle Class: Social Experience in the American City, 1760–1900* (New York: Cambridge University Press, 1989), 3.

5. Ibid.

6. "Bohemia in New York," *New York Times*, January 6, 1858.

7. *Oxford English Dictionary*, s.v. "Bohemian."

8. Félix Pyat, "Les artistes" (1834), quoted in Seigel, *Bohemian Paris*, 17 (see Introduction, note 6).

9. Quotations are from "Enlightenment" poet William Cowper and "Romantic" poet John Clare. Cowper's *The Task* (1785) and Clare's "The Gipsy's Song" (1825), quoted in Katie Trumpener, "The Time of the Gypsies: A 'People Without History' in the Narratives of the West," *Critical Inquiry* 18, no. 4 (1992): 864, 866.

10. "Bohemia in New York"; William Winter, *Old Friends: Being Literary Recollections of Other Days* (New York: Moffat, Yard and Co., 1909), 105.

11. Charles Astor Bristed, "A New Theory of Bohemians," *The Knickerbocker* 57, no. 3 (1861): 311.

12. Bristed's "The Gypsies of Art: Translated for *The Knickerbocker* from Henry Murger's 'Scenes de La Boheme'" began in March 1853. See *The Knickerbocker* 41, no. 3 (1853): 218.

13. Henri Murger, "The Bohemians of the Latin Quarter: Original Preface, 1850," in *On Bohemia: The Code of the Self-Exiled*, ed. César Graña and Marigay Graña (New Brunswick, NJ: Transaction Publishers, 1990), 45.

14. As Bristed further attests, the notion of an "American Bohemia" was first regarded as an oxymoron, especially by foreigners. According to Bristed, when "it was rumored in New York that a club had been established on the European principle, this idea "provoked much ridicule from some of the Europeans settled among us." Bristed, "A New Theory of Bohemians," 311.

15. As Renee M. Sentilles notes in her study of the Bohemian Adah Isaacs Menken, "the bohemians made the most of the French connection since it provided useful freedoms." Sentilles also suggests how embracing "France" at once allowed the Bohemians to be within and without the dominant culture "since Americans on the whole tended to both revere French culture as cultivated yet vilify it as debauched." See Renee M. Sentilles, *Performing Menken: Adah Isaacs Menken and the Birth of American Celebrity* (Cambridge: Cambridge University Press, 2003), 145.

16. "Pfaff's," *Saturday Press*, March 3, 1860 (hereafter cited as *SP*). The *SP* is now available online through Lehigh University's Digital Library. For this important new resource, see Edward Whitley, "The Vault at Pfaff's: An Archive of Art and Literature by New York City's Nineteenth-Century Bohemians," http://digital.lib.leigh.edu/pfaffs/.

17. Quoted in Parry, *Garrets*, 22 (see Introduction, note 9).

18. Junius Henri Browne, *The Great Metropolis* (Hartford, CT: American Publishing, 1869), 373.

19. Winter, *Old Friends*, 64.

20. C. T. Congdon, *Reminiscences of a Journalist* (Boston: James R. Osgood and Co., 1880), 22–23.

21. Winter, *Old Friends*, 92.

22. Christine Stansell argues that "in gravitating to Pfaff's, Whitman put himself for the first time in a daily relationship with writers who aspired to a kind of world beyond Grub Street." Christine Stansell, "Whitman at Pfaff's: Commercial Culture, Literary Life and New York Bohemia at Mid-Century," *Walt Whitman Quarterly Review* 10, no. 3 (1993): 117.

23. Walt Whitman, "The Two Vaults," in *Uncollected Poetry and Prose*, vol. 2, ed. Emory Holloway (Garden City: Doubleday, Page and Co., 1921), 92–93.

24. "Pfaff's," *SP*, December 3, 1859 (reprinted from the New York correspondence of Boston's *Saturday Express*).

25. David Reynolds, *Walt Whitman's America: A Cultural Biography* (New York: Alfred A. Knopf, 1995), 377.

26. "Leaves of Grass," *SP*, August 4, 1860 (reprinted from the London *Saturday Review*, July 7).

27. Edmund Clarence Stedman became a Wall Street banker, as well as a genteel poet, in the years after he frequented Pfaff's. Yet he continued to call himself a Bohemian

in 1892: "Its citizenship is not to be shaken off, even though one becomes naturalized elsewhere." "The Nature and Elements of Poetry," *Century Illustrated Magazine* 44, no. 4 (1892): 622.

28. "Bohemia in New York."

29. Parry, *Garrets*, 20; Reynolds, *Walt Whitman's America*, 377.

30. Winter, *Old Friends*, 58. According to his obituary in the *New York Times* (April 11, 1875), Clapp was born in Massachusetts, worked as a sailor, went into the mercantile business, became a temperance advocate and abolitionist speaker, and "was for some time in Paris" before he was employed by Albert Brisbane to translate the socialistic works of Charles Fourier. He then began his reign as "King of Bohemia."

31. Winter, *Old Friends*, 57.

32. William Dean Howells, *Literary Friends and Acquaintance: A Personal Retrospect of American Authorship* (1900; repr., New York: Harper and Brothers, 1901), 70.

33. For a useful introduction to antebellum reform, see Ronald G. Walters, *American Reformers, 1815–1860* (New York: Hill and Wang, 1978).

34. On the Temperance movement, see Blumin, *Emergence of the Middle Class*, 195–203.

35. Michael Moon, *Disseminating Whitman: Revision and Corporeality in* Leaves of Grass (Cambridge, MA: Harvard University Press, 1991), 57.

36. Vigilante, "Temperance Reform," quoted in Sean Wilenz, *Chants Democratic: New York City and the Rise of the American Working Class, 1788–1850* (New York: Oxford University Press, 1984), 312.

37. Moon, *Disseminating Whitman*, 20–25.

38. The phrase is David Reynolds's. *Beneath the American Renaissance: The Subversive Imagination in the Age of Emerson and Melville* (Cambridge, MA: Harvard University Press, 1988), 67.

39. Michael Warner, "Whitman Drunk," in *Breaking Bounds: Whitman and American Cultural Studies*, ed. Betsy Erkkila and Jay Grossman (New York: Oxford University Press, 1996), 36.

40. Walt Whitman, *Franklin Evans, or The Inebriate* (1842), in *The Early Poems and the Fiction*, ed. Thomas Brasher (New York: New York University Press, 1963), 167–68.

41. Moon, *Disseminating Whitman*, 25.

42. Walt Whitman, *The Brooklyn Daily Times*, September 1858, in *I Sit and Look Out: Editorials from the Brooklyn Daily Times by Walt Whitman*, ed. Emory Holloway and Vernolian Schwarz (New York: AMS Press, 1966), 67. Interestingly, Whitman's "literary men" do not quite follow the model Eve Kosofsky Sedgwick advances in *The Epistemology of the Closet*. There, Sedgwick designates urban bohemias as the geographic and "temporal space where the young, male bourgeois literary subject was required to navigate his way through his 'homosexual panic'—seen here as a developmental stage—toward the more repressive, self-ignorant, and apparently consolidated status of the mature bourgeois paterfamilias." For Whitman, however, the literary man can never achieve even the illusion of such an "apparently consolidated status" after becoming "infected" with the "restless craving for excitement." See Eve Kosofsky Sedgwick, *The Epistemology of the Closet* (Berkeley: University of California Press, 1990), 188, 193.

43. Whitman, "The Two Vaults," 92.

44. Walt Whitman, *Leaves of Grass* (Boston: Thayer and Eldridge, 1860). All page references in the text are to this edition.

45. Horace Traubel, *With Walt Whitman in Camden*, vol. 1 (New York: Rowman and Littlefield, 1961), 214 (hereafter cited as *WWC*).

46. Stansell, "Whitman at Pfaff's," 111.

47. Michael Moon uses this phrase in his own reading of the poem. Moon, *Disseminating Whitman*, 160.

48. Reformer William K. Northall's 1851 complaint, quoted in Randall Knoper, *Acting Naturally: Mark Twain in the Culture of Performance* (Berkeley: University of California Press, 1995), 29.

49. On separate spheres and emergent bourgeois discourses, see Carroll Smith-Rosenberg, *Disorderly Conduct: Visions of Gender in Victorian America* (New York: Oxford University Press, 1985). On the limits of the ideology of "separate spheres," see *No More Separate Spheres! A Next Wave American Studies Reader*, ed. Cathy N. Davidson and Jessamyn Hatcher (Durham: Duke University Press, 2002).

50. Ronald Walters uses this phrase in reference to William Lloyd Garrison in *American Reformers*, 11.

51. Henry Clapp, *The Pioneer: or Leaves from an Editor's Portfolio* (Lynn, MA: J. B. Tolman, 1846), 13.

52. Ibid., 37.

53. Ibid., 86.

54. Henry Clapp, "A New Portrait of Paris," *SP*, December 4, 1858.

55. Henry Clapp, *Husband vs. Wife* (New York: Rudd and Carleton, 1858).

56. Clapp, *The Pioneer*, 82–84.

57. Walters, *American Reformers*, 86–99.

58. Clapp, *The Pioneer*, 62.

59. Reynolds, *Walt Whitman's America*, 377–78.

60. "The Slavery Question," *SP*, November 17, 1860.

61. Clapp, *The Pioneer*, 61.

62. Thomas Ewbank, "Slavery: Ethnologically Considered," *SP*, February 19, 1859.

63. "On the Death of the Temperance Movement," *SP*, December 11, 1850.

64. Whitman in a notebook of the mid-1850s, quoted in David Reynolds, "Politics and Poetry: *Leaves of Grass* and the Political Crisis of the 1850's," in *The Cambridge Companion to Walt Whitman*, ed. Ezra Greenspan (New York: Cambridge University Press, 1995), 88.

65. Ralph Waldo Emerson, "The Poet" (1841), in *The Portable Emerson*, ed. Carl Bode (New York: Penguin, 1981), 256.

66. Silver White, "About Vagabonds," *SP*, August 26, 1865.

67. "The World Is out of Joint," *SP*, September 22, 1860.

68. Ibid.

69. Seigel, *Bohemian Paris*, 10–11.

70. On the role of print culture in spreading middle-class "gentility," see John F. Kasson, *Rudeness and Civility: Manners in Nineteenth Century Urban America* (New York: Hill and Wang, 1990).

71. These categories appear in Matthew Hale Smith, *Sunshine and Shadow in New York* (Hartford, CT: J. B. Burr and Co., 1868).

72. "Bohemia in New York."

73. Sarah Hale, *Sketches of American Character* (1830), quoted in Daniel T. Rodgers, *The Work Ethic in Industrial America, 1850–1920* (Chicago: University of Chicago Press, 1978), 10.

74. Rodgers, *Work Ethic*, 11.

75. Ibid., 16.

76. "Bohemia in New York."

77. "Bohemian Walks and Talks," *Harper's Weekly* 2, no. 55 (1858): 35.

78. "Work," *SP*, August 12, 1865 (reprinted from the *London Saturday Review*). In his recent *Doing Nothing*, Tom Lutz exposes how, since the eighteenth century, there has been a "shadow culture advocating a kind of shirker ethic," and he includes the Pfaffians as members of this often neglected "counter-chorus" (47). Tom Lutz, *Doing Nothing: A History of Loafers, Loungers, Slackers, and Bums in America* (New York: Farrar, Straus and Giroux, 2006), 135–40.

79. Silver White, "About Vagabonds," *SP*, August 26, 1865; and George Arnold, "Cui Bono," *SP*, June 30, 1860.

80. Honoré de Balzac, "A Treatise upon the Life of Elegance," trans. Edward Howland, *SP*, October 6, 1860.

81. Pierre Bourdieu, *The Rules of Art: Genesis and Structure of the Literary Field*, trans. Susan Emanuel (Stanford: Stanford University Press, 1995), 56.

82. Balzac, "The Life of Elegance," *SP*, October 6, 1860.

83. Karl Marx, *The Eighteenth Brumaire of Louis Bonaparte,* in Karl Marx and Friedrich Engels: *Selected Works in One Volume* (New York: International Publishers, 1968), 138.

84. "Bohemia in New York"; on the "loafers" of the Bowery, see "The Central Park—How It Looks Now," *New York Times*, March 5, 1856.

85. Walt Whitman, "Sun-Down Papers," *Long Island Democrat*, November 28, 1840, in *Uncollected Poetry and Prose*, I: 45.

86. Of course, the ever-multitudinous Whitman also expressed bourgeois censorship of the loafer in his early journalism. In an 1845 article, he demanded, "How much of your leisure time do you give to loafing? What vulgar habits of smoking cigars, chewing tobacco, or making frequent use of blasphemous or obscene language?" Brooklyn *Star*, October 10, 1845, quoted in Reynolds, *Walt Whitman's America*, 106.

87. Benjamin Rush recorded these thoughts in his commonplace book from 1792; *The Autobiography of Benjamin Rush: His "Travels Through Life" together with his Commonplace Book for 1789–1813*, ed. George W. Corner (Princeton, NJ: Princeton University Press, 1948), 225.

88. William Winter, "Sketch of O'Brien," in Fitz-James O'Brien, *The Poems and Stories of Fitz-James O'Brien*, ed. William Winter (Boston: James R. Osgood and Co., 1881), xvii, xxi.

89. Francis Wolle, *Fitz-James O'Brien: A Literary Bohemian of the Eighteen-Fifties* (Boulder: University of Colorado Studies, 1944), 55.

90. César Graña, *Fact and Symbol* (New York: Oxford University Press, 1971), 10–11.

91. Balzac, "A Prince of Bohemia" (translated for the *Saturday Press*), *SP*, April 14, 1860.

92. "Bohemian Walks and Talks: The Ethnography of the Street," *Harper's Weekly* 2, no. 56 (1858): 55.

93. Ibid. This essay addresses the difficulty of developing a language of class in the U.S. context. As Amy Schrager Lang has argued, "in the quarter century following the revolutions of 1848, legislators, journalists, ministers, labor leaders, political radicals and fledgling political scientists, playwrights, and novelists would struggle to find a social vocabulary adequate to the task of naming, ordering, interpreting, and containing the effects of class difference in a period that saw not only the emergence of new social groupings and new kinds of people but one in which new class formations challenged the ideals of traditional republicanism and political democracy." See Lang, *The Syntax of Class: Writing Inequality in Nineteenth-Century America* (2003; repr. Ann Arbor: University of Michigan Press, 2006), 3–4.

94. N.E., "What Is an American Lady?" *SP*, September 9, 1865.

95. O'Brien, *Poems and Stories*, xlix.

96. Ibid., 291. Further citations in the text are to this edition. The story first appeared in *Harper's New Monthly Magazine* 11, no. 62 (July, 1855): 233–42.

97. Whitman, "Sun-Down Papers."

98. Henry Clapp, "A Night with a Mosquito," *SP*, October 30, 1858: 4.

99. Ibid.

100. Traubel, *WWC*, 2: 375.

101. Henry Clapp to Walt Whitman, March 27, 1860, in Traubel, *WWC*, 1: 237–38.

102. "Bohemian Walks and Talks," quoted in Parry, *Garrets*, 58.

103. "Bohemians," *SP*, March 3, 1860.

104. Indeed, Seigel argues that most French Bohemians thought of Bohemianism and its attendant poverty as "a temporary necessity imposed on young artists and writers, a form of life they would be only too willing to give up once their careers were launched." See Seigel, *Bohemian Paris*, 135.

105. Ada Clare, "Thoughts and Things," *SP*, February 11, 1860.

106. Howells, *Literary Friends*, 72.

107. Ada Clare, "Thoughts and Things," *SP*, February 11, 1860.

108. Ibid.

109. *Oxford English Dictionary*, s.v. "cosmopolite," "worldling."

110. Henry Clapp, "The Freedom Not to Worship," *SP*, September 8, 1860. See also "Bohemian Walks and Talks: The Sunday Law," *Harper's Weekly* 2, no. 62 (1858): 147. "The Sunday Law" also takes aim at the hypocrisy of social authorities, complaining about "a number of policemen . . . supported by a corps of reporters, [who] made a tour in Bowery and streets adjacent, looked in upon German theatres, beer-shops, and concert-rooms, drank some beer . . . thus breaking the law they were detailed to enforce."

111. Henry Clapp, "The Metropolitan Sabbath," *SP*, August 25, 1860.

112. "Pfaff's," *SP*, March 3, 1860.

113. These quotations from contemporary German American commentators appear in Kathleen Neils Conzen, "Ethnicity as Festive Culture: Nineteenth-Century German America on Parade," in *The Invention of Ethnicity*, ed. Werner Sollors (Oxford: Oxford University Press, 1989), 52, 51.

114. *New York Times*, quoted in ibid., 72. David A. Gerber also argues that German "immigrant contributions . . . proved vital to American recreational life" in his "'The Germans Take Care of Our Celebrations': Middle-Class Americans Appropriate German Ethnic Culture in Buffalo in the 1850's," in *Hard at Play: Leisure in America, 1840–1940*, ed. Kathryn Grover (Amherst: University of Massachusetts Press, 1992), 56. As Gerber reminds us, during this time, German immigrants appeared less threatening than the Irish to most Anglo-Americans. Half of the German immigrants were Protestant, and the Catholics had dispersed sectarian loyalties. Further, German immigrants were less politically active, and despite their beer gardens, they were thought to hold their liquor better and to have ordered homes and neighborhoods. Still, nativists did not distinguish between the Germans and the Irish in their effort to change the process through which one became a citizen. Ibid., 41.

115. "The Samaritans of the Police," *SP*, September 8, 1860.

116. "Bohemian Walks and Talks," *Harper's Weekly* 2, no. 60 (1858): 115.

117. "Mrs. Gurney," *SP*, August 18, 1860.

118. "Bohemian Walks and Talks," *Harper's Weekly* 2, no. 55 (1858): 35.

119. "The Sickles-Tragedy," *SP*, March 5, 1859. This editorial also poses an ironic hypothetical: "Suppose we do dishonor our wives? Suppose hundreds of us—thousands of us—do so, and do so pretty openly, too; and talk about it—boast of it, even? . . . What is woman that we are mindful of her . . . ? Isn't she, our toy, our play-thing, our slave; made to minister to our caprices, and subject herself to our tyranny?"

120. "From Olive Logan," *SP*, December 9, 1865. Logan complains, however, that the *Press* had recently copied a "narrow-minded article about 'Authoresses'" from a London review.

121. "A New Nation in Prospect," *SP*, September 23, 1865.

122. Ada Clare, "Thoughts and Things," *SP*, January 14, 1860.

123. Whitman to Traubel, November 17, 1888, *WWC* 3: 117.

124. Mary Chilton, "Leaves of Grass," *SP*, June 9, 1860.

125. Whitman, "A Memorandum at a Venture," in *Prose Works 1892*, vol. 2, ed. Floyd Stovall (New York: New York University Press, 1964), 491. For more on Whitman and his female contemporaries, see Sherry Ceniza, "Women's Response to the Leaves of Grass," in *The Cambridge Companion to Walt Whitman*, 110–134.

126. Stansell, "Whitman at Pfaff's," 112.

127. "Woman in the Kitchen," *SP*, July 21, 1860.

128. Ada Clare, "Thoughts and Things," *SP*, March 3, 1860.

129. Winter, *Old Friends*, 58.

130. Henry Clapp, "Bohemians," *SP*, March 3, 1860.

131. Henry Clapp, "A New Portrait of Paris," *SP*, November 13, 1858.

132. Silver White, "About Vagabonds," *SP*, August 26, 1865.

133. Clapp, "A New Portrait of Paris."

134. Walt Whitman, *Leaves of Grass: The First (1855) Edition* (New York: Penguin Classics, 1986), 5.

135. D.D., "Bohemia," *SP*, June 16, 1860.

136. Clapp, "A Night with a Mosquito."

137. "Correspondence," *SP*, November 6, 1858. These words are credited to Nathaniel Peabody Rogers. In quoting from Rogers, Clapp writes: "Let us have our say . . . about this matter of the persecution of the Jews; and, to be modest, we will say it in the words of another."

138. Sentilles, *Performing Menken*, 141.

139. Michael Davitt Bell, "Beginnings of Professionalism," in Sacvan Bercovitch, The *Cambridge History of American Literature*, vol. 2 (Cambridge: Cambridge University Press, 1995), 57.

140. "All About a Mocking-Bird," *SP*, January 7, 1860.

141. A Woman, "Walt Whitman," *SP*, June 23, 1860

142. "Books, Etc.," *SP*, July 7, 1860.

143. Whitman's interest in French culture may well have dated from his time in Bohemia. Certainly, later in his life he voiced prototypically Bohemian sentiments when he told Traubel: "I am aware of what our puritans think of the French; it counts for little with me . . . the main difference between us and the French in sex directions is their frankness as opposed to our hypocrisy." Traubel, *WWC* 4: 223. Indeed, Whitman also reportedly loved to recite the work of the quintessential Bohemian, Henri Murger himself, specifically a translation of Murger's "La ballade du desespere." See Roger Asselineau, "When Walt Whitman Was a Parisian," in *Walt Whitman of Mickle Street: A Centennial Collection,* ed. Geoffrey M. Sill (Knoxville: University of Tennessee Press, 1994), 273. The French returned Whitman's appreciation; the *Saturday Press* recorded positive French reviews of *Leaves*, noting, "In that Imperial country, his democracy is taking root, and will live." *SP*, November 17, 1860.

144. Betsy Erkkila, *Whitman the Political Poet* (Oxford: Oxford University Press, 1989), 155–56.

145. Ibid, 179.

146. Whitman, "Two Vaults," 92–93. According to Sculley Bradley and Harold W. Blodgett, these lines were written in a notebook dating from 1861–62. *Leaves of Grass: A Norton Critical Edition*, ed. Sculley Bradley and Harold W. Blodgett (New York: W. W. Norton, 1973), 660–61.

147. Erkkila, *The Political Poet*, 176.

148. Whitman, *Democratic Vistas* (1871), in *Complete Poetry and Selected Prose*, ed. James E. Miller Jr. (Boston: Houghton Mifflin, 1959), 492.

149. Erkkila, *The Political Poet*, 176.

150. Indeed, during this period, Whitman and his family rented out the top part of their Brooklyn house and lived in the basement of the home. As biographer Roy Morris

Jr. notes, "Whitman was spending an inordinate amount of time underground, just then." Roy Morris Jr., *The Better Angel: Walt Whitman in the Civil War* (Oxford: Oxford University Press, 2000), 25.

151. Walt Whitman, *Walt Whitman's Leaves of Grass: The First (1855) Edition*, ed. Malcolm Cowley (New York: Penguin Classics, 1986), 5.

152. Ibid., 6.

153. "Salut au Monde" itself posits international interchange in the service of American identity: After saluting the world, the poet declares, "Toward you all, in America's name." Whitman, *Leaves of Grass: A Norton Critical Edition*, 148.

154. Whitman, *Leaves of Grass: The First (1855) Edition*, 114.

155. Walter Grunzweig, "For America—For All the Earth": Walt Whitman as an International(ist) Poet," in *Breaking Bounds: Whitman and American Cultural Studies*, ed. Betsy Erikkila and Jay Grossman (New York: Oxford University Press, 1996), 238.

156. Jonathan Arac, "Whitman and the Problem of the Vernacular," in Erkkila and Grossman, *Breaking Bounds*, 54. Arac does not discuss Whitman's and Baudelaire's shared Bohemianism.

157. Charles Baudelaire, *Oeuvres*, vol. 1, ed. Yves Gérard Le Dantec, quoted in Walter Benjamin, *Charles Baudelaire: A Lyric Poet in the Era of High Capitalism*, trans. Harry Zohn (London: Verso, 1983), 34.

158. Charles Baudelaire's journal, *My Heart Laid Bare*, is quoted in Seigel, *Bohemian Paris*, 106–15.

159. Whitman, "Sparkles from the Wheel," quoted in Alan Trachtenberg, "Whitman's Lesson of the City," in Erkkila and Grossman, *Breaking Bounds*, 172.

160. Baudelaire, *My Heart Laid Bare*, quoted in Seigel, *Bohemian Paris*, 114.

161. Traubel, *WWC*, 2: 375.

162. Henry Clapp to Walt Whitman, March 27, 1860, in Traubel, *WWC* 1:237.

163. Whitman in Traubel, *WWC* 1: 237.

164. Charles Baudelaire, "Further Notes on Edgar Poe," in *The Painter of Modern Life and Other Essays*, ed. and trans. Jonathan Mayne (New York: Da Capo Press, 1964), 94.

165. Walt Whitman, "Edgar Poe's Significance," in *Specimen Days and Collect* (Philadelphia: David McKay, 1882), 158. The phrase "myriad rushing Broadway" is from "The Vault at Pfaff's."

166. Baudelaire, "Further Notes on Edgar Poe," 101. These phrases occur in Whitman, *Democratic Vistas*, 462–500.

167. Howells, *Literary Friends*, 68.

168. Ibid., 69.

169. Bayard Taylor, "Bostonians," *The Golden Era*, September 23, 1860 (reprinted from the New York *Tribune*).

170. Winter, *Old Friends*, 105.

171. Howells, *Literary Friends*, 76.

172. Winter, *Old Friends*, 106.

173. Ralph Waldo Emerson to James T. Fields (date not specified), quoted in Annie Fields, *Authors and Friends* (Boston: Houghton Mifflin, 1897), 85.

174. Richard Brodhead, *The School of Hawthorne*, 55.

175. Ibid, 55.

176. Howells, *Literary Friends*, 11.

177. Figaro [Henry Clapp], "Dramatic Feuilleton," *SP*, February 3, 1866.

178. Charles Baudelaire, "The Painter of Modern Life," in *The Painter of Modern Life*, 29.

179. "To Whom It May Concern," *SP*, November 6, 1858. Such words oppose those of Hawthorne's outburst in which he confidently—though anxiously—distinguishes himself from the popular "trash" produced by "the damned mob of scribbling women." Nathaniel

Hawthorne to W. B. Ticknor, January 1855, quoted in Jane Tompkins, *Sensational Designs: The Cultural Work of American Fiction, 1790–1860* (Oxford: Oxford University Press, 1985), 217.

180. "Editorial Correspondence," *SP*, November 13, 1858.

181. "To All Cultivated Persons," *SP*, December 25, 1858.

182. "Dramatic Feuilleton," *SP*, November 20, 1858.

183. For a discussion of the evolution of the words "genteel" and "gentility," see Kasson, *Rudeness and Civility*, 34.

184. Charles Astor Bristed, *The Upper Ten Thousand: Sketches of American Society* (New York: Stringer and Townsend,1852), 35.

185. Ibid., 37.

186. *Mechanic's Free Press*, September 13, 1828, and *The Working Man's Advocate*, May 18, 1844, quoted in Blumin, *Emergence of the Middle Class*, 123, 125.

187. Ronald Story, *The Forging of an Aristocracy: Harvard and the Boston Upper Class, 1800–1870* (Middletown, CT: Wesleyan University Press, 1980), 196.

188. Frederic Cople Jaher, *The Urban Establishment: Upper Strata in Boston, New York, Charleston, Chicago, and Los Angeles* (Chicago: University of Illinois Press, 1982), 75.

189. Ibid.

190. Story, *Forging of an Aristocracy*, 3.

191. Jaher, *Urban Establishment*, 66.

192. C. C. Felton, "Pierce's History of Harvard College," *Christian Examiner* 15 (January 1934): 330, quoted in Story, *Forging of an Aristocracy*, 117.

193. Theodore Parker, "The Position and Duties of the American Scholar: An Address Delivered at Waterville, August 8, 1849," in *The Works of Theodore Parker*, vol. 7, ed. Frances P. Cobbe (London: Trubner and Co., 1864), 221, quoted in Story, *The Forging of an Aristocracy*, 91.

194. Simon Greenleaf, quoted in Story, *The Forging of an Aristocracy*, 77.

195. Representative Henry Wilson, quoted in ibid., 140–41.

196. "College Discipline," *SP*, December 8, 1860.

197. "Poor Punch!," *SP*, January 22, 1859.

198. "Edward Everett and His Critics," *SP*, August 11, 1860.

199. R.R., "The Sage," *SP*, December 1, 1860.

200. Howells, *Literary Friends*, 70.

201. Henry Adams to Henry James, 18 November, 1903, quoted in Jaher, *The Urban Establishment*, 75–76.

202. Jaher, *The Urban Establishment*, 6.

203. George Ticknor to George S. Hillard, July 17, 1848, and Henry Lee to H. Lee Jr., January 3, 1853, quoted in Jaher, *The Urban Establishment*, 67.

204. *SP*, August 11, 1860 (reprinted from the *Gloucester Telegraph*, August 8).

205. Jaher, *The Urban Establishment*, 245.

206. Bristed, *The Upper Ten Thousand*, 43.

207. Adam Count de Gurowski, "Minor Experiences in America," *SP*, August 25, 1860.

208. Jaher, *The Urban Establishment*, 67.

209. Celia Thaxter, "The Representative Art," *Atlantic Monthly* 5, no. 32 (1860): 690.

210. Jaher, *The Urban Establishment*, 233.

211. "New York Society," *SP*, December 24, 1859.

212. Whitman, *Democratic Vistas*, 469.

213. Traubel, *WWC* 2: 375.

214. Howells, *Literary Friends*, 70.

215. Ibid.

216. Howells, *Literary Friends*, 70.

217. Winter, *Old Friends*, 80–81.

218. *New York Sunday Courier*, quoted in "The Siege of Bohemia," *Golden Era*, February 14, 1863.

219. James L. Ford, *The Literary Shop and Other Tales* (New York: Geo. H. Richmond and Co., 1894), 8–9.

220. *The Round Table*, quoted in "The Siege of Bohemia," *Golden Era*, February 14, 1863.

221. Christine Stansell, "Whitman at Pfaff's," 114. Stansell's argument partially replicates that of E. C. Stedman, a "genteel" New York poet and sometime associate of the Bohemians, who eventually become a Wall Street banker. According to Stedman, higher pay for literary and journalistic work would have obviated the need for a Bohemia; writing at the turn of the nineteenth century, a time when new mass market magazines provided writers with more generous remunerations, Stedman insisted: "If any of the [Bohemians] were living now . . . they would be in society, have cheerful homes, belong to clubs, have stable if not handsome incomes—in short, lead the lives of other successful professional men. If there had been a *Century*, a *Cosmopolitan*, and a score of other paying magazines, I suppose that Clapp, Arnold and O'Brien and the rest would have been as 'conservative' as our modern authors and would have dined above-stairs, and not under the pavement." Stedman, quoted in Algernon Tassin, "The Magazine in America," *Bookman* 42, no. 4 (1915): 411.

222. Stansell, "Whitman at Pfaff's," 115.

223. "Bohemian Walks and Talks," *Harper's Weekly* 2, no. 60 (1858): 115; Charles Eliot Norton to James Russell Lowell in *Letters of Charles Eliot Norton*, vol. 1, ed. Sara Norton and Mark Howe (Boston: Houghton Mifflin, 1913), 135; A Woman, "Walt Whitman," *SP*, June 23, 1860.

224. Sylvia Beach to Henry Clapp, June 7, 1860, quoted in Ceniza, "Women's Response," 124. Beach was writing specifically of Whitman's poetry, and her letters are part of the Feinberg Collection, Library of Congress.

225. William Winter uses the phrase "the gypsies are all gone" in reference to the end of the first New York Bohemia. *Old Friends*, 106.

226. "About Bohemians," *New York Leader*, quoted in Parry, *Garrets*, 60; *The Round Table*, January 2, 1864, quoted in Tice L. Miller, *Bohemians and Critics: American Theatre Criticism in the Nineteenth Century* (Metuchen, NJ: Scarecrow Press, 1981), 16.

227. *Wilmington* (NC) *Herald*, quoted in Parry, *Garrets*, 60.

Chapter 2

1. John McCrackan to his sister Mary, February 13, 1852, in Roger W. Lotchin, *San Francisco: From Hamlet to City, 1846–1856* (New York: Oxford University Press, 1974), 292.

2. *Alta Californian*, August 27, 1853, quoted in Lotchin, *San Francisco*, 286.

3. As southern states began seceding, the *Golden Era* frequently emphasized that California was "far remote from the existing scenes which are transpiring among our brethren beyond the Rocky mountains and on the Atlantic border." After the war began, most California papers editorialized on behalf of the Union, but also tempered their responses to the conflict; like the *Golden Era*, the press recognized that "our community is composed of citizens from every other state" and thus urged "a spirit of kindness and forbearance." *Golden Era*, December 18, 1860 (hereafter cited as *GE*).

4. Bret Harte, "Bohemian Days in San Francisco," in Bret Harte, *A Treasure of the Redwoods and Other Tales* (Boston: Houghton Mifflin, 1903), 134.

5. I use the term "bourgeois" to designate the complex of social and economic forces that these Bohemians defined themselves against. Harte and the San Francisco Bohemians

did not themselves use this term, but, as this chapter will demonstrate, no other term is sufficiently broad. Both as the Marxist referent for capitalist power and as a term connoting conventional, middle-class values, "bourgeois" best encompasses the aspects of modernity that these Bohemians most frequently questioned.

6. For a summary of such critiques of Bohemianism, especially as fashioned by Soviet writers, see Parry, *Garrets*, xxvii (see Introduction, note 9). For a more recent version, made with reference to the Pfaffians, see Reynolds, *Walt Whitman's America*, 378 (see Chapter 1, note 25).

7. I borrow these terms from Raymond Williams, *Marxism and Literature* (New York: Oxford University, 1977), 121–28. Williams argues that "in authentic historical analysis it is necessary at every point to recognize the complex interrelations between movements and tendencies both within and beyond a specific and effective dominance"—including that of "bourgeois culture." "Residual" and "emergent" social practices and ideologies can exert oppositional pressure on the status quo, yet often are or become "wholly or largely incorporated into the dominant culture" (121–22).

8. Sacvan Bercovitch expresses the hope that "the current dissensus in academic criticism may help to bring alive the experiences of disruption and discontinuity that characterize American literary history." Bercovitch, *Rites of Assent*, 374 (see Introduction, note 19).

9. As Gary Scharnhorst details, "the *re*canonization of American literature has led to a virtual *de*canonization of Harte." Gary Scharnhorst, "Whatever Happened to Bret Harte?" in *American Realism and the Canon*, ed. Tom Quirk and Gary Scharnhorst (Newark: University of Delaware Press, 1994), 201.

10. Parry, *Garrets*, 212.

11. On Harte's early life, see Richard O'Connor, *Bret Harte: A Biography* (Boston: Little, Brown, 1966), 9–47.

12. E. J. Edwards, "New News of Yesterday," *New York Mail*, February 5, 1912, quoted in George R. Stewart, *Bret Harte: Argonaut and Exile* (1935; repr., Port Washington, NY: Kennikat Press, 1959), 18. Harte was connected to the governors of Connecticut through his mother's line.

13. Harte described this boyhood adventure in an article for the *Golden Era*, November 4, 1860, quoted in O'Connor, *Bret Harte*, 15.

14. Bret Harte, Diary, December 31, 1857 (Bancroft Manuscript Collection, University of California, Berkeley, CA), quoted in Gary Scharnhorst, *Bret Harte* (New York: Twayne Publishers, 1992), 3.

15. Ibid.

16. Charles A. Murdock, "Bret Harte in Humboldt," *Overland Monthly* 60, no. 3 (1902): 301.

17. Bret Harte, "Indiscriminate Massacre of Indians," *Northern Californian*, February 29, 1860, quoted in O'Connor, *Bret Harte*, 45.

18. This was the recollection of Charles A. Murdock, a friend of Harte's from Humboldt County, in his memoir *A Backward Glance at Eighty* (San Francisco: Paul Elder and Company, 1921), 79.

19. On Lawrence and the *Golden Era* (which was subtitled "A California Family Newspaper Devoted to Literature, Agriculture, the Mining Interest, Local and Foreign Intelligence, Commerce, Education, and the Fine Arts"), the most complete account remains Franklin Walker, *San Francisco's Literary Frontier* (Seattle: University of Washington Press, 1939), 116–46.

20. Shortly after Harte joined the paper, Lawrence editorialized that "Bret's . . . contribution may justly be considered among the classics of modern prose composition." "The Golden Era This Week," *GE*, October 7, 1860.

21. Walter Benjamin, *Charles Baudelaire: A Lyric Poet in the Era of High Capitalism* (London: Verso, 1997).

22. Ibid., 36, 39.

23. Ibid., 37, 39.

24. Ibid., 55.

25. My account of English and American spectators is indebted to Dana Brand's excellent survey. Dana Brand, *The Spectator and the City in Nineteenth-Century American Literature* (Cambridge: Cambridge University Press, 1991).

26. Jürgen Habermas's influential concept of the "public sphere" informs most recent accounts of the eighteenth-century spectator. See Brand, *The Spectator and the City*; Terry Eagleton, *The Function of Criticism: From the Spectator to Post-Structuralism* (London: Verso, 1984), 9–27.

27. Eagleton, *The Function of Criticism*, 26.

28. *The Spectator* 1, no. 69: 294, quoted in Brand, *The Spectator and the City*, 36; Brand, *The Spectator and the City*, 37.

29. Brand, *The Spectator and the City*, 38.

30. Charles Dickens, *The Sketches by Boz* (New York: The University Society, 1908), 58.

31. Nathaniel Parker Willis, *The Rag Bag: A Collection of Ephemera* (New York: Charles Scribner, 1855), 47, quoted in Brand, *The Spectator and the City*, 76–77.

32. Brand, *The Spectator and the City*, 77.

33. Ibid., 78.

34. Benjamin, *Charles Baudelaire*, 171.

35. *GE*, August 12, 1860.

36. I borrowed this list of spectatorial signatures from Wyn Kelley, *Melville's City: Literary and Urban Form in Nineteenth-Century New York* (Cambridge: Cambridge University Press, 1996), 69. She includes "the bohemian" in her own list, apparently regarding this signature as part of the same spectatorial phenomenon. To the contrary, I argue that, in most instances, "the bohemian" is a related, but ultimately distinct literary identity.

37. *Spectator* 1, no. 69: 294, quoted in Brand, *The Spectator and the City*, 36.

38. "The Projected Fair of the Mechanics' Institute," *Call*, April 14, 1864, quoted in *Clemens of the Call: Mark Twain in San Francisco*, ed. Edgar M. Branch (Berkeley: University of California Press, 1969), 104.

39. Bret Harte, "The Bohemian at the Fair," *GE*, September 9, 1860. The performance of *The Bohemian Girl* is announced in "Dramatic and Musical," *GE*, September 9, 1860.

40. Bret Harte, "The Bohemian at the Fair," *GE*, September 9, 1860.

41. Ibid.

42. Thomas Richards, *The Commodity Culture of Victorian England: Advertising and Spectacle, 1851–1914* (Stanford, CA: Stanford University Press, 1990), 2.

43. Karl Marx, "The Fetishism of Commodities and the Secret Thereof," *Capital*, vol. 1 in *The Marx-Engels Reader*, ed. Robert C. Tucker (New York: W. W. Norton, 1978), 321.

44. Harte, "The Bohemian at the Fair," *GE*, September 9, 1860. Elsewhere, Harte's ironic take on the developing commodity culture approaches a twentieth-century level of disgust: he refers derisively to ads seen at a local restaurant "that advise me confidentially to lose no time after refreshing my inner man, to clothe myself at Heuston, Hastings & Co., and thus complete my earthly mission." Bret Harte, "Bohemian Papers: On Restaurants," *GE*, February 1, 1861.

45. John F. Kasson, *Civilizing the Machine: Technology and Republican Values in America, 1776–1900* (Harmondsworth: Penguin, 1976), 162.

46. Guides to the Philadelphia exposition emphasized the sublimity of the Corliss engine. I have borrowed the phrase "sublime machine" from William Leiss, "Technology and Degeneration: The Sublime Machine," in *Degeneration: The Dark Side of Progress*, ed. J. Edward Chamberlin and Sander L. Gilman (New York: Columbia University Press, 1985), 145.

47. William Dean Howells, "A Sennight of the Centennial," *Atlantic Monthly* 38 (1876): 86.

48. In a Marxist critique of capitalism, any form of property is itself an alienation—in Lukacs's terms, it is a reification of the self. Like other American romantics, however, Harte believed that reading and writing were relatively unalienated forms of labor and that literary property ennobled rather than depleted individual identity. On Thoreau's "attempt to devise a conception of reading and writing as unalienated labor," see M. T. Gilmore, "*Walden* and the Curse of Trade," in *Ideology and Classic American Literature*, ed. Sacvan Bercovitch and Myra Jehlen (Cambridge: Cambridge University Press, 1982), 302.

49. Harte, "Wanted—A Printer," *GE*, January 27, 1861.

50. It is useful to compare Harte's romantic view of print with what Michael Warner has identified as the rationalistic "print ideology" of eighteenth-century America. According to Warner, this print ideology "valorized the general above the personal and construed the opposition between the two in the republican terms of virtue and interest" (Warner, 5) Using Ben Franklin as the ultimate example and proponent of this ideology, Warner argues that Franklin sought to efface the personal in the effort to become, quite literally, a man of letters. Indeed, as Warner reminds us, Franklin modeled his own prose on that of the English *Spectator*, purposefully imitating its "form," the "arrangement of thoughts," and even the thoughts themselves. In this way, Franklin entered the public sphere of print culture, thus seeking an uncanny degree of spectatorial detachment. For this Franklin, it is the separation of print from the individual self that endows the medium with an exemplary, representative civic value. Alternatively, Harte's Bohemian spectator seeks to reembody thought, using the experience of print and typesetting to eroticize the circulation of ideas and to promote a kind of Whitmanian "adhesiveness" between individuals and even social classes. For Harte, only embodied thought adequately constitutes civic life. See Michael Warner, "Franklin and the Letters of the Republic," in *The New American Studies: Essays from Representations*, ed. Philip Fisher (Berkeley: University of California Press, 1991), 3–23.

51. Bret Harte, "The Bohemian at the Fair," *GE*, September 16, 1860.

52. Charles Baudelaire. "The Painter of Modern Life," in *The Painter of Modern Life and Other Essays*, ed. and trans. Jonathan Mayne (New York: Da Capo Press, 1964), 9.

53. O'Connor, *Bret Harte*, 70.

54. Ibid.

55. Bret Harte, "Town and Table Talk: A la Bohemian," *GE*, August 12, 1860.

56. On the expanding role of women in the Protestant churches during the mid-nineteenth century, see Ann Douglas, *The Feminization of American Culture* (New York: Doubleday, 1977).

57. O'Connor, *Bret Harte*, 59–63.

58. Bret Harte, "Bohemian Feuilleton," *GE*, February 24, 1861. Harte was not the only one to link the cause of the war effort with that of Bohemia. A group of Northern war journalists referred to themselves as a "Bohemian Brigade." James M. Perry describes this journalism, though he does not say much about how the term "Bohemian Brigade" functioned for these journalists or if it figured in their dispatches. Apparently this was a name some war correspondents had given themselves early in the war in the western campaign, where they all were assigned the same Room 45 of a hotel in Cairo, Illinois. See James M. Perry, *A Bohemian Brigade* (New York: John Wiley and Sons, 2000), 71. Further, in 1863, one edition of a magazine entitled *The Bohemian* appeared out of Richmond, Virginia (see Chapter 4 for more on this periodical). In this magazine, a section called "Bohemiana" offers a Southern version of the Bohemian spectator, insisting, "He does not profess to be wiser than the rest of the world, but he does claim to be more observant than most men." *The Bohemian* (Richmond, VA, 1863).

59. Bret Harte, "Fixing Up an Old House," in *The Writings of Bret Harte*, vol. 20, ed. Charles Meeker Kozlay (Boston: Houghton Mifflin, 1914), 129. The article first appeared in *The Californian*, July 16, 1864.

60. Bret Harte, "Seeing the Steamer Off," in *Gabriel Conroy; Bohemian Papers; Stories of and for the Young*, vol. 2 (Boston: Houghton Mifflin, 1903), 244. First published in the *Golden Era*, several of Harte's "Bohemian Papers" are included in this edition of his collected works. Franklin Walker argues that the republished "Bohemian Papers" are "the pick of the lot." Walker, *San Francisco's Literary Frontier*, 128.

61. Harte, "Neighborhoods I Have Moved From," in *Gabriel Conroy; Bohemian Papers*, vol. 2, 248–51.

62. Ibid., 250.

63. Lynn Wardley makes this observation about Charlotte Perkins Gilman's 1892 "The Yellow Wallpaper." Lynn Wardley, "Relic, Fetish, Femmage: The Aesthetics of Sentiment in the Work of Stowe," *Yale Journal of Criticism* 5 (1992): 184.

64. On late-nineteenth-century fears of emasculation, see T. J. Jackson Lears, *No Place of Grace: Antimodernism and the Transformation of American Culture, 1880–1920* (Chicago: University of Chicago Press, 1983).

65. "Farm, Garden and Household," *GE*, November 18, 1860.

66. To be sure, the many voluntary associations that sprang up in nineteenth-century America often translated many of ideals of the middle-class "private sphere" into a form of community service and involved male and female participation (though such organizations were often segregated by gender). Many of these associations, including Temperance and Bible, Tract, Missionary and Sunday School societies, attempted to foster community (though they often worked to bolster the hegemony and social leadership of the bourgeoisie and to "uplift" immigrants and the working-classes). On such associations, see Blumin, *Emergence of the Middle Class* (see Chapter 1, note 4).

67. Burton J. Bledstein, *The Culture of Professionalism: The Middle Class and the Development of Higher Education in America* (New York: W. W. Norton, 1976), 56–65.

68. Bret Harte, "Seeing the Steamer Off," 243–44.

69. Harte, "Neighborhoods I Have Moved From," 252.

70. Bret Harte, "Bohemian Papers: Melons," *GE*, October 5, 1862.

71. In numerous *Golden Era* columns, Harte parodies the popular "city mysteries" genre, a genre which flourished in the wake of Eugene Sue's *Mysteries of Paris* (1846). See, for example, "The Bohemian's Sensation Play," *GE*, November 25, 1860.

72. Lawrence W. Levine, *Highbrow/Lowbrow: The Emergence of Cultural Hierarchy in America* (Cambridge, MA: Harvard University Press, 1988), 192–200.

73. "O.G," *GE*, July 1, 1860. Based on the style of the writing, George Rippey Stewart believes that this article was one of Harte's first assignments for the *Golden Era*, though Harte's authorship remains in doubt. George Rippey Stewart, *A Bibliography of the Writings of Bret Harte in the Magazines and Newspapers* (Berkeley: University of California Press, 1933), 137. In implicit contrast to the bourgeois opera house, the "Cheap Shows," according to Harte, provided a more "Bohemian" atmosphere: "The strong point of the establishment was the air of complete abandonment and *insouciance* which pervaded it." Bret Harte, "The Bohemian Does the Cheap Shows," *GE*, October 14, 1860.

74. Bret Harte, "Bohemian Papers: City Improvements," *GE*, February 15, 1863. Indeed, as Mary Ryan has shown, this credo continued to inform urban planning in San Francisco. Following the Civil War, the city sought to reserve the land that would become Golden Gate Park and sold the project to taxpayers and local entrepreneurs by representing it as "a direct moneyed return on investment"; as the Park Commissioners' report of 1872 argued, "In all other cities where public parks have been made the increase in the amount received from taxation, on the enhanced value of property resulting from Park improvements is largely in excess of the interest on the money expended." San

Francisco Park Commissioners, *The First Biennial Report, 1870–1871* (San Francisco: n.p., 1874), 72, quoted in Mary P. Ryan, *Civic Wars: Democracy and Public Life in the American City During the Nineteenth Century* (Berkeley: University of California Press, 1997), 205.

75. Harte, "Bohemian Papers: City Improvements," February 15, 1863.

76. Bercovitch famously defines the "American Jeremiad" (first imported to America from the Old World by Puritan clergy) as both a lament over the decline of the community from a state of higher purity and as a reaffirmation of collective destiny. See Sacvan Bercovitch, *The American Jeremiad* (Madison: University of Wisconsin Press, 1978).

77. Ryan, *Civic Wars*, 209.

78. Harte,"Bohemian Papers: City Improvements," *GE*, February 15, 1863.

79. Indeed, the irony of Harte's statement increases when juxtaposed to a similar one from Ben Franklin's "Dogood" papers: "I am not without Hopes, that communicating my small Stock in this Manner, by Peace-meal to the Publick, may be at least in some Measure useful." Unlike Harte's Bohemian Papers, these letters reveal an unjaundiced faith in the power of the printed word. Benjamin Franklin, *The Papers of Benjamin Franklin*, vol. 1 (New Haven, CT: Yale University Press, 1959), 13, quoted in Warner, "Franklin and the Letters," 10.

80. Harte, "Bohemian Papers: A Rail at the Rail," *GE*, April 12, 1863.

81. On the changing fortunes of bourgeois ideals of "sincerity," see Karen Halttunen, *Confidence Men and Painted Women: A Study of Middle-Class Culture in America, 1830–1870* (New Haven, CT: Yale University Press, 1982).

82. Harte, "Bohemian Papers: A View from a Back Window," *GE*, March 8, 1863.

83. Harte, "The Bohemian on Balls," *GE*, October 28, 1860.

84. "The Nomads of San Francisco," *GE*, February 17, 1861.

85. "Hotel Ethics," *GE*, February 22, 1863.

86. George F. Parsons, "What Is Bohemianism?" *Overland Monthly* (November, 1868): 426, 429.

87. Bret Harte, "Bohemian Feuilleton: Hotel Life," *GE*, April 21, 1861.

88. See Jean-Christophe Agnew, "The Consuming Vision of Henry James," in *The Culture of Consumption: Critical Essays in American History, 1880–1980*, ed. Richard Wightman Fox and T. J. Jackson Lears (New York: Pantheon Books, 1983), 79.

89. To be sure, as recent scholarship has emphasized, in manifold ways the separate spheres binary "was more a class, race, and national ideology than a universal social practice." *Sentimental Men: Masculinity and the Politics of Affect in American Culture*, ed. Mary Chapman and Glenn Hendler (Berkeley: University of California Press, 1999), 3.

90. Bret Harte, "Bohemian Papers: On Restaurants," *GE*, February 1, 1863.

91. Reflecting on restaurants, Harte admits, "There are moments in a man's life when free agency becomes a bore and it is pleasant to have others think for you." Ibid.

92. Bret Harte, "The Bohemian Concerning," *GE*, November 11, 1860.

93. By the 1850s, the discourse of racial Anglo-Saxonism was flourishing in many social, political, and scientific circles, and some felt that the presence of German immigrants would dilute America's Anglo-Saxon stock. Yet, as Matthew Frye Jacobson has argued, "By longstanding tradition in the high discourse of race, the Anglo-Saxon and Teutonic traditions were closely aligned; indeed, by many accounts Anglo-Saxons traced their very genius to the forests of Germany." See Matthew Frye Jacobson, *Whiteness of a Different Color: European Immigrants and the Alchemy of Race* (Cambridge, MA: Harvard University Press, 1998), 46.

94. See Ronald Takaki, *A Different Mirror: A History of Multicultural America* (Boston: Little, Brown, 1993), 215.

95. Bret Harte, "Bohemian Papers: "The Mission Dolores," *GE*, March 22, 1863.

96. Indeed, the belief that the Mexicans would eventually "give way" was expressed in the U.S. Senate during debates over the Mexican War. For example, one Senator from

New York, Daniel S. Dickinson, supported the war, arguing that, "like their doomed brethren, who were once spread over the several States of the Union, they are destined, by laws above human agency, to *give way* to a stronger race from this continent or another [my emphasis]." *Congressional Globe*, 30th Cong., 1st Sess. (Dickinson, January 12, 1848), quoted in Reginald Horsman, *Race and Manifest Destiny: The Origins of American Racial Anglo-Saxonism* (Cambridge, MA: Harvard University Press, 1981), 243–44.

97. Anne K. Mellor, *English Romantic Irony* (Cambridge, MA: Harvard University Press, 1980), 14.

98. Harte mocks notions of Anglo-American "progress" in other Bohemian sketches. In "A Rail at the Rail," Harte ironically begins, "I wish it to be understood at the beginning of this article, that I am a Friend of Progress." *GE*, April 12, 1863.

99. This phrase comes from Leo Marx, *The Machine in the Garden: Technology and the Pastoral Ideal in America* (New York: Oxford University Press, 1964), 32.

100. Nathaniel Hawthorne, *American Notebooks*, ed. Randall Stewart (New Haven, CT: Yale University Press, 1932), 104.

101. Ironically enough, Thomas O. Larkin—a local businessman and former consul in Mexican California who had once championed Manifest Destiny—also waxed nostalgic for a more pastoral California in an 1856 letter: "Times are hard here, becoming harder. I begin to yearn after the times prior to July 1846 [the date when American occupation of what would become San Francisco began] and all their beautiful pleasures and the flesh pots of those days—halcyon days they were." Thomas O. Larkin to Stearnes, April 24, 1856, quoted in Lotchin, *San Francisco*, 301. Later nostalgic pastorals of Spanish California include Helen Hunt Jackson's *Ramona* (1884) and Gertrude Atherton's *Before the Gringo Came* (1894) and *The Californians* (1898).

102. On Virgil's first eclogue, see Marx, *The Machine in the Garden*, 19–24. In a later essay, Harte himself describes Spanish California as being filled with "peaceful, pastoral days." See Bret Harte, "The Argonauts of '49" (1872), in *Selected Stories and Sketches* (Oxford: Oxford University Press, 1995), 278.

103. These phrases are from the Reverend Walter Colton's *The Land of Gold; or, Three Years in California* (Cincinnati, OH: A. S. Barnes and Co., 1850), 412, quoted in Eric J. Sunquist, "The Literature of Expansion and Race," in *The Cambridge History of American Literature*, vol. 2, *1820–1865*, ed. Sacvan Bercovitch (New York: Cambridge University Press, 1995), 172.

104. Bret Harte, "Bohemian Papers: The Angelus," *GE*, October 19, 1862.

105. Bret Harte, "The Legend of Monte del Diablo," in *The Writings of Bret Harte*, vol. 1, *Roaring Camp Edition* (Boston: Houghton Mifflin, 1871), 382–97.

106. The purposeless ramble was, of course, also one of the dominant tropes of the spectatorial tradition.

107. Bret Harte, "Bohemian Days in San Francisco," in *A Treasure of the Redwoods and Other Tales* (Boston: Houghton Mifflin, 1903), 136.

108. Victor M. Valle and Rodolfo D. Torres, *Latino Metropolis* (Minneapolis: University of Minnesota Press, 2000), 67–68.

109. Harte, "Bohemian Days in San Francisco," 138.

110. Harte, "The Argonauts of '49," 278.

111. Harte, "Bohemian Days in San Francisco," 146.

112. In another Bohemian column, Harte defines his own cosmopolitan aspirations by introducing his friend "Brick," someone who supposedly "did Hong Kong, Calcutta, Alexandria, Rome, Venice, Genoa, Basle, Baden, Paris and London before he was missed from Montgomery Street—who has seen everything and done everything; smoked opium in China, chewed betel nut in India, ate hasheesh in Syria," and so on. This man, Harte writes, "has a right to walk with the Bohemian." "The Bohemian at the Fair," *GE*, September 16, 1860.

113. Harte, "Bohemian Days in San Francisco," 138.

114. Nathaniel Hawthorne, "Preface," *The Blithedale Romance* (1852; repr., New York: W. W. Norton, 1978), 2.

115. Harte, "Bohemian Days in San Francisco," 147.

116. Ibid., 138.

117. *American Monthly Magazine and Critical Review* 2 (1818), 443, quoted in Stuart Creighton Miller, *The Unwelcome Immigrant: The American Image of the Chinese, 1785–1882* (Berkeley: University of California Press, 1969), 92.

118. *New York Herald*, November 24, 1840, quoted in Horsman, *Race and Manifest Destiny*, 227.

119. "City News," *GE*, December 16, 1860.

120. Harte became nationally famous in 1870, largely because of a poem called "Plain Language from Truthful James," also known as the "Heathen Chinee." As Ronald Takaki has noted, this poem "helped to crystallize and focus anti-Chinese anxieties and paranoia." As Takaki also notes, the irony was that Harte "regarded himself as a friend of the Chinese" and, further, that the poem had sought to demonstrate the hypocrisy of anti-Chinese attitudes: the very white man who discovers the "heathen Chinee" cheating at cards was himself trying to cheat "Ah Sin." Still, the poem recycles stereotypical images of Chinese deceptiveness (even as it equates such dishonesty with that of Ah Sin's white opponent) and thus has some of the ambivalent racial signification of his earlier columns. On the "Heathen Chinee," see Ronald Takaki, *Iron Cages: Race and Culture in Nineteenth-Century America* (New York: Alfred A. Knopf, 1979), 222–29. Perhaps out of guilt for the anti-Chinese sentiment the poem galvanized, Harte reportedly told a friend that it was "the worst poem I ever wrote, possibly the worst poem anyone ever wrote." S. R. Elliott, "Glimpses of Bret Harte," *The Reader* 10, no. 2 (1907): 124.

121. Harte, "Bohemian Days in San Francisco," 146–47.

122. Bret Harte, "Town and Table Talk: The Bohemian at the Fair," *GE*, September 23, 1860.

123. Bret Harte, "A Boy's Dog," in "Bohemian Papers," *The Writings of Bret Harte*, vol. 14 (Boston: Houghton Mifflin, 1903), 201–2.

124. Of course, the "Heathen Chinee's" "child-like" smile turns out to be more cunning than simple, and one stereotype is exchanged for another over the course of that poem. Yet, the Bohemian Paper "John Chinaman" does not, to my mind, bear any signs of irony when recording an instance of the title character's "simplicity." Harte notes that "a sad and civil young Chinaman" had brought him his shirt with most of the buttons missing. Harte then says: "In a moment of unguarded irony I informed him that unity would at least have been preserved if the buttons were removed altogether. . . . I thought I had hurt his feelings, until the next week, when he brought me my shirts with a look of intelligence, and the buttons carefully and totally erased." Harte never indicates that this was anything but simplicity, though it is easy enough to see an "Ah Sin" like manipulation of white expectation— the "look of intelligence" might thus signify a knowingly subversive literalization of Harte's ironic comment. The latter reading, though embroiling "John" in the stereotype of Chinese cunning, at least has the virtue of granting him a greater understanding and, perhaps, an Ah Sin–like ability to protect himself from white control. See Bret Harte, "Bohemian Papers: John Chinaman," *GE*, April 5, 1863.

125. Josiah Royce used this phrase to describe Harte's tales, believing that the "perverse romanticism" of Harte's stories had a negative influence on the state. Josiah Royce, *California: The Conquest in 1846 to the Second Vigilance Committee in San Francisco* (Boston: Houghton Mifflin, 1914), 345. I myself am using Royce's phrase perversely, as a positive rather than negative appraisal.

126. Bret Harte, "The Bohemian Concerning," *GE*, November 11, 1860.

127. Ibid.

128. In several of his sketches, Harte wrote in the "Bad Boy" or "Bad Girl" genre that Twain would bring to fruition. Also anticipating Huck was one "Hooker McFinn" from a *Golden Era* story by Sally Sorrel. "Let any fellow what aint afeared to have a good time, knock my top over," is the motto of this "Vulgar Little Boy." See *GE*, October 12, 1862.

129. "Bohemian Days in San Francisco," 142. Though Harte distinguishes the "Bohemianism" of gamblers from the more "innocent" variety—presumably that of the Bohemian literati—and even wonders whether or not he was correct to apply the term to the gambling world, both usages would have been appropriate; they often intersected. The notion of an artistic "Bohemia" emerged alongside or shortly after that of a more sinister variety, and the metaphor of a gypsylike existence was also applied to the "twilight zone between ingenuity and criminality." Seigel, *Bohemian Paris*, 4. Indeed, Thackeray's *Vanity Fair* uses the term "Bohemians" (the first text to use the word in English, according to the *Oxford English Dictionary*) to describe Becky's shady gambling associates. Murger himself sought to distinguish his artistic Bohemia from the other variety, announcing at the very outset of his original preface to his sketches: "The Bohemians of whom it is a question in this book have no connection with the Bohemians whom melodramatists have rendered synonymous with robbers and assassins. Neither are they recruited from among the dancing-bear leaders, sword swallowers, gilt watch-guard vendors, street lottery keepers and a thousand other vague and mysterious professionals whose main business is to have no business at all, and who are always ready to turn their hands to anything except the good." Henri Murger, "The Bohemians of the Latin Quarter," 42 (see Introduction, note 1). The sort of criticism that the Pfaffians attracted in New York and that, as we will see, Mark Twain also generated in San Francisco suggests that many Bohemian journalists often appeared to occupy a similar netherworld. Harte himself provides a clue to the perceived affinity between journalists, gypsies, urban gamblers, and confidence men; as part of his answer to the bourgeois "Coralie," Harte writes: "You say your father says that Bohemians are Gipsies, and that Gipsies steal? Well, my dear, he meant that Bohemians lived by their wits—or rather by the dullness of others" "The Bohemian Concerning," *GE*, November 4, 1860.

130. Bret Harte, "The Work on Red Mountain," *GE*, December 9 and 16, 1860.

131. Bret Harte, "The Story of M'Liss," in *The Outcasts of Poker Flat and Other Tales* (New York: Signet Classics, 1961), 96.

132. Bret Harte to James R. Osgood, April 2, 1873, quoted in Scharnhorst, *Bret Harte*, 6.

133. Lee Mitchell, "Bierstadt's Settings, Harte's Plots," in *Reading the West: New Essays on the Literature of the American West*, ed. Michael Kowalewski (Cambridge: Cambridge University Press, 1996), 122.

134. J. David Stevens, "She War a Woman": Family Roles, Gender, and Sexuality in Bret Harte's Western Fiction," *American Literature* 69, no. 3 (1997): 572. As Stevens notes, Harte's tales are often read as "sentimental," a vexed term that has, until recently, been used to dismiss many of his literary productions (along with those of many contemporary female writers). Others, including Stevens, have reexamined Harte's use of the sentimental, and view it neither as the expression of conventional pieties nor as excessive and disproportionate. Indeed, it is precisely Harte's sentimentalism that critics like Stevens and June Howard seek to uphold as a ground of subversion; according to Howard, Harte only "fails to confine emotion to its proper sphere" if one cannot conceive of nurturing miners or, in other instances, of love between men. See June Howard, "What Is Sentimentality?" *American Literary History* 11, no. 1 (1999): 75–76. Interestingly, the *Golden Era* railed against "sentimentalism," but the periodical exclusively associated the term with false and hypocritical expressions of emotion: "Have you heard the rich hoarder, who never

put a dollar in the poor box, say, 'God help the poor?' That was sentimentalism." "Sentimentalism," *GE*, December 23, 1860.

135. The proofreader allegedly objected to the representation of "Cherokee Sal," a prostitute, and to the vulgarities of the miners, not to any perceived religious parable—though one might imagine that it is precisely the "moral" or religious reading of the tale that could offend as an instance of blasphemy. See Scharnhorst, *Bret Harte*, 23.

136. For such a reading of "The Luck," see O'Connor, *Bret Harte*, 100.

137. Stevens, "She War a Woman," 575–76.

138. Margaret B. Wright, "Bohemian Days," *Scribner's Monthly* 16 (1878): 127.

139. Harte, "Melons."

140. "The Siege of Bohemia," *GE*, February 14, 1863.

141. "Ada Clare," *GE*, March 20, 1864.

142. Walker, *San Francisco's Literary Frontier*, 133. While Webb and Harte planned their defection, another Webb column entitled "The Bohemians in Court" further dramatized the charming roguishness of the *Golden Era* Bohemians. The sketch offers a literary hoax (perhaps loosely based on an actual event) to highlight their antics and enhance their collective celebrity. According to Webb, "A Bohemian knocked down a man who makes and dispenses drinks, for some reason or other—probably because he demanded pay for them—and the consequence was an arrest and a scene in the Police Court room." Flaunting prototypical Bohemian rashness and insolvency (or, perhaps, the indignity of commercial transactions) the column goes on to describe a court scene in which fellow Bohemians stand up for their one of their own. The parade of eccentricity ensues: "Fitz Hugh Ludlow, better known by the soubriquet of the "Hasheesh Infant," came into court . . . bearing a huge book under his arm—Darwin's *Origin of the Species*," a book that seems to function as a kind of Bohemian talisman endowed with the power to affront traditional pieties. Serving as an ironic character reference, Webb's "Ludlow" then announces that the defendant "was a Bohemian by nature and profession," a statement that, in part because of its questionable value to the defense, only underscores Bohemian marginality. The absurdity increases as Colonel Lawrence takes the stand. Webb's Lawrence proceeds to engage in fatuous puffery, extolling the virtues of the *Golden Era* and delighting in his Bohemian coterie. Beyond introducing such pivotal Bohemian figures, this sketch proposes an allegory of the Bohemian condition at large. As the trial unfolds, the various Bohemians succeed so well in embroidering the truth and in representing the plaintiff as such a vile miscreant that the Judge resolves to sentence the Bohemian for *not* inflicting a more thorough beating. In sum, even the Bohemians' cherished verbal and critical abilities prove wayward and possibly self-defeating. Further, the Bohemian in question forfeits bail by arriving late to his sentencing, it being "after the night of the Russian ball." The Bohemians, the sketch insists, cannot or will not accommodate themselves to any disciplinary structure. *C'est la vie de bohème* of *The Golden Era* as advertised by Webb. Inigo [Charles Webb], "Things: The Bohemians in Court," *GE*, February 22, 1863.

143. Inigo, "Things," *GE*, November 15, 1863.

144. Inigo, "Things," *GE*, November 8, 1863.

145. Harte, "About the Inigo Boy," *GE*, November 15, 1863.

146. The *Californian* brandished this phrase on its masthead.

147. "Things," *GE*, November 8, 1863.

148. Twain used this phrase to describe himself in a letter to his family. Mark Twain to Mrs. Jane Clemens and Mrs. Moffett, August 19, 1863, in *Mark Twain's Letters*, vol. 1, ed. Albert Bigelow Paine (New York: Harper and Brothers, 1917), 92.

149. Amigo [Albert S. Evans], "Our San Francisco Correspondence," *Gold Hill Evening News*, January 29, 1866.

150. Amigo [Albert S. Evans], "Our San Francisco Correspondence," *Gold Hill Evening News*, January 22, 1866.

151. Justin Kaplan, *Mark Twain and His World* (New York: Simon and Schuster, 1974), 56. Twain's "official" biography also invokes Bohemianism to describe his years in San Francisco. Relying on extensive interviews with Twain, his biographer, Albert Bigelow Paine, entitles this chapter of Twain's life "Bohemian Days." Paine, *Mark Twain: A Biography*, vol. 1 (New York: Harper and Brothers, 1912), 257–62.

152. Dan De Quille, "Mark Twain and Dan De Quille Hors de Combat," *GE*, May 1, 1864.

153. Mark Twain, "Those Blasted Children," *GE*, March 27, 1864.

154. Mark Twain, "Early Rising: As Regards Excursions to the Cliff House," *GE*, July 3, 1864. Though to greater comic effect, Twain's sketch replays one of Harte's earlier Bohemian feuilletons; Harte writes: "When the novelty of early rising wears off and the habit commences, I look upon its greatest claim as lost. A man never again experiences that momentary exaltation which a change from any bad habit brings at first." Harte too subverts Franklin's adage, though with a more incisive, class-based critique of the bourgeois credo; according to Harte, the notion that early risers eventually become " 'healthy, wealthy, and wise' " was "a happy future, that when a child, I sincerely believed to be in store especially for milkmen and newspaper carriers." Harte, "Bohemian Feuilleton," *GE*, April 7, 1861.

155. Mark Twain, "The Great Prize Fight Between His Excellency Gov. Stanford and Hon. F. F. Low, Governor Elect of California," *GE*, October 11, 1863.

156. Mark Twain, "What Have the Police Been Doing?" *GE*, Jan. 21, 1866; "The Moral Phenomenon," *Californian*, August 25, 1866.

157. Following Justin Kaplan, we might say, in effect, that the "Hartford literary gentleman [already] lived inside the Sage-brush Bohemian," and that, for Twain, the desire to conform uneasily coexisted with the desire to rail or "laugh from the outside." Justin Kaplan, *Mr. Clemens and Mark Twain* (New York: Simon and Schuster, 1966), 18. Twain himself famously promoted such visions of his dual self, and a story from the Paine biography (most likely related by Twain) mythologizes his inner conflict as an expression of Bohemian-Bourgeois opposition. According to this story, the eleven-year-old Twain promised his mother on his father's deathbed that he would be a "faithful and industrious man, and upright, like his father." Later that night, however, Twain ostensibly walked in his sleep for the first time. (See Paine, *Mark Twain*, 75.) Paine does not interpret this scene, but Van Wyck Brooks grasps the significance Twain most likely glimpsed: "He became, and his immediate manifestation of somnambulism is the proof of it, a dual personality"—one split between the demands of his bourgeois culture (now located in his superego, evidently the product of Oedipal repression) and the primal rebelliousness of a true artist (the Bohemian as the anarchic, creative id). Whether or not this scene ever occurred, it nonetheless reflects Twain's own recognition of his conflicting impulses, as well as his investment in the romantic myth of the embattled Bohemian artist. See Van Wyck Brooks, *The Ordeal of Mark Twain* (New York: E. P. Dutton, 1920), 42.

158. Mark Twain to Edward House, January 14, 1884, quoted in Kaplan, *Mark Twain and His World*, 56.

159. Like Kaplan, Mark Knoper also points to the duality of Twain's persona; however, Knoper rightly sees this doubleness as inhering within Bohemian subjectivity itself. According to Knoper, Twain's "self-professed bohemianism in San Francisco aptly situates him: as a middle-class male seemingly disaffected from his origins, as an explorer of the boundaries of bourgeois life, as a person radically ambivalent about bourgeois culture and its contradictions as well as its excluded others." As Knoper argues, Twain's subcultural experiences often reinscribed forms of social dominance: working-class male subcultures bonded while ogling female theatrical performers; male literary bohemians defined their work against the "sentimental" fictions of successful female writers; minstrel

entertainments (a source for Twain's own burlesque patterns) appropriated African American "signifying" to mock bourgeois masculinity and valorize aspects of "blackness" while confirming white supremacy. Similarly, present in Harte's "Bohemian" persona, such doubleness defined—and limited—the oppositional energies of Twain's "Sage-Brush Bohemian." Mark Knopler, *Acting Naturally: Mark Twain and the Culture of Performance* (Berkeley: University of California Press, 1995), 41.

160. Mark Twain to Charles Warren Stoddard, April 23, 1867, in *Mark Twain's Letters*, vol. 2, *1867–1868*, ed. Edgar Marquess Branch (Berkeley: University of California Press, 1990), 30.

161. Mark Twain to Thomas Bailey Aldrich, January 28, 1861, in *Mark Twain's Letters*, vol. 1, ed. Albert Bigelow Paine, 182–83.

162. "Etc," *Overland Monthly* 1, no. 4 (October 1868): 387.

163. Henri Murger, "The Bohemians of the Latin Quarter," 45.

Chapter 3

1. Roche, *Life of John Boyle O'Reilly*, 10.

2. O. B. Bunce, "Literary Eccentrics," *Appleton's Journal of Literature, Science and Art* 3, no. 57 (1870): 494.

3. Charles Carroll, "Good Bohemians," *Appleton's Journal: A Monthly Miscellany* 3, no. 19 (1877): 336.

4. Ibid., 337

5. Ibid.

6. Ibid. Of course, the "Good Bohemian" continued to vie with the "Bad Bohemian" in the popular imagination. In 1911, the painter Everett Shinn still felt the need to distinguish between the two varieties: "In the popular acceptance of the term ["Bohemian"] it isn't a particularly fine thing to be. Most people when they employ the word do so more or less as a term of contempt. To them it signifies loose morals and loose living. In that sense I don't suppose anyone—perhaps a few very youthful individuals—would care to have the name applied to themselves." But he insists that "in its best sense," Bohemia is "nothing but an informal meeting of minds" (though he then rushes to specify that "by informal I don't necessarily mean undignified"). Quoted in Louis Baury, "The Message of Bohemia," *The Bookman* 34, no. 3 (1911): 260.

7. Carroll, "Good Bohemians," 338.

8. L. H. Bickford and Richard Stillman Powell, *Phyllis in Bohemia* (New York: Herbert S. Stone, 1897), 9.

9. Theodore Dreiser, *A Book About Myself* (New York: Boni and Liveright, 1922), 138. In her work on French Bohemianism, Mary Gluck distinguishes between the Murger-derived "sentimental bohemia," which was based on (more or less) "realistic tales about the lives and tribulations of artists and tended to appeal to middle-class literary sensibilities," and a "second, less familiar version" that she terms "ironic bohemia." The latter involved "parodic gestures and ironic public performances of experimental artists and aimed to differentiate the artist of modernity from his middle-class counterparts." As this study demonstrates, it was the "sentimental" version that proved especially compelling to late-nineteenth-century Americans. Gluck, *Popular Bohemia*, 15 (see Introduction, note 7).

10. Mary Heaton Vorse, "Bohemia as It Is Not," *The Critic* 43, no. 2 (1903): 177–78.

11. Philip Fisher, *Hard Facts: Setting and Form in the American Novel* (New York: Oxford University Press, 1987), 9.

12. John Moran, "Studio-Life in New York," *Art Journal* 5 (1879): 343–45.

13. Leo Marx, *The Machine in the Garden*, 23 (see Chapter 2, note 99).

14. Ibid., 22.

15. George Barry Mallon, "The Hunt for Bohemia," *Everybody's Magazine* 12, no. 1 (1905): 189.

16. "The Art-Schools of New York," *Scribner's Monthly* 16, no. 6 (1878): 761–62.

17. Mary Warner Blanchard, *Oscar Wilde's America: Counterculture in the Gilded Age* (New Haven, CT: Yale University Press, 1998), xii.

18. "Art and Art-Life in New York," *Lippincott's* 3 (June 1882): 597.

19. *New York Times*, March 5, 1882.

20. Elizabeth Oakes Smith, "Studio of an Artist," *Baldwin's Monthly* 8 (1874): 2.

21. Roger B. Stein, "Artifact as Ideology: The Aesthetic Movement in Its American Context," in Doreen Bolger Burke and others, *In Pursuit of Beauty: Americans and the Aesthetic Movement* (New York: Metropolitan Museum of Art, 1986), 23. For some late-nineteenth-century American painters, "art" absorbed and even transcended the natural. Whereas, in 1855, the landscape painter Asher B. Durand enjoined American artists to inhabit "the STUDIO of Nature," later painters sought to make their studio spaces into temples of art (Durand, "Letter 1," *The Crayon* 1 [January 3, 1855]: 2). As Nicolai Cikovsky Jr. notes, painters like William Merritt Chase "replaced landscape subjects with figural and still-life ones . . . and, above all, they replaced devotion to Nature with devotion to Art." Nicolai Cikovsky Jr., "William Merritt Chase's Tenth Street Studio," *Archives of American Art Journal* 16, no. 2 (1976): 9.

22. Earl Shinn and Francis Hopkinson Smith, *The Book of the Tile Club* (Boston: Houghton Mifflin, 1887), 13.

23. Daniel T. Rodgers, *The Work Ethic in Industrial America, 1850–1920* (Chicago: University of Chicago Press, 1974), 125.

24. Interestingly, the "Bad Bohemian" had been adept at separating the very qualities that the postbellum economy increasingly wedged apart, severing creativity from steady labor and divorcing convictions from "his engagements." Noah Porter, the new President of Yale, discussed the prototypical "Bad Bohemian" in 1871: "The Bohemian . . . is a person of no mean qualifications, but smart rather than solid, and apt rather than trustworthy. . . . He does not hesitate to write leaders at the same time in the organs of two opposing parties—for and against protection, or whatever question divides the parties of the day. He is ready for hire to applaud and to defame any man, and to extol and depress the same man in two successive weeks, according to his engagement." The Bohemian, in Porter's estimation, was essentially a journalistic confidence man and consummate political operative. Noah Porter, *Books and Reading* (New York: Charles Scribner and Sons, 1871), 353–54.

25. C. F. Peters, "Little Glimpses of Some Well Known Artists: Second Series," *The Bohemian* 13 (Deposit, NY, 1906): 18–19.

26. C. M. Fairbanks, "The Social Side of Artist Life," *The Chautauquan* 13 (September 1891): 747.

27. Margaret Stirling, "The Artist's Last Picture," *Peterson's Magazine* 78, no. 1 (1880): 25.

28. As the title of the story suggests, the painter is stricken with illness and must paint one last painting to save his family from being left penniless upon his death. Though insofar as anyone expresses the moral of the story, it is not that these Bohemians should have been more disciplined and thrifty; "the trouble was," in the words of a doctor, that "he was too happy. Such happiness never lasts" (27).

29. Marx, *Machine in the Garden*, 23.

30. "Young Artists' Life in New York," *Scribner's Monthly* 19, no. 3 (1880): 364.

31. John Moran, "Studio-Life in New York," 343–45.

32. Frances Hodgson Burnett, "A Story of the Latin Quarter," *Scribner's Monthly* 18 (May 1879): 23.

33. Theodore Dreiser, *Newspaper Days* (1931; repr., Philadelphia: University of Pennsylvania Press, 1991), 170.

34. Ibid., 240.
35. "Young Artist's Life in New York," 357.
36. Moran, "Studio-Life in New York," 343–45.
37. Charles De Kay, *The Bohemian: A Tragedy of Modern Life* (New York: Scribners, 1878), 34.
38. Eva Katherine Clapp, "The Old and the New Bohemia," *The New Bohemian* (April 1896): 137.
39. Ellen Glasgow, *Phases of an Inferior Planet* (New York: Harper and Brothers, 1898), 112.
40. Henry James, "Collaboration," in *Henry James: Complete Stories, 1892–1898* (New York: Library of America, 1996), 234.
41. Moran, "Studio-Life in New York," 343–45.
42. Fairbanks, "The Social Side of Artist Life," 748.
43. "A Bohemian," *Lippincott's* 3 (April 1882): 393.
44. Ibid., 395.
45. Ibid., 397, 399, 400, 403.
46. Stephen Crane, *The Third Violet* (New York: D. Appleton and Co., 1897), 32.
47. Crane, "The Art-Students' League Building" in *Stephen Crane: Tales, Sketches, and Reports*, ed. Fredson Bowers (Charlottesville: University of Virginia Press, 1973), 313–14.
48. Dreiser, *A Book About Myself*, 122–23.
49. Edgar Fawcett, "The Gilded Cage," *The Independent* 45, no. 2352 (1893): 26–27.
50. Aline Gorren, "American Society and the Artist," *Scribner's* 26 (1899): 633.
51. Shinn and Smith, *A Book of the Tile Club*, 9.
52. Louis Baury, "The Story of the Tile Club," *Bookman* 35 (June 1912): 386.
53. Shinn and Smith, *A Book of the Tile Club*, 9. *Lippincott's* "Art and Art Life in New York" further publicized the Tiler's disavowal of high society: "The Fifth-Avenue mansion, with its glare and glitter, its frescoes, French cooks, and army of servants, may be well enough for the gay worldling, but entails too much worry and vexation of spirit for the modest Tiler. He courts it not." "Art and Art Life in New York," *Lippincott's* 3 (June 1882): 603. For the nicknames of the Tilers, see Baury, "The Story of the Tile Club," 386, 391.
54. Shinn and Smith, *A Book of the Tile Club*, 50.
55. Ibid., 53–54.
56. Sarah Burns, *Inventing the Modern Artist: Art and Culture in Gilded Age America* (New Haven, CT: Yale University Press, 1996), 63.
57. Shinn and Smith, *A Book of the Tile Club*, 57.
58. M. H. Dunlop, *Gilded City: Scandal and Sensation in Turn-of-the-Century New York* (New York: Perennial, 2000), 96.
59. Chase ultimately contradicted his own aesthetic ideology when explaining his need to sell his collection of art objects in 1896. Heavily in debt, Chase announced that he was giving up the studio in order to concentrate on his painting. Ibid., 105.
60. Though celebrating "rarefied aesthetic atmosphere" in his guide through the studios, John Moran implies that the need for art to generate art embroils the painter in the derivative and betrays the absence of the "vital Art element" in the painter himself: "One man . . . must have beautiful things around him, since he is largely dependent on external impression; while another, being intensely subjective, does not acquire or need the immediate presence of picturesque or decorative accessories." Moran, "Studio Life in New York," 343.
61. W. A. Cooper, "Artists in Their Studios," *Godey's Magazine* 130 (1895): 296.
62. Quoted in Nicolai Cikovsky Jr., "William Merritt Chase's Tenth Street Studio," 8.

63. Charles Dudley Warner, *The Golden House* (New York: Harper and Brothers, 1894), 3.

64. Dunlop, *Gilded City*, 106.

65. James L. Ford, "Bohemia Invaded," in *Bohemia Invaded and Other Stories* (New York: Frederick A. Stokes Co., 1895), 6, 7, 8, 15.

66. James L. Ford, "Seeing the Real New York: Trip No. 4—Bohemia," *The Cosmopolitan* 40, no. 6 (1906): 712–18.

67. Bickford and Powell, *Phyllis in Bohemia*, 91, 233.

68. H.C. Bunner, *The Midge* (New York: Charles Scribner's Sons, 1886), 153.

69. H.C. Bunner, "The Bowery and Bohemia," in *Jersey Street and Jersey Lane: Urban and Suburban Sketches by H. C. Bunner* (New York: Scribner's Sons, 1893), 76–77.

70. O. Henry, "A Philistine in Bohemia," in *The Complete Works of O. Henry* (New York: Doubleday, 1953), 1348–52.

71. William Dean Howells, *The Coast of Bohemia* (New York: Harper and Brothers, 1893).

72. William Dean Howells, "Introductory Sketch," *The Coast of Bohemia*, 2nd ed. (New York: Harper and Brothers, 1899), 5.

73. Clarence Cook, *The House Beautiful* (New York: Scribner's Sons, 1881), 22.

74. Clarence Cook, "Studio Suggestions for Decoration," *The Monthly Illustrator* 4 (June 1895): 235.

75. Dunlop, *Gilded City*, 101.

76. Ibid., 102.

77. See Helen M. Sweeny, "Was She Right?" *Catholic World* 59, no. 349 (1894): 37. In this story, a "well-bred Bohemian" named Christine has a "tent-like structure" in her home that she calls her "cozy corner."

78. James L. Ford, "The Froth of New York Society," *Munsey's Magazine* 21 (1899): 953.

79. Clara Davidson, "A Bohemian Love-Story," *New Peterson Magazine* 1, no. 2 (1893): 133–38.

80. "Young Artist's Life in New York," 363–64.

81. Fairbanks, "The Social Side of Artist Life," 747.

82. John Sloan, quoted in Baury, "The Message of Bohemia," 273–74.

83. Baury, "The Message of Bohemia," 274.

84. Mallon, "The Hunt for Bohemia," 189.

85. Fairbanks, "The Social Side of Artist Life," 750.

86. George Cary Eggleston, *Recollections of a Varied Life* (New York: Henry Holt and Company, 1910), 177.

87. Edmund Pendleton, *A Conventional Bohemian* (New York: D. Appleton and Co., 1886). Constance, the titular conventional Bohemian, cultivates a salon, and "Bohemian though most of the men who surrounded her were, her innate dignity imposed on them a salutary restraint" (2).

88. James L. Ford, "The Froth of New York Society," 954.

89. Henry James, "The Sweetheart of M. Briseaux" (1873), in *A Landscape Painter and Other Tales: 1864–1874* (New York: Penguin, 1990).

90. "Jonna E. Wood and Her Work," *Current Literature* 17, no. 1 (1895): 13.

91. William Dean Howells, "Introductory Sketch," in *The Coast of Bohemia*, 2nd ed., vi. In this sketch, Howells also records that a student at the Synthesis of Art Studies later told him: "Well, anyone could see that it was studied altogether from the outside, that it wasn't at all the *spirit* of the Synthesis" (v).

92. Quoted in Helen Damon-Moore, *Magazines for the Millions: Gender and Commerce in the* Ladies' Home Journal *and the* Saturday Evening Post, *1880–1910* (Albany: State University of New York Press, 1994), 85.

93. Quoted in Damon-Moore, *Magazines for the Millions*, 83.

94. Damon-Moore, *Magazines for the Millions*, 92.

95. Ruth Ashmore, "The Girl Who Is Employed," *Ladies' Home Journal* 13, no. 1 (1895): 24.

96. On the emergence of new heterosocial entertainments in the wake of the Victorian era, see Lewis A. Erenberg, *Steppin' Out: New York Nightlife and the Transformation of American Culture, 1890–1930* (Chicago: University of Chicago Press, 1981).

97. Alice Preston, "The Things of Girls," *Ladies' Home Journal* 22, no. 2 (1905): 32.

98. Katherine Ferguson, "The Autobiography of a Girl," *Ladies' Home Journal* 17, no. 6 (1900).

99. Radford Pyke, "What Men Like in Women," *Cosmopolitan* 31, no. 6 (1901): 611.

100. Harold Van Santvoord, "An Impending Evil," *Life* 8, no. 207 (1886): 383.

101. Emilie Ruck De Schell, "Is Feminine Bohemianism a Failure?" *The Arena* 20, no. 104 (1898): 70, 74–75.

102. "The Story of an Artist's Model . . . A New York Trilby," *New York World*, October 13, 1895, quoted in Burns, *Inventing the Modern Artist*, 88.

103. Burns, *Inventing the Modern Artist*, 87–88.

104. Evelyn Nesbit, *Tragic Beauty: The Lost 1914 Memoirs of Evelyn Nesbit*, ed. Deborah Dorian Paul (www.Lulu.com, 2006), 44. According to Paul, *Tragic Beauty* brings together all of the existing portions of the manuscript that Evelyn Nesbit submitted to her publishers, John Long Ltd. of London, in 1914.

105. F. H. Lancaster, "Out of Bohemia," *The Bohemian* (Boston: The Bohemian Publishing Co., 1903): 28–34.

106. Variations on this plot recur in the literature of the period. Like Phyllis, "Stella" is quickly reconciled to bourgeois matrimony after a brief foray into Bohemia in W. Carey Wonderly, "When Stella Lived in Bohemia," *The Bohemian* 13 (Deposit, NY, 1906).

107. O. Henry, "Extradited from Bohemia," in *The Complete Works of O. Henry*, vol. 2 (New York: Doubleday and Co., 1953).

108. Mellie A. Hopkins, "Female Bohemian Life in Boston," *The Californian* 2, no. 7 (1880): 26-29. On the "Boston marriage," see Sarah Deutsch, *Women and the City: Gender, Space, and Power in Boston, 1870–1940* (Oxford: Oxford University Press, 2000), 109.

109. Robert W. Chambers, *Outsiders: An Outline* (New York: Frederick A. Stokes Co., 1899).

110. Christine Stansell, *American Moderns: Bohemian New York and the Creation of a New Century* (New York: Metropolitan Books, 2000), 34.

111. Robert W. Chambers, *The Common Law* (New York: D. Appleton and Co., 1911).

112. Joanne Meyerowitz, "Sexual Geography and Gender Economy: The Furnished Room Districts of Chicago, 1890–1930," in *Unequal Sisters: A Multi-Cultural Reader in U.S. Women's History*, ed. Vicki L. Ruiz and Ellen Carol DuBois (New York: Routledge, 1994), 197.

113. Ellen Glasgow, *The Descendant* (New York: Harper and Brothers, 1897).

114. Susan A. Glenn, *Female Spectacle: The Theatrical Roots of Modern Feminism* (Cambridge: Harvard University Press, 2000), 4.

115. Susan Goodman, *Ellen Glasgow: A Biography* (Baltimore: Johns Hopkins University Press, 2003), 13–14.

116. Theodore Dreiser, *The "Genius"* (1915, repr., New York: World Publishing Co., 1946).

117. Richard Lingeman, *Theodore Dreiser: An American Journey*, vol. 2 (New York: G. P. Putnam's Sons, 1990), 23.

118. Theodore Dreiser to H. L. Mencken, August 8, 1909, in *Dreiser-Mencken Letters: The Correspondence of Theodore Dreiser and H. L. Mencken, 1907–1945*, vol. 1, ed. Thomas P. Riggio (Philadelphia: University of Pennsylvania Press, 1986), 28–29.

119. Theodore Dreiser to Charles G. Ross, August 16, 1909, in *Letters of Theodore Dreiser*, vol. 1, ed. Robert H. Elias (Philadelphia: University of Pennsylvania Press, 1959), 94–95.

120. *The Bohemian* (October 1909): 531. Dreiser relocated the magazine to New York City (where it was published by the Bohemian Publishing Company) and quickly changed the rhetorical stance of the magazine. The editorial section of the August issue, published just before Dreiser took over, rhapsodizes about Bohemia in the flowery terms common to other fin-de-siècle Bohemian magazines, many of which were themselves more genteel than otherwise (see Chapter 5). The previous New York editors had opined, "My Bohemian would be for the happy mortals who look upon life a little differently from their fellows. It would be for those who know the art of living—for connoisseurs of the emotions—for all lovers of the whimsical; for the Peter Pantheists; for those whose love of art is intuitive; for those who would cherish a sin or a sorrow, a victory or a struggle, not for the thing itself, but for its art or its virtuosity." *The Bohemian* (Deposit, NY: The Outing Press), August 1909.

121. "The Superior Sex," *The Bohemian* (October 1909): 420.

122. "At the Sign of the Lead Pencil," *The Bohemian* (November 1909): 555.

123. Harriman appears in "Our Gallery of the World," *The Bohemian* (November 1906). Goldman is featured in ibid. (December 1906).

124. Quoted in Benjamin McArthur, *Actors and American Culture, 1880–1920* (Philadelphia: Temple University Press, 1984), 160.

125. Quoted in Glenn, *Female Spectacle*, 31.

126. Glenn, *Female Spectacle*, 6.

127. Belle Livingstone, *Belle of Bohemia: The Memoirs of Belle Livingstone* (London: John Hamilton Ltd., 1927), 48.

128. Jonathan Freedman, "The Moment of Henry James," in *The Cambridge Companion to Henry James*, ed. Jonathan Freedman (Cambridge: Cambridge University Press, 1998), 7.

129. "Shall Our Young Men Study in Paris? Written by an American Girl After Two Years of Parisian Art Study," *The Arena* (1895): 133–34.

130. Gertrude Christian Fosdick, *Out of Bohemia: A Story of Paris Student Life* (New York: George H. Richmond and Co., 1894).

131. Robert W. Chambers, *In the Quarter* (Chicago: F. T. Neely, 1894).

132. Freedman, "The Moment of Henry James," 7.

133. Henry James, *The Ambassadors* (1903; repr., New York: Penguin Books, 1986).

134. Henry James, "Preface to the New York Edition of *The American*," *The American* (1907; repr., New York: W. W. Norton, 1978).

135. Henry James, from Preface to *The Golden Bowl*, in *Henry James: The Future of the Novel*, ed. Leon Edel (New York: Vintage, 1956), 70.

136. Though she does not discuss Little Bilham and his representative Americanness, Sarah Wilson argues that, especially in James's late work, "Americanness figures in his writing as a means of producing newness, difference and complexity." Wilson, "Americanness Becomes Modernism in James's *The Ambassadors*," *Studies in the Novel* 36, no. 4 (2004): 510.

137. Kevin Kohan, "Rereading the Book in Henry James's *The Ambassadors*," *Nineteenth Century Literature* 54, no. 3 (1999): 375.

138. Leon Edel, *Henry James: A Life* (New York: Harper and Row, 1985), 454.

139. Ross Posnock, *The Trial of Curiosity: Henry James, William James and the Challenge of Modernity* (Oxford: Oxford University Press, 1991), 231.

140. "Trilby," *Outlook* 50, no. 14 (1894): 553.

141. Dreiser, *Newspaper Days*, 545–46.

142. Ibid., 547.

143. After describing this visit, Dreiser concludes: "And so this romance ended for me. At the time, of course, I did not know it. . . . By the time I was finally capable of maintaining her economically, my earlier mood had changed. That hour which we have known . . . had gone forever." This romantic idyl, linked by association to the youthful Bohemia of *Trilby*, could never translate into a fulfilling bourgeois marriage. Still, later in his career, Dreiser again endorsed the romantic mythos of Bohemia through his middle-aged financial "Titan," the hero of his "Trilogy of Desire," Frank Cowperwood. After seeing a production of Puccini's *La Bohème*, Cowperwood muses, "That makeshift studio world may have no connection with the genuine professional artist, but it's very representative of life." Dreiser thus advances a more capacious definition of realism that allows for the relevance of "Bohemia." Dreiser, *The Stoic* (1914; repr. New York: Signet Classics, 1965), 408.

144. *Trilbyana: The Rise and Progress of a Popular Novel* (New York: The Critic Co., 1895), 22.

145. Jonathan Freedman, *The Temple of Culture: Assimilation and Anti-Semitism in Literary Anglo-America* (Oxford: Oxford University Press, 2000), 90.

146. *Trilbyana*, 19.

147. Freedman, *The Temple of Culture*, 92.

148. Ibid..

149. Kohan, "Rereading the Book," 399.

150. James, *The Ambassadors*, 97.

151. In the years following the publication of *The Ambassadors*, advertising did in fact come to be the proponent of (in Jonathan Freedman's words) "aestheticized consumerism (or consumerist aestheticism)." Indeed, as Freedman observes, "this process seems to have begun in the home, although not, as with [the aesthetic] writers in the living room or dining room, but rather in the bathroom." This location, we may surmise, might well be the province of the "vulgar" item produced in Woollett. Jonathan Freedman, *Professions of Taste: Henry James, British Aestheticism, and Commodity Culture* (Stanford, CA: Stanford University Press, 1990), 109.

152. James, "Preface to *The Golden Bowl*," 61.

153. "Trilby a Future Metropolis," *New York Times*, May 23, 1897.

Chapter 4

1. Christine Stansell, *American Moderns: Bohemian New York and the Creation of a New Century* (New York: Metropolitan Books, 2000), 335.

2. This term has appeared in pop-cultural periodicals. See, for example, *Entertainment Weekly*, June 27 and July 4, 2008: 118.

3. David Brooks, *Bobos in Paradise: The New Upper Class and How They Got There* (New York: Simon and Schuster, 2000). Powers's book also calls attention to this process of mutual cooptation: Ann Powers, *Weird Like Us: My Bohemian America* (New York: Simon and Schuster, 2000).

4. Jackson Lears, "The Golden Age," review of *American Moderns* by Christine Stansell, *New Republic* (August 21, 2000): 36.

5. *Annals of the Bohemian Club*, vol. 2, *1880–1887* (San Francisco: Press of the Hicks-Judd Co., 1900), 40. These lines were written by the journalist and club member James F. Bowman.

6. *Annals of the Bohemian Club*, vol. 1, *1872–1880*, 159.

7. Ibid., 163. These words are from a "dream" written by poet and club member Charles Warren Stoddard, June 30, 1878.

8. *Annals, 1880–1887*, 15; see Kevin Starr, *Americans and the California Dream, 1850–1915* (New York: Oxford University Press, 1973).

9. *Annals, 1872–1880*, 40. These words were from a newspaper article on the club, written April 13, 1872 (though quoted in the *Annals*, the *Annals* do not give the complete citation).

10. *Annals, 1872–1880*, 20, 21, 26.

11. G. William Domhoff, *The Bohemian Grove and Other Retreats* (New York: Harper and Row, 1974), 54. Thus, virtually from its beginnings, the club became elite. Yet Domhoff's study, which examines the sociology of the club in the mid-twentieth century, also observes that the club became increasingly conservative in its cultural agenda and in its representative artist-members.

12. Oscar Wilde, quoted in *San Francisco Examiner*, April 11, 1882; see John van der Zee, *The Greatest Men's Party on Earth: Inside the Bohemian Grove* (New York: Harcourt Brace Jovanovich, 1974), 28.

13. *Annals, 1872–1880*, 187–88.

14. Seigel, *Bohemian Paris*, 5 (see Introduction, note 6).

15. The phrase "bourgeois playing at being bourgeois" belongs to T. J. Clark. See T. J. Clark, *Image of the People: Gustave Courbet and the Revolution of 1848* (1973; repr., Princeton, NJ: Princeton University Press, 1982), 34.

16. César Graña, *Bohemian Versus Bourgeois* (New York: Basic Books, 1964).

17. *Annals, 1880–1887*, 17–19.

18. Domhoff, *Bohemian Grove*, 33.

19. B. E. Lloyd, *Lights and Shades in San Francisco* (San Francisco: A. L. Bancroft and Co., 1876), 486. However, the guidebook's subsequent praise of Bohemianism, both within and without the club, suggests that Lloyd was somewhat facetious when he characterized local artists and writers as a class of unfortunates. The guidebook thus enacts the contemporary shift in perspective toward Bohemianism.

20. T. J. Jackson Lears, *No Place of Grace: Antimodernism and the Transformation of American Culture, 1889–1920* (Chicago: University of Chicago Press, 1981).

21. *Annals, 1872–1880*, 237.

22. George M. Beard, *American Nervousness: Its Causes and Consequences* (New York: G. P Putnam's Sons, 1881), 7.

23. Ibid., 23.

24. Edward Wakefield, "Nervousness: The National Disease of America," *McClure's Magazine* 2 (February 1884): 305.

25. Tom Lutz, *American Nervousness, 1903: An Anecdotal History* (Ithaca, NY: Cornell University Press, 1991), 15, 22. Just as admitting the haute bourgeoisie within the purview of Bohemia verges on the paradoxical, so the phrase "therapeutic dissent" risks being an oxymoron. The extent to which "therapy" fosters or curtails "opposition" has been widely debated. Critics of the modern "ideology of the therapeutic" most often charge that it endangers dissent; whether minimizing the larger social causes of psychological distress, molding the individual to meet normative demands, or reducing countercultural movements to desires for self-fulfillment, a therapeutic ethos potentially forestalls social change—the need for which may well create the internal voids and conflicts that psychological therapies attempt, more or less ineffectively, to bridge. In such critical views, the "triumph of the therapeutic" is synonymous with "evasive banality" or "weightlessness," and has become the hallmark of a late-capitalist "culture of narcissism." In addition to Lears's *No Place of Grace*, some of the most influential critiques of a therapeutic ethos include Christopher Lasch, *The Culture of Narcissism: American Life in an Age of Diminishing Expectations* (New York: W. W. Norton, 1978); and Philip Reiff, *The Triumph of the Therapeutic: Uses of Faith After Freud* (New York: Harper and Row, 1966). Other critics maintain that even the most facile of therapeutic modes "often show

evidence of praiseworthy human desires for change." See Mark Edmundson, *Nightmare on Main Street: Angels, Sadomasochism, and the Culture of the Gothic* (Cambridge, MA: Harvard University Press, 1997), 77.

26. See Horace Bushnell's 1848 Phi Beta Kappa address "Work and Play," quoted in Michael Oriard, *Sporting with the Gods: The Rhetoric of Play in American Culture* (Cambridge: Cambridge University Press, 1991), 11. On Bushnell and Beecher's attitudes toward leisure and work, also see Daniel T. Rodgers, *The Work Ethic in Industrial America, 1850–1920* (Chicago: University of Chicago Press, 1974), 94–99.

27. "Editor's Study," *Harper's Monthly* 89 (October 1894): 799–801. As research in social history has demonstrated, any wider examination of a late-nineteenth-century "leisure ethic" should not view it as a strictly bourgeois phenomenon. In addition to the growth of a pseudoaristocratic "leisure class" amongst America's haute bourgeoisie, the working classes championed their right to leisure, and "eight hours for what we will" became an important labor slogan. Though many social historians view new bourgeois emphases on leisure (particularly "cultivated" leisure or mass-cultural entertainments) as an attempt at social control, as a means of assuaging proletarian discontent, others insist that leisure activities expressed and developed a working-class consciousness. Resisting "top-down" models of social transformation, several historians argue that working-class recreations, in turn, profoundly influenced bourgeois ethics of leisure and morality alike. For studies of the relationship between recreational practice and working-class life, see Roy Rozenzweig, *Eight Hours for What We Will: Workers and Leisure in an Industrial City, 1870–1920* (Cambridge: Cambridge University Press, 1983); Kathy Peiss, *Cheap Amusements: Working Women and Leisure in Turn-of-the-Century New York* (Philadelphia: Temple University Press, 1986); Francis G. Couvares, *The Remaking of Pittsburgh: Class and Culture in an Industrializing City, 1877–1919* (Albany: State University of New York Press, 1984); and John F. Kasson, *Amusing the Million: Coney Island at the Turn of the Century* (New York: Hill and Wang, 1978). On interactions between "high" and "low" life and their decisive cultural impact, see Lewis A. Erenberg, *Steppin' Out: New York Nightlife and the Transformation of American Culture, 1890–1930* (Chicago: University of Chicago Press, 1981). On the work-leisure question and its class articulations, the work of Daniel T. Rodgers is indispensable.

28. These are the adjectives used in a description of the club published in *Harper's Magazine* in 1883, in the context of a larger piece on San Francisco. The article also specifies that this is "the association which perhaps comprises more than any other the best intelligence of San Francisco." William Henry Bishop, "San Francisco," *Harper's Monthly Magazine* 66 (1883): 819.

29. *Annals, 1872–1880*, 240–46.

30. The "Ode to Care" was written by Dr. H. J. Stewart for the 1889 Midsummer Jinks. *Annals of the Bohemian Club*, vol. 3, *1887–1895*, 96.

31. Annals, *1880–1887*, 127.

32. Victor Turner, *The Ritual Process: Structure and Anti-Structure* (Ithaca, NY: Cornell University Press, 1969).

33. Hamilton Wright Mabie, "Culture and Work," *Outlook* 58, no. 4 (January 1898): 217.

34. Lines from Newton J. Tharp's "Sire's Announcement" for the 1905 Midsummer Jinks, quoted in Porter Garnett, *The Bohemian Jinks: A Treatise* (San Francisco: Bohemian Club, 1908), 67.

35. *Annals, 1887–1895*, 126.

36. *Annals, 1872–1880*, 109.

37. I have borrowed these phrases and analytic conceptions from Fredric Jameson's discussion of the romance and "magical narratives." Fredric Jameson, *The Political Un-*

conscious: Narrative as a Socially Symbolic Act (Ithaca, NY: Cornell University Press, 1981), 144–49.

38. At the turn of the century, a wide range of self-declared "Bohemias" promoted similar rhetoric, constructing Bohemia as a realm of rest and rejuvenation. For example, see the poem "In Bohemia": "Out of the toilsome heat and glare / Into the dews and night-cool air! . . . Out of the desert wide and white / Into the opalescent light / Of fair Bohemia!" Elgin H. Ray, "In Bohemia," *The New Bohemian* (October 1895): 11.

39. *Annals, 1887–1895*, 256.

40. Ibid.

41. *Annals, 1872–1880*, 141.

42. *Annals, 1880–1887*, 40.

43. For example, a Mr. W. W. Morrow, a future representative in Congress and Judge of the United States Circuit Court, sired a Thanksgiving jinks and issued a "proclamation" to "the children of this free and independent nation of Bohemia." *Annals, 1872–1880*, 180.

44. On changing definitions of childhood, see George Boas, *The Cult of Childhood* (London: Warburg Institute, 1966).

45. James Fenimore Cooper, *The Last of the Mohicans* (1826; repr., New York: Charles Scribner's Sons, 1919), 72; Theodore Russell to Charles Russell, May 30, 1838, quoted in E. Anthony Rotundo, *American Manhood: Transformations in Masculinity from the Revolution to the Modern Era* (New York: Basic Books, 1993), 58.

46. For accounts of this genre, see Stephen Mailloux, "The Rhetorical Use and Abuse of Fiction: Eating Books in Late Nineteenth-Century America," *boundary 2* 17, no. 1 (1990): 133–57; Bill Brown, *The Material Unconscious: American Amusement, Stephen Crane, and the Economies of Play* (Cambridge, MA: Harvard University Press, 1996), 167–98; and Oriard, *Sporting with the Gods*, 396–406.

47. William Dean Howells, *A Boy's Town* (New York: Harper and Brothers, 1890), 67.

48. With reference to the late nineteenth century, Nancy Glazener argues that "children became the emblems of an antidote to socialization even though—which is to say, precisely because—the juridical and educational apparatuses designed to discipline them had become more extensive and intrusive in recent decades." Nancy Glazener, *Reading for Realism: The History of a U.S. Literary Institution, 1850–1910* (Durham, NC: Duke University Press, 1997), 172.

49. Howells, *A Boy's Town*, 151.

50. "Sire's Invocation to His Children," 1881, in *Annals, 1880–1887*, 40.

51. Annie Payson Call, *Power Through Repose* (Boston: Little, Brown, 1900), 89–91. Of course, it is unclear to what extent all club members embraced "the child" as a therapeutic ideal. Despite being a member of the club, Jack London continued to differentiate between the Bohemian and the Bourgeois according to the former's relatively childlike behavior. Partly set in Carmel (an artist colony that functioned as a retreat from San Francisco for many contemporaries), London's *The Valley of the Moon* contains thinly disguised versions of many prominent Bohemian Club members from both the more "Bohemian" and the more "Bourgeois" crowds. London's "rampant bohemian[s]" are characterized by "their excessive jollity, their childlike joy, and the childlike things they did," including frolicking beach games. In contrast, the "bourgeois . . . aristocracy of art and letters" was allegedly "sober and conventional." London thus draws the familiar dichotomy between the childlike Bohemian and the Bourgeois adult—the very binarism that the Bohemian Club sought to undo, at least at the level of its rhetoric. Jack London, *The Valley of the Moon* (1913; repr., Santa Barbara, CA: Peregrine Smith, 1978), 393, 406.

52. Harriet Beecher Stowe, "The Economy of the Beautiful," in *Household Papers and Stories* (Boston: Houghton Mifflin, 1896).

53. See Mary P. Ryan, *Cradle of the Middle Class: The Family in Oneida County, New York, 1790–1865* (Cambridge: Cambridge University Press, 1981).

54. Mark Carnes, *Secret Ritual and Manhood in Victorian America* (New Haven: Yale University Press, 1989).

55. *Annals, 1872–1880*, 231.

56. The poet Charles Warren Stoddard used these phrases in an ode to the midsummer encampment. *Annals, 1872–1880*, 163.

57. Rotundo, *American Manhood*, 37, 39, and, for a larger discussion of "Boy Culture" and young men's associations, see 31–74.

58. *Annals, 1880–1887*, 45.

59. As Andreas Huyssen reminds us, "the imaginary femininity of male authors, which often grounds their oppositional stance vis-à-vis bourgeois society, can easily go hand in hand with the exclusion of real women from the literary enterprise and with the misogyny of bourgeois patriarchy itself." The same can be said of the imaginary femininity of the other "Bourgeois-Bohemians" of the club. See Andreas Huyssen, *After the Great Divide: Modernism, Mass Culture, Postmodernism* (Bloomington: University of Indiana Press, 1986), 45.

60. Carroll Smith-Rosenberg's seminal essay, "The Female World of Love and Ritual" explores the intense homosocial ties that prevailed among women. Speculating that "much of the emotional stiffness and distance that we associate with Victorian marriage" could be "a structural consequence of contemporary sex-role differentiation and gender-role socialization," Smith-Rosenberg explores the extent to which female relationships served as a primary emotional focus for nineteenth-century middle-class women. Based on the fraternal model, male homosociality appears to have functioned analogously. See Carroll Smith-Rosenberg, *Disorderly Conduct: Visions of Gender in Victorian America* (New York: Oxford University Press, 1985), 75.

61. *Annals, 1872–1880*, 137.

62. Joanne Dobson uses the phrase "human connectedness" to describe the sentimentalism of nineteenth-century women writers. Joanne Dobson, "The American Renaissance Reenvisioned," in *The (Other) American Traditions: Nineteenth-Century Women Writers*, ed. Joyce W. Warren (New Brunswick, NJ: Rutgers University Press, 1994). As June Howard reminds us, however, the sentimental should not be viewed as being synonymous with the feminine or the domestic (or rather, we should analyze the process, begun as early as the late eighteenth century, by which sentimentality and domesticity merged in critical analyses). From Adam Smith to the Scottish Common Sense philosophers, "sentiment" in both male and female was seen as crucial to social and economic life. Though the nineteenth century increasingly recruited the sentimental for the "private sphere," associations like the Bohemian Club manifest the extent to which seemingly "feminine" notions of sensibility still permeated organizations that would have been classified as part of the "public sphere." June Howard, "What Is Sentimentality?" *American Literary History* 2 (Spring 1999): 63–81. Chapman and Hendler's *Sentimental Men* also encourages critics to examine how "sentimental men straddle the ideological boundaries between public and private spheres." Mary Chapman and Glenn Hendler, *Sentimental Men: Masculinity and the Politics of Affect in American Culture* (Berkeley: University of California Press, 1999), 9.

63. *Annals, 1887–1895*, 214. This quote was voiced by the "High Priest" during the 1893 Cremation of Care.

64. Eve Kosofsky Sedgwick, *The Epistemology of the Closet* (Berkeley: University of California Press, 1990), 193.

65. Ibid.

66. *Annals, 1880–1887*, 24–25.

67. Charles Warren Stoddard, *For the Pleasure of His Company: An Affair of the Misty City* (1903; repr., San Francisco: Gay Sunshine Press, 1987).

68. George Sterling to Ambrose Bierce, July 6, 1909, in M. E. Grenander, "Ambrose Bierce and Charles Warren Stoddard: Some Unpublished Correspondence," *Huntington Library Quarterly* 23, no. 3 (1960), 291; Jack London to George Sterling, September 27, 1907, in *Letters from Jack London*, ed. King Hendricks and Irving Shepard (London: Macgibbon and Kee), 251; Roger Austen, *The Double Life of Charles Warren Stoddard* (Amherst: University of Massachusetts Press, 1991), 159.

69. Lloyd, *Lights and Shades*, 483, 486. For more on the general tensions between "brotherhood" and domesticity, see Mary Ann Clawson, *Constructing Brotherhood: Class, Gender, and Fraternalism* (Princeton, NJ: Princeton University Press, 1989), 185–87.

70. "Freshness of Feeling," *The Outlook* 54 (September 5, 1896): 423; Burns, *Inventing the Modern Artist*, 170; Grant Allen, "Women's Intuition," *The Forum* 9 (May 1890): 333–40.

71. On the influence of these Victorian thinkers in America, see Roger Stein, *John Ruskin and Aesthetic Thought in America, 1840–1900* (Cambridge, MA: Harvard University Press, 1967); John Henry Raleigh, *Matthew Arnold and American Culture* (Berkeley: University of California Press, 1961).

72. *Annals, 1872–1880*, 34. Even in *Guy Mannering* itself, the "High Jinks" is performed by a group of lawyers who seek to experience traditional folk customs. Scott's model is thus all the more specific to Bohemian Club festivities. On Scott's influence on the historical romance, see Lears, *No Place of Grace*, 98–107, and George Dekker, *The American Historical Romance* (Cambridge: Cambridge University Press, 1986).

73. Richard H. Brodhead, "Regionalism and the Upper Class," in *Rethinking Class: Literary Studies and Social Formations*, ed. Wai Chee Dimock and Michael T. Gilmore (New York: Columbia University Press, 1994), 157–58.

74. Matthew Arnold, "Sweetness and Light," in *Selected Prose* (1869; repr., London: Penguin Books, 2001), 207–8.

75. *Annals, 1872–1880*, 170.

76. William Dean Howells, *A Traveller from Altruria* (1894), in *The Altrurian Romances* (Bloomington: Indiana University Press, 1968), 51.

77. Ibid., 52.

78. *Annals, 1880–1887*, 45.

79. Call, *Power Through Repose*, 144.

80. Beard, *American Nervousness*, 276–77.

81. *Annals, 1880–1887*, 51. Despite the similarity in names, the reference is not to Charles Eliot Norton (nor is it to Charles William Eliot). Yet as an influential purveyor of genteel "culture," Norton would most likely also have been regarded by club members as an inhabitant of the "Elysian Field." On Norton's influence on genteel culture, see Jonathan Freedman, *Professions of Taste: Henry James, British Aestheticism, and Commodity Culture* (Stanford, CA: Stanford University Press, 1990), 86–93.

82. Jonathan Freedman, *The Temple of Culture: Assimilation and Anti-Semitism in Literary Anglo-America* (Oxford: Oxford University Press, 2000), 94.

83. Porter Garnett attributes these words to Will Irwin (without providing a specific citation); Garnett, *The Bohemian Jinks*, 8.

84. *Annals, 1887–1895*, 151.

85. Ibid.

86. Sire Newton J. Tharp, " Sire's Announcement" for the Midsummer Jinks "The Quest of the Gorgon" (1905), quoted in Garnett, *The Bohemian Jinks*, 67–68.

87. Herman Scheffauer, " Sire's Announcement" for the Midsummer Jinks "The Sons of Baldur" (1908), quoted in Garnett, *The Bohemian Jinks*, 93–94.

88. For a history of nineteenth- and early-twentieth-century attitudes, as well as state and federal policies toward the wilderness, I have relied on Roderick Nash, *Wilderness and the American Mind* (New Haven: Yale University Press, 1967).

89. Henry David Thoreau, *The Maine Woods* (New York: Thomas Y. Crowell and Co., 1909), 205.

90. William Cullen Bryant, "The Utility of Trees," in *The Life and Works of William Cullen Bryant*, vol. 6, ed. Parke Godwin (New York: D. Appleton and Co., 1884), 405.

91. *U.S. Statutes at Large*, quoted in Nash, *Wilderness*, 102; Olmsted Papers, Box 32, quoted in Nash, *Wilderness*, 106; Frederick Law Olmsted, *A Consideration of the Justifying Value of a Public Park* (Boston: Tolman and White, 1881), 19.

92. John Muir. "The Wild Parks and Forest Reservations in the West," *Atlantic Monthly* 81 (1898): 15.

93. *Special Report of the New York Forest Commission on the Establishment of an Adirondack State Park*, New York Senate Doc. 19 (January 28, 1891), 29, quoted in Nash, *Wilderness*, 120.

94. George Sterling, "The Triumph of Bohemia"(1907), quoted in Garnett, *The Bohemian Jinks*, 78–92. Jack London allegedly based "Brissenden" in *Martin Eden* on Sterling, then one of California's most prominent poets.

95. Thomas Cole, "Lament of the Forest," *Knickerbocker Magazine* 17 (1841): 518–19, quoted in Nash, *Wilderness*, 97.

96. *Congressional Record*, 49th Cong., 2nd Sess., 18 (December 14, 1886), 154, quoted in Nash, *Wilderness*, 115.

97. P. B. Van Trump, "Mt. Tahoma," *Sierra Club Bulletin* 1 (1894): 115, quoted in Nash, *Wilderness*, 158.

98. Discussing the price of the grove, the historiographer ponders, "What was a thousand [more] dollars compared to the beauty and majesty of these God-given trees, this noble river, these boskey glades and babbling brooks? This indeed, was the pearl of all groves, fit tabernacle in which to perform the rites of Bohemia." *Annals, 1880–1887*, 93.

99. Charles Dudley Warner, "The Adirondacks Verified, Part VI," *Atlantic Monthly* 41, no. 248 (June 1878): 755.

100. Bangor and Aroostook Railroad Company, *In the Maine Woods* (Bangor: 1911), 7, quoted in Nash, *Wilderness*, 155.

101. This circular was issued on November 24, 1877, by the "Sire," one Barbour Lathrop. Lathrop was a self-described "newspaper man," and this was "in contradistinction to the title of 'journalist' which others arrogated." *Annals, 1872–1880*, 144–47.

102. Henry Ward Beecher, *Star Papers; or, Experiences of Art and Nature* (New York: J. B. Ford and Company, 1873), 263.

103. See Robert C. Fuller, *Americans and the Unconscious* (New York: Oxford University Press, 1986), 31. Several other studies connect mind-cure and turn-of-the-century psychology. See especially Nathan G. Hale Jr., *Freud and the Americans: The Beginnings of Psychoanalysis in the United States, 1876–1917* (New York: Oxford University Press, 1971).

104. William James, *The Varieties of Religious Experience: A Study in Human Nature* (1902; repr., New York: Longmans, Green, and Co., 1905), 511, 515.

105. Ibid., 483, 513, 515.

106. Ibid., 289, 523.

107. Christmas Jinks from 1881, in *Annals, 1880–1887*, 56.

108. *Annals, 1887–1895*, 214.

109. *Annals, 1872–1880*, 143.

110. See the *Annals* and Garnett, *The Bohemian Jinks*, for excerpts from and descriptions of these jinks.

111. Garnett, *The Bohemian Jinks*, 32.

112. Lears, *No Place of Grace*, 166.

113. Charles K. Field, "The Man in the Forest," quoted in Garnett, *The Bohemian Jinks*, 46–52.

114. P. Robertson, "Gypsy Jinks," quoted in *Annals, 1887–1895*, 262–68.

115. *Annals, 1887–1895*, 191.

116. On Hollywood's fascination with Buddhism, see Orville Schell, *Virtual Tibet: Searching for Shangri-La from the Himalayas to Hollywood* (New York: Metropolitan Books, 2000).

117. Johan Huizinga, *Homo Ludens: A Study of the Play Element in Culture* (1944; repr., Boston: Beacon Press, 1950), 13.

118. Will Irwin, Prologue to "The Hamadryad Jinks" (1904).

119. Bryan Hooker, quoted in Lears, *No Place of Grace*, 171. Though not focusing on the "Jinks," Anthony W. Lee also seeks to explain the appeal of the figure of the ethnic Other to members of the Bohemian Club. He notes that representations of the Chinese and Chinatown in effect triangulated relations between Bohemian and Bourgeois members. Artist Bohemians painted Chinatown, Bourgeois-Bohemians bought the paintings, and both united as voyeuristic flâneurs. See Lee, *Picturing Chinatown: Art and Orientalism in San Francisco* (Berkeley: University of California Press, 2001), 68.

120. G. Stanley Hall, *Adolescence*, vol. 2 (New York: D. Appleton, 1904), 342.

121. William James, *Psychology: Briefer Course* (1892; repr., New York: Fawcett Publications, 1963), 196.

122. Fredric Jameson, *The Political Unconscious: Narrative as a Socially Symbolic Act* (Ithaca, NY: Cornell University Press, 1981), 291.

123. James, *Psychology*, 196.

124. See Peter Stallybrass and Allon White, *The Politics and Poetics of Transgression* (Ithaca, NY: Cornell University Press, 1986), 188–89.

125. Ibid., 194.

126. Jameson, *Political Unconscious*, 291.

127. Stallybrass and White, *Politics of Transgression*, 188–89.

128. Northrop Frye, *The Anatomy of Criticism* (Princeton, NJ: Princeton University Press, 1957), 193.

129. Frank Norris, *Blix*, in *The Complete Works of Frank Norris: Blix, Moran of the Lady Letty, and "Essays on Authorship* (New York: P. F. Collier and Son, 1899), 22.

130. Frank Norris, "A Plea for Romantic Fiction," *Boston Evening Transcript*, December 18, 1901.

131. Frank Norris, *The Octopus* (1901), in *Frank Norris: Novels and Essays* (New York: Library of America, 1986), 26. All references in the text are to this edition.

132. Mark Seltzer, *Bodies and Machines* (New York: Routledge, 1992), 25–35.

133. Ibid., 29.

134. Alan Trachtenberg, *The Incorporation of America: Culture and Society in the Gilded Age* (New York: Hill and Wang, 1982), 231.

135. *Rand, McNally and Co.'s Handbook of the World's Columbian Exposition* (Chicago: Rand, McNally and Co., 1893), 25.

136. Robert W. Rydell, "The Culture of Imperial Abundance: World's Fairs in the Making of American Culture," in *Consuming Visions: Accumulation and Display of Goods in America, 1880–1920*, ed. Simon J. Bonner (New York: W. W. Norton, 1989), 198.

137. David Harvey, *The Condition of Postmodernity: An Enquiry into the Origins of Cultural Change* (Cambridge, MA: Blackwell, 1990), 301–2.

138. On the spectator and the brute, see June Howard, *Form and History in American Literary Naturalism* (Chapel Hill: University of North Carolina Press, 1988).

139. Harvey, *The Condition of Postmodernity*, 300. The late-nineteenth-century aesthetic movement anticipated the type of "postmodern" eclecticism that Harvey describes. As Roger B. Stein has argued, the aesthetic movement functioned (however inadvertently)

to justify British and American imperialism by dehistoricizing past stylistic choices: "one need not know—or care—how art functioned in past cultures to draw upon the decorative forms and patterns of those worlds." Roger B. Stein, "Artifact as Ideology: The Aesthetic Movement in Its American Context," in Doreen Bolger Burke and others, *In Pursuit of Beauty: Americans and the Aesthetic Movement* (New York: Metropolitan Museum of Art, 1986), 27.

140. Elaborating on Marxist concepts, Henri Lefebvre notes, "Primary nature includes the forest, the sea, the desert; second nature envelops the city and machines, but also the elaborated body, a 'worked' body that is inseparable from its urban setting and its urban ornamentation." Lefebvre, "Towards a Leftist Cultural Politics," in *Marxism and the Interpretation of Culture*, ed. Cary Nelson and Lawrence Grossberg (Urbana: University of Illinois Press, 1988), 82.

141. Many denizens of turn-of-the-twenty-first century Silicon Valley now "cremate care" annually at a week-long festival called Burning Man. Located in the desert one hundred miles north of Reno, Burning Man attracted 23,000 people in 1999, many of them (according to *Forbes* magazine) Silicon Valley engineers, software developers, executives, digital artists, lawyers, and professors. The festival climaxes with "the burn" on the final Saturday night. Participants gather around a 40-foot-tall sculpture of a man, circling the effigy as it goes up in flames. Anyone willing to pay the $250 price of admission may attend (and the festival currently has low-income tickets available). So far, the festival has resisted corporate sponsorship ("we're not against commerce . . . what we are against is the commodification of culture," declares the founder of the festival). Much like the Bohemian Club, Burning Man offers itself as pure play; like the earlier institution, however, lines between work and play are frequently traversed, and *Forbes* even calls Burning Man "cyberculture's *de rigueur* power-networking retreat of the year." See Josh McHugh, "Burning Passion," *Forbes* (October 4, 1999): 99–101. (McHugh also analogizes Burning Man to the Bohemian Grove.) The different themes of the yearly festival are also reminiscent of the Jinks: past themes have included Fertility, Time, Hell, Outer Space, the Body, and Beyond Belief. See www.burningman.com.

Chapter 5

1. L. H. Bickford and Richard Stillman Powell's *Phyllis in Bohemia* (1897), 9.

2. I borrow this phrase from Alan Trachtenberg, *The Incorporation of America: Culture and Society in the Gilded Age* (New York: Hill and Wang, 1982). Trachtenberg references William Dean Howells, who coined the phrase "our deeply incorporated civilization." Trachtenberg, *Incorporation*, 185.

3. Louis Baury, "The Message of Bohemia," *The Bookman* 34, no. 3 (1911): 258.

4. Mary Heaton Vorse, "Bohemia as It Is Not," *The Critic* 43, no. 2 (1903): 177–78.

5. Edmund Clarence Stedman, "The Nature and Elements of Poetry," *Century Illustrated Magazine* 64, no. 4 (1892): 622.

6. Gelett Burgess, "A Map of Bohemia," *The Lark* (March 1, 1896).

7. William Dean Howells, *The Coast of Bohemia* (New York: Harper and Brothers, 1893), 28–29.

8. Frederick Jackson Turner, "The Significance of the Frontier in American History," in *The Frontier in American History* (New York: Henry Holt and Co., 1920). Turner first read this paper at the meeting of the American Historical Association in Chicago, July 12, 1893.

9. Turner, "The Significance of the Frontier," 37. Turner assigned individualism a narrow priority over equality as an "American ideal," but he shared Howells's sense of the early society of the Middle West as a community in which "liberty and equality flourished . . . as perhaps never before in history." With the closing of the frontier and the "incorporation" of agriculture and industry, however, Turner recognized that American

individualism had come into increasing conflict with egalitarian democracy. Still, Turner was skeptical of any "reaction against individualism and in favor of drastic assertion of the powers of government." Turner, *The Frontier*, 153–54; 306–7.

10. Turner, *The Frontier*, 15.

11. See Trachtenberg, *Incorporation*, 32.

12. William Dean Howells. "A Bit of Altruria in New York," October 24, 1893, *Letters of an Altrurian Traveller* III, in *The Altrurian Romances*, ed. Clara and Rudolf Kirk (Bloomington: Indiana University Press, 1968), 227. Howells represents "Altruria" as a further evolution of American ideals. It is a utopian land that combines political, social, and economic forms of equality—unlike the United States, which Howells argues offers only political equality, and even that only to white males. The "bit of Altruria" that Howells identifies in New York is Central Park, and, in the park, a "ragged bison pair" on display provides a grim reminder of what America might have been.

13. William Dean Howells, "The Editor's Study," *Harper's Monthly* (May 1886), in *W. D. Howells as Critic*, ed. Edwin H. Cady (London: Routledge, 1973), 80; "The Editor's Study," *Harper's Monthly* (September 1887), in *Howells as Critic*, 115.

14. William Dean Howells, *Literary Friends and Acquaintance: A Personal Retrospect of American Authorship* (1900; repr., Bloomington: Indiana University Press, 1968), 63.

15. William Dean Howells, *A Modern Instance* (1882; repr., Boston: Houghton Mifflin, 1957), 18.

16. Ibid., 142.

17. William Dean Howells, *A Hazard of New Fortunes* (1890; repr., New York: Meridian Books, 1994), 85.

18. Howells uses this phrase to describe Beaton in *Hazard*, 103. It applies equally to Bartley.

19. Howells, "Editor's Study," *Harper's New Monthly Magazine* 77 (July 1888): 315.

20. "Young Artists' Life in New York," *Scribner's Monthly* 19, no. 3 (1880): 357.

21. *Cosmopolitan* and *Munsey's*, quoted in Matthew Schneirov, *The Dream of a New Social Order: Popular Magazines in America, 1893–1914* (New York: Columbia University Press, 1994), 98. Richard Ohmann also argues that these publications "assumed and helped promote an interest in New York as a cultural magnetic field, influential throughout American society. By placing the reader there, and by furnishing monthly bulletins on the city's events and 'seasons,' *Munsey's* especially made him or her a canny participant in its social flow." Richard Ohmann, *Selling Culture: Magazines, Markets, and Class at the Turn of the Century* (New York: Verso, 1996), 231.

22. Howells himself continued to have mixed feelings about enshrining New York as the cultural and literary "center" of the United States. In an essay entitled "American Literary Centres," Howells argues that "New York society has not taken to our literature." He admits, "New York publishes it, criticizes it, and circulates it" but doubts if "New York society much reads it or cares for it"; consequently, "New York is therefore by no means the literary centre that Boston once was, though a large number of our literary men live in or about New York"; thus authors need not flock to New York and can instead "very wisely . . . stay at home." Howells, "American Literary Centres," *Literature and Life: Studies* (New York: Harper and Brothers, 1902), 179, 183.

23. *Brooklyn Magazine* 3 (December 1885): 96, quoted in Frank Luther Mott, *A History of American Magazines, 1885–1905* (Cambridge, MA: Harvard University Press, 1957), 83.

24. "Our Monthly Gossip," *Lippincott's Magazine* 37 (January 1886): 106.

25. *Journalist*, September 19, 1891, quoted in Mott, *A History of American Magazines, 1885–1905*, 83.

26. Schneirov, *Dream of a New Social Order*, 4.

27. George Alfred Townsend, *Campaigns of a Non-Combatant* (New York: Belock and Company, 1866), 57.

28. Howells, *A Traveler from Altruria* (1854), in *The Altrurian Romances*, 160–63.

29. Gilder used this phrase in expressing his hopes for the 1884 *Century* series on the Civil War. See Schneirov, *Dream of a New Social Order*, 45.

30. Richard Brodhead, "Literature and Culture 1865–1910," in *Columbia Literary History of the United States*, ed. Emory Elliot (New York: Columbia University Press, 1988), 474.

31. Nancy Glazener, *Reading for Realism: The History of a U.S. Literary Institution, 1850–1910* (Durham, NC: Duke University Press, 1997), 193.

32. Ibid., 204.

33. The Northern newsmen in the armies called themselves a "Bohemian Brigade." George Alfred Townshend, for one, embraced a Bohemian ethos and reflected in 1866: "For be it known, I loved Bohemia! This roving commission, these vagabond habits, this life in the open air among the armies, the white tents, the cannon and the drums, they were my Elysium, my heart!" Townsend, *Campaigns of a Non-Combatant*, 95. On the "Bohemian Brigade," see Louis M. Starr, *Bohemian Brigade: Civil War Newsmen in Action* (Madison: University of Wisconsin Press, 1987), 62.

34. *The Bohemian* (Richmond, VA: G. W. Gary, 1863).

35. George Alfred Townsend, *Bohemian Days: Three American Tales* (New York: H. Campbell and Co., 1880), 18. Townsend was a journalist who served as a foreign correspondent for the *New York Mercury*, and his column was occasionally republished in San Francisco's *The Golden Era* (just at the time Bret Harte was writing his Bohemian columns). His column was called "Bohemian Life Abroad" (see *The Golden Era*, August 23, 1863). In *Bohemian Days*, he claimed that his "The Rebel Colony in Paris" was written in 1864 (and that it was read to several of the subjects of the tale at the time), but it was not published in book form until 1880.

36. Charles De Kay, *The Bohemian: A Tragedy of Modern Life* (New York: Charles Scribner's Sons, 1878).

37. Albert Parry, *Garrets and Pretenders: A History of Bohemianism in America* (1933; repr., New York: Dover Publications, 1960), 87.

38. C. C. Cummings, "Origin of the Bohemian Character," *Fort Worth Bohemian* 1, no. 2 (1899): 7 (hereafter cited as *FWB*).

39. "The Vine Clad Bohemian Nest," *FWB* 1, no. 1 (1899): 3.

40. Quoted in "Jottings," *FWB* 1, no. 2 (1900): 5.

41. "Our Portrait Gallery," ibid., 13–14.

42. "Jottings," *FWB* 3, no. 3 (1902): 7.

43. "Jottings," *FWB* 1, no. 2 (1900): 5.

44. Henrie C. L. Gorman, "Fort Worth Past and Present," *FWB* 1, no. 1 (1899): 69.

45. "Our Literary Club in Bohemia," ibid., 4.

46. Leon Mead, "In Bohemia," *FWB* 1, no. 4 (1900): 136–38.

47. "Our Portrait Gallery," *FWB* 1, no. 1 (1899): 5–13. A similar club (though all-male) also existed in Worcester, Massachusetts. Founded in 1897, the club's original constitution announced: "The object of the Bohemians shall be to bring together men of congenial tastes and comradeship for sociability and exchange of ideas upon such subjects as may suggest themselves, especially those pertaining to art, literature, and music." Club members included teachers, attorneys, physicians, a city engineer and amateur painter, a church rector, and a clerk of State Mutual Life Insurance Company; club talks included "Some Queer Things in Music," "The Early Amusements of Worcester," "Wireless Telegraphy," and "The Worcester School Board" (all from 1899). See Octavo I, "The Bohemians: Records," Worcester Bohemian Society, Records, 1897–1978, American Antiquarian Society, Worcester, MA. A letter dated October 14, 1898, praised their Bohemia, and "the

door that . . . led to converse sweet and gentle meditation." See Correspondence, 1897–1954: Worcester Bohemian Society, Records, 1897–1978, American Antiquarian Society.

48. Parry, *Garrets*, 173.

49. "Jottings," *FWB* 2, no. 2 (1900–1901): 4.

50. "Jottings," *FWB* 1, no. 4 (1900): 4.

51. The term "professional-managerial class" or "PMC" is controversial. According to Janice Radway's summary of the debate surrounding the term, difficult questions remain as to whether "the PMC is a distinct class, a class faction, or a contradictory location within class relations." Still, Radway uses the term in her own analysis of the Book-of-the-Month Club, as does Richard Ohmann in his study of turn-of-the-century mass circulation magazines. As both argue, this "class" or "class faction" mediates between capital and labor, and is more or less affiliated with one or the other—in most analyses, it is primarily aligned with the capitalist class. Members of the PMC include doctors, lawyers, mid- to upper-level corporate managers and government officials, and teachers, as well as less strictly professionalized "brain workers" (to use a then-current term), such as writers, editors, and advertising men. The line between knowledge-based PMC work and other "lower-level" middle-class occupations was and is blurry, however, and "culture" and other forms of both formal and informal education have helped many to cross this status divide. See Janice Radway, *A Feeling for Books: The Book of the Month Club, Literary Taste and Middle-Class Desire* (Chapel Hill: University of North Carolina Press, 1997), 387.

52. Jonathan Freedman, *Professions of Taste: Henry James, British Aestheticism, and Commodity Culture* (Stanford, CA: Stanford University Press, 1990), 112–13.

53. Ohmann, *Selling Culture*, 160.

54. Gorman, "Fort Worth Past and Present," 69.

55. "Jottings," *FWB* 2, no. 3 (1901): 5.

56. Mott, *A History of American Magazines*, 72.

57. "Jottings," *FWB* 2, no. 2 (1900–1901): 6.

58. Blurbs from the *Saturday Review*, Atlanta, Georgia; the *Fort Worth Evening Times*; and the *New Albany Gazette*, New Albany, Mississippi, quoted in "Jottings," *FWB* 2, no. 1 (1900): 6. Blurbs from the *Sunny South* and the *Fort Worth Labor Journal*, quoted in "Jottings," *FWB* 1, no. 4 (1900): 5. The *Vehicle Fashion* and the *Beau Monde*, quoted in "Jottings," *FWB* 2, no. 4 (1901): 8–9.

59. As Ohmann notes, magazines "had become the major form of repeated cultural experience for the people of the United States." He elaborates that in 1865, there may have been one copy of a magazine each month to every ten people in the country. By 1905, there were three copies for every four people, or about four to every household. Ohmann, *Selling Culture*, 29.

60. "Jottings," *FWB* 3, no. 4 (1902): 5.

61. "Jottings," *FWB* 4, no. 1 (1902): 2.

62. "Jottings," *FWB* 2, no. 2 (1900–1901): 6.

63. "Editorial," *The New Bohemian: A Modern Monthly* (Cincinnati, OH: Bohemian Publishing Co., January 1896): 38 (hereafter cited as *NB*). The name or names of the editorial staff were never recorded in the magazine. Mott says that the paper was edited by Walter S. Hurt, and he describes it as "local and amateur"—precisely, I would add, the negative terms that the periodical strove to revalue. Mott, *A History of American Magazines*, 95. Some Bohemian publications were designed for young amateur writers: one example is *The Amateur Bohemian* (Oakland, CA, 1896–98).

64. The *New York Press*, quoted in *NB* (July 1896): 62.

65. "A Night in Bohemia," *NB* (October 1895): 19.

66. "Editorial," *NB* (May 1896): 229.

67. "Editorial," *NB* (January 1896): 38.

68. "Editorial," *NB* (May 1896): 231.

69. "Generous Greetings," *NB* (June 1896): 297.

70. *NB* (February 1896): 77.

71. "Publisher's Desk," *Munsey's* (January 1894), quoted in Schneirov, *Dream of a New Social Order*, 85.

72. *Review of Reviews* 5 (June 1892): 609.

73. Hopes for the West to reinvigorate a staid Eastern culture also informed several East Coast periodicals' assessments of *The New Bohemian* itself. The *New York Press* confirmed *The New Bohemian*'s self-representation as a Western Bohemian opposed to an Eastern Bourgeois, arguing: "The chief charm of *The New Bohemian* is its living, local color, and the frank ferocity of its editorial attitude toward the effete East in literature . . . I think it is a good thing that the West is fermenting or fulminating in this fashion. The East has grown cliquey, provincial, bourgeois." Quoted in *NB* (July 1896): 62.

74. *NB* (July 1896): 62.

75. Larzer Ziff, *The American 1890s: Life and Times of a Lost Generation* (New York: Viking Press 1966), 132.

76. "Editorial," *NB* (July 1896): 60.

77. Gelett Burgess, quoted in Ziff, *1890s*, 139.

78. "Between the Covers," *NB* (May 1896): 226.

79. "Editorial," *NB* (November 1895): 38. The *New Bohemian* frequently discussed other "little magazines," and its favorable reviews of *The Philistine*, *M'lle New York*, and *The Lark* further reveal its allegiance to the so-called little riot of decadence. For example, under the heading "Between the Covers," *The New Bohemian* characterized Elbert Hubbard's *The Philistine* thus: "A recent luminary on our eastern horizon, it has risen into view with comet-like velocity. . . . Here is a Philistine who revels in the rumpus, and cringes not at the frown of the gods and goddesses on the literary Olympus who have allowed their Augean stables to infect the heavens." See "Between the Covers," *NB* (October 1895): 38. Here, the heavy alliteration, combined with the self-conscious conjunction of elevated and colloquial diction, further aligns the *New Bohemian* with other little magazines. In its review of James Gibbon Huneker's *M'lle New York*, the *New Bohemian* waxed decadent once again: "It is impossible to describe her; to appreciate her, one must look upon her alluring curves and hear her audacious challenge." See "Between the Covers" (October 1895): 37. Elsewhere, playing with *M'lle New York*'s "too too" arty diction, The *New Bohemian* referred to the former's "brilliant blasphemy, her palpitant pasquinade, her riotous risqué." *NB* (August 1896): 125.

80. Based in Chicago (though started by Harvard alumni), the *Chap-Book* was the most eminent of these little magazines. It did not explicitly affiliate itself with "Bohemia," however, and thus has not been a focus for this study. Still, the *Chap-Book* did (with all due irony) connect itself to regional boosterism. For example, reporting that the "As Seen by Him" column in *Vogue* turned out to be written by Hamlin Garland, the magazine editorialized that it was "regrettable that so much of the clever work of our western authors should make for the fame of the East, and I look forward—with hope and confidence—to the establishment in Chicago of maps, bicycle factories, publishing houses, and department stores, where the native literary talent will find not only opportunity, but fame as well." Protesting both Garland's perceived betrayal of his region and his sellout to the commodity culture detailed in *Vogue*, the *Chap-Book* ironically recognized that for the West to have "culture" and retain its writers, it would have to expand its commercial interests. "Notes," *The Chap-Book* (April 1896): 485.

81. Freedman, *Professions of Taste*, 112–13. On the other hand, a young Willa Cather (still a resident of Nebraska) complained about "the vague idea floating through this country that there ought to be a great 'western school' of literature" and "that Chicago

should become a sort of Athens, and that Kansas City should become the seat of culture and art as well as of pork packing." She insisted that this notion had "spoiled Hamlin Garland" (before the *Chap-Book* revealed his connection to *Vogue*) and she lamented the "bohemian . . . nastiness and flippery" of the *Chap-Book*. See Willa Cather, "The Chicago *Chap-Book* and Hobart Chatfield-Taylor," *Nebraska State Journal* (May 26, 1895): 12, in *The World and the Parish: Willa Cather's Articles and Reviews*, vol. 1, *1893–1902*, ed. William M. Curtin (Lincoln: University of Nebraska Press, 1970), 155.

82. Interestingly enough, however, the only student publication blurbed by the *New Bohemian* hailed from New England—specifically from Amherst College in Massachusetts. According to the *Amherst Student*, *The New Bohemian* "comes up to the stand." See "Taffy," *NB* (February 1896). On the larger connections between the little magazines and university culture, see Glazener, *Reading for Realism*, 237. Glazener argues that these overlapping sites of literary authority ultimately challenged the dominance of what she calls "the *Atlantic* group."

83. Freedman, *Professions of Taste*, 114.

84. "The Old and New Bohemia," *NB* (April 1896): 143.

85. These blurbs all appear in the *New Bohemian*. "Generous Greetings," *NB* (June 1896): 296–97; "A Few Bouquets," *NB* (May 1896): 233.

86. "Editorial," *NB* (August 1896): 122; "Editorial," *NB* (June 1896): 294.

87. "The Passing Show," *NB* (May 1896): 219. *The Chap-Book* itself specified that it did not always "sympathize with Mr. Beardsley's point of view." See "Notes," *The Chap-Book* (November 1, 1895): 509. One of the first self-consciously decadent little magazines, Boston's *The Mahogany Tree* of 1892, also sought to distinguish the "Decadent" from the "Bohemian" in part. Defining the Decadent (positively) in relation to the Bohemian, the periodical insisted that the former was "a more ethereal sort of a person and one who absolutely must live in luxury and idleness to be perfect, but his morals are similar to those of a Bohemian. That is, he has no morals." Of course, as we have seen, many "Bohemians" disagreed with this assessment of their moral decadence. *The Mahogany Tree*, quoted in David Weir, *Decadent Culture in the United States: Art and Literature in the American Grain, 1890–1926* (Albany: State University of New York Press, 2008), 58–59.

88. *The Medical Gleaner*, quoted in "Gentle Jollies," *NB* (January 1896): 40.

89. The Wichita *Eagle*, quoted in "Bits of Blarney," *NB* (August 1896): 127; Cincinnati's *Our Companion*, quoted in "Blush Provokers," *NB* (July 1896): 62.

90. The Memphis *Commercial Appeal*, quoted in "Spare these Blushes," *NB* (December 1895): 40. By contrast, the *Atlantic*, the standard bearer of the genteel and publisher of serialized novels, fulminated against the "literary quick lunch" that accommodated itself to the hectic schedule of commercial life. Samuel McChord Crothers, *Atlantic Monthly* 86 (November 1900): 654–63.

91. "Editorial," *NB* (August 1896): 122.

92. On the development of a professional ethos in American culture, see Burton J. Bledstein, *The Culture of Professionalism* (New York: W. W. Norton, 1976). On literary professionalism, see Christopher P. Wilson, *The Labor of Words: Literary Professionalism in the Progressive Era* (Athens: University of Georgia Press, 1985). As early as 1877, the *National Review* notes, "Writing for the magazines has become a profession, employing a considerable number of trained experts." Quoted in John Tebbel and Mary Ellen Zuckerman, *The Magazine in America, 1741–1990* (Oxford: Oxford University Press, 1991), 61. Yet as the new popular magazines increasingly relied upon commissioned articles and stories, this profession became a precarious one. An estimate in 1900 concluded that 20,000 Americans were writing or trying to write, for publication, and most were unsuccessful. Tebbel and Zuckerman, *The Magazine in America*, 70.

93. "Editorial," *NB* (February 1896): 78. At times, despite its Western boosterism, the *New Bohemian* was almost as wary of Chicago as it was of the East, referring to Chicago as a "despotic literary center." Ibid., 81.

94. The quoted phrases appear in "Editorial," *NB* (March 1896): 119–22.

95. Eva Katherine Clapp, "The Old and New Bohemia," *NB* (April 1896): 144.

96. "Editorial," *NB* (February 1896): 78.

97. "Editorial," *NB* (April 1896): 171.

98. "Editorial," *NB* (July 1896): 56.

99. Glazener, *Reading for Realism*, 216.

100. In his review of scholarship on Bohemianism, "The Strange Career of American Bohemia," Daniel Borus identifies Bohemia with the female aesthetic culture discussed in Mary Warner Blanchard's *Oscar Wilde's America: Counterculture in the Gilded Age*. He notes that one of the strengths of Blanchard's book is that it discovers "a bohemia in a time when and in places where it was not thought to have existed" (379). That time was the Gilded Age, and many of those places were Midwestern. Yet the aesthetic women and groups that Blanchard discusses do not appear to have self-identified as "Bohemian." Blanchard herself recognizes that the terms "aesthetic" and "Bohemian" were intertwined but not entirely interchangeable: "The aesthetic vogue in America was part of and distant from this life of bohemia. Bohemia arose from a specific locale (Montmartre, Union Square, or later Greenwich Village), but the identification with bohemia in the 1870s and 1880s symbolized in many ways a detached, exotic realm. . . . This artistic exoticism was inherent in popular aestheticism in America, part of the counterpoint to mainstream life" (Blanchard, 167). As Blanchard suggests, there are multiple points of contact between contemporary aestheticism and Bohemianism (along with "Decadence"); in my research, I have tried to discover what those who explicitly invoked the term "Bohemian" meant by this term, as well as the many places where contemporaries sought to locate this "detached, exotic realm." Elsewhere in his article, Borus recognizes the need for precision when speaking of this capacious category. Daniel H. Borus, "The Strange Career of American Bohemia," *American Literary History* 14, no. 2 (2002): 376–88; Mary Warner Blanchard, *Oscar Wilde's America: Counterculture in the Gilded Age* (New Haven, CT: Yale University Press, 1998).

101. "Jottings," *FWB* 2, no. 4 (1901): 5.

102. "Jottings," *FWB* 3, no. 3 (1902): 9.

103. "Jottings," *FWB* 4, no. 1 (1902): 3.

104. "Jottings," *FWB* 3, no. 4 (1902): 6.

105. *El Paso News*, quoted in "Jottings," *FWB* 4, no. 1 (1902): 6; *American Home Journal*, quoted in "Jottings," *FWB* 4, no. 3 (1903): 5.

106. *FWB* 1, no. 4 (1900): 124.

107. *Ladies' Home Journal* (April 1893): 18; ibid. (February 1896): 16, quoted in Ohmann, *Selling Culture*, 270–71.

108. Laura A. Smith, "The Girl Who Lives in a Small Town," *Ladies' Home Journal* 23, no. 8 (1906): 24.

109. Eva Katherine Clapp, "The Old and the New Bohemia," *NB* (April 1896): 137, 145.

110. Eve Brodlique, "Song: Bohemia's Land," *NB* (February 1896): 42.

111. On such modernist cross-dressing, see Carroll Smith-Rosenberg, *Disorderly Conduct: Visions of Gender in Victorian America* (Oxford: Oxford University Press, 1985), 288.

112. "The Borders of Bohemia," *NB* (August 1896): 120.

113. "The Borders of Bohemia," *NB* (May 1896): 216.

114. "The Borders of Bohemia," *NB* (June 1896):,282.

115. "Editorial," *NB* (August 1896): 121–122; see Barbara Welter, "The Cult of True Womanhood, 1820-1860," *American Quarterly* 18 (Summer 1966): 151–74.

116. "Editorial," *NB* (August 1896): 121.

117. Ibid., 122.

118. Ibid., 121.

119. Roger B. Stein, "Artifact as Ideology: The Aesthetic Movement in Its American Context," in Doreen Bolger Burke and others, *In Pursuit of Beauty: Americans and the Aesthetic Movement* (New York: Metropolitan Museum of Art, 1986), 28. Stein discusses Cincinnati's role in the Aesthetic movement, and quotes from William H. Fry, *Wood-Carving: A Short Paper* (Cincinnati, 1897), in "Artifact as Ideology," 35.

120. "The Borders of Bohemia," *NB* (July 1896): 54.

121. David Hollinger, *In the American Province: Studies in the History and Historiography of Ideas* (Bloomington: Indiana University Press, 1985), ix.

122. As mentioned in Chapter 3, *Everybody's Magazine* referred to Bohemia as a "neutral ground between propriety and license."

123. Anthony Giddens, *The Consequences of Modernity* (Stanford, CA: Stanford University Press, 1990), 64.

124. Howells, *A Hazard of New Fortunes*, 267.

125. *The Bohemian* 1, no. 1 (Boston: Bohemian Publishing Co., 1900): 1. The periodical continued through 1901. The almanac *Bohemia: A Symposium of Literary and Artistic Expressions by Men and Women Distinguished in Journalism, Art, Romance, Finance, Diplomacy, Politics, and Statecraft* (Philadelphia: International League of Press Clubs, 1904) surveyed local, national, and international topics and thus implicitly suggested the breadth of "Bohemia." However, it also reassured readers that Bohemia was safe for the bourgeois and that it "desires to conform to all the healthful decencies of life, to all social ordinances which are truly refining" (379).

126. *Buffalo Bohemian* (March 1893): 28. Despite these anxieties about the provincialism of the city, many concurred with an article from the *New England Magazine* (also dated 1893) that the city, "The Queen of the Lakes," had "in store a mighty future." See "The City of Buffalo," *New England Magazine* (April 1893): 257. By 1890, Buffalo had become a center for trade and commerce and there were sixty millionaires living in the city (along with thousands of poor). As in other contemporary cities, the Buffalo urban elite sponsored a symphony orchestra and a historical society, built music halls and libraries. The *Bohemian* was part of this effort to "uplift" the city. For information on Buffalo, see Louis Palkan Rudnick, *Mabel Dodge Luhan: New Woman, New Worlds* (Albuquerque: University of New Mexico Press, 1984), 3–6. A leading figure in the Greenwich Village of the second decade of the twentieth century, Dodge came from an affluent Buffalo family.

127. Emily Selinger, "My Occult Wife," *The Bohemian* 1, no. 3 (April 1893): 33.

128. "Salutatory," *The Bohemian* 1, no. 1 (February 1893): 2. Alan Trachtenberg uses the phrase "Central Park of the Imagination" to describe Howellsian realism. As envisioned by Olmsted, Central Park, much like Howells's fictions, strove to provide a "communal spectacle of a revived Republic." Trachtenberg, *Incorporation*, 200.

129. *The Bohemian* (March 1893): 28.

130. Ibid., 41.

131. *Bohemia Nugget* (January 27, 1899): 1.

Chapter 6

1. Walt Whitman, *Democratic Vistas* (1871), in *Complete Prose Works* (Boston: Small, Maynard, 1901), 249–50.

2. Ralph Waldo Emerson, "The Poet" (1841), in *The Portable Emerson*, ed. Carl Bode (New York: Penguin, 1981), 262.

3. William Reimer, *Bohemia: The East Side Cafes of New York* (New York: Caterer Publishing Co., 1903), 3.

4. James Jeffrey Roche, *Life of John Boyle O'Reilly: Together with his Complete Poems and Speeches* (New York: Cassell Publishing Co., 1891), 10.

5. Charles F. Warwick, "In Bohemia," *Bohemia* (Philadelphia, 1904).

6. Myra Jehlen, "The Novel and the Middle Class in America," in *Ideology and Classic American Literature*, ed. Sacvan Bercovitch and Myra Jehlen (Cambridge: Cambridge University Press, 1986), 139.

7. Ralph Waldo Emerson, Journal 8 (July 11, 1922), in *Journals of Ralph Waldo Emerson, 1820–1872*, vol. 1, ed. Edward Waldo Emerson and Waldo Emerson Forbes (Boston: Houghton Mifflin, 1909), 162.

8. O'Reilly was a dedicated Irish Nationalist who had been arrested for treason in Ireland and sent to a penal colony in Australia in 1867. He escaped in 1869, and began a literary career in Boston. He edited the Boston *Pilot* and served as president of the Papyrus Club and the Boston Press Club. When he died in 1890, the genteel George Parsons Lathrop downplayed O'Reilly's revolutionary spirit, insisting that when his friend "uttered terrible theories looking towards the destruction of human society as it now exists, . . . those theories were only a sort of rendrock, intended merely to blow up the granite walls of inert prejudice, and make an opening for broader paths of progress and enlightenment." *The Critic* (August 1890): 82. Contemporaries thus took O'Reilly's poetic statement, "I'd rather live in Bohemia than in any other land; / For only there are the values true," as an ode to genteel ideality, and embraced it as such; but in the context of O'Reilly's life and political thought, his words have a more pointed political resonance.

9. "Shall Our Young Men Study in Paris? Written by an American Girl After Two Years of Parisian Art Study," *The Arena* 13 (1895): 131.

10. Ibid., 133–34.

11. Robert W. Chambers, *In the Quarter* (Chicago: F. T. Neely, 1894), 148.

12. Charles Sears Baldwin, "False Gypsies," *Atlantic Monthly* 91, no. 1 (1903): 415–17.

13. Edward Alsworth Ross, *The Old World in the New: The Significance of Past and Present Immigration to the American People* (New York: Century Co., 1913), 138.

14. Willa Cather, "The Bohemian Girl," in *Stories, Poems, and Other Writings* (New York: Library of America, 1992), 123. References in text are to this edition. Cather expressed ambivalence about artistic "Bohemianism" on several occasions. In 1896, Cather insisted: "Artists have never been close observers of the conventionalities of life because it requires too much time and that way lies an artificial regularity. But to openly defy the accepted conventionalities of any generation requires an even greater expenditure of time and that way lies anarchy. For the business of an artist's life is not Bohemianism for or against, but ceaseless and unremitting labor." Willa Cather, "Murger's Bohemia," *Journal* (May 3, 1896), in *The World and the Parish: Willa Cather's Articles and Reviews, 1893–1902*, ed. William M. Curtin (Lincoln: University of Nebraska Press, 1970), 295.

15. *Handbook for Scout Masters* (New York: National Council Boy Scouts of America, 1914), 102, quoted in Mark Seltzer, *Bodies and Machines* (New York: Routledge, 1992), 150.

16. Henry James, *The Portrait of a Lady* (1908; repr., New York: Penguin Books, 1986), 564, 636. Cather's best-known "Bohemian girl," Antonia, *does* remain tied to her Nebraskan home; she even becomes the proverbial Earth mother, her own fecundity metonymizing that of the land, and, in so doing, claiming it as her own.

17. As John Higham notes, Scandinavian immigrants enjoyed a "relative exemption from nativist attack." John Higham, *Send These to Me: Immigrants in Urban America* (Baltimore: Johns Hopkins University Press, 1984), 106.

18. Reimer, *Bohemia*, 3.

19. George Barry Mallon, "The Hunt for Bohemia," *Everybody's Magazine* 12, no. 1 (1905): 189.

20. Charles F. Peters, "When New York Dines a la Boheme," *The Bohemian* 6 (Deposit, NY: Bohemian Publishing Co., 1903): 78.

21. Arthur Ransome's travelogue *Bohemia in London* (1907) also refers would-be Bohemians to ethnic restaurants. He recommends a "tiny Morrish café: Dark hair, dark eyes, sallow-skinned faces everywhere, here and there a low-caste Englishman, and sometimes, if you are lucky, a Bohemian in emerald corduroy, lolling broadly on his chair" (124). In England, as in the United States, Bohemia provided a bridge between the "foreign" and the "domestic."

22. Reimer, *Bohemia*, 13–15.

23. Hutchins Hapgood, *Types from the City Streets* (New York: Funk and Wagnalls Co., 1910), 189–90.

24. Not all representations of "Bohemian" restaurants were so affirmative. In *Predestined* (1910), Stephen French Whitman sardonically describes the scene at a "Bohemian resort," an "Italian restaurant, called 'Benedetto's," where the protagonist "consumed a soup redeemed from tastelessness by grated parmesan" and observes the uncouth patrons through the thick tobacco smoke: "their feet twisted behind chair-legs, their elbows on the table, all arguing with gesticulations. . . . Felix soon wearied of the 'shop talk' that he heard at Benedetto's. There great names were ignored, or else uneasily disparaged, while New York authors so obscure as to be unknown to Felix were vehemently extolled." Stephen French Whitman, *Predestined: A Novel of New York Life* (New York: Charles Scribner's Sons, 1910), 240–44.

25. Henry James, *The American Scene* (1907), in *Collected Travel Writings: Great Britain and America* (New York: Library of America, 1993), 427. James does not himself use the word "Bohemia" to describe this cultural geography. When the word "Bohemian" appears in *The American Scene*, it is as a synonym for the "quaintly aesthetic," and modifies the bric-a-brac inspired by the Aesthetic movement of the 1870s and 1880s. Ibid., 359.

26. The artist F. Luis Mora described a similar spot, noting that it constituted his "ideal of true Bohemia": "'For that', he says, 'I should take you, I think, into some German restaurant—some quiet place where the light was soft. In it I would show you two calm, settled Teutons at a side table lingering with unhurried pleasure over their tall steins. . . . And that would be Bohemia. As I regard it, it would be the highest possible type of Bohemia—one founded upon a great sympathy, a pervading harmony." Quoted in Louis Baury, "The Message of Bohemia," *The Bookman* 34, no. 3 (November 1911): 265.

27. Roger Abrahams, "Equal Opportunity Eating: A Structural Excursus on Things of the Mouth," in *Ethnic and Regional Foodways in the United States: The Performance of Group Identity*, ed. Linda Keller Brown and Kay Mussell (Knoxville: University of Tennessee Press, 1984).

28. Reimer, *Bohemia*, 4, 12.

29. Onoto Watanna, "The Wife of Shimadzu," *Smart Set* 7, no. 1 (1902): 141–47.

30. James L. Ford, *Bohemia Invaded and Other Stories* (New York: Frederick A. Stokes and Company, 1885), 2.

31. In "Seeing the Real New York: Trip No. 4—Bohemia," Ford once again satirized the "invaders" of Bohemia, but this time, like Watanna in "The Wife of Shimadzu," he saw the ethnic proprietor as the one who had placed Bohemianism "on a strictly business basis." In his story, a guide brings interested tourists into "Bohemian Hall: Table d'hôte with wine, fifty cents," taking them past "tables that were for the most part stained with wine and scented with garlic." The tourists then are "welcomed by the proprietor, whose greasy countenance shone with the ecstatic joy of one who is making money out of an institution that was once but another name for poverty, and at his invitation they proceeded to inspect his famed Bohemian Hall and the various groups of patrons who were there in pursuit of that free and joyous life that Murger has so well described." James L. Ford, "Seeing the Real New York: Trip No. 4—Bohemia," *Cosmopolitan* 40, no. 6 (1906): 712.

32. *American Illustrator* (May 1903), quoted in Dominika Ferens, *Edith and Winnifred Eaton: Chinatown Missions and Japanese Romances* (Urbana: University of Illinois Press, 2002), 122.

33. Though the "Wife of Shimadzu" encourages cross-cultural contact for her own commercial gain, the wife is vehemently against interracial "mixture of blood." After spotting "the feature traits of the Eurasian" in a woman at her restaurant, she expels the "despicable woman" from the establishment.

34. Interestingly, Watanna's sister, Sui Sin Far (who openly acknowledged her own biracial, Chinese American identity) saw in the "Bohemian" a liminal identity "exempt from the conventional restrictions imposed upon either the white or Chinese woman" (62); still, though glimpsed in the story "Its Wavering Image" (1912), this Bohemian identity is ultimately untenable for Pan, her racially mixed protagonist: after Pan is exploited by a white journalist in search of local color, she finally decides to identify more fully with her Chinese heritage. Thus, in Far as in Watanna, a Bohemian identity/cultural space fails adequately to mediate inter-ethnic tensions. Sui Sin Far, *Mrs. Spring Fragrance and Other Writings*, ed. Amy Ling and Annette White-Parks (Chicago: University of Illinois Press, 1995).

35. James Huneker, *New Cosmopolis: A Book of Images* (New York: Charles Scribner's Sons, 1915), 3, 6, 19–20.

36. Robert Haven Schauffler, "The Island of Desire," *Outlook* (March 23, 1912): 666–73.

37. John Frow, *Time and Commodity Culture* (Oxford: Oxford University Press, 1997), 95.

38. Schauffler, "The Island of Desire," 668.

39. Maria Sermolino, *Papa's Table d'Hôte* (Philadelphia: J. B. Lippincott Co., 1952). References in the text are to this volume.

40. James's responses to the Lower East Side have often been read as expressions of genteel antimodernism, yet Ross Posnock argues that *The American Scene* instead expresses "James' enthusiasm for the indeterminate, open-ended quality of the present moment," an enthusiasm that "is particularly striking in the context of the patrician orthodoxy's disgust with modern cosmopolitan democratic culture." Ross Posnock, *The Trial of Curiosity: Henry James, William James, and the Challenge of Modernity* (Oxford: Oxford University Press, 1991), 145. For many Anglo-American moralists, of course, Bohemia remained a zone of corruption. In "Tackling the Downtown Problem in New York" (May 16, 1912), for example, *The New York Observer* records the battle between "Presbyterianism, represented by the activities of the Labor Temple," and the "cheap Bohemia all about us, which is very attractive to the young people in our community—and in most cases, quite within their means."

41. Reimer, *Bohemia*, 7.

42. Ibid., 13.

43. Susan Kalcik, "Ethnic Foodways in America: Symbol and the Performance of Identity," in Brown and Mussell, eds., *Ethnic and Regional Foodways*, 41.

44. John Higham, *Strangers in the Land: Patterns of American Nativism, 1860–1925* (New York: Atheneum, 1965), 120–21.

45. In *American Moderns*, Stansell notes the attraction that the Lower East Side began to have for journalists and would-be Bohemians like Hapgood. "By its very nature," she writes, "bohemia invited the adoption of a transnational identity" (23).

46. Abrahams, "Equal Opportunity Eating," 34–35.

47. Reimer, *Bohemia*, 28.

48. Clarence E. Edwords, *Bohemian San Francisco: Its Restaurants and Their Most Famous Recipes. The Elegant Art of Dining* (San Francisco: Paul Elder and Co., 1913), 3, 73.

49. Arnold Genthe, *As I Remember* (New York: Reynal and Hitchcock, 1936), 54–55.

50. Norris says that "Condy had joined a certain San Francisco club of artists, journalists, musicians, and professional men that is one of the institutions of the city, and, in fact, famous throughout the United States." And, if we were to doubt the club to which Norris refers, he has Condy receive a letter addressed to "Conde Rivers, Esq., Bohemian Club, San Francisco, Cal." Frank Norris, *Blix: Moran of the Lady Letty: Essays on Authorship* (New York: P. F. Collier and Son, 1899), 22–23.

51. Indeed, *Bohemian San Francisco* maintains, "Bohemianism is the protest of naturalism against the too rigid, and, oft-times, absurd restrictions established by Society." Somewhat paradoxically, the pamphlet insists that even elaborately prepared foods convey this "naturalism" (6).

52. Frank Norris, "The Third Circle," in *Stories of the New and Old West* (New York: Doubleday, 1928), 1–10.

53. Edwords, *Bohemian San Francisco*, 54–56. The guidebook gives credence to Sau-ling Cynthia Wong's incisive observation: "early on, the Chinese learned that the fastest way to a racist's heart might be through his stomach." As Wong records: "from doing 'women's work' in white establishments, early Chinese Americans moved on to opening their own restaurants, which offered one of the few avenues to an independent livelihood free from white competition." She also notes, "the primary clientele changed from fellow Chinese to whites apparently during the early decades of the Exclusion period. Since then the restaurant trade has continued to be the economic mainstay of Chinese immigrants." Such restaurant trade has been controversial within the Chinese American community, and, as Wong reports, the writer Frank Chin protested what he saw as "food pornography." Wong glosses this term, noting, "food pornographers (of whatever nativity) are the ones who capitalize on their 'foreignness.'" Sau-ling Cynthia Wong, *Reading Asian American Literature: From Necessity to Extravagance* (Princeton, NJ: Princeton University Press, 1993), 55–58.

54. bell hooks, *Black Looks: Race and Representation* (Boston: South End Press, 1992), 24.

55. Edwords, *Bohemian San Francisco*, 54.

56. Norris, "The Third Circle," 1.

57. The phrase "Show Place and Forbidden Things" is from Arnold Genthe and Will Irwin, *Pictures of Old Chinatown* (New York: Moffat, Yard, and Co., 1908), 33.

58. Charles Sears Baldwin, "Bohemia," *The Dial* 80 (June 1926). Here Baldwin (the author of "False Gypsies") insists, "Bohemia has no sea-coast because it has no geography—except for those who trade. . . . Bohemia has, indeed, a commercial geography; but it has no other."

59. As Arnold Genthe recollects, Coppa's allowed even "the most impecunious artist" to have "a five-course dinner including a bottle of native wine, all for fifty cents." Further, even "if one had no money, one could eat at Coppa's anyway" since Coppa "was generous with credit, knowing that when better days came the debt would be paid." By way of payment, local artists even festooned the walls of Coppa's with an elaborate mural, one that included a series of self-portraits under the heading "Bohemia's Hall of Fame." Many of the most notable San Francisco Bohemian artists (and members of the Club) participated, including Xavier Martinez, Porter Garnett, Robert Aitken and Gelett Burgess. Largely because of this mural, the restaurant quickly became a popular tourist attraction. Genthe, *Pictures*, 55; see also Edwords, *Bohemian San Francisco*, 36–38; Oscar Lewis, *Bay Window Bohemia: An Account of the Brilliant Artistic World of Gaslit San Francisco* (New York: Doubleday and Co., 1956), 100–105.

60. Johnson's book was published in 1912, and Cahan's was first published in 1913 as "Autobiography of an American Jew" in *McClure's*. It was expanded and revised for book publication as *The Rise of David Levinsky* (New York: Harper and Brothers, 1917).

61. Sussman and Goldstein's Café on the Lower East Side served as Cahan's unofficial office, and it was here that he first received a note from Howells asking to make his acquaintance. See Ronald Sanders, *The Downtown Jews: Portraits of an Immigrant Generation* (New York: Harper and Row, 1969), 190.

62. Hapgood, *Types*, 120.

63. Hutchins Hapgood, *The Spirit of the Ghetto: Studies of the Jewish Quarter in New York* (New York: Funk and Wagnalls Co., 1902), 47.

64. Ibid., 40.

65. Jonathan Freedman, *The Temple of Culture: Assimilation and Anti-Semitism in Literary Anglo-America* (Oxford: Oxford University Press, 2000), 54.

66. From Henry James's contention that America stood for the worship of the "Almighty dollar" to the assessment of a Jewish writer who concluded, "The New World stands for three things: money and money and again money," contemporary commentators reinforced the notion that America was the capitalist nation par excellence. Many Jewish immigrants shared the belief that America dispossessed the Jew of his or her "entire Old World soul," replacing a "deep-rooted tradition, a system of culture and tastes and habits" with crass materialism; in this view, the Jew became, according to the title of Marcus Ravage's 1917 account, *An American in the Making*. Quotations from this unidentified Jewish writer and Marcus Ravage appear in Irving Howe, *World of Our Fathers* (New York: Harcourt Brace Jovanovich, 1976), 75–76. But, then again, the Jew has long been made to symbolize the workings of the capitalist marketplace. In fin-de-siècle America, such anti-Semitic accounts as *The New York Jew* (1888) continued to insist that Jews embodied the capitalist imperative: with their "lust for money . . . the spirit of gain and the desire for domination chase every other idea from their mentality, together with every affection, which is, as we know, the characteristic sign of obsession." Thus, Jews allegedly took their capitalism to the point of pathology and inflicted it on the country at large. (Quotations from *The New York Jew*, written by an anonymous author, appear in Freedman, *The Temple of Culture*, 68.) In March 1913, the very month before Cahan's first draft of "Autobiography of an American Jew" was featured in *McClure's*, this same magazine published "The Jewish Invasion of America," an article that similarly stressed the pivotal role of the Jewish capitalist. The essay included such sensational (and grossly exaggerated) subheadings as "The Conquest of the Clothing Trades," "Business Completely Transformed by the Jews," "Jews the Greatest Owners of Land," "The Jewish Middleman in Real Estate," "Jews Control the Big Department Stores," and so on. It was the Jews, such accounts insisted, who were remaking America in their own image, ever escalating the nation's capitalist development. Burton J. Hendrick, "The Jewish Invasion of America," *McClure's Magazine* 60, no. 5 (March 1913): 125–28.

67. Waldo Frank, *Our America* (New York, 1919).

68. Hapgood, *Types*, 18.

69. Norris, "A Plea for Romantic Fiction" (1901), in Frank Norris, *Novels and Essays* (New York: The Library of America, 1986), 1166.

70. Hapgood, *Spirit of the Ghetto*, 37, 306; Hapgood, *Types*, 18.

71. Hapgood, *Spirit of the Ghetto*, 42.

72. Ibid., 36, 40.

73. Hapgood's various equations of high and low, Anglo-American and Hebraic only partly correspond to those of Matthew Arnold, whose writings famously upheld "Culture" as an antidote to "Philistinism." For Arnold, Jews were arguably the ultimate exemplars of the Philistine middle-class consciousness: they were, implicitly, the purveyors of "Hebraism" and, as such, represented "strictness of conscience" and "plain, capital intimations of the universal order." In this context, the term "capital" names the very economic system with which Jews have so long been identified, both within and

without the United States. Conversely, when Hapgood refers to the "Hebraic," it suggests an idealism that seems to have more "sweetness and light" (or at least "light") than Arnold's formulation implies. On the other hand, however, Arnold's conception of a transcendent sphere of "Culture" depended upon, in Jonathan Freedman's words "the culturally fraught idiom of the alien *within*," an idiom that was commonly used to designate the figure of the Jew (Freedman, *Temple of Culture*, 47). In Arnold's famous formulation from *Culture and Anarchy* (1883): "Therefore, when we speak of ourselves as divided into Barbarians, Philistines, and Populace, we must be understood always to imply that within each of these classes there are a certain number of aliens, if we may so call them,—persons who are mainly led, not by their class spirit, but by a general humane spirit, by the love of human perfection" (quoted in Freedman, *Temple of Culture*, 47). These aliens thus allegedly transcended class and, perhaps, ethnicity. Hapgood does not seem to have been as interested in the transcendence of class, given his predilection for borrowing its vocabulary in his literary analysis, but he shared Arnold's sense of being an alien within, and he even more concretely spelled out how this made for an identification with Jews.

74. Werner Sollors, *Beyond Ethnicity: Consent and Descent in American Culture* (Oxford: Oxford University Press, 1986), 171.

75. Abraham Cahan, *The Rise of David Levinsky* (1917; repr., New York: Penguin Books, 1993), 456.

76. As Phillip Barrish argues, Levinsky's continual self-criticism can itself be seen as an effort to generate cultural capital or "distinction," in Bourdieu's sense of the term; accordingly, Levinsky "can exhibit one dimension or moment of his self as recognized, and recognized as separate, by another—thereby elevated—dimension of his self." Extending such a reading, the very act of devaluing himself in relation to the literary liquor dealer would paradoxically allow him to accrue more cultural capital. See Phillip Barrish, "'The Genuine Article': Ethnicity, Capital, and *The Rise of David Levinsky*," *American Literary History* 5, no. 4 (1993): 647.

77. *Discourses of Keidansky* (1903), quoted in Howe, *World of Our Fathers*, 235. Keidansky, a Jewish immigrant from Boston, further describes the cafés as a place where "people feel free, act independently, speak as they think, and are not ashamed of their feelings."

78. Cahan, *Bletter fun Mein Leben*, quoted and translated in Sanders, *Downtown Jews*, 252. Cahan also ironizes attempts of Jewish Bohemians to profit from the Jewish bourgeoisie while simultaneously asserting their superiority. In *Levinsky*, a Jewish violinist enters Levinsky's office with "bohemian self-importance." Levinsky notes: "The implication was that, while I had succeeded as a prosaic, pitiable cloak-manufacturer, he had conquered the world by the magic of his violin and compositions. . . . The upshot of the interview was that I sent a check to the treasurer of the free conservatory of which Octavius was one of the founders." *Levinsky*, 445.

79. Carrie Tirado Bramen, "The Urban Picturesque and the Spectacle of Americanization," *American Quarterly* 52, no. 3 (2000): 472.

80. Indeed, since the capitalists of the cloak-manufacturing industry were themselves predominantly Jewish, it is probable that it was *their* power that constituted the greater threat to the uptown Anglo-American bourgeoisie. As Ronald Sanders notes, "the old-stock bourgeoisie of New York, though not normally inclined to favor labor unions, were in this crisis [the cloakmakers' strike of 1890] sympathetic to the claims of an oppressed, slum, immigrant population against a group of bosses who also happened to be immigrants, but who were economic and social upstarts as well." Sanders, *The Downtown Jews*, 117.

81. Susan K. Harris, "Problems of Representation in Turn-of-the-Century Immigrant Fictions," in *American Realism and the Canon*, ed. Tom Quirk and Gary Scharnhorst (Newark: University of Delaware Press, 1994), 135.

82. In "The Consuming Vision of Henry James," Jean-Christophe Agnew argues that James's fictional practice demonstrates the extent to which the act of consumption informed both material life and intellectual cognition. Other critics have since generalized this consuming vision, arguing that it is a definitive feature of turn-of-the-century realism. See Jean-Christophe Agnew, "The Consuming Vision of Henry James," in *The Culture of Consumption: Critical Essays in American History, 1880–1980*, ed. Richard Wightman Fox and T. J. Jackson Lears (New York: Pantheon, 1984), 67–100.

83. Werner Sollors has remarked on the structural similarities between Cahan's and Johnson's novels, though he does not address their shared use of "Bohemia." Sollors, *Beyond Ethnicity*, 168–73.

84. This Bohemia has not been included in previous surveys of U.S. Bohemianism. In her history of early-twentieth-century Bohemian New York, for example, Christine Stansell claims that the "demographics of the city" in the first decades of the century "made for few black candidates for bohemia." With the Greenwich Village of 1910 and later as the center of her New York Bohemia, Stansell notes how few African Americans were professionally and socially involved with the Villagers before the 1920s. She does note that James Weldon Johnson was "a subscriber to the *Masses*, the flagship paper of modern radicalism published from Greenwich Village" and that (presumably because of this) he "was sufficiently aware of bohemia to draw the Tenderloin into analogy: the black neighborhood was a magnet for 'colored Bohemians,' he wrote in 1912." Cook and Rogers's musical drama, however, uses the term "Black Bohemia" as well, and it was written in 1911. The first edition of the revitalized *Masses* appeared in December at the end of 1912, and so it is doubtful that Johnson's use of the term in his novel (published in 1912) was influenced by the Village Bohemians. See Stansell, *American Moderns*, 67.

85. James Weldon Johnson, *Black Manhattan* (New York: Alfred A. Knopf, 1930), 74, 78.

86. W. E. B. Du Bois, whose vision of "double consciousness" is echoed in Johnson's conception of a "dual personality," was particularly critical of connections between art and libertinism and of an art that *represented* libertinism. Regarding such art as pandering to white interest in the "primitive," an interest that flowered during the 1920s, Du Bois wrote of Claude McKay's 1928 *Home to Harlem*: "After the dirtier parts of its filth I feel distinctly like taking a bath. . . . It looks as though McKay has set out to cater to that prurient demand on the part of white folk for a portrayal in Negroes of that utter licentiousness which conventional civilization holds white folk back from enjoying—if enjoyment it can be called." Quoted from *Black American Prose Writers of the Harlem Renaissance*, ed. Harold Bloom (New York: Chelsea House, 1994), 109. McKay, however, did not view African American "primitivism" as the projection of white fantasies—he saw it as a way of critiquing Western culture and of celebrating African American vitality. See Claude McKay, *Home to Harlem*; Robert A. Coles and Diane Isaacs, "Primitivism as a Therapeutic Pursuit," in *The Harlem Renaissance: Re-Valuations*, ed. Amritjit Singh (New York: Garland Publishing, 1989).

87. James H. Dormon, "Shaping the Popular Image of Post-Reconstruction American Blacks: The 'Coon Song' Phenomenon of the Gilded Age," *American Quarterly* 40, no. 4 (1988): 456.

88. Matthew Arnold, *Culture and Anarchy* (1869; repr., Oxford: Oxford University Press, 2006), 81; ibid., 39.

89. Paul Laurence Dunbar to Alice Ruth Moore (April 19, 1896), in *The Paul Laurence Dunbar Reader*, ed. Jay Martin and Gossie H. Hudson (New York: Dodd, Mead and Co., 1975), 434.

90. Johnson, *Black Manhattan*, 74.

91. Johnson, *Along This Way* (1933; repr., New York: Penguin Books, 1990), 152.

92. Johnson, *The Autobiography of an Ex-Colored Man* (1912; repr., New York: Penguin Books, 1990), 71–72.

93. W. E. B. Du Bois, "The Conservation of Races" (1897) in *A W. E. B. Du Bois Reader*, ed. Andrew G. Paschal (New York: Collier Books, 1993), 26.

94. Robert B. Stepto, *From Behind the Veil: A Study of Afro-American Narrative* (Urbana: University of Illinois Press, 1979), 122–27.

95. Ibid., 125. Stepto's notion of "symbolic space," or what he also refers to as "symbolic geography," draws on Victor Turner, and it is defined as the literary representation of "a region in time and space offering spatial expressions of social structures and ritual grounds on the one hand, and of *communitas* and *genius loci* on the other. The distinction between the two pairings has to do quite simply with time: social structures and ritual grounds exist in time, while spatial expressions of *communitas* and *genius loci* are, as Turner says of *communitas* alone, 'moments in and out of time.'" For Stepto, "the Club" becomes a symbolic geography akin to the "Black Belt," one that exists (as a narrative and social location) both within and without a specific time and place and that thus functions as an expression "of 'race-spirit' or 'race-message' (Du Bois's terms)." Stepto, *From Behind the Veil*, 66.

96. Sara Blair, "Cultural Geography and the Place of the Literary," *American Literary History* 10, no. 3 (1998): 557.

97. Stepto, *From Behind the Veil*, 125.

98. Will Marion Cook, with Alex Rogers, *Black Bohemia* (1911; electronic edition by Alexander Street Press, L.L.C., 2005), 3–4.

99. Johnson, *Black Manhattan*, 93.

100. Ibid., 118.

101. Ibid., 115.

102. Ibid., 111.

103. Such discourses, based on a racializing of Gabriel Tarde's *The Laws of Imitation* (1890), argued that blacks could only achieve a superficial patina of civilized behavior at best, since "the race habit of a thousand generations or more is not lightly set aside by the voluntary or enforced imitation of visible models, and there is always a strong tendency to reversion." See Charles Ellwood, "The Theory of Imitation in Social Psychology," quoted in Eric Sunquist, *To Wake the Nations: Race in the Making of American Literature* (Cambridge, MA: Harvard University Press, 1993), 254.

104. An exception to this rule was Bob Cole's *A Trip to Coontown* (1898). As Johnson recounts in *Black Manhattan*, Cole had previously worked with the white managers Voelckel and Nolan on the hit show *Oriental America*. He protested that he had not received an adequate salary and gathered up his sheet music and walked out. He was then arrested, and declared before the magistrate, "These men have amassed a fortune from the product of my brain, and now they call me a thief; I won't give it up." He lost this court battle but then began to plan his own musical. It was *A Trip to Coontown* and, Johnson writes, it was the "first Negro show to make a complete break from the minstrel pattern, the first that was not a mere potpourri, the first to be written with continuity and to have a cast of characters working out the story of a plot from beginning to end; and therefore, the first Negro musical comedy. It was, furthermore, the first coloured show to be organized, produced, and managed by Negroes." It ran for three seasons. *Black Manhattan*, 101–2.

105. Johnson, *Black Manhattan*, 103.

106. Johnson, *Along This Way*, 152.

107. Cristina L. Ruotolo, "James Weldon Johnson and the Autobiography of an Ex-Colored Man," *American Literature* 72, no. 2 (2000): 256.

108. Johnson, *Along This Way*, 153; *The Autobiography of an Ex-Colored Man*, 73.

109. Ruotolo, "James Weldon Johnson," 256.

110. Johnson, *Black Manhattan*, 117; *Along This Way*, 150, 152.

111. Will Marion Cook, "Clorindy, the Origin of the Cakewalk," in *Anthology of the Afro-American in the Theater*, ed. Lindsay Patterson (New York: Publishers Co., 1967), 55; Ernest Hogan, quoted in Sunquist, *To Wake the Nations*, 284; Johnson, *Along This Way*, 153, 154.

112. Ford, "Seeing the Real New York: Trip No. 4—Bohemia," 712.

113. Stepto, *From Behind the Veil*, 127.

114. In describing such dynamics, Johnson may have inadvertently given fodder to the contemporary vice squads that sought to suppress several institutions in black Bohemia that fostered interracial sociability. Singling out the Marshall Hotel at 129 West 53rd Street, the Committee of Fourteen noted that it was "patronized largely by white women and colored men" who held "questionable orgies and revels . . . nightly." Quoted in Mary J. Sacks, *Before Harlem: The Black Experience in New York City Before World War I* (Philadelphia: University of Pennsylvania Press, 2006), 65, 188.

115. Sunquist, *To Wake the Nations*, 279.

116. Shephard Edmonds, an African American musician and former slave, quoted in Sunquist, *To Wake the Nations*, 278.

117. In his well-known study, Henry Louis Gates connects the African American folk figure of the Signifying Monkey to rhetorical strategies that enable "the black person to move between two [racially defined] discursive universes." Henry Louis Gates Jr., *The Signifying Monkey: A Theory of Afro-American Literary Criticism* (New York: Oxford University Press, 1988). Referencing Gates, Sunquist also draws on the concept of signifying in his discussion of the cakewalk.

118. Johnson, *Black Manhattan*, 105.

119. Ibid., 94, 111, 119.

120. Johnson, *Along This Way*, 149.

121. Ibid., 150.

122. Ibid.

123. R. C. Simmons, "Europe's Reception to Negro Talent," *Colored American Magazine* (November 1905), quoted in Ruotolo, "James Weldon Johnson," 258.

124. Johnson, *Second Book of Negro Spirituals*, in *Books of American Negro Spirituals, 1925–1926* (New York: Viking, 1969), 16.

125. Johnson, *Along This Way*, 328.

126. Jeffrey Melnick, *A Right to Sing the Blues: African Americans, Jews, and American Popular Song* (Cambridge, MA: Harvard University Press, 1999), 148–49.

127. Melnick imagines that Johnson's later translation of "the white men who affixed their own names as the composers" (from his earlier discussion) into the "Jewish musicians" who "fused and developed" ragtime represented a "generally positive outlook on the production of racially mixed cultural products." Melnick, *A Right to Sing the Blues*, 150. At the least, the shift in Johnson's rhetoric acknowledges the ambiguities and complexities of black-Jewish relations at the turn of the century, relations that in many ways rearticulated the color line (and even enabled Jews to configure themselves as "white" ethnics) but that also resulted in some more positive political and cultural alliances. Indeed, at the same time that Tin Pan Alley was creating its "melting pot" music, the Yiddish *Forward* (one of the central organs of the "East Side Bohème") was arguing, "if one is talking about American music today, one is really talking about Negro music." The *Forward*, quoted in Melnick, *A Right to Sing the Blues*, 146.

128. Robert Hughes, *Contemporary American Composers* (1900), quoted in Ruotolo, "James Weldon Johnson," 254.

129. Johnson, *Along This Way*, 150. Later in his career, as a contributing editor to the African American weekly the *New York Age* from 1914 to 1923, Johnson wrote many essays protesting American imperialism and explicitly connected it with U.S. racial politics, both at home and abroad. He maintained that the United States committed "mod-

ern piracy" and "highway robbery" in Latin America and Haiti, and he claimed that those nations were being "Jim Crowed" by the Wilson administration. After his time as a songwriter in black Bohemia, Johnson had worked as a U.S. consul from 1906 to 1913, and, as Lawrence J. Oliver demonstrates, it was during his years in Puerto Cabello and Corinto that Johnson experienced how the color line "extended across the segregated South into the nation's interactions with Latin America and the Caribbean." Lawrence J. Oliver, "'Jim Crowed' in Their Own Countries: James Weldon Johnson's New York *Age* Essays on Colonialism during the Wilson Years," in *Critical Essays on James Weldon Johnson*, ed. Kenneth M. Price and Lawrence J. Oliver (New York: G. K. Hall and Co., 1997), 210. According to Johnson, the whole question of American imperialism was "involved in our own national and local Negro problem," and he vigorously protested U.S. imperialist violence. He testified before Congress in support of Haitian independence and helped establish the Society for the Independence of Haiti and Santo Domingo (Oliver, "'Jim Crowed,'" 216). Indeed, Du Bois called Johnson's diplomacy "one of the greatest single achievements done in colored America." Focusing on Johnson's diplomacy and the largely neglected *Age* essays, Oliver argues that Johnson's "transnational and intercultural perspective" begs inclusion in "our cultural mapping of the 'black Atlantic'" (Oliver, "'Jim Crowed,'" 219). The "black Atlantic" is Paul Gilroy's term for the "continually crisscrossed . . . movements of black people—not only as commodities but engaged in various struggles toward emancipation, autonomy, and citizenship." See Paul Gilroy, *The Black Atlantic: Modernity and Double Consciousness* (Cambridge, MA: Harvard University Press, 1993), 16. Johnson's essays from the *Age* are cited in Oliver, "'Jim Crowed,'" 211, 212, 213.

130. I borrow the term "contact zone" from Mary Louise Pratt. As Pratt explains, this coinage "is an attempt to invoke the spatial and temporal copresence of subjects previously separated by geographic and historical disjunctures, and whose trajectories now intersect." Foregrounding "co-presence, interaction, interlocking understandings and practices, often within radically asymmetrical relations of power," this term aptly describes what happens in the many disparate Bohemias that I have discussed in this chapter. See Pratt, *Imperial Eyes: Travel Writing and Transculturation* (London: Routledge, 1992), 7.

131. Paul Gilroy, *The Black Atlantic*, 15; Blair, "Cultural Geography and the Place of the Literary," 556.

Chapter 7

1. Charles Carroll, "Good Bohemians," *Appleton's Journal: A Monthly Miscellany* 3, no. 19 (1877): 337.

2. Hutchins Hapgood, "The New Bohemia" (1913), Hapgood Collection, Collection of American Literature, Beinecke Rare Book and Manuscript Library, Yale University.

3. During this period, Bohemias continued to exist in other parts of the nation, notably in Chicago. There on Fifty-Seventh Street, in the dilapidated spaces that had been abandoned in the wake of the World's Fair of 1893, many Bohemians gathered (though a number would soon move to Greenwich Village). Those affiliated with the Chicago Bohemian scene included Floyd Dell, Margaret Anderson, Harriet Monroe, Carl Sandburg, Vachel Lindsay, Theodore Dreiser, and Sherwood Anderson. Chicago was the home of a little theatre movement that predated that of the Village, and such important modernist periodicals as *Poetry* and *The Little Review* emerged in Chicago. See Steven Watson, *Strange Bedfellows: The First American Avant-Garde* (New York: Abbeville Press, 1991), 16–27. During this period, Harlem was also emerging as a vibrant cultural center, though the term "black Bohemia" does not seem to have traveled from midtown Manhattan to Harlem. Hapgood, the Bohemian flâneur who frequented the Lower East Side at the turn of the century, wanted to make inroads into the African American literary community. In

his memoirs, he writes of approaching W. E. B. Du Bois, asking him for "introductions to some of the more expressive of the race." According to Hapgood, Du Bois declined: "'The Negroes,' he said, 'do not wish to be written about by white men, even when they know that they will be treated sympathetically. Perhaps especially then, they do not desire it.'" Hapgood notes that Du Bois was so "proud and truthful" that he gave up on the idea. In the 1920s, however, Harlem Renaissance writer Claude McKay became a part of the Village milieu, coediting *The Liberator*, the periodical that grew out of *The Masses*, and, according to Langston Hughes, one could meet "the bohemians of both Harlem and the Village" at parties given by Renaissance writer Wallace Thurman. See Hutchins Hapgood, *A Victorian in the Modern World* (1939; repr., Seattle: University of Washington Press, 1972), 344–45; Langston Hughes, *The Big Sea* (1940, repr., New York: Hill and Wang, 1993), 249.

4. Hapgood, "The New Bohemia," 1–2.

5. Ibid., 2–3.

6. Mabel Dodge Luhan, *Movers and Shakers* (1936, repr., Albuquerque: University of New Mexico Press, 1985), 37.

7. According to Max Eastman, the "spirit" that many of the Bohemians hoped to find was decidedly secular. With regard to Hutchins Hapgood, Eastman noted that this "Sentimental Rebel" harbored a strong "Christian sentiment bereft of Deity yet carried to a bellicose extreme." Max Eastman, *Enjoyment of Living* (New York: Harper and Brothers, 1948), 424–25.

8. Alfred Kazin, *On Native Grounds: An Interpretation of Modern American Prose Literature* (New York: Harcourt, Brace and Co., 1942), 166.

9. See Robert E. Humphrey, *Children of Fantasy: The First Rebels of Greenwich Village* (New York: Ronald Press, 1978); Christine Stansell, *American Moderns: Bohemian New York and the Creation of a New Century* (New York: Metropolitan Books, 2000).

10. These phrases are quoted from an obituary written for Thomas A. Janvier, a writer who, along with H. C. Bunner and James L. Ford, had helped to establish the link between the Village and Old World Bohemia. See *Outlook* 104, no.10 (June 28, 1913): 416.

11. "Greenwich Village," *The Dial* 57, no. 679 (1914): 239. On the phrase "Greenwich Villagism," see Max Eastman, "Bunk About Bohemia," *Modern Monthly* 8 (May 1934): 201.

12. Luhan, *Movers and Shakers*, 68–69.

13. On 42 Washington Square South, see Robert A. Rosenstone, *Romantic Revolutionary: A Biography of John Reed* (Cambridge, MA: Harvard University Press, 1975), 82. That so many of Reed's first Bohemian compatriots were also recently graduated from Harvard raises the question whether early-twentieth-century college life (at Harvard and elsewhere) fostered or mirrored Bohemianism. *The Dial*, for one, insisted that it did just that. According to *The Dial*, part of what drew the Village into the orbit of the Parisian Latin Quarter was its affinity with undergraduate student cultures. "In the Latin Quarter, where students have been for generations as much a part of the life as poets, they are lumped together as a matter of long-established custom," *The Dial* noted, all the while recognizing that, "In the Village . . . there is a feeling that college is one of those established institutions that . . . are the most contemptibly and irremediably bourgeois." Still *The Dial* supported "those who perceive the similarities between Bohemians and undergraduates, between the communal spirit of Greenwich Village and . . . that of Stanford, or Wisconsin, or Princeton," maintaining that both college life and Bohemia "are conscious attempts to create a little world apart, to found a convention less oppressive than that of middle-class society." "Greenwich Village," 239–40. While contemporary accounts suggest that in point of fact, many colleges reinforced preexisting bourgeois social hierarchies (both on and off campus), it is true that Reed happened to be at Harvard at a time when college "rebels" had an increasing

impact on student life (and their intent was not to form a "little world apart" but rather to open up the university to the outside world). John Reed, "Almost Thirty" (1917) in *Adventures of a Young Man* (San Francisco: City Lights Books, 1975), 135–37. On Reed and other contemporary undergraduate "rebels" and their difference from prototypical "college men" of the time, see Helen Lefkowitz Horowitz, *Campus Life: Undergraduate Cultures from the End of the Eighteenth Century to the Present* (Chicago: University of Chicago Press, 1987).

14. "The Day in Bohemia," reprinted in Luhan, *Movers and Shakers*, 173, 174.

15. Henri Murger, *Scenes de la Vie de Bohème*, trans. Elizabeth Ward Hugus (Salt Lake City, UT: Peregrine Smith Books, 1988), 9.

16. Floyd Dell, *Love in Greenwich Village* (New York: George H. Doran Co., 1926), 15.

17. Dell, "Rents Were Low in Greenwich Village" (1947), in *The Greenwich Village Reader: Fiction, Poetry and Reminiscences, 1872–2002*, ed. June Skinner Sawyers (New York: Cooper Square Press, 2001), 260.

18. Dell, *Love in Greenwich Village*, 33.

19. Hapgood, *A Victorian*, 318.

20. Dell, "Rents Were Low in Greenwich Village," 260.

21. Hapgood, *A Victorian*, 318.

22. Dell, *Love in Greenwich Village*, 23.

23. Hippolyte Havel, "The Spirit of the Village," *Greenwich Village: A Fortnightly* (January 20, 1915), in *The Greenwich Village Reader*, 85.

24. Ibid., 83–86. With their emphasis on collective agency and new invention, Havel's words echo those of a fellow anarchist, the French geographer Élisée Reclus. According to Kristin Ross, Reclus was the first to use the term "social geography." A participant in one of the landmark events of French Bohemianism, the Paris Commune of 1871, Reclus later insisted, "Geography is not an immutable thing. It is made, it is remade every day; at each instant, it is modified by men's actions." See Ross, *The Emergence of Social Space: Rimbaud and the Paris Commune* (Minneapolis: University of Minnesota Press, 1988), 91.

25. Dell, "Rents Were Low in Greenwich Village," 261.

26. Dell, *Homecoming: An Autobiography* (New York: Farrar and Rinehart, 1933), 325.

27. Watson, *Strange Bedfellows*, 230–31.

28. Dell, *Love in Greenwich Village*, 20, 29–30. In *Love in Greenwich Village*, Dell refers to Henrietta Rodman as "Egeria."

29. Henri Murger, "The Bohemians of the Latin Quarter: Original Preface, 1850," in *On Bohemia: The Code of the Self-Exiled*, ed. César Graña and Marigay Graña (New Brunswick, NJ: Transaction Publishers, 1990), 49.

30. Dell, *Love in Greenwich Village*, 31.

31. Hapgood, "The New Bohemia"; Dell, *Love in Greenwich Village*, 31.

32. Robert K. Sarlos, "Jig Cook and Susan Glaspell: Rule Makers and Rule Breakers" in *1915: The Cultural Moment*, ed. Adele Keller and Lois Rudnick (New Brunswick, NJ: Rutgers University Press, 1991), 251.

33. George Cram Cook, quoted in Susan Glaspell, *The Road to the Temple* (New York: Frederick A. Stokes Co., 1927), 252. Randolph Bourne, another prominent Village intellectual, also used this phrase in his essay "Transnational America": "All our idealisms must be those of future social goals in which all can participate, the good life of personality lived in the environment of Beloved Community." Quoted in Casey Nelson Blake, *Beloved Community: The Cultural Criticism of Randolph Bourne, Van Wyck Brooks, Waldo Frank, and Lewis Mumford* (Chapel Hill: University of North Carolina Press, 1990), 1.

34. Hapgood, *A Victorian*, 394.

35. Hutchins Hapgood, "Cristine," c. 1918, Hapgood Collection, quoted in Watson, *Strange Bedfellows*, 224.

36. John Quinn, quoted in Watson, *Strange Bedfellows*, 228.

37. Malcolm Cowley, *Exile's Return* (1934; repr., New York: Penguin Books, 1976), 59. The line of poetry quoted by Cowley to encapsulate "the idea of living for the moment" is from "First Fig" (1922) by Villager and Provincetown actress Edna St. Vincent Millay, and thus is particularly appropriate to the New Bohemia, specifically to the Provincetown Players.

38. Hapgood, *A Victorian*, 422.

39. Alfred Stieglitz to Spencer Kellog, 17 December 1913, Alfred Stieglitz Archive, Yale University, cited in Edward Abrahams, "Alfred Stieglitz's Faith and Vision," in Keller and Rudnick, *1915*, 191.

40. Abrahams, "Stieglitz's Vision," 186.

41. Hapgood, *A Victorian*, 336.

42. Hutchins Hapgood, "Life at the Armory," *New York Globe*, February 17, 1913, quoted in Watson, *Strange Bedfellows*, 172.

43. Luhan, *Movers and Shakers*, 37.

44. "Cubists and Futurists Are Making Insanity Pay," *New York Times*, March 16, 1913.

45. Milton W. Brown, "The Armory Show and Its Aftermath," in Keller and Rudnick, *1915*, 170.

46. Quoted in Abrahams, "Stieglitz's Vision," 191.

47. Eastman, *Enjoyment of Living*, 396.

48. Ibid., 390.

49. Ibid., 394.

50. Ibid., 402.

51. Eugene V. Debs, quoted in Ross Wetzsteon, *The Republic of Dreams: Greenwich Village, the American Bohemia, 1910–1960* (New York: Simon and Schuster, 2002), 59.

52. Rebecca Zurnier, "*The Masses* and Modernism," in Keller and Rudnick, *1915*, 202–3.

53. Eastman, *Enjoyment of Living*, 411.

54. Eastman, *Venture* (New York: Albert and Charles Boni, 1927), 36, 40–41.

55. Eastman, *Enjoyment of Living*, 406–7.

56. Ibid., 421.

57. Anonymous jingle, in *May Days: An Anthology of Verse from Masses-Liberator*, ed. Genevieve Taggard (New York: Boni and Liveright, 1925), quoted in Leslie Fishbein, *Rebels in Bohemia: The Radicals of The Masses, 1911–1917* (Chapel Hill: University of North Carolina Press, 1982), 184.

58. Ibid., 419. One of Eastman's very first editorials for *The Masses* was a protest against lynching; the magazine "purveyed racist stereotypes in cartoons and poetry," however. See Eugene E. Leach, "The Radicals of *The Masses*," in Keller and Rudnick, *1915*, 42.

59. E. Ralph Cheney, "Costly Luxuries," *The Masses* 8 (May 1916): 22, quoted in Fishbein, *Rebels in Bohemia*, 187.

60. Eastman, *Enjoyment of Living*, 414–15.

61. Max Eastman, "Bunk About Bohemia," *Modern Monthly* 8 (May 1934): 202, 200.

62. Ibid., 202–203.

63. Parry, quoted in ibid., 203.

64. Ibid., 204, 203.

65. For example, Parry writes of *The New Masses* that it suffered from "rigidity of dogma": "It inherited the flaming revolt of the old *Masses*, but it misses the belly-filling

laughter and romantic moods with which that revolt was so adroitly seasoned and made attractive to outsiders." Albert Parry, *Garrets and Pretenders: A History of Bohemianism in America* (1933; repr., New York: Dover Publications, 1960), 356–57.

66. Ibid., 200–201.

67. Eastman, "Bunk About Bohemia," 203. This view of Bohemia further connected Eastman and Trotsky. As Alan M. Wald notes, Trotsky himself shared this vision: "In 1938 Trotsky wrote that 'generally speaking, art is the expression of man's need for a harmonious and complete life, that is to say, his need for those major benefits of which a society of classes has deprived him. That is why a protest against reality, either conscious or unconscious, active or passive, optimistic or pessimistic, always forms part of a really creative work.'" Alan M. Wald, *The New York Intellectuals: The Rise and Decline of the Anti-Stalinist Left from the 1930s to the 1980s* (Chapel Hill: University of North Carolina Press, 1987), 92.

68. Luhan, *Movers and Shakers*, 81–83. Dodge includes the newspaper headline and interview in her memoir.

69. Eastman, *Venture*, 210–11.

70. Bill Haywood, in *Rebel Voices: An I.W.W. Anthology*, ed. Joyce L. Kornbluh (Ann Arbor: University of Michigan Press, 1964), 1.

71. Luhan, *Movers and Shakers*, 188.

72. Ray Stannard Baker, "The Revolutionary Strike," *American Magazine* (May 1912): 24.

73. Luhan, *Movers and Shakers*, 203, 205.

74. Hapgood quotes from his *Globe* column in *A Victorian*, 351.

75. Elizabeth Gurley Flynn, *The Rebel Girl: An Autobiography, 1906–1926* (1955; repr., New York: International Publishers, 1994), 169.

76. Gerald W. McFarland, *Inside Greenwich Village: A New York City Neighborhood, 1898–1918.* (Amherst: University of Massachusetts Press, 2001), 201.

77. John Reed, quoted in Fishbein, *Rebels in Bohemia*, 187.

78. John Reed, quoted in Daniel Aaron, *Writers on the Left: Episodes in American Literary Communism* (1961; repr., New York: Columbia University Press, 1992), 25.

79. Eastman, *Enjoyment of Living*, 548; Art Young in the New York *Sun* and John Sloan in the New York *World*, quoted in *Enjoyment of Living*, 555–56.

80. Eastman, *Enjoyment of Living*, 548.

81. Fishbein, *Rebels in Bohemia*, 26.

82. Eastman, *Enjoyment of Living*, 465.

83. Ada Clare, "Thoughts and Things," *SP*, February 11, 1860; "The Borders of Bohemia," *NB* (August 1896): 120.

84. See June Sochen, *The New Woman in Greenwich Village, 1910–1920* (New York: Quadrangle Books, 1972).

85. "Feminists Ask for Equal Chance," *New York Times*, February 21, 1914.

86. "Emma Goldman's Defense," *The Masses* (June 1916), quoted in *Echoes of Revolt: The Masses, 1911–1917*, ed. William L. O'Neill (1966; repr., Chicago: Elephant Paperbacks 1989), 211–12.

87. "Talk on Feminism Stirs Great Crowd," *New York Times*, February 18, 1914.

88. "Feminists Ask for Equal Chance," *New York Times*, February 21, 1914.

89. Advertisement by Alice Carpenter, Zona Gale, Anna Strunsky Walling, Marie Jenney Howe, and Vira Boarman Whitehouse, *The Masses*, February 1916, p. 1, cited in Sochen, *The New Woman*, 80.

90. Mari Jo Buhle, *Women and American Socialism, 1870–1920* (Urbana: University of Illinois Press, 1983), 262.

91. Dell, "Confessions of a Feminist Man," *The Masses* (March 1914), in *Echoes of Revolt*, 197–98.

92. Dell, "Adventures in Anti-Land," *The Masses* (October–November 1915), in O'Neill, *Echoes of Revolt*, 199–200.
93. Hapgood, "The New Bohemia," 4–5.
94. Luhan, *Movers and Shakers*, 235, 241, 238.
95. Hapgood, *A Victorian*, 320.
96. Neith Boyce, "Feminism," *Life* (June 4, 1914): 1030.
97. Neith Boyce, "The Wife of a Genius," *Harper's Weekly* (December 12, 1914): 566–68.
98. Dell, "Feminism for Men," *Masses* 5, no. 10 (July 1914): 19–20.
99. Ibid.
100. Eastman, *Enjoyment of Living*, 521.
101. Ellen Kay Trimberger, "Feminism, Men and Modern Love," in *Powers of Desire: The Politics of Sexuality*, ed. Ann Snitow, Christine Stansell, and Sharon Thompson (New York: Monthly Review Press, 1983), 133.
102. Edward Carpenter, *Love's Coming of Age* (New York: 1911), quoted in Trimberger, "Feminism, Men, and Modern Love," 133.
103. Ellen Kay Trimberger, ed., *Intimate Warriors: Portraits of a Modern Marriage 1899–1944 with Selected Works by Neith Boyce and Hutchins Hapgood* (New York: Feminist Press, 1991), 3.
104. Hutchins Hapgood to his mother, 15 May 1898 and Neith Boyce, "Autobiography," in the Hapgood Collection, Beinecke Rare Book and Manuscript Library, quoted in Trimberger, "Introduction," *Intimate Warriors*, 5.
105. Trimberger, *Intimate Warriors*, 7.
106. Hapgood, *The Story of a Lover* (1914), in Trimberger, *Intimate Warriors*, 160.
107. Ibid., 146.
108. Neith Boyce to Hutchins Hapgood, 1907, quoted in Trimberger, *Intimate Warriors*, 205.
109. Hapgood, *The Story of a Lover* (1914), in Trimberger, *Intimate Warriors*, 163.
110. René Girard, *Deceit, Desire and the Novel: Self and Other in Literary Structure* (Baltimore: Johns Hopkins University Press, 1965), 17.
111. Hapgood, *The Story of a Lover* (1914), in Trimberger, *Intimate Warriors*, 162.
112. Ibid., 162–63.
113. Ibid., 165, 174.
114. Mabel Dodge to Neith Boyce, letter dated 1913, quoted in Ellen Kay Trimberger, "The New Woman and the New Sexuality," in Keller and Rudnick, *1915*, 110.
115. Mabel Dodge, "A Quarrel," *The Masses* 8, no. 9 (September 1916): 16–17.
116. Floyd Dell, *Sweet-and-Twenty*, in *King Arthur's Socks and Other Village Plays by Floyd Dell* (New York: Alfred A. Knopf, 1922), 97, 99.
117. Wetzsteon, *Republic of Dreams*, 253.
118. Floyd Dell, "The Kitten and the Masterpiece," *Love in Greenwich Village*, 56, 72.
119. Floyd Dell, "Why Mona Smiled," *The Masses* 5, no. 9 (June 1914): 16–17.
120. Louise Bryant to Sara Bard Field, June 12, 1916, quoted in Nancy F. Cott, *The Grounding of Modern Feminism* (New Haven: Yale University Press, 1987), 44.
121. Hapgood, *A Victorian*, 395.
122. Neith Boyce and Hutchins Hapgood, *Enemies* (1920), first published in *The Provincetown Plays*, ed. George Cram Cook and Frank Shay (Cincinnati, OH: Stewart Kidd and Company, 1921), in Trimberger, *Intimate Warriors*, 191, 195.
123. Cott, *Grounding of Modern Feminism*, 45.
124. Annette Wynne, "Her Veins Are Lit with Strange Desire," in *May Days*, 170, quoted in Mari Jo Buhle, *Women and American Socialism*, 263.
125. Mari Jo Buhle, *Women and American Socialism*, 263.

126. Bernadine Kielty Scherman, *Girl From Fitchburg* (New York: Random House, 1964), 60, quoted in Judith Schwarz, *Radical Feminists of Heterodoxy: Greenwich Village, 1912–1940* (Norwich, VT: New Victoria Publishers, 1986), 34.

127. Jan Seidler Ramirez, "The Tourist Trade Takes Hold," in *Greenwich Village: Culture and Counterculture*, ed. Rick Beard and Leslie Cohen Berlowitz (New Brunswick, NJ: Rutgers University Press, 1993), 383.

128. Anna Alice Chapin, *Greenwich Village* (New York: Dodd, Mead and Co., 1917), 209–10.

129. Ramirez, "The Tourist Trade," 382.

130. Dell, *Love in Greenwich Village*, 297.

131. James L. Ford, "Seeing the Real New York: Trip No. 4—Bohemia," *The Cosmopolitan* 40, no. 6 (1906): 712–18.

132. Ramirez, "The Tourist Trade," 374, 378.

133. Guido Bruno, "The Village Paper," from *Fragments from Greenwich Village* (New York: Privately published, 1921), in *The Greenwich Village Reader*, 197.

134. Ramirez, "The Tourist Trade," 375–376.

135. *Greenwich Village: A Semimonthly Edited by Guido Bruno, His Garret on Washington Square*, vol. 2 (June 23, 1915): cover page.

136. Ibid., 140–41.

137. Eastman, *Enjoyment of Living*, 418.

138. Djuna Barnes, "Greenwich Village as It Is," *Pearson's Magazine*, October 1916 (repr., New York: Phoenix Bookshop, 1978), 4–5.

139. Dell, *Love in Greenwich Village*, 299.

140. Jan Ramirez and Rick Beard, "Greenwich Thrillage: Village Commerce," in *Greenwich Village: Culture and Counterculture*, 338.

141. Dell, *Love in Greenwich Village*, 300. The humor magazine *Puck* ridiculed the phenomenon of "Professional Bohemians" as early as 1916. In one piece, an organization called the "Washington Square Chapter of the Professional Bohemians" resolves to "eschew sleep and the conventional periods and places of dining, to the end that we shall be seen in as large numbers as possible at unearthly hours in certain obscure and uncomfortable retreats to be hereafter decided upon." And this because, "The editors of our leading periodicals feel keenly the need of an efficiently organized group of Bohemians" whose antics might provide journalists with ready copy. "Professional Bohemians: Washington Square Chapter," *Puck* 79, no. 2039 (April 1, 1916): 13.

142. Dell, "The Fall of Greenwich Village," 301.

143. Charles Baudelaire, *Oeuvres*, vol. 1, ed. Yves Gérard Le Dantec, quoted in Walter Benjamin, *Charles Baudelaire: A Lyric Poet in the Era of High Capitalism*, trans. Harry Zohn (London: Verso, 1983), 34. Harry Zohn's translation of Baudelaire reads: "I played the hypocrite and mimicked loftiness, I who sell my thought and want to be an author."

144. Dell, *Love in Greenwich Village*, 298.

145. Chapin, *Greenwich Village*, 229.

146. Ibid., 232–33.

147. Ibid., 213–14.

148. *New York Tribune* (November 14, 1915), quoted in McFarland, *Inside Greenwich Village*, 208.

149. *The Ink-Pot* (October 1916), quoted in Ramirez, "The Tourist Trade," 382. Of course, as Ramirez notes, Bohemia quickly became fodder for the emerging motion picture industry. Plots often centered on the ingénue who followed *The Forbidden Path* (the title of a film from 1918) into Bohemia (387).

150. "When the Village Robs the Cradle," *New York Times*, February 18, 1923.

151. Lewis Erenberg, "Village Nightlife, 1910–1950," in *Greenwich Village: Culture and Counterculture*, 360–61.

152. Nathan Miller, *New World Coming: The 1920s and the Making of Modern America* (New York: Scribner's, 2003), 259. As Miller notes, one "major reason for the cult of youth was the increased size of the generation between sixteen and thirty years old" (259). Miller also notes that through the cult of youth, "elements of the free love ethic of Greenwich Village bohemia, including a faint tolerance for premarital sex, the acknowledgment of female sexuality, and the acceptance of birth control, had infiltrated American culture" (260).

153. Cowley, *Exile's Return*, 64–65.

154. Sinclair Lewis, *Babbitt* (1922; repr., New York: The New American Library, 1961), 223.

155. I again borrow this phrase from Seigel, *Bohemian Paris*.

156. Charles Sears Baldwin, "Bohemia," *The Dial* 80 (June 1926): 469.

157. Corrine Lowe, *Ladies' Home Journal* (March 1920): 28; *Vogue* (June 1, 1927): 88–89, cited in Ramirez, "The Tourist Trade," 379, 381.

158. George Chauncey, "Long-Haired Men and Short-Haired Women: Building a Gay World in the Heart of Bohemia," in *Greenwich Village: Culture and Counterculture*, 156–59.

159. Dell, "Rents Were Low in Greenwich Village," 264

160. Ramirez, "The Tourist Trade," 388.

161. Ed Falkowski, "Guido Bruno—Romantic Ghost," *The Bookman* 69, no. 2 (1929): 168.

162. "When the Village Robs the Cradle," *New York Times*, February 18, 1923.

163. Dell, "Rents Were Low in Greenwich Village," 64, 266.

164. Cowley, *Exile's Return*, 61–62.

165. I borrow this felicitous phrase from Edith Wharton, *The Custom of the Country* (1913; repr., New York: Penguin Books, 1987), 157. In the novel, a character speaks of "the permitted diversion, . . . a kind of superior Bohemia, where one may be respectable without being bored."

166. Thomas Bender, *New York Intellect* (New York: Knopf, 1987), 245, quoted in Stansell, *American Moderns*, 321.

167. Stansell, *American Moderns*, 321.

168. Dell, *Love in Greenwich Village*, 320.

169. Ibid., 303.

170. Dell, *Homecoming*, 283.

171. Trimberger, "Feminism, Men, and Modern Love," 147.

172. William Barrett, "The Village: Bohemia Gone Bourgeois," *New York Times*, April 4, 1954.

173. Eastman, *Venture*, 77.

174. Brooks, *Bobos in Paradise*, 10–11.

175. Eastman, *Enjoyment of Living*, 456. Eastman had been courting Huntington as an investor for *The Masses*, but he did not "get any money from him": "I got, on the contrary, a feeling of remorse that throughout that whole delightful twelve hours of friendship, instead of giving myself to it for its own sake, I had kept wondering what I would get for it for *The Masses*."

176. Brooks, *Bobos in Paradise*, 46.

177. F. Scott Fitzgerald, quoted in William O'Neill, *The Last Romantic: A Life of Max Eastman* (1978; repr., New Brunswick, NJ: Transaction Publishers, 1991), 122. O'Neill also details Eastman's changing views on the USSR.

178. Liza Featherstone, "Retail Workers Fight Back," posted October 17, 2006, http://www.thenation.com/blogs/notion/130472 (accessed March 15, 2009).

179. See http://www.bohemian.org/nvannuys/bnvhome.htm (accessed March 7, 2009); http://www.bohemiatucson.com (accessed March 7, 2009); http://www.americantowns.com/fl/orlando/organization/bohemia_society_of_the_arts_and_sciences (accessed March 7, 2009); http://www.myspace.com/newbohemia (accessed May 21, 2007; site now discontinued); and, for another example of a self-defined Bohemian on myspace.com, see http://www.myspace.com/fecklessbohemian (accessed March 7, 2009). Further, in cities throughout the United States, sociologist Richard Lloyd has identified the presence of what he terms "Neo-Bohemias"—places where there is a "symbiosis" between "the activities of contemporary artists (and affiliated lifestyle aesthetes) and central features of postindustrial urbanism." Like the Village of the years following 1910, these areas market their Bohemian ambiance, often relying on "young cultural producers and aspirants" to staff the bars, coffeehouses, clubs, and restaurants that fuel the economy of Neo-Bohemia. Richard Lloyd, *Neo-Bohemia: Art and Commerce in the Post-Industrial City* (New York: Routledge, 2006), 15, 138.

180. As the *New York Times* reported, however, several high school productions of *Rent* have already been canceled due to objections about the show's morality. Patrick Healy, "'Rent' the High School Musical? Not in Some Communities," *New York Times*, February 20, 2009.

Index